LEEDS POLYTECHNIC LIBRARY

Beckett Park
Leeds S6 3QS

KU-546-823

LEEDS BECKETT UNIVERSITY
LIBRARY
DISCARDED

1700120749

Dewey Decimal Classification and Relative Index

Dewey Decimal Classification and Relative Index

Devised by Melvil Dewey

EDITION 20

Edited by

John P. Comaromi, Editor

Julianne Beall, Assistant Editor

Winton E. Matthews, Jr., Assistant Editor

Gregory R. New, Assistant Editor

VOLUME 3

Schedules 600–999

FOREST PRESS

A Division of
OCLC Online Computer Library Center, Inc.
ALBANY, NEW YORK
1989

LEEDS POLYTECHNIC

1700120749

BP ✓

128308   26.9.90

28.9.90   L.185

Copyright 1876, 1885, 1911, 1913, 1915, 1919
by Melvil Dewey
Copyright 1888, 1891, 1894, 1899
by Library Bureau
Copyright 1922, 1927, 1932, 1942, 1952, © 1958
by Lake Placid Club Education Foundation
Copyright 1951, © 1965, 1971
by Forest Press, Inc.
Vol. 2 © 1967 by Forest Press, Inc.
© 1979 by Forest Press
A Division of the Lake Placid Education Foundation
© 1989
OCLC Online Computer Library Center, Inc.

All rights reserved. No part of this publication may be reproduced, stored in a retrieval
system, or transmitted, in any form or by any means, electronic, mechanical, photocopying,
recording or otherwise, without the prior written permission of the publisher.

DDC, FOREST PRESS, DEWEY DECIMAL CLASSIFICATION, and DEWEY
DECIMAL CLASSIFICATION, ADDITIONS, NOTES AND DECISIONS are registered
trademarks of OCLC Online Computer Library Center, Inc.

Library of Congress Cataloging-in-Publication Data
Dewey, Melvil, 1851-1931.
    Dewey decimal classification and relative index / devised by
Melvil Dewey. -- Ed. 20 / edited by John P. Comaromi, Julianne
Beall, Winton E. Matthews, Jr., Gregory R. New.
    Contents: v. 1. Introduction. Tables -- v. 2-3. Schedules -- v.4. Relative
index. Manual.
    1. Classification, Dewey decimal. I. Comaromi, John P. (John Phillip),
1937- . II. Beall, Julianne, 1946- . III. Matthews, Winton E. IV. New,
Gregory R. V. Forest Press. VI. Title.
Z696.D519 1989   025.4'31--dc19   88-24629

∞

The paper used in this publication meets the minimum requirements
of American National Standard for Information Science - Permanence
of Paper for Printed Library Materials. ANSI Z39.48-1984.

ISBN: (set) 0-910608-37-7; v. 1 0-910608-38-5; v. 2 0-910608-39-3;
v. 3 0-910608-40-7; v. 4 0-910608-41-5

Contents

Volume 1

Contents

Volume 2

Volume 3

Volume 4

Schedules

Use of the Schedules

Full instructions on the use of the Schedules are found in the Introduction to the Dewey Decimal Classification in Volume 1.

The first three digits of a DDC number are normally found at the top of the page.

A number in square brackets [ ] is not currently in use.

A number in parentheses ( ) is an option to standard usage.

600

---

600   Technology (Applied sciences)

See also 303.483 for technology as a cause of cultural change, 306.46 for sociology of technology, 338.1–338.4 for economic aspects of industries based on specific technologies, 338.926 for technology transfer, 338.927 for appropriate technology

See Manual at 300 vs. 600; 500 vs. 600

601   Philosophy and theory

602   Miscellany

[.72]   Patents

> Do not use; class in 608

.75   Trademarks and service marks

> Class here comprehensive works on trademarks generally used for products rather than services

> Class interdisciplinary works on trademarks and service marks in 929.9

.9   **Commercial miscellany**

> Class interdisciplinary commercial miscellany in 380.1029; commercial miscellany of products and services used in individual and family living in 640.29, of manufactured products in 670.29

603   Dictionaries, encyclopedias, concordances

604   Technical drawing, hazardous materials technology, history and description with respect to kinds of persons

.2   **Technical drawing**

> Class here engineering graphics, drafting illustrations

> Class drafting illustrations in a specific subject with the subject, using notation 0221 from Table 1, e.g., map drawing 526.0221, drafting in electronics 621.3810221

> *For architectural drawing, see 720.284*

.22   Arrangement and organization of drafting rooms, preservation and storage of drawings

.24   Specific drafting procedures and conventions

> Use of this number for comprehensive works on drafting procedures and conventions discontinued; class in 604.2

.242   Production illustration

     Nontechnical graphic representations

.243   Lettering, titling, dimensioning, shades, shadows

.245   Projections

     Orthographic, isometric, spherical

     Including perspectives

.25   Preparation and reading of copies

     Examples: blueprints, photostats

     See also 686.42 for printing blueprints

[.6]   **Waste technology**

     Relocated to 628.4

.7   **Hazardous materials technology**

     Methods of extracting, manufacturing, processing, utilizing, handling, transporting, storing solids, liquids, gases of corrosive, explosive, flammable, infectious, radioactive, toxic nature

     Class comprehensive works on and social aspects of hazardous materials safety in 363.17; technology of a specific hazardous material with the technology, e.g., of explosives 662.2; safety techniques for a specific application of hazardous materials with the application outside 300, using notation 0289 from Table 1, e.g., safety techniques in working with hazardous paving materials 625.80289 (*not* 363.179)

     See Manual at 363.176 vs. 604.7; 660.2804 vs. 604.7

.8   **History and description with respect to kinds of persons [*formerly* 609]**

     Add to base number 604.8 the numbers following —08 in notation 081–089 from Table 1, e.g., novices 604.880909, students and learners 604.88375 [*both formerly* 607.33]

605   Serial publications

606   Organizations

[.8]   **Management of technology**

     Relocated to 658

607   Education, research, related topics

.01–.03   Treatment in areas, regions, places in general; in ancient world

     Add to base number 607.0 notation 1 or 3 from Table 2, e.g., in ancient Rome 607.037

[.04–.09]   Treatment in specific continents, countries, localities in modern world

     Do not use; class in 607.4–607.9

.1 **Schools and courses**

.2 **Industrial research**

Class here products research; historical, descriptive, experimental research

Add to base number 607.2 notation 1 or 3–9 from Table 2, e.g., products research in China 607.251

Class product planning in management in 658.5038, management of research for new and improved products in 658.57

.3 **Other aspects of education and research**

[.33] Students, learners, apprentices, novices

Apprentices relocated to 331.55, novices to 604.880909, students and learners to 604.88375

.34–.39 Specific aspects

Add to base number 607.3 the numbers following —07 in notation 074–079 from Table 1, e.g., museums, collections, exhibits 607.34

See also 381.1 for commercial aspects of fairs and expositions; 900 for fairs and expositions of civilization, e.g., the 1964–1965 New York World's Fair 909.826074747243

.4–.9 **Education, research, related topics in specific continents, countries, localities in modern world**

Add to base number 607 notation 4–9 from Table 2, e.g., education and research in Japan 607.52

608 **Inventions and patents**

Do not use for history and description of technology with respect to kinds of persons; class in 604.8

See Manual at 608 vs. 609

[.09] Historical, geographical, persons treatment

Do not use; class in 608.7

.7 **Historical, geographical, persons treatment**

Add to base number 608.7 notation 01–9 from Table 2, e.g., patents from Brazil 608.781

Class history of inventions in 609

609 **Historical, geographical, persons treatment**

Class here history of inventions, technological aspects of industrial archaeology

History and description with respect to kinds of persons relocated to 604.8

Class historical and geographical treatment of production and economic aspects of industrial archaeology in 338.09, historical aspects of industrial archaeology in 900

See Manual at 300 vs. 600: Comprehensive works; 608 vs. 609

610   Medical sciences   Medicine

610.19
Health psychology

Class home care of the sick and infirm in 649.8

For veterinary medicine, see 636.089

See Manual at 591 vs. 610; 362.1–362.4 vs. 610; 362.17 vs. 610; 616 vs. 610

SUMMARY

610.1–.9	[Standard subdivisions, medical personnel, nursing]
611	**Human anatomy, cytology (cell biology), histology (tissue biology)**
.01	Anatomic embryology, cytology (cell biology), histology (tissue biology)
.1	Cardiovascular organs
.2	Respiratory organs
.3	Digestive tract organs
.4	Lymphatic and glandular organs
.6	Urogenital organs
.7	Motor and integumentary organs
.8	Nervous system Sense organs
.9	Regional and topographical anatomy
612	**Human physiology**
.01–.04	[Biophysics, biochemistry, control processes, tissue and organ culture, physiology of specific activities]
.1	Blood and circulation
.2	Respiration
.3	Digestion
.4	Secretion, excretion, related functions
.6	Reproduction, development, maturation
.7	Motor functions and integument
.8	Nervous functions Sensory functions
.9	Regional physiology
613	**Promotion of health**
.04	Promotion of health of specific sex and age groups
.1	Environmental factors
.2	Dietetics
.3	Beverages
.4	Personal cleanliness and related topics
.5	Artificial environments
.6	Special topics
.7	Physical fitness
.8	Substance abuse (Drug abuse)
.9	Birth control and sex hygiene
614	**Forensic medicine, incidence of disease, public preventive medicine**
.1	Forensic medicine (Medical jurisprudence)
.4	Incidence of and public measures to prevent disease
.5	Incidence of and public measures to prevent specific diseases and kinds of diseases
.6	Disposal of the dead

615		**Pharmacology and therapeutics**
	.1	Drugs (Materia medica)
	.2	Inorganic drugs
	.3	Organic drugs
	.4	Practical pharmacy
	.5	Therapeutics
	.6	Methods of administering medication
	.7	Pharmacodynamics
	.8	Specific therapies and kinds of therapies
	.9	Toxicology

616		**Diseases**
	.001–.009	Standard subdivisions
	.01–.09	[General topics]
	.1	Diseases of the cardiovascular system
	.2	Diseases of the respiratory system
	.3	Diseases of the digestive system
	.4	Diseases of the blood-forming, lymphatic, glandular systems Diseases of the endocrine system
	.5	Diseases of the integument, hair, nails
	.6	Diseases of the urogenital system Diseases of the urinary system
	.7	Diseases of the musculoskeletal system
	.8	Diseases of the nervous system and psychiatric disorders
	.9	Other diseases

617		**Surgery and related topics**
	.001–.008	Standard subdivisions of surgery
	.01–.09	[General topics]
	.1	Wounds and injuries
	.2	Results of injuries
	.3	Orthopedics
	.4	Surgery by systems
	.5	Regional medicine Regional surgery
	.6	Dentistry
	.7	Ophthalmology
	.8	Otology and audiology
	.9	Operative surgery and special fields of surgery

618		**Other branches of medicine Gynecology and obstetrics**
	.01–.09	[Standard subdivisions and special topics of gynecology and obstetrics]
	.1	Gynecology
	.2	Obstetrics
	.3	Diseases and complications of pregnancy
	.4	Childbirth (Parturition) Labor
	.5	Complicated labor
	.6	Normal puerperium
	.7	Puerperal diseases
	.8	Obstetrical surgery
	.9	Pediatrics and geriatrics

619		**Experimental medicine**
	.5	Fowl
	.7	Dogs
	.8	Cats
	.9	Other mammals

[.23]	Medicine as a profession, occupation, hobby
	Do not use; class in 610.69

.28 Auxiliary techniques and procedures; apparatus, equipment, materials

Class here comprehensive works on biomedical engineering, medical instrumentation

Class biological instrumentation in 574.028

.6 Organizations, management, professions

.65 Group practice

Class the economics of group practice in 338.7–338.8

.69 Medical personnel

Class medical personnel (other than nurses) of a specific specialty with the specialty, using notation as directed, e.g., obstetricians 618.2023; critical appraisal and description of work, individual and collected biographies with the specialty using notation 092 from Table 1, e.g., biography of psychiatrists 616.890092

See Manual at 610.69

.695 Specific kinds of medical personnel

Nature of duties, characteristics of professions

Class here medical missionaries

Class medical records librarians in 651.504261, medical secretaries in 651.3741

For nursing personnel, see 610.73069

.695 2 Physicians

.695 3 Medical technicians and assistants

.696 Medical relationships

Examples: relationships between medical personnel and patients, between medical personnel and the public, within medical professions

.7 Education, research, nursing, related topics

.72 Research

.724 Experimental research

Class experimental medicine in 619

.73 Nursing and services of medical technicians and assistants

Class here general medical nursing

Patient education by nurses relocated to 615.507

See Manual at 610.73

SUMMARY

.730 1   Philosophy and theory of nursing

.730 2   Miscellany of nursing

[.730 23]   Nursing as a profession, occupation, hobby

Do not use; class in 610.73069

.730 3–.730 5   Standard subdivisions of nursing

.730 6   Nursing organizations and personnel

Class management of services of nurses in 362.173068

.730 69   Nursing personnel

Nature of duties, characteristics of the profession, relationships

See Manual at 610.69

.730 692   Professional nurses and nursing

Including associate-degree nurses and nursing, nurse practitioners

.730 693   Practical nurses and nursing

Example: registered nursing assistants (Canada)

.730 698   Auxiliary personnel

Examples: aides, attendants, orderlies, volunteers

.730 699   Relationships of nurses

Examples: relationships between nurses and patients, between nurses and the public, within the nursing profession

.730 7–.730 9   Standard subdivisions of nursing

>   610.732–610.736 Nursing

Class comprehensive works in 610.73

.732   Private duty nursing

.733   Institutional nursing and ward management

Class nonmedical aspects of ward management in 362.173068

.734   Public health nursing

Class here Red Cross nursing

.734 3	Community and district nursing
	Example: work of visiting nurses
.734 6	Occupational health nursing (Industrial nursing)
.734 9	Disaster nursing
.736	Specialized nursing

Unless other instructions are given, observe the following table of precedence, e.g., pediatric surgical nursing 610.73677 (*not* 610.7362)

Surgical, obstetrical, gynecologic nursing	610.7367
Pediatric nursing	610.7362
Geriatric nursing	610.7365
Nursing of specific diseases	610.7369
Psychiatric and neurologic nursing	610.7368
Intensive (Critical), emergency, long-term, terminal care nursing	610.7361

For public health nursing, see 610.734

.736 1	Intensive (Critical), emergency, long-term, terminal care nursing
.736 2	Pediatric nursing
.736 5	Geriatric nursing
.736 7	Surgical, obstetrical, gynecologic nursing
.736 77	Surgical nursing

Including ophthalmic nursing, orthopedic nursing

Class nursing for obstetrical and gynecologic surgery in 610.73678, nursing for cancer surgery in 610.73698

.736 78	Obstetrical and gynecologic nursing
.736 8	Psychiatric and neurologic nursing
	Example: nursing for mentally retarded people
.736 9	Nursing with respect to specific diseases

For psychiatric and neurologic nursing, see 610.7368

.736 91	Cardiovascular diseases
.736 92	Respiratory diseases
.736 98	Cancer
.736 99	Communicable diseases
.737	Services of medical technicians and assistants
[.737 023]	Work of medical technicians and assistants as a profession, occupation, hobby

Do not use; class in 610.6953

.9	**Historical, geographical, persons treatment**

See Manual at 610.9

611   Human anatomy, cytology (cell biology), histology (tissue biology)

Use 611.001–611.009 for standard subdivisions for human anatomy, cytology, histology; for human anatomy alone

For pathological anatomy, see 616.07

See Manual at 573.6 vs. 611; 611 vs. 612

SUMMARY

611.01	**Anatomic embryology, cytology (cell biology), histology (tissue biology)**
.1	**Cardiovascular organs**
.2	**Respiratory organs**
.3	**Digestive tract organs**
.4	**Lymphatic and glandular organs**
.6	**Urogenital organs**
.7	**Motor and integumentary organs**
.8	**Nervous system Sense organs**
.9	**Regional and topographical anatomy**

.01   Anatomic embryology, cytology (cell biology), histology (tissue biology)

> Class here specific systems, organs, regions

.013   Anatomic embryology

.018   Cytology (Cell biology) and histology (tissue biology)

.018 1   Cytology (Cell biology)

.018 15   Pathology (Cytopathology)

.018 16   Physiological genetics

>   611.018 2–611.018 9 Histology (Tissue biology)

> Class here histogenesis, histophysiology, histopathology, tissue regeneration

> Class comprehensive works in 611.018

.018 2   Connective tissue

> Examples: adipose, areolar, collagenous, elastic, reticular tissues; pigmented cells; fibers, ground substances

> Class cartilaginous tissue in 611.0183

.018 3   Cartilaginous tissue

> Contains elastic, fibrous, hyaline cartilage

.018 4   Osseous (Bone) tissue

> Examples: spongy and compact bone tissues, endosteum, periosteum

> Including red and yellow bone marrow (medulla)

.018 5	Blood and lymph elements

Examples: blood plasma, red corpuscles (erythrocytes), white corpuscles (leucocytes), platelets (thrombocytes), lymph plasma, lymphocytes

.018 6	Muscular tissue

Contains smooth (nonstriated, involuntary), skeletal (striated, voluntary), cardiac (striated, involuntary) muscle tissues

.018 7	Epithelial tissue

Examples: serous and mucous membranes; simple columnar, simple squamous, stratified squamous epithelia

.018 8	Nerve tissue

Examples: neurons, interstitial nerve tissue (neuroglia, neurilemma, satellite cells), meninges, sheaths

.018 9	Histology (Tissue biology) of specific systems, organs, regions

Add to base number 611.0189 the numbers following 611 in 611.1–611.9, e.g., the histology of the thymus gland 611.018943; however, class specific tissues of specific systems, organs, regions in 611.0182–611.0188

> ## 611.1–611.9 Gross anatomy

Class here comprehensive works on gross anatomy and tissue structure

Class comprehensive works in 611, tissue structure in 611.0182–611.0189

See Manual at 612.1–612.8

.1	**Cardiovascular organs**
.11	Pericardium
.12	Heart

Including ventricles, auricles, endocardium, myocardium

For pericardium, see 611.11

.13	Arteries

Class here comprehensive works on blood vessels

Class blood vessels of a specific system or organ with the system or organ, e.g., cerebral blood vessels 611.81

For veins, see 611.14; capillaries, 611.15

.14	Veins
.15	Capillaries
.2	**Respiratory organs**
.21	Nose and nasal accessory sinuses

.22	Larynx
	Including epiglottis, glottis, laryngeal muscles
.23	Trachea and bronchi
.24	Lungs
.25	Pleura
.26	Diaphragm
.27	Mediastinum
.3	**Digestive tract organs**
.31	Mouth
.313	Tongue
	Including muscles of the tongue [*formerly also* 611.734]
.314	Teeth
.315	Palate
.316	Salivary glands
.317	Lips
.318	Cheeks
.32	Pharynx, tonsils, esophagus
.33	Stomach
	Including the pylorus
	Class here comprehensive works on gastrointestinal organs
	For intestine, see 611.34
.34	Intestine
.341	Small intestine
	Contains duodenum, jejunum, ileum
.345	Cecum and vermiform appendix
.347	Large intestine
	Including colon, sigmoid flexure (sigmoid colon)
	For cecum and vermiform appendix, see 611.345; rectum, 611.35
.35	Rectum and anus
	See also 611.96 for perineum
.36	Biliary tract
	Contains liver, gall bladder, bile ducts
.37	Pancreas and islands of Langerhans

.38   Peritoneum

Including mesentery, omentum

.4   Lymphatic and glandular organs

Class glandular organs of a specific system with the system, e.g., salivary glands 611.316

.41   Spleen

Class here comprehensive works on the anatomy of the blood-forming (hematopoietic or hemopoietic) system

Class bone marrow in 611.0184

.42   Lymphatic system

For lymphatic glands, see 611.46

.43   Thymus gland

.44   Thyroid and parathyroid glands

.45   Adrenal glands

.46   Lymphatic glands

.47   Carotid, pituitary, pineal glands

.49   Breasts

.6   Urogenital organs

.61   Kidneys and ureters

Class here comprehensive works on anatomy of urinary organs

For bladder and urethra, see 611.62

.62   Bladder and urethra

.63   Testicles, prostate, scrotum

Class here comprehensive works on male genital organs

For penis, see 611.64

.64   Penis

.65   Ovaries and fallopian tubes

Class here comprehensive works on female genital organs

For uterus, see 611.66; vagina, hymen, vulva, 611.67

.66   Uterus

Including the cervix of the uterus

.67   Vagina, hymen, vulva

.7	**Motor and integumentary organs**
.71	Bones

For the ossicles, see 611.85

.711	Of the spinal column
.712	Of the chest

Example: ribs

For the sternum, see 611.713

.713	Sternum
.715	Of the brainpan

For the mastoid processes, see 611.85

.716	Of the face
.717	Of the upper extremities

Contains scapulas, clavicles, humeri, radii, ulnas, carpal and metacarpal bones, phalanges and sesamoid bones of hands

Class comprehensive works on bones of the extremities in 611.718

.718	Of the lower extremities

Contains hip bones, femurs, patellas, tibias, fibulas, tarsal and metatarsal bones, phalanges and sesamoid bones of feet

Class here comprehensive works on bones of the extremities

For bones of the upper extremities, see 611.717

.72	Articulations (Ligaments and joints)
.73	Muscles

Class muscles of a specific system or organ with the subject, e.g., heart muscles 611.12

.731	Of the back
.732	Of the head
.733	Of the neck
[.734]	Of the tongue

Relocated to 611.313

.735	Of the chest
.736	Of the abdomen and pelvis
.737	Of the upper extremities

Contains muscles of shoulders, arms, forearms, hands

.738   Of the lower extremities

         Contains muscles of hips, buttocks, thighs, legs, feet

         Class here comprehensive works on muscles of extremities

         For muscles of upper extremities, see 611.737

.74   Connective tissue

         Examples: tendons, fasciae

         Class bursae and sheaths of tendons in 611.75

         For ligaments, see 611.72

.75   Bursae and sheaths of tendons

.77   Integument

         For hair and nails, see 611.78

.78   Hair and nails

.8   **Nervous system**   **Sense organs**

         Class here neuroanatomy

.81   Brain

         Class here the central nervous system

         For spinal cord, see 611.82

.82   Spinal cord

.83   Nerves and ganglia

         Class nerves of a specific system or organ with the system or organ, e.g., optic nerves 611.84

.84   Eyes

         Class here the orbit

.85   Ears

         Including the mastoid processes, ossicles

.86   Olfactory organs

.87   Gustatory organs

.88   Tactile organs

.9   **Regional and topographical anatomy**

         Including back

         Class specific systems or organs in a region in 611.1–611.8

.91   Head

         For the face, see 611.92

.92	Face

> *See also 611.317 for lips, 611.318 for cheeks*

.93	Neck
.94	Thorax
.95	Abdomen

Epigastric through lumbar regions

.96	Perineum and pelvic region
.97	Upper extremities
.98	Lower extremities

Class here comprehensive works on the extremities

> *For the upper extremities, see 611.97*

612   Human physiology

Class here comprehensive works on anatomy and physiology

Use 612.001–612.009 for standard subdivisions

Class physiological psychology in 152

> *For human anatomy, cytology (cell biology), histology (tissue biology), see 611; pathological physiology, 616.07*

> *See Manual at 611 vs. 612; 612 vs. 616*

SUMMARY

612.01–.04	**[Biophysics, biochemistry, control processes, tissue and organ culture, physiology of specific activities]**
.1	**Blood and circulation**
.2	**Respiration**
.3	**Digestion**
.4	**Secretion, excretion, related functions**
.6	**Reproduction, development, maturation**
.7	**Motor functions and integument**
.8	**Nervous functions Sensory functions**
.9	**Regional physiology**

.01	Biophysics and biochemistry
.014	Biophysics
.014 2	Physical phenomena in humans

Including the human aura when scientifically considered

> *See also 133.8 for the aura as a manifestation of psychic power*

.014 21	Bioenergetics

> *For body heat, see 612.01426; bioelectricity, 612.01427*

.014 26	Body heat
	Including regulation
	Class here production, maintenance
.014 27	Bioelectricity
	Including electrophysiology
.014 4	Effects of terrestrial agents
	Including aerospace physiology
	Class space physiology in 612.0145
.014 41	Mechanical forces
.014 412	Gravitational forces
.014 414	Acceleration and deceleration
.014 415	Pressure
	Including submarine physiology
.014 42	Electricity
.014 44	Visible light
.014 45	Sound and related vibrations
.014 452	Subsonic vibrations
.014 453	Sound
.014 455	Ultrasonic vibrations
.014 46	Thermal forces
.014 462	Heat and high temperatures
.014 465	Cold and low temperatures

For cryogenic temperatures, see 612.014467

.014 467	Cryogenic temperatures
.014 48	Radiation (Radiobiology)
	Class here dosimetry

Add to base number 612.01448 the numbers following 574.1915 in 574.19151–574.19157, e.g., gamma radiation 612.014486; however, class visible light in 612.01444

.014 5	Extraterrestrial biophysics

Class here bioastronautics, space physiology

Add to base number 612.0145 the numbers following 574.191 in 574.1913–574.1917, e.g., gravitation 612.014532

Class aerospace physiology in 612.0144, space medicine in 616.980214

.015	Biochemistry

Class metabolism in 612.39

.015 01	Philosophy and theory

Class theoretical biochemistry in 612.01582

.015 02	Miscellany
.015 028	Auxiliary techniques and procedures; apparatus, equipment, materials

Class analytical biochemistry in 612.01585

.015 1	Enzymes

Add to base number 612.0151 the numbers following 574.1925 in 574.19253–574.19258, e.g., saccharolytic enzymes 612.01514

.015 2	Fluids, inorganic constituents, pigments
.015 22	Fluids

Example: water

Including electrolytic balance, fluid balance

See Manual at 612.3923 vs. 612.01522

.015 24	Inorganic constituents

Example: minerals

Class inorganic fluids in 612.01522, inorganic pigments in 612.01528

.015 28	Pigments

Class biochemistry of skin pigmentation in 612.7927

.015 4	Biosynthesis

Add to base number 612.0154 the numbers following 574.1929 in 574.19293–574.19297, e.g., biosynthesis of proteins 612.01546

.015 7	Organic compounds

Add to base number 612.0157 the numbers following 547.7 in 547.72–547.79, e.g., carbohydrates 612.01578; however, class enzymes in 612.0151, vitamins in 612.399, hormones in 612.405

Class organic fluids in 612.01522, organic pigments in 612.01528

.015 8	Theoretical, physical, analytical biochemistry

Class physical, theoretical, analytical biochemistry of a specific constituent with the subject, e.g., physical chemistry of carbohydrates 612.01578

.015 82	Theoretical biochemistry
.015 83	Physical biochemistry
.015 85	Analytical biochemistry

.02	Control processes and tissue and organ culture
.022	Control processes
	Including biological rhythms, homeostasis
.028	Tissue and organ culture
.04	Physiology of specific activities

Class here comprehensive works on the physiology of physical movements in relation to multiple physiological systems

Class the physiology of physical movements in relation to a specific system with the system, e.g., the musculoskeletal system 612.76

.042	Work
.044	Sports

Class here recreation

> ### 612.1–612.8 Specific functions, systems, organs

Class comprehensive works in 612

See Manual at 612.1–612.8

.1   **Blood and circulation**

Class circulation in a specific system or organ with the system or organ, e.g., the brain 612.824

For lymph and lymphatics, see 612.42

.11   Blood

Class the spleen in 612.41, bone marrow in 612.491

For blood chemistry, see 612.12

.111	Red corpuscles (Erythrocytes)
.111 1	Biochemistry
	Including hemoglobins
.111 2	Counts and counting
.112	White corpuscles (Leucocytes)
.112 1	Biochemistry
.112 2	Biophysics
.112 7	Counts and counting
.115	Coagulation (Clotting)

Including the role of fibrin, fibrinoplastin, plasma, thrombin in clotting

.116   Plasma

For the role of plasma in clotting, see 612.115

.117	Platelets and hemoconia
.118	Biophysics and biological properties
.118 1	Biophysics
	Physical properties and phenomena, effect of physical agents
	Including hemorrheology (study of blood flow)
	Class biophysics of specific components or functions in 612.111–612.117
.118 2	Biological properties
[.118 22]	Immunity (Immunology)
	Relocated to 616.079
.118 25	Blood types (groups) and typing
.12	Blood chemistry
	Including carbohydrates, cholesterol, enzymes, lipids, minerals
	Class chemistry of specific components or functions in 612.111–612.117, biological properties in 612.1182
.13	Blood vessels and vascular circulation
	For vasomotors, see 612.18
.133	Arteries and arterial circulation
.134	Veins and venous circulation
.135	Capillaries and capillary circulation
.14	Blood pressure
.17	Heart
.171	Biophysics
	Including contraction and dilation of heart cavities, valvular activity, recording methods
	For blood pressure, see 612.14
.173	Biochemistry
.178	Innervation
.18	Vasomotors
	Nerves causing dilation (vasodilators) and constriction (vasoconstrictors) of blood vessels

.2	**Respiration**

Including comprehensive works on physiology of the nose

Class physiology of the nose as an olfactory organ in 612.86

.21	Biophysics

Including respiratory movements, rhythm, sounds

.22	Biochemistry

Including oxygen supply, gas exchange, carbon dioxide removal

.26	Tissue (Internal) respiration
.28	Innervation of respiratory apparatus
.3	**Digestion**

Class here nutrition

Class dietetics in 613.2

.31	Mouth and esophagus

Including ingestion and start of digestion

.311	Teeth

Including mastication

.312	Tongue and tonsils

Class here comprehensive works on physiology of the tongue

Class physiology of the tongue as a gustatory organ in 612.87

.313	Salivary glands and saliva
.315	Esophagus
.32	Stomach and gastric secretions

Class here comprehensive works on gastrointestinal organs and secretions

For intestine and intestinal secretions, see 612.33

.33	Intestine and intestinal secretions

For large intestine, see 612.36

.34	Pancreas and pancreatic secretions
.35	Biliary tract

Contains liver, gall bladder, bile and bile ducts

.36	Large intestine and defecation
.38	Absorption

Transfer of digested food from the alimentary canal into the blood stream

Class absorption in a specific part of the alimentary canal with the part, e.g., intestine 612.33

.39   Metabolism

Class metabolism of drugs in 615.7, of toxic substances in 615.9; metabolism within a specific function, system, or organ with the function, system, or organ, e.g., the metabolism of plasma 612.116

.391   Hunger and thirst mechanisms

.392   Metabolism of inorganic substances

Class here minerals

.392 3   Water

See Manual at 612.3923 vs. 612.01522

.392 4   Elements

Examples: iron, phosphorus, sulfur

.392 6   Compounds other than water

Example: salts

.396   Carbohydrate metabolism

.397   Lipid metabolism

Including fats

.398   Protein metabolism

.399   Vitamins

.4   Secretion, excretion, related functions

Class here the endocrine system

Use 612.4001–612.4009 for standard subdivisions

Class glands and glandular activity in a specific system or organ with the system or organ, e.g., salivary glands 612.313

For mammary glands and lactation, see 612.664

.405   Hormones

.41   Spleen

Class here comprehensive works on the blood-forming (hematopoietic or hemopoietic) system

Class the physiology of bone marrow in 612.491

.42   Lymph and lymphatics

.43   Thymus gland

.44   Thyroid and parathyroid glands

.45   Adrenal glands

.46	Excretion
	Class here the urinary system
	For defecation, see 612.36
.461	Urine
.463	Kidneys
.467	Ureters, bladder, urethra
.49	Bone marrow and carotid, pituitary, pineal glands
	Use of this number for other glands discontinued; class in 612.4
.491	Bone marrow
.492	Carotid, pituitary, pineal glands
.6	**Reproduction, development, maturation**
	Class here comprehensive medical works on sex
	Interdisciplinary works on sex relocated to 306.7
	Class a specific aspect of sex with the aspect, e.g., sexual disorders 616.69
.600 1–.600 9	Standard subdivisions
.61	Male reproductive system
	Including function in sexual activity
	For climacteric, see 612.665
.62	Female reproductive system
	Including function in sexual activity
	Class pregnancy in 612.63, menstruation in 612.662
	For climacteric, see 612.665
.63	Pregnancy and childbirth
	Including placenta
	Class comprehensive works on pregnancy and childbirth in 618.2, physiology of embryo in 612.64
.64	Physiology of embryo and fetus
	Class here comprehensive works on embryology
	Use 612.64001–612.64009 for standard subdivisions
	For anatomic embryology, see 611.013
.640 1	Development of specific systems, organs, regions
	Add to base number 612.6401 the numbers following 611 in 611.1–611.9, e.g., development of the eye 612.640184
.646	Development of embryo

| .647 | Development of fetus |

> 612.65–612.67 Postnatal development

Class comprehensive works in 612.6; postnatal development of a specific system, organ, region with the system, organ, region, e.g., postnatal development of teeth 612.311

| .65 | Child development |
| .652 | Development of newborn (neonate) |

First month of postnatal development

| .654 | Development from infancy to beginning of puberty |

From second month of postnatal development

| .66 | Adult development and maturity |

For aging, see 612.67

| .661 | Puberty and development prior to attainment of full maturity |
| .662 | Menstruation |

Including menarche

.663	Full maturity
.664	Mammary glands and lactation
.665	Climacteric

Including menopause

| .67 | Aging |

Class here physical gerontology

See also 616.078 for death

.68	Longevity factors
.7	**Motor functions and integument**
.74	Muscles

Class locomotion, exercise, rest in 612.76; muscles of a specific system or organ with the system or organ, e.g., eye muscles 612.846

| .741 | Biophysics |

Including contractions, elasticity, irritability, tonus

| .743 | Innervation |
| .744 | Biochemistry |

Including fatigue products

.75   Bones, joints, connective tissues

           Class bone marrow in 612.491; locomotion, exercise, rest in 612.76

           For mastoid processes, ossicles, see 612.854

.76   Locomotion, exercise, rest

           Including body mechanics

           Class the total physiology of physical movements (including muscle contractions, breathing, blood flow, digestion during exercise) in 612.04

.78   Voice and speech

           Class here organs of speech

.79   Integument   Skin

.791   Biophysics of the skin

           Including absorbency, contractions, irritability, resistivity, tonus

.792   Biochemistry of the skin

.792 1   Glands and glandular secretions

           Example: perspiration

.792 7   Pigmentation

.798   Innervation of the skin

.799   Hair and nails

.8   **Nervous functions   Sensory functions**

           Class here neurophysiology, psychophysiology

           See Manual at 152 vs. 612.8

SUMMARY

612.801–.809		**Standard subdivisions**
	.81	**Nerves and nerve fibers**
	.82	**Brain**
	.83	**Spinal cord**
	.84	**Eyes and vision**
	.85	**Ears and hearing**
	.86	**Nose and smelling**
	.87	**Tongue and tasting**
	.88	**Other sense organs and sensory functions**
	.89	**Autonomic nervous system**

.801   Philosophy and theory

           Use of this number for principles of innervation discontinued; class in 612.8

.804   Special topics

.804 2   Neurochemistry

           Including cerebrospinal fluid

.804 3	Biophysics of the nervous system

.81   **Nerves and nerve fibers**

Class here peripheral nervous system

Class innervation and neural activity in a specific system or organ with the system or organ, e.g., heart innervation 612.178

For autonomic nervous system, see 612.89

.811   Motor and sensory nerves

.813   Biophysics

Including electrophysiology

Class biophysics of a specific kind of nerve with the nerve, e.g., biophysics of cranial nerves 612.819

For irritability, see 612.816

.814   Biochemistry

Class biochemistry of a specific kind of nerve with the nerve, e.g., biochemistry of motor nerves 612.811

.816   Irritability

.819   Cranial and spinal nerves

.82   **Brain**

Class here central nervous system; physiology of memory, of thinking

For spinal cord, see 612.83

See also 153 for psychology of memory and thinking

.821   Sleep phenomena

Physiology of the brain during sleep and dreams

See Manual at 154.6 vs. 612.821

.822   Biochemistry and biophysics

Class biochemistry and biophysics of a specific part of the brain with the part, e.g., biophysics of the cerebrum 612.825

.824   Circulation

Class circulation in a specific part of the brain with the part, e.g., circulation in the cerebellum 612.827

.825   Cerebrum

Including cerebral hemispheres, convolutions, corpus striatum, cortex, rhinencephalon

Class here prosencephalon (forebrain)

For cerebral commissures and peduncles, see 612.826; diencephalon, 612.8262

.825 2   Localization of motor functions

27

.825 5	Localization of sensory functions
.826	Diencephalon and brain stem
	Including cerebral commissures and peduncles
	For medulla oblongata, see 612.828
.826 2	Diencephalon
	Including geniculate bodies, hypothalamus, thalamus
.826 4	Mesencephalon (Midbrain)
	Including corpora quadrigemina
.826 7	Pons Variolii
.827	Cerebellum
.828	Medulla oblongata
.83	Spinal cord

>   612.84–612.88 Sense organs and sensory functions

Class comprehensive works in 612.8

.84	Eyes and vision
	Class here physiological optics, eyeballs
.841	Fibrous tunics, conjunctivas, anterior chambers
	Including corneas, scleras
.842	Uveas
	Contains choroids, ciliary bodies, irises
.843	Optic nerves and retinas
.844	Aqueous humors, crystalline lenses, vitreous bodies
.846	Movements
	Class here ocular neuromuscular mechanism
.847	Eyelids and tear ducts
	Class conjunctivas in 612.841
.85	Ears and hearing
.851	External ears
.854	Middle ears
	Including eustachian tubes (auditory tubes), mastoid processes, ossicles, tympanic membranes

.858   Internal ears

Including cochleas, labyrinths, semicircular canals, vestibules

.86   Nose and smelling

Class here chemical senses

Class comprehensive works on physiology of the nose in 612.2

For tasting, see 612.87

.87   Tongue and tasting

Class comprehensive works on physiology of the tongue in 612.312

.88   Other sense organs and sensory functions

Examples: sense of movement (motion), tactile and proprioceptive organs and senses

Including pain sensations and reactions

.89   Autonomic nervous system

Contains sympathetic and parasympathetic nervous systems

.9   Regional physiology

Including back

Add to base number 612.9 the numbers following 611.9 in 611.91–611.98, e.g., physiology of face 612.92

Class physiology of specific systems and organs in specific regions in 612.1–612.8

613   Promotion of health

Former heading: General and personal hygiene

Including inherited diseases as a factor

Class here measures to promote health and prevent disease taken by the individual and his medical advisers, comprehensive medical works on personal and public measures to promote health and prevent disease

Class public measures to promote health and prevent disease in 614, personal preventive measures applied to specific diseases or groups of diseases in 616–618, child rearing in 649

See Manual at 613 vs. 615.8

SUMMARY

613.04	**Promotion of health of specific sex and age groups**
.1	**Environmental factors**
.2	**Dietetics**
.3	**Beverages**
.4	**Personal cleanliness and related topics**
.5	**Artificial environments**
.6	**Special topics**
.7	**Physical fitness**
.8	**Substance abuse (Drug abuse)**
.9	**Birth control and sex hygiene**

.04	Promotion of health of specific sex and age groups

.042   Promotion of health of specific sex groups

.042 3   Males

.042 32   Boys under twelve

.042 33   Young men

Aged twelve through twenty

.042 34   Adult men

.042 4   Females

.042 42   Girls under twelve

.042 43   Young women

Aged twelve through twenty

.042 44   Adult women

.043   Promotion of health of specific age groups

Class promotion of health of specific age groups of specific sexes in 613.042

.043 2   Infants and children

Through age eleven

Class here pediatric preventive measures

.043 3   Young adults

Aged twelve through twenty

.043 4   Mature adults

Examples: college-age, middle-aged persons

For persons in late adulthood, see 613.0438

.043 8   Persons in late adulthood

Former heading: Adults aged 65 and over

Class here geriatric preventive measures

[.081–.084]   Persons of specific sex and age groups

Do not use; class in 613.04

.1   **Environmental factors**

Class here acclimation

For artificial environments, see 613.5

.11   Weather and climate

For seasonal changes, see 613.13; humidity, 613.14

.111   Cold weather and climate

Example: arctic climate

.113   Hot weather and climate

Example: tropical climate

.12   Physiographic and other regions

Examples: mountains, seashore

.122   Health resorts

.13   Seasonal changes

.14   Humidity

.19   Air and light

.192   Breathing

.193   Sun bathing

.194   Nudism

.2   **Dietetics**

Comprehensive works on diet and physical fitness relocated to 613.7

Class human nutritional requirements considered in relation to physiological processes and the role of nutrients in the body in 612.3; diet therapy in 615.854; dietetics for pregnant women in 618.24; diets to prevent a specific disease with the disease, using notation 05 from the tables under 616.1–616.9, 617, 618.1–618.8

For beverages, see 613.3

See also 616.39 for conditions resulting from nutritional deficiencies, 641.563 for cooking for preventive and therapeutic diets, 649.3 for domestic aspects of feeding children

See Manual at 613.2 vs. 641.3, 363.8

.24   Weight-gaining programs

.25   Weight-losing programs

.26 Specific dietary regimens

Example: regimens involving specific foods

Including breast feeding

Class interdisciplinary works on breast feeding in 649.33, regimens involving specific nutritive elements in 613.28

For weight-gaining programs, see 613.24; weight-losing programs, 613.25

.262 Vegetarian

.28 Specific nutritive elements

Examples: diets high and low in carbohydrates, fats, proteins, salt

Class weight modification programs involving specific nutritive elements in 613.24–613.25

.3 Beverages

Class personal aspects of preventing alcohol abuse in 613.81

.4 Personal cleanliness and related topics

Class personal grooming in 646.7

.41 Bathing

.48 Clothing and cosmetics

.482 Clothing

.488 Cosmetics

.5 Artificial environments

In enclosed spaces

Examples: homes, offices

Including indoor temperatures and air conditioning

.6 Special topics

Class here personal safety

Class personal safety in a specific field with the subject, using notation 0289 from Table 1, e.g., personal safety in welding 671.520289

.62 Industrial and occupational health

See Manual at 613.62 vs. 363.11

.66 Self-defense

.67 Military and camp health

.68 Travel health

Example: shipboard health

.69   Survival

            After accidents and disasters, in other unfavorable circumstances

            For self-defense, see 613.66

.7   Physical fitness

            Class here comprehensive works on diet and physical fitness [*formerly* 613.2]

            For breathing, see 613.192

.704   Special topics

            ─────────────

>   613.704 2–613.704 5 Specific age and sex groups

            Class comprehensive works in 613.704, physical yoga of specific age and sex groups in 613.7046

.704 2   Physical fitness of children

.704 3   Physical fitness of young adults

                Aged twelve through twenty

.704 4   Physical fitness of adults

                Class physical fitness of adult women in 613.7045

.704 46   Physical fitness of persons in late adulthood

                    Class physical fitness of men in late adulthood in 613.70449

.704 49   Physical fitness of adult men

                    Class here physical fitness of males

                    Class physical fitness of boys in 613.7042, of young men (aged twelve to twenty) in 613.7043

.704 5   Physical fitness of adult women

                Class here physical fitness of females

                Class physical fitness of girls in 613.7042, of young women (aged twelve to twenty) in 613.7043

.704 6   Physical yoga

                Class here hatha yoga

                Class exercises from the martial arts traditions in 613.7148

[.708 1–.708 4]   Persons of specific sex and age groups

                    Do not use; class in 613.7042–613.7045

.71   Exercise [*formerly also* 796.4] and sports activities

Class here aerobic exercise, comprehensive works on exercise and sports activities for fitness and for improvement in the shape of the body

Class physical yoga in 613.7046, exercises to aid childbirth in 618.24, exercise and sports activities to improve the shape of the body in 646.75, parental supervision of children's exercise and sports activities in 649.57

See Manual at 613.71 vs. 646.75, 796

[.710 247 96]   For persons occupied with athletics and sports

Do not use; class in 613.711

[.710 887 96]   Treatment with respect to persons occupied with athletics and sports

Do not use; class in 613.711

.711   Fitness training for sports

Including fitness training for specific sports not provided for below, e.g., football

Class here promotion of health of athletes

Class specific kinds of fitness training with the kind, e.g., weight lifting 613.713; fitness training for specific sports listed below with the sport, e.g., swimming 613.716

.713   Weight lifting [*formerly also* 796.41]

See Manual at 613.71 vs. 646.75, 796

.714   Calisthenics [*formerly also* 796.41] and isometric exercises

Class here gymnastic exercises [*formerly also* 796.41]

Standard subdivisions are added for calisthenics and isometric exercises, or for calisthenics alone

See also 613.713 for weight lifting, 613.715 for aerobic dancing, 613.716 for aquatic exercises

.714 8   Exercises from the martial arts traditions

Examples: aikido, karate exercises

Class here fitness training for the martial arts, T'ai chi ch'üan exercises

See also 796.8 for the martial arts as sports

.714 9   Isometric exercises

.715   Aerobic dancing

.716   Aquatic exercises and swimming

.717   Running and walking

.717 2   Running

.717 6   Walking

.78   Correct posture

.79   Relaxation, rest, sleep

.8   **Substance abuse (Drug abuse)**

Limited to personal preventive aspects

Examples: abuse of analgesics, depressants, inhalants, sedatives, tranquilizers

Class here appeals to the individual to avoid substance abuse for health reasons

Class interdisciplinary works on substance abuse in 362.29, comprehensive medical works on addictive and disorienting drugs in 615.78, comprehensive medical works on substance abuse as a disease in 616.86

.81   Alcohol

Class here personal aspects of prevention of alcoholism

.83   Narcotics, hallucinogens, psychedelics, cannabis

Use of this number for comprehensive works on personal aspects of preventing drug abuse discontinued; class in 613.8

.835   Cannabis

Class here specific kinds of cannabis, e.g., hashish, marijuana

.84   Stimulants and related substances

Examples: amphetamine, ephedrine; cocaine

Class nicotine in 613.85

.85   Tobacco

.9   **Birth control and sex hygiene**

.907   Education, research, related topics

Class sex education of children in the home in 649.65

.94   Birth control (Contraception)

Including artificial insemination, measures to increase the likelihood of having a child of the desired sex

Class here family planning

Class interdisciplinary works on birth control and family planning in 363.96

.942   Surgical methods

Limited to personal health aspects

Examples: tubal sterilization, vasectomy

Class comprehensive works on surgical methods of birth control for males in 617.463; for females in 618.1, e.g., tubal sterilization 618.12059

.943	Chemical, rhythm, mechanical methods
.943 2	Chemical
	Limited to personal health aspects
	Example: pills (oral contraceptives)
	Class the pharmacodynamics of chemical contraceptives in 615.766
.943 4	Rhythm
.943 5	Mechanical
	Example: intrauterine devices
.95	Sex hygiene
	Class manuals of sexual technique in 613.96
[.950 81–.950 84]	Sex hygiene of specific age and sex groups
	Do not use; class in 613.951–613.955
.951	Sex hygiene of children and young adults
	Through age twenty
	Class sex hygiene of boys and young men in 613.953, of girls and young women in 613.955
.952	Sex hygiene of adult men
	Class here sex hygiene of males
	Class sex hygiene of boys and young men (through age twenty) in 613.953
.953	Sex hygiene of boys and young men
	Through age twenty
.954	Sex hygiene of adult women
	Class here sex hygiene of females
	Class sex hygiene of girls and young women (through age twenty) in 613.955
.955	Sex hygiene of girls and young women
	Through age twenty
.96	Manuals of sexual technique

614 Forensic medicine, incidence of disease, public preventive medicine

Former heading: Public health and related topics

Class social provision for public health services other than those concerned with incidence and prevention of disease in 362.1, public safety programs in 363.1, environmental problems and services in 363.7

SUMMARY

.1   **Forensic medicine (Medical jurisprudence)**

Examples: determination of time and cause of death; of cause, nature and extent of injury

Including forensic dentistry, psychiatry, toxicology

.4   **Incidence of and public measures to prevent disease**

Class here epidemiology

For incidence of and public measures to prevent specific diseases and kinds of diseases, see 614.5

See also 351.774 for premarital examinations and certification, 351.816 for registration and certification of births and deaths

See Manual at 614.4; 614.4–614.5 vs. 362.1–362.4

.409   Historical, geographical, persons treatment of epidemiology

Class geographical treatment of incidence of diseases in 614.42, history of epidemics in 614.49

.42   Incidence

Rate, range, or amount of occurrence

Class here health surveys, medical geography

.422   Treatment by areas, regions, places in general

Add to base number 614.422 the numbers following —1 in notation 11–19 from Table 2, e.g., diseases in the tropics 614.4223

.423–.429   Treatment by specific continents, countries, localities

Add to base number 614.42 notation 3–9 from Table 2, e.g., diseases in the United States 614.4273

.43   Disease carriers (Vectors) and their control

Class diseases transmitted by vertebrates other than humans in 614.56

.432   Insects

.432 2   Flies

.432 3   Mosquitoes

.432 4   Lice and fleas

.433   Arachnids

Examples: mites, ticks

.434   Birds

.438   Rodents

.44   Public preventive medicine

For specific preventive measures, see 614.45–614.48

> 614.45–614.48 Specific preventive measures

Class comprehensive works in 614.44

.45   Isolation

Prevention of the spread of disease in homes, hospitals, schools, public places through isolation

For quarantine, see 614.46

.46   Quarantine

Isolation procedures at frontiers and ports of entry

Class comprehensive works on isolation in 614.45

.47   Immunization

Public measures for preventing disease through protective inoculation

.48   Disinfection, fumigation, sterilization

.49   History of epidemics

Add to base number 614.49 notation 1–9 from Table 2, e.g., history of epidemics in the United Kingdom 614.4941

.5   **Incidence of and public measures to prevent specific diseases and kinds of diseases**

Class incidence of and public measures to prevent mental and emotional illnesses and disturbances in 362.2

See Manual at 614.5; 614.4–614.5 vs. 362.1–362.4

SUMMARY

614.51	Salmonella and bacillary diseases, cholera, dysentery, epidemic diarrhea, influenza
.52	Eruptive diseases (Exanthems) and rickettsial diseases
.53	Protozoan diseases
.54	Miscellaneous diseases
.55	Parasitic diseases
.56	Zoonoses
.57	Bacterial and viral diseases
.59	Diseases of regions, systems, organs; other diseases

.51	Salmonella and bacillary diseases, cholera, dysentery, epidemic diarrhea, influenza
.511	Salmonella diseases
.511 2	Typhoid fever (Enteric fever)
.511 4	Paratyphoid fever
.512	Bacillary diseases

> *For bacillary dysentery, see 614.516*

.512 3	Diphtheria
.512 5	Botulism
.512 8	Tetanus
.514	Cholera

> *See Manual at 616.932 vs. 616.33*

.516	Amebic and bacillary dysentery
.517	Epidemic diarrhea
.518	Influenza

> Including acute influenzalike diseases in epidemic form

.52	Eruptive diseases (Exanthems) and rickettsial diseases
.521	Smallpox (Variola major) and attenuated forms
.522	Scarlet fever (Scarlatina)
.523	Measles (Rubeola)
.524	German measles (Rubella)
.525	Chicken pox (Varicella)
.526	Rickettsial diseases

> Add to base number 614.526 the numbers following 616.922 in 616.9222–616.9226, e.g., Q fever 614.5265

.53	Protozoan diseases

> Add to base number 614.53 the numbers following 616.936 in 616.9362–616.9364, e.g., malaria 614.532

> *For amebic dysentery, see 614.516*

.54	Miscellaneous diseases

> Limited to the diseases provided for below

.541	Yellow fever
.542	Tuberculosis
.543	Whooping cough (Pertussis)
.544	Mumps (Epidemic parotitis)

.545   Puerperal septicemia and pyemia

> Class comprehensive works on incidence of and public measures to prevent septicemia and pyemia in 614.577

.546   Leprosy (Hansen's disease)

.547   Venereal diseases

> Class Acquired Immune Deficiency Syndrome (AIDS) in 614.5993

.547 2   Syphilis

.547 8   Gonorrhea

.549   Poliomyelitis

.55   Parasitic diseases

> Add to base number 614.55 the numbers following 616.96 in 616.962–616.969, e.g., schistosomiasis 614.553; however, class trichinosis in 614.562

.56   Zoonoses

> Class incidence of and public measures to prevent a specific zoonosis not provided for here with the disease, e.g., Q fever 614.5265

.561   Anthrax

> Variant names: charbon, splenic fever
>
> Example: Woolsorters' disease

.562   Trichinosis

.563   Rabies (Hydrophobia)

.564   Glanders (Equinia)

.565   Undulant fever (Brucellosis)

.566   Parrot fever (Psittacosis)

.57   Bacterial and viral diseases

.571   Dengue fever

.573–.575   Bacterial and other viral diseases

> Add to base number 614.57 the numbers following 616.92 in 616.923–616.925, e.g., tularemia 614.5739
>
> *For bacterial blood diseases, see 614.577*

.577   Bacterial blood diseases

> Examples: erysipelas, pyemia, septicemia
>
> Class puerperal septicemia and pyemia in 614.545

.59   Diseases of regions, systems, organs; other diseases

.591–.598   Diseases of regions, systems, organs

Add to base number 614.59 the numbers following 616 in 616.1–616.8, e.g., heart disease 614.5912, nutritional diseases 614.5939; however, class epidemic diarrhea in 614.517; allergies affecting specific regions, systems, organs in 614.5993; tumors (neoplasms) of regions, systems, organs in 614.5999

See Manual at 614.5939 vs. 363.82

.599   Other diseases

.599 2   Gynecological, obstetrical, pediatric, geriatric disorders

Class puerperal septicemia and pyemia in 614.545

.599 3   Diseases of the immune system

Examples: allergies; autoimmune diseases; immune deficiency diseases, e.g., acquired immune deficiency syndrome (AIDS)

.599 6   Dental diseases

Including fluoridation of water supply

.599 7   Eye diseases

.599 8   Ear diseases

.599 9   Tumors (Neoplasms)

Benign and malignant

Class public programs to control cancer-causing agents in 363.179, to control carcinogens in food in 363.192

.6   Disposal of the dead

Class social aspects and services in 363.75

615   Pharmacology and therapeutics

See Manual at 615

SUMMARY

.1   **Drugs (Materia medica)**

Substances used for diagnosis, cure, mitigation, treatment, or prevention of disease

Class here pharmacology

Class drug therapy in 615.58

> *For specific drugs and groups of drugs, see 615.2–615.3; practical pharmacy, 615.4; physiological and therapeutic action of drugs, 615.7*
>
> *See Manual at 615.1 vs. 615.7*

.11   Pharmacopeias

Add to base number 615.11 notation 3–9 from Table 2, e.g., pharmacopeias of Japan 615.1152

[.12]   Dispensatories

Relocated to 615.13

.13   Formularies

Class here dispensatories [*formerly* 615.12]

Add to base number 615.13 notation 3–9 from Table 2, e.g., formularies of the United States 615.1373

.14   Posology

Including incompatibilities

Class here dosage determination, prescription writing

.18   Drug preservation technique

Class here packaging designed to preserve drug quality and potency

.19   Pharmaceutical chemistry

Development, manufacture, analysis of drugs

.190 01   Philosophy and theory

.190 02   Miscellany

[.190 028 7]   Testing and measurement

Do not use; class in 615.1901

.190 03–.190 09   Standard subdivisions

.190 1   Analysis

[.190 15–.190 18]   Chemical analysis and assay methods

Numbers discontinued; class in 615.1901

[.191]   Manufacture and preparation

Number discontinued; class in 615.19

> ### 615.2–615.3 Specific drugs and groups of drugs

General aspects: pharmaceutical chemistry, preservation, general therapeutics

Class comprehensive works in 615.1, a specific drug or group of drugs affecting a specific system in 615.7

See Manual at 615.2–615.3; 615.2–615.3 vs. 615.7

.2   **Inorganic drugs**

Add to base number 615.2 the numbers following 546 in 546.2–546.7, e.g., calomel 615.2663

Class radiopharmacy (the use of radioactive medicines) in 615.842

.3   **Organic drugs**

See Manual at 615.2–615.3

.31   Synthetic drugs

Add to base number 615.31 the numbers following 547.0 in 547.01–547.08, e.g., sulfonamides 615.3167

Class a specific synthetic drug not provided for here with the drug, e.g., synthetic vitamins 615.328

.32   Drugs of plant origin

Class enzymes of plant origin in 615.35

.321   Pharmacognosy

Class here herbals, minimally processed alkaloids; comprehensive works on crude drugs and simples (products that serve as drugs with minimal processing, e.g., medicinal teas, baking soda, royal jelly)

For drugs derived from specific plants, see 615.323–615.327

.322   Drugs derived from bryophytes

Add to base number 615.322 the numbers following 588 in 588.1–588.3, e.g., drugs derived from Musci 615.3222

.323–.327   Drugs derived from specific plants

Add to base number 615.32 the numbers following 58 in 583–587, e.g., belladonna 615.32379

For drugs derived from bryophytes, see 615.322; drugs derived from thallophytes, 615.329

.328   Vitamins

Including synthetic vitamins, vitamins of animal origin

Class here vitamin therapy [*formerly also* 615.854]

.329   Drugs derived from thallophytes

Class here antibiotics

Add to base number 615.329 the numbers following 589 in 589.1–589.9, e.g., streptomycin 615.32992

.34   Fish-liver oils

.35   Enzymes

Examples: chymotrypsin, diastase, papain, pepsin, trypsin

.36   Drugs of animal origin

Class here hormones

Class each drug of animal origin not provided for here with the subject, e.g., fish-liver oils 615.34

.362   Thyroid and parathyroid extracts

.363   Pituitary hormones

Example: ACTH (adrenocorticotrophic hormone) [*formerly also* 615.364]

.364   Adrenal hormones

Examples: adrenalin, aldosterone, cortisone

ACTH (adrenocorticotrophic hormone) relocated to 615.363

For sex hormones, see 615.366

.365   Insulin

.366   Sex hormones

.367   Liver extracts

.37   Serums and immunological drugs

.372   Vaccines, bacterins, serobacterins

.373   Toxins and toxoids

.375   Antitoxins, toxin-antitoxins, convalescent serums

.39   Human blood products and their substitutes

Examples: gamma globulins, plasma substitutes

Including blood and blood plasma transfusion [*formerly* 615.65]

For convalescent serums, see 615.375

See also 362.1784 for blood and blood plasma banks

.4   **Practical pharmacy**

Preparing prescriptions and dispensing drugs

See Manual at 615.4

.42   Solutions and extracts

               Examples: collodions, decoctions, elixirs, glycerites, infusions, syrups, tinctures

.43   Pills, capsules, tablets, troches, powders

.45   Ointments and emulsions

.5   **Therapeutics**

               Class here comprehensive works on iatrogenic diseases, patient compliance, placebo effect

               Class therapies applied to specific diseases or groups of diseases in 616–618; specific occurrences of iatrogenic diseases, patient compliance, placebo effect with the occurrence, e.g., drug interactions not anticipated by a doctor 615.7045, surgical complications and sequelae 617.01

               For specific therapies and kinds of therapies, see 615.8; first aid, 616.0252

.507   Education, research, related topics

               Class here patient education by nurses [*formerly* 610.73], comprehensive works on patient education

               Class patient education on a specific topic with the topic, e.g., patient education about diabetes mellitus 616.462007

.53   General therapeutic systems

               Including eclectic and botanic medicine

               Class here Ayurveda (''Hindu medicine'')

               Class drug therapy regardless of system in 615.58

               See also 615.32 for botanic remedies

               See Manual at 615.53

.530 28   Auxiliary techniques and procedures; apparatus, equipment, materials

               Class methods of administering medication in 615.6

.531   Allopathy

               System of therapy based on the theory that the best cure is a treatment having effects that are opposite to the effects of the disease

               Class allopathy as a synonym for orthodox or standard medical practice in medical numbers other than 615.531

.532   Homeopathy

.533   Osteopathy

               As a therapeutic system

               Class osteopathy as a medical science in medical numbers other than 615.533, e.g., osteopathic medical education 610.7, osteopathic discussion of thyroid diseases 616.44

.534   Chiropractic

> *See Manual at 615.534*

.535   Naturopathy

[.537]   Eclectic and botanic medicine

> Number discontinued; class in 615.53

.54   Pediatric and geriatric therapeutics

.542   Pediatric therapeutics

> Class a specific aspect of pediatric therapeutics with the subject, e.g., medical gymnastics 615.824

.547   Geriatric therapeutics

> Class a specific aspect of geriatric therapeutics with the subject, e.g., acupuncture 615.892

.58   Drug therapy

> Class here chemotherapy
>
> Class general therapeutics of a specific drug or group of drugs in 615.2–615.3
>
> *For methods of administering medication, see 615.6*

.6   **Methods of administering medication**

> Examples: external, inhalatory, oral, rectal methods; parenteral methods (e.g., intra-arterial, intradermal, intramuscular, intravenous, subcutaneous injections); administering medication through serous and mucous membranes
>
> Use this number only for works that focus narrowly on methods of administering medication
>
> Class methods of administering a specific drug or group of drugs in 615.2–615.3; general works on a specific type of therapy with the therapy, e.g., drug therapy 615.58, inhalatory therapy 615.836, parenteral therapy 615.855

[.61–.64]   Oral, rectal, parenteral, inhalatory medication

> Numbers discontinued; class in 615.6

[.65]   Blood and blood plasma transfusions

> Relocated to 615.39

[.66–.67]   Medication through serous and mucous membranes; external medication

> Numbers discontinued; class in 615.6

.7   Pharmacodynamics

Physiological and therapeutic action of drugs

Class here pharmacokinetics

> *For toxicology, see 615.9*
>
> *See Manual at 612.1–612.8; 615.1 vs. 615.7; 615.2–615.3 vs. 615.7; 615.7 vs. 615.9; 615.7 vs. 616–618*

.704   Special effects and actions of drugs

Class here adverse reactions, toxic reactions

Class drug allergies in 616.975

.704 2   Side effects

[.704 3]   Aftereffects

Number discontinued; class in 615.704

.704 5   Interactions

.71   Drugs affecting the cardiovascular system

.711   Heart stimulants

.716   Heart depressants

.718   Drugs affecting the blood and blood-forming organs

.72   Drugs affecting the respiratory system

Examples: cough remedies, expectorants

.73   Drugs affecting the digestive system and metabolism

.731   Emetics

.732   Cathartics (Laxatives, Purgatives)

.733   Anthelmintics

.734   Digestants

.735   Demulcents

.739   Drugs affecting metabolism

.74   Drugs affecting the lymphatic and glandular systems

.75   Antipyretics (Febrifuges)

.76   Drugs affecting the urogenital system

.761   Drugs affecting the urinary system

Examples: diuretics, antidiuretics

.766   Drugs affecting the reproductive system

.77	Drugs affecting the motor and integumentary systems
.771	Drugs affecting the bones
.773	Drugs affecting the muscles
.778	Drugs affecting the skin
.779	Drugs affecting nails and hair
.78	Drugs affecting the nervous system

Class here psychopharmacology, comprehensive medical works on addictive and disorienting drugs

Class interdisciplinary works on drug addiction in 362.29, comprehensive medical works on addictions as diseases in 616.86, works on personal aspects of preventing drug addiction in 613.8

For antipyretics, see 615.75

See also 178 for the ethics of using addictive and disorienting drugs

.781	Anesthetics
.782	Sedative-hypnotic drugs

Example: barbiturates

.782 2	Narcotics
.782 7	Cannabis

Example: marijuana

.782 8	Alcohol
.783	Analgesics

Including comprehensive works on drugs used as both analgesics and antipyretics

Class antipyretic use in 615.75

.784	Antispasmodics (Anticonvulsants)
.785	Stimulants
.788	Psychotropic drugs
.788 2	Tranquilizers

Examples: chlorpromazine, diazepam, meprobamate

.788 3	Hallucinogenic and psychedelic drugs
.8	**Specific therapies and kinds of therapies**

Class comprehensive works in 615.5, drug therapy in 615.58, surgery in 617

See Manual at 613 vs. 615.8; 615.8

.804	Special topics
.804 3	Therapies directed toward a specific objective

Example: resuscitation

.82	Physical therapies

Class here physiotherapy, therapeutic manipulations and exercises

For phototherapy and related therapies, see 615.83; radiotherapy and electrotherapy, 615.84; hydrotherapy and balneotherapy, 615.853

.822	Mechanotherapy and therapeutic massage

Example: acupressure

Class here comprehensive works on massage

Class reducing and slenderizing massage in 646.75

.824	Medical gymnastics
.83	Therapies of light, heat, sound

Including ultrasonic therapy

.831	Phototherapy
.831 4	Heliotherapy
.831 5	Ultraviolet-radiation therapy
.832	Thermotherapy
.832 2	Infrared-radiation therapy
.832 3	Diathermy (Thermopenetration)
.832 5	Fever therapy
.832 9	Cryotherapy
.834	Climatotherapy
.836	Aerotherapy and inhalation therapy

Examples: oxygen and carbon dioxide therapies, pneumatotherapy

.84	Radiotherapy and electrotherapy
.842	Radiotherapy (Radiation therapy, Actinotherapy)

For phototherapy, see 615.831

.842 2	X-ray therapy
.842 3	Radium therapy
.842 4	Radioactive isotope therapy

Class radium therapy in 615.8423

.845	Electrotherapy

Example: electronic therapy

Including magnetic therapy

.85	Miscellaneous therapies

Limited to the therapies provided for below

.851	Mental and activity therapies
	For faith healing, see 615.852
.851 2	Hypnotherapy (Suggestion therapy)
.851 5	Activity (Occupational) therapies
	For biblio- and educational therapies, see 615.8516
[.851 52]	Occupational therapy
	Number discontinued; class in 615.8515
.851 53	Recreational therapy
.851 54	Music therapy
.851 55	Dance therapy
.851 56	Art therapy
.851 6	Biblio- and educational therapies
.852	Religious therapy (Hierotherapy, Faith healing)
	Including psychic and spiritualistic surgery
.853	Hydrotherapy and balneotherapy
.854	Dietotherapy
	Vitamin therapy relocated to 615.328
	See Manual at 615.854
.855	Parenteral therapy
.856	Controversial and spurious therapies
	Class here quackery
	Specific controversial or spurious therapies relocated to the kind of therapy, e.g., controversial dietotherapy 615.854
.88	Empirical and historical remedies
	Class here home remedies
	For ancient and medieval remedies, see 615.899
	See Manual at 615.8809
.882	Folk medicine
	See Manual at 615.8809; 615.882
.886	Patent medicines
.89	Other therapies
.892	Acupuncture
	Class here comprehensive works on acupuncture and acupressure
	Class acupressure in 615.822

.899   Ancient and medieval remedies

See Manual at 615.8809

.9   Toxicology

Class here poisons and poisoning

Class forensic toxicology in 614.1, effects of poisons on specific systems and organs in 616–618

See Manual at 615.7 vs. 615.9

.900 1   Philosophy and theory

.900 2   Miscellany

[.900 287]   Testing and measurement

Do not use; class in 615.907

.900 3–.900 9   Standard subdivisions

.902   Industrial toxicology

Including toxicology of pollution

Class here environmental toxicology

Class toxic reactions and interactions of drugs in 615.704, toxicology of food additives in 615.954

.905   Prevention of poisoning

.907   Tests, analysis, detection of poisons and poisoning

Class here diagnoses and prognoses of poisoning

The topics listed under 616.075 Diagnoses and prognoses are all included here

.908   Treatment of poisoning

.91   Gaseous poisons

Example: asphyxiating gases

Class here lethal gases

.92   Inorganic poisons

Class gaseous inorganic poisons in 615.91, radiation poisoning in 616.9897

.921   Acids

Class specific acids in 615.925

.922   Alkalis

Class specific alkalis in 615.925

.925   Specific inorganic poisons

Add to base number 615.925 the numbers following 546 in 546.2–546.7, e.g., mercurial poisons 615.925663

.94　　　　Animal poisons

.942　　　　Venoms

Examples: bee, scorpion, snake, spider venoms

.945　　　　Poisonous food animals

Example: poisonous fish

Including mammalian organs; food animals made poisonous by microorganisms, e.g., shellfish made poisonous by red tides

.95　　　　Organic poisons

Class gaseous organic poisons in 615.91

For animal poisons, see 615.94

.951　　　　Synthetic and manufactured poisons

Add to base number 615.951 the numbers following 547.0 in 547.01–547.08, e.g., ethers 615.95135

.952　　　　Plant and plant-derived poisons

Add to base number 615.952 the numbers following 58 in 583–589, e.g., opium 615.9523122, bacterial food poisons 615.95299

Class food animals made poisonous by plants in 615.945

.954　　　　Food poisons

Including toxicology of food additives

Class poisonous food animals in 615.945; plant and plant-derived poisons in 615.952, e.g., bacterial food poisons 615.95299

616　Diseases

Class here internal medicine

Class wounds and injuries, surgical treatment of diseases, diseases by body region, diseases of teeth, eyes, ears in 617; gynecological, obstetrical, pediatric, geriatric diseases in 618

For incidence of and public measures to prevent disease, see 614.4; therapeutics, 615.5

See Manual at 612 vs. 616; 615.7 vs. 616–618; 616 vs. 610; 616 vs. 616.075; 616.01; 616.01 vs. 616.9; 617 vs. 616; 617.4 vs. 616; 618.92 vs. 616, 618.32

SUMMARY

616.001–.009	**Standard subdivisions**
.01–.09	**[General topics]**
.1	**Diseases of the cardiovascular system**
.2	**Diseases of the respiratory system**
.3	**Diseases of the digestive system**
.4	**Diseases of the blood-forming, lymphatic, glandular systems Diseases of the endocrine system**
.5	**Diseases of the integument, hair, nails**
.6	**Diseases of the urogenital system Diseases of the urinary system**
.7	**Diseases of the musculoskeletal system**
.8	**Diseases of the nervous system and mental disorders**
.9	**Other diseases**

.001   Philosophy and theory

> *See Manual at 616 vs. 610*

.002   Miscellany

> *See Manual at 616 vs. 610*

[.002 3]   Work with diseases as a profession, occupation, hobby

> Do not use; class in 610.69

[.002 87]   Testing and measurement

> Do not use; class in 616.075

.003–.007   Standard subdivisions

> *See Manual at 616 vs. 610*

.008   History and description with respect to kinds of persons

> *See Manual at 616 vs. 610*

.008 3   Young people

> Class diseases of infants and children up to puberty in 618.92

.008 4   Persons in specific stages of adulthood

[.008 46]   Late adulthood

> Do not use; class in 618.97

.009   Historical, geographical, persons treatment

> *See Manual at 616 vs. 610*

.009 2   Persons

> Class life with a physical disease in 362.19, with a mental disorder in 616.890092

SUMMARY

616.01	**Medical microbiology**	
.02	**Special topics**	
.04	**Special medical conditions**	
.07	**Pathology**	
.08	**Psychosomatic medicine**	
.09	**Case histories**	

.01   Medical microbiology

Study of pathogenic microorganisms and their relation to disease

Class here drug resistance in microorganisms

Class resistance to specific drugs in 615

See Manual at 616.01; 616.01 vs. 616.9

.014   Bacteria

Add to base number 616.014 the numbers following 589.9 in 589.92–589.99, e.g., Enterobacteriaceae 616.0145

For rickettsiae, see 616.0192

.015   Fungi

.016   Protozoa

.019   Ultramicrobes

.019 2   Rickettsiae

.019 4   Viruses

.02   Special topics

.024   Domestic medicine

Diagnosis and treatment of ailments without direction of physician

Including advice on when to go to a doctor

For first aid, see 616.0252

See also 649.8 for home care of sick and infirm

.025   Medical emergencies

Class intensive care in 616.028

.025 2   First aid

.028   Intensive (Critical) care

.029   Terminal care

.04   Special medical conditions

.042   Genetic (Hereditary) diseases

Class amniocentesis to diagnose genetic diseases in 618.32042

.043 Congenital diseases

Including teratology

Class congenital diseases of genetic origin in 616.042

See Manual at 618.92 vs. 616, 618.32

.047 Manifestations of disease

Symptoms as problems in their own right

Examples: edemas, fevers, infections, shock

Class here symptomatology [*formerly* 616.072]; pathology, diagnosis, treatment of symptoms of various etiologies

Class interpretation of symptoms for diagnosis and prognosis in 616.075; symptoms of a specific disease or class of diseases with the disease, e.g., symptoms of heart diseases 616.12

.047 2 Pain

Headaches of unknown origin relocated to 616.8491

Class headaches in 616.8491

.047 3 Inflammation

.07 Pathology

Use for detailed descriptions of diseased conditions, causes and manifestations, diagnostic techniques. For works lacking detail, prefer 616 over 616.07

Class forensic pathology in 614.1

For cytopathology, see 611.01815; histopathology, 611.0182–611.0189; medical microbiology, 616.01

.071 Etiology

Class social factors contributing to the spread of a disease in 362.1042, genetic diseases in 616.042

[.072] Symptomatology

Relocated to 616.047

.075 Diagnosis and prognosis

Including ocular diagnosis

Class here differential diagnosis

Class nonprofessional diagnosis in 616.024

See Manual at 616 vs. 616.075

.075 1 Medical history taking

.075 4	Physical diagnosis
	Including thermography
	Class here comprehensive works on diagnostic imaging
	For radiological diagnosis, see 616.0757
	See Manual at 616.0757
.075 43	Ultrasonic diagnosis
	Class here sonography (echography)
.075 44	Sound
.075 45	Optical diagnosis
	Class here endoscopy
	Class microscopy in 616.0758
.075 47	Electrical diagnosis
.075 48	Magnetic diagnosis
	Class here nuclear magnetic resonance (NMR) imaging
.075 6	Chemical diagnosis
	Example: immunodiagnosis
	Class here clinical chemistry
	Class radioimmunoassay in 616.0757
.075 61	Blood analysis
.075 63	Analysis of gastroenteric contents
.075 66	Urinalysis
	Class radioscopic urinalysis in 616.0757
.075 7	Radiological diagnosis
	Diagnosis involving use of X-rays, radioactive materials, other ionizing radiations
	Examples: radioimmunoassay, radioscopic urinalysis
	Class here comprehensive works on tomography, on medical radiology
	For radiotherapy, see 615.842
	See Manual at 616.0757
.075 72	Roentgenology (X-ray examination)
	Including computerized axial (computed) tomography (CAT, CT), fluoroscopy
	Use of this number for comprehensive works on tomography discontinued; class in 616.0757
	See Manual at 616.0757

.075 75	Radioisotope scanning

Often called nuclear medicine

Including positron emission tomography (PET)

See also 616.07548 for nuclear magnetic resonance imaging

.075 8	Microscopy in diagnosis

Class here biopsies

.075 81	Bacteriological examination
.075 82	Cytological examination
.075 83	Histological and histochemical examination
.075 9	Autopsy (Post-mortem examination)

Class forensic autopsy in 614.1

.078	Death

Class interdisciplinary works on human death in 306.9

.079	Immunity (Immunology) [*formerly also* 612.11822]

Including interferon, reticuloendothelial system

Class here immunogenetics

Failures of immunity relocated to 616.97, autoimmunity to 616.978

Class immunodiagnosis in 616.0756

See Manual at 591.29 vs. 616.079

.079 2	Antigens
.079 3	Antibodies
.079 5	Immune reactions

Examples: agglutination, precipitation

Class here serology

.08	Psychosomatic medicine

This number is largely limited to the psychosomatic aspects of the diseases defined in 616.1–616.7, 616.9

Class comprehensive works on psychological and psychosomatic aspects of disease in 616.0019, psychosomatic symptoms considered as problems in their own right in 616.047, mental disorders and their somatic manifestation in 616.89, diseases caused by stress in 616.98

See also 616.8525 for hypochondriacal neuroses

.09	Case histories

> **616.1–616.9 Specific diseases**

All notes under 616.01–616.08 are applicable here

Except for additions, changes, deletions, exceptions shown under specific
entries, add to the notation for each term identified by * as follows:

001	Philosophy and theory
002	Miscellany
[0023]	The specialty as a profession, occupation, hobby
	Do not use; class in 023
[00287]	Testing and measurement
	Do not use; class in 075
003–006	Standard subdivisions
007	Education, research, related topics
[00724]	Experimental research
	Do not use; class in 027
008	History and description with respect to kinds of persons
0083	Young people
	Class diseases of infants and children up to puberty in 618.92
0084	Persons in specific stages of adulthood
[00846]	Late adulthood
	Do not use; class in 618.97
009	Historical, geographical, persons treatment
0092	Persons
	Class life with a physical disease in 362.19, with a mental disorder in 616.890092
01	Microbiology
	Add to 01 the numbers following 616.01 in 616.014–616.019, e.g., fungi 015
	When the cause of a disease or class of diseases is known to be a single type of microorganism, use 01 without further subdivision for works about the type of microorganism
	See Manual at 616.1–616.9: Add table: 071 vs. 01
02	Special topics
023	Personnel
	Nature of duties, characteristics of profession, relationships
	Do not use for the technology of the operations that the personnel perform, e.g., techniques used by a cardiological paramedic 616.12 (*not* 616.120233)
0232	Physicians
0233	Technicians and assistants
024	Domestic medicine
	Class a specific kind of therapy in 06, e.g., drug therapy 061
	For first aid, see 0252
025	Medical emergencies
	Class here comprehensive works on emergency therapy for specific diseases or kinds of diseases
	Class intensive care in 028; a specific kind of emergency therapy in 06, e.g., emergency drug therapy 061
0252	First aid
027	Experimental medicine

(continued)

> **616.1–616.9 Specific diseases (continued)**

028   Intensive care
        Class a specific kind of therapy in 06, e.g., drug therapy 061

029   Terminal care
        Class a specific kind of therapy in 06, e.g., drug therapy 061

03   Rehabilitation
        Restoration of a sick or disabled person by therapy and by training for participation in the activities of a normal life within the limitations of disabilities
        Class comprehensive works on rehabilitation in 617.03, rehabilitative therapy in 06

04   Special classes of diseases

042   Genetic (Hereditary) diseases
        When a specific type of genetic disease has an indirect etiology, class with the system showing the most visible manifestations, e.g., mental retardation caused by hereditary metabolic disorders 616.8588042, not 616.39042

043   Congenital diseases
        Class congenital diseases of genetic origin in 042

05   Preventive measures
        By the individual and by medical personnel
        Class comprehensive works in 613, public measures for preventing specific diseases in 614.5

06   Therapy
        Class here rehabilitative therapy; specific kinds of therapy used in domestic medicine, medical emergencies, intensive care, terminal care
        Class comprehensive works on therapy in 615.5; comprehensive works on therapy for specific diseases or kinds of diseases in domestic medicine in 024, in medical emergencies in 025, in intensive care in 028, in terminal care in 029; comprehensive works on rehabilitative therapy and training for persons with a specific disease or kind of disease in 03; comprehensive works on therapy and pathology (07) of a specific disease or kind of disease in the number for the disease or kind of disease, without adding from the add table, e.g., cause, course, and cure of heart disease 616.12 (*not* 616.1206)

061   Drug therapy

062–069   Other therapies
        Add to 06 the numbers following 615.8 in 615.82–615.89, e.g., X-ray therapy 06422, rehabilitative activity therapies 06515

07   Pathology
        Add to 07 the numbers following 616.07 in 616.071–616.079, e.g., etiology 071, diagnosis 075
        Class social factors contributing to the spread of a disease in 362.19
        See Manual at 616.1–616.9: Add table: 071 vs. 01

08   Psychosomatic medicine

09   Case histories

Class comprehensive works in 616

See Manual at 612.1–612.8

> ### 616.1–616.8 Diseases of specific systems and organs

Class comprehensive works in 616, diseases of the immune system in 616.97, tumors (neoplasms) of specific systems and organs in 616.992, tuberculosis of specific systems and organs in 616.995

See Manual at 616.1–616.8

.1   ***Diseases of the cardiovascular system**

Cardiopulmonary resuscitation (CPR) is classed in 616.1025

Class diseases of the blood-forming system in 616.41

SUMMARY

616.11		**Diseases of the endocardium and pericardium**
.12		**Diseases of the heart**
.13		**Diseases of the blood vessels**
.14		**Diseases of the veins and capillaries**
.15		**Diseases of the blood**

.11   *Diseases of the endocardium and pericardium

.12   *Diseases of the heart

Example: cor pulmonale

Class here cardiology; necrosis and other degenerative diseases of the heart

For diseases of the endocardium and pericardium, see 616.11

.122   *Angina pectoris

.123   *Coronary diseases (Ischemic heart diseases)

Comprehensive works on heart attacks are classed in 616.123025; works on heart attacks in the sense of myocardial infarction are classed in 616.1237

Class heart attacks not caused by narrowing or blocking of the coronary arteries with the cause, e.g., heart attacks caused by congestive heart failure 616.129025

For angina pectoris, see 616.122

See Manual at 616.123028

.123 2   *Coronary arteriosclerosis

.123 7   *Myocardial infarction

.124   *Myocarditis

Class here comprehensive works on diseases of the myocardium

For myocardial infarction, see 616.1237

.125   *Valvular diseases

*Add as instructed under 616.1–616.9

.127   *Rheumatic heart diseases

              Class rheumatic valvular diseases in 616.125

.128   *Arrhythmia

              Including allorhythmia

              Class implantation of heart pacers in 617.412059, their functioning in
              617.4120645

.129   *Heart failure

.13   *Diseases of the blood vessels

              Class here angiology; diseases of the blood vessels in a specific region, e.g.,
              the abdominal and pelvic cavities

              Class diseases of the blood vessels in a specific system or organ with the
              system or organ, e.g., cerebrovascular diseases 616.81

              For diseases of the veins and capillaries, see 616.14

.131   *Peripheral vascular diseases

              For cerebrovascular diseases, see 616.81

.132   *Hypertension

              Essential and renal

.133   *Aneurysms

.135   *Arterial embolisms and thromboses

              For pulmonary embolisms and thromboses, see 616.249

.136   *Arteriosclerosis

              Class here atherosclerosis

.138   *Diseases of the aorta

.14   *Diseases of the veins and capillaries

.142   *Phlebitis and thrombophlebitis

.143   *Varicose veins (Varix)

.145   *Venous embolisms and thromboses

.148   *Diseases of capillaries

              Including telangiectasis, telangitis

.15   *Diseases of the blood

              Class here hematology

              For bacterial blood diseases, see 616.94

*Add as instructed under 616.1–616.9

.151	*Diseases of erythrocytes

Class here hemoglobin disorders

For anemia, see 616.152; polycythemia, 616.153

.152	*Anemia

Example: thalassemia

.152 7	*Sickle cell anemia
.153	*Polycythemia
.154	*Diseases of leucocytes

Including agranulocytosis

.156	*Reticulosis
.157	*Hemorrhagic diseases

Class here comprehensive works on disorders of blood coagulation

For arterial embolisms and thromboses, see 616.135; venous embolisms and thromboses, 616.145

.157 2	*Hemophilia
.2	**Diseases of the respiratory system**

Including apnea

Class here dyspnea

.200 1–.200 3	Standard subdivisions

As modified under 616.1–616.9

.200 4	Special topics

Add to base number 616.2004 the numbers following 0 in notation 01–09 from table under 616.1–616.9, e.g., diagnosis of respiratory diseases 616.200475

.200 5–.200 9	Standard subdivisions

As modified under 616.1–616.9

.201	*Croup
.202	*Respiratory allergies

Class here hay fever

Class asthma in 616.238

.203	*Influenza
.204	*Whooping cough (Pertussis)
.205	*Common cold (Coryza)
.208	*Hyperventilation (Overbreathing)

*Add as instructed under 616.1–616.9

.21   *Diseases of the nose, larynx, accessory organs

Class otorhinolaryngology, comprehensive works on diseases of the eyes, ears, nose, throat in 617.51

For laryngology, see 616.22

.212   *Of nose, nasopharynx, accessory sinuses

Class here rhinology

Class the common cold in 616.205

.22   *Diseases of larynx, glottis, vocal cords, epiglottis

Class here laryngology

.23   *Diseases of trachea and bronchi

Examples: bronchiectasis, tracheitis

Class bronchopneumonia in 616.241

.234   *Bronchitis

.238   *Bronchial asthma

Class here comprehensive works on asthma

Class cardiac asthma in 616.12

.24   *Diseases of the lungs

Class here comprehensive works on diseases of lungs and bronchi

Class diseases of bronchi in 616.23, pulmonary tuberculosis in 616.99524

.241   *Pneumonia

Including Legionnaires' disease

See also 616.245 for necropneumonia

.244   *Pneumoconiosis

Diseases caused by dust and other particles

Examples: asbestosis, black lung disease, byssinosis (brown lung disease), pulmonary abscesses, silicosis

.245   *Necropneumonia

.248   *Emphysema

.249   *Pulmonary embolisms and thromboses

.25   *Diseases of the pleura

Class pleural pneumonia in 616.241

.27   *Diseases of the mediastinum

.3   *Diseases of the digestive system

Class allergies of the digestive system in 616.975

*Add as instructed under 616.1–616.9

SUMMARY

616.31	**Diseases of the mouth and throat**
.32	**Diseases of the pharynx and esophagus**
.33	**Diseases of the stomach**
.34	**Diseases of the intestine**
.35	**Diseases of the rectum and anus**
.36	**Diseases of the biliary tract**
.37	**Diseases of the pancreas**
.38	**Diseases of the peritoneum**
.39	**Nutritional and metabolic diseases**

.31   *Diseases of the mouth and throat

Class the oral region (a broader concept than the mouth as a digestive organ) in 617.522, diseases of the teeth and gums in 617.63

For laryngology, see 616.22; diseases of the pharynx, 616.32

.312   *Trench mouth (Vincent's angina)

.313   *Mumps (Epidemic parotitis)

.314   *Diseases of the tonsils

.316   *Diseases of the salivary glands

.32   *Diseases of the pharynx and esophagus

.33   *Diseases of the stomach

Example: gastroptosis

Class here gastroenteritis, comprehensive works on gastroenterology (gastrointestinal diseases)

For diseases of the intestine, see 616.34; typhoid fever, 616.9272; cholera, 616.932; dysenteries, 616.935

See Manual at 616.932 vs. 616.33

.332   *Functional disorders

Examples: dyspepsia, disorders of secretion, gastric indigestion

.333   *Gastritis

.334   *Gastric ulcers

Class peptic ulcers in 616.343

.34   *Diseases of the intestine

.342   *Functional disorders

Including obstructions

.342 3   *Malabsorption

.342 7   *Diarrhea

.342 8   *Constipation

*Add as instructed under 616.1−616.9

.343	*Peptic ulcers

Class here comprehensive works on gastric and peptic ulcers

For gastric ulcers, see 616.334

.343 3	*Duodenal ulcers
.343 4	*Gastrojejunal ulcers
.344	*Enteritis

Examples: duodenitis, jejunitis

.344 5	*Ileitis

Including Crohn's disease

.344 7	*Colitis
.35	*Diseases of the rectum and anus

Class here proctology

.36	*Diseases of the biliary tract
.362	*Diseases of the liver
.362 3	*Hepatitis
.362 4	*Cirrhosis
.362 5	*Jaundice
.365	*Diseases of the gall bladder and bile duct
.37	*Diseases of the pancreas

Including cystic fibrosis

Class diseases of pancreatic internal secretion in 616.46

.38	*Diseases of the peritoneum
.39	*Nutritional and metabolic diseases

Inborn (inherited) errors of metabolism are classed in 616.39042

Class nutritional and metabolic diseases of a specific system or organ with the system or organ, e.g., metabolic bone diseases 616.716

For endocrinology, see 616.4

>	616.392–616.396 Deficiency diseases

Class comprehensive works in 616.39

.392	*Beriberi
.393	*Pellagra
.394	*Scurvy

*Add as instructed under 616.1–616.9

.395	*Rickets
.396	Other deficiency diseases and states

Examples: emaciation, fatty degeneration, kwashiorkor

Class anorexia nervosa in 616.85262

For multiple deficiency states, see 616.399

.398	*Obesity

Contains nutritional and endocrinal obesity

Food addiction is classed in 616.39808

Class appetite and eating disorders as neuroses in 616.8526

.399	Other nutritional and metabolic diseases

Including multiple deficiency states

.399 5	*Diseases of protein metabolism

Example: amyloidosis

.399 7	*Diseases of lipid metabolism
.399 8	*Diseases of carbohydrate metabolism
.399 9	*Gout
.4	***Diseases of the blood-forming, lymphatic, glandular systems *Diseases of the endocrine system**

Class here endocrinology

Class endocrinal obesity in 616.398; diseases of glands in a specific system or organ with the system or organ, e.g., diseases of female sex glands 618.1

.41	*Of the blood-forming (hematopoietic) system

Spleen and bone marrow disorders

For anemia, see 616.152

.42	*Of the lymphatic system

Examples: lymphatitis, lymphomatosis

Class Hodgkin's disease in 616.99446

>	616.43–616.48 Of endocrine system

Class comprehensive works in 616.4

.43	*Of the thymus gland
.44	*Of the thyroid and parathyroid glands
.442	*Goiter
.443	*Hyperthyroidism

*Add as instructed under 616.1–616.9

.444   *Hypothyroidism

> *For myxedema, see 616.858848*

.445   *Hyperparathyroidism and hypoparathyroidism

.45   *Diseases of the adrenal glands

> Examples: Addison's disease, Cushing's syndrome, hyperadrenalism, hypoadrenalism

.46   *Diseases of pancreatic internal secretion (Diseases of the islands of Langerhans)

.462   *Diabetes mellitus

> Class here comprehensive works on diabetes
>
> *For diabetes insipidus, see 616.47*

.466   *Hypoglycemia

.47   *Diseases of the pituitary gland

> Examples: diabetes insipidus, dwarfism, gigantism
>
> Including acromegaly, Simmond's disease

.48   *Diseases of other glands

> Example: hyperpinealism
>
> Including polyglandular disorders

.49   *Diseases of the male breast

> Class comprehensive works on diseases of the breast in 618.19

.5   ***Diseases of the integument, hair, nails**

> Examples: photosensitivity diseases, sunburn
>
> Class here dermatology
>
> Class comprehensive works on allergies of the skin in 616.973, dermatological manifestations of food and drug allergies in 616.975
>
> Class venereal diseases in 616.951

.51   *Papular eruptions

> Including urticaria (hives)
>
> Class here dermatitis
>
> *For vesicular and pustular eruptions, see 616.52; contact allergies, 616.973*

.52   *Vesicular and pustular eruptions

> Example: herpes simplex type 1 (cold sores, fever blisters)
>
> Class herpes simplex type 2 (genital herpes) in 616.9518

*Add as instructed under 616.1–616.9

.521   *Eczema

           Including atopic dermatitis

.522   *Shingles (Herpes zoster)

.523   *Boils and carbuncles (Furuncles)

.524   *Impetigo

.526   *Psoriasis

.53   *Diseases of sebaceous glands

           Examples: acne, blackheads, seborrhea, wens

.54   *Skin hypertrophies, scalp diseases, related disorders

           For pigmentary changes, see 616.55

.544   *Skin hypertrophies

           Examples: callosities, corns, ichthyosis, keratosis, scleroderma, warts (verrucae), xeroderma

.545   *Skin ulcerations

           Examples: decubitus ulcers (bedsores)

.546   *Diseases of scalp, hair, hair follicles

           Examples: baldness (alopecia), dandruff, excessive hairiness (hypertrichosis)

.547   *Diseases of nails

.55   *Pigmentary changes

           Examples: albinism, moles, pigmentary nevi

           Including comprehensive works on nevi

           Class capillary nevi in 616.99315

.56   *Diseases of sweat glands

           Examples: anhidrosis, heat rash, prickly heat

.57   *Parasitic skin diseases

           Examples: athlete's foot, mange, ringworm, scabies, yaws

.58   Chilblains, frostbite, chapping

.6   *Diseases of the urogenital system   *Diseases of the urinary system

           Class here urology

\>   616.61–616.64 Diseases of the urinary system

           Class comprehensive works in 616.6

*Add as instructed under 616.1–616.9

.61   *Of kidneys and ureters

Class here nephrology

Subdivisions are added for kidneys and ureters, for kidneys alone

Class renal hypertension in 616.132, kidney stones in 616.622, kidney dialysis in 617.461059

.612   *Nephritis

Examples: Bright's disease, glomerulonephritis

.613   *Pyelitis (Pyelonephritis) and pyelocystitis

.614   *Renal failure

.62   *Of bladder and urethra

For diseases of the male urethra, see 616.64

.622   *Kidney stones (Urinary calculi)

Renal and vesical calculi

.623   *Cystitis

.624   *Urethritis

.63   *Urinary manifestations

Limited to manifestations of diseases of the urogenital system

Examples: albuminuria, hematuria, proteinuria

Class interpretation of symptoms for diagnosis and prognosis in 616.6075; psychosomatic enuresis in 616.849; urinary manifestations of a specific disease or of disease in a specific organ with the disease or organ, e.g., urinary manifestations of renal failure 616.614

See also 616.07566 for urinalysis in diagnosis of diseases in general

.633   *Pyuria

.635   *Uremia

.64   *Diseases of the male urethra

.65   *Diseases of the genital system

Class here *diseases of the male genital system, *diseases of the prostate gland

Class diseases of the female genital system in 618.1; diseases of a specific male genital organ not provided for here with the organ, e.g., diseases of the male urethra 616.64

.66   *Diseases of the penis

.67   *Diseases of the scrotum

.68   *Diseases of the testicles and accessory organs

*Add as instructed under 616.1–616.9

.69   *Sexual disorders

        Class here male sexual disorders

        Class sexual personality disorders in 616.8583, female sexual disorders in 618.17

.692   *Impotence and infertility

        Class here comprehensive works on male and female infertility, on impotence

        Class impotence as a psychological disorder in 616.85832; female infertility, artificial insemination in 618.178

.693   *Male climacteric disorders

        Class comprehensive works on climacteric disorders in 618.175

.694   *Hermaphroditism

.7   *Diseases of the musculoskeletal system

        See Manual at 617.3 vs. 616.7, 617.5

.71   †Of bones

        Class here chronic diseases of the skeletal system

        Class correction of deformities of the skeletal system (orthopedics), treatment of chronic diseases of the skeletal system in 617.3

        For diseases of the spine, see 616.73

.712   †Osteitis

        Examples: osteitis deformans, osteochondritis, periostitis

.715   †Osteomyelitis

.716   †Disorders of metabolic origin

        Example: osteoporosis

        For rickets, see 616.395

.72   *Diseases of the joints

        For gout, see 616.3999

.722   *Arthritis

.722 3   *Osteoarthritis (Hypertrophic arthritis)

.722 7   *Rheumatoid arthritis

        Class ankylosing spondylitis in 616.73

*Add as instructed under 616.1–616.9

†Add as instructed under 616.1–616.9, except class treatment of chronic diseases in 617.3

.723   *Rheumatism

Class here rheumatology

Class a specific rheumatic disease with the disease, e.g., rheumatoid arthritis 616.7227, rheumatic fever 616.991

.73   *Diseases of the spine

Example: ankylosing spondylitis

.74   *Diseases of the muscles

Class diseases of muscles in a specific system or organ with the system or organ, e.g., diseases of the heart 616.12

.742   *Muscular rheumatism

.743   *Myositis

.744   *Neuromuscular diseases

Class neuromuscular diseases resulting from disorders of the central nervous system in 616.83

.744 2   *Myasthenia gravis

.748   *Progressive muscular dystrophy

.75   *Diseases of tendons and fasciae

.76   *Diseases of bursae and sheaths of tendons

.77   *Diseases of connective tissue

Including Ehlers-Danlos syndrome, Marfan syndrome, systemic lupus erythematosus

Class here collagen diseases

For rheumatoid arthritis, see 616.7227; diseases of tendons and fasciae, 616.75

.8   **Diseases of the nervous system and mental disorders**

Class here neuropsychiatry

Use 616.8001–616.8009 for standard subdivisions

SUMMARY

616.801–.809	**Standard subdivisions of neurology, of brain diseases**
.81	**Cerebrovascular diseases**
.82	**Meningeal diseases**
.83	**Other organic diseases of the central nervous system**
.84	**Manifestations of neurological diseases and mental disorders**
.85	**Miscellaneous diseases of the nervous system and mental disorders**
.86	**Substance abuse (Drug abuse)**
.87	**Diseases of the cranial, spinal, peripheral nerves**
.88	**Diseases of the autonomic (sympathetic and parasympathetic) nervous system**
.89	**Mental disorders**

*Add as instructed under 616.1–616.9

.801–.803	Standard subdivisions of neurology, of brain diseases
	As modified under 616.1–616.9
.804	Special topics in neurology, in brain diseases

Add to base number 616.804 the numbers following 0 in notation 01–09 from table under 616.1–616.9, e.g., diagnosis of brain diseases 616.80475

Class manifestations of neurological diseases as problems in their own right in 616.84

.805–.809	Standard subdivisions of neurology, of brain diseases
	As modified under 616.1–616.9

>   616.81–616.84 Neurology   Brain diseases

Class comprehensive works in 616.8, diseases of nerves in a specific system or organ with the system or organ, e.g., neuromuscular diseases 616.74

For diseases of the cranial, spinal, peripheral nerves, see 616.87; of the autonomic nervous system, 616.88

.81	*Cerebrovascular diseases
	Examples: apoplexy (stroke)
.82	*Meningeal diseases
	Example: meningitis
.83	Other organic diseases of the central nervous system

Examples: amytrophic lateral sclerosis, Friedreich's ataxia, tardive dyskinesia

Class here diseases of basal ganglia, of the spinal cord

For chorea, see 616.851; epilepsy, 616.853; senile dementia, 616.8983

.831	*Alzheimer's disease
.832	*Encephalitis
.833	*Parkinson's disease (Paralysis agitans)
.834	*Multiple sclerosis
.835	*Poliomyelitis
.836	*Cerebral palsy
.837	*Paraplegia

Neurological aspects only

Class comprehensive works on neurological and surgical aspects in 617.58

*Add as instructed under 616.1–616.9

.838   *Locomotor ataxia (Tabes dorsalis)

                  Class comprehensive works on syphilis in 616.9513, general paresis in
                  616.892

.84   Manifestations of neurological diseases and mental disorders

                  Symptoms as problems in their own right

                  Class here pathology, diagnosis, treatment of symptoms

                  Class interpretation of symptoms for diagnosis and prognosis of
                  neurological disease in 616.80475, of mental disorders in 616.89075;
                  migraine in 616.857; diagnostic and prognostic interpretation of symptoms
                  of a specific disease or class of diseases with the disease, e.g., of
                  schizophrenia 616.8982075

.841   Dizziness (Vertigo)

.842   Paralysis

[.844]   Spinal irritation

                  Number discontinued; class in 616.84

.845   Convulsions

.849   Miscellaneous symptoms

                  Limited to coma, enuresis, pain, reflex disturbances, and the symptoms
                  provided for below

                  Use of this number for other symptoms discontinued; class in 616.84

.849 1   *Headache

                  Example: cluster headache

                  Including headaches of unknown origin [*formerly* 616.0472]

                  For migraine, see 616.857

.849 8   Sleep disturbances

                  Example: insomnia

.85   Miscellaneous diseases of the nervous system and mental disorders

                  Only those named below

SUMMARY

616.851	**Chorea**	
.852	**Neuroses**	
.853	**Epilepsy**	
.855	**Speech and language disorders**	
.856	**Cutaneous sensory disorders**	
.857	**Migraine**	
.858	**Disorders of personality and intellect**	

.851   *Chorea

*Add as instructed under 616.1–616.9

| .852 | †Neuroses |

Class neurotic aspects of a specific disease with the disease, e.g., of asthma 616.238

For speech and language disorders, see 616.855

See also 616.856 for cutaneous sensory disorders

| .852 1 | †Traumatic neuroses |

Examples: compensation and occupation neuroses, posttraumatic stress disorder

.852 12	†War neuroses (Combat fatigue)
.852 2	†Anxiety, phobic, obsessive-compulsive neuroses
.852 23	†Anxiety neuroses
.852 25	†Phobic neuroses

Example: agoraphobia

| .852 27 | †Obsessive-compulsive neurosis |

Example: compulsive gambling

| .852 3 | †Dissociative reactions |
| .852 32 | †Amnesia and fugue |

Subdivisions are added for amnesia and fugue, for amnesia alone

| .852 36 | †Dual and multiple personalities |
| .852 4 | †Hysterical neuroses |

For dissociative reactions, see 616.8523

| .852 5 | †Hypochondriacal neuroses |
| .852 6 | †Eating disorders |

Class here appetite disorders

.852 62	†Anorexia nervosa
.852 63	†Bulimia
.852 7	†Depressive neuroses

Class here comprehensive works on depression

Class postpartum depression in 618.76

For neurasthenia, see 616.8528; manic-depressive psychoses, 616.895

| .852 8 | †Neurasthenia (Asthenic reactions) |

Chronic fatigue and depression

Class comprehensive works on depression in 616.8527

| .853 | *Epilepsy |

*Add as instructed under 616.1–616.9

†Add as instructed under 616.1–616.9, except use 0651 also for psychotherapies

.855	†Speech and language disorders

Class here comprehensive works on communicative disorders, on voice disorders

Class comprehensive works on learning and communicative disorders in 616.85889

.855 2	*Neurological language disorders (Aphasias)

Diminution or loss of faculty of language in any of its forms due to cerebral lesions, e.g., agnosia, agrammatism, agraphia, apraxia

For written language disorders, see 616.8553

.855 3	†Written language disorders

Class here dyslexia

.855 4	†Stammering and stuttering
.856	*Cutaneous sensory disorders

Examples: anesthesia, hyperesthesia, hypesthesia, paresthesia

.857	*Migraine
.858	Disorders of personality and intellect
.858 2	†Sociopathic personality disorders

Class here self-destructive tendencies, violent behavior

Class sexual disorders in 616.8583, substance abuse in 616.86

For other sociopathic neuroses and suicidal compulsions, see 616.8584

.858 22	†Family violence and abuse

Examples: child abuse, spouse abuse

Class incest, sexual abuse of children in 616.8583

.858 3	†Sexual disorders

Including incest, sexual abuse of children

.858 32	†Frigidity and impotence

Class comprehensive works on impotence in 616.692

.858 33	†Nymphomania and satyromania
.858 34	†Homosexuality
.858 35	†Sadism and masochism
.858 4	Other sociopathic neuroses and suicidal compulsions
.858 42	†Kleptomania
.858 43	†Pyromania

*Add as instructed under 616.1–616.9

†Add as instructed under 616.1–616.9, except use 0651 also for psychotherapies

.858 44	Homicidal and suicidal compulsions
.858 445	†Suicidal compulsions
.858 45	†Compulsive lying and †defrauding
.858 5	Borderline and narcissistic personality disorders
.858 52	†Borderline personality disorder
.858 8	*Mental deficiency and learning disabilities

Class here feeblemindedness, mental retardation

.858 84	Due to deformity, injury, disease
.858 842	*Down's syndrome
.858 843	*Hydrocephalus
.858 844	*Microcephaly
.858 845	*Cerebral sphingolipidosis

Former heading: Amaurotic idiocy

Example: Tay-Sachs disease

.858 848	*Myxedema

Example: congenital myxedema (cretinism)

.858 89	*Learning disabilities

Regardless of level of intelligence

Class here comprehensive works on learning and communicative disorders

Class communicative disorders in 616.855; learning disabilities associated with a specific disorder with the disorder, e.g., minimal brain dysfunction 616.8589

.858 9	*Attention deficit disorder and *hyperactivity (hyperkinesia)

Class here minimal brain dysfunction

.86	‡Substance abuse (Drug abuse)

Examples: abuse of analgesics, depressants, inhalants, sedatives, tranquilizers

Class here addiction, habituation, intoxication

Class interdisciplinary works on substance abuse in 362.29, comprehensive medical works on addictive and disorienting drugs in 615.78, personal measures to prevent substance abuse in 613.8, food addiction in 616.39808

.861	‡Alcohol

Class here alcoholism

*Add as instructed under 616.1–616.9

†Add as instructed under 616.1–616.9, except use 0651 also for psychotherapies

‡Add as instructed under 616.1–616.9, except use 0651 also for psychotherapies and do not use 05; class prevention in 613.8 or its subdivisions

[.862] Effect of metallic intoxication on nervous system and mental condition

Number discontinued; class in 616.8

.863 ‡Narcotics, hallucinogens, psychedelics, cannabis

Use of this number for comprehensive works on drug abuse discontinued; class in 616.86

.863 2 ‡Narcotics

Opium and its derivatives and synthetic equivalents

Class here specific narcotics, e.g., heroin, morphine

.863 4 ‡Hallucinogens and ‡psychedelics

Class here specific hallucinogens and psychedelics, e.g., LSD, mescaline, PCP

Class cannabis in 616.8635

.863 5 ‡Cannabis

Class here specific kinds of cannabis, e.g., hashish, marijuana

.864 ‡Stimulants and related substances

Class here specific kinds of stimulants, e.g., amphetamine, ephedrine

Class nicotine in 616.865

.864 7 ‡Cocaine

Class here specific forms of cocaine, e.g., crack

.865 ‡Tobacco

.87 *Diseases of the cranial, spinal, peripheral nerves

Examples: disorders of taste and smell, neuralgias, neuritis, sciatica

Class neurofibromatosis in 616.99383

For herpes zoster, see 616.522; cutaneous sensory disorders, 616.856; diseases of the autonomic system, 616.88

.88 *Diseases of the autonomic (sympathetic and parasympathetic) nervous system

*Add as instructed under 616.1–616.9

‡Add as instructed under 616.1–616.9, except use 0651 also for psychotherapies and do not use 05; class prevention in 613.8 or its subdivisions

.89   *Mental disorders

Class here comparative abnormal behavior of animals [*formerly also* 156.7], abnormal and clinical psychologies [*formerly also* 157], psychiatry

Class manifestations of mental disorders in 616.84 when considered as symptoms so serious that they become problems in their own right; puerperal mental disorders in 618.76; physical manifestations of mental disorders involving a specific system with the system, using 08 from the table under 616.1–616.9 if appropriate, e.g., psychosomatic ulcers 616.3408

For neuroses, see 616.852; disorders of personality and intellect, 616.858

See Manual at 150.195 vs. 616.89

[.890 083 5]   With respect to young adults

Do not use; class in 616.89022

.890 22   Mental disorders of young adults

Aged twelve to twenty

[.890 6]   Therapy

Do not use; class in 616.891

.891   Therapy

.891 2   Shock therapy

Examples: insulin and other drug shock therapies

.891 22   Electric shock therapy (Electroconvulsive therapy)

.891 3   Physical therapies

For electric shock therapy, see 616.89122; psychosurgery, 617.481

.891 4   Psychotherapy

For group and family psychotherapy, see 616.8915; mental and activity therapies, 616.8916; psychoanalysis, 616.8917

.891 42   Behavior therapy (Behavior modification therapy)

.891 43   Gestalt therapy

.891 44   Milieu therapy

Utilization of the environment for treatment

.891 45   Transactional analysis

.891 5   Group and family psychotherapy

.891 52   Group psychotherapy

.891 523   Psychodrama

.891 56   Family psychotherapy

Including marital psychotherapy

*Add as instructed under 616.1–616.9

.891 6 Mental and activity therapies

Add to base number 616.8916 the numbers following 615.851 in 615.8512–615.8516, e.g., hypnotherapy 616.89162

.891 7 Psychoanalysis

[.891 701 9] Psychological principles of psychoanalysis

Do not use; class in 150.195 unless applied to therapy, in which case class in 616.8917

.891 8 Drug therapy

Class drug shock therapy in 616.8912

> 616.892–616.898 Psychoses

Class here functional psychoses, organic psychoses

Class comprehensive works in 616.89; puerperal psychoses in 618.76; a specific organic psychosis not provided for here with the subject, e.g., psychosis due to brain tumors 616.99281

.892 *General paresis (Neurosyphilis)

Class comprehensive works on syphilis in 616.9513, locomotor ataxia in 616.838

.895 †Manic-depressive psychoses

Including depressive reactions, involutional psychoses

Class here manic, depressive, circular and alternating manic-depressive psychoses

Class comprehensive works on depression in 616.8527

.897 †Paranoia and paranoid conditions

.898 Schizophrenia, autism, senile dementia

.898 2 †Schizophrenia and †autism

.898 3 †Senile dementia

See also 616.831 for Alzheimer's disease

.9 **Other diseases**

Class here communicable diseases not otherwise provided for

See Manual at 616.01 vs. 616.9

*Add as instructed under 616.1–616.9

†Add as instructed under 616.1–616.9, except use 0651 also for psychotherapies

SUMMARY

.901–.903   Standard subdivisions of communicable diseases

As modified under 616.1–616.9

.904   Special topics in communicable diseases

Add to base number 616.904 the numbers following 0 in notation 01–09 from table under 616.1–616.9, e.g., diagnosis of communicable diseases 616.90475

.905–.909   Standard subdivisions of communicable diseases

As modified under 616.1–616.9

>   616.91–616.96 Communicable diseases

Class comprehensive works in 616.9; a specific communicable disease not provided for here with the disease, e.g., mumps 616.313

.91   *Eruptive diseases (Exanthems)

For eruptive fevers, see 616.9223

.912   *Smallpox (Variola major)

.913   *Attenuated forms of smallpox

Examples: alastrim (amaas, Cuban itch, variola minor), cowpox (variola vaccinia)

.914   *Chicken pox (Varicella)

.915   *Measles (Rubeola)

.916   *German measles (Rubella)

.917   *Scarlet fever (Scarlatina)

.92   *Bacterial and viral diseases

Examples: Lyme disease, toxic shock syndrome

Class a specific bacterial disease or group of bacterial diseases not provided for here with the disease or group of diseases, e.g., bacterial blood diseases 616.94

.921   *Dengue fever

*Add as instructed under 616.1–616.9

.922	*Rickettsial diseases
.922 2	*Epidemic (Louse-borne) and murine (flea-borne) typhus
	Including Brill's disease
.922 3	*Rickettsialpox and tick typhus
	Including boutonneuse fever
	Class here eruptive fevers, spotted fevers
	For North Queensland tick typhus, see 616.9226
.922 4	*Tsutsugamushi disease (Scrub typhus, Japanese river fever)
.922 5	*Q fever
.922 6	Bullis fever, North Queensland tick typhus, trench fever
.923	*Pasteurella and related diseases
.923 2	*Bubonic plague
.923 9	*Tularemia
.924	*Colorado tick fever and relapsing fevers
.924 2	*Colorado tick fever
.924 4	*Relapsing fevers
.925	*Viral diseases
	Including comprehensive works on herpesvirus diseases
	Class a specific viral disease or group of viral diseases with the disease or group of diseases, e.g., shingles 616.522, herpes simplex 2 (genital herpes) 616.9518
.927	*Salmonella diseases
.927 2	*Typhoid fever (Enteric fever)
.927 4	*Paratyphoid fever
.928	*Yellow fever
.93	Bacillary and protozoan diseases, cholera, dysenteries
.931	*Bacillary diseases
	For bacillary dysentery, see 616.9355
.931 3	*Diphtheria
.931 5	*Botulism
.931 8	*Tetanus
.932	*Cholera
	See Manual at 616.932 vs. 616.33

*Add as instructed under 616.1–616.9

.935   *Dysenteries

.935 3   *Amebic dysentery

.935 5   *Bacillary dysentery (Shigella diseases)

.936   *Protozoan diseases

                     For amebic dysentery, see 616.9353

.936 2   *Malaria

.936 3   *Trypanosomiasis

                     Examples: African sleeping sickness, e.g., Gambian and Rhodesian
                     trypanosomiasis; Chagas' disease (South American trypanosomiasis)

.936 4   *Leishmaniasis

                     Examples: cutaneous leishmaniasis (oriental sores), mucocutaneous
                     leishmaniasis (forest yaws), visceral leishmaniasis (kala-azar)

.94   *Bacterial blood diseases

.942   *Erysipelas

.944   *Septicemia and pyemia

.95   Venereal diseases and zoonoses

                     For tularemia, see 616.9239

.951   *Venereal diseases

                     Class acquired immune deficiency syndrome (AIDS) in 616.9792

.951 3   *Syphilis

                     *For locomotor ataxia, see 616.838; general paresis
                     (neurosyphilis), 616.892*

.951 5   *Gonorrhea

.951 8   Other venereal diseases

                     Examples: chancroid, herpes simplex type 2 (genital herpes),
                     lymphogranuloma venereum

.953   *Rabies (Hydrophobia)

.954   *Glanders (Equinia)

.956   *Anthrax

                     Variant names: charbon, splenic fever

                     Example: Woolsorters' disease

.957   *Undulant fever (Brucellosis)

.958   *Parrot fever (Psittacosis)

.959   *Zoonoses

                     Class a specific zoonosis with the disease, e.g., Q fever 616.9225

*Add as instructed under 616.1–616.9

.96   *Parasitic diseases

Class here medical parasitology

For parasitic skin diseases, see 616.57

.962   *Diseases due to endoparasites

For diseases due to worms, see 616.963–616.965

\>   616.963–616.965 Diseases due to worms

Class here medical helminthology

Class comprehensive works in 616.962

.963   *Diseases due to flukes (Trematoda)

Example: schistosomiasis (bilharziasis)

.964   *Diseases due to tapeworms (Cestoda)

Examples: hydatid diseases (echinococcosis)

.965   *Diseases due to roundworms (Nematoda)

.965 2   *To filariae

Examples: elephantiasis, onchocerciasis, wuchereriasis

Class here filariasis

.965 4   To other nematodes

Including ascariasis, enterobiasis, hookworm infestations (ancyclostomiasis), trichinosis

.968   *Diseases due to ectoparasites

Class here medical entomology

Class a specific entomological disease with the disease, e.g., Colorado tick fever 616.9242

.969   *Diseases due to fungi

Including fungal allergies

Class here medical mycology

.97   *Diseases of the immune system

Former heading: Allergies and autoimmune diseases

Class here failures of immunity [*formerly also* 616.079], comprehensive works on allergies

Class a specific allergy not provided for here with the subject, e.g., hay fever 616.202

.973   *Contact allergies

Class here dermatological allergies

*Add as instructed under 616.1–616.9

.975   *Food and drug allergies

 Class here allergies of the digestive system

.977   *Physical allergies

 Hypersensitivity to physical agents, e.g., heat, sunlight, cold, humidity

.978   *Autoimmune diseases

 Diseases caused by immune reactions to the body's own tissues

 Class here autoimmunity [*formerly* 616.079]

 Class systemic lupus erythematosus in 616.77

.979   *Immune deficiency diseases

.979 2   *Acquired immune deficiency syndrome (AIDS)

.98   Noncommunicable diseases

 Class here environmental medicine, diseases due to stress

 Use 616.98001–616.98009 for standard subdivisions

 Class noncommunicable diseases of a specific organ or system with the subject, e.g., mental disorders 616.89

 For tumors, see 616.992

.980 2   Specialized medical fields

 Example: travel medicine

 For industrial and occupational medicine, see 616.9803

.980 21   Aerospace medicine

.980 213   Aviation medicine

.980 214   Space medicine

.980 22   Submarine medicine

 Class diseases due to compression and decompression in 616.9894

.980 23   Military medicine

 For naval medicine, see 616.98024

.980 24   Naval medicine

.980 3   Industrial and occupational medicine

 See also 613.62 for industrial and occupational health

.988   *Diseases due to climate and weather

 Class here medical climatology and meteorology

 Add to base number 616.988 the numbers following −1 in notation 11–13 from Table 2, e.g., diseases due to tropical climate 616.9883

*Add as instructed under 616.1–616.9

.989   *Diseases due to physical agents

                Examples: heat exhaustion, hypothermia

                Diseases due to light are predominantly dermatological and are classed in
                616.5

.989 2   *To motion

.989 3   *To altitude

                Example: mountain sickness

.989 4   *To compression and decompression

.989 6   *To sound and other vibrations

.989 7   *To radiation

                Class here comprehensive medical works on radiation sickness and
                injuries

.99   Tumors and miscellaneous communicable diseases

                Only those named below

                Use of this number for other diseases discontinued; class in 616.9

.991   *Rheumatic fever

.992   †Tumors (Neoplasms and neoplastic diseases)

                Medical and surgical treatment

                Class here oncology

                Add to base number 616.992 the numbers following 611 in 611.1–611.9,
                e.g., tumors of teeth and surrounding tissues 616.992314 [*formerly*
                617.63], tumors of eyes 616.99284 [*formerly* 617.7]; tumors of ears
                616.99285 [*formerly* 617.8]; then add further as instructed under
                618.1–618.8

                For benign tumors, see 616.993; malignant tumors, 616.994

                See Manual at 616.992 vs. 616.994

.993   †Benign tumors (neoplasms)

                Medical and surgical treatment

                Example: adenomas [*formerly also* 616.994]

                Add to base number 616.993 the numbers following 611 in 611.1–611.9,
                e.g., neurofibromatosis (Recklinghausen's disease) 616.99383, benign
                skin tumors 616.99377; then add further as instructed under 618.1–618.8

*Add as instructed under 616.1–616.9
†Add as instructed under 618.1–618.8

.994   †Cancers (Malignant tumors [neoplasms])

                Medical and surgical treatment

                Class here carcinomas

                Adenomas relocated to 616.993

                See Manual at 616.992 vs. 616.994

.994 1   †Of cardiovascular organs and blood

.994 11–.994 15   Of cardiovascular organs

                Add to base number 616.9941 the numbers following 611.1 in
                611.11–611.15, e.g., cancer of heart 616.99412; then add further
                as instructed under 618.1–618.8

.994 18   †Of the blood

                Including erythrocytes, plasma, platelets

                For cancer of leucocytes, see 616.99419

.994 19   †Leukemia

                Cancer of leucocytes

.994 2–.994 9   Cancers (Malignant tumors [neoplasms]) of other organs and of regions

                Add to base number 616.994 the numbers following 611 in
                611.2–611.9, e.g., cancer of lymphatic glands (Hodgkin's disease)
                616.99446; then add further as instructed under 618.1–618.8

.995   *Tuberculosis

                Add to base number 616.995 the numbers following 611 in 611.1–611.9,
                e.g., tuberculosis of the teeth and surrounding tissues 616.995314
                [*formerly* 617.63], tuberculosis of the eyes 616.99584 [*formerly* 617.7],
                tuberculosis of the ears 616.99585 [*formerly* 617.8], pulmonary
                tuberculosis 616.99524; then add further as instructed, under
                616.1–616.9

                See Manual at 616.995

.998   *Leprosy (Hansen's disease)

*Add as instructed under 616.1–616.9
†Add as instructed under 618.1–618.8

617   Miscellaneous branches of medicine   Surgery

Only those branches named below

Comprehensive works on major, minor, emergency surgery are classed in
617.024–617.026; on surgery by instrument and technique in 617.05; on surgical
pathology in 617.07; on operative surgery and special fields of surgery in 617.9

Except where contrary instructions are given, all notes under 616.01–616.08 and in
the table under 616.1–616.9 are applicable here

Except for additions, changes, deletions, exceptions shown under specific entries,
add to notation for each term identified by * as follows:

001–007	Standard subdivisions	
	As modified under 616.1–616.9	
008	History and description with respect to kinds of persons	
0083	Young people	
	Class dentistry for infants and children in 617.645; surgery for infants and children up to puberty in 617.98; regional medicine, ophthalmology, otology, audiology for infants and children up to puberty in 618.92097	
0084	Persons in specific stages of adulthood	
[00846]	Late adulthood	
	Do not use; class in 618.97, except class surgery in 617.97	
0088	Occupational and religious groups	
0088355	Military personnel	
	Class military surgery in 617.99	
[009]	Historical, geographical, persons treatment	
	Do not use; class in 09	
01	Surgical complications and sequelae	
	Examples: complicating preconditions, e.g., heart problems; surgical infections	
02	Special topics	
023	Personnel	
	Nature of duties, characteristics of profession, relationships	
0232	Physicians	
0233	Technicians and assistants	
024	Domestic medicine	
	For first aid, see 0262	
026	Emergencies	
0262	First aid	
027	Experimental medicine	
028	Intensive care	
03	Rehabilitation	
	Restoration of a sick or disabled person by therapy and by training for participation in the activities of a normal life within the limitations of disabilities	
	Including self-help devices for persons with disabilities	
	Class rehabilitative therapy in 06	
04	Special classes of diseases	
042	Genetic diseases	
043	Congenital diseases	
	Class congenital diseases of genetic origin in 042	
044	Wounds and injuries	
05	Preventive measures and surgery	

(continued)

617   Miscellaneous branches of medicine   Surgery (continued)

052   Preventive measures
By the individual and by medical personnel
Class comprehensive works on prevention in 613, public
measures for preventing specific diseases in 614.5

059   Surgery
Including surgery utilizing specific instruments or techniques,
e.g., catheterization, cryosurgery, laser surgery, microsurgery
For surgical complications and sequelae, see 01
See Manual at 617: Add table: 059

0592   Cosmetic and restorative plastic surgery, transplantation of
tissue and organs, implantation of artificial organs

06   Therapy
Class here rehabilitative therapy
Class comprehensive works on rehabilitative therapy and training
for persons with a specific disease or kind of disease in 03
For surgery, see 059
See Manual at 617: Add table: 06

061   Drug therapy

062–069   Other therapies
Add to 06 the numbers following 615.8 in 615.82–615.89, e.g.,
X-ray therapy 06422, rehabilitative activity therapies 06515

07   Pathology
Add to 07 the numbers following 616.07 in 616.071–616.079,
e.g., physical diagnosis 0754

08   Psychosomatic medicine

09   Historical, geographical, persons treatment
Add to 09 notation 01–9 from Table 2, e.g., the subject in India
0954

*See Manual at 615.7 vs. 616–618; 617 vs. 616; 618.9209 vs. 617; 618.977
vs. 617*

SUMMARY

617.001–.008	**Standard subdivisions of surgery**	
.01–.09	[General topics]	
.1	Wounds and injuries	
.2	Results of injuries	
.3	Orthopedics	
.4	Surgery by systems	
.5	Regional medicine	Regional surgery
.6	Dentistry	
.7	Ophthalmology	
.8	Otology and audiology	
.9	Operative surgery and special fields of surgery	

.001   Philosophy and theory of surgery

.002   Miscellany of surgery

[.002 3]   Surgery as a profession, occupation, hobby

Do not use; class in 617.023

[.002 8]	Auxiliary techniques and procedures; apparatus, equipment, materials
	Do not use; class in 617.9, except class testing and measurement in 617.075
.003–.007	Standard subdivisions of surgery
.008	History and description of surgery with respect to kinds of persons
.008 3	Young people
	Class surgery for infants and children up to puberty in 617.98
.008 4	Persons in specific stages of adulthood
[.008 46]	Late adulthood
	Do not use; class in 617.97
.008 8	Occupational and religious groups
[.008 835 5]	Military personnel
	Do not use; class in 617.99
[.009]	Historical, geographical, persons treatment of surgery
	Do not use; class in 617.09
.01	Surgical complications and sequelae
	Examples: complicating preconditions, e.g., heart problems; surgical infection
.02	Special topics
.023	Personnel
	Nature of duties, characteristics of profession, relationships
	Do not use for the technology of the operations that the personnel perform, e.g., physical diagnosis by a surgeon 617.0754 (*not* 617.0232)
.023 2	Surgeons
.023 3	Surgical technicians and assistants
.024	Minor surgery
	Class here outpatient surgery
.025	Major surgery
.026	Emergency surgery
.026 2	First aid
.03	Rehabilitation
	Restoration of a sick or disabled person by therapy and by training for participation in the activities of a normal life within the limitations of disabilities
	Including self-help devices for persons with disabilities
	Class rehabilitative therapy in 617.06

.05	Surgery by instrument and technique

> Examples: cryosurgery, laser surgery, microsurgery

.06	Nonsurgical therapy

> Class here rehabilitative therapy

> Add to base number 617.06 the numbers following 615.8 in 615.82–615.89, e.g., X-ray therapy 617.06422, rehabilitative activity therapies in 617.06515

> Class comprehensive works on rehabilitative therapy and training in 617.03

.07	Pathology

> Add to base number 617.07 the numbers following 616.07 in 616.071–616.079, e.g., physical diagnosis 617.0754

.08	Psychosomatic medicine
.09	Historical, geographical, persons treatment of surgery

> Add to base number 617.09 notation 01–9 from Table 2, e.g., collective biographies of surgeons 617.0922

> ### 617.1–617.5 Surgery

Class comprehensive works in 617, surgical treatment of tumors in 616.992–616.994

For operative surgery and special fields of surgery, see 617.9

.1	**Wounds and injuries**

Class here traumatology

Use 617.1001–617.1009 for standard subdivisions

Class wounds and injuries of specific systems, regions, organs in 617.4–617.5

Class results of injuries in 617.2

.102	Special topics
.102 6	Emergencies
.102 62	First aid

> Class first aid for a specific type of wound or injury with the type, e.g., first aid for crash wounds 617.1028

.102 7	Athletic injuries

> Class here sports medicine

> Class a specific branch of sports medicine with the subject, e.g., promotion of health of athletes 613.711

.102 8	Crash injuries

> Injuries resulting from transportation accidents

.103	Rehabilitation

Restoration of a sick or disabled person by therapy and by training for participation in the activities of a normal life within the limitations of disabilities

Including self-help devices for persons with disabilities

Class rehabilitative therapy in 617.106

.106	Nonsurgical therapy

Class here rehabilitative therapy

Add to base number 617.106 the numbers following 615.8 in 615.82–615.89, e.g., therapeutic massage 617.10622, rehabilitative activity therapies 615.8+515

Class comprehensive works on rehabilitative therapy and training in 617.103

.107	Pathology

Add to base number 617.107 the numbers following 616.07 in 616.071–616.079, e.g., physical diagnosis 617.10754

.11	*Burns and scalds

Class burns and scalds resulting from injuries from electricity and radiation in 617.12

.12	*Injuries from electricity and radiation
.122	*From electricity
.124	*From radiation

Class comprehensive medical works on radiation sickness and injuries in 616.9897

.13	*Abrasions and contusions
.14	*Wounds

For abrasions and contusions, see 617.13

.140 6	Therapy

Class removal of foreign bodies from wounds in 617.146

.143	*Incisions, lacerations, punctures
.145	*Gunshot wounds
.146	Removal of foreign bodies from wounds
.15	Fractures

Add to base number 617.15 the numbers following 611.71 in 611.711–611.718, e.g., fracture of femur 617.158

.16	*Dislocations

*Add as instructed under 617

.17	*Sprains and strains
.18	*Asphyxiation
	Examples: choking, drowning, hanging, strangulation, suffocation
.19	*Blast injuries
.2	**Results of injuries**
	See also 617.103 for rehabilitation, 617.106 for rehabilitative therapy
.21	Traumatic and surgical shock
.22	Inflammation, infection, fever
.3	**Orthopedics**
	Correction of deformities
	Class here treatment of chronic diseases of the skeletal system
	Class plastic surgery of bones in 617.4710592
	For fractures, see 617.15
	See Manual at 617.3 vs. 616.7, 617.5
.300 1	Philosophy and theory
.300 2	Miscellany
.300 28	Auxiliary techniques and procedures; apparatus, equipment, materials
	Class orthopedic appliances in 617.307
.300 3–.300 9	Standard subdivisions
.307	Orthopedic appliances
	See Manual at 617.307 vs. 617.9
.37	*Deformities
	For deformities of the extremities, see 617.39
.371	*Head and neck
.374	*Chest
.375	*Spine
	Example: scoliosis
.376	*Hip and pelvis
.39	*Deformities of the extremities
	Class amputations in 617.58
.397	*Upper extremities
.398	*Lower extremities
	See also 617.585 for podiatry

*Add as instructed under 617

> ### 617.4–617.5 Surgery by systems and regions

> Class here wounds and injuries of specific systems, regions, organs; surgery of specific organs

> Class comprehensive works in 617

.4   **Surgery by systems**

For respiratory system, see 617.54

See Manual at 612.1–612.8; 617.4 vs. 616

.41   *Cardiovascular system

.412   *Heart

Implantation of heart pacers is classed in 617.412059, their functioning in 617.4120645

.413   *Arteries

Class here comprehensive works on surgery of blood vessels (vascular surgery)

Class surgery of blood vessels in a specific system or organ with the system or organ, e.g., cerebrovascular surgery 617.481

For veins, see 617.414; capillaries, 617.415

.414   *Veins

.415   *Capillaries

.43   *Digestive system

Including bariatric surgery

Class surgery of specific organs of digestive system in 617.5

.44   *Glands and lymphatic system

Including bone marrow

Class surgery of a specific gland with the gland, e.g., thyroid gland 617.539

.46   *Urogenital system

Class gynecological and obstetrical surgery in 618

.461   *Kidneys, adrenal glands, ureters

Class here comprehensive works on surgery of urinary organs

Subdivisions may be added for surgery of kidneys

Hemodialysis, peritoneal dialysis are classed in 617.461059

For bladder and urethra, see 617.462

.462   *Bladder and urethra

*Add as instructed under 617

.463   *Male genital organs

.47   *Motor and integumentary systems

For amputations, see 617.58

.471   *Bones

Class chronic diseases of the skeletal system in 616.71

See also 617.44 for bone marrow

.471 044   Wounds and injuries

For fractures, see 617.15

.472   *Joints

Surgery of joints of the extremities relocated to 617.58

For jaws, see 617.522

See also 616.72 for nonsurgical medical aspects of joints

.472 044   Wounds and injuries

For dislocations, see 617.16

.473   *Muscles

.473 044   Wounds and injuries

For sprains and strains, see 617.17

.474   *Tendons

.475   *Bursae

.477   *Integument

Class here surgery of the skin

.477 9   *Hair

Including removal, transplantation

.48   *Nervous system

Class here neurosurgery

Class ophthalmological surgery in 617.71; otological surgery in 617.81–617.88; surgery of nerves of a specific system or organ with the system or organ, e.g., neuromuscular surgery 617.473

.481   *Brain

Including psychosurgery, topectomy

.482   *Spinal cord

Including surgical treatment of spina bifida

.483   *Nerves

*Add as instructed under 617

.5   Regional medicine   Regional surgery

Class nonsurgical medicine of specific systems or organs in specific regions in 616

See Manual at 617.3 vs. 616.7, 617.5; 617.5

SUMMARY

617.51	**Head**
.52	**Face**
.53	**Neck**
.54	**Thorax (Chest) and respiratory system**
.55	**Abdominal and pelvic cavities**
.56	**Back**
.57	**Upper extremities**
.58	**Lower extremities**

.51   *Head

Class here otorhinolaryngology, comprehensive works on diseases of eyes, ears, nose, throat

Class ears in 617.8

For face, see 617.52; throat, 617.531

.514   *Skull

.52   *Face

Class eyes in 617.7

.522   *Oral region

Including lips, tongue, jaws, parotid gland

Class the mouth as a digestive organ in 616.31, teeth in 617.6

See Manual at 617.522 vs. 617.605

.522 5   *Palate

.523   *Nose

Class here comprehensive works on nose and throat

Class comprehensive works on diseases of eyes, ears, nose, throat in 617.51

For throat, see 617.531

.53   *Neck

.531   *Throat

For pharynx, see 617.532; larynx and trachea, 617.533

.532   *Pharynx

Including tonsils

*Add as instructed under 617

.533	*Larynx and trachea

Including epiglottis, vocal cords

.539	*Thyroid and parathyroid glands
.54	*Thorax (Chest) and respiratory system

Class surgery of heart in 617.412, of nose in 617.523, of larynx and trachea in 617.533

.542	*Lungs
.543	*Pleura
.544	*Bronchi
.545	*Mediastinum
.546	*Thymus gland
.547	*Diaphragm
.548	*Esophagus
.549	*Male breast

Class comprehensive works on surgery of the breast in 618.19

.55	*Abdominal and pelvic cavities

For urogenital system, see 617.46

.551	*Spleen
.553	*Stomach

Including pylorus

.554	*Intestine
.554 1	*Small intestine

Contains duodenum, jejunum, ileum

.554 5	*Cecum and vermiform appendix
.554 7	*Large intestine

Including colon, sigmoid flexure (sigmoid colon)

For cecum and vermiform appendix, see 617.5545; rectum, 617.555

.555	*Rectum, anus, perineum
.556	*Biliary tract

Contains liver, gall bladder, bile ducts

.557	*Pancreas and islands of Langerhans

*Add as instructed under 617

.558	*Peritoneum

Including mesentery, omentum

.559	*Abdominal hernias
.56	*Back

Class shoulders in 617.572, hips in 617.581

.564	*Backache
.57	*Upper extremities
.572	*Shoulders
.574	*Arms, elbows, wrists
.575	*Hands
.58	*Lower extremities

Class here surgery of joints of the extremities [*formerly also* 617.472], comprehensive works on the extremities, on amputations

For upper extremities, see 617.57

See also 616.72 for nonsurgical medical aspects of joints

.581	*Hips
.582	*Thighs and knees
.584	*Legs and ankles

Leg: segment of inferior limb between knee and ankle

.585	*Feet

Class here podiatry (chiropody)

.6	***Dentistry**
.600 9	Historical, geographical, persons treatment
.601	Oral hygiene and preventive dentistry

Class here dental hygiene

Class surgical complications and sequelae in 617.605

.605	Surgery

Including surgical complications and sequelae

Class preventive measures in 617.601, orthodontics in 617.643, cavities in 617.67

See Manual at 617.522 vs. 617.605

[.605 9]	Surgical therapy

Number discontinued; class in 617.605

*Add as instructed under 617

[.609]   Historical, geographical, persons treatment

           Do not use; class in 617.6009

.63   *Dental diseases

           Tumors of teeth and surrounding tissues relocated to 616.992314, tuberculosis of teeth and surrounding tissues to 616.995314

.632   *Of gums and tooth sockets

           Including alveolar abscesses, gingivitis, periodontitis, pyorrhea

           Class here periodontics

.634   *Of tooth tissues

           Examples: diseases of cementum, dentine, enamel

           For cavities, see 617.67

.634 2   *Of dental pulp

           Class here endodontics

.64   Orthodontics and pedodontics

.643   *Orthodontics

.645   *Pedodontics

           Class a specific aspect of pedodontics with the aspect, e.g., periodontics 617.632

.66   *Extractions

           Class here exodontics

.67   *Cavities (Caries)

.672   Preparation and treatment

.675   Fillings and inlays

           Examples: amalgam, cement, porcelain, plastic fillings and inlays

.69   Prosthetic dentistry (Prosthodontics)

.690 28   Auxiliary techniques and procedures; apparatus, equipment

           Class materials in 617.695

.692   Dentures, crowns, bridges

.695   Materials

.7   **Ophthalmology**

           Treatment of ocular diseases, correction of refractive errors

           Tumors of eyes relocated to 616.99284, tuberculosis of eyes to 616.99584

[.704 4]   Wounds and injuries

           Do not use; class in 617.713

*Add as instructed under 617

[.705 9]	Surgical therapy
	Do not use; class in 617.71
[.707]	Pathology
	Do not use; class in 617.71
.71	Pathology and surgery of eyes

Class pathology and surgery of specific diseases and parts of eyes with the disease or part, e.g., diagnosis of glaucoma 617.741075

| .712 | *Loss of function |

Blindness and partial blindness

See also 617.75 for disorders of refraction and accommodation, color blindness

| .713 | *Wounds and injuries |
| .715 | Diagnosis and prognosis |

Add to base number 617.715 the numbers following 616.075 in 616.0751–616.0759, e.g., physical diagnosis 617.7154

| .719 | Diseases of corneas and scleras |

See also 362.1783 for eye banks

| .719 001–.719 009 | Standard subdivisions |
| .72 | *Diseases of uveas |

Contains diseases of choroids, ciliary bodies, irises

| .73 | *Diseases of optic nerves and retinas |

Class diseases of ocular neuromuscular mechanism in 617.762

| .74 | *Diseases of eyeballs |

For diseases of corneas and scleras, see 617.719; of uveas, 617.72; of retinas, 617.73

| .741 | *Glaucoma |
| .742 | *Diseases of crystalline lenses |

Class here cataracts

| .746 | *Diseases of vitreous bodies |
| .75 | Disorders of refraction and accommodation, color blindness |

Class here optometry

Use of this number for other functional disorders of vision discontinued; class in 617.7

See also 617.712 for blindness and partial blindness

*Add as instructed under 617

.752	Optical work	
	Setting and adjusting lenses, mechanical work of opticians	
.752 2	Eyeglasses	
	Other than contact lenses, intraocular lenses	
	See also 617.7523 for contact lenses, 617.7524 for intraocular lenses	
.752 3	Contact lenses	
.752 4	Intraocular lenses	
.755	Disorders of refraction and accommodation	
	Examples: astigmatism, hyperopia, myopia, presbyopia	
	For aniseikonia, see 617.758	
.758	Aniseikonia	
.759	Color blindness	
.76	Diseases of ocular muscles and lacrimal mechanisms	
.762	*Of ocular neuromuscular mechanism	
	Examples: binocular imbalance, diplopia, strabismus	
	Class here orthoptics	
.764	*Of lacrimal glands and ducts	
.77	Diseases of conjunctivas and eyelids	
.771	*Of eyelids	
.772	*Trachoma	
.773	*Conjunctivitis	
	For trachoma, see 617.772	
.78	*Diseases of orbits	
.79	Prosthetic ophthalmology	
	Fitting of artificial eyes	

.8   ***Otology and audiology**

Class here loss and impairment of function (deafness and hearing impairment)

Tumors of ears relocated to 616.99285, tuberculosis of ears to 616.99585

.81	*Diseases of external ears
	For diseases of auricles, see 617.82; of auditory canals, 617.83
.82	*Diseases of auricles
.83	*Diseases of auditory canals

*Add as instructed under 617

.84   *Diseases of middle ears

> *For diseases of tympanic membranes, see 617.85; of eustachian tubes, 617.86; of mastoid processes, 617.87*

.842   *Of ossicles

.85   *Diseases of tympanic membranes

.86   *Diseases of eustachian tubes (auditory tubes)

.87   *Diseases of mastoid processes

.88   *Diseases of internal ears and the aural nervous system

.882   *Diseases of internal ears

> Example: Menière's disease

> Including diseases of cochleas (labyrinths), semicircular canals, vestibules

.886   *Diseases of the aural nervous system

> Including sensorineural deafness

.89   Correction of impaired hearing

> Example: use of hearing aids

> Class treatment of diseases of specific parts of the hearing apparatus in 617.81–617.88

.9   **Operative surgery and special fields of surgery**

> Class here auxiliary techniques and procedures; apparatus, equipment, materials; comprehensive works on surgical appliances, on prosthetic equipment

> Class a specific appliance or piece of equipment with its specific use, e.g., dentures 617.692

> *See Manual at 617.307 vs. 617.9*

>   617.91–617.96 Surgical techniques, procedures, apparatus, equipment, materials

> Class comprehensive works in 617.9; except for anesthesiology class techniques, procedures, apparatus, equipment, materials of surgery of a specific system, organ, region with surgical therapy of the subject, e.g., preoperative care in neck surgery 617.53059

.91   Operative surgery

> *For anesthesiology, see 617.96*

.910 01   Philosophy and theory

.910 02   Miscellany

*Add as instructed under 617

.910 028	Auxiliary techniques and procedures
	Class surgical instruments, apparatus, equipment, materials in 617.9178
.910 03–.910 09	Standard subdivisions
.910 1	Asepsis and antisepsis
.917	Operating room
.917 2	Preparation of the operating room
.917 8	Surgical instruments, apparatus, equipment, materials
	For surgical dressings, see 617.93
.919	Preoperative and postoperative care
.93	Surgical dressings and their use
.95	Cosmetic and restorative plastic surgery, transplantation of tissue and organs, implantation of artificial organs

Class plastic surgery and transplantation of tissue of specific systems, regions, organs in 617.4–617.5, transplantation of specific organs and implantation of artificial substitutes for specific organs in 617.4, in all cases using subdivision 0592 under 617

See also 362.1783 for tissue and organ banks

.950 01–.950 09	Standard subdivisions
.96	Anesthesiology

Methods and techniques of inducing anesthesia, management of accidents and complications resulting from it

Class acupuncture as an anesthetic in 615.892

.960 4	Special topics
.960 41	Complications and sequelae
.960 42	Emergencies

Class resuscitology in 615.8043

> 617.962–617.966 Types of anesthesia

Class comprehensive works in 617.96, anesthesiology regardless of type for specific kinds of surgery in 617.967

.962	General anesthesia
	Examples: inhalation, intravenous, rectal anesthesias
.964	Regional anesthesia
	Examples: caudal, epidural (peridural), saddle block, spinal anesthesias
.966	Local anesthesia

.967   Anesthesiology for specific kinds of surgery

General, regional, local anesthesia

Add to base number 617.967 the numbers following 617 in 617.1–617.9, e.g., dental anesthesia 617.9676

For anesthesiology for gynecology and obstetrics, see 617.968

.968   Anesthesiology for gynecology and obstetrics

.968 1   Gynecology

.968 2   Obstetrics

>   617.97–617.99 Special fields of surgery

Class comprehensive works in 617.9; specific surgical techniques regardless of field in 617.91–617.96; surgery of a specific organ, system, disorder regardless of field with the subject, e.g., fractures 617.15

.97   *Geriatric surgery

.98   *Pediatric surgery

.99   *Military surgery

618   Other branches of medicine   Gynecology and obstetrics

See Manual at 615.7 vs. 616–618

SUMMARY

618.01–.09	**[Standard subdivisions and special topics of gynecology and obstetrics]**
.1	**Gynecology**
.2	**Obstetrics**
.3	**Diseases and complications of pregnancy**
.4	**Childbirth (Parturition) Labor**
.5	**Complicated labor**
.6	**Normal puerperium**
.7	**Puerperal diseases**
.8	**Obstetrical surgery**
.9	**Pediatrics and geriatrics**

.01   Philosophy and theory of gynecology and obstetrics

.02   Miscellany of gynecology and obstetrics

[.028 7]   Testing and measurement

Relocated to 618.0475

.03   Dictionaries, encyclopedias, concordances of gynecology and obstetrics

.04   Special topics of gynecology and obstetrics

Add to base number 618.04 the numbers following 0 in notation 01–09 from table under 618.1–618.8, e.g., testing and measurement 618.0475 [*formerly* 618.0287], emergencies 618.0425; however, class gynecology and obstetrics as a profession, occupation, hobby in 618.023

*Add as instructed under 617

.05–.07	Standard subdivisions of gynecology and obstetrics
.08	History and description of gynecology and obstetrics with respect to kinds of persons
.083	Young people

Class gynecology for girls up to puberty in 618.92098

.084	Persons in specific stages of adulthood
[.084 6]	Late adulthood

Do not use; class 618.978

.09	Historical, geographical, persons treatment of gynecology and obstetrics

Class life with a disease in 362.198

> ### 618.1–618.8 Gynecology and obstetrics

Medical and surgical

Except where contrary instructions are given, all notes under 616.01–616.08 and in the table under 616.1–616.9 are applicable here

Except for additions, changes, deletions, exceptions shown under specific entries, add to the notation for each term identified by * as follows:

001–008	Standard subdivisions
	As modified under 616.1–616.9
009	Historical, geographical, persons treatment
0092	Persons
	Class life with a disease in 362.198
01–04	Microbiology, special topics, rehabilitation, special classes of diseases
	Add to 0 the numbers following 0 in notation 01–04 from table under 616.1–616.9, e.g., medical emergencies 025
05	Preventive measures and surgery
052	Preventive measures
	By the individual and by medical personnel
	Class comprehensive works on prevention in 613, public measures preventing specific diseases in 614.5992
059	Surgery
	Including surgical complications and sequelae; surgery utilizing specific instruments or techniques, e.g., catheterization, cryosurgery, laser surgery, microsurgery
06	Therapy
	Class here rehabilitative therapy
	Class comprehensive works on rehabilitative therapy and education for living with handicaps and disabilities in 03
	For surgery, see 059
061	Drug therapy
062–069	Other therapies
	Add to 06 the numbers following 615.8 in 615.82–615.89, e.g., X-ray therapy 06422
07	Pathology
	Add to 07 the numbers following 616.07 in 616.071–616.079, e.g., physical diagnosis 0754

(continued)

> **618.1-618.8 Gynecology and obstetrics (continued)**

08   Psychosomatic medicine
09   Case histories

Class comprehensive works in 618

.1   ***Gynecology**

Including endocrine gynecology, endometriosis

Class tumors of genital system in 616.99265

For puerperal diseases, see 618.7; pediatric gynecology, 618.92098

.11   *Diseases of the ovaries

.12   *Diseases of the Fallopian tubes (oviducts)

.13   *Diseases of the perimetrium (Periuterine diseases)

.14   *Diseases of the uterus

Class here diseases of the uterine cervix

For diseases of the perimetrium, see 618.13

[.140 59]   Surgery

Do not use; class in 618.145

.142   *Infections

Examples: cervicitis, endometritis, pyometra

For leukorrhea, see 618.173

See also 618.1 for endometriosis

.143   *Erosions

.144   *Malformations

Examples: atrophies, hypertrophies, prolapse of uterus

.145   Surgery

.145 3   Hysterectomies

.145 8   Dilation and curettage

See also 618.88 for surgical abortion

.15   *Diseases of the vagina

For leukorrhea, see 618.173

.16   *Diseases of the vulva

*Add as instructed under 618.1-618.8

| .17 | *Functional and systemic disorders |
| .172 | *Menstruation disorders |

Examples: amenorrhea, dysmenorrhea, menorrhagia, oligomenorrhea, premenstrual syndrome (PMS)

| .173 | *Leukorrhea |
| .175 | *Menopause disorders |

Class here comprehensive works on climacteric disorders

Class male climacteric disorders in 616.693, involutional psychoses in 616.895

| .178 | *Infertility |

Including artificial insemination

Embryo transplant ("test-tube baby") is classed in 618.178059

Class comprehensive works on male and female infertility in 616.692

| .19 | *Diseases of the breast |

Class here comprehensive works on diseases of the male and female breast

Class tumors of the breast in 616.99249, surgery of the male breast in 617.549

For diseases of the male breast, see 616.49; diseases of lactation, 618.71

| .2 | ***Obstetrics** |

For diseases, disorders, management of pregnancy, parturition, puerperium, see 618.3–618.8

| [.205 2] | Preventive measures |

Do not use; class 618.24

| [.205 9] | Surgical therapy |

Do not use; class in 618.8

| [.207 5] | Diagnosis |

Do not use; class in 618.22

| .22 | Diagnosis |

Use of this number for symptomatology discontinued; class in 618.2

| .24 | Prenatal care and preparation for childbirth |

Examples: dietetics for pregnant women, exercises to aid childbirth

| .25 | *Multiple pregnancy and childbirth |

*Add as instructed under 618.1–618.8

>   **618.3–618.8 Diseases, disorders, management of pregnancy, parturition, puerperium**

        Class comprehensive works in 618.2

.3   ***Diseases and complications of pregnancy**

.31   Extrauterine pregnancy (Ectopic pregnancy)

        Examples: abdominal, cervical, ovarian, tubal pregnancies

.32   *Fetal disorders

        Examples: fetal degeneration, calcification

        Class here perinatal medicine

        Amniocentesis to diagnose genetic diseases is classed in 618.32042

        Class neonatal medicine in 618.9201

           For childbirth, see 618.4

           See Manual at 618.92 vs. 616, 618.32

.326   *Diseases of specific systems and organs

.326 1   *Of the cardiovascular system

.326 8   *Of the nervous system

        Including drug dependence

[.33]   Spontaneous abortion

        Relocated to 618.392

.34   *Diseases of the placenta and amniotic fluid

.39   Miscarriage and premature delivery

.392   Spontaneous abortion [*formerly* 618.33] and miscarriage

        Before fetus is viable

.397   Premature delivery

        After fetus is viable and before full term

.4   **Childbirth (Parturition)**   **Labor**

        Class a specific aspect not provided for here with the aspect, e.g., Caesarean section 618.86

.42   Presentations

        Position of fetal body during labor

.45   Natural childbirth

        Childbirth without use of analgesics

*Add as instructed under 618.1–618.8

.5	**Complicated labor**
.51	Maternal complications

Difficult labor due to anomalies of expellant forces and mechanical obstructions

.53	Fetal complications

Difficult labor due to size of fetus

.54	Uterine hemorrhage
.56	Placental complications
.58	Complications from umbilical cord
.6	**Normal puerperium**

Postpartum management and care

.7	***Puerperal diseases**

Example: Sheehan's syndrome

.71	*Diseases of lactation
.73	*Puerperal metritis and peritonitis
.74	*Puerperal septicemia and pyemia
.75	*Puerperal eclampsia
.76	*Puerperal mental disorders

Example: postpartum depression

.77	*Hemic disorders
.79	Maternal death
.8	**Obstetrical surgery**

Class embryo transplant ("test-tube baby") in 618.178059

.82	Version and extraction

Class embryo transplant ("test-tube baby") in 618.178059

.83	Embryotomy and craniotomy

Mutilation of fetus to facilitate delivery when impossible by natural means

.85	Minor surgery

Examples: episiotomy, repair of lacerations of genital tract, symphyseotomy, vaginiperineotomy

.86	Caesarean section
.87	Surgical removal of placenta
.88	Surgical abortion

*Add as instructed under 618.1–618.8

.89   Asepsis and antisepsis

.9   Pediatrics and geriatrics

.92   Pediatrics

Diseases of infants and children up to puberty

Including sudden infant death syndrome (crib death, cot death)

Class medicine for young people who have reached puberty in 616.00835; pediatric aspects of wounds and injuries in 617.1, of results of injuries in 617.2; pediatric orthopedics in 617.3

For pedodontics, see 617.645; pediatric surgery, 617.98

See Manual at 618.92 vs. 616, 618.32

.920 001–.920 008   Standard subdivisions

As modified under 616.1–616.9

.920 009   Historical, geographical, persons treatment

.920 009 2   Persons

Class life with a physical disease in 362.19892, with a psychiatric disorder in 618.92890092

.920 01–.920 09   General topics

Add to base number 618.920 notation 01–09 from table under 616.1–616.9, e.g., diagnosis 618.920075; however, class pediatric preventive measures in 613.0432, pediatric therapeutics in 615.542

.920 1   Newborn infants (Neonates)

In first month after birth

Class perinatal medicine in 618.32

.920 11   Premature infants

.920 12   Full-term infants

.920 9   Special branches of medicine

Class sports medicine in 617.1027, orthopedics in 617.3, pedodontics in 617.645, surgery in 617.98

See Manual at 618.9209 vs. 617

.920 97   Regional medicine, ophthalmology, otology, audiology

.920 975   Regional medicine

Add to base number 618.920975 the numbers following 617.5 in 617.51–617.58, e.g., disorders of the face 618.9209752

.920 977–.920 978   Ophthalmology, otology, audiology

Add to base number 618.92097 the numbers following 617 in 617.7–617.8, e.g., trachoma in children 618.92097772

.920 98	Gynecology
.920 981	Specific diseases

> Add to base number 618.920981 the numbers following 618.1 in 618.11–618.19, e.g., diseases of the uterus 618.9209814

.921–.929　Specific diseases

> Add to base number 618.92 the numbers following 616 in 616.1–616.9, e.g., cardiac diseases in children 618.9212
>
> Class orthopedic diseases in 617.3, dental diseases in 617.645, other diseases not provided for here in 618.9209

.97　*Geriatrics

> Diseases of persons in late adulthood

[.970 5]　Preventive measures

> Do not use; class in 613.0438

[.970 6]　Therapy

> Do not use; class in 615.547

.976–.978　Specific diseases

> Add to base number 618.97 the numbers following 61 in 616–618, e.g., geriatric mental illness 618.97689; however, class geriatric aspects of wounds and injuries in 617.1, of results of injuries in 617.2; geriatric orthopedics in 617.3; geriatric surgery in 617.97
>
> *See Manual at 618.977 vs. 617*

619　Experimental medicine

Class experimental medicine with respect to pharmacology and therapeutics in 615, with respect to specific diseases in 616–618; animal experimentation with respect to anatomy and physiology in 591–599, human experimentation with respect to anatomy and physiology in 611–612

.5　**Fowl**

.7　**Dogs**

.8　**Cats**

.9　**Other mammals**

.93　Rodents and rabbits

> Examples: guinea pigs, hamsters, mice, rats

.98　Primates

> Examples: apes, monkeys, humans

*Add as instructed under 616.1–616.9

620   Engineering and allied operations

Class here manufacturing of products of various branches of engineering

Class comprehensive works on manufacturing in 670

For chemical engineering, see 660

SUMMARY

620.001–.009	[Standard subdivisions and general topics]
.1	Engineering mechanics and materials
.2	Sound and related vibrations
.3	Mechanical vibration
.4	Engineering for specific kinds of geographical environments, fine particle and remote control technology
.8	Human-factors and safety engineering
621	**Applied physics**
.04	[Energy and plasma engineering]
.1	Steam engineering
.2	Hydraulic-power technology
.3	Electric, electronic, magnetic, communications, computer engineering; lighting
.4	Heat engineering and prime movers
.5	Pneumatic, vacuum, low-temperature technologies
.6	Fans, blowers, pumps
.8	Machine engineering
.9	Tools and fabricating equipment
622	**Mining and related operations**
.1	Prospecting and exploratory operations
.2	Excavation techniques
.3	Mining for specific materials
.4	Mine environment
.5	Mine drainage
.6	Mine transport systems
.7	Ore dressing
.8	Mine health and safety
623	**Military and nautical engineering**
.04	General topics
.1	Fortifications
.2	Mine laying, mine clearance, demolition
.3	Engineering of defense
.4	Ordnance
.5	Ballistics and gunnery
.6	Military transportation technology
.7	Communications, vehicles, sanitation, related topics
.8	Nautical engineering and seamanship
624	**Civil engineering**
.1	Structural engineering and underground construction
.2	Bridges
.3	Specific types of bridges
.4	Tubular and box-girder bridges
.5	Suspension bridges
.6	Arch bridges
.7	Compound bridges
.8	Movable bridges

625	Engineering of railroads, roads, highways
.1	Railroads
.2	Railroad rolling stock
.3	Inclined, mountain, ship railroads
.4	Rapid transit systems
.5	Cable and aerial railways
.6	Surface rail and trolley systems
.7	Roads
.8	Artificial road surfaces
627	**Hydraulic engineering**
.04	[Hydrodynamics and recreational waters]
.1	Inland waterways
.2	Harbors, ports, roadsteads
.3	Port installations
.4	Flood control
.5	Reclamation, irrigation, related topics
.7	Underwater operations
.8	Dams and reservoirs
.9	Other hydraulic structures
628	**Sanitary and municipal engineering Environmental protection engineering**
.1	Water supply
.2	Sewers and sewage
.3	Sewage treatment and disposal
.4	Waste technology, public toilets, street cleaning
.5	Pollution technology and industrial sanitation engineering
.7	Sanitary engineering for rural and sparsely populated areas
.9	Other branches of sanitary and municipal engineering
629	**Other branches of engineering**
.04	Transportation engineering
.1	Aerospace engineering
.2	Motor land vehicles, and cycles
.3	Air-cushion vehicles (Ground-effect machines, Hovercraft)
.4	Astronautics
.8	Automatic control engineering

.001   Philosophy and theory

.001 1   Systems

Class interdisciplinary works on systems in 003; works covering systems of agriculture, home economics, or management in addition to engineering in 601.1; design of engineering systems in 620.0042; manufacturing systems in 670.11

.001 13   Computer modeling and simulation

Class computer-aided design in 620.00420285

.001 171   Large-scale systems

Class here analysis of large, complex systems [*formerly* 620.72]

[.001 53]	Physical principles in engineering

Do not use; class comprehensive works in 621, engineering mechanics in 620.1, sound engineering in 620.2, electrical and magnetic engineering in 621.3, optical engineering in 621.36, electronic engineering in 621.381, heat engineering in 621.402, nuclear engineering in 621.48

.002	Miscellany
[.002 87]	Testing and measurement

Do not use; class in 620.0044

[.002 88]	Maintenance and repair

Do not use; class in 620.0046

[.002 89]	Safety engineering

Relocated to 620.86

.003	Dictionaries, encyclopedias, concordances
.004	Design, testing, measurement, quality, maintenance, repair
.004 2	Engineering design

Class here design of large, complex systems [*formerly* 620.72]

.004 202 85	Computer-aided design (CAD)

Class comprehensive works on computer-aided design and computer-aided manufacturing (CAD/CAM) in 670.285

[.004 22]	Analysis

Number discontinued; class in 620

[.004 25]	Design

Number discontinued; class in 620.0042

.004 4	Testing and measurement

Including inspection, simulation

Class interdisciplinary works on measurement in 530.8

.004 5	Quality

Examples: interchangeability, maintainability, precision

Class testing and measurement for quality in 620.0044, maintenance in 620.0046

.004 52	Reliability
.004 54	Durability

.004 6	Maintenance and repair

Class here interdisciplinary works on maintenance and repair

Class maintenance and repair in a specific subject with the subject, using notation 0288 from Table 1, e.g., clock and watch repair 681.110288

.005–.008	Standard subdivisions
.009	Historical, geographical, persons treatment
.009 1	Treatment by areas, regions, places in general

Class engineering to overcome problems of specific kinds of geographical environments in 620.41

.009 2	Persons

Class persons treatment of engineers known primarily as entrepreneurs in 338.76

.1   Engineering mechanics and materials

Use 620.1001–620.1009 for standard subdivisions of engineering mechanics and materials, of engineering mechanics alone

SUMMARY

620.103–.107	**Engineering (Applied) mechanics**
.11	**Engineering materials**
.12	**Wood**
.13	**Masonry materials**
.14	**Ceramic and allied materials**
.16	**Metals**
.17	**Ferrous metals**
.18	**Nonferrous metals**
.19	**Other engineering materials**

>   620.103–620.107 Engineering (Applied) mechanics

Class comprehensive works in 620.1

For fine particle technology, see 620.43

See also 531 for mechanics as a subject in physics

See Manual at 621 vs. 530

.103	Applied statics

Class applied solid statics in 620.1053, applied fluid statics in 620.1063

.104	Applied dynamics

Class applied solid dynamics in 620.1054, applied fluid dynamics in 620.1064

.105   Applied solid mechanics

Class structural theory in 624.17

For mechanical vibration, see 620.3

See also 621.811 for physical principles of machinery

.105 3   Statics

.105 4   Dynamics

.106   Applied fluid mechanics

Class here applied hydromechanics, comprehensive works on fluid-power technology

Class steam engineering in 621.1, hydraulic-power technology in 621.2, hydraulic engineering in 627

For applied gas mechanics, see 620.107

.106 3   Statics

.106 4   Dynamics

Including cavitation, pressure surge, water hammer

Class here flow

See also 621.4022 for convective transport, heat convection

.107   Applied gas mechanics

Class here applied aeromechanics

Class steam engineering in 621.1, pneumatic and vacuum technology in 621.5, aeromechanics of flight in 629.1323, air-conditioning engineering in 697.93

.107 3   Statics

.107 4   Dynamics

.11   Engineering materials

Class comprehensive works on materials, manufacture of materials in 670

For specific kinds of materials, see 620.12–620.19

SUMMARY

620.110 287	**Testing and measurement**
.112	**Resistance and other specific properties of materials, nondestructive testing**
.116	**Porous materials**
.117	**Organic materials**
.118	**Composite materials**

.110 287   Testing and measurement

Do not use for nondestructive testing; class in 620.1127

.112   Resistance and other specific properties of materials, nondestructive testing

Class here failure, strength of materials

Class properties and nondestructive testing of porous, organic, composite materials in 620.116–620.118

SUMMARY

620.112 1	**Resistance to thermal forces**
.112 2	**Resistance to decay, decomposition, deterioration**
.112 3	**Resistance to mechanical deformation (Mechanics of materials)**
.112 4	**Resistance to specific mechanical stresses**
.112 5	**Properties affecting permanent deformation**
.112 6	**Resistance to fracture (Fracture mechanics)**
.112 7	**Nondestructive testing**
.112 9	**Other properties**

>   620.112 1–620.112 6 Resistance to specific forces

Class comprehensive works in 620.112

.112 1   Resistance to thermal forces

Class resistance to thermal radiation in 620.11228

See also 620.11296 for thermal properties

.112 15   Changes in temperature

Examples: cyclical and sudden changes

.112 16   Low and cryogenic temperatures

.112 17   High temperatures

.112 2   Resistance to decay, decomposition, deterioration

Physicochemical actions not basically thermal or mechanical

Including action of pests

.112 23   Biodegradation, corrosion, weathering

Examples: rot, rust

.112 28   Resistance to radiations

.112 3   Resistance to mechanical deformation (Mechanics of materials)

Fatigue relocated to 620.1126

For resistance to specific mechanical stresses, see 620.1124; resistance to fracture, 620.1126

.112 302 87   Testing and measurement

Including strain gauges

.112 32   Temporary deformation (Elasticity)

Including elastic limit

.112 33	Permanent deformation (Plasticity)
	Including creep, plastic flow
	For properties affecting permanent deformation, see 620.1125
.112 4	Resistance to specific mechanical stresses
	Class resistance to change of form, regardless of stress, in 620.1125; resistance to fracture, regardless of stress, in 620.1126
.112 41	Tension
.112 42	Compression
.112 43	Torsion (Twisting)
.112 44	Flexure (Bending)
.112 45	Shearing
.112 48	Vibrations
.112 5	Properties affecting permanent deformation
	Examples: impact strength, rigidity, shock resistance; ductility, malleability
.112 6	Resistance to fracture (Fracture mechanics)
	Including brittleness, hardness
	Class here fatigue [*formerly* 620.1123]; fatigue, fracture, rupture strength; crack resistance, resistance to penetration and breaking
.112 7	Nondestructive testing
.112 72	Radiographic (X-ray) testing
.112 73	Tracer testing
.112 74	Ultrasonic testing
.112 78	Magnetic testing
.112 9	Other properties
.112 92	Mechanical properties
	Examples: adhesiveness, roughness, texture; friction, wear resistance
	See also 620.44 for surface technology
.112 94	Acoustical properties
.112 95	Optical properties
	Examples: luminescence, photoelasticity, refractivity
.112 96	Thermal properties
	Example: heat conductivity
	See also 620.1121 for resistance to thermal forces

.112 97	Electric, electronic, magnetic properties
.112 972	Semiconductivity
.112 973	Superconductivity
.112 99	Microphysical properties

Examples: atomic, molecular, nuclear, crystallographic properties

Including microstructure

For electronic properties, see 620.11297

> ### 620.116–620.118 Porous, organic, composite materials

Class comprehensive works in 620.11, a specific kind of porous, organic, composite material in 620.12–620.19

.116   *Porous materials

Class porous organic materials in 620.117, porous composite materials in 620.118

.117   *Organic materials

Class organic composite materials in 620.118

.118   *Composite materials

Class specific composite materials with the predominant component in 620.12–620.19, e.g., ferroconcrete 620.137

> ### 620.12–620.19 Specific kinds of materials

Add to each subdivision identified by * as follows:
    0287   Testing and measurement
                        Do not use for nondestructive testing; class in 7
        1–9   Specific properties and nondestructive testing
                Add the numbers following 620.112 in 620.1121–620.1129, e.g., nondestructive testing 7

Class comprehensive works in 620.11; porous, organic, composite materials in 620.116–620.118; manufacturing and chemical properties of specific kinds of materials with the materials, e.g., wood 674

.12   *Wood

Including laminated wood

Class here physical properties [*formerly also* 674.132]

.13   Masonry materials

For brick, tile, terra-cotta, see 620.142

.130 287   Testing and measurement

Do not use for nondestructive measurement; class in 620.130427

*Add as instructed under 620.12–620.19

.130 4	Special topics
.130 42	*Specific properties and nondestructive testing
.132	*Natural stones
.135	*Cement

Class here masonry adhesives [*formerly* 620.15]

.136	*Concrete

For reinforced and prestressed concrete, see 620.137; concrete blocks, 620.139

.137	*Reinforced and *prestressed concrete
.139	Artificial stones

Examples: cinder and concrete blocks

.139 028 7	Testing and measurement

Do not use for nondestructive measurement; class in 620.1390427

.139 04	Special topics
.139 042	*Specific properties and nondestructive testing
.14	Ceramic and allied materials

Class masonry materials in 620.13

.140 287	Testing and measurement

Do not use for nondestructive measurement; class in 620.140427

.140 4	Special topics
.140 42	*Specific properties and nondestructive testing
.142	Brick, tile, terra-cotta
.143	*Refractory materials

Example: fireclays

Class refractory metals in 620.16

For asbestos, see 620.195

.144	*Glass

Including fiber glass

.146	Porcelain and enamel
[.15]	Masonry adhesives

Relocated to 620.135

*Add as instructed under 620.12–620.19

.16	*Metals

Class here alloys

For ferrous metals, see 620.17; nonferrous metals, 620.18

.17	*Ferrous metals

Class here iron, steel

.18	Nonferrous metals

Class here nonferrous alloys

.180 287	Testing and measurement

Do not use for nondestructive measurement; class in 620.180427

.180 4	Special topics
.180 42	*Specific properties and nondestructive testing
.182	*Copper

Class here brass, Muntz metal; bronzes, gunmetal; copper-aluminum alloys; copper-beryllium alloys

.183	*Lead
.184	Zinc and cadmium
.184 2	*Zinc

For brass, Muntz metal, see 620.182

.184 6	*Cadmium
.185	*Tin

For bronzes, gunmetal, see 620.182

.186	*Aluminum

For copper-aluminum alloys, see 620.182

.187	*Magnesium
.188	*Nickel
.189	Other metals
.189 1	*Mercury
.189 2	Precious, rare-earth, actinide-series metals

Add to base number 620.1892 the numbers following 669.2 in 669.22–669.29, e.g., uranium 620.1892931

.189 3	Metals used in ferroalloys

For nickel, see 620.188

*Add as instructed under 620.12–620.19

.189 302 87	Testing and measurement
	Do not use for nondestructive measurement; class in 620.18930427
.189 304	Special topics
.189 304 2	*Specific properties and nondestructive testing
.189 32	Titanium, manganese, vanadium
.189 322	*Titanium
.189 33	*Cobalt
.189 34	Chromium, molybdenum, tungsten
.189 35	Zirconium and tantalum
.189 352	*Zirconium
.189 4	*Beryllium
	For copper-beryllium alloys, see 620.182
.189 5	Antimony, arsenic, bismuth
.189 6	Alkali and alkaline-earth metals
	Examples: barium, calcium, lithium, potassium, sodium, strontium
.189 602 87	Testing and measurement
	Do not use for nondestructive measurement; class in 620.18960427
.189 604	Special topics
.189 604 2	*Specific properties and nondestructive testing
.189 9	Miscellaneous rare metals
	Limited to gallium, germanium, hafnium, indium, niobium, selenium, tellurium, thallium
.19	Other engineering materials
.191	Soils and related materials
	Examples: aggregates, gravel, clay, sand
	Class interdisciplinary works on soils in 631.4, foundation soils in 624.151
.191 028 7	Testing and measurement
	Do not use for nondestructive measurement; class in 620.1910427
.191 04	Special topics
.191 042	*Specific properties and nondestructive testing

*Add as instructed under 620.12–620.19

.192	Polymers

For elastomers, see 620.194

.192 028 7	Testing and measurement

Do not use for nondestructive measurement; class in 620.1920427

.192 04	Special topics
.192 042	*Specific properties and nondestructive testing
.192 3	*Plastics

Class here plastic laminating materials

.192 4	*Gums and *resins
.193	Nonmetallic elements

Examples: carbon, hydrogen, nitrogen, oxygen, phosphorus, silicon, sulfur; inert gases

Class phosphor bronze in 620.182

.193 028 7	Testing and measurement

Do not use for nondestructive measurement; class in 620.1930427

.193 04	Special topics
.193 042	*Specific properties and nondestructive testing
.194	*Elastomers

Class here rubber

.195	Insulating materials

Examples: asbestos, corkboard, diatomaceous earth, kapok, rock wool

Including dielectric materials

.195 028 7	Testing and measurement

Do not use for nondestructive measurement; class in 620.1950427

.195 04	Special topics
.195 042	*Specific properties and nondestructive testing
.196	Bituminous materials

Examples: synthetic and natural asphalt, tar

.196 028 7	Testing and measurement

Do not use for nondestructive measurement; class in 620.1960427

.196 04	Special topics

*Add as instructed under 620.12–620.19

.196 042	*Specific properties and nondestructive testing
.197	Organic fibrous materials

        Examples: paper, paperboard, rope, textiles

.197 028 7	Testing and measurement

        Do not use for nondestructive measurement; class in 620.1970427

.197 04	Special topics
.197 042	*Specific properties and nondestructive testing
.198	Other natural and synthetic minerals

        Examples: corundum, feldspar, gems, graphite, oil, quartz, water

.199	Adhesives and sealants

        Class here comprehensive works on laminating materials

        For masonry adhesives, see 620.135; plastic laminating materials, 620.1923

.199 028 7	Testing and measurement

        Do not use for nondestructive measurement; class in 620.1990427

.199 04	Special topics
.199 042	*Specific properties and nondestructive testing
.2	**Sound and related vibrations**

        See also 534 for physics of sound

        See Manual at 621 vs. 530

>   620.21–620.25 Applied acoustics (Acoustical engineering)

        Class comprehensive works in 620.2; electroacoustical communications in 621.3828; interdisciplinary works on architectural acoustics in 729.29, engineering works on architectural acoustics in 690.2

.21	General topics of applied acoustics

        Examples: analysis and synthesis [*formerly* 534.4], sources of sound

.23	Noise and countermeasures
.25	Acoustics in specific physical environments

        Example: underwater acoustics

.28	Applied ultrasonics and subsonics

        For ultrasonic testing of materials, see 620.11274

*Add as instructed under 620.12–620.19

.3	**Mechanical vibration**

Class effects of vibrations on materials in 620.11248

For sound and related vibrations, see 620.2

.302 87	Measurement [*formerly* 620.32] and testing
.31	Generation and transmission
[.32]	Measurement

Relocated to 620.30287

.37	Effects and countermeasures
.4	**Engineering for specific kinds of geographical environments, fine particle and remote control technology**
.41	Engineering for specific kinds of geographical environments

Class a specific technology with the technology, using notation 091 from Table 1 when the environment is not inherent in the subject, e.g., ergonomics for deserts 620.8209154, nautical engineering 623.8

.411–.417	Specific kinds of terrestrial environments

Add to base number 620.41 the numbers following —1 in —11–17 from Table 2, e.g., ocean engineering 620.4162; however, class engineering of estuaries in 627.124

Class hydraulic engineering in 627

.419	Extraterrestrial environments
.43	Fine particle technology

Example: dust

Class here powder technology

Including liquid particle technology

.44	Surface engineering
.46	Remote control and telecontrol
[.7]	**Engineering of large, complex systems**

Number discontinued; class in 620

[.72]	Analysis and design of large, complex systems

Analysis relocated to 620.001171, design to 620.0042

.8	**Human-factors and safety engineering**

Class here work environment engineering

Class a specific application with the application, e.g., engineering of the home kitchen work environment 643.3

See also 628 for environmental protection engineering

.82   Human-factors engineering

Variant names: biotechnology, design anthropometry, ergonomics

[.85]   Environmental health engineering

Relocated to 628

.86   Safety engineering [*formerly also* 620.00289]

Class safety engineering of a specific technology with the technology, using notation 0289 from Table 1, e.g., safety in machine engineering 621.80289

621   Applied physics

Mechanical, electrical, electronic, electromagnetic, heat, light, nuclear engineering

Standard subdivisions are added for mechanical engineering

Class applied mechanics in 620.1, applied acoustics in 620.2, a specific application with the application, e.g., military engineering 623

See Manual at 621 vs. 530

SUMMARY

621.04	[Energy and plasma engineering]
.1	Steam engineering
.2	Hydraulic-power technology
.3	Electric, electronic, magnetic, communications, computer engineering; lighting
.4	Heat engineering and prime movers
.5	Pneumatic, vacuum, low-temperature technologies
.6	Fans, blowers, pumps
.8	Machine engineering
.9	Tools and fabricating equipment

.04   Special topics

.042   Energy engineering

Class here engineering of alternative, renewable energy sources

Class interdisciplinary works on energy in 333.79

.044   Plasma engineering

See also 530.44 for plasma as a subject in physics

>   **621.1–621.2 Fluid-power technologies**

Class comprehensive works in 620.106

.1   **Steam engineering**

>   621.15–621.16 Specific kinds of steam engines

Class comprehensive works in 621.1, marine steam engines in 623.8722

For steam locomotives, see 625.261; steam tractors and rollers, 629.2292

.15 Portable engines

Class comprehensive works on specific structural types of steam engines in 621.16

.16 Stationary engines

Class here comprehensive works on specific structural types of steam engines

Class portable engines of specific structural types in 621.15

.164 Reciprocating engines

.165 Turbines

.166 Other stationary engines

Example: rotary engines

.18 Generating and transmitting steam

Class generating steam in specific kinds of steam engines in 621.15–621.16, in central stations in 621.19

> 621.182–621.183 Generation

Class comprehensive works in 621.18

.182 Fuels and fuel consumption

.183 Boilers and boiler furnaces

Including accessories [*formerly* 621.184], mechanical stokers, chimneys

[.184] Thermodynamics, design, construction

Number discontinued; class in 621.18

Accessories relocated to 621.183

.185 Transmitting steam

Including insulation, pressure regulators, safety valves, steam pipes

.19 Central stations

.194 Boiler operations (Boiler-house practices)

Including feed-water treatment

.197 Accessories

Including condensers, cooling towers, superheaters

.199 Cogeneration of electric power and heat

Class interdisciplinary works on cogeneration of electricity and heat in 333.793

.2 **Hydraulic-power technology**

Class hydraulic control in 629.8042

.204		Special topics
.204 2		Specific liquids
.204 22		Water
.204 24		Hydraulic fluids
		Other than water

.21   **Water mills**

Including waterwheels, water lifting devices

.24   **Turbines**

.25   **Pumps and accumulators**

.252   Pumps

Class comprehensive works on pumps in 621.69

.254   Accumulators

.26   **Hydraulic transmission**

Use of this number for comprehensive works on hydraulic-power machinery and appliances discontinued; class in 621.2

Class specific liquids in hydraulic transmission in 621.2042

For rams, see 621.27

.27   Rams

.3   Electric, electronic, magnetic, communications, computer engineering; lighting

Including superconductivity

Standard subdivisions are added for electromagnetic engineering, for combined electric and electronic engineering, for electrical engineering alone

See also 537 for physics of electricity and electromagnetism

SUMMARY

621.302 8		**Auxiliary techniques and procedures; apparatus, equipment, materials**
	.31	**Generation, modification, storage, transmission of electric power**
	.32	**Lighting**
	.33	**Electric power transmission for railroads**
	.34	**Magnetic engineering**
	.36	**Applied optics and paraphotic engineering**
	.37	**Testing and measurement of electrical quantities**
	.38	**Electronics and communications engineering**
	.39	**Computers**

.302 8   Auxiliary techniques and procedures; apparatus, equipment, materials

Class electrical equipment in 621.31042

.302 87   Testing and measurement

Class electrical testing and measurement in 621.37

.31   Generation, modification, storage, transmission of electric power

Class here alternating current [*formerly also* 537.63]

SUMMARY

621.310 4	[Electrical machinery and equipment]
.312	Generation, modification, storage
.313	Generating machinery and converters
.314	Transformers
.315	Capacitors (Condensers)
.316	Details and parts of generators
.317	Control devices
.319	Transmission

.310 4   Special topics

.310 42   Electrical machinery and equipment

Including eddy currents, shaft currents

Class a specific application with the subject, e.g., refrigerators 621.57

For electric motors, see 621.46

.312   Generation, modification, storage

For equipment for generation, modification, control, see 621.313–621.317

.312 1   Generation

Class here central and auxiliary power plants, mechanical generation

For direct energy conversion, see 621.3124

.312 13   Specific kinds of mechanical generation

Use of this number for comprehensive works on mechanical generation discontinued; class in 621.3121

.312 132   Steam-powered generation

Class here comprehensive works on generation from fossil fuels

For generation by internal combustion engines, see 621.312133; nuclear steam-powered generation of electricity, 621.483

.312 133   Generation by internal combustion engines

.312 134   Hydroelectric generation

Including tidal generation

Class engineering of dams for hydroelectric power in 627.8

.312 136   Wind-powered generation

.312 4	Direct energy conversion
	For direct nuclear generation, see 621.3125
.312 42	Electrochemical energy conversion
	Class comprehensive works on electrochemical engineering in 660.297
.312 423	Primary batteries
.312 424	Secondary batteries (Storage batteries)
.312 429	Fuel cells
.312 43	Thermoelectric generation
	Including thermionic converters
	Class generation of electricity from solar radiation in 621.31244
.312 44	Generation of electricity from solar radiation
	Class here photovoltaic generation, use of solar batteries and cells
.312 45	Magnetohydrodynamic generation
.312 5	Direct nuclear generation
	Including radioisotope-powered generators
[.312 52]	Nuclear steam-powered generation of electricity
	Relocated to 621.483
[.312 56]	Direct nuclear generation
	Number discontinued; class in 621.3125
.312 6	Modification and storage
	Examples: operation of transformer, converter substations
	Class storage of electrical energy by chemical methods in 621.312424

> 621.313–621.317 Machinery and equipment for generation, modification, control

Class comprehensive works in 621.31042

.313	Generating machinery and converters
	Including static generators [*formerly also* 537.23]
	Class here comprehensive works on generators and motors
	For details and parts of generators, see 621.316; electric motors, 621.46
.313 2	Direct-current machinery
	Examples: dynamos, converters to alternating current

.313 3	Alternating-current machinery
	Class here synchronous machinery
	For synchronous generators, see 621.3134; synchronous converters to direct current, 621.3135; asynchronous machinery, 621.3136
.313 4	Synchronous generators
.313 5	Synchronous converters to direct current
	For rectifiers, see 621.3137
.313 6	Asynchronous machinery
	For rectifiers, see 621.3137
.313 7	Rectifiers
.314	Transformers
.315	Capacitors (Condensers) [*formerly also* 537.242]
.316	Details and parts of generators
	Contains armatures and armature winding, brushes, commutators, contactors, electromagnets (field cores)
	Class a specific part not provided for here with the subject, e.g., transformers 621.314
.317	Control devices
	Class here protective devices [*formerly also* 621.319], power electronics, switching equipment
	Examples: circuit breakers, fuses, grounding devices, lightning arresters, meters, relays, rheostats
	Class switches at service end of line in 621.31924
.319	Transmission
	Including access to power lines [*formerly also* 634.93], power failure
	Class here electrification [*formerly* 621.394]
	Protective devices relocated to 621.317
	Class interdisciplinary works on electrification, on power failure in 333.7932
	For electric power transmission for railroads, see 621.33
[.319 011]	Systems
	Do not use; class in 621.3191
.319 1	Systems
	Class lines and circuitry in 621.3192
.319 12	Direct-current systems

.319 13	Alternating-current systems
	Including high-tension systems
.319 15	Composite current systems
	Direct and alternating currents combined
.319 16	Polycyclic current systems
.319 2	Circuitry [*formerly also* 537.61, 537.63] and lines (Networks)
.319 21	Physical phenomena in circuits
	Examples: heat losses in lines, transients
.319 22	Overhead lines and their components
.319 23	Underground lines and their components
.319 24	Apparatus at service end of line
	Examples: extension cords, junctions, outlets, sockets, switches
	Class here interior wiring
	For exterior service wiring and its components, see 621.31925
.319 25	Exterior service wiring and its components
.319 3	Equipment and components
	Class equipment for generation, modification, control in 621.313–621.317, use in lines and circuitry in 621.3192
.319 32	Uninsulated wires
.319 33	Insulated wires
.319 34	Cables
.319 37	Insulators and insulation
.32	**Lighting**
	Class here electric lighting
.321	**Principles of lighting**
	Former heading: Illumination
.321 1	Layouts, calculations, photometry
.321 2	Direct lighting
.321 3	Indirect and semi-indirect lighting
.321 4	Floodlighting
	Class here directed lighting
	Class exterior floodlighting in 621.3229
[.321 5]	Transillumination
	Number discontinued; class in 621.321

.322   **Lighting in specific situations**

Use of this number for comprehensive works on lighting discontinued; class in 621.32

Class specific forms of lighting in 621.323–621.327; lighting of airports, 629.1365

For public lighting, see 628.95

.322 5–.322 8   Interior lighting

Add to base number 621.322 the numbers following 72 in 725–728, e.g., lighting for libraries 621.32278

Class comprehensive works in 621.322

.322 9   Exterior lighting

Examples: advertising and display lighting, garden and patio lighting

---

>   **621.323–621.327 Specific forms of lighting**

Class comprehensive works in 621.32

.323   Nonelectrical lighting

Examples: candles, oil-burning devices, torches

For gas lighting, see 621.324

.324   Gas lighting

>   **621.325–621.327 Electric lighting**

Class comprehensive works in 621.32

.325   Arc lighting

Electric-discharge lighting in which light is produced by consumable electrodes or by vapors emanating from consumable electrodes

Class here enclosed arc lighting [*formerly* 621.327]

.326   Incandescent lighting

.327   Vapor (Luminous-tube) lighting

Enclosed arc lighting relocated to 621.325

.327 3   Fluorescent lighting

.327 4   Mercury-vapor lighting

.327 5   Neon lighting

.327 6   Sodium-vapor lighting

.33   Electric power transmission for railroads

.34 Magnetic engineering

Class here artificial magnets and magnetic induction [*formerly also* 538.2], electromagnets

Class electromagnets as parts of generators in 621.316, of electric motors in 621.46

Use 621.3 for comprehensive works on electromagnetic technology

See also 538 for physics of magnetism

.36 Applied optics and paraphotic engineering

Class manufacture of optical instruments in 681.4, interdisciplinary works on photography in 770

For lighting, see 621.32

See also 535 for optics and light as subjects in physics

See Manual at 621.36 vs. 621.381045, 621.3827

.361 Industrial and engineering spectroscopy

.361 2 Infrared spectroscopy

.361 3 Visible (Chromatic) spectroscopy

Including Raman spectroscopy

.361 4 Ultraviolet spectroscopy

Including vacuum ultraviolet spectroscopy

.361 5 Radio-frequency and microwave spectroscopy

.361 6 X-ray and gamma-ray spectroscopy

.361 7 Magnetic resonance spectroscopy

> 621.362–621.364 Paraphotic technology

Class comprehensive works in 621.36, paraphotic spectroscopy in 621.361, paraphotic photography in 621.3672

.362 Infrared technology

.364 Ultraviolet technology

.366 Laser technology [*formerly also* 535.58]

Light amplification by stimulated emission of radiation

For laser communications, see 621.3827

See Manual at 621.36 vs. 621.381045, 621.3827

.366 1 Solid-state lasers

.366 2 Fluid-state lasers

For gaseous-state lasers, see 621.3663

.366 3	Gaseous-state lasers
.366 4	Chemical and dye lasers
.367	Technological photography and photo-optics

Including spectrography, stroboscopic photography

Class here image processing, optical data processing

> For photoelectrical and photoelectronic devices, see 621.381542; optical communications, 621.3827

> See Manual at 006.37 vs. 006.42, 621.367, 621.391, 621.399; 778.3 vs. 621.367

.367 2	Infrared and ultraviolet photography
.367 3	Radiography (X-ray and gamma-ray photography)
.367 5	Holography
.367 8	Remote sensing technology

> For photogrammetry, see 526.982

.369	Other branches of applied optics
.369 2	Fiber optics [formerly also 535.89]

> See also 621.381045 for optoelectronics

> See Manual at 621.36 vs. 621.381045, 621.3827

.369 3	Integrated optics
.37	Testing and measurement of electrical quantities

Instruments and their use

Class testing and measurement of a specific apparatus, part, or function with the subject, using notation 0287 from Table 1, e.g., testing overhead lines 621.319220287

.372	Units and standards of measurement

Including calibration of electrical instruments

.373	Recording meters

Class meters recording specific electrical quantities in 621.374

.374	Instruments for measuring specific electrical quantities

Use of this number for comprehensive works on measuring electric quantities discontinued; class in 621.37

.374 2	For measuring resistance, capacitance, inductance

Examples: bridges, ohmmeters, resistance boxes, shunts

Including comprehensive works on electrical bridges (bridge circuits)

> For frequency bridges, see 621.3747

.374 3   For measuring potential

                Examples: electrometers, potentiometers, voltage detectors, voltmeters

.374 4   For measuring current

                Examples: ammeters, ampere-hour meters, coulometers, galvanometers, milliammeters, voltameters

.374 5   For measuring energy

                Examples: demand meters, electric supply meters, watt-hour meters

.374 6   For measuring power

                Examples: electrodynamometers, volt-ammeters, wattmeters

.374 7   For measuring frequency

                Examples: frequency bridges, oscillographs

                Class electric phasemeters in 621.3749

.374 9   For measuring phase

                Examples: power-factor meters, synchroscopes

[.379]   Electrical instruments for measurement of nonelectrical quantities

                Relocated to 681.2

.38   Electronics and communications engineering

SUMMARY

621.381	**Electronics**
.382	**Communications engineering**
.383	**Telegraphy**
.384	**Radio and radar**
.385	**Telephony**
.386	**Telephone terminal equipment**
.387	**Telephone transmission and nonterminal equipment**
.388	**Television**
.389	**Sound recording, security, related systems**

[.380 282]   Electroacoustical apparatus and equipment

                Relocated to 621.38284

[.380 283]   Antennas

                Relocated to 621.3824

[.380 4]   Special topics

                Special topics of communications engineering relocated to 621.382

[.380 44]   Audiovisual engineering

                Relocated to 621.3897

.381   Electronics

Including x-ray and gamma-ray circuitry [*formerly also* 537.5353] and tubes [*formerly also* 537.5355]

Class here microelectronics, shortwave and long-wave electronics

Class signal processing in 621.3822, electronic noise and interference in 621.38224; a specific application with the subject, e.g., laser technology 621.366, radio engineering 621.384

See also 537.5 for physics aspects

See Manual at 621.381

SUMMARY

621.381 01–.381 09	**Standard subdivisions**
.381 3	**Microwave electronics**
.381 5	**Components and circuits**

.381 011   Systems [*formerly* 621.3811]

.381 028 7   Measurement [*formerly* 621.381043] and testing

.381 04   Special topics

[.381 042]   Analysis, synthesis, design

Number discontinued; class in 621.381

[.381 043]   Measurement

Relocated to 621.3810287

.381 044   Power and energy in electronic systems

.381 045   Optoelectronics

See also 621.3692 for fiber optics

See Manual at 621.36 vs. 621.381045, 621.3827

.381 046   Packaging

[.381 1]   Systems

Relocated to 621.381011

.381 3   Microwave electronics

.381 302 18   Standards [*formerly* 621.38137]

.381 302 87   Testing and measurement [*formerly* 621.38137]

.381 31   Wave propagation and transmission

Including interference

.381 32   Circuits

Analysis, design, constituent parts, functions

Add to base number 621.38132 the numbers following 621.38153 in 621.381532–621.381537, e.g., amplifiers 621.381325

.381 33	Components and devices
	Class use of components in specific circuits in 621.38132
.381 331	Wave guides
.381 332	Cavity resonators
.381 333	Klystrons
.381 334	Magnetrons
.381 335	Traveling-wave tubes
.381 336	Masers [*formerly also* 537.5344]
	Microwave amplification by stimulated emission of radiation
[.381 336 1–.381 336 2]	Specific kinds of masers
	Numbers discontinued; class in 621.381336
[.381 37]	Standards; testing and measurement
	Standards relocated to 621.38130218, testing and measurement to 621.38130287
.381 5	Components and circuits
	Analysis, design, functions, manufacture
	Class here integrated, microelectronic, thin-film circuits [*all formerly* 621.38173]; analog, digital, semiconductor circuits; circuits and components common to electronics and communications engineering
	Use of this number for comprehensive works on shortwave and long-wave electronics discontinued; class in 621.381
	Class microwave components and circuits in 621.3813, components and circuits of a specific branch of communications engineering in 621.383–621.389, very large scale integration in 621.395
	See Manual at 621.381
.381 502 18	Standards [*formerly* 621.381548]
[.381 502 87]	Testing and measurement
	Do not use; class in 621.381548

>   621.381 51–621.381 52 Components

Class comprehensive works in 621.3815, use of components in specific circuits in 621.38153, devices not intrinsic to circuits in 621.38154

.381 51	Electronic tubes
	Use of this number for comprehensive works on components discontinued; class in 621.3815
.381 512	Vacuum tubes

[.381 512 2–.381 512 8]	Specific kinds of vacuum tubes
	Numbers discontinued; class in 621.381512
.381 513	Gas tubes
[.381 513 2–.381 513 8]	Specific kinds of gas tubes
	Numbers discontinued; class in 621.381513
.381 52	Semiconductors

.381 52   Class here miniaturization and thin-film production technology [*both formerly* 621.3817], microelements and thin-film components [*both formerly* 621.38171], crystal devices, optoelectronic devices

.381 522   Diodes

Examples: junction, light-emitting, tunnel (Esaki), Zener diodes; varactors

.381 528   Transistors and thyristors

Example: phototransistors

.381 528 2   Junction transistors

.381 528 4   Field-effect transistors

.381 528 7   Thyristors

.381 53   Printed circuits and circuits for specific functions

Use of this number for comprehensive works on circuits discontinued; class in 621.3815

[.381 530 4]   Semiconductor circuits

Number and its subdivisions discontinued; class in 621.3815

.381 531   Printed circuits [*formerly* 621.38174]

Including microlithography

>   621.381 532–621.381 537 Circuits for specific functions

Class comprehensive works in 621.3815

.381 532   Converters (Rectifiers and inverters), filters, interference eliminators

.381 532 2   Converters (Rectifiers and inverters)

.381 532 4   Filters

.381 533   Oscillators

Class use of oscillators in pulse circuits in 621.381534

.381 534	Pulse circuits
	Examples: pulse generators, counting circuits
	Including pulse processes
	Class modulation, demodulation, detection of pulses in 621.3815365
.381 535	Amplifiers and feedback circuits
	Class operational amplifiers in 621.395
.381 536	Modulators, demodulators, detectors
	Class here modulation, demodulation, detection
.381 536 2	Amplitude
	Including attenuators
.381 536 3	Frequency
	See also 621.3815486 for frequency synthesizers
.381 536 4	Phase
	Including phase-locked loops
.381 536 5	Pulse
.381 537	Switching, control, trigger circuits, relays
	Logic circuits relocated to 621.395
.381 537 2	Switching theory
	Class switching theory in logic circuit design in 621.395
.381 54	Supplementary components
	Devices not intrinsic to circuits
	Class here electronic instrumentation (applications of electronics)
	Class instrumentation in a specific field with the field, e.g., electronic control 629.89
.381 542	Photoelectric and photoelectronic devices
	Examples: photoconductive, photoemissive, photovoltaic cells; electric eyes; photomultipliers; cathode-ray, electron-ray tubes; phototubes

.381 548	Testing and measuring components
	Examples: bridges (bridge circuits); signal, square-wave, sweep generators; thermisters
	Class here testing and measuring electronic circuits and components, instruments for testing and measuring electronic signals
	Standards of electronic circuits and components relocated to 621.38150218; electronic gauges, indicators, meters, probes of general utility to 681.2
	Class testing and measuring a specific circuit or component with the circuit or component, using notation 0287 from Table 1, e.g., testing amplifiers 621.3815350287
.381 548 3	Oscilloscopes
	Including oscillographs
.381 548 6	Frequency synthesizers
[.381 6]	X-ray and gamma-ray electronics
	Number discontinued; class in 621.381
[.381 7]	Microelectronics
	Use of this number for microelectronics discontinued; class in 621.381
	Miniaturization and thin-film production technology relocated to 621.38152
[.381 71]	Microelements and thin-film components
	Relocated to 621.38152
[.381 73]	Integrated, microelectronic, thin-film circuits
	Integrated, microelectronic, thin-film circuits relocated to 621.3815; very large scale integration to 621.395
[.381 74]	Printed circuits
	Relocated to 621.381531
[.381 792]	Electronic eavesdropping devices
	Relocated to 621.38928
[.381 9]	Special developments
	Number discontinued; class in 621.381
[.381 95]	Computers
	Relocated to 621.39
[.381 952]	Turing machines
	Relocated to 511.3

[.381 959 4]	Turing and infinite-state machines
	Relocated to 511.3
.382	Communications engineering

Telegraphy relocated to 621.383. In addition, the following subdivisions are reused: 621.3823, 621.3824, 621.3825, 621.3827, 621.3828

Class here special topics in communications engineering [*formerly* 621.3804]; analog, digital, electronic communications; communications systems; telecommunications

Unless other instructions are given, class complex subjects with aspects in two or more subdivisions of this schedule in the one coming last, e.g., signal processing in acoustical communications 621.3828 (*not* 621.3822)

Class components and circuits common to electronics and communications engineering in 621.3815, e.g., amplifiers 621.381535, switching circuits 621.381537; data communications engineering in 621.3981

For specific communications systems, see 621.383–621.389

See Manual at 621.382 vs. 621.3981, 004.6

.382 2	Signal processing

Class here information theory

See Manual at 621.3822 vs. 003.54

.382 23	Signal analysis and theory
.382 24	Noise and interference

Including electromagnetic compatibility and incompatibility

Class here electronic noise and interference

.382 3	Miscellaneous topics

Limited to studios, transmission facilities, and the topics provided for below

.382 32	Power and energy in communications systems
.382 34	Recording devices

Use for works covering recording devices of two or more communications systems, e.g. video recorders and sound recorders

Examples: discs, tapes

Class video recorders in 621.38833, sound recorders in 621.38932

.382 35	Facsimile transmission

By wire or radio wave

Example: radiofacsimile [*formerly* 621.3842]

Class here telefacsimile

.382 38	Space communications
	See also 621.3825 for satellite relay
.382 4	Antennas [*formerly* 621.380283] and propagation
.382 5	Relay communication
	Class here satellite relay
.382 54	Satellite antennas and propagation
.382 7	Optical communications

Transmission of sound, visual images, other information by light

Including optical disc technology

Class here laser communications [*formerly* 621.3896]

Class opticoacoustic communications in 621.3828

See Manual at 621.36 vs. 621.381045, 621.3827

.382 75	Optical-fiber communication

Class here guided-light communication

.382 8	Acoustical communications

Audio systems covering broadcasting and transmission as well as recording and reproduction of sound

Including acousto-optical communications

Class here electroacoustical communications

Class audio systems limited to recording and reproduction of sound in 621.3893

.382 84	Specific devices

Class here electroacoustical apparatus and equipment [*formerly* 621.380282]

Examples: microphones, speakers

Class antennas in 621.3824

>   621.383–621.389 Specific communications systems

Class comprehensive works in 621.382

.383	Telegraphy [*formerly also* 621.382]
	For radiotelegraphy, see 621.3842
.384	Radio and radar

Class here broadcast radio, comprehensive works on radio and television

For television, see 621.388

SUMMARY

621.384 01–.384 09	**Standard subdivisions**
.384 1	**Specific topics in general radio**
.384 2	**Radiotelegraphy**
.384 5	**Radiotelephony**
.384 8	**Radar**

.384 021 8   Standards [*formerly* 621.38417]

.384 028 7   Measurement [*formerly* 621.38417] and testing

.384 028 8   Maintenance and repair

> Class maintenance and repair of receiving sets in 621.384187

> 621.384 1–621.384 5 Radio

Class comprehensive works in 621.384

.384 1   Specific topics in general radio

> Use of this number for comprehensive works on radio, on radio and television discontinued; class in 621.384

SUMMARY

621.384 11	**Wave propagation and transmission**
.384 12	**Circuits**
.384 13	**Components and devices**
.384 15	**Systems by wave type, satellite and relay systems**
.384 16	**Amateur (Ham) radio**
.384 18	**Radio receiving sets**
.384 19	**Special developments**

.384 11   Wave propagation and transmission

> Including interference
>
> *See also 384.5452 for allocation of frequencies*

.384 12   Circuits

> Analysis, design, components, functions
>
> Examples: filters, interference eliminators [*both formerly* 621.384133], amplifiers, modulation circuits, oscillators, rectifiers
>
> Class a specific application with the subject, e.g., receiving set circuits 621.38418

.384 13   Components and devices

.384 131   Transmitters

> Design, circuits, components

.384 132   Tubes

> Class use of tubes in specific circuits in 621.38412

.384 133	Miscellaneous supplementary devices

Limited to condensers (capacitors), grounding devices, inductors, microphones, resistors, testing equipment

Filters and interference eliminators relocated to 621.38412

.384 134	Semiconductor devices

Class use of semiconductor devices in specific circuits in 621.38412

.384 135	Antennas
[.384 136]	Radio receiving sets

Relocated to 621.38418

.384 15	Systems by wave type, satellite and relay systems

> 621.384 151–621.384 153 Systems by wave type

Class comprehensive works in 621.38415, satellite and relay systems of a specific wave type in 621.384156

.384 151	Shortwave systems

Examples: very-high-frequency (VHF), ultrahigh frequency (UHF)

For frequency-modulation systems, see 621.384152

.384 152	Frequency-modulation (FM) systems

Including stereo-multiplex systems

.384 153	Long-wave systems

Examples: amplitude modulation (AM), very-low-frequency (VLF), single-sideband systems

.384 156	Satellite and relay systems
.384 16	Amateur (Ham) radio

Class here comprehensive works on amateur and citizens band radio

Use of this number for comprehensive works on radio stations discontinued; class in 621.384

For citizens band radio, see 621.38454

See Manual at 621.38416 vs. 621.38454

[.384 162–.384 164]	Clear-channel, regional, broadcasting stations

Numbers discontinued; class in 621.384

[.384 165]	Mobile radio stations

Relocated to 621.3845

[.384 166]	Amateur (Ham)
	Number discontinued; class in 621.38416
[.384 168]	Portable radio stations
	Relocated to 621.3845
[.384 17]	Standards and measurement
	Standards relocated to 621.3840218, standards of receiving sets to 621.384180218, measurement to 621.3840287, measurement of receiving sets to 621.384180287, allocation of frequency to 384.5452
.384 18	Radio receiving sets [*formerly* 621.384136]
.384 180 218	Standards [*formerly* 621.38417]
.384 180 287	Measurement [*formerly* 621.38417] and testing
[.384 180 288]	Maintenance and repair
	Do not use; class on 621.384187
[.384 185–.384 186]	Assembling and installation
	Numbers discontinued; class in 621.38418
.384 187	Maintenance and repair
.384 19	Special developments
.384 191	Direction and position finding
	Including radio beacons, radio compasses, loran
.384 196	Radio control
	Variant names: remote control, telecontrol
.384 197	Space communication
.384 2	Radiotelegraphy
	Class here specific instruments and apparatus of radiotelegraphy [*formerly* 621.3843]
	Radiofacsimile relocated to 621.38235
[.384 3]	Specific instruments and apparatus of radiotelegraphy
	Relocated to 621.3842
.384 5	Radiotelephony
	Including portable radio stations [*formerly* 621.384168], e.g., walkie-talkies
	Class here mobile radio stations [*formerly* 621.384165], specific instruments and apparatus of radiotelephony [*formerly* 621.3846], comprehensive works on radio transmission in telephony
	For radio relays, see 621.38782
	See Manual at 621.3845 vs. 621.38782

.384 54	Citizens band radio

Class comprehensive works on amateur and citizens band radio in 621.38416

See Manual at 621.38416 vs. 621.39454

.384 56	Cellular telephone systems (Cellular radio)

Variant names: cellular radio, portable telephone systems

[.384 6]	Specific instruments and apparatus of radiotelephony

Relocated to 621.3845

.384 8	Radar
[.384 81]	Fundamentals

Number discontinued; class in 621.3848

.384 83	Specific instruments and devices

Examples: antennas, receivers, transmitters

.384 85	Systems

Examples: continuous, monopulse, pulse-modulated

.384 86	Stations
.384 88	Scanning patterns
.384 89	Special developments
.384 892	Racon
.384 893	Shoran
.385	Telephony

Class here telephone systems based on wires, cables, lasers, optical fibers

Class cellular telephone systems in 621.38456, data communications engineering in 621.3981

For radiotelephony, see 621.3845; telephone equipment and transmission, 621.386–621.387

.385 1	Network analysis
.385 7	Automatic and semiautomatic switching systems

Example: direct distance dialing

>   621.386–621.387 Telephone equipment and transmission

Class comprehensive works in 621.385

.386	Telephone terminal equipment

Dialing, transmitting, receiving equipment

.386 7	Telephone answering and message recording devices

.386 9	Pay telephones
.387	Telephone transmission and nonterminal equipment
	Example: switches
.387 8	Transmission
.387 82	Long-distance systems
	Including radio relays
	See Manual at 621.3845 vs. 621.38782
.387 83	Local systems
.387 84	Transmission lines and cables
	Including poles, auxiliary line equipment
.388	Television
.388 001	Philosophy and theory
.388 002	Miscellany
.388 002 18	Standards [*formerly* 621.3887]
.388 002 87	Measurement [*formerly* 621.3887] and testing
.388 002 88	Maintenance and repair
	Maintenance and repair covering broadcast and transmission equipment as well as receiving sets
	Class maintenance and repair of receiving sets in 621.38887
.388 003–.388 009	Standard subdivisions
.388 02	Black-and-white television
.388 04	Color television
.388 1	Wave propagation and transmission
	Including definition, resolution, interference
	Use of this number for fundamentals discontinued; class in 621.388
[.388 11]	Wave propagation and transmission
	Number discontinued; class in 621.3881
[.388 12–.388 13]	Circuits and optics
	Numbers discontinued; class in 621.388
.388 3	Components and devices
.388 31	Transmitters
.388 32	Tubes, transistors, semiconductor diodes

.388 33	Video recorders and video recordings
	Use of this number for comprehensive works on television supplementary devices discontinued; class in 621.3883
[.388 330 288]	Maintenance and repair
	Do not use; class in 621.388337
.388 332	Video recordings
	Examples: cassettes, discs
	Use of this number for video recorders discontinued; class in 621.38833
[.388 332 028 8]	Maintenance and repair
	Maintenance and repair of video recorders and video recordings relocated to 621.388337
.388 337	Maintenance and repair of video recorders and video recordings [*formerly* 621.3883320288]
.388 34	Cameras and components
.388 35	Antennas
[.388 36]	Television receiving sets
	Relocated to 621.3888
.388 5	Communication systems
.388 53	Satellite television
.388 57	Cable television
.388 6	Stations
	Class here studios
.388 62	Broadcasting stations
.388 63	Closed-circuit stations
.388 64	Mobile stations
[.388 7]	Standards and measurement
	Standards relocated to 621.38800218, measurement to 621.38800287
.388 8	Television receiving sets [*formerly* 621.38836]
[.388 802 88]	Maintenance and repair
	Do not use; class 621.38887
[.388 85–.388 86]	Assembly and installation
	Numbers discontinued; class in 621.3888
.388 87	Maintenance and repair
[.388 872–.388 874]	Of black-and-white and color sets
	Numbers discontinued; class in 621.38887

[.388 9]	Special developments
	Number discontinued; class in 621.388
.389	Sound recording, security, related systems
	Example: underwater devices
.389 2	Public address, security, related systems
	Examples: announcing, calling, paging systems
.389 28	Security electronics

Including electronic eavesdropping devices [*formerly* 621.381792] and other surveillance systems and countermeasures

Class here alarm systems

.389 3   Sound recording and reproducing systems

Audio systems limited to recording and reproduction of sound

Class comprehensive works on acoustical communications, on audio systems covering transmission as well as recording and reproduction in 621.3828; telephone message recording in 621.3867

.389 32   Recorders and recordings

Examples: compact disc, cylinder, disc, film records and recorders

.389 324   Tape recorders and recordings

Example: cassettes

.389 33   Reproducers

Example: jukeboxes

Class here phonographs

Class combination recorders-reproducers in 621.38932

.389 332   High-fidelity systems (Hi-fi)

For stereophonic systems, see 621.389334

.389 334   Stereophonic systems

Including quadraphonic systems [*formerly* 621.389336]

[.389 336]   Quadraphonic systems

Relocated to 621.389334

.389 4   Language translators

.389 5   Sonar

Use of this number for underwater devices discontinued; class in 621.389

[.389 52]   Projectors and hydrophones

Number discontinued; class in 621.389

[.389 53]	Sonar
	Number discontinued; class in 621.3895
[.389 6]	Laser communications
	Relocated to 621.3827
.389 7	Audiovisual engineering [*formerly* 621.38044]
.39	Computers [*formerly* 621.38195]

This schedule was first published as a separate in 1985

Class here electronic digital computers, central processing units, computer reliability, general computer performance evaluation

Unless other instructions are given, class complex subjects with aspects in two or more subdivisions of 621.39 in the one coming last, e.g., circuitry of computer internal storage in 621.3973 (*not* 621.395)

Use of this number for other branches of electrical engineering discontinued; class in 621.3

Class selection and use of computer hardware, works treating both hardware and either programming or programs in 004; specific applications with the subject, e.g., use of computers to regulate processes automatically 629.895

See Manual at 004–006 vs. 621.39

[.390 287]	Testing and measurement
	Do not use; class in 621.392
.391	General works on specific types of computers

Including optical computers

Class here specific types of processors, e.g., multiprocessors

Class programmable calculators in 681.14

See Manual at 006.37 vs. 006.42, 621.367, 621.391, 621.399

>	621.391 1–621.391 6 Digital computers

Class comprehensive works in 621.39

See Manual at 004.11–004.16

.391 1	Digital supercomputers
.391 2	Digital mainframe computers
	For digital supercomputers, see 621.3911
.391 4	Digital minicomputers

Class comprehensive works on digital minicomputers and microcomputers in 621.3916

.391 6	Digital microcomputers

Class here personal computers, comprehensive works on minicomputers and microcomputers

.391 9	Hybrid and analog computers
.392	Systems analysis and design, computer architecture

Including hardware description languages

See Manual at 004.21 vs. 004.22, 621.392

[.393]	Rural electrification

Relocated to 333.7932

[.394]	Electrification

Relocated to 621.319

.395	Circuitry

Class here logic circuits [*formerly also* 621.381537], very large scale integration (VLSI) [*formerly also* 621.38173], logic design of circuits

[.396]	Electric heating

Relocated to 621.4028

.397	Storage
.397 3	Internal storage (Main memory)

Examples: magnetic-core memory

Class here random-access memory (RAM), read-only memory (ROM)

Class compact disk read-only memory (CD-ROM) in 621.3976

.397 32	Semiconductor memory

Class here bipolar, metal-oxide-semiconductor (MOS), thin-film memory

.397 6	External (Auxiliary) storage

Examples: hard and floppy disks; compact disk read-only memory (CD-ROM); magnetic tapes (cartridges, cassettes, reel-to-reel tapes), tape and disk drives

.397 63	Magnetic bubble memory
.397 67	Optical storage devices

Class storage of pictorial data in optical storage devices in 621.367

.398	Interfacing and communications devices, peripherals
.398 1	Interfacing and communications devices

Class here data communications engineering

See Manual at 004.6; 621.382 vs. 621.3981, 004.6

.398 14	Analog-to-digital and digital-to-analog converters
	Example: modems

.398 4	Peripherals
	Class peripheral storage in 621.3976

For peripherals combining input and output functions, see 621.3985; input peripherals, 621.3986; output peripherals, 621.3987

.398 5	Peripherals combining input and output functions
	Class here computer terminals
	Class tape and disk devices in 621.3976

.398 6	Input peripherals
	Examples: card readers, keyboards

.398 7	Output peripherals
	Examples: monitors (video display screens)
	Computer output microform devices relocated to 681.6, computer output printers to 681.62

See also 621.399 for computer graphics

.399	Devices for special computer methods
	Examples: devices for computer graphics, pattern recognition

See Manual at 006.37 vs. 006.42, 621.367, 621.391, 621.399

.4	**Heat engineering and prime movers**
	Class here engines, power plants, propulsion systems
	Use 621.4001–621.4009 for standard subdivisions

For steam engineering, see 621.1; hydraulic-power technology, 621.2

SUMMARY

621.402–.406	[Heat engineering and turbines]
.42	Stirling engines, air motors and propulsion
.43	Internal-combustion engines and propulsion
.44	Geothermal engineering
.45	Wind engines and propulsion
.46	Electric and related propulsion
.47	Solar-energy engineering
.48	Nuclear engineering

.402	Heat engineering
	Class a kind of heat engineering with the kind, e.g., geothermal engineering in 621.44, heating buildings in 697

For low-temperature technology, see 621.56

See also 536 for physics of heat

.402 011	Thermal systems [*formerly* 621.4028]
.402 1	Thermodynamics
.402 2	Heat transfer

Conduction, convection, radiation, heat exchange

Heat exchangers relocated to 621.4025

.402 3	Fuels and combustion

Class pollution by-products of combustion in 628.532

.402 4	Insulation
.402 5	Equipment

Examples: heat exchangers [*formerly also* 621.4022], furnaces, heat engines, heat pipes, heat pumps

Class solar furnaces in 621.477

.402 8	Specific heat systems

Not provided for elsewhere

Examples: electric heating [*formerly* 621.396]; distribution, storage systems

Comprehensive works on thermal systems relocated to 621.402011

Class a specific aspect of a specific heat system with the aspect, e.g., heat transfer in electric heating 621.4022

.406	Turbines

Class here turbomachines

.42	Stirling engines, air motors and propulsion

Example of air motor: rotary vane positive expansion motors

For wind engines and propulsion, see 621.45

.43	Internal-combustion engines and propulsion

Class generation of electricity by internal combustion engines in 621.312133

>   621.433–621.436 Specific internal-combustion engines

Class comprehensive works in 621.43, parts and accessories of specific engines in 621.437

.433	Gas turbines and free-piston engines

Standard subdivisions are added for gas turbines and free-piston engines and for gas turbines alone

For turbojet engines, see 621.4352

[.433 2]	Simple gas turbines

Number discontinued; class in 621.433

.433 5	Free-piston engines
.434	Spark-ignition engines
	Nondiesel piston engines
	Example: rotary spark-ignition engines
	Class here reciprocating spark-ignition engines
.435	Jet and rocket engines
.435 2	Jet engines and propulsion
	Including turbojet engines
.435 6	Rocket engines and propulsion (Rocketry)
.436	Diesel and semidiesel engines
	Class here compression-ignition engines
[.436 028 8]	Maintenance and repair
	Do not use; class in 621.4368
.436 1	General topics
	Examples: breathing, combustion, compression, cooling, exhaust, injection
.436 2	Design and construction
.436 8	Operation, maintenance, repair
.437	Parts and accessories of internal-combustion engines
	Examples: carburetors, connecting rods, cylinders, governors, ignition devices, pistons, valves
.44	Geothermal engineering
	Including prospecting for sources of geothermal energy, utilization of differences in ocean temperature
.45	Wind engines and propulsion
	Class wind-powered generation of electricity in 621.312136
.453	Windmills
.46	Electric and related propulsion
	Class here electric motors
[.462]	Electric motors
	Number discontinued; class in 621.46
.465	Ion motors
.466	Plasma motors

.47   Solar-energy engineering

Class engineering of secondary sources of solar energy with the secondary source, e.g., wind energy 621.45

For generation of electricity from solar radiation, see 621.31244

.471   General topics

Examples: heat storage, radiation, thermodynamics

.473   Solar engines and propulsion

.477   Solar furnaces

.48   Nuclear engineering

Fission and fusion technology

Class direct nuclear generation of electricity in 621.3125

See also 539.7 for nuclear physics

[.481]   Generation of thermal power

Use of this number for radioisotope-powered generators discontinued; class in 621.48

Nuclear generation of thermal power relocated to 621.483

.483   Nuclear reactors, power plants, by-products

Class here nuclear steam-powered generation of electricity [*formerly* 621.31252], nuclear generation of thermal power [*formerly* 621.481], fission reactors

For fusion reactors, power plants, by-products, see 621.484

.483 015 3   Physical principles

Class reactor physics in 621.4831

[.483 028 9]   Safety measures

Do not use; class in 621.4835

.483 1   Reactor physics

Including critical size

Class here physics of reactor cores

Class physics of a specific component, material, process with the subject, using notation 0153 from Table 1, e.g., nuclear reactions in fuel elements 621.483350153975

.483 2   Design, construction, shielding, siting

.483 23   Shielding

.483 3   Materials

.483 32   Structural materials

.483 35	Fuel element materials
	Fuels and cladding
.483 36	Coolants
.483 37	Moderators
.483 4	Specific types of reactors

Classified by neutron energy, moderator, fuel and fuel conversion, coolant

Examples: breeder reactors

Class a specific aspect of a specific type with the aspect, e.g., shielding of fast reactors 621.48323

| .483 5 | Operation, control, safety measures |
| .483 7 | Radioactive isotopes |

Class here comprehensive technological works on radioisotopes

Class a specific application with the subject, e.g., radioactive isotope therapy 615.8424

| .483 8 | Waste technology |

General aspects: treatment, disposal, utilization of radioactive waste

| .484 | **Fusion (Thermonuclear) reactors, power plants, by-products** |

Examples: tokamaks

.485	Nuclear propulsion
.5	**Pneumatic, vacuum, low-temperature technologies**
.51	Pneumatic technology

Class here air compression technology, air compressors

For compressed-air transmission, see 621.53; pneumatic conveying and cleaning, 621.54; fans, blowers, pumps, 621.6; pneumatic control, 629.8045

| .53 | Compressed-air transmission |
| .54 | Pneumatic conveying and cleaning |

Including carriers, cleaners, sandblasters

| .55 | Vacuum technology [*formerly also* 533.5] |

Including vacuum pumps [*formerly* 621.692]

See also 533.5 for vacuum physics

.56		Low-temperature technology

Class here refrigeration

For refrigerators and freezers, see 621.57; ice manufacture, 621.58; cryogenic technology, 621.59

See also 536.56 for physics of low temperatures

.560 11   Systems [*formerly* 621.567]

.563   Heat pumps

.564   Refrigerants and coolants

[.567]   Systems

Relocated to 621.56011

.57   Refrigerators and freezers

.58   Ice manufacture

.59   Cryogenic technology

Technology of temperatures below -100°C or -148°F

Including liquefaction and solidification of gases having low boiling points

.6   **Fans, blowers, pumps**

.61   Fans and blowers

For rotary fans and blowers, see 621.62; centrifugal fans and blowers, 621.63

.62   Rotary fans and blowers

.63   Centrifugal fans and blowers

>   621.64–621.69 Pumps

Class comprehensive works in 621.69, hydraulic pumps in 621.252

.64   Hand pumps

.65   Reciprocating pumps

.66   Rotary pumps

.67   Centrifugal pumps

.69   Pumps   Pneumatic pumps

Class hydraulic pumps in 621.252

For hand pumps, see 621.64; reciprocating pumps, 621.65; rotary pumps, 621.66; centrifugal pumps 621.67

.691   Jet pumps

[.692]	Vacuum pumps

Relocated to 621.55

.699   Density and direct-fluid-pressure displacement pumps

.8   Machine engineering

Class a specific kind of machinery not provided for here with the kind, e.g., hydraulic machinery 621.2; a specific use of machinery with the use, e.g., gears in clocks 681.112

SUMMARY

621.801–.809	Standard subdivisions
.81	General topics
.82	Machine parts
.83	Gears, ratchets, cams
.84	Valves and pistons
.85	Power transmission systems
.86	Materials-handling equipment
.87	Cranes, derricks, elevators
.88	Fasteners
.89	Friction and its elimination (Tribology)

[.801 53]   Physical principles

Relocated to 621.811

.802 87   Testing and measuring

Class here strength tests of mechanisms

[.802 88]   Maintenance and repair

Relocated to 621.816

.81   General topics

.811   Physical principles [*formerly also* 621.80153]

Examples: kinematics, vibration

Class here principles of simple machines [*formerly also* 531.8]

.812   Speed and power control devices

.815   Machine design

.816   Maintenance and repair [*formerly also* 621.80288]

Including balancing

.82   Machine parts

For gears, ratchets, cams, see 621.83; valves, pistons, 621.84

.821   Journals

.822   Bearings

Examples: ball, roller, sliding bearings

Class journals in 621.821

.823	Shafts and shafting

Example: axles

Class bearings in 621.822

For journals, see 621.821

.824	Springs
.825	Couplings, clutches, universal joints
.827	Connecting rods, cranks, eccentrics
.83	Gears, ratchets, cams
.833	Gears and gearing
.833 1	Spur gears
.833 2	Bevel and skew bevel gears
.833 3	Worm and spiral gears
.837	Ratchets and ratchet wheels
.838	Cams
.84	Valves and pistons

Variant names for valves: cocks, faucets, taps

Standard subdivisions are added for valves and pistons and for valves alone

.85	Power transmission systems

Class power transmission systems for materials-handling equipment in 621.86; a specific machine part of a transmission system with the part, e.g., shafts 621.823

.852	By belt
.853	By rope
.854	By wire
.859	By chain
.86	Materials-handling equipment

For cranes, derricks, elevators, see 621.87

.862	Hoisting equipment

For specific kinds of hoisting equipment, see 621.863–621.865

>   621.863–621.865 Specific kinds of hoisting equipment

Class comprehensive works in 621.862

.863	Chain hoists, fork lifts, tackles
.864	Windlasses, winches, capstans

.865	Power shovels
.867	Conveying equipment

For telpherage, see 621.868

.867 2	Pipes and pipelines

Including pipe laying

Class pipelines for transporting coal in 662.624, petroleum in 665.544, industrial gases in 665.744; manufacturing pipes of a specific material with the material, e.g., metal pipes 671.832

.867 5	Belt conveyors
.867 6	Escalators
.868	Telpherage

Examples: chair lifts, ski tows

Class here comprehensive works on people movers

For escalators, see 621.8676; elevators, 621.877

.87	Cranes, derricks, elevators
.872	Derricks

Class cranes in 621.873

.873	Cranes
.877	Elevators

Including jacks

.88	Fasteners

See also 621.97 for fastening equipment

.882	Screws, nuts, bolts
.883	Cotters and cotter pins
.884	Nails and rivets
.885	Sealing devices
.89	Friction and its elimination (Tribology)

Including lubrication, lubricants, wear

For bearings, see 621.822

.9	**Tools and fabricating equipment**

Use 621.9001–621.9009 for standard subdivisions

Class a specific use with the use, e.g., lathes in woodworking 684.08

.902	Machine tools
.902 3	Numerical control

.904	Pneumatic tools
.908	Hand tools
.91	Planing and milling tools

See also 671.35 for machining metal

.912	Planers, shapers, slotters
.914	Crushing tools
.92	Grinding and abrading tools
.922	Lapping tools

Examples: buffing, polishing tools

.923	Emery wheels and grindstones
.924	Filing tools
.93	Cutting, sawing, disassembling tools

Examples: axes, crowbars, saws, shears, slicers, trimmers

.932	Knives
.94	Turning tools

Class turning tools used for perforating and tapping in 621.95

.942	Lathes
[.943]	Chucks

Relocated to 621.992

.944	Gear-cutting, pipe-threading, screw-cutting tools

For tapping tools, see 621.955

[.945]	Boring tools

Relocated to 621.952

.95	Perforating and tapping tools

For punching tools, see 621.96

.952	Drilling tools

Class here boring tools [*formerly* 621.945]

.954	Reaming and broaching tools
.955	Tapping tools

See also 621.84 for taps (valves)

.96	Punching tools

Class die punches in 621.984

.97	Fastening and joining equipment

Class fasteners in 621.88

.972	Screwdrivers and wrenches
.973	Hand hammers
.974	Power hammers
.977	Welding and soldering equipment
.978	Riveting equipment
.98	Pressing, molding, impressing equipment
.982	Bending tools
.983	Straightening tools
.984	Molding and impressing equipment

Examples: molds, dies, stamps

.99	Other tools and equipment
.992	Holding, guiding, safety equipment

Examples: chucks [*formerly* 621.943], clamps, guards, jigs, shields, vises

[.994]	Measuring tools

Relocated to 681.2

622 Mining and related operations

SUMMARY

622.1	Prospecting and exploratory operations
.2	Excavation techniques
.3	Mining for specific materials
.4	Mine environment
.5	Mine drainage
.6	Mine transport systems
.7	Ore dressing
.8	Mine health and safety

[.028 9]	Safety measures

Do not use; class safety measures regardless of technique employed or mineral extracted in 622.8

.1	**Prospecting and exploratory operations**

> 622.12–622.17 General topics

Class comprehensive works in 622.1, general topics applied to specific materials in 622.18, to treasure in 622.19

.12   Surface exploration

Examples: biogeochemical, geobotanical, geological prospecting

.13   Geochemical prospecting

Including mineral surveys (qualitative and quantitative measurement of mineral content)

Class biogeochemical prospecting in 622.12

.14   Mine surveys

Determination of size, depth, shape of mines

.15   Geophysical exploration

.152   Gravitational prospecting

.153   Magnetic prospecting

.154   Electrical prospecting

Examples: galvanic-electromagnetic, resistivity, self-potential prospecting

.159   Other methods of prospecting

Examples: gas-detection, geothermal, radioactivity prospecting

.159 2   Seismic prospecting

Variant name: acoustical, vibration prospecting

.17   Underwater prospecting

.18   Prospecting for specific materials

Add to base number 622.18 the numbers following 553 in 553.2–553.9, e.g., for petroleum 622.1828; however, prospecting for water relocated from 622.187 to 628.114

Standard subdivisions are added to subdivisions for specific materials even if only one type of prospecting is used, e.g., seismic exploration for petroleum in Texas 622.182809764

.19   Prospecting and exploring for treasure

Underground and underwater treasure hunting

Class archaeological methods and equipment in 930.1028

.2   Excavation techniques

Class here subsurface mining

Class extraction techniques for specific materials in 622.3

See also 622.4–622.8 for nonextractive mining technologies

[.202 89]   Safety measures

Do not use; class safety measures regardless of technique employed in 622.8

>   622.22–622.28 Underground mining

                  Class comprehensive works in 622.2

.22   In-situ processing

                  Class here leach mining wells, solution mining

                      See Manual at 622.7, 622.22 vs. 669, 662.6

.23   Underground blasting and drilling

.24   Underground boring

.25   Underground shafts and shaft sinking

.26   Underground tunnels and tunneling

.28   Underground supporting structures and their erection

                  Class here control of roof and wall failure (rock failure) [*formerly* 622.8]

.29   Surface and underwater mining

.292   Surface mining [*formerly* 622.3]

                  Class here open-pit, strip mining [*formerly* 622.31]

                  Class reclamation after surface mining in 631.64

.292 7   Alluvial mining [*formerly* 622.32]

                  Examples: hydraulic, placer mining

.295   Underwater mining

                  Class here off-shore mining, mineral extraction from ocean floor

.3   **Mining for specific materials**

                  Class here extraction techniques of specific materials

                  Use of this number for comprehensive works on types of mining discontinued; class in 622

                  Surface mining relocated to 622.292, dressing of specific mineral ores to 622.7

                  Class prospecting for specific materials in 622.18; nonextractive mining technologies relating to specific materials in 622.4–622.8, e.g., mine safety technology 622.8

[.31]   Open-pit and strip mining

                  Relocated to 622.292

[.32]   Alluvial mining

                  Relocated to 622.2927

.33   Carbonaceous materials

.331–.337	Coal, graphite, solid and semisolid bitumens

Add to base number 622.33 the numbers following 553.2 in 553.21–553.27, e.g., coal 622.334; however, bituminous shale relocated from 622.333 to 622.3383

.338	Oil, oil shales, tar sands, natural gas

Use 622.338 for extraction of petroleum in the broad sense covering oil and gas, 622.3382 for petroleum in the narrow sense limited to oil

Class interdisciplinary works on petroleum in 553.28, comprehensive technical works in 665.5

.338 1	Drilling techniques

Including use of drilling muds (drilling fluids)

.338 19	Offshore drilling

Class here comprehensive works on offshore petroleum extraction

Class a specific aspect of offshore petroleum extraction with the aspect, e.g., offshore enhanced oil recovery 622.3382

.338 2	Oil

Including tertiary recovery, well blowouts

Class here reservoir engineering; enhanced, secondary, tertiary recovery; well flooding

Oil shale relocated to 622.3383

Class techniques of drilling for oil in 622.3381

.338 27	Specific enhanced oil recovery methods

Examples: enhanced recovery by use of bacteria, carbon dioxide, heat, water

.338 3	Oil shale [*formerly* 622.3382] and tar sands

Variant names for oil shale: bituminous shale [*formerly* 622.333], black shale; for tar sands: bituminous sands, oil sands

Class extraction of oils from oil shale and tar sands in 665.4

.338 5	Gas

Class techniques of drilling for gas in 622.3381

.339	Fossil gums and resins
.34	Metals and their ores
.341	Iron and iron ores

> 　　　　　　622.342–622.349 Nonferrous metals and their ores

Class comprehensive works in 622.34

.342	Gold, silver, platinum

.342 2	Gold
.342 3	Silver
.342 4	Platinum
.343–.349	Other nonferrous metals and their ores

> Add to base number 622.34 the numbers following 553.4 in 553.43–553.49, e.g., uranium ores 622.34932

.35–.39   Other materials

> Add to base number 622.3 the numbers following 553 in 553.5–553.9, e.g., gem diamonds 622.382; however, water extraction relocated from 622.37 to 628.114

> **622.4–622.8 Nonextractive mining technologies**

> Class here nonextractive mining technologies relating to specific materials

> Class comprehensive works in 622

.4   **Mine environment**

> *For mine drainage, see 622.5; mine health and safety, 622.8*

.42   Ventilation and air conditioning

> *For temperature control, see 622.43*

.43   Temperature control

.47   Illumination

.473   Portable lamps

.474   Electric lighting systems

.48   Electricity

> Class electricity applied to a specific operation with the operation, e.g., temperature control 622.43

.49   Sanitation

.5   **Mine drainage**

.6   **Mine transport systems**

> Haulage and hoisting

.65   Hand and animal haulage

.66   Mechanical haulage

> Example: mine railroads

> Class vertical haulage in 622.68

.67   Direct- and gear-driven hoists

.68	Elevators
	Including skips
.69	Surface transportation
	General aspects: loading, unloading, transshipment
.7	**Ore dressing**
	Class here dressing of specific mineral ores [*formerly* 622.3]
	See Manual at 622.7, 622.22 vs. 669, 662.6
.73	Crushing and grinding
.74	Sizing
	Example: screening

> 622.75–622.77 Ore concentration

Variant names: beneficiation, ore separation

Class comprehensive works in 622.7

.75	Mechanical separation
.751	Gravity concentration
.752	Flotation
.77	Magnetic and electrostatic (inductive charging) separation
.79	Milling plants
	Class specific milling-plant operations in 622.73–622.77
.8	**Mine health and safety**
	Control of roof and wall failure (rock failure) relocated to 622.28
	Class interdisciplinary works on mine safety in 363.119622
	For sanitation, see 622.49
.82	Control of gas and explosions
	Class here comprehensive works on fire control, on respiratory safety
	For dust control, see 622.83
.83	Dust control
.89	Rescue operations

623 Military and nautical engineering

See Manual at 355 vs. 623

SUMMARY

623.04		**General topics**
	.1	**Fortifications**
	.2	**Mine laying, mine clearance, demolition**
	.3	**Engineering of defense**
	.4	**Ordnance**
	.5	**Ballistics and gunnery**
	.6	**Military transportation technology**
	.7	**Communications, vehicles, sanitation, related topics**
	.8	**Nautical engineering and seamanship**

.04   General topics

.042   Optical and paraphotic engineering

.043   Electronic engineering

.044   Nuclear engineering

.045   Mechanical engineering

.047   Construction engineering

> ### 623.1–623.7 Military engineering

Class comprehensive works in 623, general topics in 623.04, naval engineering in 623.8

.1   Fortifications

Class here forts and fortresses

Class artistic aspects in 725.18

.109   Historical and persons treatment

Geographical treatment relocated to 623.19

[.12]   Permanent fortifications

Number discontinued; class in 623.1

.15   Temporary fortifications

.19   Geographical treatment [*formerly also* 623.109]

Add to base number 623.19 notation 1–9 from Table 2, e.g., forts in France 623.1944

.2   Mine laying, mine clearance, demolition

.26   Mine laying and mine clearance

See also 623.45115 for manufacture of mines

.262   On land

.263   In water

.27   Demolition

.3   Engineering of defense

Class warning systems in 623.737

See also 623.4 for ordnance

.31   Against invasion

Examples: countermining, flooding, mechanical barriers, moats, traps

Class artistic aspects of moats in 725.18

For fortifications, see 623.1; mine laying and demolition, 623.2

[.37]   [Warning systems]

Relocated to 623.737

.38   Protective construction

Example: air raid shelters

.4   Ordnance

Class combat ships in 623.82

For combat vehicles, see 623.74

SUMMARY

623.402 88	**Maintenance and repair**
.41	**Artillery**
.42	**Specific pieces of artillery**
.43	**Gun mounts**
.44	**Small arms and other weapons**
.45	**Ammunition and other destructive agents**
.46	**Accessories**

.402 88   Maintenance and repair [*formerly* 623.48]

.41   Artillery

For specific pieces of artillery, see 623.42; artillery projectiles, 623.4513

.412   Field artillery

Including railroad-borne artillery

.417   Coast artillery

.418   Naval artillery

.419   Space artillery

Use of this number for other artillery discontinued; class in 623.41

[.419 4]   [Space artillery]

Number discontinued; class in 623.419

.42	Specific pieces of artillery
	Examples: cannons, howitzers, mortars, crew-served rocket launchers
	Including mortars for launching chemical projectiles [*formerly* 623.445]
.43	Gun mounts
.44	Small arms and other weapons
	Class here side arms
	Class artistic aspects of arms and armor in 739.7, vehicle-mounted small arms with the specific vehicle, e.g., on armored cars 623.7475
	See also 623.455 for small arms ammunition
.441	Weaponry of prefirearm origin
	Examples: armor, bayonets, bows and arrows, catapults, knives, maces, shields, spears, swords, tomahawks
.442	Portable firearms
	For pistols and revolvers, see 623.443
.442 4	Automatic firearms
	Examples: automatic rifles, machine and submachine guns
	Class automatic pistols and revolvers in 623.443
.442 5	Rifles, muskets, carbines
.442 6	Portable rocket launchers (Bazookas)
.443	Pistols and revolvers
.445	Chemical weapons
	Examples: flame throwers; rifle attachments for launching smoke and gas canisters
	Mortars for launching chemical projectiles relocated to 623.42
	Class artillery for launching chemical projectiles in 623.41, chemical delivery devices in 623.4516
	For chemical agents, see 623.4592
.446	Destructive radiation weapons
	Examples: laser weapons, thermal weapons
	Class here destructive radiations [*formerly* 623.4595]
.447	Destructive vibration weapons
	Example: ultrasonic weapons
	Class here destructive vibrations [*formerly* 623.4596]

.45   Ammunition and other destructive agents

SUMMARY

.451   Charge-containing devices

Class here bombs, missiles, projectiles

For tactical rockets, see 623.4543

See also 623.455 for small arms ammunition

.451 1   Grenades, mines, nuclear weapons

Class grenades and mines with special types of charges in 623.4516–623.4518

.451 14   Rifle and hand grenades

.451 15   Mines

.451 19   Nuclear weapons

Examples: artillery projectiles, bombs

For nuclear missiles, see 623.4519

.451 3   Artillery projectiles

Class artillery projectiles with special types of charges in 623.4516–623.4518, nuclear artillery projectiles in 623.4519

.451 4   Antipersonnel devices

Example: booby traps

Class here shrapnel devices

Specific antipersonnel devices other than booby traps relocated to the subject, e.g., antipersonnel hand grenades 623.45114

\>   623.451 6–623.451 8 Devices with special types of charges

Class comprehensive works in 623.451

For nuclear weapons, see 623.45119

.451 6   Chemical and biological devices

Projectiles and related devices containing gas, incendiary materials, microbes, smoke

Standard subdivisions are added for chemical and biological devices and for chemical devices alone

Class chemical agents in 623.4592, biological agents in 623.4594

.451 7	High-explosive devices

Examples: blockbusters, high-explosive-antitank (HEAT) projectiles, torpedoes

For bangalore torpedoes, see 623.4545

.451 8	Armor-piercing devices
.451 9	Guided missiles

Nuclear and nonnuclear missiles

Class here storage and launching equipment, launch vehicles; strategic missiles, comprehensive works on rockets

.451 91	Air-to-air guided missiles
.451 92	Air-to-surface guided missiles
.451 93	Air-to-underwater guided missiles
.451 94	Surface-to-air guided missiles

Class here antimissile missiles, interceptor missiles

.451 95	Ballistic missiles (Surface-to-surface guided missiles)
.451 952	Short range ballistic missiles
.451 953	Intermediate range ballistic missiles
.451 954	Long range ballistic missiles

Class here intercontinental ballistic missiles

.451 96	Surface-to-underwater guided missiles
.451 97	Underwater guided missiles

Underwater-to-air, underwater-to-surface, underwater-to-underwater

.451 98	Space guided missiles
.452	Explosives
.452 6	Burning and deflagrating explosives

Examples: cordite, guncotton, gunpowder, smokeless powder

Class here propellant explosives

.452 7	High explosives

Examples: dynamite, nitroglycerin, TNT (trinitrotoluene)

.454	Detonators, rockets, demolition charges
.454 2	Detonators

Examples: fuses, percussion caps, primers

.454 3	Tactical rockets
	Unguided nuclear and nonnuclear rockets
	Class comprehensive works on rocket weapons, on rocket-propelled guided missiles in 623.4519
.454 5	Demolition charges
	Examples: bangalore torpedoes, destructors, shaped charges
	Class shaped charges in bombs, missiles, projectiles in 623.451
.455	**Small arms ammunition**
	Examples: bazooka rockets, bullets, cartridges
.459	**Nonexplosive agents**
	Class here detection of nonexplosive agents
.459 2	Chemical agents
	Example: tear gas
	Class here poisons and gases
.459 4	Biological agents
[.459 5]	Destructive radiations
	Relocated to 623.446
[.459 6]	Destructive vibrations
	Relocated to 623.447
.46	**Accessories**
	Examples: sighting and range apparatus
[.48]	Maintenance and repair
	Relocated to 623.40288
.5	**Ballistics and gunnery**
.51	**Ballistics**
.513	Motion of projectiles within the bore (Interior ballistics)
.514	Motion of projectiles after leaving gun tube (Exterior ballistics)
.516	Effect of projectiles on targets (Terminal ballistics)
.55	**Gunnery**
	For recoil, see 623.57
.551	Land gunnery
.553	Naval gunnery
.555	Aircraft gunnery
.556	Spacecraft gunnery

.557	Target selection and detection

Class siting and range apparatus in 623.46, application to specific types of gunnery in 623.551–623.556

.558	Firing and fire control

Class application to specific types of gunnery in 623.551–623.556

For target selection and detection, see 623.557

.57	Recoil
.6	**Military transportation technology**

For vehicles, see 623.74

.61	Land transportation

For roads, see 623.62; railroads and their rolling stock, 623.63; bridges, 623.67; tunnels, 623.68

.62	Roads
.63	Railroads and their rolling stock
.631	The way

Earthwork and track

.633	Rolling stock
.64	Naval facilities

Examples: artificial harbors, docks, naval bases

Class artistic aspects of naval facilities in 725.34

.66	Air facilities

Class here air bases, airports, comprehensive works on military aerospace engineering

Add to base number 623.66 the numbers following 629.136 in 629.1361–629.1368, e.g., airstrips 623.6612

Class artistic aspects of air facilities in 725.39

For military astronautics, see 623.69; aircraft, 623.746

.67	Bridges
.68	Tunnels
.69	Space facilities

Class here comprehensive works on military astronautics

For spacecraft, see 623.749

.7   **Communications, vehicles, sanitation, related topics**

SUMMARY

623.71	**Intelligence and reconnaissance topography**
.72	**Photography and photogrammetry**
.73	**Communications technology**
.74	**Vehicles**
.75	**Sanitation and safety engineering**
.76	**Electrical engineering**
.77	**Camouflage and concealment**

.71   Intelligence and reconnaissance topography

Standard subdivisions are added for intelligence and reconnaissance topography and for intelligence alone

Including sketching and map making

For photography and photogrammetry, see 623.72

.72   Photography and photogrammetry

.73   Communications technology

Class comprehensive works on military electronics in 623.043

.731   Visual signals

.731 2   Semaphore, heliograph, flag signals

.731 3   Pyrotechnical devices

.731 4   Electrooptical devices

Example: blinkers

.732   Wire telegraphy

.733   Wire telephony

.734   Radio communication and radar

.734 1   Shortwave radio

.734 2   Radiotelegraphy

Class shortwave radiotelegraphy in 623.7341

.734 5   Radiotelephony

Class shortwave radiotelephony in 623.7341

.734 8   Radar

.735   Television

.737   Warning systems [*formerly* 623.37]

Class here air-raid warning systems

.74 Vehicles

Support vehicles, combat vehicles and their ordnance

Class railroad rolling stock in 623.633

For nautical craft, see 623.82

See Manual at 629.046 vs 385.388

SUMMARY

623.741	**Lighter-than-air aircraft**
.742	**Free balloons**
.743	**Airships (Dirigibles)**
.744	**Barrage balloons**
.746	**Aircraft Heavier-than-air aircraft**
.747	**Motor land vehicles**
.748	**Air-cushion vehicles**
.749	**Spacecraft**

.741 Lighter-than-air aircraft

For specific types of lighter-than-air aircraft, see 623.742–623.744

> 623.742–623.744 Specific types of lighter-than-air aircraft

Class comprehensive works in 623.741

.742 Free balloons

Class here comprehensive works on military balloons

.743 Airships (Dirigibles)

.743 5 Rigid airships

.743 6 Semirigid airships

.743 7 Nonrigid airships

.744 Barrage balloons

.746 Aircraft   Heavier-than-air aircraft

Class lighter-than-air aircraft in 623.741

.746 04 Special topics

> 623.746 042–623.746 047 General types of heavier-than-air aircraft

Class here piloting general types of heavier-than-air aircraft

Class comprehensive works in 623.746, comprehensive works on piloting in 623.746048

.746 042 Propeller-driven airplanes

.746 044 Jet planes

.746 045 Rocket planes

.746 047	Vertical-lift (VTOL) aircraft
	Example: helicopters
.746 048	Piloting

Class piloting of a specific type of heavier-than-air aircraft with the aircraft, e.g., piloting jet planes 623.746044, piloting fighters 623.7464

.746 049	Components

Examples: engines, escape equipment

Including instrumentation (avionics)

Class components of a specific type of aircraft with the aircraft, e.g., components of jet planes 623.746044, of fighters 623.7464

For aircraft ordnance, see 623.7461

.746 1	Aircraft ordnance

For charge-containing devices, see 623.451

>   623.746 2–623.746 7 Heavier-than-air aircraft for specific uses

Class here piloting heavier-than-air aircraft for specific uses

Class comprehensive works in 623.746, comprehensive works on piloting in 623.746048, aircraft ordnance regardless of type of aircraft in 623.7461, pilotless aircraft regardless of type in 623.7469

.746 2	Trainers
.746 3	Bombers and fighter-bombers
.746 4	Fighters
.746 5	Personnel and cargo transports
.746 6	Rescue aircraft
.746 7	Reconnaissance aircraft
.746 9	Pilotless aircraft (Guided aircraft)
	Variant name: drones
	Reconnaissance and combat
.747	**Motor land vehicles**
.747 2	For transporting personnel
	Class armored personnel carriers in 623.7475
.747 22	Jeeps and similar vehicles
.747 23	Buses
.747 24	Ambulances
.747 4	For transporting supplies

.747 5	For combat

Examples: armored cars, other armored vehicles

.747 52	Tanks
.748	Air-cushion vehicles
.748 2	Overland air-cushion vehicles
.748 4	Overwater air-cushion vehicles
.748 5	Amphibious air-cushion vehicles
.749	Spacecraft
.75	Sanitation and safety engineering

Class here health engineering

.751	Water supply
.753	Sewage treatment and disposal
.754	Garbage and refuse treatment and disposal
.76	Electrical engineering
.77	Camouflage and concealment
.8	**Nautical engineering and seamanship**

Nautical engineering: engineering of ships and boats and their component parts

Class here naval engineering, comprehensive works on military water transportation

Class harbors, ports, roadsteads in 627.2

For naval facilities, see 623.64

SUMMARY

623.81	**Naval architecture**	
.82	**Nautical craft**	
.83	**Shipyards**	
.84	**Hulls of nautical craft**	
.85	**Engineering systems of nautical craft**	
.86	**Equipment and outfit of nautical craft**	
.87	**Power plants of nautical craft**	
.88	**Seamanship**	
.89	**Navigation**	

.81	Naval architecture

Variant names: marine architecture, naval design

Observe the following table of precedence, e.g., design of steel plates for battleship in 623.81252 (*not* 623.817765 or 623.81821)

Design of craft	623.812
Design in specific materials	623.818
Design tests	623.819
Structural analysis and design	623.817

.810 287   Measurement

Class design testing in 623.819

.812   Design of craft

Class here hydrodynamics of hulls [*formerly* 623.8144]

.812 04   Design of general types of craft

Add to base number 623.81204 the numbers following 623.820 in
623.8202–623.8205, e.g., design of submersible craft 623.812045

.812 1–.812 9   Design of specific kinds of craft

Add to base number 623.812 the numbers following 623.82 in
623.821–623.829, e.g., design of sailboats 623.81223

[.814]   Design of specific parts and details

Relocated to 623.84–623.87

[.814 4]   Hulls

Hydrodynamics of hulls relocated to 623.812

.817   Structural analysis and design

Add to base number 623.817 the numbers following 624.17 in
624.171–624.177, e.g., structural analysis 623.8171, wreckage studies
623.8176

.818   Design in specific materials

Add to base number 623.818 the numbers following 624.18 in
624.182–624.189, e.g., design in steel 623.81821

.819   Design tests

.82   Nautical craft

Class shipyards in 623.83, overwater hovercraft in 629.324

For naval architecture, see 623.81; parts and details, 623.84–623.87

SUMMARY

623.820 01–.820 09	**Standard subdivisions**
.820 1–.820 7	**[Models and miniatures, general types of craft, craft of specific materials]**
.821	**Ancient and medieval craft**
.822	**Modern wind-driven ships**
.823	**Small and medium power-driven ships**
.824	**Power-driven merchant and factory ships**
.825	**Power-driven warships**
.826	**Support warships and other government ships**
.827	**Nonmilitary submersible craft**
.828	**Other power-driven ships**
.829	**Hand-propelled and towed craft**

.820 01   Philosophy and theory

.820 02   Miscellany

.820 022	Illustrations
[.820 022 8]	Models and miniatures

> Do not use; class models and miniatures of all types of craft in 623.8201

.820 028	Auxiliary techniques and procedures; apparatus, equipment, materials
.820 028 8	Maintenance and repair [*formerly* 623.8208]
.820 03–.820 09	Standard subdivisions
.820 1	Models and miniatures

> Class ships in bottles in 745.5928

.820 104	Models and miniatures of general types of craft

> Add to base number 623.820104 the numbers following 623.820 in 623.8202–623.8205, e.g., models of sailing craft 623.8201043

.820 11–.820 19	Models and miniatures of specific types of craft

> Add to base number 623.8201 the numbers following 623.82 in 623.821–623.829, e.g., models of battleships 623.820152

> 623.820 2–623.820 5 General types of craft

Class comprehensive works in 623.82, general types of craft in specific materials in 623.8207, specific types of craft in 623.821–623.829

.820 2	Small craft

> Class small sailing craft in 623.8203; small submersible craft in 623.8205; small power-driven craft in 623.823

.820 23	Pleasure craft

> Example: yachts

.820 26	Working craft
.820 3	Sailing ships
.820 4	Power-driven ships

> Examples: hydrofoils, steamships

> Class power-driven submersible craft in 623.8205; small power-driven craft in 623.823

.820 5	Submersible craft
.820 7	Craft of specific materials

> Class works limited to hulls of specific materials in 623.84

[.820 8]	Maintenance and repair

> Relocated to 623.8200288

.821   Ancient and medieval craft

         Examples: biremes, caravels, galleys, triremes

>   623.822–623.829 Modern craft

         Class comprehensive works in 623.82

.822   Modern wind-driven ships

         Including rotor ships

.822 3   Pleasure craft

         Example: sailing yachts

.822 4   Merchant ships

         Example: clipper ships

.822 5   Warships

.822 6   Work ships

         Example: research ships

         For merchant ships, see 623.8224

>   623.823–623.828 Power-driven craft

         Class comprehensive works in 623.8204

.823   Small and medium power-driven ships

         Class small and medium power-driven craft not provided for here in 623.824–623.828

.823 1   Motorboats

         Class here speedboats

.823 13   Outboard motorboats

.823 14   Inboard motorboats

         Examples: hydroplanes, motor yachts

.823 15   Inboard-outboard motorboats

.823 2   Tugboats and towboats

.823 4   Ferryboats

.824   Power-driven merchant and factory ships

         Class trawlers in 623.828

.824 3   Passenger ships

         Class ferryboats in 623.8234

.824 32   Ocean liners

.824 36	Inland-waterway ships
	Example: river steamers
.824 5	Cargo ships
	Examples: bulk carriers, freighters, tankers
.824 8	Factory ships
	Examples: whaleboats and ship canneries
.825	Power-driven warships
	For support warships, see 623.826
.825 1	Naval ordnance
	Armor, weapons
	For naval artillery, see 623.418; charge-containing devices, 623.451

> 623.825 2–623.825 8 Specific types of combat warships

Class comprehensive works in 623.825, naval ordnance in 623.8251

.825 2	Battleships
.825 3	Cruisers
.825 4	Destroyers and destroyer escorts
.825 5	Aircraft carriers
.825 6	Landing craft
.825 7	Submarines
.825 72	Diesel-engine and electric-motor powered submarines
.825 74	Nuclear-powered submarines
.825 8	Light combat craft
	Example: torpedo boats
.826	Support warships and other government ships
.826 2	Minelayers and minesweepers
.826 3	Police boats, revenue cutters, coast guard craft
.826 4	Hospital ships and military transports
.826 5	Military supply ships
.827	Nonmilitary submersible craft
	Examples: bathyscaphes, bathyspheres
.828	Other power-driven ships
	Examples: lightships [*formerly* 627.923], dredgers, drilling ships, icebreakers, trawlers

.829   Hand-propelled and towed craft

> Examples: barges, canoes, coracles, lifeboats, rafts, rowboats, scows, towed canalboats

.83   Shipyards

> Including dry docks, floating dry docks [both *formerly also* 627.35]

>   623.84–623.87 Parts and details of nautical craft

> Class here design of specific parts and details [*formerly* 623.814]

> Class comprehensive works in 623.82

.84   Hulls of nautical craft

> Class hydrodynamics of hulls in 623.812

.842   Lofting

.843   Metalwork

.843 2   Welding and riveting

.843 3   Ship fitting

.844   Carpentry

.845   Construction with masonry, ceramics, allied materials

> Add to base number 623.845 the numbers following 624.183 in 624.1832–624.1838, e.g., concrete hulls 623.8454

.848   Resistant construction

> Examples: corrosion-, fire-resistant construction

.85   Engineering systems of nautical craft

> Use 623.85001–623.85009 for standard subdivisions

> *For power plants, see 623.87*

.850 1   Mechanical systems

.850 3   Electrical systems

.850 4   Electronic systems

.852   Electric lighting

.853   Air conditioning and temperature controls

.853 5   Cooling

> Including refrigeration

.853 7   Heating and air conditioning

.854   Water supply and sanitation

.854 2   Potable water

.854 3		Seawater

Used for sanitation and fire fighting

.854 6   Sanitation

Class seawater for sanitation in 623.8543

.856   Communication systems

Add to base number 623.856 the numbers following 623.73 in 623.731–623.737, e.g., flag systems 623.85612

.86   Equipment and outfit of nautical craft

Including flares, other portable lights

Class use of equipment and outfit in 623.88

.862   Gear and rigging

Examples: anchors, cordage, masts, rope, rudders, sails, spars

.863   Nautical instruments

.865   Safety equipment

Examples: fire fighting, lifesaving equipment

Class comprehensive works on marine safety technology in 623.888

.866   Furniture

.867   Cargo-handling equipment

Class cargo handling in 623.8881

See also 627.34 for onshore cargo-handling equipment

.87   Power plants of nautical craft

Class here marine engineering

.872   Specific kinds of engines

Use of this number for comprehensive works on engines discontinued; class in 623.87

.872 2   Steam engines

.872 3   Internal-combustion engines

Inboard and outboard

Add to base number 623.8723 the numbers following 621.43 in 621.433–621.437, e.g., diesel engines 623.87236

.872 6   Electric engines

.872 7   Solar engines

.872 8   Nuclear engines

.873   Engine auxiliaries

Examples: boilers, piping, propellers, pumps, shafting

.874	Fuels
.88	Seamanship

For navigation, see 623.89

[.880 289]	Safety measures

Do not use; class in 623.888

.881	Handling general types of craft

Add to base number 623.881 the numbers following 623.820 in 623.8202–623.8205, e.g., handling small craft 623.8812

Class handling specific types of craft in 623.882, safety and related topics in handling general types of craft in 623.888

.882	Handling specific types of craft

Add to base number 623.882 the numbers following 623.82 in 623.821–623.829, e.g., handling power-driven merchant ships 623.8824

Class safety and related topics in handling specific types of craft in 623.888

.888	Specific topics

Class here marine safety technology

For safety equipment, see 623.865

.888 1	Loading and unloading of nautical craft

Class here cargo handling

.888 2	Knotting and splicing ropes and cables

Class here interdisciplinary works on knotting and splicing

Class a specific application with the subject, e.g., knotting in camping 796.545

.888 4	Prevention of collision and grounding

Including rules of the road

.888 5	Wreckage studies

Class wreckage studies in marine architecture in 623.8176

.888 6	Fire fighting technology

See also 623.865 for manufacture of fire fighting equipment

.888 7	Rescue operations
.89	Navigation

Selection and determination of course

Class navigation procedures to prevent collision and grounding in 623.8884

.892   Geonavigation

For electronic aids to geonavigation, see 623.893

.892 021 2   Tables, formulas, specifications

Class tide and current tables in 623.8949

.892 2   Piloting and pilot guides

Positioning craft by visual observation of objects of known position

For piloting in and pilot guides to specific marine harbors and shores, see 623.8929

.892 209   Historical and persons treatment

Class geographical treatment in specific oceans and intercontinental seas in 623.89223–623.89227, in specific inland waters in 623.89229, in specific marine harbors and shores in 623.8929

.892 23–.892 27   Piloting in and pilot guides to specific oceans and intercontinental seas

Add to base number 623.8922 the numbers following −16 in notation 163–167 from Table 2, e.g., pilot guides to North Sea 623.8922336

.892 29   Piloting in and pilot guides to specific inland waters

Add to base number 623.89229 notation 4–9 from Table 2, e.g., pilot guides to Great Lakes 623.8922977

.892 3   Dead reckoning

.892 9   Piloting in and pilot guides to specific marine harbors and shores

Class here approach and harbor piloting and pilot guides

.892 909   Historical and persons treatment

Class geographical treatment in 623.89291–623.89299

.892 91–.892 99   Geographical treatment

Add to base number 623.8929 notation 1–9 from Table 2, e.g., harbor piloting for Scandinavia 623.892948; however, class approach and harbor piloting and pilot guides dealing comprehensively with specific oceans and intercontinental seas in 623.89223–623.89227

.893   Electronic aids to geonavigation

Class here comprehensive works on aids to geonavigation

For nonelectronic aids to geonavigation, see 623.894

>   623.893 2–623.893 3 Direction- and position-finding devices

Class comprehensive works in 623.893

.893 2   Radio aids

Examples: compasses, loran, radio

.893 3	Microwave aids

Examples: racon, radar, shoran

.893 8	Sounding devices

Sonar, other echo and sound-ranging devices

.894	Nonelectronic aids to geonavigation

.894 2	Lighthouses

Class interdisciplinary works on lighthouses in 387.155, construction of lighthouses in 627.922

.894 3	Lightships

Class construction of lightships in 623.828

.894 4	Beacons, buoys, daymarks

Class construction of beacons, buoys, daymarks in 627.924

.894 5	Light lists

.894 9	Tide and current tables

624 Civil engineering

Including engineering of landscape architecture

Class here construction engineering

Class specific branches of civil engineering in 625–629, construction of buildings in 690

For military construction engineering, see 623.047

See Manual at 624.1 vs. 624; 690 vs. 624

SUMMARY

624.01–.09	Standard subdivisions
.1	Structural engineering and underground construction
.2	Bridges
.3	Specific types of bridges
.4	Tubular and box-girder bridges
.5	Suspension bridges
.6	Arch bridges
.7	Compound bridges
.8	Movable bridges

[.029 9]	Estimates of labor, time, materials

Do not use; class 624.1042

.068 5	Management of production [*formerly also* 658.5]

.1 Structural engineering and underground construction

Class a specific application with the application, e.g., structural engineering of dams 627.8

See Manual at 624.1 vs. 624

SUMMARY

.101　　　　　　Philosophy and theory

　　　　　　　　Class structural analysis and design in 624.17

[.102 99]　　　　　　Estimates of labor, time, materials

　　　　　　　　　Do not use; class in 624.1042

.104　　　　　　Special topics

.104 2　　　　　　Estimates of labor, time, materials

　　　　　　　　　Class interdisciplinary works on quantity surveying in 692.5

.15　　　　　　Foundation engineering and engineering geology

.151　　　　　　Engineering geology

　　　　　　　　Class here properties of soils that support structures (foundation soils)

.151 09　　　　　　Historical, geographical, persons treatment

　　　　　　　　　Class soil surveys in 624.1517

.151 3　　　　　Rock and soil mechanics

.151 32　　　　　Rock mechanics

.151 36　　　　　Soil mechanics

　　　　　　　　　Including drainage properties, permeability; permafrost

.151 362　　　　　　Consolidation

.151 363　　　　　　Stabilization

.151 4　　　　　Soil content analysis

.151 7　　　　　Soil surveys

　　　　　　　　　Add to base number 624.1517 notation 1–9 from Table 2, e.g., soil survey of Japan 624.151752

　　　　　　　　　Class general soil surveys not focusing on engineering problems in 631.47

>　　　624.152–624.158 Foundation engineering

　　　Class comprehensive works in 624.15, engineering geology of foundations in 624.151

.152   Excavation

Including blasting, shoring

Class here earthwork

Class embankment in 624.162

.153   Foundation materials

Add to base number 624.153 the numbers following 620.1 in 620.12–620.19, e.g., iron 624.1537

Class foundation materials for specific types of foundations in 624.154–624.158

>   624.154–624.158 Specific types of foundations

Class comprehensive works in 624.15

.154   Pile foundations

.156   Floating foundations

Examples: cantilever and platform foundations

.157   Underwater foundations

Including caissons, cofferdams

See also 627.702 for underwater construction operations

.158   Pier foundations

.16   Supporting structures other than foundations

Examples: abutments, piers

.162   Embankments

.164   Retaining walls

.17   Structural analysis and design

Class here interdisciplinary works on structural analysis and design, structural theory

Class a specific application with the application, e.g., structural analysis of aircraft 629.1341

.171   Structural analysis

Class analysis of specific structural elements in 624.1772–624.1779

For loads, see 624.172, stresses and strains, 624.176

.171 2   Graphic statics

.171 3   Static determinacy and indeterminacy

Including statically indeterminate structures

.171 4   Deflections

.171 5	Moments and moment distribution

>   **624.172–624.176 Loads, stresses, strains**

Class comprehensive works in 624.171; loads, stresses, strains of specific structural elements in 624.1772–624.1779

.172	Loads

For wind loads, see 624.175

.175	Wind loads
.176	Stresses and strains (Deformation)

Produced by loads, winds, vibrations, impacts, blasts, temperature changes

Class here wreckage studies

.176 2	Earthquake engineering
.177	Structural design and specific structural elements

Class analysis in 624.171

.177 1	Structural design

For design of specific structural elements, see 624.1772–624.1779; design in specific materials, 624.18

>   **624.177 2–624.177 9 Design and construction of specific structural elements**

Class here specific structural elements in metal [*formerly* 624.182]

Class comprehensive works in 624.17, design of specific structural elements in specific materials other than metal in 624.18

.177 2	Beams, girders, cylinders, columns, slabs
.177 23	Beams and girders
.177 3	Trusses and frames
.177 4	Cables, wires, bars, rods
.177 5	Arches and domes
.177 6	Shells and plates
.177 62	Shells
.177 65	Plates
.177 9	Sandwich and honeycomb constructions

Class specific sandwich and honeycomb constructions in 624.1772–624.1776

.18	Design and construction in specific materials

.182	Metals

Specific structural elements in metal relocated to 624.1772–624.1779

.182 1	Iron and steel (Ferrous metals)
.182 2–.182 9	Nonferrous metals

Add to base number 624.182 the numbers following 620.18 in 620.182–620.189, e.g., construction in aluminum 624.1826

.183	Masonry, ceramic, allied materials
.183 2	Stone

Including artificial stone, e.g., concrete blocks

.183 3	Cement
.183 4	Concrete

Class concrete and cinder blocks in 624.1832

See also 721.0445 for visual concrete

.183 41	Reinforced concrete (Ferroconcrete)

Class a specific concrete structural element of reinforced concrete in 624.18342–624.18349

.183 412	Prestressed concrete
.183 414	Precast concrete
.183 42–.183 49	Specific concrete structural elements

Add to base number 624.1834 the numbers following 624.177 in 624.1772–624.1779, e.g., concrete shells 624.183462

.183 6	Brick and tile
.183 8	Glass
.184	Wood and laminated wood
.189	Other materials

Add to base number 624.189 the numbers following 620.19 in 620.191–620.199, e.g., design in plastics 624.18923

.19	Underground construction

Class here ventilation

Class subsurface mining in 622.2, construction of underground waste disposal facilities in 628.44566

.192	Mountain tunnels
.193	Tunnels

For mountain tunnels, see 624.192; underwater tunnels, 624.194

Class artistic aspects in 725.98

.194	Underwater tunnels

.2	**Bridges**

Class artistic aspects in 725.98

For specific types of bridges, see 624.3

[.202 88]	Maintenance and repair

Do not use; class in 624.28

.25	Structural analysis and design
.252	Loads, stresses, strains

Class loads, stresses, strains of specific structural elements and materials in 624.257

.253	Floor systems
.254	Foundations
.257	Structural elements and materials

For floor systems, see 624.253; foundations, 624.254

.28	Construction, maintenance, repair
.283	Floor systems

Class here comprehensive works on floor systems of bridges

For structural analysis and design of floor systems, see 624.253

.284	Foundations

Class here comprehensive works on foundations of bridges

For structural analysis and design of foundations, see 624.254

.3	**Specific types of bridges**

For tubular bridges, see 624.4; arch bridges, 624.6; compound bridges, 624.7; movable bridges, 624.8

> 624.32–624.35 Long-span bridges

Class comprehensive works in 624.3

For suspension bridges, see 624.5

.32	Trestle bridges
.33	Continuous bridges

Bridges consisting of beams, girders, or trusses extending uninterruptedly over more than two supports

For trestle bridges, see 624.32

.35	Cantilever bridges

.37	Girder and beam bridges

Examples: covered-, lattice-, plate-girder bridges; Bailey bridges

Class long-span girder and beam bridges in 624.32–624.35

For box-girder bridges, see 624.4; plate-girder suspension bridges, 624.5

.38	Truss bridges

Class long-span truss bridges in 624.32–624.35

.4   Tubular and box-girder bridges

.5   Suspension bridges   -

Examples: plate-girder suspension bridges

[.52–.55]	Early and modern suspension bridges

Numbers discontinued; class in 624.5

.6   Arch bridges

Class here truss arch bridges

.63	Of masonry
.67	Of metal

.7   Compound bridges

Class a specific type of compound bridge with the type, e.g., plate-girder suspension bridges 624.5

.8   Movable bridges

.82	Bascule bridges
.83	Swing bridges

Variant names: swing drawbridges, swivel bridges

.84	Vertical lift bridges
.86	Transporter bridges
.87	Pontoon bridges

625   Engineering of railroads, roads, highways

General aspects: planning, analysis, design, construction

Class military transportation engineering in 623.6, tunnel engineering in 624.193, bridge engineering in 624.2

SUMMARY

625.1	**Railroads**
.2	**Railroad rolling stock**
.3	**Inclined, mountain, ship railroads**
.4	**Rapid transit systems**
.5	**Cable and aerial railways**
.6	**Surface rail and trolley systems**
.7	**Roads**
.8	**Artificial road surfaces**

.1   **Railroads**

Including comprehensive works on special-purpose railroads

Class here comprehensive works on broad-, narrow-, standard-gage railroads

Class electrification of railroads in 621.33

> *For railroad rolling stock, see 625.2; special-purpose railroads, 625.3–625.6*

.100 1   Philosophy and theory

.100 2   Miscellany

[.100 228]   Models and miniatures

Do not use; class in 625.19

[.100 288]   Maintenance and repair

Do not use; class in 625.17

.100 3–.100 9   Standard subdivisions

.103   Monorail railroads

Class elevated monorail systems in 625.44

.11   Surveying and design

Examples: final location surveys; determination of grades, switchbacks, right-of-way

---

>   625.12–625.16 Permanent way

Class comprehensive works in 625.1

.12   Earthwork

.122   Engineering geology

Including surveys, tests, analysis of foundation soils; soil and rock mechanics

.123   Roadbed preparation

Example: excavation

.13   Protective structures

         Examples: snow fences, permanent snowsheds, retaining walls

.14   Track

         For rails and rail fastenings, see 625.15; track accessories, 625.16

.141   Ballast

.143   Ties (Sleepers) and tie plates

.144   Track laying

         Class laying of monorail tracks in 625.146, of tracks over ice cover in 625.147

.146   Monorail tracks

.147   Tracks over ice cover

.15   Rails and rail fastenings

.16   Track accessories

.163   Turnouts and crossings

         Including frogs, switches, sidings

.165   Control devices

         Examples: signals, signs

.17   Maintenance and repair

         Example: snow removal operations

.18   Railroad yards (Terminal layouts)

.19   Model and miniature railroads and trains

.2   **Railroad rolling stock**

         Class here comprehensive works on specific types of cars, on rolling stock for roads with two running rails

         Class rolling stock for special-purpose railroads in 625.3–625.6

         See Manual at 629.046 vs. 388

[.202 28]   Models and miniatures

         Do not use; class in 625.19

\>   625.21–625.26 For roads with two running rails

         Class comprehensive works in 625.2

.21   Running gear

         Examples: axles, bearings, springs, wheels

         Class here running gear for specific types of cars

>   625.22–625.24 Specific types of cars

Class comprehensive works in 625.2, running gear for specific types of cars in 625.21, accessory equipment for specific types of cars in 625.25

.22   Work cars (Nonrevenue rolling stock)

Examples: cabooses, handcars, railroad snowplows

.23   Passenger-train cars

Examples: coaches; baggage, dining, sleeping cars

.24   Freight cars

Examples: boxcars, gondola cars, refrigerator cars, tank cars

.25   Accessory equipment

Examples: brakes, buffers, couplings

Class here accessory equipment for specific types of cars

.26   Locomotives

Class running gear in 625.21, accessory equipment in 625.25

.261   Steam locomotives

.262   Gas-turbine locomotives

.263   Electric locomotives

For diesel electric locomotives, see 625.2662

.265   Air-compression-powered locomotives

.266   Diesel and semidiesel locomotives

.266 2   Diesel-electric locomotives

.266 4   Diesel-hydraulic locomotives

.27   Mechanical operation

.28   Monorail rolling stock

>   **625.3–625.6 Special-purpose railroads**

Class here roadbeds, tracks and accessories, rolling stock

Class comprehensive works in 625.1, mine railroads in 622.66

.3   **Inclined, mountain, ship railroads**

.32   Funicular railroads

.33   Rack railroads

.39   Ship railroads

.4	**Rapid transit systems**

Including guided-way systems

For surface systems, see 625.6

.42	Underground railways (Subways)

.44	Elevated railroads

Including elevated monorail systems

.5	**Cable and aerial railways**

For funicular railroads, see 625.32

.6	**Surface rail and trolley systems**

Light interurban and local

.65	Roadbeds, tracks, accessories

.66	Streetcars and trolleys

Including horse-drawn streetcars

.7	**Roads**

Class here highways, streets

Class grade crossings (road crossings of railroads) in 625.163

For artificial road surfaces, see 625.8

[.702 88]	Maintenance and repair

Do not use; class in 625.76

[.702 89]	Safety measures

Do not use; class in 625.7042

.704	Special topics
.704 2	Safety engineering

.72	Surveying and design

.723	Surveying

Example: final location surveys

Class soil surveys in 625.732

.725	Design

Including determination of bankings, grades

.73	Earthwork

.732	Engineering geology

Including surveys, tests, analysis of foundation soils; soil and rock mechanics

.733	Foundation preparation
	Including excavation
.734	Drainage
	Including conduits, dikes, ditches, gutters, pipes
	For culverts, see 625.7342
.734 2	Culverts
.735	Subsurface highway materials
.74	Dirt roads
	Stabilized and unstabilized
	Including soil stabilization processes
	For surfacing dirt roads, see 625.75
.75	Surfacing dirt roads
.76	Maintenance and repair
	Class maintenance and repair not provided for here with the subject, using notation 0288 from Table 1, e.g., maintenance of roadside areas 625.770288, maintenance and repair of forestry roads in 634.93
.761	Damages and their repairs
	Examples: resurfacing, shoulder maintenance
.763	Snow and ice control measures
	Examples: use of snowplows, snow fences
	Class here municipal snow and ice removal [*formerly* 628.466]
.77	Roadside areas
	Examples: parking turnouts, picnic areas, rest areas
	Including planting and cultivation of roadside vegetation
.79	Ice crossings, traffic control equipment, protective roadside barriers
	For public lighting for roads, see 628.95
.792	Ice crossings
	Class here ice and snow-compacted roads
.794	Traffic control equipment
	Examples: markings, signals, signs
.795	Protective roadside barriers
	Examples: dividers, fences
	Class snow fences in 625.763, curbs in 625.888

.8   **Artificial road surfaces**

General aspects: design, construction, materials

Class here comprehensive works on paving

Class paving surfaces not provided for here with the surface, e.g., airport runways 629.13634

[.802 88]   Maintenance and repair

Do not use; class in 625.76

>   625.81–625.86 Pavements in specific materials

Class comprehensive works in 625.8, sidewalks in specific materials in 625.881–625.886

.81   Flagstones

.82   Brick and stone

Including gravel and crushed stone pavements

For flagstones, see 625.81

.83   Wood

.84   Concretes

For bituminous concrete, see 625.85

.85   Bituminous materials

Examples: asphalts, tar, bituminous concrete

For macadam, see 625.86

.86   Macadam and telford surfaces

.88   Sidewalks and auxiliary pavements

.881–.886   Sidewalks in specific materials

Add to base number 625.88 the numbers following 625.8 in 625.81–625.86, e.g., brick sidewalks 625.882

.888   Curbs

.889   Auxiliary pavements

Examples: driveways, parking aprons

For curbs, see 625.888

[626]   [Unassigned]

Most recently used in Edition 14

627   Hydraulic engineering

The branch of engineering dealing with utilization and control of natural waters of the earth

Class here hydraulic structures, water resource engineering

Class comprehensive works on ocean engineering in 620.4162, water supply engineering in 628.1

SUMMARY

627.04	[Hydrodynamics and recreational waters]
.1	Inland waterways
.2	Harbors, ports, roadsteads
.3	Port installations
.4	Flood control
.5	Reclamation, irrigation, related topics
.7	Underwater operations
.8	Dams and reservoirs
.9	Other hydraulic structures

.04   Special topics

.042   Hydrodynamics of waterways and water bodies

.046   Recreational waters

.1   **Inland waterways**

Class dredging and related operations in 627.7

.12   Rivers and streams

Class canalized rivers in 627.13

.122   Silt and sediment

General aspects: measurement, analysis, preventive measures

.123   Water diversions

Example: construction of barrages

.124   River mouths and estuaries

.125   Applied dynamics of rivers and streams

.13   Canals

Class here canalized rivers, comprehensive works on canals

Class tunnels carrying canals in 624.193, bridges carrying canals in 624.2, irrigation canals in 627.52

[.130 288]   Maintenance and repair

Do not use; class in 627.136

.131   Surveying and design

.132	Earthwork

Examples: clearing and grubbing, rock cutting

.133	Bank protection and reinforcement
.134	Water supply for canals
.135	Auxiliary devices
.135 2	Locks, gates, sluices
.135 3	Lifts, inclines, ramps
.136	Maintenance and repair

> 627.137–627.138 Specific types of navigation canals

Class comprehensive works in 627.13, engineering and construction details of specific types of canals in 627.131–627.136

.137	Ship canals
.138	Barge canals
.14	Lakes
[.17]	Subsurface water

Relocated to 628.114

.2   **Harbors, ports, roadsteads**

Class dredging and related operations in 627.7

For port installations, see 627.3

.22	Anchorages and mooring grounds

Including supertanker berthing areas

Class freestanding mooring and berthing structures in 627.32

.23	Channels and fairways
.24	Protective structures

Examples: breakwaters, jetties, seawalls

.3   **Port installations**

Class artistic aspects in 725.34

For navigation aids, see 627.92

> 627.31–627.34 Specific types of structures and equipment

Class comprehensive works in 627.3, specific types of structures in small craft installations in 627.38

.31	Docks

Class here piers, quays, wharves

[.312–.313]	Specific kinds of docks

Numbers discontinued; class in 627.31

.32	Freestanding mooring and berthing structures
.33	Port buildings
.34	Cargo-handling equipment

See also 623.867 for shipboard cargo-handling equipment

[.35]	Other terminal facilities

Number discontinued; class in 627.3

Dry docks, floating dry docks relocated to 623.83

.38	Small-craft installations (Marinas)
.4	**Flood control**

Including flood wreckage studies

Class here use of dams and reservoirs for flood control [*formerly* 627.8]

Class construction of dams and reservoirs for flood control in 627.8; flood control for and wreckage studies of a specific type of structure with the structure, e.g., flood wreckage studies of bridges 624.2

.42	Flood barriers

Examples: dikes, levees, seawalls

.44	Water storage

In ponds, lakes, reservoirs

.45	Water diversion

Through enlargement of natural channels and construction of auxiliary channels

.5	**Reclamation, irrigation, related topics**

Class here comprehensive works on soil erosion and its control

Class erosion of agricultural soils and its control in 631.45, reclamation of agricultural soils in 631.6, revegetation and surface mine reclamation in 631.64

.52	Irrigation

Class here construction and use of irrigation canals

Use of this number for comprehensive works on land reclamation, on soil erosion and its control discontinued; class in 627.5

Class engineering of dams and reservoirs for irrigation in 627.8

.54	Drainage and reclamation from sea
	Including polders
.56	Artificial recharge of groundwater [*formerly also* 628.114]
	Former heading: water reclamation
	Class comprehensive works on engineering of groundwater in 628.114
.58	Shore protection and reclamation
	Examples: dune stabilization, seawall construction
	Class here beach erosion and its control
	Class inland dune stabilization in 631.64

.7   Underwater operations

.700 1	Philosophy and theory
.700 2	Miscellany
[.700 288]	Maintenance and repair
	Do not use; class in 627.705
.700 3–.700 9	Standard subdivisions

>   627.702–627.705 General topics

Class comprehensive works in 627.7

.702	Underwater construction
.703	Salvage operations
.704	Research operations
.705	Maintenance and repair operations
.72	Diving
	Class here interdisciplinary works on diving
	For diving sports, see 797.2
.73	Dredging
.74	Blasting
.75	Drilling

.8   Dams and reservoirs

Class here engineering of dams and reservoirs for specific purposes

Use of dams and reservoirs for flood control relocated to 627.4

Class a specific use of dams and reservoirs with the use, e.g., water storage and conservation 628.132

.802 8	Auxiliary techniques and procedures; apparatus, equipment
	Class materials in 627.81

.81   Materials, earthwork, planning, surveying

Class materials, earthwork, planning, surveying for specific kinds of dams in 627.82–627.85; for reservoirs in 627.86; for auxiliary structures in 627.88

>   627.82–627.85 Specific kinds of dams

Class comprehensive works in 627.8, ancillary structures of specific kinds of dams in 627.88

.82   Masonry dams

.83   Earth- and rock-fill dams

.84   Movable dams

Examples: bear-trap, shutter (wicket) dams

.85   Metal dams

.86   Reservoirs

Including silting control

Class ancillary structures of reservoirs in 627.88

.88   Ancillary structures

.882   Sluices, gates, penstocks

.883   Spillways and weirs

.9   Other hydraulic structures

.92   Navigation aids

Class use of navigation aids in 623.894

.922   Lighthouses

[.923]   Lightships

Relocated to 623.828

.924   Light beacons, buoys, daymarks

.98   Offshore structures

Example: drilling platforms

Class here artificial islands

Class use of offshore structures with the use, e.g., use of drilling platforms in petroleum extraction 622.33819

For freestanding mooring and berthing structures, see 627.32

628   Sanitary and municipal engineering   Environmental protection engineering

Class here environmental health engineering [*formerly also* 620.85], public sanitation technology

Class interdisciplinary works on environmental protection on 363.7, military sanitary engineering in 623.75; a specific aspect of municipal engineering not provided for here with the subject, e.g., road and street engineering in 625.7, laying gas pipelines 665.744

For plumbing, see 696.1

See Manual at 300 vs. 600; 363

SUMMARY

628.1	Water supply
.2	Sewers and sewage
.3	Sewage treatment and disposal
.4	Waste technology, public toilets, street cleaning
.5	Pollution technology and industrial sanitation engineering
.7	Sanitary engineering for rural and sparsely populated areas
.9	Other branches of sanitary and municipal engineering

[.091 734]   Treatment in rural regions

Do not use; class in 628.7

.1   Water supply

Class here comprehensive works on water supply, sewers, sewage

Class water supply for rural and sparsely populated areas in 628.72

For sewers and sewage, see 628.2

SUMMARY

628.102 87	Measurement
.11	Sources
.13	Storage and conservation
.14	Collection and distribution systems
.15	Mains and service pipes
.16	Testing, analysis, treatment, pollution

.102 87   Measurement

Class testing in 628.161

.11   Sources

Including waste water

Class here protection and engineering evaluation of sources

Class interdisciplinary works on sources, on evaluation of sources in 553.7; economic and social evaluation of adequacy, development requirements, conservation of sources in 333.91; hydraulic engineering in 627

See also 628.132 for reservoirs

.112	Lakes, rivers, springs

Class artesian wells in 628.114

.114	Groundwater (Subsurface water) [*formerly also* 627.17]

Including prospecting for water [*formerly also* 622.187], artesian wells, prevention of seawater intrusion

Class here water extraction [*formerly also* 622.37], wells

Artificial recharge of groundwater relocated to 627.56

.116	Seawater

Class desalinization in 628.167

[.119]	Waste water

Number discontinued; class in 628.11

.13	Storage and conservation

Including storage tanks, water towers

.132	Reservoirs

Including evaporation control

Class engineering of reservoirs for water supply, comprehensive works on protection of reservoirs in 627.86

.14	Collection and distribution systems

Class storage in collection and distribution systems in 628.13

For mains and service pipes, see 628.15

.142	Collection systems

.144	Distribution systems

.144 028 7	Testing and measurement

Class here measurement of consumption [*formerly also* 628.17]

.15	Mains and service pipes

Class here aqueducts

.16	Testing, analysis, treatment, pollution

See Manual at 363.61

SUMMARY

628.161	**Testing and analysis**
.162	**Treatment**
.164	**Mechanical treatment**
.165	**Aeration and deaeration**
.166	**Chemical treatment**
.167	**Desalinization**
.168	**Pollution and countermeasures**

.161　　　　Testing and analysis

> Class here testing and measurement of pollution [*formerly* 628.1680287]

.162　　　　Treatment

> Class here comprehensive works on treatment of water supply and sewage, treatment of sewage effluent for reuse
>
> *For mechanical treatment, see 628.164; chemical treatment, 628.166; desalinization, 628.167; sewage treatment, 628.3*

.162 2　　　Coagulation (Flocculation), screening, sedimentation (settling)

.164　　　　Mechanical treatment

> Examples: filtration, membrane (osmotic) processes
>
> Class membrane processes for desalinization in 628.1674
>
> *For screening, sedimentation, see 628.1622*

.165　　　　Aeration and deaeration

> *See also 628.1662 for ozone treatment*

.166　　　　Chemical treatment

> *For coagulation, see 628.1622; aeration and deaeration, 628.165*

.166 2　　　Disinfection

> Examples: chlorination, copper sulfate treatment, ozone treatment, ultraviolet radiation
>
> Including dechlorination

.166 3　　　Fluoridation

> Class interdisciplinary works on fluoridation in 614.5996, defluoridation in 628.1667

.166 6　　　Demineralization processes

> Example: softening
>
> Class desalinization in 628.167

.166 7　　　Defluoridation

.167　　　　Desalinization

.167 2　　　By distillation

.167 23　　　Using nuclear energy

.167 25　　　Using solar energy

.167 3　　　By electrolysis

.167 4　　　By membrane processes

.167 42　　　Electrodialysis

.167 44　　　Reverse osmosis

.167 46　　　Piezodialysis

.167 5	By freezing
.167 6	With gas hydrates
.168	Pollution and countermeasures

Comprehensive works on liquid wastes relocated to 628.43

Class interdisciplinary works on water pollution and countermeasures in 363.7394; prevention of natural pollution of water sources in 628.11; pollution countermeasures that consist of routine water-supply or water-supply and sewage treatment in 628.162, of sewage treatment in 628.3

[.168 028 7]	Testing and measurement

Relocated to 628.161

.168 09	Historical, geographical, persons treatment

Class here pollution in specific areas [*formerly* 628.1686], technological countermeasures in specific areas [*formerly* 628.1688]

Class pollution surveys in specific areas in 363.73209

.168 2	Pollution from sewage and domestic wastes
.168 23	From detergents
.168 25	From sanitary landfills
.168 3	Pollution from industrial waste

Class countermeasures by originating industry with the industry, e.g., engineering control of acid mine drainage by coal companies 622.5

For pollution from radioactive wastes, see 628.1685

.168 31	Thermal pollution
.168 32	Acid mine drainage
.168 33	Oil spills

Including disposal of cleanup debris

.168 36	Waste from chemical and related industries
.168 37	Waste from manufacturing industries
.168 4	Pollution from agricultural waste
.168 41	Soil improvement wastes

Examples: fertilizers, irrigation return flow

.168 42	Pesticides
.168 46	Animal wastes

Including feedlot runoff

.168 5	Pollution from radioactive wastes

[.168 6]	Pollution in specific areas
	Relocated to 628.16809
[.168 8]	Abatement programs
	Abatement programs relocated to 363.73946, technological countermeasures in specific areas to 628.16809
[.17]	Water requirements and use
	Water requirements relocated to 333.9112, water use to 333.9113, measurement of consumption to 628.1440287

.2   Sewers and sewage

Class road drainage in 625.734

For sewage treatment and disposal, see 628.3

[.202 88]	Maintenance and repair
	Do not use; class in 628.24
.21	Sewer systems for handling precipitation

Including overflows

Class here urban drainage

Use of this number for comprehensive works on sewerage systems discontinued; class in 628.2

.212	Separate storm sewer systems
.214	Combined sewer systems
.23	Ventilation and deodorization of sewers
.24	Design, construction, maintenance, repair of sewers
.25	Appurtenances of sewers

Examples: catch basins, house connections, manholes, ventilators

.29	Pumping stations

.3   Sewage treatment and disposal

Class creation, treatment, disposal of sewage in a specific technology with the technology, e.g., treatment of food-processing sewage by food processors 664.096

For unsewered sewage disposal, see 628.742

See Manual at 363.61

>	628.32–628.35 Treatment

Class comprehensive works in 628.3

.32	Disinfection

.34	**Primary treatment**

Examples: centrifugation, primary sedimentation, screening, skimming

Class comprehensive works on a specific process that is used also in both primary and secondary treatment in 628.351–628.354

.35	**Secondary and tertiary treatment**

Class here aeration, biological treatment

> **628.351–628.354 Secondary treatment**

Class comprehensive works in 628.35

.351	**Oxidation ponds**

Variant names: sewage lagoons, stabilization ponds

Including oxidation ditches

Use of this number for comprehensive works on aeration, on biological treatment discontinued; class in 628.35

.352	**Filtration**

Examples: sand and trickling filters

.353	**Secondary sedimentation**
.354	**Activated sludge process**
.357	**Tertiary treatment**

Examples: nitrogen removal

Removal of mineral nutrients, of specific minerals relocated to 628.358

Class comprehensive works on a specific process that is used in secondary and tertiary treatment in 628.351–628.354

For demineralization, see 628.358

.358	**Demineralization**

Class here removal of mineral nutrients, of specific minerals [*both formerly* 628.357]

.36	**Disposal**

For disposal into water, see 628.39

.362	**Sewage effluent disposal**

Class artificial recharge of groundwater in 627.56, treatment for reuse as water supply in 628.162

.362 3	**Sewage irrigation**

.364   Sewage sludge disposal

Example: sanitary landfills

For underground disposal of sludge, see 628.366; incineration of sludge, 628.37; utilization of sludge, 628.38

.366   Underground disposal of sludge

Including storage

.37   Incineration of sludge

Former heading: Disposal by destruction

.38   Utilization of sludge

Class a specific use with the use, e.g., use as fertilizer 631.869

.39   Disposal of sewage, sewage effluent, sewage sludge into water

.4   Waste technology [*formerly also* 604.6], public toilets, street cleaning

Class here industrial waste treatment and disposal by type of industry [*formerly* 628.54]

Use of this number for public sanitation discontinued; class in 628

Class interdisciplinary works on waste in 363.728; pollution from wastes in 628.5; waste technology for rural and sparsely populated areas in 628.74; creation, control, utilization of waste in a specific technology with the technology, e.g., waste control in pulp and paper technology 676.042, use of scrap metal 669.042

For gaseous wastes, see 628.53

.42   Toxic and hazardous wastes

Class toxic and hazardous liquid wastes in 628.43, solid wastes in 628.44, gaseous wastes in 628.53

.43   Liquid wastes [*formerly* 628.168]

Class liquid wastes released into bodies of water in 628.168

For sewers and sewage, see 628.2

.44   Solid wastes (Refuse)

.440 4   Special topics

.440 42   Specific kinds of solid wastes

See Manual at 628.44042 vs. 363.7288, 628.445

.442   Collection

.445   Treatment and disposal

See Manual at 628.44042 vs. 363.7288, 628.445

> 628.445 6–628.445 9 Disposal

Class comprehensive works in 628.445

.445 6   Disposal on land and underground

Use of this number for comprehensive works on reduction discontinued; class in 628.445

.445 62   In open dumps

.445 64   In sanitary landfills

.445 66   Underground disposal

Other than in sanitary landfills

Including construction of facilities, storage

.445 7   Incineration

.445 8   Conversion into useful products

Class here recycling technology

Class specific conversion technology with the technology, e.g., converting household garbage into fertilizer 668.6377

.445 9   Disposal into water

.45   **Public toilets**

.46   **Street cleaning**

[.462]   Sprinkling and sweeping

Number discontinued; class in 628.46

[.466]   Municipal snow and ice removal

Relocated to 625.763

.5   Pollution technology and industrial sanitation engineering

Class here industrial pollution

Standard subdivisions may be used for combined treatment of pollution technology and industrial sanitary engineering, or for pollution technology alone

Class interdisciplinary works on pollution in 363.73; water pollution in 628.168; engineering causes of pollution in a specific technology and reengineering a specific technology to control pollution with the technology, e.g., engineering to control pollution in petroleum refineries 665.53

For noise, see 620.23

.509 173 4   Rural regions

Class here pollution in rural and sparsely populated areas [*formerly* 628.7]

.51   Industrial sanitation engineering

Class here industrial plant sanitation

.52   Specific kinds of pollutants

General aspects: movement through the environment, control measures

Example: pesticides [*formerly also* 628.7462]

Class specific kinds of water pollutants in 628.168, air pollutants in 628.53, soil pollutants in 628.55

.53   Air pollution

Class here gaseous wastes, the immediate dispersal of pollutants from the source

Class air quality surveys in 363.73922

.532   By products of combustion

Class here smog

Use of this number for comprehensive works on fumes, gases discontinued; class in 628.53

.535   By radioactive substances

Example: radon

.536   By microbes

[.54]   Industrial waste treatment and disposal by type of industry

Relocated to 628.4

.55   Soil pollution

.7   **Sanitary engineering for rural and sparsely populated areas**

Pollution in rural and sparsely populated areas relocated to 628.5091734

Class pest control in rural and sparsely populated areas in 628.96091734

See Manual at 628.7

.72   Water supply

.74   Waste technology

.742   Unsewered sewage disposal

Including septic tanks

.744   Solid waste technology

Class agricultural solid waste technology in 628.746

.746   Agricultural waste technology

Class water pollution from agricultural wastes in 628.1684; utilization of agricultural wastes in a specific technology with the technology, e.g., for biogas 665.776

[.746 1]	Utilization of animal wastes for soil improvement

Comprehensive works relocated to 631.86, manufacture of fertilizers from animal wastes to 668.636, animal manures not used for soil improvement to 628.7466

[.746 2]	Pesticides

Relocated to 628.52

.746 6	Animal wastes

Class here animal manures [*formerly* 628.7461]

.9   Other branches of sanitary and municipal engineering

.92   Fire-safety and fire-fighting technology

Class interdisciplinary works on fire hazards and their control in 363.37, forest fire technology in 634.9618

.922   Fire-safety technology

Including fire escapes

Class here fire prevention

.922 2   Flammability studies and testing

Class development of fire resistance in products in 628.9223

.922 3   Fireproofing and fire retardation

Examples: fire doors, fire retardants

Class here development of fire resistance in products

Class development of fire resistance in a specific product with the product, e.g., textiles 677.689, buildings 693.82

.922 5   Fire detection and alarms

.925   Fire-fighting technology

Class here use of equipment and supplies, comprehensive works on their manufacture

Class fire-fighting technology for airports in 629.1368; manufacture of specific kinds of equipment and supplies with the kind, e.g., fire engines 629.225, fire resistant clothing 687.16, fire stations 690.519

.925 2   Extinction with water

Examples: hydraulic systems, sprinkler systems

.925 4   Extinction with chemicals

.95   Public lighting

Examples: lighting for parks, roads

Class lighting of airports in 629.1365

.96   Pest control

Class here comprehensive works on pest control technology

Class interdisciplinary works on pest control in 363.78, control of agricultural pests in 632.6

For control of plant pests, see 628.97

.963   Aquatic invertebrates

Class aquatic insects in 628.9657

For mollusks and molluscoids, see 628.964

.964   Mollusks and molluscoids

.965   Terrestrial invertebrates

.965 7   Insects

.967   Cold-blooded vertebrates

.968   Birds

.969   Mammals

.969 3   Rodents

.969 7   Land carnivores

Examples: stray cats and dogs

.97   Control of plant pests

629   Other branches of engineering

General aspects: planning, analysis, design, construction, operation

See Manual at 629.046 vs. 388

SUMMARY

629.04	**Transportation engineering**
.1	**Aerospace engineering**
.2	**Motor land vehicles, and cycles**
.3	**Air-cushion vehicles (Ground-effect machines, Hovercraft)**
.4	**Astronautics**
.8	**Automatic control engineering**

.04   Transportation engineering

Unless other instructions are given, class complex subjects with aspects in two or more subdivisions of this schedule in the number coming last in the schedule, e.g., land vehicles 629.049 (*not* 629.046)

Class military transportation technology in 623.6, operation of transportation equipment for recreational purposes in 796–797, technical problems peculiar to transportation of a specific commodity with the commodity, e.g., slurry transportation of coal 662.624

[.040 289]   Safety measures

Do not use; class in 629.042

.042   Health and safety engineering

Including control devices, e.g., markings, signals, signs

.045   Navigation

For celestial navigation, see 527

.046   Transportation equipment

Class here vehicles

See Manual at 629.046 vs. 388

.047   Stationary transportation facilities

Class here trafficways

Class transportation buildings in 690.53

>   629.048–629.049 Engineering of transportation in specific mediums

Class comprehensive works in 629.04

For aerospace engineering, see 629.1

.048   Water transportation engineering

For nautical engineering and seamanship, see 623.8; inland waterways, 627.1; harbors, ports, roadsteads, 627.2; overwater air-cushion vehicles, 629.324

.049   Land transportation engineering

Class pipes and pipelines in 621.8672

For railroads, roads, highways, see 625; motor land vehicles, cycles, 629.2; overland air-cushion vehicles, 629.322; nonmotor land vehicles, 688.6

.1   **Aerospace engineering**

For astronautics, see 629.4

SUMMARY

629.11	**Mechanics and operation of aerospace flight**
.12	**Aerospace vehicles and stationary facilities**
.13	**Aeronautics**
.14	**Portable flight vehicles**

.11   Mechanics and operation of aerospace flight

Class mechanics and operation of a specific type of aerospace flight with the type, e.g., astromechanics 629.411

.12   Aerospace vehicles and stationary facilities

Class a specific facility with the facility, e.g., air-cushion vehicles 629.3

.13   Aeronautics

Use 629.13001–629.13009 for standard subdivisions

SUMMARY

629.130 1–.130 9	**Standard subdivisions of flight**
.132	**Principles of aerial flight**
.133	**Aircraft types**
.134	**Aircraft components and general techniques**
.135	**Aircraft instrumentation and systems (Avionics)**
.136	**Airports**

.130 1   Philosophy and theory of flight

[.130 153 36]   Aeromechanics of flight

Do not use; class in 629.1323

[.130 155 15]   Aviation meteorology

Do not use; class in 629.1324

.130 2–.130 8   Standard subdivisions of flight

.130 9   Historical, geographical, persons treatment of flight [*formerly also* 629.132509]

Record of flying activities in all types of aircraft

Class flight guides in 629.13254

.130 91   Transoceanic flights

Add to base number 629.13091 the numbers following 551.46 in 551.461–551.469, e.g., transpacific flights 629.130915

Do not use for other regional treatment; class in 629.1309

.130 92   Fliers

.132   Principles of aerial flight

SUMMARY

629.132 2	**Aerostatics**
.132 3	**Aerodynamics**
.132 4	**Aviation meteorology**
.132 5	**Flying and related topics**
.132 6	**Automatic control**

.132 2   Aerostatics

.132 3   Aerodynamics

Including aircraft noise

Class here comprehensive works on aeromechanics

Use 629.1323001–629.1323009 for standard subdivisions

For aerostatics, see 629.1322; weather aerodynamics, 629.1324

.132 303   Subsonic aerodynamics

.132 304	Transonic aerodynamics
	Including sonic booms
.132 305	Supersonic aerodynamics
.132 306	Hypersonic aerodynamics
.132 31	Gliding and soaring
.132 32	Airflow
	Example: turbulence
	For boundary layers, see 629.13237
.132 322	Incompressible airflow
.132 323	Compressible airflow
.132 327	Air pockets (Air holes)
.132 33	Lift and thrust
.132 34	Drag (Air resistance)
.132 35	Pressure distribution and aerodynamic load
.132 36	Stability and control
.132 362	Aeroelasticity, flutter, vibration
.132 364	Moments of inertia
	Examples: pitch, roll, yaw
	Including restoring torques and damping
.132 37	Boundary layers
.132 38	Propulsion principles
.132 4	Aviation meteorology
	Weather conditions and aerodynamics
.132 5	Flying and related topics
	Class flying kites and model airplanes in 796.15, air sports in 797.5
[.132 509]	Historical, geographical, persons treatment of flight
	Relocated to 629.1309
.132 51	Navigation
.132 52	Piloting
	Class here comprehensive works on flight operations, on piloting airplanes
	For navigation, see 629.13251
[.132 520 92]	Pilots
	Do not use; class in 629.13092

.132 521	General topics

Use of this number for comprehensive works on on piloting airplanes discontinued; class in 629.13252

Class general topics of specific types of aircraft in 629.132522–629.132528

.132 521 2	Takeoff
.132 521 3	Landing
.132 521 4	Piloting under adverse conditions

Examples: nighttime, bad weather, disablement of craft

.132 521 6	Piloting commercial craft [*formerly also* 629.1325240423]
.132 521 7	Piloting private craft [*formerly also* 629.1325240422]
.132 522	Piloting lighter-than-air aircraft
.132 523–.132 528	Piloting specific types of heavier-than-air aircraft

Add to base number 626.13252 the numbers following 629.1333 in 629.13333–629.13338, e.g., piloting of helicopters 629.1325252; however, piloting private craft relocated from 629.1325240422 to 629.1325217, piloting commercial craft from 629.1325240423 to 629.1325216

Class comprehensive works on piloting airplanes in 629.13252, hang gliding in 629.14

.132 54	Flight guides (Pilot guides)

Class here charts, logbooks, maps

Add to base number 629.13254 notation 1–9 from Table 2, e.g., pilot guides to Spain 629.1325446

.132 55	Wreckage studies
.132 6	Automatic control

Former heading: Command systems

Of manned and guided aircraft

See also 629.1352 for automatic pilots

.133	Aircraft types

Class components and general techniques of specific aircraft types in 629.134

.133 021 8	Standards [*formerly also* 629.13457]
[.133 022 8]	Models and miniatures

Do not use; class models and miniatures of all types of aircraft in 629.1331

[.133 028 7]	Testing and measurement

Do not use; class testing and measurement of all types of aircraft in 629.1345

[.133 028 8]		Maintenance and repair

Do not use; class maintenance and repair of all types of aircraft in 629.1346

.133 028 9   Safety measures

Class safety equipment in 629.13443

.133 1   Models and miniatures

Add to base number 629.1331 the numbers following 629.133 in 629.1332–629.1333, e.g., models of helicopters 629.1331352

Class flying model aircraft in 796.15

.133 2   Lighter-than-air aircraft

.133 22   Free and captive balloons

Class dirigible balloons in 629.13324

.133 24   Airships (Dirigibles)

For specific types of airships, see 629.13325–629.13327

>   629.133 25–629.133 27 Specific types of airships

Class comprehensive works in 629.13324

.133 25   Rigid airships

.133 26   Semirigid airships

.133 27   Nonrigid airships

.133 3   Heavier-than-air aircraft

.133 32   Kites

.133 33   Gliders

Class hang gliders in 629.14

.133 34   Airplanes

For rocket planes, see 629.13338

.133 340 4   Special topics

.133 340 42   General topics

.133 340 422   Private airplanes

.133 340 423   Commercial airplanes

.133 340 426   Short takeoff and landing (STOL) airplanes

.133 343   Propeller-driven airplanes

Piston and turboprop

Including ultralight airplanes

Class propeller-driven seaplanes in 629.133347, propeller-driven amphibious planes in 629.133348

.133 347	Seaplanes
.133 348	Amphibious planes
.133 349	Jet airplanes
.133 35	Vertical-lift (VTOL) craft

Examples: autogiros, convertiplanes, flying jeeps

.133 352	Helicopters
.133 36	Orthopters (Ornithopters)
.133 38	Rocket planes
.134	Aircraft components and general techniques

For aircraft instrumentation and systems, see 629.135

SUMMARY

629.134 1	**Analysis and design**
.134 2	**Manufacturing and assembling**
.134 3	**Parts**
.134 4	**Interiors and special equipment**
.134 5	**Tests and measurements**
.134 6	**Maintenance and repair**

[.134 028 7]	Testing and measurement

Do not use; class in 629.1345

[.134 028 8]	Maintenance and repair

Do not use; class in 629.1346

.134 1	Analysis and design

Class analysis and design of parts in 629.1343, of interiors and special equipment in 629.1344

.134 2	Manufacturing and assembling

Class manufacturing and assembling of parts in 629.1343, of interiors and special equipment in 629.1344

.134 3	Parts
.134 31	Airframes

Class a specific component part with the component, e.g., fuselages 629.13434

.134 32	Airfoils

Including wing accessories

Class here wings

For control surfaces, see 629.13433; propellers, vertical lift rotors, 629.13436

.134 33	Control surfaces

Examples: ailerons, flaps, rudders

.134 34	Fuselages
.134 35	Engines and fuels
	Including pollution control
.134 351	Fuels
	Class here propellants
	Class fuels and propellants for specific engines in 629.134352–629.134355
.134 352	Reciprocating and compound engines
	Piston and compound piston-turbine engines
	Class comprehensive works on reciprocating, compound, gas-turbine, jet engines in 629.13435
.134 353	Gas-turbine and jet engines
	Standard subdivisions are added for gas-turbine and jet engines, for gas-turbine engines alone, for jet engines alone
.134 353 2	Turboprop engines
.134 353 3	Turbojet engines
.134 353 4	Turboramjet engines
.134 353 5	Ramjet engines
.134 353 6	Pulse-jet engines
.134 353 7	Fan-jet engines
.134 354	Rocket engines
.134 355	Nuclear power plants
.134 36	Propellers and vertical lift rotors
.134 37	Rigging and bracing equipment
.134 38	Other equipment
.134 381	Takeoff and landing gear
	See also 678.32 for manufacture of tires
.134 386	Escape equipment
	Examples: capsule cockpits, parachutes, pilot ejection seats
.134 4	Interiors and special equipment
.134 42	Comfort equipment
	Examples: air conditioning, heating, pressurization, soundproofing, ventilating equipment
.134 43	Safety equipment
	Examples: fire prevention equipment, life rafts, safety belts

.134 45	Interiors
	Including cabins
.134 5	Tests and measurements
	Class wreckage studies in 629.13255
.134 52	Ground tests and inspection
	Including wind and shock tunnels
.134 53	Flight tests
.134 57	Measurements
	Standards relocated to 629.1330218
.134 6	Maintenance and repair
	Class maintenance and repair of a specific part with the part, using notation 0288 from Table 1, e.g., maintenance of interiors 629.134450288
.135	**Aircraft instrumentation and systems (Avionics)**
.135 1	Navigation instrumentation
	Examples: air-mileage and air-position indicators, radio compasses (direction finders)
	Including landing and navigation lights
.135 2	Flight instrumentation
	Examples: automatic pilots; air-speed, vertical-speed, turn and bank indicators; accelerometers, altimeters, Machmeters; directional gyros, gyrohorizons
.135 3	Power-plant monitoring instrumentation
.135 4	Electrical systems
.135 5	Electronic systems
.136	**Airports**
	Class here commercial land airports
.136 1	Specific types other than commercial land airports
	Example: floating airports (seadromes)
	Class details of specific types of airports in 629.1363–629.1368
.136 12	Airstrips
[.136 13]	Commercial land airports
	Number discontinued; class in 629.136
.136 16	Heliports

>   629.136 3–629.136 8 Details of airports

Class comprehensive works in 629.136

.136 3	Runways
.136 34	Pavements
.136 35	Drainage systems
.136 37	Snow removal and compaction
[.136 4]	Airport terminal buildings

Relocated to 690.539

.136 5	Lighting systems
.136 6	Air traffic control systems

Radar control and radar devices

.136 8	Fire fighting equipment
.14	Portable flight vehicles

Units intended to be carried by a single person

Including hang gliders and gliding

Class hang gliding as a sport in 797.55

.2   **Motor land vehicles, and cycles**

SUMMARY

629.201–.209	**Standard subdivisions**
.22	**Types of vehicles**
.23	**Design, materials, construction**
.24	**Chassis**
.25	**Engines**
.26	**Bodies**
.27	**Other equipment**
.28	**Tests, driving, maintenance, repair**
.29	**Specialized land vehicles**

.202 8	Auxiliary techniques and procedures; apparatus and equipment

Class materials in 629.232

.202 89	Safety measures

Class safety engineering of motor land vehicles in 629.2042

.204	Special topics
.204 2	Safety engineering of motor land vehicles

Class here comprehensive works on motor land vehicle and highway safety engineering

For highway safety engineering, see 625.7042

.22	Types of vehicles

Class here three-wheel vehicles

Class specific details in 629.23–629.28

[.220 228]	Models and miniatures

Do not use; class models and miniatures of all types of vehicles in 629.221

[.220 287]	Testing and measurement

Do not use; class testing and measurement of all types of vehicles in 629.282

[.220 288]	Maintenance and repair

Do not use; class maintenance and repair of all types of vehicles in 629.287

.220 289	Safety measures

Class safety accessories in 629.276

.220 4	Special topics
.220 42	Off-road vehicles

Examples: all-terrain vehicles, snowmobiles

For dune buggies, see 629.222

.221	Models and miniatures

Add to base number 629.221 the numbers following 629.22 in 629.222–629.229, e.g., models of racing cars 629.2218

> 629.222–629.228 Gasoline-, oil-, man-powered vehicles

Class comprehensive works in 629.22

.222	Passenger automobiles

Including dune buggies, sport cars, station wagons

Class racing cars in 629.228

.222 2	Specific named passenger automobiles

Arrange alphabetically by name or make of car

Use of this number for comprehensive works on passenger automobiles for private transportation discontinued; class in 629.222

.222 3	For public transportation
.222 32	Taxicabs and limousines
.222 33	Buses
.222 34	Ambulances

.223   Light trucks

Examples: pickup trucks

Including customized vans

.224   Trucks (Lorries)

Class here tractor trailers

For light trucks, see 629.223

.225   Work vehicles

Examples: bulldozers, tractors

Class automotive materials-handling equipment in 621.86, steam tractors in 629.2292

For trucks, see 629.224

.226   Motorized homes, campers, trailers (caravans)

Class here comprehensive works on recreational vehicles (RVs)

Class construction of towed mobile homes in 690.879; a specific kind of recreational vehicle not provided for here with the vehicle, e.g., dune buggies 629.222

For tractor trailers, see 629.224

See Manual at 629.226 vs. 643.2, 690.879, 728.79

.227   Cycles

.227 1   Monocycles

.227 2   Bicycles

Mopeds and motor bicycles relocated to 629.2275

Class tandem bicycles in 629.2276

.227 3   Tricycles

.227 5   Motorcycles and motorscooters

Including mopeds and motor bicycles [*both formerly* 629.2272], minibikes

.227 6   Tandem bicycles

.228   Racing cars

Conventional and converted

Including karts, hot rods

.229   Other types of vehicles

.229 2   Steam-powered vehicles

Including steam tractors and steamrollers

.229 3   Electric-powered vehicles

.229 4   Air-compression-powered vehicles

.229 5   Solar energy-powered vehicles

.229 6   Nuclear-powered vehicles

.23   Design, materials, construction

Class materials for, design and construction of parts in 629.24–629.27

.231   Analysis and design

Including anthropometric and safety design

.232   Materials

.234   Manufacturing techniques

Including factory inspection

> 629.24–629.27 Parts

Class comprehensive works in 629.2

.24   Chassis

.242   Supporting frames

.243   Springs and shock absorbers

.244   Transmission devices

.244 6   Automatic transmission devices

.245   Rear axles, differentials, drive shafts

.246   Brakes

Including brake fluids

.247   Front axles and steering gear

.248   Wheels

Including rims, hubcaps, bearings

.248 2   Tires

See also 678.32 for manufacture of tires

.25   Engines

Class here pollution control

Use 629.25001–629.25009 for standard subdivisions

Most works covering automobile engines as a whole focus on spark-ignition engines and are classed in 629.2504

> 629.250 1–629.250 9 Specific types of engines

Class comprehensive works in 629.25

.250 1	Steam engines
.250 2	Electric power plants
.250 3–.250 6	Internal-combustion engines

> Add to base number 629.250 the numbers following 621.43 in 621.433–621.436, e.g., diesel engines 629.2506

.250 7	Air-compression engines
.250 8	Solar engines
.250 9	Nuclear power plants

> **629.252–629.258 Parts and auxiliary systems of internal-combustion engines**

Class here comprehensive works on specific kinds of parts and auxiliary systems of automotive engines

Class comprehensive works in 629.25, a specific part and auxiliary system of noninternal-combustion engines in 629.259

.252	Motor parts of internal-combustion engines

Including mufflers (silencers)

.252 8	Emission control devices
.253	Fuel systems and fuels of internal-combustion engines
.253 3	Carburetors and carburetion
.253 8	Fuels
.254	Ignition, electrical, electronic systems of internal-combustion engines

Standard subdivisions are added for ignition, electrical, electronic systems, for ignition systems alone, for electrical systems alone

Class specific uses of electrical and electronic systems with the use, e.g., electronic fuel injection 629.253, electric starters 629.257

.254 2	Batteries
.254 8	Auxiliary electrical systems

For lighting equipment, see 629.271

.254 9	Electronic systems
.255	Lubricating systems and lubricants of internal-combustion engines
.256	Cooling systems of internal-combustion engines

Including antifreeze solutions

.257	Starting devices of internal-combustion engines
.258	Throttles and spark control devices of internal-combustion engines

.259		Parts and auxiliary systems of other kinds of power plants
.259 2		Of steam engines
.259 3		Of electric power plants
.259 4		Of air-compression engines
.259 5		Of solar engines
.259 6		Of nuclear power plants
.26	Bodies	

Including convertible tops, doors, fenders, interior and exterior decoration, running boards, seats, windows, windshields

.27	Other equipment
.271	Lighting equipment
.273	Panel instrumentation
.275	Hardware

Examples: handles, hinges, locks

.276	Safety accessories

Examples: air bags, bumpers, mirrors, seat belts, windshield wipers and washers

.277	Comfort, convenience, entertainment equipment

Examples: air conditioners, ashtrays, glove compartments, heaters, radios, tape players, telephones, televisions, two-way radios

.28	Tests, driving, maintenance, repair
.282	Tests and related topics

For factory inspection, see 629.234

.282 4	Road tests (Performance tests)
.282 5	Periodic inspection and roadability tests
.282 6	Wreckage studies

Determination of mechanical failure through examination of remains

.283	Driving (Operation)

General aspects: methods of driving, factors in safe driving

Class here driving private passenger automobiles

For driving vehicles other than internal-combustion passenger vehicles, see 629.284

.283 04	Special topics
.283 042	Driving off-road vehicles

Examples: all-terrain vehicles, snowmobiles

[.283 2]	Driving private passenger automobiles
	Use of this number discontinued; class in 629.283
.283 3	Driving public transportation vehicles
.283 32	Taxicabs and limousines
.283 33	Buses
.283 34	Ambulances
.284	Driving vehicles other than internal-combustion passenger vehicles

Add to base number 629.284 the numbers following 629.22 in 629.223–629.229, e.g., driving trucks 629.2844

.286	Services provided by garages and service stations

See also 690.538 for garage and service station buildings

For maintenance and repair, see 629.287

.287	Maintenance and repair

Add to base number 629.287 the numbers following 629.22 in 629.2204–629.229, e.g., repair of motorcycles 629.28775

Arrange alphabetically by trade name under each type of vehicle

(Option: Arrange all vehicles regardless of type alphabetically by trade name)

Class works on car tune-ups limited to maintenance and repair of the engine in 629.25; maintenance and repair of a specific part with the part, using notation 0288 from Table 1, e.g., maintenance of bodies 629.260288

.29	Specialized land vehicles

Use of this number for other topics discontinued; class in 629.2

For overland air-cushion vehicles, see 629.322

.292	Nonsurface motor land vehicles

Examples: subterranean, ocean-floor vehicles

.295	Vehicles for extraterrestrial surfaces

Example: moon cars

.3	**Air-cushion vehicles (Ground-effect machines, Hovercraft)**
.31	General topics

Class general topics applied to specific types of vehicles in 629.32

.313	Lift systems
.314	Propulsion systems
.317	Structural analysis and design
.32	Types of vehicles

.322   Overland air-cushion vehicles

Class amphibious air-cushion vehicles in 629.325

.324   Overwater air-cushion vehicles

Class amphibious air-cushion vehicles in 629.325

.325   Amphibious air-cushion vehicles

.4   **Astronautics**

SUMMARY

629.401–.409	**Standard subdivisions**
.41	**Space flight**
.43	**Unmanned space flight**
.44	**Auxiliary spacecraft**
.45	**Manned space flight**
.46	**Engineering of unmanned spacecraft**
.47	**Astronautical engineering**

[.401 521]   Astromechanics

Do not use; class in 629.411

.409 2   Astronautical engineers

Class astronauts in 629.450092

.41   Space flight

Class preparation for flight to a specific celestial body with the flight, e.g., preparation for manned lunar flight 629.454

For unmanned space flight, see 629.43; manned space flight, 629.45

.411   Astromechanics

.411 1   Gravitation

.411 3   Orbits

[.411 4]   Perturbations

Use of this number discontinued; class in 629.411

.415   Planetary atmospheres

Including exit and reentry problems

.415 1   Aerodynamics

.415 2   Atmospheric thermodynamics

.416   Space phenomena and environments affecting flight

Examples: meteoroids, radiations

.418   Weightlessness

General aspects: phenomena, effects, countermeasures

.43	Unmanned space flight
.432	Launching
.433	Guidance and homing
.434	Flight of artificial satellites

Class satellite flight for a specific purpose with the purpose, e.g., weather satellites 551.6354

.435	Astronautical exploratory and data-gathering operations
.435 2	Ionospheric and near-space
.435 3	Lunar
.435 4	Planetary

Add to base number 629.4354 the numbers following 523.4 in 523.41–523.48, e.g., Venusian probes 629.43542

.437	Communications and tracking
.44	Auxiliary spacecraft
.441	Space shuttles
.442	Space stations

Class here space colonies

.445	Space laboratories
.45	Manned space flight

Use 629.45001–629.45009 for standard subdivisions

Class auxiliary spacecraft in 629.44

.450 1	Projected accounts

Class projected accounts of flight to a specific celestial body in 629.454–629.455

.450 7	Selection and training of astronauts
.452	Launching and takeoff
.453	Guidance, homing, navigation
.454	Circumterrestrial and lunar flights
.454 2	Preflight activities

Examples: flight planning, preparation, training

.454 3	Takeoff and in-flight activities
.454 4	Approach, orbiting, landing
.454 5	Retakeoff and return flight

.455	Planetary flights

Class here flights to planetary satellites

Add to base number 629.455 the numbers following 523.4 in 523.41–523.48, e.g., flights to Mars 629.4553; then add 0* and to the result add the numbers following 629.454 in 629.4542–629.4545, e.g., landing on Mars 629.455304

.457	Communications and tracking
.458	Piloting and related activities
.458 2	Piloting
.458 3	Rendezvous with other spacecraft
.458 4	Extravehicular activities

Example: space walks

.458 5	Rescue operations
.458 8	Atmospheric entry and landing
.46	Engineering of unmanned spacecraft

Example: artificial satellites

[.460 4]	Special topics

Use of this number discontinued; class in 629.4

[.460 44]	Environmental control

Relocated to 629.467

.461–.468	Analysis, design, construction, materials, parts, systems, facilities

Add to base number 629.46 the numbers following 629.47 in 629.471–629.478, e.g., environmental control 629.467 [*formerly also* 629.46044]

.47	Astronautical engineering

Class here comprehensive works on spacecraft

For auxiliary spacecraft, see 629.44; engineering of unmanned spacecraft, 629.46

[.470 4]	Special topics

Use of this number discontinued; class in 629.47

[.470 44]	Environmental control

Relocated to 629.477

.471	Structural analysis and design of spacecraft
.472	Spacecraft materials and components
.473	Spacecraft construction

*Add 00 for standard subdivisions; see instructions at beginning of Table 1

.474	Spacecraft engineering systems

For propulsion systems, see 629.475; life-support systems, 629.477

.474 2	Flight operations systems

Examples: piloting, guidance, homing, navigation, landing systems

.474 3	Communication and tracking systems
.474 4	Auxiliary power systems
.474 43	Nuclear power systems
.474 45	Electric and magnetohydrodynamic power systems
.475	Propulsion systems

Engines, fuels, auxiliary equipment and instrumentation

.475 2	Chemical propulsion
.475 22	Liquid propellant
.475 24	Solid propellant
.475 3	Nuclear propulsion
.475 4	Photon propulsion
.475 5	Electric and magnetohydrodynamic propulsion

Examples: plasma and ion propulsion

.477	Environmental control [*formerly also* 629.47044] and life-support systems
.477 2	Space suits
.477 3	Food and water supply
.477 4	Sanitation and sterilization

Including control of wastes

.477 5	Control of temperature, humidity, air supply and pressure
.478	Terrestrial facilities

Examples: launch complexes, space ports; spacecraft maintenance, ground testing, repair facilities

.8	**Automatic control engineering**

Class here automatons that are not computer controlled

Class a specific application with the application, e.g., numerical control of machine tools 621.9023

See Manual at 003.5 vs. 629.8

.801	Philosophy and theory

Class control theory in 629.8312

.804	Special topics

.804 2	Hydraulic control
	Including fluidics
.804 3	Electric control
	Electronic control relocated to 629.89
	Class computer control in 629.89
.804 5	Pneumatic control

.82   **Open-loop systems**

Mechanisms in which outputs have no effect on input signals

Example: vending machines

Class computer control of open-loop systems in 629.89

.83   **Closed-loop (Feedback) systems**

Mechanisms which maintain prescribed relationships between the controlled outputs and the inputs

Class computer control of closed-loop systems in 629.89

.830 1   Philosophy and theory

Class control theory in 629.8312

[.830 288]   Maintenance and repair

Do not use; class in 629.8318

.831   **General principles**

Class general principles of specific mechanisms and systems in 629.832–629.836

.831 2   Control theory

Mathematical design, analysis, synthesis

Including optimal control

Class here comprehensive works on control theory

Class interdisciplinary works on control theory in 003.5, control theory for open-loop systems in 629.82

.831 3   Circuitry

.831 4   Feedback characteristics

.831 5   System components

Examples: amplifiers, error correctors, error detectors

.831 7   Construction and assembly

.831 8   Maintenance and repair

> 629.832–629.836 Specific mechanisms and systems

General aspects: components, circuitry, construction

Class comprehensive works in 629.83

.832   Linear mechanisms and systems

.832 3   Servomechanisms

.833   Multiple-loop mechanisms and systems

.836   Nonlinear mechanisms and systems

Example: adaptive control systems

.89   Computer control

Class here electronic control [*formerly* 629.8043], comprehensive works on computer control

Computer control of factory operations for manufacture of products listed in 670–680 is classed in 670.427

[.891]   Sequential machines

Relocated to 511.3

.892   Robots

Former heading: Automatons

Unless it is redundant, add to base number 629.892 the numbers following 00 in 004–006, e.g., use of digital microcomputers 629.892416, but use of digital computers 629.892 (*not* 629.8924)

Use of this number for automatons that are not computer controlled discontinued; class in 629.8

.895   Computerized process control

Use of computers to keep conditions of continuous processes as close as possible to desired values or within a desired range by controlling continuous variables such as temperature or pressure

Unless it is redundant, add to base number 629.855 the numbers following 00 in 004–006, e.g., use of digital microcomputers 629.895416, but use of digital computers 629.895 (*not* 629.8954)

Use of this number for comprehensive works on computer control discontinued; class in 629.89

630 Agriculture and related technologies

Class here farming, farms, comprehensive works on plant crops

See also 306.349 for agricultural sociology, 307.72 for rural sociology, 333.76 for agricultural land economics, 338.1 for agricultural economics, 900 (with use of notation 009734 from table under 930–990) for rural conditions and civilization

See Manual at 580–590 vs. 630, 641.3

SUMMARY

630.1–.9	**Standard subdivisions**
631	**Specific techniques; apparatus, equipment, materials**
632	**Plant injuries, diseases, pests**
633	**Field and plantation crops**
634	**Orchards, fruits, forestry**
635	**Garden crops (Horticulture) Vegetables**
636	**Animal husbandry**
637	**Processing dairy and related products**
638	**Insect culture**
639	**Hunting, fishing, conservation, related technologies**

[.15] Scientific principles

> Do not use; class in 630.21–630.29

.2 Miscellany and scientific principles

.201 Special treatment

.201 1–.201 2 Tabulated, illustrative, related materials

> Add to base number 630.201 the numbers following —02 in notation 021–022 from Table 1, e.g., agricultural pictures 630.20122

.201 7 Humorous treatment

.201 8 Audiovisual treatment

.202 Synopses and outlines

> Use of this number for manuals discontinued; class in 630

.203–.207 Other miscellany

> Add to base number 630.20 the numbers following —02 in notation 023–028 from Table 1, e.g., directories 630.205

.208 Auxiliary techniques and procedures [*both formerly* 631]

> Class here auxiliary techniques and procedures for field crops [*both formerly* 633.0028]

> Add to base number 630.208 the numbers following —028 in notation 0285–0289 from Table 1, e.g., safety measures 630.2089

> Class apparatus, equipment, materials in 631

.209   Commercial miscellany [*formerly also* 380.141029, 381.41029, 382.41029]

> Add to base number 630.209 the numbers following —029 in notation 0294–0299 from Table 1, e.g., product directories 630.2094

.21–.29   Scientific principles

> Add to base number 630.2 the numbers following 5 in 510–590, e.g., agricultural meterology 630.2515; however, agricultural genetics relocated from 630.2751 to 631.523

> Class miscellany in 630.201–630.209

.71   Schools and courses

.717   Extension work for young people

631   Specific techniques; apparatus, equipment, materials

Topics common to plant and animal husbandry or limited to plant culture

Class here apparatus, equipment, materials for field crops [*all formerly* 633.0028]; cultivation, harvesting, related topics of field and plantation crops [*all formerly* 633.08]

Use of this number for comprehensive works on crops and their production discontinued; class in 630

Auxiliary techniques and procedures relocated to 630.208

Class techniques, apparatus, equipment, materials of specific plant crops in 633–635; of animal husbandry in 636.01–636.08

> *For plant injuries, diseases, pests, see 632*

SUMMARY

631.2	Use of agricultural structures	
.3	Use of agricultural tools, machinery, apparatus, equipment	
.4	Soil science	
.5	Cultivation and harvesting	
.6	Clearing, drainage, revegetation	
.7	Water conservation	
.8	Use of fertilizers and soil conditioners	

.2   **Use of agricultural structures**

> Class construction of agricultural structures with the structure, e.g., barns 690.8922

.21   Farmhouses

.22   General-purpose buildings

> Class here barns

> Class housing for domestic animals in 636.0831

[.23]   Granaries, grain elevators, silos

> Use of granaries and grain elevators relocated to 633.10468, of silos to 633.20868

.25	Machine and equipment sheds
.27	Fences, hedges, walls
.28	Roads, bridges, dams

.3   Use of tools, machinery, apparatus, equipment

Class comprehensive works on manufacture of tools, machinery, apparatus, equipment in 681.7631; manufacture of a specific article with the article, e.g., tractors 629.225

See also 631.2 for use of agricultural structures

.304	Workshops
[.31]	Soil-working tools and machines

Relocated to 631.51

[.33]	Use of planting and sowing equipment

Relocated to 631.53

.34	Use of equipment for care and shelter of plants

Use of equipment for a specific purpose relocated to the purpose, e.g., greenhouses 631.583

[.35]	Use of harvesting equipment

Comprehensive works relocated to 631.55, use of grain harvesting equipment to 633.1045

[.36]	Use of equipment in preparation for storage and transport

Relocated to 631.56

.37	Use of power and power machinery

Class a specific use of power and power machinery with the use, e.g., combines 633.1045

.371	Kinds of power

Examples: human, animal, mechanical, electric power

.372	Tractors
.373	Transport equipment

Examples: trucks, wagons

.4   Soil science

Class here interdisciplinary works on soils [*formerly also* 553.6]

Class soil formation in 551.305, petrology of soils in 552.5, engineering use of soils in 624.151

For clearing and drainage, see 631.6; use of fertilizers and soil conditioners, 631.8

[.401 2]		Classification of soils
		Do not use; class in 631.44
[.401 5]		Scientific principles
		Do not use; class in 631.4
[.409]		Historical, geographical, persons treatment
		Do not use; class in 631.49

.41 **Soil chemistry**

Class gas content in 631.433

For soil fertility, acidity, alkalinity, see 631.42

.416 Inorganic chemistry

Example: salinity

See also 631.82 for soil conditioners

.417 Organic chemistry

Including humus

Class here soil biochemistry

.42 **Soil fertility, acidity, alkalinity**

.422 Fertility

Class use of fertilizers in 631.8

.43 **Soil physics**

Including soil micromorphology

.432 Moisture and hydromechanics

.433 Gas content and mechanics

.436 Thermal phenomena

.44 **Soil classification**

.45 **Soil erosion and its control**

Class here soil conservation, comprehensive works on soil and water conservation

For revegetation, see 631.64; water conservation, 631.7

.451 Conservation tillage

Example: mulch tillage

For tillage for water conservation, see 631.586

.452 Crop rotation and cover crops

Class comprehensive works on crop rotation in 631.582

.455 Contouring and terracing

.456	Strip cropping
.46	Soil biology

For biochemistry, see 631.417

.47	Soil and land use surveys

Soil types, agricultural utilization of land in specific areas

Add to base number 631.47 notation 01–9 from Table 2, e.g., soil survey of Gonzales County, Texas 631.47764257

See Manual at 631.47 vs. 631.49

.49	Historical, geographical, persons treatment

Add to base number 631.49 notation 01–9 from Table 2, e.g., soil science in China 631.4951

For soil and land use surveys, see 631.47

See Manual at 631.47 vs. 631.49

.5	**Cultivation and harvesting**
.51	Soil working (Tillage)

Before and after planting

Class here use of soil-working tools and machines [*formerly also* 631.31]

Class soil working in special methods of cultivation in 631.58

For conservation tillage, see 631.451

.52	Production of propagational organisms and new varieties

Example of propagational organism: seedlings

Class here nursery practice

.521	Seeds
.523	Development of new varieties

Including plant introductions

Class here agricultural genetics [*formerly also* 630.2751], germ plasm, hybrids

.526	Bulbs and tubers
.53	Plant propagation

Class here use of planting and sowing equipment [*formerly also* 631.33], comprehensive works on plant breeding

For production of propagational organisms and new varieties, see 631.52; grafting, pruning, training, 631.54

.531	Propagation from seeds
.532	Propagation from bulbs and tubers

.533	Propagation from suckers, runners, buds

Class propagation from tubers in 631.532, from cuttings in 631.535

.534	Propagation by layering
.535	Propagation from cuttings and slips
.536	Propagation by transplanting
[.537]	Propagation from nursery stock

Number discontinued; class in 631.53

.54	Grafting, pruning, training

Most works on grafting and pruning will be classed in 634.044 and cognate numbers in 634.1–634.8

.541	Grafting
.542	Pruning
[.544]	Forcing

Relocated to 631.583

[.545]	Retarding

Relocated to 631.583

.546	Training on poles, trellises, walls
.55	Harvesting

Examples: mowing, reaping

Class here use of harvesting equipment [*formerly also* 631.35]

Class operations subsequent to harvesting in 631.56

.558	Yields

See Manual at 631.558 vs. 338.1

.56	Operations subsequent to harvesting

Examples: cleaning, husking, packing

Class here use of equipment in preparation for storage and transport [*formerly also* 631.36]

.567	Grading
.568	Storage

.57   Varieties and kinds of organisms used in agriculture

Use for description of organisms that contain little or no information on how to grow them

Most works on varieties and kinds of plants will be classed in 633–635, usually using 7 from table under 633–635, e.g., varieties of grain crops 633.1047

Class physiology and anatomy of agricultural plants in 581, development of new varieties in 631.523

.58   Special cultivation methods

See also 333.76 for special methods of cultivation as topics in land economics, 338.162 for them as topics in agricultural economics

.581   Reduced cultivation methods

Class here minimum tillage, surface tillage

.581 2   Fallowing

.581 4   No-tillage

.581 8   Shifting cultivation (Slash-and-burn agriculture)

.582   Crop rotation

Class crop rotation to control erosion in 631.452

.583   Controlled-environment agriculture

Including forcing [*formerly* 631.544], retarding [*formerly* 631.545]

Class here use of greenhouses [*formerly also* 631.34]

Most works on use of greenhouses are classed in 635.0483 (greenhouse gardening) and cognate numbers in 635.1–635.9

.584   Organic farming

Class a specific aspect with the aspect, e.g., compost 631.875

.585   Soilless culture (Hydroponics)

.586   Dry farming

Class here tillage for water conservation

.587   Irrigation [*formerly also* 631.7]

Use only for works describing what is done on the farm, e.g., installation of center-pivot sprinkler systems

Class comprehensive works on irrigation, works on obtaining irrigation water from off-farm sources in 627.52; digging wells in 628.114

For sewage irrigation, see 628.3623

.6   Clearing, drainage, revegetation

.61   Clearing

.62   Drainage

Class comprehensive works on drainage, on off-farm drainage projects in 627.54

.64   Revegetation

Including inland dune stabilization, surface mine reclamation

Class comprehensive works on reclamation in 627.5, reforestation in 634.956

.7   **Water conservation**

Irrigation relocated to 631.587

For tillage for water conservation, see 631.586

.8   **Use of fertilizers and soil conditioners**

Including growth regulators

Class here comprehensive works on agricultural chemicals

Class comprehensive works on soil fertility in 631.422

For pesticides, see 632.95

See also 668.62 for manufacture of fertilizers

.809   Historical, geographical, persons treatment of use of fertilizers [*formerly* 631.819] and soil conditioners

.81   Nutritive principles, complete fertilizers, methods of application

Use of this number for comprehensive works on fertilizers discontinued; class in 631.8

Class nutritive principles and methods of application of specific fertilizers in 631.83–631.87

.811   Nutritive principles

.813   Complete fertilizers

.816   Methods of application

[.819]   Historical, geographical, persons treatment

Relocated to 631.809

.82   Soil conditioners

Example: for control of salinity

.821   For control of acidity

Example: lime

.825   For control of alkalinity

.826   For texture

Example: peat

> 631.83–631.87 Specific kinds of fertilizers

Class comprehensive works in 631.8

.83   Potassium fertilizers

.84   Nitrogen fertilizers

.841   Ammonium, urea, cyanamide fertilizers

For ammonium nitrate, see 631.842

.842   Nitrate fertilizers

Example: ammonium nitrate

.843   Slaughterhouse (Abattoir) residues

For bone meal, see 631.85

.847   Biological methods of soil nitrification

Use of nitrifying bacteria, nitrifying crops

.85   Phosphorus fertilizers

Including bone meal

.86   Organic fertilizers

Including other organic fertilizers [*formerly* 631.87]

Class here utilization of animal wastes for soil improvement [*formerly also* 628.7461], animal manures

For slaughterhouse residues, see 631.843; vegetable manures and converted household garbage, 631.87

.861   Farm manure

.866   Guano

.869   Sewage sludge

.87   Vegetable manures and converted household garbage

Other organic fertilizers relocated to 631.86

.874   Green manures

.875   Compost

.877   Converted household garbage

632   Plant injuries, diseases, pests

Class here injuries, diseases, pests of field and plantation crops [*formerly* 633.089], pathology of agricultural plants, comprehensive works on plant and animal injuries, diseases, pests

Class comprehensive works on physiology and pathology of agricultural plants in 581.1; use of agricultural plants in studies of basic pathological processes in 581.2; injuries, diseases, pests of specific crops and groups of crops in 633–635

For veterinary medicine, see 636.089

.1   **Injuries and damages caused by environmental forces**

.11   Low temperatures injury

.12   High temperatures and drought injury

.14   Hail damage

.15   Lightning injury

.16   Wind and rain damage

.17   Flood damage

.18   Fire injury

.19   Air pollution and radiation injury

.2   **Galls and pathological development**

.3   **Diseases**

Class protozoan diseases in 632.631

For fungus diseases, see 632.4; viral and rickettsial diseases, 632.8

.32   Bacterial diseases

.4   **Fungus diseases**

Add to base number 632.4 the numbers following 589.2 in 589.22–589.25, e.g., rusts 632.425, smuts 632.427

.5   **Harmful plants**

Class here plant pests

.52   Parasites

.58   Weeds

.6   **Pests   Animal pests**

Add to base number 632.6 the numbers following 59 in 592–599, e.g., snails 632.643; however, class insect pests in 632.7

Class pest control service and interdisciplinary works on pests in 363.78, comprehensive works on pest control technology, on specific topics of pest control and of animal pest control in 632.95

For plant pests, see 632.5; pest control materials, 632.9

.7   Insect pests

Add to base number 632.7 the numbers following 595.7 in 595.71–595.79, e.g., locusts 632.726

.8   Viral and rickettsial diseases

.9   General topics of pest, harmful-plant, disease control

Class control of specific pests, of specific animal pests, of harmful plants, of diseases in 632.2–632.7

.93   Plant quarantine

.94   Spraying, dusting, fumigating

Use of this number for comprehensive works on control methods and apparatus discontinued; class in 632.9

.95   Pest control materials (Pesticides)

.950 4   Special topics

.950 42   Undesired effects and their control

.951   Insecticides, rodenticides, vermicides

.952   Fungicides and algicides

.953   Bactericides

.954   Herbicides

.96   Biological control

> ## 633–635 Specific plant crops

Add to notation for each term identified by * as follows:
1–6   Cultivation and harvesting
    Add the numbers following 631.5 in 631.51–631.56, e.g., harvesting 5
    For special cultivation methods, see 8
7   Varieties and kinds
    Special topics of specific varieties and kinds relocated to the topic, e.g., irrigation of a variety 87
8   Special cultivation methods, fertilizers, soil conditioners
81–87   Special cultivation methods
    Add to 8 the numbers following 631.58 in 631.581–631.587, e.g., irrigation 87
89   Fertilizers and soil conditioners
    Add to 89 the numbers following 631.8 in 631.81–631.87, e.g., compost 8975
9   Injuries, diseases, pests
    Add to 9 the numbers following 632 in 632.1–632.9, e.g., injuries from low temperatures 911

Class comprehensive works in 630

See Manual at 633–635

633   Field and plantation crops

Large-scale production of crops intended for agricultural purposes and industrial processing other than preservation

Class truck farming in 635; a specific plantation or field crop not provided for here with the crop, e.g., bananas 634.772

SUMMARY

633.001–.009		[Standard subdivisions]
	.1	Cereal grains (Cereals)
	.2	Forage crops
	.3	Legumes, other forage crops
	.5	Fiber crops
	.6	Sugar, syrup, starch crops
	.7	Alkaloidal crops
	.8	Other crops grown for industrial processing

.001   Philosophy and theory

.002   Miscellany

[.002 8]   Auxiliary techniques and procedures; apparatus, equipment, materials

Auxiliary techniques and procedures for field crops relocated to 630.208; apparatus, equipment, materials for field crops to 631

.003–.009   Standard subdivisions

[.08]   Cultivation, harvesting, related topics of field and plantation crops

Relocated to 631

[.089]   Injuries, diseases, pests of field and plantation crops

Relocated to 632

.1   Cereal grains (Cereals)

Class cereal crops grown for forage in 633.25

.104   *Cultivation, harvesting, related topics

.104 5   Harvesting

Class here use of grain harvesting equipment [*formerly also* 631.35]

.104 68   Storage

Including use of granaries and grain elevators [*formerly also* 631.23]

.11   *Wheat

.12   *Buckwheat

.13   *Oats

.14   *Rye

*Add as instructed under 633–635

.15	*Corn	

Variant names: Indian corn, maize

.16	*Barley

.17	Millets, grain sorghums, upland and wild rice

.171	*Millets (Panicum and related genera)

.171 7	Varieties and kinds

Examples: broomcorn millet, panic grass, proso

.174	*Grain sorghums

Class sweet sorghums in 633.62

.174 7	Varieties and kinds

Examples: broomcorn, durra (Jerusalem corn), kafir corn, shallu

.178	Wild rice

.179	Upland rice [*formerly* 633.18]

.18	*Rice

Class here paddy rice

Upland rice relocated to 633.179

See also 633.178 for wild rice

.2 Forage crops

Class here forage grasses, Pooideae grasses

Use 633.2001–633.2009 for standard subdivisions

Class forage legumes and other forage crops in 633.3

.202	Pasture and its grasses

Class comprehensive works on ranches and farms devoted to livestock in 636.01, pasture use of forests in 634.99, specific pasture grasses in 633.21–633.28

.208	*Cultivation, harvesting, related topics of forage crops

.208 68	Storage

Including comprehensive works on use of silos [*formerly also* 631.23]

Class use of silos for grain storage in 633.10468

.21	*Bluegrasses (Poa)

.22	*Orchard grass

Variant name: cocksfoot

*Add as instructed under 633–635

.23	*Bent grasses
.237	Varieties and kinds
	Example: redtop
.24	*Timothy
.25	Cereal grasses

Add to base number 633.25 the numbers following 633.1 in 633.11–633.18, e.g., rye grasses 633.254

.26	Sedges

Former heading: other Cyperaceae

.27	Panicoideae grasses

For corn, see 633.255; millets, 633.2571; sorghums, 633.2574

.28	Other Pooideae grasses
.3	**Legumes, other forage crops**

Class here grain legumes, forage legumes

Class comprehensive works on legumes in 635.65

.304	*Cultivation, harvesting, related topics
.31	*Alfalfa

Variant name: lucerne

.32	*Trifolium clovers
.327	Varieties and kinds

Examples: alsike, crimson, red, white clover

.33	*Cowpeas

Variant name: black-eyed peas

.34	*Soybeans

Variant name: soja

.35	*Vetches
.36	Lespedeza and related legumes
.364	*Lespedeza

Variant name: bush clover

.366	*Sweet clovers
.367	*Lupines
.368	*Peanuts

Variant name: groundnuts

*Add as instructed under 633–635

.369	*Field peas (Pisum arvense)
	Variant name: Austrian winter peas
.37	Other legumes
.372	*Kidney beans
	Variant names: navy, pea beans
.374	*Trefoils (Lotus)
.39	Other forage crops
[.4]	**Edible roots and tubers**
	Edible roots relocated to 635.1
[.49]	Edible tubers
	Relocated to 635.2
.5	**Fiber crops**

―――――

> 633.51–633.56 Soft fibers

Class comprehensive works in 633.5

.51	*Cotton
.52	*Flax
.53	*Hemp (Cannabis sativa)
	See also 633.79 for marijuana
.54	*Jute
.55	*Ramie
.56	Other soft fibers
	Examples: chingma (China jute), kenaf (ambari hemp), sunn
.57	Hard fibers
	For other hard fibers, see 633.58
.571	*Manila hemp
	Variant name: abaca
.576	*Pineapple fibers
.577	*Sisal (Agave fibers)
.58	Other hard fibers
	Examples: coconut (coir), esparto, jipijapa, raffia, reed, rush fibers
	Including bamboo, willow (osier), other basketwork and wickerwork plants

*Add as instructed under 633–635

.6   **Sugar, syrup, starch crops**

Standard subdivisions are added for sugar, syrup, starch crops; for sugar crops alone; and for syrup crops alone

.61   *Sugar cane

.62   *Sorgo

Variant name: sweet sorghums

.63   *Sugar beets

.64   *Sugar maples

.68   Starch crops

Examples: arrowroot, sago palm, taro

.682   *Cassava (Manioc)

.7   **Alkaloidal crops**

.71   *Tobacco

.72   *Tea

.73   *Coffee

.74   *Cacao

Representative products: cocoa, chocolate

.75   *Poppies (Papaver somniferum)

.76   *Kola nuts (Cola nuts)

.77   *Maté

Variant name: Paraguay tea

.78   *Chicory

.79   *Marijuana

Class here hashish

See also 633.53 for hemp

.8   **Other crops grown for industrial processing**

.81   Perfume-producing plants

.82   Flavoring-producing plants

Examples: hops, mints, sassafras, vanilla, wintergreen

For spices, see 633.83; alliaceous plants, 635.26; aromatic and sweet herbs, 635.7

*Add as instructed under 633–635

.83   Spices

     Examples: allspice, cinnamon, clove, ginger, nutmeg

     Class here sweet spices

      For hot spices, see 633.84

.84   Hot spices

     Examples: black pepper, chili, horseradish, mustard, paprika

.85   For nonvolatile oils

     Class here oilseed plants

     Class coconuts in 634.61, olives in 634.63

.851   *Oil palm

.853   *Rapeseed

.86   For dyes

.87   For tannin

     Example: canaigre

.88   For medicines

     Add to base number 633.88 the numbers following 58 in 583–589, e.g., digitalis 633.88381; however, class poppies in 633.75

.89   For other purposes

.895   For rubber and resins

.895 2   *Rubber trees (Hevea brasiliensis)

.895 9   Turpentine

     Use of this number for other resin-producing plants discontinued; class in 633.895

.898   For insecticides

634 Orchards, fruits, forestry

     Class here comprehensive works on tree crops

     Standard subdivisions are added for orchards, fruits, forestry; for orchards alone; and for fruits alone

     Class trees grown for plantation crops in 633, ornamental trees in 635.977

      For pepos, see 635.61; tomatoes, 635.642

*Add as instructed under 633–635

SUMMARY

634.04	**Cultivation, harvesting, related topics of orchards, of fruit**
.1	**Pomaceous fruits**
.2	**Drupaceous fruits**
.3	**Citrus and moraceous fruits**
.4	**Other fruits**
.5	**Nuts**
.6	**Tropical and subtropical fruits**
.7	**Berries and herbaceous tropical and subtropical fruits**
.8	**Grapes**
.9	**Forestry**

.04   *Cultivation, harvesting, related topics of orchards, of fruit

---

>   **634.1−634.6 Orchards and their fruits**

Class comprehensive works in 634

.1   **Pomaceous fruits**

.11   *Apples

.13   *Pears

.14   *Quinces

.15   *Medlars (Mespilus germanica)

.16   *Loquats

         Variant name: Japanese medlars

.2   **Drupaceous fruits**

.21   *Apricots

.22   *Plums

.227   Varieties and kinds

         Example: damson

.23   *Cherries

.25   *Peaches

.257   Varieties and kinds

         Example: nectarines

.3   **Citrus and moraceous fruits**

.304   *Citrus fruits [*formerly* 634.35]

         Class specific citrus fruits in 634.31−634.34

.31   *Oranges

.32   *Grapefruit

*Add as instructed under 633−635

.33	Citron group
.331	*Citrons
.334	*Lemons
.337	*Limes
.34	*Kumquats
[.35]	Citrus fruits
	Relocated to 634.304
.36	*Moraceous fruits
	For figs, see 634.37; mulberries, 634.38; breadfruit, 634.39
.37	*Figs
.38	*Mulberries
.39	*Breadfruit

.4 Other fruits

Class tropical and subtropical fruits not provided for here in 634.6

.41	Annonaceous fruits
	Examples: cherimoya, custard apples, papaws
.42	Myrtaceous and passifloraceous fruits
.421	*Guavas
.425	*Passion fruit
.43	Sapotaceous fruits
	Examples: sapodilla plums (chicozapote), star apples
.44	Anacardiaceous fruits
	Examples: mangoes, Spanish plums
	Class cashew nuts in 634.573
.45	*Persimmons
.46	Leguminous fruits
	Examples: carob (locusts, Saint-John's-bread), tamarinds
	Class garden legumes in 635.65

.5 Nuts

.51	*Walnuts
.52	*Pecans
	Use of this number for hickory nuts discontinued; class in 634.5

*Add as instructed under 633–635

.53	*Chestnuts
.54	*Filberts
.55	*Almonds
.57	Cashew nuts, pistachios, Brazil nuts

> Use of this number for other nuts discontinued; class in 634.5

.573	*Cashew nuts
.574	*Pistachios
.575	*Brazil nuts

.6 Tropical and subtropical fruits

> Not provided for elsewhere
>
> *For herbaceous tropical and subtropical fruits, see 634.77*

.61	*Coconuts
.62	*Dates
.63	*Olives
.64	*Pomegranates
.65	Papayas, avocados, mangosteens

> Use of this number for other tropical and subtropical tree fruit discontinued; class in 634.6

.651	*Papayas
.653	*Avocados

> Variant name: alligator pears

.655	*Mangosteens

.7 Berries and herbaceous tropical and subtropical fruits

> Class here comprehensive works on small fruits
>
> Class a specific small fruit not provided for here with the fruit, e.g., mulberries 634.38, grapes, 634.8

.71	Cane fruits (Rubus)
.711	*Raspberries
.713	*Blackberries
.714	*Loganberries
.717	*Dewberries
.718	*Boysenberries

*Add as instructed under 633–635

.72	Ribes
.721	*Currants
.725	*Gooseberries
.73	Huckleberries and blueberries
.732	*Huckleberries
.737	*Blueberries (Vaccinium)
.74	Other bush fruits

Examples: barberries, buffalo berries, elderberries, juneberries

.75	*Strawberries
.76	*Cranberries
.77	Herbaceous tropical and subtropical fruits

Class comprehensive works on tropical and subtropical fruit in 634.6

.772	*Bananas
.773	*Plantains
.774	*Pineapples
.775	Cactus fruits
.8	**Grapes**

Class here viticulture

.81	Soil working (Tillage)
.82	Injuries, diseases, pests

Add to base number 634.82 the numbers following 632 in 632.1–632.9, e.g., fungus diseases 634.824

.83	Varieties and kinds

Specific aspects of specific varieties and kinds relocated to the aspect, e.g., fungus diseases of muscadines 634.824

.88	Cultivation and harvesting

Add to base number 634.88 the numbers following 631.5 in 631.52–631.58, e.g., harvesting grapes 634.885; however, class varieties in 634.83

For tillage, see 634.81

*Add as instructed under 633–635

.9   **Forestry**

SUMMARY

634.901–.909	**Standard subdivisions**
.92	**Forest management**
.93	**Access and safety features**
.95	**Silviculture**
.96	**Injuries, diseases, pests**
.97	**Kinds of trees**
.98	**Forest exploitation and products Logging and lumber**
.99	**Agroforestry**

[.906 85]   Management of production

>   Do not use; class 634.92

.906 88   Management of distribution (Marketing)

>   Class here marketing methods [*formerly* 634.954]

>   •   634.92–634.96 General topics

Class comprehensive works in 634.9, general topics applied to specific kinds of trees in 634.97

For exploitation and products, see 634.98

.92   Forest management

Class here production management in forestry

Use of this number for forest economy discontinued; class in 634.9

Class comprehensive works on management in forestry in 634.9068, production management of a specific aspect of forestry with the aspect, e.g., of logging 634.98

.928   Production planning and mensuration

Use of this number for comprehensive works on forest management discontinued; class in 634.92

.928 3   Production planning

Former heading: Regulation

.928 5   Mensuration and estimation

.93   Access and safety features

Examples: bridges, lookout towers, roads, trails

Access to power lines relocated to 621.319

.95   Silviculture

[.952]   Harvesting methods

Relocated to 634.98

.953   Maintenance cuttings

Examples: improvement cuttings, thinnings, prunings

[.954]	Marketing methods

Relocated to 634.90688

.955	Brush disposal methods
.956	Forestation

Class here afforestation, reforestation, breeding

.956 2	Seeds and seeding
.956 4	Nursery practice
.956 5	Cultivation at permanent site
.96	Injuries, diseases, pests

Add to base number 634.96 the numbers following 632 in 632.1–632.9, e.g., forest fire technology 634.9618

.97	Kinds of trees

Class here general topics of forestry applied to specific kinds of trees

Add to notation for each subdivision identified by † as follows:
2–6   General topics
        Add the numbers following 634.9 in 634.92–634.96, e.g., reforestation 56
        For exploitation and products, see 8
7   Varieties and kinds
        General topics of a specific variety or kind relocated to the topic, e.g., reforestation of a variety 56
8   Exploitation and products   Logging and lumber
[82]   Logging
        Number discontinued; class in 8
83   Pulpwood
        Use of this number for logs discontinued; class in 8
[85–87]   Minor products
        Relocated to 634.985–634.987

.972	Dicotyledons

Class here hardwoods

Use of this number for comprehensive works on angiosperms, on deciduous trees discontinued; class in 634.97

Class deciduous gymnosperms in 634.975

For other dicotyledons, see 634.973

.972 1	†Oak
.972 2	†Maple
.972 3	†Poplar
.972 4	†Chestnut
.972 5	†Beech
.972 6	†Birch

†Add as instructed under 634.97

| .972 7 | †Linden |
| .972 77 | Varieties and kinds |

Examples: basswood (American linden), lime (European linden)

| .972 8 | †Elm |
| .973 | Other dicotyledons |

Add to base number 634.973 the numbers following 583 in 583.1–583.9, e.g., locust trees 634.973322

| .974 | Monocotyledons |

Add to base number 634.974 the numbers following 584 in 584.1–584.9, e.g., palm trees 634.9745

| .975 | Gymnosperms |

> 634.975 1–634.975 8 Coniferous trees

Class comprehensive works in 634.975, specific conifers not provided for here in 634.97592

.975 1	†Pine
.975 2	†Spruce
.975 3	†Hemlock
.975 4	†Fir
.975 5	†Cypress
.975 6	†Cedar
.975 7	†Larch
.975 8	†Sequoia
.975 9	Other gymnosperms

Add to base number 634.9759 the numbers following 585 in 585.1–585.9, e.g., tamaracks 634.97592

| .98 | Forest exploitation and products   Logging and lumber |

Class here harvesting methods [*formerly also* 634.952], comprehensive works on lumbering

Class exploitation and utilization of specific kinds of trees in 634.97; trees cultivated for products other than lumber or pulp with the product, e.g., turpentine trees 633.8959, pecan trees 634.52

For sawmill operations, see 674.2

| [.982] | Logging |

Number discontinued; class in 634.98

†Add as instructed under 634.97

.983   Pulpwood

Use of this number for comprehensive works on logs discontinued; class in 634.98

>   634.985–634.987 Exploitation of minor forest products

Use only for products that have not been cultivated

Class here minor products of specific kinds of trees [*formerly* 634.97, with use of 85–87 from table under 634.97]

Class comprehensive works in 634.987

.985   Barks

.986   Saps

.987   Minor forest products

Examples: fruits, seeds, nuts

For barks, see 634.985; saps 634.986

.99   Agroforestry

Forestry in combination with other farming

Including flood control, grazing, range management

Use of this number for other aspects of forestry discontinued; class in 634.9

Class a specific aspect of agroforestry with the aspect, e.g. logging 634.98

[.999]   Farm forestry

Number discontinued; class in 634.99

635   **Garden crops (Horticulture)**   **Vegetables**

Vegetables: crops grown primarily for human consumption without intermediate processing other than preservation

Class here home gardening, truck farming

Class orchards in 634

SUMMARY

635.04	**Cultivation, harvesting, related topics**
.1	**Edible roots**
.2	**Edible tubers and bulbs**
.3	**Edible leaves, flowers, stems**
.4	**Cooking greens and rhubarb**
.5	**Salad greens**
.6	**Edible garden fruits and seeds**
.7	**Aromatic and sweet herbs**
.8	**Mushrooms and truffles**
.9	**Flowers and ornamental plants**

.04   *Cultivation, harvesting, related topics

*Add as instructed under 633–635

> **635.1–635.8 Edible crops**

Class comprehensive works in 635

.1   **Edible roots [*formerly also* 633.4]**

Class cassava in 633.682

.11   *Beets

.12   Turnips and related crops

.125   *Turnips

.126   *Rutabagas

Variant names: Russian turnips, swedes, Swedish turnips

.128   *Celeriac

Variant names: celery root; knob, root, turnip celery

.13   *Carrots

.14   *Parsnips

.15   *Radishes

.16   *Salsify

.2   **Edible tubers [*formerly also* 633.49] and bulbs**

Class taro in 633.68

.21   *Potatoes

.22   *Sweet potatoes

.23   *Yams (Dioscorea)

.24   *Jerusalem artichokes

.25   *Onions

.26   Alliaceous plants

Examples: chives, garlic, leeks, shallots

For onions, see 635.25

.3   **Edible leaves, flowers, stems**

For cooking greens and rhubarb, see 635.4; salad greens, 635.5

See Manual at 635.3 vs. 635.4, 635.5

.31   *Asparagus

.32   *Artichokes

See also 635.24 for Jerusalem artichokes

*Add as instructed under 633–635

.34   *Cabbages

>   Class here comprehensive works on cultivation of Brassica oleracea
>
>   *For cauliflower and broccoli, see see 635.35; Brussels sprouts, 636.36*

.347   Varieties and kinds

>   Examples: kale (collards), kohlrabi

.35   *Cauliflower and *broccoli

.36   *Brussels sprouts

.4   Cooking greens and rhubarb

>   *See Manual at 635.3 vs. 635.4, 635.5*

.41   *Spinach

.42   *Chard

.48   *Rhubarb

.5   Salad greens

>   *See Manual at 635.3 vs. 635.4, 635.5*

.51   *Dandelions

.52   *Lettuce

.53   *Celery

>   *See also 635.128 for celeriac*

.54   *Chicory

.55   *Endives

.56   Sorrel and cresses

.6   Edible garden fruits and seeds

.61   Pepos

>   Class here melons
>
>   *For squashes and pumpkins, see 635.62; cucumbers, 635.63*

.611   *Muskmelons

.611 7   Varieties and kinds

>   Examples: casaba, honeydew melons; cantaloupes

.615   *Watermelons

.62   *Squashes and *pumpkins

.63   *Cucumbers

*Add as instructed under 633–635

.64	Other fruits
.642	*Tomatoes
.643	*Sweet peppers

Variant name: bell, green peppers

.646	*Eggplants
.648	*Okra
.65	Garden legumes

Class here comprehensive works on legumes in agriculture

Class legumes as field crops in 633.3, leguminous fruit in 634.46

.651	*Broad beans
.652	*Kidney beans

Variant names: snap, string, wax beans

.653	*Lima beans
.655	*Soybeans

Variant name: soja

.656	*Peas (Pisum sativum)

Variant name: English peas, garden peas

.657	*Chick-peas

Variant names: chestnut beans, chich, dwarf peas, garavance, garbanzo

.658	*Lentils
.659	Other garden legumes
.659 2	*Black-eyed peas

Variant name: cowpeas

.659 6	*Peanuts

Variant name: groundnuts

.67	Corn

Variant names: Indian corn, maize

.672	*Sweet corn
.677	*Popcorn
.7	**Aromatic and sweet herbs**

Class here herb gardens

.8	**Mushrooms and truffles**

*Add as instructed under 633–635

.9   **Flowers and ornamental plants**

Class here floriculture

See Manual at 582.1 vs. 635.9

SUMMARY

635.902 8	**Auxiliary techniques and procedures**
.91	**Specific techniques; apparatus, equipment, materials**
.92	**Injuries, diseases, pests**
.93	**General and taxonomic groupings**
.94	**Groupings by means of propagation**
.95	**Groupings by environmental factors**
.96	**Groupings by purpose**
.97	**Other groupings**
.98	**Special methods of cultivation**

.902 8   Auxiliary techniques and procedures [*formerly* 635.91]

.91   Specific techniques; apparatus, equipment, materials

Add to base number 635.91 the numbers following 631 in 631.2–631.8, e.g., pruning 635.91542; however, class special methods of cultivation in 635.98

Auxiliary techniques and procedures relocated to 635.9028

Class cultivation, harvesting, fertilizers, soil conditioners of specific groupings of ornamental plants in 635.93–635.97

.92   Injuries, diseases, pests

Add to base number 635.92 the numbers following 632 in 632.1–632.9, e.g., fungus diseases 635.924

Class injuries, diseases, pests of specific groupings of plants in 635.93–635.97

>   635.93–635.97 Groupings of plants

Unless other instructions are given, class complex subjects with aspects in two or more subdivisions of this schedule in the number coming first in the schedule, e.g., succulent houseplants 635.955 (*not* 635.965)

Class comprehensive works in 635.9

.93   General and taxonomic groupings

.931   By life duration

Class specific families, genera, species regardless of life duration in 635.933–635.939

For perennials, see 635.932

.931 2   *Annuals

.931 4   *Biennials

.932   *Perennials

*Add as instructed under 633–635

.933–.939	Taxonomic groupings

Add to base number 635.93 the numbers following 58 in 583–589, e.g., cactus 635.93347; however, class comprehensive works on dicotyledons in 635.9, taxonomic groupings of trees in 635.9773–635.9775

.94	Groupings by means of propagation
.942	*From seeds
.944	From *bulbs and *tubers
.946	*From runners and *by layering
.948	From *cuttings and *slips
.95	Groupings by environmental factors
.951	Native habitats

Add to base number 635.951 notation 4–9 from Table 2, e.g., ornamentals native to Scotland 635.951411

.952	By climatic factors

Other than temperate zone

Examples: alpine, arctic, tropical plants

Use of this number for temperate-zone plants discontinued; class in 635.9

Class alpine (rock) gardens in 635.9672

.953	By seasonal and diurnal factors

Examples: winter-flowering plants, morning- and night-blooming plants

.954	By light factors

Examples: plants favoring shade, sunshine

.955	By soil factors

Examples: plants favoring dry, rich, sandy soils

Including succulent plants

Works on succulent plants emphasizing cactus are classed in 635.93347

.96	Groupings by purpose
.962	*For flower beds
.963	For *borders and *edgings
.964	For ground cover

Class here grass

.964 2	*Turf

Class lawns in 635.9647

.964 7	*Lawns

*Add as instructed under 633–635

.965   *For houseplants

Including window-box gardening

Class comprehensive works on container gardening in 635.986, bonsai in 635.9772

.966   *For cutting

Class flower arrangement in 745.92

.967   For special kinds of gardens

For window-box gardening, see 635.965

.967 1   Roof, balcony, patio gardening

Class comprehensive works on container gardening in 635.986

.967 2   *Rock gardens (Alpine gardens)

Class alpine plants in 635.952

.967 4   *Water gardens

.967 6   *Wild flower gardens

Class wild flowers of a specific native habitat in 635.951

.968   For fragrance and color

.969   *For nurseries

Class here nursery practice

.97   Other groupings

.973   *Everlastings

.974   *Vines

Class here climbing plants

.975   *Foliage plants

.976   *Shrubs and *hedges

.977   Trees

Class here potted trees

Class comprehensive works on container gardening in 635.986

.977 2   *Bonsai

Class bonsai of specific families, genera, species in 635.9773–635.9775

.977 3–.977 5   Taxonomic groupings

Add to base number 635.977 the numbers following 58 in 583–585, e.g., elms 635.9773962; however, use 635.977 for comprehensive works on dicotyledonous trees

*Add as instructed under 633–635

.98	Special methods of cultivation

Class special methods of cultivation of specific groupings of plants in 635.93–635.97

.982	Controlled-environment gardening

For bell-jar gardening, see 635.985

.982 3	*Greenhouse gardening
.982 4	*Terrariums
.985	*Bell-jar gardening
.986	*Container gardening

Class here pot gardening

.987	Organic gardening

Class a specific aspect with the aspect, e.g., compost 635.91875

636   Animal husbandry

Class culture of nondomesticated animals in 639

See Manual at 800 vs. 591, 636, 398.245

SUMMARY

636.001–.009	Standard subdivisions
.01–.08	[Ranches and farms, young of animals, production and maintenance, animals for specific purposes, veterinary sciences]
.1	Equines Horses
.2	Ruminants and Tylopoda Bovines Cattle
.3	Smaller ruminants Sheep
.4	Swine
.5	Poultry Chickens
.6	Birds other than poultry
.7	Dogs
.8	Cats
.9	Other mammals

.001	Philosophy and theory
[.001 575 1]	Genetics

Relocated to 636.0821

.002	Miscellany
[.002 77]	Ownership marks

Do not use; class in 636.0812

.003–.009	Standard subdivisions

*Add as instructed under 633–635

.01	Ranches and farms

Class here soil and water management on ranches and farms devoted to animal husbandry

Class production of forage crops in 633.2, development of pasturage in 633.202, pasture use of forests in 634.99, housing for animals in 636.0831, grazing in 636.084

.07	Young of animals

Class production and maintenance, rearing for specific purposes, veterinary medicine of young animals in 636.08

.08	Production and maintenance, animals for specific purposes, veterinary sciences

SUMMARY

636.081	Selection, judging, ownership marks
.082	Breeding
.083	Care and maintenance
.084	Feeding
.085	Feeds and applied nutrition
.086	Specific field crop feeds
.087	Other specific feeds
.088	Animals for specific purposes
.089	Veterinary sciences Veterinary medicine

> 636.081–636.087 Production and maintenance

Class comprehensive works in 636, production and maintenance of animals for specific purposes in 636.088

.081	Selection, judging, ownership marks
.081 1	Judging
.081 2	Ownership marks

Class here branding

.082	Breeding
.082 1	Genetics [*formerly also* 636.0015751]

Including germ plasm, source species

.082 2	Breeding records

Examples: herdbooks, pedigrees, studbooks

.082 4	Breeding and reproduction methods
.082 41	Inbreeding and line breeding
.082 42	Outbreeding

For crossbreeding, see 636.08243

.082 43	Crossbreeding
	Class here hybrids
.082 45	Artificial insemination
.083	Care and maintenance
	Including predator control, transporting animals
	For feeding, see 636.084; veterinary sciences, 636.089
	See also 179.3 for ethical aspects of animal care
.083 1	Housing
	Example: cages
	Including stockyards
.083 2	Animal hospitals and auxiliary care of sick and injured animals
.083 3	Individual tending
	Examples: dipping, grooming, shearing
.083 7	Harnesses and accessories
.084	Feeding
	Example: grazing
	Class pasture use of forests in 634.99
	For feeds and applied nutrition, see 636.085
.085	Feeds and applied nutrition
.085 2	Applied nutrition
.085 5	Feeds
	For specific feeds, see 636.086–636.087
.085 51	Green fodder
.085 52	Silage
.085 54	Dry fodder
.085 57	Formula feed

>	636.086–636.087 Specific feeds
	Class comprehensive works in 636.0855
.086	Specific field crop feeds
.087	Other specific feeds
.087 4	Fruits
.087 5	Garden crops
.087 6	Meat, fish, eggs

.087 7	Mineral additives

.088 Animals for specific purposes

Class here production, maintenance, training

Class veterinary sciences of animals for specific purposes in 636.089

See Manual at 636.088

.088 1	Breeding stock

.088 2 Draft animals (Beasts of burden)

Class comprehensive works on work animals in 636.0886

.088 3 Food animals

Class animals raised for eggs and milk in 636.08842

.088 4 Animals raised for special products

For food animals, see 636.0883

.088 42 For eggs and milk

.088 44 For hide and fur

For hair, see 636.08845

.088 45 Hair and feathers

Examples: bristles, wool

.088 5 Laboratory animals

.088 6 Work animals

Examples: guarding, herding, hunting

For draft animals, see 636.0882; sport, stunt, exhibition animals, 636.0888

.088 7 Pets

Class here obedience training

Class reminiscences about and true accounts of a person's pets or favorite animals in 808.883; reminiscences and accounts in a specific literature with the literature using notation 803 from Table 3−B or cognate numbers under the appropriate language; other accounts and stories of pets not intended to illustrate agricultural techniques with the appropriate literary form in 800

See Manual at 800 vs. 591, 636, 398.245

.088 8 Sport, stunt, exhibition animals

Examples: circus, fighting, racing, show animals

Class comprehensive works on work animals in 636.0886

.088 9 Zoo animals

Use of this number for animals raised for other purposes discontinued; class in 636.088

[.088 92]	For multiple purposes
	Number discontinued; class in 636
[.088 99]	Zoo animals
	Number discontinued; class in 636.0889
.089	Veterinary sciences Veterinary medicine

Add to base number 636.089 the numbers following 61 in 610–619, e.g., veterinary viral diseases 636.0896925

Class animal hospitals and auxiliary care of sick and injured animals in 636.0832

.1   Equines   Horses

Use 636.1001–636.1009 for standard subdivisions

.101–.108   Ranches and farms, young horses, production and maintenance, horses for specific purposes, veterinary sciences

Add to base number 636.10 the numbers following 636.0 in 636.01–636.08, e.g., training horses for sports and exhibition 636.10888; however, class draft horses in 636.15; training of riders and drivers, comprehensive works on training horses and their riders and drivers in 798

> 636.11–636.17 Specific breeds and kinds of horses

Class comprehensive works in 636.1

.11   Oriental horses

Examples: Barb, Persian, Tartar, Turkish

.112   Arabian horses

.12   Racehorses and trotters

Class a specific breed with the breed, e.g., Thoroughbred 636.132

.13   Saddle (Riding) horses

Examples: American saddle horse, Palomino, Tennessee Walking Horse

For Oriental horses, see 636.11

.132   Thoroughbred

.133   Quarter horse

.14   Carriage horses (Heavy harness horses)

Examples: Cleveland bay, Hackney, Yorkshire coach horse

Class here comprehensive works on harness horses

For draft horses, see 636.15; light harness horses, 636.17

.15   Draft horses

> Examples: Belgian, Clydesdale, Percheron, Shire, Suffolk (Suffolk punch)

.16   Ponies

> Examples: Hackney, Shetland, Welsh ponies

.161   Ranches and farms, young ponies, production and maintenance, ponies for specific purposes, veterinary sciences

> Add to base number 636.161 the numbers following 636.0 in 636.01–636.08, e.g., housing 636.161831

.17   Light harness horses

> Examples: Morgan, Standardbred

.18   Other equines

> Examples: asses, mules; zebras

.2   **Ruminants and Tylopoda   Bovines   Cattle**

> Use 636.2001–636.2009 for standard subdivisions
>
> *For smaller ruminants, see 636.3*

.201–.208   Ranches and farms, young of animals, production and maintenance, animals for specific purposes, veterinary sciences

> Add to base number 636.20 the numbers following 636.0 in 636.01–636.08, e.g., heifers 636.207; however, class cattle for specific purposes in 636.21

.21   Cattle for specific purposes

> Class here production, maintenance, training
>
> Add to base number 636.21 the numbers following 636.088 in 636.0881–636.0889, e.g., raising cattle for beef 636.213, for milk 636.2142; however, class milking and milk processing in 637.1
>
> Class specific breeds of cattle for specific purposes in 636.22–636.28

>   636.22–636.28 Specific breeds of cattle

> Class comprehensive works in 636.2

.22   British breeds of cattle

.222   English beef breeds

> Examples: Hereford, Shorthorn, Sussex

.223   Scottish, Welsh, Irish beef breeds

> Examples: Aberdeen Angus, black Welsh, Galloway, Kyloe

.224   Channel Island dairy breeds

> Contains Alderney, Guernsey, Jersey

.225	Scottish and Irish dairy breeds
	Examples: Ayrshire, Dexter shorthorn, Kerry
.226	Dual-purpose breeds
	Examples: Devon, English longhorn, Polled Durham
.23	German, Dutch, Danish, Swiss breeds of cattle
.232	Beef breeds
.234	Dairy breeds
	Examples: Brown Swiss, East Friesian, Holstein-Friesian, Oldenburg
.236	Dual-purpose breeds
.24	French and Belgian breeds of cattle
.242	Beef breeds
.244	Dairy breeds
.246	Dual-purpose breeds
.27	Other European breeds of cattle
.28	Non-European breeds of cattle
.29	Other larger ruminants and Tylopoda
.291	Zebus
.292	Bison
	Variant names: American buffalo, buffalo
	See also 636.293 for water buffalo
.293	Other Bovoidea
	Example: water buffalo
.294	Cervoidea and Giraffoidea
	Examples: deer, reindeer
.295	Camels
.296	Tylopoda
	Contains alpacas, llamas, vicuñas
	For camels, see 636.295
.3	**Smaller ruminants Sheep**
	Use 636.3001–636.3009 for standard subdivisions
	Class Traguloidea in 636.97355

.301–.308   Ranches and farms, young of animals, production and maintenance, animals for specific purposes, veterinary sciences

> Add to base number 636.30 the numbers following 636.0 in 636.01–636.08, e.g., sheep ranches 636.301; however, class sheep for specific purposes in 636.31

.31   Sheep for specific purposes

> Class here production, maintenance, training

> Add to base number 636.31 the numbers following 636.088 in 636.0881–636.0889, e.g., raising sheep for mutton 636.313, for wool 636.3145

> Class specific breeds of sheep for specific purposes in 636.32–636.38

>   636.32–636.38 Specific breeds of sheep

> Class comprehensive works in 636.3

.32   British breeds of sheep

.33   German, Dutch, Swiss breeds of sheep

.34   French and Belgian breeds of sheep

.35   Italian breeds of sheep

.36   Merino breeds

> Class here Spanish breeds of sheep

.366   Spanish Merino breeds

.367   Other European Merino breeds

.368   Non-European Merino breeds

.37   Other European breeds of sheep

.38   Non-European breeds of sheep

> *For non-European Merino breeds, see 636.368*

.381   American breeds

.385   Asian breeds

.386   African breeds

.39   Goats

> Use 636.39001–636.39009 for standard subdivisions

.390 1–.390 8   Ranches and farms, young of goats, production and maintenance, goats for specific purposes, veterinary sciences

> Add to base number 636.390 the numbers following 636.0 in 636.01–636.08, e.g., breeding 636.39082; however, class goats for specific purposes in 636.391

.391   Goats for specific purposes

Class here production, maintenance, training

Add to base number 636.391 the numbers following 636.088 in 636.0881–636.0889, e.g., raising goats for hair 636.39145

Class specific breeds of goats for specific purposes in 636.392–636.398

.392–.398   Specific breeds of goats

Add to base number 636.39 the numbers following 636.3 in 636.32–636.38, e.g., Angora goats 636.3985

.4   **Swine**

Use 636.4001–636.4009 for standard subdivisions

.401–.408   Farms, young pigs, production and maintenance, swine for specific purposes, veterinary sciences

Add to base number 636.40 the numbers following 636.0 in 636.01–636.08, e.g., housing 636.40831; however, class swine for food in 636.4, for other specific purposes in 636.41

.41   Swine for specific purposes other than food

Class here production, maintenance, training

Add to base number 636.41 the numbers following 636.088 in 636.0881–636.0889, e.g., swine production for bristles 636.4145; however, swine production for food discontinued from 636.413 to 636.4

Class specific breeds of swine for specific purposes in 636.42–636.48

>   636.42–636.48 Specific breeds of swine

Class comprehensive works in 636.4

.42–.47   European breeds of swine

Add to base number 636.4 the numbers following 636.3 in 636.32–636.37, e.g., British breeds 636.42

.48   Non-European breeds of swine

.482   Poland China

.483   Duroc

Variant name: Duroc-Jersey

.484   American breeds

Examples: Cheshire, Chester White, Hampshire, mule-foot, razorback, Victoria

For Poland China, see 636.482; Duroc, see 636.483

.485   Asian breeds

.486   African breeds

.489   Oceanic breeds

.5   Poultry   Chickens

> Class here comprehensive works on raising birds
>
> Use 636.5001−636.5009 for standard subdivisions
>
> *For birds other than poultry, see 636.6*

.501−.508   Farms, young poultry, production and maintenance, poultry for specific purposes, veterinary sciences

> Add to base number 636.50 the numbers following 636.0 in 636.01−636.08, e.g., chicken breeding 636.5082; however, class poultry for specific purposes in 636.51

.51   Poultry for specific purposes

> Class here production, maintenance, training
>
> Add to base number 636.51 the numbers following 636.088 in 636.0881−636.0889, e.g., raising chickens for meat 636.513, for eggs 636.5142
>
> Class specific breeds of chickens for specific purposes in 636.52−636.58, poultry other than chickens for specific purposes in 636.59

> **636.52−636.58 Specific breeds of chickens**
>
> Class comprehensive works in 636.5

.52−.57   European breeds of chickens

> Add to base number 636.5 the numbers following 636.3 in 636.32−636.37, e.g., Leghorn chickens 636.55
>
> Class diminutive varieties in 636.587

.58   Non-European breeds and special varieties of chickens

> **636.581−636.584 American breeds**
>
> Class comprehensive works in 636.58, diminutive varieties in 636.587

.581   Bucks County, Dominique, Java, Jersey Blue, Winnebago

.582   Plymouth Rock

.583   Wyandotte

.584   Rhode Island Red

.585   Asian breeds

> Class diminutive varieties in 636.587

.587   Diminutive varieties

.587 1   Bantam

.587 2	Cornish
.59	Other poultry
.592	Turkeys

Use 636.592001–636.592009 for standard subdivisions

.592 01–.592 08	Farms, young turkeys, production and maintenance, turkeys for specific purposes, veterinary sciences

Add to base number 636.5920 the numbers following 636.0 in 636.01–636.08, e.g., raising turkeys for meat 636.5920883

.593	Guinea fowl
.594	Pheasants
.595	Peafowl
.596	Pigeons
.597	Ducks
.598	Geese

.6   Birds other than poultry

Class comprehensive works on birds in 636.5

.61	Birds raised for feathers
.63	Game birds
.68	Song and ornamental birds

Examples: mynas, toucans

For peafowl, see 636.595

.681	Swans
.686	Finches, parrots, hawks

Use of this number for comprehensive works on cage and aviary birds discontinued; class in 636.68

.686 2	Finches

Example: canaries

.686 4	Budgerigars

Variant names: lovebirds; grass, shell parrakeets

Class comprehensive works on parrakeets in 636.6865

.686 5	Parrots

Examples: cockatoos, lories, macaws

Class here comprehensive works on parrakeets

For budgerigars, see 636.6864

.686 9	Hawks

Use of this number for other cage and aviary birds discontinued; class in 636.68

.7   Dogs

.700 1	Philosophy and theory
.700 2	Miscellany
.700 22	Illustrations, models, miniatures [*all formerly* 636.77]
.700 3–.700 9	Standard subdivisions
.701–.708	Puppies, production and maintenance, dogs for specific purposes, veterinary sciences

Add to base number 636.70 the numbers following 636.0 in 636.01–636.08, e.g., housing 636.70831

.71	Breeds

For specific breeds, see 636.72–636.76

>   636.72–636.76 Specific breeds and groups of dogs

Class comprehensive works in 636.71, the toy of any breed in 636.76

See Manual at 636.72–636.76

.72	Nonsporting dogs

Variant name: utility group

Contains Bichon Frise, Boston terrier, bulldog, Chinese Shar-Pei, chow chow, Dalmatian, French bulldog, Keeshond, Lhasa apso, poodle (miniature and standard), Schipperke, Tibetan spaniel, Tibetan terrier

Class comprehensive works on terriers in 636.755

.73	Working and herding dogs

Contains Akita, Alaskan malamute, Bernese mountain dog, boxer, bull mastiff, Doberman pinscher, Great Dane, Great Pyrenees, Komondor, Kuvasz, mastiff, Newfoundland, Portuguese water dog, Rottweiler, Saint Bernard, Samoyed, schnauzer (standard and giant), Siberian husky

Class miniature schnauzer in 636.755; miniature pinscher in 636.76

.737	Herding dogs

Contains Australian cattle dog, bearded collie, Belgian malinois, Belgian tervuren, bouvier des Flandres, briard, collie, German shepherd (German police dog), puli, Welsh corgi; named breeds of sheepdogs

.75	Sporting dogs, hounds, terriers
.752	Sporting dogs

Contains Brittany vizsla, Weimaraner, wirehaired pointing griffon; named breeds of pointers, retrievers, setters, spaniels

.753	Hounds

Contains Basenji, beagle, Borzoi, dachshund, harrier, Rhodesian ridgeback, saluki, whippet; named breeds of hounds

.755	Terriers

Including miniature Schnauzer

Class Boston and Tibetan terriers in 636.72, toy terriers in 636.76

.76	Toy dogs

Contains Affenpinscher, Brussels griffon, Chihuahua, English toy spaniel, Italian greyhound, Japanese chin, Maltese, Mexican Hairless (Xoloizuintli), miniature pinscher, Papillon, Pekingese, Pomeranian, pug, Shih Tzu, silky terrier, toy Manchester terrier, toy poodle, Yorkshire terrier

Class miniature poodle in 636.72; miniature schnauzer in 636.755

[.77]	Illustrations, models, miniatures

Relocated to 636.70022

.8   Cats

.800 1	Philosophy and theory

.800 2	Miscellany

.800 22	Illustrations, models, miniatures [*all formerly* 636.87]

.800 3–.800 9	Standard subdivisions

.801–.808	Kittens, production and maintenance, cats for specific purposes, veterinary sciences

Add to base number 636.80 the numbers following 636.0 in 636.01–636.08, e.g., breeding cats 636.8082; however, use 636.8 for pet cats

---

> 636.82–636.83 Domestic cats

Class comprehensive works in 636.8

.82	Short-haired domestic cats

.822	Common short-haired cats

.823	Manx cat

.825	Asian short-haired cats

Examples: Burmese, Siamese

.826	Other short-haired cats

Examples: Abyssinian, Russian blue

.83	Long-haired domestic cats

Examples: Angora (coon cat), chinchilla, Himalayan, Persian

[.87] Illustrations, models, miniatures

Relocated to 636.80022

.89 Nondomestic cats

Examples: cheetahs, ocelots

.9 Other mammals

.91 Monotremes and marsupials

.93–.98 Placental mammals

Add to base number 636.9 the numbers following 599 in 599.3–599.8, e.g., elephants 636.961; however, class Equidae in 636.1, Ruminantia (except Traguloidea) in 636.2, Tylopoda in 636.296, Felidae in 636.8

637 Processing dairy and related products

Class comprehensive works on dairy farming in 636.2142

SUMMARY

.1 Milking and milk processing

> 637.12–637.14 Cows' milk

Class comprehensive works in 637.1

.12 Milking and inspection of cows' milk

.124 Milking

.124 028 Auxiliary techniques, procedures; materials

Class milking machinery and equipment in 637.125

.125 Milking machinery and equipment

.127 Testing [*formerly also* 637.1410287] and inspection

Former heading: Quality and purity determinations

.127 6 Butterfat tests

.127 7 Bacterial counts

[.13] Processing of cows' milk

Relocated to 637.14

.14 Processing [*formerly* 637.13] and forms of cows' milk

> 637.141–637.146 Whole milk

Class comprehensive works in 637.14

.141   Fresh whole milk

Including comprehensive works on pasteurization, homogenization, vitamin D treatment

Class pasteurization, homogenization, vitamin D treatment of products other than fresh whole milk with the product, e.g., of cream 637.148

.141 028 7   Measurement

Testing relocated to 637.127

.142   Concentrated liquid forms of whole milk

.142 2   Evaporated milk

[.142 3]   Plain condensed milk

Number discontinued; class in 637.142

.142 4   Sweetened condensed milk

.143   Dried whole milk

.146   Cultured whole milk

.147   Skim milk

[.147 1–.147 2]   Fresh and concentrated skim milk

Numbers discontinued; class in 637.147

.147 3   Dried skim milk

.147 6   Cultured skim milk

Class here yogurt

.148   Cream

.17   Milk other than cows' milk

.2   Butter processing

.22   Quality determinations

[.23]   Processing

Number discontinued; class in 637.2

.24   By-products

Class here buttermilk

.3   Cheese processing

Including by-products

.32   Quality determinations

[.33]	Processing
	Number discontinued; class in 637.3
.35	Varieties
.352	Cream cheese
.353	Ripened soft cheeses
	Examples: Brie, Camembert, Gorgonzola, Limburger, Neufchâtel
.354	Hard cheeses
	Examples: cheddar, Parmesan, Swiss
.356	Sour milk cheeses
	Example: cottage cheese
.358	Cheese foods
.4	**Manufacture of frozen desserts**
	Examples: ice cream, frozen custards, sherbets
.5	**Egg processing**
	Class raising hens for eggs in 636.5142, other poultry for eggs in 636.59
.54	Chicken eggs
.541	Fresh eggs
.543	Dried whole eggs
.547	Dried egg whites
.548	Dried egg yolks
.59	Other kinds of eggs
	Add to base number 637.59 the numbers following 636.59 in 636.592–636.598, e.g., duck eggs 637.597

638   Insect culture

.1	**Bee keeping (Apiculture)**
.11	Apiary establishment
.12	Varieties of bees
	Class a specific aspect of a specific variety of bee with the aspect, e.g., apiary establishment 638.11
.13	Pasturage for bees
.14	Hive management
.140 28	Auxiliary techniques and procedures
	Class apparatus, equipment, materials in 638.142

.142	Equipment and supplies

Examples: hive sections, hives, protective equipment, smokers

.144	Supplementary feeding of bees
.145	Queen rearing
.146	Swarming control
.15	Injuries, diseases, pests
.16	Honey processing

Class here comprehensive works on hive products

For wax, see 638.17

.17	Wax
.2	**Silkworms**
.3	**Resin- and dye-producing insects**
.5	**Other insects**
.57	Specific insects

Add to base number 638.57 the numbers following 595.7 in 595.71–595.79, e.g., praying mantises 638.5725

639   Hunting, fishing, conservation, related technologies

Class sport hunting and fishing in 799

SUMMARY

639.01–.09	Standard subdivisions	
.1	Hunting and trapping	
.2	Commercial fishing, whaling, sealing	
.3	Culture of cold-blooded vertebrates	Of fish
.4	Culture and harvest of mollusks	
.5	Culture and harvest of crustaceans	
.7	Culture and harvest of other invertebrates	
.8	Aquiculture	
.9	Conservation of biological resources	

.029	Commercial miscellany [*formerly also* 380.143029, 380.1431029, 381.43029, 381.431.029, 382.43029, 382.431029]
.091 6	Treatment in air and water

Aquiculture relocated to 639.8

.091 62	Treatment in oceans and seas

Mariculture relocated to 639.8

.1	**Hunting and trapping**

.11   Fur-bearing and other mammals

Add to base number 639.11 the numbers following 599 in 599.1–599.8, e.g., deer hunting and trapping 639.117357

For whaling, see 639.28; sealing, 639.29

See also 636.08844 for fur farming

.12   Birds

> 639.122–639.124 Of specific habitats

Class comprehensive works in 639.12, specific kinds of birds regardless of habitat in 639.128

.122   Land birds

.123   Shore birds

.124   Waterfowl

.128   Specific kinds

Add to base number 639.128 the numbers following 598 in 598.3–598.9, e.g., pheasants 639.128617

.13   Amphibians

.14   Reptiles

Add to base number 639.14 the numbers following 597.9 in 597.92–597.98, e.g., hunting alligators 639.148

.2   **Commercial fishing, whaling, sealing**

Class here works on fisheries encompassing culture as well as capture, on fisheries encompassing invertebrates as well as fish

Class culture of fish in 639.3, fisheries for invertebrates in 639.4

See also 639.8 for aquiculture, 799.1 for sport fishing

[.200 1–.200 9]   Standard subdivisions of commercial fishing, whaling, sealing

Relocated to 639.201–639.209

.201–.209   Standard subdivisions of commercial fishing, whaling, sealing [*formerly* 639.2001–639.2009]; of commercial fishing

> 639.21–639.22 Fishing in specific types of water

Class comprehensive works in 639.2, fishing for specific kinds of fish regardless of kind of water in 639.27

.21   Fishing in fresh water

.22   Fishing in salt and brackish waters

.27   Fishing for specific kinds of fish

>   Add to base number 639.27 the numbers following 597 in 597.2–597.5, e.g., salmon fishing 639.2755

.28   Whaling

.29   Sealing

.3   Culture of cold-blooded vertebrates   Of fish

[.300 1–.300 9]   Standard subdivisions of culture of cold-blooded vertebrates

>   Relocated to 639.01–639.09

.301–.309   Standard subdivisions of culture of cold-blooded vertebrates [*formerly* 639.3001–639.3009], of fish

---

>   639.31–639.34 Fish culture

Class comprehensive works in 639.3

For culture of specific kinds of fish, see 639.372–639.375

.31   Fish culture in fresh water

Class culture in freshwater aquariums in 639.344

.311   In natural and artificial ponds

Including fish hatcheries

.312   In lakes

.313   In rivers and other streams

.32   Fish culture in salt and brackish waters

Class culture in marine aquariums in 639.342

.34   Fish culture in aquariums

.342   Marine aquariums

.344   Freshwater aquariums

.37   Culture of amphibians and specific kinds of fish

.372–.375   Culture of specific kinds of fish

Add to base number 639.37 the numbers following 597 in 597.2–597.5, e.g., trout hatcheries 639.3755

.376–.378   Amphibians

Add to base number 639.37 the numbers following 597 in 597.6–597.8, e.g., frog farming 639.3789

Class comprehensive works in 639.376

.39   Reptiles

> Add to base number 639.39 the numbers following 597.9 in 597.92–597.98, e.g., snake farming 639.396

.4   **Culture and harvest of mollusks**

> Class here comprehensive works on culture and harvest of invertebrates
>
> *For culture and harvest of crustaceans, see 639.5; of other invertebrates, 639.7*

.41   Oysters

[.411]   Edible oysters

> Number discontinued; class in 639.41

.412   Pearl oysters

.42   Mussels

.44   Clams

.48   Other mollusks

> Add to base number 639.48 the numbers following 594 in 594.1–594.5, e.g., squid 639.4858

.5   **Culture and harvest of crustaceans**

.54   Specific crustaceans

> Add to base number 639.54 the numbers following 595.384 in 595.3841–595.3844, e.g., lobsters 639.541
>
> Use of this number for comprehensive works on edible crustaceans discontinued; class in 639.5

.7   **Culture and harvest of other invertebrates**

> *For insect culture, see 638*

.73   Protozoa, Parazoa, Coelenterata, Echinodermata and related phyla

> Add to base number 639.73 the numbers following 593 in 593.1–593.9, e.g., sponges 639.734

.75   Worms

> Add to base number 639.75 the numbers following 595.1 in 595.12–595.18, e.g., earthworms 639.7546

.8   **Aquiculture [*formerly* 639.0916]**

> Class here mariculture [*formerly* 639.09162]
>
> Class aquiculture of specific animal with the animal, e.g., of oysters 639.41

.89   Of plants

.9   **Conservation of biological resources**

Class here game keeping, wildlife conservation

Class interdisciplinary works on conservation of biological resources in 333.9516

>   639.92–639.96 Conservation of animals

Class comprehensive works in 639.9, conservation of specific kinds of animals in 639.97

.92   Habitat improvement for animals

.93   Animal species population control

.95   Reserves and refuge areas for animals

.96   Control of injuries, diseases, predators of animals

.97   Specific kinds of animals

Add to base number 639.97 the numbers following 59 in 592–599, e.g., protective measures for birds 639.978

.99   Plant conservation

640   Home economics and family living

Class here management of home and personal life, domestic arts and sciences

Class personal health in 613

SUMMARY

640.1–.9	[Standard subdivisions and specific aspects of household management]
641	Food and drink
642	Meals and table service
643	Housing and household equipment
644	Household utilities
645	Household furnishings
646	Sewing, clothing, management of personal and family living
647	Management of public households (Institutional housekeeping)
648	Housekeeping
649	Child rearing and home care of sick and infirm

.202   Synopses and outlines

Use of this number for manuals discontinued; class in 640

Helpful hints and miscellaneous recipes relocated to 640.41

[.288]   Maintenance and repair

Do not use; class in 643.7

[.297]   Evaluation and purchasing manuals

Do not use; class in 640.73

.4   **Specific aspects of household management [*formerly also* 640.68]**

      Class comprehensive works on household management in 640

.41   Helpful hints and miscellaneous recipes [*formerly* 640.202]

.42   Management of money

      Including records of household expenditures

      Class here accounting, budgeting, expenditure control

      Class evaluation and purchasing guides in 640.73

      See Manual at 332.024 vs. 640.42

.43   Management of time and energy

.46   Household employees

      Duties, hours, selection, training

      Class management of institutional household employees in 647.2

.49   Survival housekeeping

      Housekeeping in presence of unfavorable circumstances and provisioning in anticipation of disaster, e.g., threat of nuclear attack

      Class personal survival after accidents, disasters, other unfavorable circumstances in 613.69

[.68]   Household management

      Use of this number for comprehensive works on household management discontinued; class in 640

      Specific aspects of household management relocated to 640.4

.71   Schools and courses

[.714]   Adult education

      Relocated to 640.715

.715   Adult education [*formerly* 640.714]

.73   Evaluation and purchasing guides

      Class here consumer education for home and personal needs

      Class interdisciplinary evaluation and purchasing guides and works on consumer education in 381.33; comprehensive works on managing household money in 640.42; evaluation and purchasing guides for specific products and services with the subject, using notation 0297 from Table 1, e.g., manual on evaluating automobiles 629.2220297

641   Food and drink

For meals and table service, see 642

SUMMARY

641.01	**Philosophy and theory**
.1	**Applied nutrition**
.2	**Beverages (Drinks)**
.3	**Food**
.4	**Food preservation and storage**
.5	**Cooking**
.6	**Cooking specific materials**
.7	**Specific cooking processes and techniques**
.8	**Cooking specific kinds of composite dishes**

.01   Philosophy and theory

.013   Gastronomy and pleasures of eating

.1   Applied nutrition

Class nutrition in the promotion of health in 613.2; nutritive values of beverages 641.2, of specific foods in 641.33–641.39

.104   Special topics

.104 2   Calories

Including calorie counters

.12   Proteins

.13   Carbohydrates

.14   Fats and oils

.16   Water

.17   Minerals

.18   Vitamins

.2   Beverages (Drinks)

Class here interdisciplinary works on production, manufacture, preservation, preparation, use

Class a specific aspect with the subject, e.g., manufacture (commercial preparation) 663

.21   Alcoholic beverages

For wine, see 641.22; brewed and malted beverages, 641.23; distilled liquor, 641.25

.22	Wine

Class here grape wine

See also 641.23 for sake (rice wine)

.222	Specific kinds of grape wine

Add to base number 641.222 the numbers following 663.22 in 663.222–663.224, e.g., champagne 641.2224

Use of this number for comprehensive works on grape wine discontinued; class in 641.22

.229	Nongrape wine

Example: cider

.23	Brewed and malted beverages

Examples: pulque, sake

Class here ale, beer

Class malt whiskey in 641.252

.25	Distilled liquor

Examples: mescal, tequila, potato whiskey, vodka

.252	Whiskey

Use 641.25 for potato whiskey

.253	Brandy
.255	Compound liquors

Examples: absinthe, cordials, gin, liqueurs

.259	Rum

Use of this number for other distilled liquor discontinued; class in 641.25

.26	Nonalcoholic beverages

Class specific nonalcoholic beverages and kinds of beverages in 641.3

.3	**Food**

Class here interdisciplinary works on food

Use of this number for comprehensive works on food and beverages discontinued; class in 641

Class interdisciplinary works on composite dishes in 641.8; a specific aspect with the subject, e.g., manufacture (commercial preparation) 664

See Manual at 580–590 vs. 630, 641.3; 613.2 vs. 641.3, 363.8

.300 1	Philosophy and theory
.300 2	Miscellany
[.300 297]	Evaluation and purchasing manuals

Do not use; class in 641.31

.300 3–.300 9		Standard subdivisions
.302		Health foods

Including organically grown foods

> 641.303–641.309 Classes of food by origin

Class comprehensive works in 641.3

.303		Food from vegetables
.306		Food from animals
.309		Mineral food
.31		Evaluation and purchasing manuals

Class applied nutrition in 641.1, evaluation and purchasing manuals of specific food in 641.33–641.39

.33–.37   Food derived from plant crops and domesticated animals

Add to base number 641.3 the numbers following 63 in 633–637, e.g., flavorings 641.3382, legumes 641.3565, meat 641.36, chicken meat 641.365

Do not use 641.333 for legumes

For honey, see 641.38

.38   Honey

.39   Game and seafood

Add to base number 641.39 the numbers following 641.69 in 641.691–641.696, e.g., oysters 641.394

Use of this number for other foods discontinued; class in 641.3

> **641.4–641.8 Food preservation, storage, cooking**

Class comprehensive works in 641.3

.4   **Food preservation and storage**

Class comprehensive works on food preservation in 664.028

> 641.41–641.47 Preservation techniques for fruit and vegetables, for food as a whole

Class comprehensive works in 641.4, preservation techniques for meat and allied foods in 641.49

.41   Preliminary treatment

.42   Canning

.44   Drying and dehydrating

Including freeze-drying

.45   Low-temperature techniques

.452   Cold storage

.453   Deep freezing

> *For freeze-drying, see 641.44*

.46   Brining, pickling, smoking

.47   Use of additives

.48   Storage

.49   Meat and allied food

> Class storage of meat and allied food in 641.48

.492   Red meat

> Add to base number 641.492 the numbers following 641.4 in 641.41–641.47, e.g., canning red meat 641.4922

.493   Poultry

> Add to base number 641.493 the numbers following 641.4 in 641.41–641.47, e.g., freezing poultry 641.49353

.494   Seafood

> Add to base number 641.494 the numbers following 641.4 in 641.42–641.47, e.g., brining seafood 641.4946

.495   Other animal flesh

> Examples: frogs, turtles, snails, insects

.5   **Cooking**

Preparation of food with and without use of heat

Unless other instructions are given, observe the following table of precedence, e.g., outdoor cooking for children 641.5622 (*not* 641.578)

For special situations, reasons, ages	641.56
Quantity, institutional, travel, outdoor cooking	641.57
Money-saving and timesaving cooking	641.55
With specific appliances, utensils, fuels	641.58
For specific meals	641.52–.54
By specific types of persons	641.51
Characteristic of specific geographical environments, ethnic cooking	641.59

Class menus and meal planning in 642

> *For cooking specific materials, see 641.6; specific cooking processes and techniques, 641.7; cooking of composite dishes, 641.8*

SUMMARY

641.501–.509	**Standard subdivisions**
.51	**Cooking by specific types of persons**
.52	**Breakfast**
.53	**Cooking luncheon, brunch, elevenses, tea, supper, snacks**
.54	**Dinner**
.55	**Money-saving and timesaving cooking**
.56	**Cooking for special situations, reasons, ages**
.57	**Quantity, institutional, travel, outdoor cooking**
.58	**Cooking with specific fuels, appliances, utensils**
.59	**Cooking characteristic of specific geographical environments, ethnic cooking**

[.502 4]   Works for specific types of users

         Do not use; class in 641.51

.508 3–.508 4   Persons of specific ages

         Class cooking for persons of specific ages in 641.562

.508 7   Handicapped and gifted persons

         Class cooking for sick persons in 641.5631

[.508 82]   Cooking with respect to religious groups

         Relocated to 641.567

.509   Historical, geographical, persons treatment

         Class here collections of recipes from specific restaurants

         Class cooking characteristic of specific geographical environments in 641.59

.51   Cooking by specific types of persons

.512   Beginner cooking

         Easy dishes

.512 3   Children's cooking

         Class cooking of food for consumption by children in 641.5622

.514   Gourmet cooking

>   641.52–641.54 Cooking specific meals

         Class comprehensive works in 641.5

.52   Breakfast

.53   Cooking luncheon, brunch, elevenses, tea, supper, snacks

.54   Dinner

.55   Money-saving and timesaving cooking

.552	Money-saving cooking
	Including leftovers
.555	Timesaving cooking
	Class here make-ahead meals
.56	Cooking for special situations, reasons, ages
.561	For one or two persons
.562	For persons of specific ages
.562 2	For infants and children
	Class cooking to be performed by children in 641.5123
.562 7	For persons in late adulthood
.563	For health, appearance, personal reasons
	Including cooking for pregnant women
	Unless other instructions are given, class complex subjects with aspects in two or more subdivisions of this schedule in the number coming first in the schedule, e.g., low-carbohydrate, low-calorie cooking for persons with diabetes 641.56314 (*not* 641.5635 or 641.5638)
.563 1	For sick persons
	Class cooking for overweight persons in 641.5635
.563 11	For persons with heart disease
.563 14	For persons with diabetes
.563 2	Cooking with specified vitamin and mineral content
	Example: salt-free cooking
.563 4	High-calorie cooking
.563 5	Low-calorie cooking
	Class here cooking for overweight persons
.563 6	Vegetarian cooking
	See also 641.65 for cooking vegetables
.563 7	Health-food cooking
	Use 641.563 for comprehensive works on health cooking
.563 8	Carbohydrate, fat, protein cooking
	Including low-carbohydrate, low-fat
.564	For various specific times of year
	Class here seasonal cooking
	Class cooking for special occasions in 641.568

.566	For Christian church limitations and observances
	Examples: Christmas, Lent
	Class here cooking for Christian groups
.567	For religious limitations and observances
	Class here cooking with respect to religious groups [*formerly* 641.50882], cooking for days of feast and fast
	Add to base number 641.567 the numbers following 29 in 292–299, e.g., Jewish cooking 641.5676
	For cooking for Christian church limitations and observances, see 641.566
.568	For special occasions
	Examples: holidays, birthdays, parties, celebrations
	Class cooking for special religious occasions in 641.567
.57	Quantity, institutional, travel, outdoor cooking
	Example: cooking for armed services
	Class here short-order cooking
.571	For schools
.572	For hotels and restaurants
[.573]	For armed services
	Number discontinued; class in 641.57
.575	For travel
	Including airline, bus, camper (caravan) cooking
	For cooking for railroad dining cars, see 641.576
[.575 2]	For motor buses
	Number discontinued; class in 641.575
.575 3	For ships
[.575 4]	For airlines
	Number discontinued; class in 641.575
.576	For railroad dining cars
.577	For canteens
	Temporary or mobile facilities for serving food
.578	Outdoor cooking
	Class here cookouts
	Class cooking in campers (caravans) in 641.575
.578 2	Camp cooking

.578 4	Cooking at an outdoor grill

Class here cooking at outdoor barbecues

Class comprehensive works on techniques of barbecuing in 641.76

.579	For hospitals and other medical facilities
.58	Cooking with specific fuels, appliances, utensils

Examples: convection-oven cooking, wood-stove cooking

Class outdoor cooking in 641.578

.583	With oil
.584	With gas
.585	With alcohol-based fuels
.586	With electricity

Cooking with electric ranges and appliances, e.g., skillets, frying pans, roasters, grills, toasters, waffle irons

Class convection-oven cooking in 641.58, microwave cooking in 641.5882, electric slow cooking in 641.5884

.587	With steam and pressure
.588	Slow and fireless cooking
.588 2	Microwave cooking
.588 4	Electric slow cooking
.589	With specific utensils

Examples: foils, specially coated utensils, blenders

Class cooking with specific utensils using specific fuels in 641.583–641.588

.59	Cooking characteristic of specific geographical environments, ethnic cooking

Including international cooking

Class historical and geographical treatment of general cooking in 641.509

See also 641.509 for collections of recipes from specific restaurants

.591	Cooking characteristic of areas, regions, places in general

Add to base number 641.591 the numbers following —1 in notation 11–19 from Table 2, e.g., arctic and cold-weather cooking 641.5911, tropical and hot-weather cooking 641.5913

.592	Ethnic cooking

Add to base number 641.592 notation 03–9 from Table 5, e.g., Afro-American cooking 641.59296073; however, class Jewish cooking in 641.5676; cooking of ethnic groups dominant in their areas in 641.593–641.599

.593–.599   Cooking characteristic of specific continents, countries, localities

Add to base number 641.59 notation 3–9 from Table 2, e.g., Southern cooking 641.5975

Class ethnic cooking of nondominant aggregates in 641.592

.6   **Cooking specific materials**

Class specific kinds of composite dishes featuring specific materials in 641.8

.61   Cooking preserved foods

Add to base number 641.61 the numbers following 641.4 in 641.42–641.46, e.g., cooking using frozen foods 641.6153

Class home preservation in 641.4, cooking using specific preserved foods in 641.63–641.69

.62   Cooking with beverages

Class home preparation of beverages in 641.87; cooking with a specific nonalcoholic beverage with the product from which it is derived, e.g., with chocolate 641.6374, with apple juice 641.6411

.622   Wine

.623   Beer and ale

.625   Spirits

>   641.63–641.69 Specific food

Class comprehensive works in 641.6

.63–.67   Cooking food derived from plant crops and domesticated animals

Add to base number 641.6 the numbers following 63 in 633–637, e.g., flavorings 641.6382, legumes 641.6565, meat 641.66, chicken meat 641.665; however, class ices and sherbets in 641.863

Do not use 641.633 for legumes

Class comprehensive works on cooking with beverages in 641.62, vegetarian cooking in 641.5636

For cooking with honey, see 641.68

.68   Cooking with honey

.69   Cooking game and seafood

Use of this number for cooking other foods discontinued; class in 641.6

.691   Game

.692   Fish

Class here seafood

For mollusks, see 641.694; crustaceans, 641.695

.694   Mollusks

        Examples: clams, mussels, octopuses, oysters, snails, squid

        Class here shellfish

        For crustaceans, see 641.695

.695   Crustaceans

        Examples: crabs, lobsters, shrimp

.696   Reptiles, amphibians, insects

        Examples: frogs, snakes, turtles

.7   **Specific cooking processes and techniques**

        Class specific processes applied to specific materials in 641.6, to specific kinds of composite dishes in 641.8

.71   Baking and roasting

.73   Boiling, simmering, stewing, steaming

.76   Broiling, grilling, barbecuing

        Class here comprehensive works on techniques of barbecuing

        Class cooking at outdoor grills in 641.5784

.77   Frying, sautéing, braising

.79   Preparation of cold dishes

        Including chilled dishes

.8   **Cooking specific kinds of composite dishes**

        Class here interdisciplinary works on composite dishes

.81   Side dishes and sauces

        Other than those listed in 641.83–641.86

        Including fondues, garnishes

.812   Appetizers, hors d'oeuvres, pâtés, relishes, savories

.813   Soups

.814   Sauces and salad dressings

.815   Breads and bread-like foods

        Examples: biscuits (United States), crackers, crepes, hot cakes, pancakes, rolls, waffles

        Class main dishes based on breads and bread-like foods in 641.82, sandwiches in 641.84, pastries in 641.865

.82	Main dishes
	Examples: quiche, soufflé
.821	Casserole dishes
.822	Pasta dishes
.823	Stews
.824	Meat and cheese pies
	Including pizza, meat loaf
	Class cooking sausage in 641.66
.83	Salads
.84	Sandwiches
	Example: submarine sandwiches
.85	Preserves and candy
.852	Jam, jelly, marmalade
.853	Candy
	Variant name: sweets (United Kingdom)
.86	Desserts
	Class here comprehensive works on sweets (United States)
	For preserves and candy, see 641.85
.862	Ice cream and ice milk
.863	Ices and sherbet
	Variant name: water ices
.864	Puddings and gelatins
.865	Pastries
.865 2	Pies and tarts
.865 3	Cakes
	Including cake decoration
	See also 641.8659 for coffee cakes
.865 4	Cookies
	Variant name: biscuits (United Kingdom)
.865 9	Danish, French, related pastries
	Examples: coffee cakes, cream puffs, eclairs
.87	Beverages
	Class interdisciplinary works on beverages in 641.2
.872	Wine

.873   Alcoholic brewed beverages

         Class here beer and ale

.874   Alcoholic beverages

         Including bartenders' manuals

         Class here comprehensive works on mixed drinks

         Class bottled and canned mixed drinks in 663.1

         For wine, see 641.872; alcoholic brewed beverages, 641.873

.875   Nonalcoholic beverages

         Examples: carbonated and malted drinks, juices, punches

         For nonalcoholic brewed beverages, see 641.877

.877   Nonalcoholic brewed beverages

         Examples: cocoa, coffee, teas

         Including concentrates and substitutes

642   Meals and table service

>   **642.1–642.5 Meals in specific situations**

         Class here comprehensive works on meals and table services in specific situations

         Class comprehensive works in 642, table service in 642.6

.1   **Meals for home and family**

         Including TV dinners

.3   **Meals for camp, picnic, travel**

.4   **Meals for social and public occasions**

         Including banquets, box lunches, catered meals

         Class here meals and catering for social and public occasions

         Class picnics in 642.3, catering which includes restaurant operation in 647.95

.5   **Meals in public and institutional eating places**

         Examples: in cafeterias, hospitals, schools

         Class here meals in restaurants and hotels

         Class meals for social and public occasions in 642.4, operation of public eating places in 647.95

> **642.6–642.8 Table service**

Class here table service in specific situations

Class comprehensive works in 642.6, comprehensive works on meals and table services in specific situations in 641.1–642.5

.6   Serving at table

Examples: place setting, seating guests, carving

Class here comprehensive works on table service

For table furnishings, see 642.7, for table decorations, see 642.8

.7   Table furnishings

Examples: dinnerware, glassware, silverware, table linens

For table decorations, see 642.8

.8   Table decorations

643   Housing and household equipment

Works for owner-occupants or renters covering activities of members of household

[.028 8]   Maintenance and repair

Do not use; class in 643.7

.1   Housing

For special kinds of housing, see 643.2

See also 728 for comprehensive works on design and construction of houses, 690.8 for construction of houses

See Manual at 643.1 vs. 363.5

[.102 88]   Maintenance and repair

Do not use; class in 643.7

[.102 97]   Evaluation and purchasing manuals

Do not use; class in 643.12

.12   Selecting, renting, buying homes

Including site selection, supervision of construction

Class here evaluation and purchasing guides

Class moving in 648.9

See also 333.338 for economics of home acquisition, 346.043 for law of real property

.16   Household security

Example: burglarproofing

.2   **Special kinds of housing**

Examples: apartments, condominiums, mobile homes, modular and prefabricated houses, vacation homes

Class single-family houses in 643.1; a specific aspect of a special kind of housing with the subject, e.g., renovating vacation homes 643.7

See Manual at 629.226 vs. 643.2, 690.879, 728.79

>   **643.3–643.5 Specific areas and their equipment**

Class comprehensive works in 643.1; household utilities in 644, household furnishings in 645; home construction of household articles made of fabric in 646.21; home workshops in 684.08; manufacture of household appliances in 683.8, of household furnishings in 684

.3   **Kitchens and their equipment**

Including kitchen linen

Class use of food storage and preparation equipment in 641.4–641.8, dishwashing equipment in 648.56

.4   **Eating and drinking areas and their equipment**

Examples: dining rooms, breakfast rooms, bars

Class table furnishings in 642.7

.5   **Other areas and their equipment**

Examples: attics, basements, other storage areas

.52   Bathrooms

.53   Bedrooms

Including bedclothing, e.g., blankets

.54   Living rooms

.55   Recreation areas

Indoor and outdoor

Examples: patios, porches, swimming pools

.58   Study and work areas

Example: dens

.6   **Appliances and laborsaving installations**

Class here maintenance and repair by members of household

Class appliances and installations for specific areas in 643.3–643.5, for a specific purpose with the purpose, e.g., sewing machines 646.2044

[.604]	Special topics

Number discontinued; class in 643.6

Appliances and laborsaving installations for handicapped persons relocated to 643.6087

.608 7	Handicapped [*formerly* 643.604], ill, gifted persons
.7	**Renovation, improvement, remodeling**

Class here comprehensive works on maintenance and repair in home economics, on maintenance and repair by members of household

Class renovation, improvement, remodeling of specific areas and their equipment in 643.3–643.5; maintenance and repair of a specific topic in home economics with the topic using notation 0288 from Table 1, e.g., of appliances 643.60288

See Manual at 643.7 vs. 690

644   Household utilities

Works for owner-occupants or renters covering activities by members of household

See Manual at 647.96–647.99 vs. 658.2, T1—0682

.1	**Heating**
.3	**Lighting**

Class lighting fixtures as furnishings in 645.5

.5	**Ventilation and air conditioning**
.6	**Water supply**

645   Household furnishings

Works for owner-occupants or renters covering activities by members of household

Class here comprehensive works on household furnishings and interior decoration of residential buildings

Interior decoration of residential buildings relocated to 747

Class home construction of fabric furnishings in 646.21, construction in wood and metal in 684

[.029 7]	Evaluation and purchasing manuals

Do not use; class in 645.042

.04	Special topics
.042	Evaluation and purchasing manuals

Class selection and purchase of fabrics for furnishings in 645.046, evaluation and purchasing manuals for specific kinds of furnishings with the kind, using notation 0297 from Table 1, e.g., for lighting fixtures 645.50297

.046   Fabrics

Description, selection, purchase, care, use

> ### 645.1–645.6 Interior furnishings

Class comprehensive works in 645

> ### 645.1–645.5 Specific kinds of interior furnishings

Class comprehensive works in 645

.1   **Floor covering**

Examples: carpeting, rugs, linoleum

.2   **Covering for walls and ceilings**

Examples: hangings, paint, paneling, wallpaper

.3   **Curtains and related furnishings**

Examples: draperies, shades, blinds, their accessories

Class wall hangings in 645.2

.4   **Furniture and accessories**

Including upholstery, slipcovers; arrangement for convenience and efficiency

Class artistic aspects of furniture and accessories in 749

.5   **Lighting fixtures**

.6   **Furnishings for specific rooms**

Class interior furnishings of specific kinds regardless of room in 645.1–645.5

.8   **Outdoor furnishings**

Examples: furnishings for gardens, patios, courts, balconies, roofs

646   Sewing, clothing, management of personal and family living

SUMMARY

646.1	Sewing materials and equipment
.2	Sewing and related operations
.3	Clothing and accessories
.4	Clothing and accessories construction
.5	Construction of headgear
.6	Care of clothing and accessories
.7	Management of personal and family living Grooming

.1   **Sewing materials and equipment**

General aspects: description, selection, purchase, care

Including leathers and furs

Materials, equipment used for clothing relocated to 646.3028

.11   Fabrics

Class here comprehensive works on fabrics in the home

Class fabrics for a specific use with the use, e.g., use in furnishings 645.046

.19   Sewing equipment, fasteners

Examples: needles, pins, scissors and shears, thimbles, thread

Class here notions

Class sewing machines in 646.2044

.2   **Sewing and related operations**

Class here mending, sewing of specific articles for the home

Class clothing construction in 646.4, mending of clothing in 646.6

For knitting, crocheting, tatting, see 746.43; embroidery, 746.44

.202 8   Auxiliary techniques and procedures

Class sewing apparatus, equipment, materials in 646.1, sewing machines in 646.2044

.204   Basic sewing operations

Class here darning

.204 2   Sewing by hand

.204 4   Sewing by machine

.21   Construction of home furnishings

Examples: making hangings, curtains, slipcovers, table linen, towels, bedclothes

Class basic sewing operations in 646.204, artistic and decorative aspects of construction of interior furnishings in 746.9

.25   Reweaving

.3   **Clothing and accessories**

Description, selection, purchase of clothing and accessories for utility, quality, economy, appearance, style

Class interdisciplinary works on clothing and accessories in 391

For clothing and accessories construction, see 646.4; care of clothing and accessories, 646.6

See Manual at 391 vs. 646.3, 746.92

.302 8	Materials, equipment [*both formerly* 646.1], apparatus; auxiliary techniques and procedures
[.302 88]	Maintenance and repair
	Do not use; class in 646.6
[.308 1–.308 2]	Clothing for men, and women
	Do not use; class in 646.32–646.34
.308 3	Young adult clothing
	Class clothing for young adult men aged twenty-one and over in 646.32, for young adult women aged twenty-one and over in 646.34, for children in 646.36
.308 4	Clothing for persons in specific stages of adulthood
	Class clothing of adult men regardless of age in 646.32, of adult women regardless of age in 646.34
[.308 7]	Clothing for handicapped and ill persons
	Do not use; class in 646.31
.309 11	Clothing for cold weather and frigid zones
.309 13	Clothing for hot weather and tropics

.31–.36   Clothing for handicapped and ill persons, men, women, children

Add to base number 646.3 the numbers following 646.40 in 646.401–646.406, e.g., clothing for handicapped persons 646.31

Class clothing for young adult men in 646.308351, for young adult women in 646.308352

.4   Clothing and accessories construction

Class here casual clothes, sports clothes

Class commercial manufacture of clothing in 687

For construction of headgear, see 646.5

.400 1–.400 7	Standard subdivisions
.400 8	Clothing with respect to specific kinds of persons
[.400 81–.400 82]	Clothing for men, and women
	Do not use; class in 646.402–646.404
.400 83	Young adult clothing
	Class clothing for young adult men aged twenty-one and over in 646.402, for young adult women aged twenty-one and over in 646.404, for children in 646.406
.400 84	Clothing of persons in specific stages of adulthood
	Class clothing of adult men regardless of age in 646.402, of adult women regardless of age in 646.404

[.400 87]	Clothing for handicapped and ill persons
	Do not use; class in 646.401
.401	Clothing for handicapped and ill persons

> 646.402–646.406 Clothing for men, women, children

Class comprehensive works in 646.4, construction of clothing for handicapped persons regardless of age or sex in 646.401, patterns regardless of kind of persons in 646.407, fitting and alterations regardless of kind of persons in 646.408

.402	Men's clothing

Class clothing for young adult men in 646.4008351

.404	Women's clothing

Class clothing for young adult women in 646.4008352

.406	Children's clothing

Class clothing of young men in 646.402, of young women in 646.404

.407	Patterns

General aspects: selection, purchase, use

Use of this number for construction of clothing without patterns discontinued; class in 646.4

.407 2	Patternmaking and pattern design
.408	Fitting and alterations

> 646.42–646.48 Specific kinds of clothing

Add to notation for each term identified by * the numbers following 646.4 in 646.4001–646.406, e.g., construction of the kind of clothing for handicapped persons 01

Class comprehensive works in 646.4

.42	*Underwear and hosiery
.43	*Specific kinds of garments

Not provided for elsewhere

Use of this number for comprehensive works on outer house garments discontinued; class in 646.4

.432	*Dresses
.433	*Suits, *trousers, *jackets

For outdoor jackets, e.g., windbreakers, see 646.45

*Add as instructed under 646.42–646.48

.435	*Shirts, *blouses, *tops
.437	*Skirts
.45	*Outer coats, sweaters, wraps

        Class here comprehensive works on coats

        Class suit coats in 646.433; outdoor athletic wear in 646.47, e.g., ski clothing

        See also 646.47 for evening wear

.452	*Overcoats

        Example: topcoats

.453	*Raincoats
.454	*Sweaters
.457	*Stoles, *cloaks, *jackets

        Class suit jackets in 641.433

.47	*Garments for special purposes

        Examples: athletic garments, evening and formal dress, maternity garments, wedding clothes

        Class accessories for special purposes in 646.48

        See also 646.4 for casual and sports clothes

.475	*Nightclothes
.478	*Costumes

        Examples: party, period costumes

        Class here theatrical costumes

.48	Accessories

        Examples: aprons, belts, gloves and mittens, handkerchiefs, neckwear, scarves

        Class hosiery in 646.42, headgear in 646.5, boots and shoes in 685.31, handcrafted costume jewelry in 745.5942

.5   Construction of headgear

.500 1–.500 7	Standard subdivisions
.500 8	History and description with respect to kinds of persons
[.500 81–.500 83]	Men, women, children

        Do not use; class in 646.502–646.506

.500 84	Persons in specific stages of adulthood

        Class construction of headgear for men regardless of age in 646.502, for women regardless of age in 646.504

*Add as instructed under 646.42–646.48

.500 9	Historical, geographical, persons treatment
.502	For men
.504	For women (Millinery)
.506	For children

.6   Care of clothing and accessories

Examples: mending, reweaving, storage, packing

Dyeing, bleaching, spot removal relocated to 648.1

For laundering and related operations, see 648.1

.7   Management of personal and family living   Grooming

Class here interdisciplinary works on success, successful living

Class interdisciplinary works on success in business and other public situations in 650.1

For parapsychological and occult means for achievement of well-being, happiness, success, see 131; psychological means for achievement of personal well-being, happiness, success, 158; etiquette (manners), 395

See also 362.82 for social services to families

.700 1–.700 7	Standard subdivisions of management of personal and family living
.700 8	Management of personal and family living with respect to kinds of persons
[.700 846]	Management of personal and family living for persons in late adulthood
	Do not use; class in 646.79
.700 9	Historical, geographical, persons treatment of personal and family living
.701–.703	Standard subdivisions of grooming
.704	Grooming for women, men, children
.704 2	For women
.704 4	For men
.704 6	For children
.705–.707	Standard subdivisions of grooming
.708	Grooming for specific kinds of persons
[.708 1–.708 3]	Grooming for men, women, children
	Do not use; class in 646.704
.708 4	Grooming for persons in specific stages of adulthood
	Class grooming for women regardless of age in 646.7042, for men regardless of age in 646.7044
.709	Historical, geographical, persons treatment of grooming

>   646.71–646.75 Grooming

Class comprehensive works in 646.7, clothing selection and dressing with style in 646.3, training children in grooming 649.63

See also 646.76 for charm

.71   Cleanliness

Examples: bathing, showering

.72   Care of hair, face, skin

Class here cosmetology

Use of this number for personal appearance discontinued; class in 646.7

.724   Care of hair

Example: shaving

Including care of beards

Class here barbering

.724 2   Hairdressing

Including dyeing

Class hairstyling in 646.7245

.724 5   Hairstyling

.724 8   Wigs

General aspects: cleaning, dyeing, selection, styling

.726   Care of face, skin

Including care of eyes, lips

Use of this number for comprehensive works on hair, skin, nails, on cosmetology discontinued; class in 646.72

Class manicuring and pedicuring in 646.727

.727   Manicuring and pedicuring

.75   Physique and form

Reducing, slenderizing, bodybuilding

Including massage, sauna, Turkish baths

See also 613.2 for dieting, 613.7 for physical fitness

See Manual at 613.71 vs. 646.75, 796

.76   Charm

.77   Dating and choice of mate

.78   Family living

Class here guides to harmonious family relations

For child rearing, see 649.1

.79   Guides for persons in late adulthood

Class here guides to retirement

Class family living in 646.78

See also 362.6 for social services to persons in late adulthood, 646.7008 for guides to management of personal and family living for other age brackets

647 Management of public households (Institutional housekeeping)

.068   Management

See Manual at 647.068

[.068 3]   Personnel management

Do not use; class in 647.2

>   **647.2–647.6 Employees**

Class comprehensive works on household employees in 640.46, comprehensive works on public household employees in 647.2

.2   **Indoor employees**

Class here personnel management, comprehensive works on public household employees

For outdoor employees, see 647.3; hours and duties, 647.6

.3   **Outdoor employees**

For hours and duties, see 647.6

.6   **Employee hours and duties**

.9   **Specific kinds of public households and institutions**

Class a specific aspect of public households and institutions with the aspect, e.g., laundering 648.1

.92   Multiple dwellings for long-term residents

Examples: apartments, apartment hotels, flats, tenements

Class boarding and rooming houses in 647.94

.94   Multiple dwellings for transients

See Manual at 913–919: Guidebooks

.940 25   Directories

             Class directories of specific continents, countries, localities in 647.943–647.949

.940 9   Historical, geographical, persons treatment

             Class treatment by specific continents, countries, localities in 647.943–647.949 (*not* 647.94093–647.94099)

.943–.949   Treatment by specific continents, countries, localities

             Class here directories

             Add to base number 647.94 notation 3–9 from Table 2, e.g., multiple dwellings for transients in Canada 647.9471; then add further as follows:

01	Hotels and inns
02	Motels
03	Bed and breakfast establishments
	Class here boarding and rooming houses
05	Clubs
06	Hostels
	For youth hostels, see 07
07	Youth hostels
08	Trailer camps
09	Campsites

.95   Eating and drinking places

             See Manual at 913–919: Guidebooks

.950 25   Directories

             Class directories of specific continents, countries, localities in 647.953–647.959

.950 9   Historical, geographical, persons treatment

             Class treatment by specific continents, countries, localities in 647.953–647.959 (*not* 647.95093–647.95099)

.953–.959   Treatment by specific continents, countries, localities

             Class here directories, operation of catering establishments

             Add to base number 647.95 notation 3–9 from Table 2, e.g., restaurants of Hawaii 647.95969

>   647.96–647.99 Institutional households not primarily used for residence, eating, drinking

             Class comprehensive works in 647

             See Manual at 647.96–647.99 vs. 658.2, T1—0682

.96   Miscellaneous institutional households

             Not provided for elsewhere

             Add to base number 647.96 the numbers following 725 in 725.1–725.9, e.g., office buildings 647.9623

.98   Religious institutions

Add to base number 647.98 the numbers following 726 in 726.1–726.9, e.g., Franciscan monasteries 647.98773

.99   Educational and research institutions

Add to base number 647.99 the numbers following 727 in 727.1–727.9, e.g., public libraries 647.99824

648   Housekeeping

Class here household sanitation

See Manual at 647.96–647.99 vs. 658.2, T1—0682

.1   **Laundering and related operations**

Examples: dyeing, bleaching, spot removal [*all formerly* 646.6], drying, pressing

Class dry cleaning in 667.12

.5   **Housecleaning**

Class here cleaning floors, furnishings

.56   Dishwashing

.7   **Control and eradication of pests**

.8   **Storage and preparation for storage**

.9   **Moving**

649   Child rearing and home care of sick and infirm

SUMMARY

649.1	**Child rearing**
.3	**Feeding**
.4	**Clothing and health**
.5	**Activities and recreation**
.6	**Training**
.7	**Moral and character training**
.8	**Home care of sick and infirm**

.1   **Child rearing**

Class here training, supervision

Observe the following table of precedence, e.g., infant boys 649.122 (*not* 649.132)

Exceptional children	649.15
Children of specific classes, types, relationships	649.14
Children of specific age groups	649.12
Children of specific sexes	649.13

Class specific elements of home care of children regardless of age, sex, or other characteristics in 649.3–649.7

.102 4	Works for specific types of users
	Do not add as instructed in Table 1
.102 42	Works for expectant parents
.102 43	Works for single parents
.102 45	Works for older children in family
.102 48	Works for baby sitters
.108	Child care with respect to kinds of persons
	Class care of specific kinds of children in 649.12–649.15
.12	Children of specific age groups
.122	Infants
	From birth to age two
.123	Children three to five
	Class here preschool children
.124	Children six to eleven
	Class here comprehensive works on school-age children to age fourteen
	Class school-age children twelve to fourteen in 649.125
.125	Young adults
	Ages twelve to twenty
.13	Children of specific sexes
.132	Boys
.133	Girls
.14	Children of specific classes, types, relationships
	Add to base number 649.14 the numbers following 155.44 in 155.442–155.446, e.g., the only child 649.142
.15	Exceptional children
	Add to base number 649.15 the numbers following 371.9 in 371.91–371.97, e.g., the gifted child 649.155

> **649.3–649.7 Specific elements of home care of children**

Class comprehensive works in 649.1

.3	**Feeding**
.33	Breast feeding
	Class nutritional aspects of breast feeding in 613.26

.4 **Clothing and health**

Class feeding in 649.3, home care for sick children in 649.8

.5 **Activities and recreation**

.51 Creative activities

Examples: paper work, painting, modeling, music

.55 Play with toys

Examples: dolls, games

Class sports games in 649.57

[.552–.554] With specific toys

Numbers discontinued; class in 649.55

.57 Exercise, gymnastics, sports

.58 Reading and related activities

Examples: storytelling, reading aloud to children, supervision of children's reading, listening

Including home teaching of reading

.6 **Training**

Class religious training in 291.44, Christian religious training in 248.845

For moral and character training, see 649.7

.62 Toilet training

.63 Training in grooming and self-reliance

Examples: bathing, dressing, feeding self

.64 Behavior modification, discipline, obedience

Use of this number for comprehensive works on behavior training discontinued; class in 649.6

Class a specific application with the application, e.g., behavior modification in dressing habits 649.63

.65 Sex education

.68 Home-based education

Contains developing learning ability, developing readiness for school, teaching of school subjects

Including techniques of study for parents [*formerly* 371.302813], works for parents on specific elementary school subjects [*formerly* in 372.3–372.8 with use of notation 0442 from table at 372.3–372.8]

For home teaching of reading, see 649.58

.7   **Moral and character training**

Religious training of children in the home relocated to 291.44, Christian religious training of children in the home to 248.845

.8   **Home care of sick and infirm**

650   Management and auxiliary services

This division is concerned with the art and science of conducting organized enterprises and with auxiliary skills and operations. The auxiliary skills and operations consist chiefly of communication and record keeping fundamental to management

Class here business

See Manual at 158.7 vs. 650; 650 vs. 330

SUMMARY

650.01–.09	**Standard subdivisions**
.1	**Personal success in business**
651	**Office services**
652	**Processes of written communication**
653	**Shorthand**
657	**Accounting**
658	**General management**
659	**Advertising and public relations**

.01   Philosophy and theory

.015 13   Business arithmetic [*formerly* 513.93]

.02–.09   Standard subdivisions

.1   **Personal success in business**

Including personal efficiency (management of own time and work)

Class here interdisciplinary works on success in business and other public situations

Class interdisciplinary works on success in general, on management of personal and family living in 646.7, success as an executive in 658.409

.12   Financial success

.13   Personal improvement and success in business relationships

.14   Success in obtaining jobs and promotions

>   **651–657 Auxiliary services**

Class comprehensive works in 650, advertising and public relations in 659

651   Office services

Class here problems of security and confidentiality

For processes of written communication, see 652; accounting, 657

SUMMARY

651.028	**Auxiliary techniques and procedures; materials**
.2	**Equipment and supplies**
.3	**Office management**
.5	**Records management**
.7	**Communication Creation and transmission of records**
.8	**Data processing Computer applications**
.9	**Office services in specific kinds of enterprises**

.028   Auxiliary techniques and procedures; materials

Class apparatus and equipment in 651.2

[.028 5]   Data processing   Computer applications

Do not use; class in 651.8

.2   Equipment and supplies

Description, use, maintenance

Use 651.2001–651.2009 for standard subdivisions

Class procurement of office equipment and supplies in 658.72

.202   Maintenance of equipment

.23   Furniture

.26   Processing equipment

Class a specific type of equipment with its use, e.g., typewriters 652.3

.29   Supplies and forms

.3   Office management

General aspects: planning, organizing, directing, controlling office services

Including role and function of administrative personnel

.306 83   Management of office personnel [*formerly* 658.3044]

.37   Clerical activities

Class written communication in 652, accounting in 657

.374   Secretarial and related activities

.374 1   Secretarial activities

Activities of secretaries, stenographers, typists

.374 3   Related activities

Examples: work of filers, messengers, receptionists, switchboard operators

Class work of stenographers, typists in 651.3741

.5		**Records management**

Class creation and transmission of records in 651.7

.504   Special topics

.504 2   Records management in specific types of enterprises

.504 26   In technical enterprises

.504 261   Medical

.51   Retention, maintenance, final disposition of records

.53   Filing systems and procedures

For storage, see 651.54–651.59

\>   651.54–651.59 Storage

General aspects: space, equipment, control, protection, preservation

Class comprehensive works in 651.53

.54   Storage of original documents

Examples: storage in filing cabinets, visible and rotary files

For storage of inactive files, see 651.56

.56   Storage of inactive files

Original documents in permanent (dead) storage

.58   Microreproduction of files

Active and inactive

.59   Computerization of files

.7   **Communication**   **Creation and transmission of records**

Class interdisciplinary works on communication in 302.2, managerial communication in 658.45

See Manual at 651.7 vs. 808.06665, 658.45

.73   Oral communication

Including use of telephone

.74   Written communication

Including dictating and use of dictating equipment

Use 651.74001–651.74009 for standard subdivisions

For specific types of written communication, see 651.75–651.78; processes of written communication, 652

[.740 2]   Style manuals

Relocated to 808.06665

>   651.75–651.78 Specific types of written communication

         Class comprehensive works in 651.74

.75   Correspondence

         Including layout of letters

         Style of business letters relocated to 808.066651

.752   Form letters and their use

.755   Memorandums

.759   Mail handling

         Including equipment, e.g., mail openers and sealers, postage meters, addressing machines

.77   Minutes

.78   Reports

.79   Internal communication

         Examples: electronic mail, intercom systems, messenger services, paging systems, pneumatic and mechanical conveyor systems

         Class oral internal communication in 651.73, internal written communication in 651.74

.8   **Data processing   Computer applications**

         Use in carrying out office functions

         Unless it is redundant, add to base number 651.8 the numbers following 00 in 004–006, e.g., use of digital microcomputers 651.8416, but use of digital computers 651.8 (*not* 651.84)

         Class interdisciplinary works on data processing in 004; computer applications for a specific office activity with the activity, e.g., computerization of files 651.59, word processing 652.5

.9   **Office services in specific kinds of enterprises**

         Add to base number 651.9 notation 001–999, e.g., office services in libraries 651.902

         Class specific elements of office services in specific kinds of enterprises in 651.2–651.8

652   Processes of written communication

         For shorthand, see 653

.1   **Penmanship**

         See also 745.61 for calligraphy

.3   **Typing**

Including description and maintenance of typewriters

Use 652.3001–652.3009 for standard subdivisions

.302   Specific levels of skill

Class speed and accuracy tests and drills in 652.307

.302 4   Basic (Beginning) level

.302 5   Intermediate level

.302 6   Advanced level

.307   Speed and accuracy

Class here tests, drills

.32   Typing for specific purposes

Other than general commercial and professional typing

.325   For personal use

.326   For specific kinds of enterprises

Examples: legal, medical, technical typing

.4   **Duplication of records and duplicating methods**

Office use of stencil, xerography, other methods

Class interdisciplinary works on photoduplication in 686.4

.5   **Word processing**

Unless it is redundant, add to base number 652.5 the numbers following 00 in 004–006, e.g., the use of digital microcomputers 652.5416, but the use of digital computers 652.5 (*not* 652.54)

.8   **Cryptography**

Class here interdisciplinary works on cryptography [*formerly* 001.5436]

Class cryptographic techniques used for security in computer systems in 005.82

653   Shorthand

.1   **Basic shorthand practice**

Class basic practice in a specific system with the system, e.g., Gregg shorthand transcription 653.4270424

[.13]   General principles

Number discontinued; class in 653.1

.14   Taking dictation, and transcription

.15   Speed and accuracy

Class speed and accuracy in transcription in 653.14

.18   Specific uses

Examples: court reporting, medical, personal

>   **653.2–653.4 Systems**

Class comprehensive works in 653

.2   **Abbreviated longhand systems**

Systems using conventional letters

.3   **Machine systems**

Add to base number 653.3 the numbers following 653.1 in 653.14–653.18, e.g., specific uses 653.38

.4   **Handwritten systems**

For abbreviated longhand systems, see 653.2

.41   Multilingual

.42   English-language

.421   Early forms

Systems devised before 1837

.422   Essentially nonphonetic systems

Class early nonphonetic systems in 653.421

>   653.423–653.428 Essentially phonetic systems

Class comprehensive works in 653.42, early phonetic systems in 653.421

.423   Geometric disjoined vowel systems

For Pitman systems, see 653.424

.424   Pitman systems

.424 04   Special topics

.424 042   Basic shorthand practice

Add to base number 653.424042 the numbers following 653.1 in 653.14–653.18, e.g., speed and accuracy 653.4240425

.424 2   Isaac Pitman

.424 3   Benn Pitman

.424 4   Graham

.424 5   Munson

.425   Geometric joined vowel systems

Examples: Dewey (1922), Lindsley, Pernin, Sloan

.426	Semigeometric, script-geometric, semiscript systems

Example: Malone

For Gregg systems, see 653.427

.427	Gregg systems
.427 04	Special topics
.427 042	Basic shorthand practice

Add to base number 653.427042 the numbers following 653.1 in 653.14–653.18, e.g., transcription 653.4270424

.427 2	Conventional systems
.427 3	Simplified systems
.428	Script systems

Example: Dewey (1936)

.43–.49	Systems used in other languages

Add to base number 653.4 notation 3–9 from Table 6, e.g., French-language systems 653.441

[654]   [Unassigned]

Most recently used in Edition 14

[655]   [Unassigned]

Most recently used in Edition 17

[656]   [Unassigned]

Most recently used in Edition 14

657   Accounting

See Manual at 657 vs. 658.1511, 658.1512

SUMMARY

657.04	Levels of accounting
.1	Constructive accounting
.2	Recording (Bookkeeping)
.3	Financial reporting (Financial statements)
.4	Specific fields of accounting
.6	Specific kinds of accounting
.7	Accounting for specific phases of business activity
.8	Accounting for enterprises engaged in specific kinds of activities
.9	Accounting for specific kinds of organizations

.04	Levels of accounting
.042	Elementary level
.044	Intermediate level

Including college-level accounting

.046   Advanced level

>   **657.1–657.9 Elements of accounting**

Unless other instructions are given, observe the following table of precedence, e.g., accounting for cost of inventory in a corporation engaged in manufacturing 657.867072 (*not* 657.42, 657.72, 657.95)

Accounting for enterprises engaged in specific kinds of activities	657.8
Financial reporting (Financial statements)	657.3
Accounting for specific phases of business activity	657.7
Constructive accounting	657.1
Recording (Bookkeeping)	657.2
Specific fields of accounting	657.4
Accounting for specific kinds of organizations	657.9
Specific kinds of accounting	657.6

Class comprehensive works in 657

.1   **Constructive accounting**

Development of accounting systems to fit the needs of individual organizations

.2   **Recording (Bookkeeping)**

Including secretarial bookkeeping and accounting

Class elementary accounting in 657.042

.3   **Financial reporting (Financial statements)**

Class here consolidated statements

.32   Preparing financial statements

[.33]   Understanding and analyzing financial statements

Number discontinued; class in 657.3

.4   **Specific fields of accounting**

For constructive accounting, see 657.1; bookkeeping, 657.2

.42   Cost accounting

.45   Auditing

.450 285   Data processing   Computer applications

Use in auditing

Class auditing of computer-processed accounts in 657.453

.452   Audit reports and reporting

.453   Auditing of computer-processed accounts

Including program auditing

.458   Internal (Management) auditing

.46	Tax accounting

Example: accounting for social security taxes

.47	Fiduciary accounting

Accounting for receiverships, estates, trusts

.48	Analytical (Financial) accounting

Examples: measurement of flow of funds, of profitability, of financial strength, of income, of liquidity; accounting for inflation

.6	**Specific kinds of accounting**
.61	Public accounting
.63	Private accounting
.7	**Accounting for specific phases of business activity**
.72	Current assets

Examples: accounts receivable, cash, inventory

.73	Fixed assets

Including depreciation, retirement, valuation and revaluation of land, buildings, equipment; insurance

.74	Current liabilities

Examples: accounts payable, notes payable, payroll

For tax accounting, see 657.46

.75	Fixed liabilities

Examples: bonds payable, leases, mortgages, pension plans, purchase contracts

.76	Capital accounting

Accounting for ownership equity

Including accounting for stock and dividends

For measurement of profitability, of income, see 657.48

.8	**Accounting for enterprises engaged in specific kinds of activities**

Aside from additions, changes, deletions, exceptions shown under specific entries, add to notation for each term identified by * as follows:
001–009   Standard subdivisions
01–07   Specific aspects of accounting
        Add to 0 the numbers following 657 in 657.1–657.7, e.g., cost accounting 042

.83	Service and professional activities
.832	Social services

Including churches, prisons

.832 2	*Hospitals

*Add as instructed under 657.8

.832 7	*Educational institutions
.833	Finance and real estate
.833 3	*Finance

For insurance, see 657.836

.833 5	*Real estate
.834	Professions
.835	*Government

Central and local governments and authorities

Class accounting for government corporations (except municipalities) in 657.95, accounting for specific government services other than military in 657.832–657.834, 657.836–657.839

.835 045   Government auditing

Class here manuals of government audit procedure [*formerly also* 351.72320202]

.836	*Insurance
.837	*Hotels and restaurants
.838	*Public utilities
.839	*Wholesale and retail trade
.84	Communications and entertainment media

Examples: newspapers, periodicals, publishing houses, television and radio networks and stations, theaters, motion-picture producers and theaters, sports

.86	Other activities
.861	*Labor unions
.862	*Mining
.863	*Agriculture
.867	*Manufacturing

Including printing

.869	*Construction
.9	**Accounting for specific kinds of organizations**
.904	Special topics
.904 2	Small business
.91	Individual proprietorships
.92	Partnerships

*Add as instructed under 657.8

.95	Corporations
.96	Combinations and mergers

> Class here accounting for multinational organizations

.97	Cooperatives
.98	Nonprofit organizations
.99	Branches

> Including agencies

658　　General management *including general management of professions & industry; mistakes, successes etc*

not to be confused with 658.5 - production management.

The science and art of conducting organized enterprises, projects, activities

Class here management of technology [*formerly also* 606.8]; management of services rendered by nonpublic organizations, whether or not for profit; management of public corporations; management of public agencies that themselves provide direct services (in contrast to public agencies that regulate, support, or control services provided by other organizations)

Class sociology of management in 302.35, management of enterprises engaged in specific fields of activity with the subject, using notation 068 from Table 1, e.g., management of commercial banks 332.12068

> *For public administration, see 350*

> *See also 306.36 for industrial sociology, 330 for economics*

> *See Manual at 350–354 vs. 658, T1—068; 658 and T1—068; 658, T1—068 vs. 302.35*

Specific principles of management are classed in 658.401–658.403

658.0082 women in management

SUMMARY　　*of business in USA 658.00973*

658.001–.009	**Standard subdivisions**
.02–.05	**[Management of enterprises of specific sizes, scopes, forms; data processing]**
.1	**Organization and finance**
.2	**Plant management**
.3	**Personnel management**
.4	**Executive management**
.5	**Management of production**
.7	**Management of materials**
.8	**Management of distribution (Marketing)**

.001	Philosophy and theory

managerial economics

> Including theory of organizations, principles derived from economics and other social and behavioral sciences

[.001 1]	Systems

> Do not use; class systems theory and analysis in 658.4032, operations research in 658.4034, models and simulation in 658.40352

.002	Miscellany
.0023	*Management as a career, career profiles & development*

[.002 85]	Data processing	Computer applications

Do not use; class in 658.05

.003–.009   Standard subdivisions *658.00952 Japanese man. methods wherever the location of the firm*

.02   Management of enterprises of specific sizes and scopes

Class management of enterprises of specific forms regardless of size or scope in 658.04

See Manual at 658 and T1—068

.022   Small enterprises

.022 08   History and description with respect to kinds of persons

Class here minority enterprises

.023   Big enterprises

.04   Management of enterprises of specific forms

Class initiation of specific forms of ownership organization in 658.114

See Manual at 658 and T1—068; 658.402 vs. 658.04, 658.114

>   658.041–658.046 Profit organizations

Class comprehensive works in 658, international profit organizations in 658.049

.041   Individual proprietorships

Including home-based, part-time, retirement enterprises

Class management by entrepreneurs in 658.421

.042   Partnerships

General and limited

.044   Unincorporated enterprises

Examples: joint stock companies, joint ventures

For partnerships, see 658.042; individual proprietorships, 658.041

.045   Corporations

Conversion of closely held corporations to corporations whose stocks are publicly traded (''going public'') relocated to 658.15224

Class combinations in 658.046

.046   Combinations

Examples: conglomerates, holding companies, interlocking directorates, subsidiaries, trusts

Class mergers in 658.16

.047   Cooperative organizations

.048   Nonprofit organizations *voluntary organisations*

Class international nonprofit organizations in 658.049

See also 658.047 for cooperative organizations

.049   International enterprises

Class organization of international enterprises and activities in 658.18

.05   Data processing   Computer applications

Class here use of data processing in managerial operations

Unless it is redundant, add to base number 658.05 the numbers following 00 in 004–006, e.g., use of digital microcomputers 658.05416, but use of digital computers 658.05 (*not* 658.054); however, class data security in 658.478

Class use of data processing in clerical operations in 651.8

See also 658.4032 for systems analysis in decision making

.1   **Organization and finance** *Theory of organisation (for management*

For internal organization, see 658.402 *purposes) = 658.001*

SUMMARY

658.11	**Initiation of business enterprises**
.12	**Legal administration**
.15	**Financial management**
.16	**Reorganization**
.18	**Organization of international enterprises and activities**

.11   Initiation of business enterprises

Including location   *business start up*

Class capitalization in 658.152; mergers, consolidations, acquisitions, take-overs, reorganization of ownership structure in 658.16

See Manual at 338.09 vs. 338.6042, 332.67309, 346.07, 658.11, 658.21, T1—068

.114   Forms of ownership organization *(partnership, sole trader etc)*

(management buy-outs = 658.16)

Class management of specific forms of ownership organization in 658.04

Add to base number 658.114 the numbers following 658.04 in 658.041–658.049, e.g., initiation of international enterprises 658.1149

See Manual at 658.402 vs. 658.04, 658.114

.12   Legal administration

Management of business to insure compliance with law

Including use of legal counsel

.15   Financial management [*managerial economics = 658.001*]

Procurement and use of funds to establish and operate enterprises

Class here financial decision making, financial planning, *financial analysis*

See Manual at 332 vs. 338, 658.15; 658.15 and T1—0681

SUMMARY

658.151	**Financial control**	
.152	**Management of financial operations**	
.153	**Taxes, insurance, charitable donations**	
.154	**Budgeting**	
.155	**Management of income and expense**	
.159	**Financial administration in enterprises of specific scopes and types**	

.151   Financial control

Procurement and use of financial information to evaluate performance of organizations and their specific activities and to suggest remedial measures

For budgeting, see 658.154; management of income and expense, 658.155

.151 1   Management accounting

Design and use of accounting procedures to provide internal reports needed for day-to-day management / *decision making*

Class accounting in 657, management audits in 658.4

See Manual at 657 vs. 658.1511, 658.1512

.151 2   Use of reports   *financial statements*   (*be aware of 657.3*)

Examples: balance sheets, income and expense statements, manufacturing cost statements, profit and loss statements

Class here financial reports made to directors, stockholders, top management

See Manual at 657 vs. 658.1511, 658.1512

.152   Management of financial operations (*restricted to activities below*)

[*capital budgeting = .154*]

Class here management of investment, comprehensive works on capital and its management

Class wage and salary administration in 658.32, customer credit management in 658.88

For budgeting, see 658.154; management of income and expense, 658.155

>   658.152 2–658.152 4 Capital and its management

Class comprehensive works in 658.152, capital budgets in 658.154

.152 2   Procurement of capital   *Capital formation*

Class here costs and valuation of capital

Class procurement of specific kinds of capital in 658.1524

.152 24   External sources

Examples: issue and sale of stocks and bonds; loans; gifts, grants

Including conversion of closely held corporations to corporations whose stocks are publicly traded (''going public'') [*formerly* 658.045]

Class debt management in 658.1526

.152 26   Internal sources

Examples: reserves, savings, proceeds of current operations

.152 4   Procurement and management of specific kinds of capital

.152 42   Long-term (Fixed) capital

Examples: land, buildings, heavy equipment; stocks and bonds of other companies, long-term loans receivable

Including leasing

See also 658.72 for procurement of office equipment

.152 44   Short-term (Working) capital

Examples: accounts receivable, cash, inventory, 30–90 day loans receivable

.152 6   Debt management *(the firm's own debt; creditman.—what other people owe = 658.88)*

Examples: accounts payable, bonds outstanding, notes payable

.153   Taxes, insurance, charitable donations

Class here ways that management can deal with taxes, what insurance is needed for the organization

Class interdisciplinary works on and economic aspects of business taxes in 336.207, on charitable donations in 361.765, on insurance in 368; legal aspects of business taxes in 343.068

.154   Budgeting

Including capital budgets, budgeting for specific objectives

.155   Management of income and expense   *risk management*

Including distribution of profit, dividend policy

Class here management of profit and loss, comprehensive works on risk management

Class use of income and expense statements in 658.1512, health and safety programs in 658.382, business security in 658.47, determination of prices in 658.816

For taxes, insurance, charitable donations, see 658.153

.155 2   Cost analysis and control

Class cost accounting in 657.42, managerial accounting in 658.1511, analysis and control of specific kinds of costs in 658.1553, cost-benefit analysis, cost-volume-profit analysis in 658.1554

.155 3   Kinds of costs

Examples: fixed and overhead costs; variable costs; labor, material costs

For costs of capital, see 658.1522

.155 4   Income (Revenue)

Return on investment, income from operations

Including break-even analysis, cost-benefit analysis, *cost effectiveness* cost-volume-profit analysis, profit and its promotion

.159   Financial administration in enterprises of specific types and scopes

Class specific aspects of financial administration in enterprises of specific types and scopes in 658.151–658.155, e.g., budgeting management in small business 658.154

.159 2   Small business

.159 208   History and description with respect to kinds of persons

Class here minority enterprises

.159 9   Foreign (International) enterprises

.16   Reorganization *management buy - outs*

Examples: acquisitions, consolidations, divestment, mergers, sale, take-overs

.18   Organization of international enterprises and activities

[man. of multinationals = .049] Including foreign licensing *cross cultural management*

Class initiation of international enterprises and activities in 658.1149

.2   Plant management

Management of buildings, equipment, facilities, grounds

Class here comprehensive works on energy management

Use 658.2001–658.2009 for standard subdivisions

Class procurement of plants (land, buildings, equipment) in 658.15242; specific aspects of energy management with the aspect, e.g., energy management to promote efficiency in production 658.515

See Manual at 647.96–647.99 vs. 658.2, T1—0682; 658.2 and T1—0682

.202   Maintenance

.21   Location

Including warehouse location

Class location of businesses in 658.11

See Manual at 338.09 vs. 338.6042, 332.67309, 346.07, 658.11, 658.21, T1—068

.23   Layout

.24   Lighting

.25   Heating, ventilating, air conditioning

.26   Utilities

Examples: electricity, gas, power and power distribution, water

Class lighting in 658.24; heating, ventilating, air conditioning in 658.25

.27   Equipment

Class office equipment in 651.2

For utilities, see 658.26; equipment for safety and comfort, 658.28

.28   Equipment for safety and comfort

Example: equipment for sanitation

Including equipment for noise control

.3   Personnel management

Procedures for hiring, developing, utilizing the capacities of employees

Use 658.3001−658.3009 for standard subdivisions

Class industrial relations in 331

For management of executive personnel, see 658.407

See Manual at 658.3 and T1—0683; 658.3 vs. 331

SUMMARY

658.301−.306	**[General topics]**
.31	**Elements of personnel management**
.32	**Wage and salary administration**
.38	**Personnel health, safety, welfare**

.301   Personnel planning and policy

Including information and decision making

Class here manpower planning

.302   Supervision

By immediate supervisors

Class employee development in 658.3124, development of supervisors in 658.407124

.303   Personnel management in enterprises of specific sizes

.304   Management of specific kinds of personnel

mentoring

Observe the following table of precedence, e.g., handicapped Black women professional personnel 658.3044 (*not* 658.3045, 658.3041, or 658.3042)

Occupying specific types of positions	658.3044
Exhibiting specific personal characteristics	658.3045
Belonging to nondominant racial, ethnic, national groups	658.3041
Of specific ages and sexes	658.3042

.304 1   Belonging to nondominant racial, ethnic, national groups

Class selection and hiring of minority employees in 658.3112

.304 2   Of specific ages and sexes

.304 4   Occupying specific types of positions (*salesmen* = ·81)

Examples: blue-collar and professional employees

Management of office personnel relocated to 651.30683

.304 5   Exhibiting specific personal characteristics

Examples: handicapped personnel, high-talent personnel, problem employees

.306   Job analysis and description [*evaluation* = ·3222]

[*design/redesign* = ·31423] Including position classification; specifications of personal, educational, physical, mental qualifications required of personnel in each position; restrictions on what qualifications can be required of personnel

.31   Elements of personnel management

SUMMARY

658.311	**Recruitment and selection of personnel**
.312	**Conditions of work and utilization of personnel**
.313	**Separation from service**
.314	**Motivation, morale, discipline**
.315	**Employer-employee relationships**

.311   Recruitment and selection of personnel

.311 1   Recruitment

.311 2   Selection *identifying competency (at selection stage)*

Including checklists and inventories, computerized matching, handwriting analysis, security clearance, personal and background investigations, use of polygraph (lie detector)

Class here comprehensive works on selection and placement

Use of this number for comprehensive works on selection and recruitment discontinued; class in 658.311

See also 658.3128 for placement, 658.383 for payment of moving expenses

.311 24   Interviewing *[interview techniques for candidates = 650.14]*

.311 25   Testing

Including aptitude testing

[.311 29]   In enterprises engaged in specific types of activity and for specific jobs

Selection of personnel in enterprises engaged in specific types of activity and for specific jobs relocated to the activity or job with use of notation 0683 from Table 1, e.g., selection of personnel in mining enterprises 622.0683

.312   Conditions of work and utilization of personnel

>   658.312 1–658.312 4 Conditions of work

Class comprehensive works in 658.312

For wage and salary administration, see 658.32; personnel health, safety, welfare, 658.38

.312 1   Days and hours of work

Including lunch periods and breaks

.312 2   Leaves of absence

Examples: paid vacations, sick leave

Class absenteeism in 658.314

.312 4   Education and training

Class here employee development *competency development*

.312 404   Development and administration of training programs

Including programmed instruction, teaching methods, training devices, evaluation of training programs, selection and training of training personnel

.312 42   Induction and orientation

.312 43   In-house work training

For specific tasks

Including retraining, adjustment to automation

.312 44	Other kinds of training *training following redundancy*

Examples: attitude training, rehabilitation training, safety training, training in human relations

.312 45	Training of specific classes of employees

Examples: blue-collar employees, professional employees

Class induction and orientation of specific classes of employees in 658.31242, training of specific classes of employees for specific tasks in 658.31243, other kinds of training regardless of class of employee in 658.31244, training of supervisors in 658.4071245

.312 5	Performance rating (Evaluation) *Appraisal ive. interviewing for*

Class promotion in 658.3126, demotion in 658.3127

.312 6	Promotion

Class promotion as an incentive in 658.3142

.312 7	Demotion

Class demotion as a penalty in 658.3144

.312 8	Utilization of personnel

Examples: allocation of staff to specific responsibilities, staffing patterns, work teams *(from personnel point of view. In doubt prefer .402)*

Including placement, transfer of employees from one position to another

For training, see 658.3124; motivation, 658.314

.313	Separation from service

Example: dismissal for cause

.313 2	Retirement *redundancy, outplacement*
.313 4	Layoff for retrenchment (Reduction in force)
.314	Motivation, morale, discipline *Use for productivity management*

Including absenteeism, performance surveys, prevention of misconduct, bonding of employees, turnover and its prevention

Class here promotion of creativity, efficiency, productivity

.314 2	Incentives *suggestion schemes*

Examples: promotion, recognition, status

For incentive payments, see 658.3225

.314 22	Job satisfaction

Class job enrichment in 658.31423

.314 23	Job enrichment *see 331.25 for objective assessments of job enrichment*

design and redesign

.314 4   Penalties

         Examples: demotion, fines, reprimands

         For dismissal for cause, see 658.313

         See also 658.3127 for demotion when not a penalty

.314 5   Interpersonal relations

         Promotion of effective working relationships between individuals and groups

         Including informal, day-to-day relations between superiors and subordinates

.315   Employer-employee relationships *industrial relations management; employee attitude surveys*

         Class informal relations in 658.3145

.315 1   Industrial relations counseling

         See also 658.385 for counseling of employees

.315 2   Employee representation in management (Participatory management)

         Including worker self-management *class objective studies of worker representation in 331.0112*

         Class industrial democracy in 331.0112

         See also 338.6 for worker control of industry

.315 3   Labor unions and other employee organizations

         Class role of employee organizations in grievances and appeals in 658.3155

         For collective bargaining, see 658.3154

.315 4   Collective bargaining

         Including arbitration, mediation, negotiation of contracts, strikes

.315 5   Grievances and appeals

.32   Wage and salary administration

         Class management of labor costs in 658.1553

.321   Payroll administration

         Class clerical techniques involved in maintaining payroll records in 651.37, payroll accounting procedures in 657.74

.322   Compensation plans

.322 2   Wage and salary scales

         Hourly or other periodic

         Including longevity, overtime, severance pay, *job evaluation*

.322 5 　　　　　　Incentive payments

　　　　　　　　　Examples: bonuses, piecework rates, profit sharing, stock ownership plans *, performance related pay*

　　　　　　　　　Class comprehensive works on incentives in 658.3142

　　　　　　　　　　For merit awards, see 658.3226

.322 6 　　　　　　Merit awards

.325 　　　　　　Employee benefits

.325 3 　　　　　　Pensions

.325 4 　　　　　　Insurance, workers' (workmens') compensation

　　　　　　　　　Class here other benefits not provided for elsewhere

.38 　　　　　Personnel health, safety, welfare

.382 　　　　　Health and safety programs

　　　　　　　　　Programs by management to enhance the well-being and safety of employees, to provide emergency and other forms of medical care

　　　　　　　　　Example: mental health programs

　　　　　　　　　Class here employee assistance programs

　　　　　　　　　Class interdisciplinary works on industrial safety in 363.11, comprehensive works on safety management in 658.408, safety of plant and equipment in 658.200289, safety training in 658.31244, provision of health and accident insurance in 658.3254

.382 2 　　　　　　Programs for drug abuse and alcoholism

.383 　　　　　Economic services

　　　　　　　　　Examples: discounts, food services, housing, moving expenses, transportation

.385 　　　　　Counseling services *counselling of employees*

　　　　　　　　　Class mental health programs and services in 658.382

.4 　　　Executive management *Class here negotiating skills in general →*

　　　　　　　　　Limited to those activities named below

　　　　　　　　　Class here role, function, powers, position of top and middle management; comprehensive works on the activities named below

　　　　　　　　　Class a specific executive managerial activity not provided for here with the activity in management, e.g., personnel management 658.3; application of a specific activity named below in another branch of management with the branch, e.g., production planning 658.503 *& more specific might be:*

　　　　　　　　　See Manual at 658.42 and 658.43 *.8101, .3154, .1553*

SUMMARY

658.400 1–.400 9	**Standard subdivisions**
.401–.409	**Specific executive management activities**
.42	**Top management**
.43	**Middle management**
.45	**Communication**
.46	**Use of consultants**
.47	**Business intelligence and security**

.400 1–.400 9   Standard subdivisions

SUMMARY

658.401	**Planning, policy making, control**
.402	**Internal organization**
.403	**Decision making and information management**
.404	**Project management**
.406	**Managing change**
.407	**Management of executive personnel**
.408	**Social responsibility of executive management**
.409	**Personal aspects of executive management**

> 658.401–658.409 Specific executive management activities

Unless other instructions are given, observe the following table of precedence, e.g., planning for change 658.406 (*not* 658.4012)

Personal aspects of executive management	658.409
Management of executive personnel	658.407
Internal organization	658.402
Managing change	658.406
Planning, policy making, control	658.401
Decision making and information management	658.403
Social responsibility of executive management	658.408
Project management	658.404

Class comprehensive works in 658.4, communication in 658.45, use of consultants in 658.46, business intelligence and security in 658.47

.401   Planning, policy making, control

.401 2   Planning and policy making

Formulation of objectives, goals, courses of action

Class here management by objectives, strategic management

Class decision making in 658.403, forecasting in 658.40355

.401 3   Control

Formulation of standards, evaluation of conformity of performance to standards, formulation of remedial measures

.402	Internal organization *team building* *(Management teams—658.4095)*
delegation	Examples: line, line and staff, functional; by departments
	Including decentralization, distribution and delegation of authority and responsibility
	Class sociology of executive institutions in 306.3, allocation of personnel to specific responsibilities in 658.3128

> *See also 302.3 for social interaction within groups*
>
> *See Manual at 658.402 vs. 658.04, 658.114*

.403	Decision making and information management
	Class here problem solving
	Use 658.403001–658.403009 for standard subdivisions
.403 01	Philosophy and theory of decision making
[.403 011]	Systems in decision making
	Do not use; class in 658.4032
[.403 015 1]	Mathematical techniques of decision making
	Do not use; class in 658.4033
.403 02–.403 09	Standard subdivisions of decision making
.403 2	Systems theory and analysis
	Including critical path method (CPM), network analysis, program evaluation review technique (PERT)
	Class decision theory in 658.40301, operations research in 658.4034, models (simulation) in 658.40352, decision analysis in 658.40354, forecasting and forecasts in 658.40355
.403 3	Mathematical techniques of decision making *mathematical models*
	Example: mathematical programming *quantitative techniques*
	Class here econometrics as an aid in decision making
	Class simulation in 658.40352
.403 4	Operations research
	Including probability theory, queuing theory
	Models relocated to 658.40352
	Class mathematical methods in 658.4033, simulation in 658.40352, games in 658.40353
.403 5	Other techniques of decision making
.403 52	Simulation *computer models / simulation* *[maths. models = .4033]*
	Class here models [*formerly* 658.4034]
.403 53	Games
.403 54	Decision analysis *risk analysis*

Handwritten margin notes:
delegation
658.4030285 – Decision support systems – Expert systems, knowledge-based systems

.403 55   Forecasting

.403 6   Group decision making *(M. teams in general 658.4095)*

Class specific techniques of group decision making in 658.4032–658.4035

.403 8   Information management *Info. for executive decisions*

Collection, processing, storage, retrieval of information

Class communication in 658.45   *may use for computers but prefer 658.05*

See Manual at 658.455 vs. 658.4038

.403 801 1   Information systems [*formerly* 658.40388]

[.403 88]   Information systems

Relocated to 658.4038011

.404   Project management

.406   Managing change */organisational development*

learning organisation Class here expansion, modernization, simplification, systemization

Class internal reorganization in 658.402; acquisition, merger, consolidation, take-over, divestment, sale of business organizations in 658.16; changes in a specific branch of management with the branch, e.g., changes in production 658.5

.406 2   Externally induced (Responsive) change

Examples: changes induced by social factors, technological changes

Including conversion to metric system

.406 3   Innovation by management *business process reengineering*

.407   Management of executive personnel

Add to base number 658.407 the numbers following 658.3 in 658.31–658.38, e.g., training of supervisors 658.4071245 *management training*

.408   Social responsibility of executive management

Including protection and preservation of environment

Class here comprehensive works on safety management

Class interdisciplinary works on safety in 363.1; social measures for prevention of pollution in 363.73, technology of pollution prevention in 628.5; managing welfare services for employees in 658.38, for other persons in 361.7; specific aspects of safety with the aspect, e.g., product safety 658.56

See Manual at 363.1

.409   Personal aspects of executive management

Biography 650.1 execs. and businessmen) Class here success as an executive *see also 650.1*

Class general success in business in 650.1

.409 2   Executive leadership *, assertiveness. Dealing with conflict — more specific numbers might be 658.315 or 658.4095*

.409 3	Personal efficiency
	Management by executives of their own time and work
.409 4	Personal characteristics of executives
	Examples: attitudes, life-styles, values
.409 5	The management environment *management teams*
	Examples: social pressures, work pressures, relations between executives in and out of the organization *prefer 158.7 for managerial stress*
.42	Top management

chief execs managing directors

Use of this number for comprehensive works on top and middle management discontinued; class in 658.4

Class initiation of business enterprises in 658.11, specific activities of top management with the subject, e.g., decision making by top management 658.403.

See Manual at 658.42 and 658.43

.421	Entrepreneurial management
	Class management of small business in 658.022
.422	Boards of directors and trustees
.43	Middle management
	See Manual at 658.42 and 658.43
.45	Communication *class communication in organisations in*
	As a technique of management *general in 302.2*
	Including credibility
	Class mechanics of communication in 651.7
	See Manual at 651.7 vs. 808.06665, 658.45
.452	Oral communication
	See also 808.51 for techniques of public speaking
.453	Written communication
.455	Informational programs *team/staff briefings*
	Examples: bulletin boards, house organs
	See Manual at 658.455 vs. 658.4038
.456	Conduct of meetings
	Class rules of order in 060.42
[.456 2]	Congresses and conferences
	Relocated to 060.68

[.456 3]   Meetings

               Number discontinued; class in 658.456

.46   Use of consultants

         Class here techniques of doing management consulting

         Class use of consultants in a specific branch of management with the branch, e.g., use of consultants in marketing research 658.83

.47   Business intelligence and security

         Class insurance in 658.153

.472   Security of information and ideas

         Including industrial espionage, security of trade secrets

         Class security of information stored in computers in 658.478

.473   Physical security

         Protection from theft by employees and others, from fraud, from terrorism, from other forms of crime

         Class physical security of computers in 658.478

         For protection against fires and other disasters, see 658.477

.477   Protection against fires and other disasters

.478   Computer security

.5   **Management of production** *[handwritten: industrial management when confined to activities below]*

         Planning, organizing, directing, controlling the specific functional activities of the organization *[handwritten: for productivity management see 658.314]*

[handwritten left margin: Class here operations management, product management, product policy, management services]

         Class here production management in manufacturing enterprises, comprehensive works on logistics

         Use 658.5001–658.5009 for standard subdivisions

         Management of production in construction enterprises relocated to 624.0685

         Class comprehensive works on energy management in 658.2, internal transportation (materials handling) in 658.781, physical distribution in 658.788, marketing in 658.8, factory operations engineering in 670.42; production management in enterprises engaged in a specific kind of activity other than manufacturing with the activity, using notation 0685 from Table 1, e.g., management of agricultural production 630.685

         See Manual at 658.5 and T1—0685

SUMMARY

658.503	**General production planning**
.51	**Organization of production**
.53	**Sequencing**
.54	**Work, fatigue, monotony studies**
.56	**Product control and packaging**
.57	**Research and development (R and D)**

*[handwritten bottom: * class here product management even when this is about largely about marketing (to avoid confusion decision making) but add a 950 - 658.8]*

.503	General production planning
.503 6	Decision making and use of information
.503 8	Product planning

Determination of line of products or services, quantity to be produced

Including diversification

Class development of new products in 658.575, marketing in 658.8

.51	Organization of production

For sequencing, see 658.53; work, fatigue, monotony studies, 658.54

.514	Use of technology

Including automation, man-machine ratios, modernization

Class development of technology in 658.577

.515	Promotion of efficiency *O ∝ M*

For use of technology, see 658.514

.53	Sequencing

Including dispatching, routing, scheduling

.533	Kinds of sequences

Examples: assembly-line, continuous, mixed, single-piece sequences

.54	Work, fatigue, monotony studies

Including work load

.542	Work studies

For fatigue and monotony studies, see 658.544

.542 1	Time studies
.542 3	Motion studies
.544	Fatigue and monotony studies
.56	Product control and packaging

Including product liability, recall, safety

Class comprehensive works on safety management in 658.408, product planning in 658.5038, design of products in 658.575

.562	Quality control

Control of products to ensure conformity to standards and specifications

For inspection, see 658.568

.562 015 195	Statistical methods [*formerly also* 658.568]

.564   Packaging

Including labeling

Class here interdisciplinary works on packaging

Class storage containers in 658.785, packing for shipment in 658.7884, use of packaging in sales promotion in 658.823; packaging technology in 688.8

.566   Product analysis

Determination of materials, parts, subassemblies needed; how much of each to make or buy

.567   Waste control and utilization

.568   Inspection

Comprehensive works on statistical methods of quality control relocated to 658.562015195

.57   Research and development (R and D)

.571   Fundamental research

.575   New product development *brand development = .827*

Class here comprehensive works on product development

Class decisions to develop new products in 658.5038, market research on new products in 658.83

For product improvement research, see 658.576

.575 2   Product design

Including generation of product ideas

.576   Product improvement research

.577   Equipment and process research

.7   **Management of materials**

Class here management of supplies

Class management of office supplies in 651.29; comprehensive works on energy management in 658.2, on logistics in 658.5

See Manual at 658.7 and T1—0687

.72   Procurement

Acquisition of equipment, materials, parts, subassemblies, supplies, tools

Class here procurement of office equipment and supplies, comprehensive works on procurement

Comprehensive works on evaluation of commodities to be purchased relocated to 381.33

Class procurement of land, buildings, heavy equipment in 658.15242, management of costs of materials in 658.1553

.722	Vendor selection
.723	Contracts and their negotiation
.728	Receiving

Documenting, handling, inspecting incoming items

Including expediting, tracing

.78 Internal control of materials and physical distribution

.781 Internal transportation (Materials handling)

Transportation of materials and parts within plant from one work station to another

.785 Storage (Warehouse management)

Including storage containers

Class location of warehouses in 658.21

.787 Inventory control (Stock control)

Class financial control of inventories in 658.15244

For receiving, see 658.728; storage, 658.785

.788 Physical distribution

Class here shipment

Class internal movement of materials in 658.781

.788 2 Traffic management

Selection of carrier and routing

.788 4 Packing for shipment

Class interdisciplinary works on packaging in 658.564

.788 5 Loading and unloading

.788 6 Expediting and tracing

.8   Management of distribution (Marketing) *marketing strategy ∅*

Goods and services

Class financial aspects of marketing management in 658.15, comprehensive works on logistics in 658.5

For physical distribution, see 658.788; advertising, 659.1

See Manual at 380.1 vs. 658.8; 658.8 and T1—0688; 658.8, T1—0688 vs. 659

(handwritten margin notes) class promotion in 659 (see manual 658.8 vs 659) - when promotion just means publicity

(handwritten bottom notes) ∅ usually here. If confined strictly to planning, decision making etc class in ·80 In doubt, prefer ·8.
* put most 'marketing audits' of the general type in 658·802

SUMMARY

658.800 1–.800 9		**Standard subdivisions**
	.802–.804	**[General topics of marketing management; marketing to specific kinds of buyers]**
	.81	**Sales management**
	.82	**Sales promotion**
	.83	**Market research and analysis**
	.84	**Channels of distribution**
	.85	**Personal selling (Salesmanship)**
	.86	**Marketing through wholesale channels**
	.87	**Marketing through retail channels**
	.88	**Credit management**

.800 1   Philosophy and theory *ethics, social aspects, marketing environment*

[.800 11]   Systems

> Do not use; class in 658.802

.800 2–.800 9   Standard subdivisions *of U.S. marketing 658.800973*

marketing plans
marketing audits (non-professional)

.802   General topics of marketing management *+ (see below)*

> Examples: control, decision making, information, organizing, planning, systems analysis

> Class application of elements of marketing management to marketing to specific kinds of buyers in 658.804

.804   Marketing to specific kinds of buyers *industrial marketing ∅*

> Examples: to governments and their agencies, to hospitals

> Class consumer research in 658.834

> *For marketing to foreign buyers, see 658.848*

[.805]   Marketing to foreign buyers

> Relocated to 658.848

[.809]   Marketing specific kinds of goods and services

> Relocated to specific subject with use of notation 0688 from Table 1, e.g., marketing automobiles 629.2220688

.81   Sales management *[selling techniques = 658.85]*

> ~~Class management of sales personnel in 658.3044~~ *No, class here*

> *For sales promotion, see 658.82*

.810 01   Philosophy and theory

.810 011 2   Forecasting and forecasts

> Class sales forecasting in 658.818

.810 02–.810 09   Standard subdivisions

∅ = marketing of goods & services to other businesses / industries / organisations
✕ a general term which can be .8 or .802 according to content of book.

.810 1   Sales planning *sales contracts inc. negotiation for*

         Including use of sales records and sales analysis

         Class here formulation of goals, objectives, standards for evaluation of sales performance

         For market research, see 658.83

.810 2   Organization of sales force

         For organization by area, see 658.8103; by product, 658.8104; by class and type of customer, 658.8105

.810 3   Organization of sales force by area

.810 4   Organization of sales force by product

.810 5   Organization of sales force by class and type of customer

.810 6   Organization and conduct of sales meetings

.812   Customer relations */ care ø*

         Including claims, complaints, handling of orders, inquiries, returns, servicing of products

.816   Price determination

.818   Sales forecasting

.82   Sales promotion

         Auxiliary operations designed to reinforce and supplement advertising, direct sales efforts

         Including distribution of instruction and other booklets to consumers; gifts, prizes, samples, trading stamps *'below the line'*

         Class use of credit to promote sales in 658.88

         For servicing of products, see 658.812

.823   Use of packaging

         Class here packaging as a sales promotion device

         Class interdisciplinary works on packaging in 658.564

.827   Use of brands and trademarks *branding ✳, brand development*

         Including producer and distributor brands

✳ use with caution eg 'brand management' more likely to .8 or .802 when book is basically on marketing techniques applied to brands ø don't assume 'customer' in the title puts it here eg 'customer marketing likely to be 658.8 (all ~~customer~~ marketing must be customer marketing — for 'customer' read 'consumer')

.83   Market research and analysis *test marketing*

Class here interviewing, use of consultants and research agencies, techniques of consulting in market research and analysis

Unless other instructions are given, class complex subjects with aspects in two or more subdivisions of this schedule in the number coming first in the schedule, e.g., research in Germany on consumer preferences 658.8343 (*not* 658.83943)

Do not use for the results of market research and analysis; class in 380–382

For sales forecasting, see 658.818

.830 2   Miscellany

.830 28   Auxiliary techniques and procedures; apparatus, equipment, materials

Use of this number for interviewing discontinued; class in 658.83

[.830 9]   Historical, geographical, persons treatment

Do not use; class in 658.839

.834   Consumer research   *For trends / forecasts a projections of industries a products use 338·47*

[.834 019]   Consumer psychology

Do not use; class in 658.8342

[.834 08]   Consumer research with respect to kinds of persons

Do not use; class in 658.8348

.834 2   Consumer behavior (Consumer psychology)

.8342021 consumer statistics / results of market research

Including motivation research

For consumer attitudes, preferences, reactions, see 658.8343

.834 3   Consumer attitudes, preferences, reactions

Including brand preferences *innovation diffusion*

Standard subdivisions are added for any or all of the topics named in the heading

.834 8   Specific types of consumers

Examples: Blacks, children, low-income groups, occupational groups, women

.835   Market study

Determination of extent of demand; location, nature, identification of market; extent and nature of competition; types of sales effort needed

[.838]   Market research on specific products

Relocated to specific subject with use of notation 0688 from Table 1, e.g., market research on clothing 687.0688

use for results of market research – mixed topics. Specific commodities with the subject of cars 629·222 (do not add 0688)

.839   Historical, geographical, persons treatment

Add to base number 658.839 notation 01–9 from Table 2, e.g., market research in Germany 658.83943

.84   Channels of distribution *(Distributive trades in general — 381)*

Marketing on the Internet (950–004.67)

Including auctions, direct-mail marketing, direct marketing, direct selling, fairs, markets, multilevel marketing, pyramid marketing, telemarketing, telephone selling, television selling *database marketing*

Class personal selling through specific channels in 658.85, e.g. personal selling by telephone; marketing through wholesale channels in 658.86, through retail channels in 658.87; mail-order, telephone-order houses, television selling organizations in 658.872; direct-mail advertising in 659.133

.848   Export marketing (International trade) *global marketing*

∅ see below.

Including marketing to foreign buyers [*formerly also* 658.805]

.85   Personal selling (Salesmanship)

prospecting

Techniques for the individual, regardless of channel

Including retail salesmanship

Class comprehensive works on management of telephone selling in 658.84

.86   Marketing through wholesale channels

Including jobbers, manufacturers' outlets

Class personal selling through wholesale channels in 658.85

See also 658.8705 for manufacturers' outlets as retail channels

.87   Marketing through retail channels *Prefer 381.1 for domestic trade i.e. what is traded & in what amounts*

Including apartment, garage, yard sales; shopping centers

Use 658.87001–658.87009 for standard subdivisions

Class personal selling through retail channels in 658.85

>   658.870 1–658.870 8 Retail channels by type of ownership and control

Class comprehensive works in 658.87

.870 1   Independent retail units

Class independent consumer cooperatives in 658.8707

.870 2   Corporate retail chains

Class here comprehensive works on retail chain stores

Class chain store consumer cooperatives in 658.8707

For voluntary retail chains, see 658.8703

.870 3   Voluntary retail chains

.870 4   Sideline stores and markets

∅ class here marketing to different countries. Class in .8009 marketing as carried out within other countries — 350 USSR, china etc

.870 5	Manufacturers' outlets

See also 658.86 for manufacturers' outlets as wholesale channels

.870 6	Branch stores
.870 7	Consumer cooperatives [*formerly also* 334.5068]
.870 8	Franchise businesses

> 658.871–658.879 Retail channels by merchandising pattern

Class comprehensive works in 658.87

.871	Department stores
.872	Mail-order houses and telephone-order houses

Including television selling organizations

Standard subdivisions are added for mail-order and telephone-order houses, for mail-order houses alone

See also 659.143 for television advertising

.873	Variety stores — chain stores eg M×S, Boots etc
.874	General stores
.875	Specialty shops
.876	Single-line outlets
.878	Supermarkets
.879	Discount stores
.88	Credit management . Factoring

Including account security, collections, credit investigations

.882	Mercantile credit , trade credit
.883	Consumer (Retail) credit
[.89]	Personal selling and retail marketing of specific goods and services

Relocated to specific subject with use of notation 0688 from Table 1, e.g., personal selling of insurance 368.00688

(.9)   Management of enterprises engaged in specific fields of activity

Don't use. Class with subject eg oiling trade 687.068

(Optional number; prefer specific subject with use of notation 068 from Table 1)

(.91) Enterprises other than those engaged in extraction, manufacturing, construction

(Optional number; prefer specific subject with use of notation 068 from Table 1)

Add to base number 658.91 notation 001–999, e.g., management of banks 658.913321; however, class management of political campaigns in 324.7

(.92–.99)   Enterprises engaged in extraction, manufacturing, construction

> (Optional number; prefer specific subject with use of notation 068 from Table 1)

> Add to base number 658.9 the numbers following 6 in 620–690, e.g., management of mines 658.922

659   Advertising and public relations

Class here publicity

Case studies 659.10722 –
specific types class with the type
without 0722 eg outdoor
advertising cases 659.1342

See Manual at 658.8, T1—0688 vs. 659

SUMMARY

659.1	**Advertising**
.2	**Public relations**

.1   **Advertising**

Nonpersonal presentation and promotion of ideas, goods, services, paid for by an identified sponsor

Advertising in different countries – take USA + UK as read.

SUMMARY

659.104	**Special topics**
.11	**General topics**
.13	**Kinds**
.14	**Advertising by broadcast media**
.15	**Display advertising**
.17	**Advertising by contests and lotteries**
.19	**Advertising specific kinds of organizations, products, services**

.104   Special topics   *— Truth in advertising, ethics*

.104 2   Social aspects of advertising   *– psychology, women*

.11   General topics   *Advertising management in general*

> Class application of general topics to specific kinds of advertising in 659.13–659.17, to advertising specific kinds of organizations, products, services in 659.19

.111   Planning and control   *- Economics in broadest sense - does it pay? budgets, cost control*

> Including decision making, goals, information

.112   Organization

> Managerial organization only

> *See also 338.7616591 for economics and history of advertising organizations*   *↳ this is about the economics of advertising businesses eg saatchi*

.112 2   Advertising departments

.112 5   Advertising agencies

.113   Advertising campaigns   *– as case studies, class in 659.10722*

.1014 Advertising Language (writing ads = 659.132. In doubt, prefer .132. Writing for specific medium - class with the medium eg 659.143.

352

.13   Kinds   *class here sponsorship by business of arts, sports etc*

Including specialty and entertainment advertising

.131   General kinds

Class general kinds of advertising in specific media in 659.132–659.136

.131 2   National (General) advertising   *– government advertising*

.131 4   Retail advertising

.131 5   Advertising directed to vocational uses

Examples: farm, industrial, professional, trade

See also 659.19 for advertising specific kinds of organizations, products, services

---

\>   659.132–659.136 Advertising in specific media

Class comprehensive works in 659.13

For broadcast media, see 659.14; display advertising, 659.15; contests and lotteries, 659.17

.132   Advertising in printed media

Including directory advertising

For direct advertising, see 659.133   *Writing for specific medium, class with the medium eg TV .143*

[.132 2–.132 4]   Copywriting, art, layout, typography

Numbers discontinued; class in 659.132   *Writing in general for*

.133   Direct advertising   *all media, class here*

Printed advertising delivered or handed directly to consumer

Examples: broadsides, circulars, letters, mail-order catalogs

Including direct-mail advertising

Class direct-mail marketing in 658.84

.134   Advertising by location of media

For point-of-sale advertising, see 659.157

.134 2   Outdoor advertising

Examples: billboards, on-premise signs, painted displays, roadside signs

Class outdoor transportation advertising in 659.1344

For advertising by electric signs, see 659.136

.134 4   Transportation advertising

Examples: airplane banners, car cards, traveling displays on exteriors of vehicles, station posters

.136   Advertising by electric signs

Use of this number for nonelectric spectacular signs discontinued; class in 659.13

.14   Advertising by broadcast media

.142   Radio

.143   Television

Class television selling as a channel of distribution in 658.84, television selling organizations in 658.872

.15   Display advertising

Including demonstrations

.152   Exhibitions and shows

Examples: fashion modeling, films , *cinema advertising*

.157   Point-of-sale advertising

Examples: counter, showcase, wall, window displays

.17   Advertising by contests and lotteries

Class audience participation in contests in 790.134, in lotteries in 795

.19   Advertising specific kinds of organizations, products, services

Add to base number 659.19 notation 001–999, e.g., library advertising 659.1902

Class specific kinds of advertising regardless of kind of organization, product, service in 659.13–659.17 *case studies* 659.20722 *but specific types*

.2   **Public relations** *class with type of corporations 659.285*

Planned and sustained effort to establish and maintain mutual understanding *without 0722* between an organization and its public

Use of this number for publicity discontinued; class in 659

.28   In specific kinds of organizations

International organisations 659.289

Add to base number 659.28 the numbers following 658.04 in 658.041–658.049, e.g., corporations 659.285 *corporate identity*

Class public relations in organizations producing specific kinds of products and services regardless of kind of organization in 659.29

.29   In organizations producing specific kinds of products and services

Add to base number 659.29 notation 001–999, e.g., public welfare agencies 659.293616; however, class public relations in libraries in 021.7, in local Christian parish in 254.4

660   Chemical engineering and related technologies

Class military applications in 623

For pharmaceutical chemistry, see 615.19; pulp and paper technology, 676; elastomers and elastomer products, 678

SUMMARY

660.01–.09	**Standard subdivisions**
.2–.7	**[General topics in chemical engineering, biotechnology, industrial stoichiometry]**
661	**Technology of industrial chemicals**
662	**Technology of explosives, fuels, related products**
663	**Beverage technology**
664	**Food technology**
665	**Technology of industrial oils, fats, waxes, gases**
666	**Ceramic and allied technologies**
667	**Cleaning, color, related technologies**
668	**Technology of other organic products**
669	**Metallurgy**

.01   Philosophy and theory

.011 5   Theory of communication and control

Class process control in 660.2815

.02   Miscellany

.028   Auxiliary techniques and procedures

Class materials in 660.282, apparatus and equipment in 660.283

[.028 9]   Safety measures

Do not use; class in 660.2804

.03   Dictionaries, encyclopedias, concordances

.04   Chemical technologies of specific states of matter

Add to base number 660.04 the numbers following 530.4 in 530.41–530.44, e.g., plasma technology 660.044

Class industrial gases in 665.7

.05–.09   Standard subdivisions

.2   General topics in chemical engineering

Use of this number for comprehensive works on chemical engineering discontinued; class in 660

For biochemical engineering, see 660.63; industrial stoichiometry, 660.7

.28   Specific types of chemical plant and specific activities in chemical plants

Use of this number for comprehensive works on the chemical plant and its work discontinued; class in 660

.280 4	Safety measures
	See Manual at 660.2804 vs. 604.7
.280 7	Specific types of chemical plant
.280 71	Bench-scale plants
.280 72	Pilot plants
.280 73	Full-scale plants

>   660.281–660.283 Process and materials

Class comprehensive works in 660.28; specific applications in unit operations in 660.2842, in unit processes in 660.2844

.281	Process design, assembly, control
.281 2	Process design
.281 5	Process control Computerized process control

Unless it is redundant, add to base number 660.2815 the numbers following 00 in 004–006, e.g., use of digital microcomputers 660.2815416, but use of digital computers 660.2815 (*not* 660.28154)

Class interdisciplinary works on computerized process control in 629.895

.282	Materials
.283	Process equipment

Examples: instruments, reactors

Including corrosion of equipment and its control

.284	Unit operations and unit processes
.284 2	Unit operations Transport phenomena engineering

Unit operations: operations basically physical

Class here separation processes

.284 22	Crushing, grinding, screening
.284 23	Mass transfer

Including absorption, adsorption, gas chromatography

For precipitation, filtration, solvent extraction, see 660.28424; fractional distillation, 660.28425

.284 24	Precipitation, filtration, solvent extraction
.284 245	Filtration
.284 248	Solvent extraction
.284 25	Fractional distillation

.284 26	Evaporative and drying processes
	For dehumidification of air and gas, see 660.28429
.284 27	Heat transfer
	Class a specific heat transfer process with the process, e.g., melting 660.284296
.284 29	Other unit operations
	Example: dehumidification of air and gas
.284 292	Momentum transfer and fluidization
	Including mixing
.284 293	Humidification
.284 296	Melting
.284 298	Crystallization
.284 4	Unit processes
	Operations basically chemical
	Add to base number 660.2844 the numbers following 547.2 in 547.21–547.29, e.g., fermentation 660.28449
.29	Applied physical chemistry
	Add to base number 660.29 the numbers following 541.3 in 541.33–541.39, e.g., catalytic reactions 660.2995; however, class absorption and adsorption in 660.28423; synthesis (e.g., addition, condensation, hydrolysis, oxidation, polymerization, reduction) and name reactions in 660.2844
.6	**Biotechnology**
	Application of living organisms or their biological systems or processes to the manufacture of useful products
	Former heading: Industrial biology
	See also 620.82 for human-factors engineering
.62	Industrial microbiology
	Use of microorganisms in genetic engineering relocated to 660.65
	Class a specific aspect of industrial microbiology with the aspect, e.g., fermentation 660.28449, use of microorganisms in biochemical engineering 660.63
.63	Biochemical engineering
	Former heading: Industrial biochemistry
.634	Enzyme technology
.65	Genetic engineering
	Including use of microorganisms in genetic engineering [*formerly* 660.62]
.7	**Industrial stoichiometry**

661   Technology of industrial chemicals

Production of chemicals used as raw materials or reagents in manufacture of other products

Use 661.001–661.009 for standard subdivisions

Class industrial gases in 665.7

SUMMARY

661.03–.08	**Compounds**
.1	**Nonmetallic elements**
.2	**Acids**
.3	**Bases**
.4	**Salts**
.5	**Ammonium salts**
.6	**Sulfur and nitrogen salts**
.8	**Organic chemicals**

> 661.03–661.08 Compounds

Class comprehensive works in 661; acids, bases, salts in 661.2–661.6; organic compounds in 661.8

.03   Metallic compounds

Class metallic compounds other than those of alkali and alkaline-earth metals in 661.04–661.07

.038–.039   Alkali and alkaline-earth compounds

Add to base number 661.03 the numbers following 546.3 in 546.38–546.39, e.g., sodium compounds 661.0382

.04–.07   Other compounds

Add to base number 661.0 the numbers following 546 in 546.4–546.7, e.g., sulfur compounds 661.0723

For hydrogen compounds, see 661.08

.08   Hydrogen compounds

Examples: heavy water (deuterium oxide), hydrides

.1   **Nonmetallic elements**

Class gaseous elements in 665.8, carbon in 662.9

> **661.2–661.6 Acids, bases, salts**

Class comprehensive works in 661; organic acids, bases, salts in 661.8

.2   **Acids**

.22   Sulfuric acid

.23   Hydrochloric acid

.24	Nitric acid
.25	Phosphoric acid

.3 Bases

Class here alkalis

.32	Sodas
.322	Caustic soda (Sodium hydroxide)
.323	Sodium bicarbonate
.324	Sodium carbonate
.33	Potash and other potassium alkalis
.332	Caustic potash (Potassium hydroxide)
.333	Potassium bicarbonate
.334	Potassium carbonate
.34	Ammonia and ammonium hydroxide
.35	Other alkalis

Examples: hydroxides and carbonates of cesium, francium, lithium, rubidium, alkaline-earth metals

.4 Salts

For ammonium salts, see 661.5; sulfur and nitrogen salts, 661.6

.42	Halogen salts

Contains chlorides, chlorites, chlorates, corresponding salts of other halogens

.43	Phosphorus and silicon salts

Contains phosphides, phosphites, phosphates, corresponding salts of silicon

.5 Ammonium salts

.6 Sulfur and nitrogen salts

For ammonium salts, see 661.5

.63	Sulfur salts

Contains sulfides, sulfites, sulfates

For plaster of paris, see 666.92

.65	Nitrogen salts

Contains nitrides, nitrites, nitrates

.8 Organic chemicals

Use 661.8001–661.8009 for standard subdivisions

>   661.802–661.804 Derived chemicals

       Class comprehensive works in 661.8

.802   Cellulose derivatives

.803   Coal tar chemicals

.804   Petrochemicals

       Industrial chemicals produced from petroleum or natural gas, excluding fuels, lubricants, refinery residues (bottoms)

       Class petrochemicals in the sense of all refinery products and by-products of petroleum in 665.538

.805   Synthetic chemicals

>   661.806–661.808 Special-purpose chemicals

       Class comprehensive works in 661.8

.806   Essential oils

       Class essential oils used for manufacture of perfumes in 668.54

.807   Solvents, diluents, extenders

.808   Photographic chemicals and photosensitive surfaces

       Including sensitometry

       Class here comprehensive works on organic and inorganic photographic chemicals

       Class inorganic photographic chemicals in 661.1–661.6

.81   Hydrocarbons

.814   Aliphatic hydrocarbons

.815   Alicyclic hydrocarbons

       Heterocyclic hydrocarbons discontinued because without meaning

.816   Aromatic hydrocarbons

>   661.82–661.89 Compounds based on specific elements other than carbon

Add to each subdivision identified by * the numbers following 661.81 in 661.814–661.816, e.g., aliphatic esters 661.834

Unless other instructions are given, observe the following table of precedence, e.g., phosphoric acids 661.87 (*not* 661.86)

Sulfur compounds	661.896
Phosphorus compounds	661.87
Silicon compounds	661.88
Organometallic compounds	661.895
Nitrogen compounds	661.894
Oxy and hydroxy compounds	661.82–.86
Halogenated compounds	661.891

Class comprehensive works in 661.8

>   661.82–661.86 Oxy and hydroxy compounds

Class comprehensive works in 661.8

.82   *Alcohols and phenols

           For glycerin, see 668.2

.83   *Esters

.84   *Ethers

.85   *Aldehydes and ketones

.86   *Acids

.87   *Phosphorus compounds

.88   *Silicon compounds

.89   Other compounds

.891   *Halogenated compounds

.894   *Nitrogen compounds

.895   *Organometallic compounds

.896   *Sulfur compounds

662   Technology of explosives, fuels, related products

.1   **Fireworks (Pyrotechnics)**

*Add as instructed under 661.82–661.89

.2   **Explosives**

Class nuclear explosives in 621.48

For fireworks, see 662.1

.26   Propellants

Examples: black powder (gunpowder), cordite, flashless and coated powders, nitrocellulose (guncotton), smokeless powder

Class here low (deflagrating) explosives

For rocket propellants, see 662.666

.27   High explosives

Examples: ammonium picrate and chlorate, dynamite, HMTD (hexamethylenetriperoxidediamine), nitroglycerin, nitroguanidine, PETN (pentaerythrite tetranitrate), RDX (cyclonite), tetryl, TNT (trinitrotoluene)

Including primary explosives, e.g., diazonitrophenol, lead azide and picrate, mercury fulminate

.4   **Detonators**

Examples: boosters, firing mechanisms, fuses, percussion caps, primers

Class explosives used in detonators in 662.27

.5   **Matches**

.6   **Fuels**

Class industrial oils, fats, waxes, gases as fuels in 665; other fuels not provided for here in 662.8

See also 621.4023 for combustion of fuels

See Manual at 622.7, 622.22 vs. 669, 662.6

.62   Coal

For coke, see 662.72

[.620 287]   Testing and measurement

Do not use; class in 662.622

.622   Properties, tests, analysis

.622 09   Historical and persons treatment

Class properties, tests, analysis of coal from specific places in 662.6229

.622 1–.622 5   Properties, tests, analysis of specific types of coal

Add to base number 662.622 the numbers following 553.2 in 553.21–553.25, e.g., analysis of bituminous coal 662.6224

.622 9   Properties, tests, analysis of coal from specific places

Add to base number 662.6229 notation 1–9 from Table 2, e.g., properties of Virginia coal 662.6229755

Class specific types of coal regardless of place in 662.6221–662.6225

.623   Treatment

Examples: desulfuration, sizing, washing; conversion to slurry, slurry dewatering

.624   Storage, transportation, distribution

.625   Uses

Examples: as a fuel, as a raw material

Class a specific use with the use, e.g., metallurgical use 669.81

.65   Wood and wood derivatives

Examples: sawdust, wood briquettes, wood scraps

Use of this number for nonwood briquettes discontinued; class in 662.6

Bagasse relocated to 662.88

For charcoal, see 662.74

.66   Synthetic fuels

Class synthetic fuel gases in 665.77

.662   Synthetic petroleum

.662 2   Production through hydrogenation and liquefaction of coal

Including Bergius process

Class production from coal gas in 662.6623

.662 3   Production through hydrogenation of carbonaceous gases

Example: Fischer-Tropsch processes

.666   Rocket fuels (Rocket propellants)

Liquid and solid

.669   Other liquid fuels

Examples: benzene from waste products, gasohol, other fuel alcohols

.7   Coke and charcoal

.72   Coke

.74   Charcoal

.8   Other fuels

.82   Colloidal and mud fuels

.86   High-energy boron fuels

.87   Wastes as fuels

Class here comprehensive works on the chemical technology of energy from waste materials

Class interdisciplinary works on energy from waste materials in 333.7938; waste biomass as fuel in 662.88; a specific form of energy from waste materials with the form, e.g., benzene made from waste products 662.669

.88   Biomass as fuel

Example: bagasse [*formerly* 662.65]

Class here plant biomass as fuel, comprehensive works on the chemical technology of biomass as fuel

Class interdisciplinary works on biomass as fuel in 333.9539

For wood and wood derivatives, see 662.65

See also 665.776 for industrial gases manufactured from biological wastes

.9   **Nonfuel carbons**

.92   Graphite and graphite products

.93   Adsorbent carbons

Examples: activated carbons, adsorbent charcoals, animal black, bone char, carbon black, decolorizing carbons, lampblack

663   Beverage technology

Commercial preparation, preservation, packaging

Class interdisciplinary works on beverages in 641.2, household preparation of beverages in 641.87

SUMMARY

.1   **Alcoholic beverages**

For wine and wine making, see 663.2; brewed and malted beverages, 663.3; distilled liquors, 663.5

.102 8   Auxiliary techniques and procedures; apparatus, equipment

Class materials in 663.11

.11   Materials

.12   Preliminary preparations

.13   Fermentation

.14	Packing
.15	Refrigeration and pasteurization
.16	Distillation
.17	Aging
.19	Bottling

.2   Wine and wine making

Including fermented cider

Class here grape wine

Class mead (honey wine) in 663.4, sake (rice wine) in 663.49

.200 1	Philosophy and theory
.200 2	Miscellany
.200 28	Auxiliary techniques and procedures; apparatus, equipment

Class materials in 663.201

.200 3–.200 9	Standard subdivisions
.201–.209	Materials, processes, operations

Class here materials, processes, operations for grape wine [*formerly* 663.2204]

Add to base number 663.20 the numbers following 663.1 in 663.11–663.19, e.g., fermentation 663.203

.22   Specific kinds of grape wine

Use of this number for comprehensive works on grape wine discontinued; class in 663.2

[.220 4]   Materials, processes, operations for grape wine

Relocated to 663.201–663.209

.222   White wine

Class sparkling white wine in 663.224

.223   Red wine

Including rosé

Class sparkling red wine in 663.224

.224   Sparkling wine

White and red

.3   Brewed and malted beverages

For specific kinds of brewed and malted beverages, see 663.4

.302 8   Auxiliary techniques and procedures; apparatus, equipment

Class materials in 663.31

| .31–.39 | Materials, processes, operations |
| | Add to base number 663.3 the numbers following 663.1 in 663.11–663.19, e.g., fermentation 663.33 |

.4 Specific kinds of brewed and malted beverages

Class malt whiskey in 663.52

.42 Beer and ale

.49 Sake and pulque

.5 Distilled liquors

Examples: mescal, tequila, potato whiskey, vodka

.500 1 Philosophy and theory

.500 2 Miscellany

.500 28 Auxiliary techniques and procedures; apparatus, equipment

Class materials in 663.501

.500 3–.500 9 Standard subdivisions

.501–.509 Materials, processes, operations

Add to base number 663.50 the numbers following 663.1 in 663.11–663.19, e.g., distillation 663.506

.52 Grain whiskey

Example: bourbon

.53 Brandy

.55 Compound liquors

Distilled spirits flavored with various seeds, roots, leaves, flowers, fruits

Examples: cordials (liqueurs), gin

.59 Rum

Use of this number for other distilled liquors discontinued; class in 663.5

.6 Nonalcoholic beverages

For nonalcoholic brewed beverages, see 663.9; milk, 637.1

.61 Bottled drinking water

Including carbonated water

Class here potable mineral water

.62 Mineralized and carbonated beverages

Class mineralized and carbonated water in 663.61

.63 Fruit and vegetable juices

Class fermented cider in 663.2, carbonated juices in 663.62

.64   Milk substitutes

Examples: coconut milk, nondairy coffee whiteners, soybean milk

.9   Nonalcoholic brewed beverages

Aside from additions, changes, deletions, exceptions shown under specific entries, add to notation for each term identified by * as follows:
028   Auxiliary techniques and procedures; apparatus, equipment
                    Class materials in 1
1   Materials
2   Preliminary preparations
3   Fermentation and oxidation
4   Firing, roasting, curing
5   Blending
7   Specific varieties
8   Concentrates
9   Packaging

.92   *Cocoa and *chocolate

.93   *Coffee

.94   *Tea

.96   Herb teas

Examples: catnip, maté, sassafras, other aromatic and medicinal teas

.97   Coffee substitutes

Examples: acorns, cereal preparations, chicory

664   Food technology

Commercial preparation, preservation, packaging

Class here comprehensive works on commercial food and beverage technology

Class interdisciplinary works on food in 641.3; household preservation, storage, cooking in 641.4–641.8

For processing dairy and related products, see 637; beverage technology, 663

SUMMARY

664.001–.009	**Standard subdivisions**
.01–.09	**[Materials, processes, operations, by-products]**
.1	**Sugars, syrups, their derived products**
.2	**Starches and jellying agents**
.3	**Fats and oils**
.4	**Food salts**
.5	**Flavoring aids**
.6	**Special-purpose food and aids**
.7	**Grains, other seeds, their derived products**
.8	**Fruits and vegetables**
.9	**Meats and allied foods**

*Add as instructed under 663.9

.001	Philosophy and theory
.001 15	Theory of communication and control
	Class process control in 664.02
.002	Miscellany
.002 8	Auxiliary techniques and procedures; apparatus, equipment
	Class materials in 664.01
[.002 87]	Testing and measurement
	Do not use; class in 664.07
.003–.009	Standard subdivisions
.01	Materials
	For additives, see 664.06
.02	Processes
	Class here process design, control, equipment
.022	Extraction
.023	Refining
.024	Manufacturing processes
	Not provided for elsewhere
	Including fermentation
	Class here food biotechnology, food processing with microorganisms
.028	Preservation techniques
	Class here interdisciplinary works on food preservation
	Class home preservation of foods in 641.4
.028 1	Preliminary treatment
	Example: peeling
.028 2	Canning
.028 4	Drying and dehydrating
.028 42	By slow, thermal processes
.028 43	Through pulverizing and flaking
.028 45	By freeze-drying
.028 5	Low-temperature techniques
	For freeze-drying, see 664.02845
.028 52	Cold storage
.028 53	Deep freezing

.028 6	Chemical preservation
	Examples: brining, pickling, smoking
	For chemical preservation by use of additives, see 664.0287
.028 7	Chemical preservation by use of additives
.028 8	Irradiation
.06	Additives
	Production, properties, use
	Example: food colors
	Class flavoring aids in 664.5
	For chemical preservation by use of additives, see 664.0287
.07	Tests, analyses, quality controls
	For color, contaminants, flavor, odor, texture
	Example: grading
	Class tests, analyses, quality controls of additives in 664.06
.08	By-products
.09	Packaging and waste control
.092	Packaging
.096	Waste control
	Class here pollution control
.1	**Sugars, syrups, their derived products**
	See also 664.5 for sugar substitutes
[.102 8]	Auxiliary techniques and procedures; apparatus, equipment
	Do not use; class in 664.11

>	664.11–664.13 Sugars and syrups
	Class comprehensive works in 664.1
.11	Materials, techniques, processes, operations, equipment, by-products of sugars and syrups
	Class materials, techniques, processes, operations, equipment, by-products of specific sugars and syrups in 664.12–664.13
.111	Materials
.112	Preliminary preparations
.113	Extraction and purification

.114	Concentration	
	Production of syrup	
.115	Crystallization	
	Production of sugar	
.116	Additives	
.117	Tests, analyses, quality controls	
	For color, contaminants, flavor, texture	
	Class tests, analyses, quality controls of additives in 664.116	
.118	By-products	
	Example: molasses	
	Class utilization in 664.19	
.119	Packaging and waste control	
	Class here pollution control	

>   664.12–664.13 Specific sugars and syrups

Class comprehensive works in 664.1

.12	Cane and beet sugar and syrup
.122	Cane sugar and syrup
.122 028	Auxiliary techniques and procedures; apparatus, equipment
	Class materials in 664.1221
[.122 028 7]	Testing and measurement
	Do not use; class in 664.1227
.122 1–.122 9	Materials, processes, operations, by-products

Add to base number 664.122 the numbers following 664.11 in 664.111–664.119, e.g., cane molasses 664.1228; however, class auxiliary techniques and procedures, apparatus, equipment in 664.122028

.123	Beet sugar and syrup
.13	Other sugars and syrups
	For honey, see 638.16
.132	Maple sugar and syrup
.133	Corn and sorghum sugars and syrups
.139	Jerusalem artichoke sugar and syrup

.15	Sugar products
.152	Jam, jelly, marmalade
.153	Candy

Variant name: sweets

See also 664.6 for chewing gum

.19	By-product utilization

Class a specific use with the use, e.g., molasses for rum 663.59

.2 Starches and jellying agents

> 664.22–664.23 Starches

Class comprehensive works in 664.2

.22	Cornstarch and potato starch
.23	Cassava and arrowroot starches
.25	Jellying agents

Class here pectin

For gelatin, see 664.26

.26	Gelatin

.3 Fats and oils

Class interdisciplinary works on animal fats and oils in 665.2, on vegetable fats and oils in 665.3

.32	Margarine
.34	Lard
.36	Salad and cooking oils
.362	Olive oil
.363	Cottonseed oil
.369	Other fats and oils

Examples: corn, peanut, safflower, sesame, soybean oils

Class peanut butter in 664.8056596

.37	Salad dressings

Examples: French dressing, mayonnaise

.4 Food salts

Examples: monosodium glutamate, table salt, tenderizers, sodium-free and other dietetic salts

Class comprehensive works on food flavoring aids in 664.5

.5   **Flavoring aids**

Examples: chocolate, sugar substitutes

Class here condiments

Class a specific flavoring aid not provided for here with the aid, e.g., sugar 664.1; flavoring aids in a specific kind of food with the kind of food, e.g., chocolate candies 664.153

For food salts, see 664.4

.52–.54   Essences and spices

Add to base number 664.5 the numbers following 633.8 in 633.82–633.84, e.g., vanilla extract 664.52

.55   Vinegar

.58   Composites

Examples: catsup, chutney, sauces

Class salad dressings in 664.37

.6   **Special-purpose food and aids**

Examples: chewing gum, snack food

Class food salts in 664.4, other special-purpose flavoring aids in 664.5

>   664.62–664.66 Special-purpose food

Class comprehensive works in 664.6; a specific food with the food, e.g., vegetables 664.8

.62   Baby food

.63   Low-calorie food

.64   Meatless high-protein food

Including synthetic meat

.65   Composites

Examples: complete meals, packaged ingredients for complete recipes

Class packaged ingredients for recipes based on a specific kind of food with the kind, e.g., mixes and prepared doughs for bakery goods 664.753

.66   Food for animals

Class here pet food

Class animal feed made from grains and other seeds in 664.76

.68   Leavening agents and baking aids

Examples: baking powder, baking soda, cream of tartar, yeast

.7　　Grains, other seeds, their derived products

> Class sugars and syrups from grain and other seeds in 664.1, starches and jellying agents from grain and other seeds in 664.2, fats and oils from grains and other seeds in 664.3

.72　　Milling and milling products

> *For animal feeds, see 664.76*

.720 01　　　　Philosophy and theory

.720 02　　　　Miscellany

[.720 028 7]　　　　　Testing and measurement

> Do not use; class in 664.7204

.720 03–.720 09　　Standard subdivisions

.720 1　　　　Preliminary treatment

.720 3　　　　Grinding and deflaking

.720 4　　　　Sifting, grading, quality controls

.720 7　　　　Products

> Examples: flour, meal, refined grain
>
> *See also 664.7208 for by-products*

.720 8　　　　By-products

> Examples: bran, siftings

.720 9　　　　Packaging and waste control

> Class here pollution control

.722　　Wheat

.722 7　　　　Products

> *See also 664.7228 for by-products*

.722 72　　　　Flour

.722 73　　　　Meal

.722 8　　　　By-products

> Examples: bran, siftings

.725　　Other cereal grains and their flours, meals, by-products

> Examples: buckwheat, corn, millet, oats, rice, rye

.726　　Other seeds and their flours and meals

> Examples: cottonseeds, sunflowers; flours and meals of nuts, peanuts, soybeans
>
> Class comprehensive works on commercial processing of nuts in 664.8045, of legumes in 664.80565

.75	Secondary products
.752	Bakery goods

> Examples: biscuits (United States), crackers
>
> Class mixes and prepared doughs for bakery goods in 664.753

.752 3	Breads
.752 5	Pastries

> Examples: cakes, cookies (biscuits [United Kingdom]), pies

.753	Mixes and prepared doughs

> Examples: biscuit, cake, pancake mixes

.755	Pastas

> Examples: macaroni, noodles, spaghetti, vermicelli

.756	Ready-to-eat cereals
.76	Animal feeds

> Class comprehensive works on foods for animals in 664.66

.762	Cereal grains

> Individual grains and mixtures
>
> Class formula feeds in 664.768

.763	Other seeds

> Individual seeds and mixtures
>
> Class formula feeds in 664.768

.764	Cereal grain and seed mixtures
.768	Formula feeds

> Cakes, flakes, granules, pellets, powders basically of cereal grains and other seeds and fortified with vitamins and minerals

.8	**Fruits and vegetables**

> Class a specific product derived from fruits and vegetables with the product, e.g., jams 664.152, fats and oils 664.3

.800 1	Philosophy and theory
.800 2	Miscellany
[.800 287]	Testing and measurement

> Do not use; class in 664.807

.800 3–.800 9	Standard subdivisions
.804	Specific fruits and groups of fruits

> Add to base number 664.804 the numbers following 634 in 634.1–634.8, e.g., citrus fruit 664.804304, nuts 664.8045

.805	Specific vegetables and groups of vegetables

Add to base number 664.805 the numbers following 635 in 635.1–635.8, e.g., salad greens 664.8055

.806–.809	Additives, tests, analyses, quality controls, by-products, packaging, waste control

Add to base number 664.80 the numbers following 664.0 in 664.06–664.09, e.g., packaging vegetables 664.8092

Class additives, tests, analyses, quality controls, by-products, packaging, waste control applied to specific fruits and groups of fruits in 664.804, to specific vegetables and groups of vegetables in 664.805

See also 664.81–664.88 for preservation techniques

.81–.88	Preservation techniques

Add to base number 664.8 the numbers following 664.028 in 664.0281–664.0288, e.g., deep freezing fruits 664.853

Class preservation techniques applied to specific fruits and groups of fruits in 664.804, to specific vegetables and groups of vegetables in 664.805

.9	**Meats and allied foods**
.900 1	Philosophy and theory
.900 2	Miscellany
[.900 287]	Testing and measurement

Do not use; class in 664.907

.900 3–.900 9	Standard subdivisions
.902	Preservation techniques, slaughtering, meat cutting
.902 8	Preservation techniques

Add to base number 664.9028 the numbers following 664.028 in 664.0281–664.0288, e.g., canning 664.90282

.902 9	Slaughtering and meat cutting

Standard subdivisions are used for either or both of the topics named in the heading

.906–.909	Additives, tests, analyses, quality controls, by-products, packaging, waste control

Add to base number 664.90 the numbers following 664.0 in 664.06–664.09, e.g., packaging meats and allied foods 664.9092

Class additives, tests, analyses, quality controls, by-products, packaging, waste control applied to specific meats or allied foods with the meat or food, e.g., packaging red meats 664.92992

See also 664.9028 for preservation techniques

.92   Red meat

[.920 287]   Testing and measurement

Do not use; class in 664.9297

.921–.928   Preservation techniques

Add to base number 664.92 the numbers following 664.028 in 664.0281–664.0288, e.g., canning red meat 664.922

Subdivisions are added for specific red meats, e.g., canning beef 664.922

.929   Additives, tests, analyses, quality controls, by-products, packaging, waste control

Add to base number 664.929 the numbers following 664.0 in 664.06–664.09, e.g., packaging red meat 664.92992

Subdivisions are added for specific red meats, e.g., packaging beef 664.92992

See also 664.921–664.928 for preservation techniques

.93   Poultry

[.930 287]   Testing and measurement

Do not use; class in 664.9397

.931–.938   Preservation techniques

Add to base number 664.93 the numbers following 664.028 in 664.0281–664.0288, e.g., deep freezing 664.9353

Subdivisions are added for specific kinds of poultry, e.g., deep freezing turkeys 664.9353

.939   Additives, tests, analyses, quality controls, by-products, packaging, waste control

Add to base number 664.939 the numbers following 664.0 in 664.06–664.09, e.g., poultry by-products 664.9398

Subdivisions are added for specific kinds of poultry, e.g., turkey by-products 664.9398

See also 664.931–664.938 for preservation techniques

.94   Fish and shellfish

Class here seafood

[.940 287]   Testing and measurement

Do not use; class in 664.9497

.941–.948   Preservation techniques

Add to base number 664.94 the numbers following 664.028 in 664.0281–664.0288, e.g., canning seafood 664.942

Subdivisions are not added for specific kinds of fish and shellfish, e.g., canning oysters 664.94 (*not* 664.942)

.949　　　　Additives, tests, analyses, quality controls, by-products, packaging, waste control

Add to base number 664.949 the numbers following 664.0 in 664.06–664.09, e.g., quality controls for seafood 664.9497

Subdivisions are not added for specific kinds of fish and shellfish, e.g., quality controls for catfish 664.94 (*not* 664.9497)

See also 664.941–664.948 for preservation techniques

.95　　　　Other meats and allied foods

Examples: frogs, turtles, snails, insects

665　Technology of industrial oils, fats, waxes, gases

Class here nonvolatile, lubricating, saponifying oils, fats, waxes

SUMMARY

665.028	Techniques, procedures, apparatus, equipment, materials
.1	Waxes
.2	Animal fats and oils
.3	Vegetable fats and oils
.4	Mineral oils and waxes
.5	Petroleum
.7	Natural gas and manufactured industrial gases
.8	Other industrial gases

.028　　　　Techniques, procedures, apparatus, equipment, materials

.028 2　　　Extraction

Examples: pressurizing, rendering, steam distilling

.028 3　　　Refining

Examples: bleaching, blending, coloring, fractionating, purifying

.028 7　　　Maintenance and repair

Do not use for testing and measurement; class in 665.0288

.028 8　　　Tests, analyses, quality controls

Do not use for maintenance and repair; class in 665.0287

.1　Waxes

Class polishing waxes in 667.72

For mineral waxes, see 665.4

.12　　　　Vegetable waxes

Examples: bayberry, candleberry, carnauba, laurel, myrtle waxes

.13　　　　Animal waxes

Examples: lanolin (wool wax), spermaceti

For beeswax, see 638.17

.19   Blended waxes

.2   Animal fats and oils

Examples: fish, neat's-foot, whale oils; tallow

Class here interdisciplinary works on animal fats and oils

Class animal fats and oils used in food or food preparation in 664.3

See also 665.13 for spermaceti

.3   Vegetable fats and oils

Class here comprehensive works on vegetable fats and oils

Class vegetable fats and oils used in food and food preparation in 664.3

.33   Wood oil

.332   Crude turpentine

Class turpentine oils in 661.806

.333   Tung oil (Chinese wood oil)

.35   Seed oils

For tung oil, see 665.333

.352   Linseed oil (Flaxseed oil)

.353   Castor oil

.354   Cocoa butter (Cacao butter)

.355   Coconut oil

.4   Mineral oils and waxes

Examples: natural asphalt, shale oil, tar sand

For petroleum, see 665.5

.5   Petroleum

Class here comprehensive works on petroleum and natural gas

Class synthetic petroleum in 662.662

For natural gas, see 665.7

.502 8   Auxiliary techniques and procedures; apparatus, equipment, materials

Class refinery techniques in 665.53

.53   Refinery treatment and products

Class preliminary refining of oil sands and oil shale to obtain distillable fluids in 665.4

.532   Fractional distillation

.533	Cracking processes
	Examples: thermal and catalytic cracking, hydrogenation of residual petroleum distillates
.534	Purification and blending of distillates
.538	Refinery products and by-products
	Including waste products
	For petrochemicals, see 661.804
.538 2	Highly volatile products
.538 24	Low-boiling naphthas
.538 25	Aviation fuel
	Examples: high-octane-rating gasoline, jet and turbojet fuel
	Class comprehensive works on gasoline in 665.53827
.538 27	Gasoline
	For high-octane-rating gasoline, see 665.53825
.538 3	Kerosene
	For jet and turbojet fuel, see 665.53825
.538 4	Heavy fuel oil
	Examples: absorber oil, diesel fuel, gas oil, heating oil
.538 5	Lubricating oil and grease
	Examples: paraffin wax and petrolatum
.538 8	Residues (Bottoms)
	Examples: asphalt, bunker and road oils, petroleum coke, pitch
	Class asphalt concrete in 666.893
	Unusable residues (wastes) are classed in 665.538
.538 9	Waste control
	Class here pollution control
.54	Storage, transportation, distribution
.542	Storage
.543	Transportation
	Example: by tankers
	For pipeline transportation, see 665.544
.544	Pipeline transportation
.55	Uses
	Class a specific use with the use, e.g., automobile engine lubricants 629.255

.7   **Natural gas and manufactured industrial gases**

> Class here comprehensive works on industrial gases
>
> Class industrial gases not provided for here in 665.8

.73   Processing natural gas

> Including extraction of helium

.74   Storage, transportation, distribution

.742   Storage

.743   Transportation

> *For pipeline transportation, see 665.744*

.744   Pipeline transportation

.75   Uses

> Class a specific use with the use, e.g., heating buildings 697.043

.77   Production of manufactured gases

.772   From coal and coke

> Examples: blast-furnace, carbureted-blue, city, coal, coke-oven, producer, water gases

.773   From petroleum and natural gas

> Examples: oil, refinery, reformed natural, reformed refinery, liquefied-hydrocarbon gases, e.g., butane, butene, pentane, propane, and their mixtures

.776   From biological wastes

.779   By mixing fuel gases from several sources

.78   Waste control

> Class here pollution control

.8   **Other industrial gases**

> *For ammonia, see 661.34*

.81   Hydrogen

.82   Gases derived from liquefaction and fractionation of air

.822   Noble gases

> Variant names: inert gases, rare gases
>
> Contains argon, helium, krypton, neon, radon, xenon
>
> Class extraction of helium from natural gases in 665.73

.823   Oxygen

.824   Nitrogen

.83	Halogen gases
.84	Sulfur dioxide
.85	Acetylene
.89	Carbon dioxide, ozone, hydrogen sulfide

> Use of this number for other gases discontinued; class in 665.8

666 Ceramic and allied technologies

Class here ceramic-to-metal bonding

SUMMARY

666.1	Glass
.2	Enamels
.3	Pottery
.4	Pottery processes and equipment
.5	Porcelain (China)
.6	Earthenware and stoneware
.7	Refractories and structural clay products
.8	Synthetic and artificial minerals and building materials
.9	Masonry adhesives

.1 Glass

[.102 8]	Auxiliary techniques and procedures; apparatus, equipment, materials

> Do not use; class apparatus, equipment, materials in 666.12, auxiliary techniques and procedures in 666.13

.104	Special topics
.104 2	Physicochemical phenomena occurring during glassmaking processes

> Examples: phase and structural transformations

> \> 666.12–666.14 General topics

Class comprehensive works in 666.1, general topics of specific types of glass in 666.15, general topics of products in 666.19

.12	Techniques, procedures, apparatus, equipment, materials

For auxiliary techniques and procedures, see 666.13

.121	Materials

> \> 666.122–666.129 Specific operations in glassmaking

Class comprehensive works in 666.12; tests, analyses, quality controls in 666.137

.122	Blowing
.123	Pressing

.124	Drawing
.125	Molding and casting
.126	Multiform processes

Cold-molding glass powder under pressure, and firing at high temperatures

.129	Annealing and tempering
.13	Auxiliary techniques and procedures

Add to base number 666.13 the numbers following —028 in —0285–0289 from Table 1, e.g., quality control in glassmaking 666.137

.14	Waste control

Class here pollution control

.15	Specific types of glass

See also 669.94 for metallic glass

.152	Window glass

Sheet glass that differs from plate glass primarily in being annealed more quickly and in not being ground and polished

.153	Plate glass

Class laminated plate glass in 666.154

.154	Laminated glass
.155	Heat-resistant glass
.156	Optical glass
.157	Fiber glass and foam glass
.19	Products
.192	Bottles
.2	**Enamels**
.3	**Pottery**

Class here comprehensive works on clay technology

Pottery in the narrow sense of earthenware is classed in 666.6

For specific types of pottery, see 666.5–666.6; structural clay products, 666.73

[.301–.309]	Standard subdivisions

Do not use; class in 666.31–666.39

.31–.39   Standard subdivisions

Add to base number 666.3 the numbers following —0 in notation 01–09 from Table 1, e.g., pottery dictionaries 666.33; however, class auxiliary techniques and procedures; apparatus, equipment, materials in 666.4

.4   **Pottery processes and equipment**

Add to base number 666.4 the numbers following 738.1 in 738.12–738.15, e.g., kilns 666.43

>   **666.5–666.6 Specific types of pottery**

Class comprehensive works in 666.3

.5   **Porcelain**

.58   Specific products

Examples: figurines, tableware, vases

.6   **Earthenware and stoneware**

.68   Specific products

Examples: containers, figurines, industrial products, tableware

.7   **Refractories and structural clay products**

.72   Refractory materials

Examples: alumina, asbestos, chrome, fireclays, mica, talc, zirconia

.73   Structural clay products

.732   Roofing tiles

.733   Tile drains and piping

.737   Bricks

For hollow and perforated bricks, see 666.738

.738   Hollow and perforated bricks

.8   **Synthetic and artificial minerals and building materials**

.86   Synthetic and artificial minerals

Examples: cryolite, feldspar, graphite, mica

For synthetic and artificial gems and gem minerals, see 666.88

.88   Synthetic and artificial gems and gem minerals

Examples: diamonds, garnets, rubies, sapphires

.89   Synthetic building materials

For structural clay products, see 666.73

.893   Concrete

Examples: asphalt concrete, ready-mix concrete

Class concrete blocks in 666.894

.894   Hollow concrete and cinder blocks

Class here comprehensive works on concrete blocks

For solid concrete blocks, see 666.895

.895   Solid concrete blocks

.9   **Masonry adhesives**

Class concrete in 666.893

.92   Gypsum plasters

Examples: Keene's cement, plaster of paris

.93   Lime mortars

.94   Portland cement

.95   Other cements

Examples: high-alumina cement, magnesia

667   Cleaning, color, related technologies

.1   **Cleaning and bleaching**

Of textiles, leathers, furs, feathers

.12   Dry cleaning

Including manufacture of dry-cleaning materials

.13   Laundering and finishing operations

See also 668.12 for soaps, 668.14 for detergents

.14   Bleaching

Including manufacture of bleaching materials

.2   **Dyes and pigments**

>   667.25–667.26 Dyes

Class comprehensive works in 667.2

.25   Synthetic dyes

.252   Nitro and nitroso dyes

.253   Azo-oxy and azo-tetrazo dyes

.254   Di- and triphenylmethane dyes

.256	Hydroxyketone dyes

Examples: alizarines, quinoidals

.257	Indigoid dyes

See also 667.26 for indigo

.26	Natural dyes

Example: indigo

.29	Pigments
.3	**Dyeing and printing**

For dyes, see 667.25–667.26

.31–.35	Dyeing specific textiles

Add to base number 667.3 the numbers following 677 in 677.1–677.5, e.g., dyeing nylon 667.3473

.36	Control of waste from dyeing processes

Class here pollution control

.38	Textile printing
.4	**Inks**

For printing ink, see 667.5

.5	**Printing ink**
.6	**Paints**

Class here paint removers

.62	Oil-soluble paint
.622	Oils, driers, plasticizers
.623	Pigments and extenders

For carbon black, see 662.93

.624	Diluents (Thinners)
.63	Water-soluble paint

Examples: latex paint, whitewash

.69	Special-purpose paints

Examples: fire-resistant, luminous, rust-resistant paints

.7	**Polishes, lacquers, varnishes**
.72	Polishes
.75	Lacquers

.79 Varnishes

Examples: shellac, spar varnish

Class here spirit varnishes

For japans, see 667.8

.8 **Japans**

.9 **Coating and coatings**

Methods and materials for producing protective and decorative coatings

Examples: dipping, metallizing, painting, spraying, varnishing

Including sign painting

Standard subdivisions are added for either or both of the topics named in the heading

Class a specific application with the application, e.g., painting automobiles 629.26, buildings 698.1; a specific coating with the coating, e.g., varnishes 667.79

668 Technology of other organic products

SUMMARY

668.1	Surface-active materials (Surfactants)	
.2	Glycerin	
.3	Adhesives and related products	
.4	Plastics	
.5	Perfumes and cosmetics	
.6	Agricultural chemicals and related products	
.9	Polymers	

.1 **Surface-active materials (Surfactants)**

.12 Soaps

.124 Soluble soaps

Examples: liquid concentrates, powders

.125 Insoluble soaps (Metallic soaps)

Examples: oleates and stearates of aluminum

.127 Scouring compounds

.14 Detergents and wetting agents

Nonsoap materials that manifest surface activity

Examples: fatty-alcohol sulfates, sulfated oils and hydrocarbons

.2 **Glycerin**

.3 **Adhesives and related products**

For masonry adhesives, see 666.9

>   668.31–668.37 Specific kinds of adhesives

Class comprehensive works in 668.3, products made from specific kinds of adhesives in 668.38

.31   Synthetic glue

.32   Animal glue

Example: casein glue

.33   Vegetable glue

Example: mucilage

See also 668.37 for gum

.34   Crude gelatin

.37   Gum and resin

.372   Natural gum and resin

See also 668.33 for mucilage

.374   Synthetic gum and resin

Example: epoxy resin

.38   Products made from adhesives

Example: tape

Class here sealants

.4   **Plastics [*formerly also* 547.8432]**

SUMMARY

668.404	**Special topics**	
.41	**Techniques, procedures, apparatus, equipment, materials**	
.42	**Polymerization plastics**	
.43	**Protein plastics**	
.44	**Cellulosics**	
.45	**Plastics from natural resins**	
.49	**Forms and products**	

[.402 8]   Auxiliary techniques and procedures; apparatus, equipment, materials

Do not use; class in 668.41

.404   Special topics

.404 2   Physicochemical phenomena of plastics manufacture

.41   Techniques, procedures, apparatus, equipment, materials

Class application to specific kinds of plastics in 668.42–668.45, application to forms and products in 668.49

.411   Materials

Examples: fillers, plasticizers

>   668.412–668.419 Specific operations

           Class comprehensive works in 668.41

.412   Molding and casting

.413   Extrusion

.414   Laminating

.415   Welding

.416   Reinforcing

.419   Auxiliary techniques and procedures

.419 2   Waste control

           Class here pollution control

.419 5–.419 9   Miscellaneous auxiliary techniques and procedures

           Add to base number 668.419 the numbers following —028 in —0285–0289 from Table 1, e.g., quality control in plastics manufacture 668.4197

>   668.42–668.45 Specific kinds of plastics

           Class comprehensive works in 668.4, forms and products of specific kinds of plastics in 668.49

.42   Polymerization plastics

.422   Thermosetting plastics

.422 2   Phenolics

.422 3   Ureas

.422 4   Melamines

.422 5   Polyesters

           Example: polyurethanes

           Class comprehensive works on polyurethanes in 668.4239

.422 6   Epoxies

.422 7   Silicones

.423   Thermoplastic plastics

           Examples: acetals, acetates, butyrates, polycarbonates, polyethers

.423 2   Acrylics (Polyacrylics)

.423 3   Styrenes (Polystyrenes)

.423 4	Polyolefins	
	Examples: polyethylenes, polyisobutylenes, polypropylenes	
.423 5	Polyamides (Nylons)	
.423 6	Vinyls (Polyvinyls)	
.423 7	Vinylidene chlorides	
.423 8	Polyfluoro hydrocarbons	
.423 9	Polyurethanes	

Class here comprehensive works on polyurethanes

Class polyurethane rubber in 678.72

For thermosetting polyurethanes, see 668.4225

.43   Protein plastics

Example: plastics derived from casein

.44   Cellulosics

Example: celluloid

.45   Plastics from natural resins

Example: lignin-derived plastics

For protein plastics, see 668.43

.49   Forms and products

Class plastic fibers and fabrics in 677.46–677.47

>   668.492–668.495 Specific forms

Class comprehensive works in 668.49

.492   Laminated plastic

.493   Foamed plastics

Example: structural foam

.494   Reinforced plastic

.495   Plastic films

.497   Containers

.5   **Perfumes and cosmetics**

.54   Perfumes

.542   Natural perfumes

Examples: floral oils and waters

.544   Synthetic perfumes

.55   Cosmetics

.6   Agricultural chemicals and related products

.62   Fertilizers

Add to base number 668.62 the numbers following 631.8 in 631.83–631.85, e.g., superphosphates 668.625

For organic fertilizers, see 668.63

.63   Organic fertilizers

Add to base number 668.63 the numbers following 631.8 in 631.86–631.87, e.g., manufacture of fertilizers from animal wastes 668.636 [*formerly* 628.7461], converting household garbage 668.6377

.64   Soil conditioners

Manufactured and organic

.65   Pesticides

.651   Insecticides, rodenticides, vermicides

.652   Fungicides and algicides

.653   Bactericides

.654   Herbicides (Weed killers)

.9   Polymers

Class here synthetic polymers [*formerly also* 547.8427]

Class a specific application with the application, e.g., manufacture of nylon hosiery 687.3; a specific polymer with the polymer, e.g., plastics 668.4

669   Metallurgy

Class here alloys, extractive metallurgy, process metallurgy, interdisciplinary works on metals

Class a specific aspect of metals with the aspect, e.g., chemistry 546.3, metalworking and primary metal products 671

See Manual at 622.7, 622.22 vs. 669, 662.6; 669

SUMMARY

669.01–.09	**Standard subdivisions**
.1	**Ferrous metals**
.2	**Precious, rare-earth, actinide-series metals**
.3	**Copper**
.4	**Lead**
.5	**Zinc and cadmium**
.6	**Tin**
.7	**Other nonferrous metals**
.8	**Metallurgical furnace technology**
.9	**Physical and chemical metallurgy**

[.001]	Philosophy and theory of metallurgy
	Relocated to 669.01
[.002]	Miscellany of metallurgy
	Relocated to 669.02
[.003]	Dictionaries, encyclopedias, concordances of metallurgy
	Relocated to 669.03
[.005–.009]	Standard subdivisions of metallurgy
	Relocated to 669.05–669.09
.01	Philosophy and theory of metallurgy [*formerly* 669.001], of extractive metallurgy
.02	Miscellany of metallurgy [*formerly* 669.002], of extractive metallurgy
.028	Specific kinds of techniques and procedures; apparatus, equipment
	Class materials in 669.042
.028 2	Pyrometallurgy
	Extraction by smelting, roasting, other furnace methods
	Class electrical zone melting in 669.0284
.028 3	Hydrometallurgy
	Extraction by leaching methods
.028 4	Electrometallurgy
	Including electrical zone melting, vacuum metallurgy
	Class here electrorefining, electrowinning
.03	Dictionaries, encyclopedias, concordances of metallurgy [*formerly* 669.003], of extractive metallurgy
.04	Special topics of metallurgy, of extractive metallurgy
.042	Materials
	Class here prepared ores and scrap metals
	Class furnace materials in 669.8
.05–.09	Standard subdivisions of metallurgy [*formerly* 669.005–669.009], of extractive metallurgy

---

>   **669.1–669.7 Metallurgy of specific metals and their alloys**

Class comprehensive works in 669

For physical and chemical metallurgy of specific metals and their alloys, see 669.96

.1	**Ferrous metals**
.14	Reduction and refining of ferrous ores

Do not use standard subdivisions

Comprehensive works on production of iron and steel are classed in 669.1

.141	Production of iron

For production of ingot iron, see 669.1423

.141 3	Blast-furnace practice

Class here casting as a part of the refining process, production of pig iron and crude cast iron

Class iron casting as a metalworking process in 672.25, cast iron products in 672.8

.141 4	Puddling furnace practice

Class here production of wrought iron

.141 9	Other iron alloy practices

Including production of iron powder and sponge iron

.142	Production of steel
.142 2	Open-hearth furnace practice (Siemens process)
.142 3	Bessemer converter practice

Including production of duplex-process steel, ingot iron

.142 4	Electric furnace practice

Example: arc furnace practice

.142 9	Production of crucible steel

>	**669.2–669.7 Nonferrous metals**

Class comprehensive works in 669

.2	**Precious, rare-earth, actinide-series metals**

>	669.22–669.24 Precious metals

Class comprehensive works in 669.2

.22	Gold
.23	Silver
.24	Platinum
.29	Rare-earth and actinide-series metals
.290 01–.290 09	Standard subdivisions

.290 1–.294 9 Specific metals and groups of metals

Add to base number 669.29 the numbers following 546.4 in 546.401–546.44, e.g., uranium 669.2931

.3 Copper

Class here brass, Muntz metal; bronze, gunmetal; copper-aluminum alloys; copper-beryllium alloys

.4 Lead

.5 Zinc and cadmium

.52 Zinc

For brass, Muntz metal, see 669.3

.56 Cadmium

.6 Tin

For bronze, gunmetal, see 669.3

.7 Other nonferrous metals

Examples: iridium, osmium, palladium, rhodium, ruthenium; rhenium

See also 669.24 for platinum

.71 Mercury

.72 Light, alkali, alkaline-earth metals

Standard subdivisions are added for light, alkali, alkaline-earth metals; for light metals alone

For titanium, see 669.7322; for zirconium, 669.735

.722 Aluminum

For copper-aluminum alloys, see 669.3

.723 Magnesium

.724 Beryllium

For copper-beryllium alloys, see 669.3

.725 Alkali and alkaline-earth metals

Contains barium, calcium, cesium, francium, lithium, potassium, radium, rubidium, sodium, strontium

For magnesium, see 669.723; beryllium, 669.724

.73 Metals used in ferroalloys

.732 Titanium, vanadium, manganese

.732 2 Titanium

.733 Nickel and cobalt

.733 2 Nickel

.734	Chromium, molybdenum, tungsten
.735	Zirconium and tantalum
.75	Antimony, arsenic, bismuth
.79	Miscellaneous rare metals and metalloids

Limited to gallium, hafnium, indium, niobium, polonium, thallium; germanium, selenium, tellurium

.8   Metallurgical furnace technology

Class metallurgical furnace technology used for a specific metal with the metal, e.g., nickel 669.7332

.802 8   Auxiliary techniques and procedures; apparatus, equipment, materials

Class refractory material in 669.82

.81   Fuel

.82   Refractory material

Class comprehensive works on refractory materials in 666.72

.83   Firing and heat control

.84   Fluxes and slag

.85   Physical processes

Example: heat exchange

.9   Physical and chemical metallurgy

Physical and chemical phenomena occurring during metallurgical processes; physical and chemical analyses of metals; formation of alloys

Standard subdivisions are added for either or both of the topics named in the heading

Class metalworking and manufacture of primary metal products in 671–673

.92   Chemical analysis

Including assaying

Class chemical analysis of specific metals and their alloys in 669.96

.94   Physicochemical metallurgical phenomena

Examples: alloy binary systems, intermetallic compounds, metallic glass, solid solutions, solidification

Including phase diagrams

Class physicochemical metallurgical phenomena of specific metals and their alloys in 669.96

.95	Metallography

.950 28   Specific kinds of techniques and procedures; apparatus, equipment, materials

.950 282   Microscopical metallography

                 Optical and electron metallography

.950 283   X-ray metallography

.951–.957   Of specific metals and their alloys

         Add to base number 669.95 the numbers following 669 in 669.1–669.7, e.g., aluminum 669.95722

.96   Physical and chemical metallurgy of specific metals and their alloys

         Add to base number 669.96 the numbers following 669 in 669.1–669.7, e.g., titanium 669.967322

         For metallography of specific metals and their alloys, see 669.951–669.957

670   Manufacturing

General aspects: planning, design, fabrication

Class here manufactured products

Class manufacture of products based on specific branches of engineering in 620, on chemical technologies in 660; military applications in 623; the arts in 700; manufacture of final products for specific uses not provided for elsewhere, in 680

Unless separate provision is made, class comprehensive works on products made by a specific process with the process, e.g., seasoned wood 674.38; but coated papers 676.283 (*not* 676.235)

SUMMARY

670.1–.9	Standard subdivisions
671	Metalworking processes and primary metal products
672	Iron, steel, other iron alloys
673	Nonferrous metals
674	Lumber processing, wood products, cork
675	Leather and fur processing
676	Pulp and paper technology
677	Textiles
678	Elastomers and elastomer products
679	Other products of specific kinds of materials

.285   Data processing   Computer applications

         Class here computer-aided design/computer-aided manufacture (CAD/CAM), comprehensive works on computer use in the management of manufacturing and computer-aided design or computer-aided manufacture

         Class computer-aided design (CAD) in 620.00420285, computer use in the management of manufacturing in 658.05, computer-aided manufacture (CAM) in 670.427

         See Manual at 670.285 vs. 670.427

.4   **Special topics**

.42   Factory operations engineering

Class here shop and assembly-line technology

For tools and fabricating equipment, see 621.9; packaging technology, 688.8

[.420 685]   Management of factory operations

Do not use; class in 658.5

.423   Machine-shop practice

.425   Inspection technology

.427   Mechanization and automation of factory operations

Class here assembling machines, computer-aided manufacture (CAM), computer control of factory operations

Class computer-aided design (CAD) in 620.00420285; comprehensive works on computer control in 629.89; computer-aided design/computer-aided manufacture (CAD/CAM), computer integrated manufacturing systems (CIM) in 670.285; automated machine-shop practice in 670.423; automated inspection technology in 670.425

See Manual at 670.285 vs. 670.427

.427 2   Robots

Unless it is redundant, add to base number 670.4272 the numbers following 00 in 004–006, e.g., use of digital microcomputers 670.4272416, but use of digital computers 670.4272 (*not* 670.42724)

.427 5   Computerized process control

Unless it is redundant, add to base number 670.4275 the numbers following 00 in 004–006, e.g., use of digital microcomputers 670.4275416, but use of digital computers 670.4275 (*not* 670.42754)

Class comprehensive works on computerized process control in 629.895

[.685]   Management of production

Do not use; class in 658.5

>   **671–679 Manufacture of products from specific materials**

Class here manufacture of primary products

Class comprehensive works in 670; manufacture of ceramic products in 666, of plastic products in 668.49

See Manual at 671–679 vs. 680

671   **Metalworking processes and primary metal products**

Class metallurgy and interdisciplinary works on metals in 669

For iron, steel, other iron alloys, see 672; nonferrous metals, 673

SUMMARY

> ### 671.2–671.7 Specific metalworking processes

Class comprehensive works in 671, specific processes applied to specific primary products in 671.8

.2 **Foundry practice (Casting)**

See also 671.32–671.34 for hot-working operations

.202 8   Auxiliary techniques and procedures; materials

Class apparatus and equipment in 671.22

.22   Foundry equipment

.23   Patternmaking and moldmaking

.24   Melting

.25   Specific methods of casting

.252   Sand casting

.253   Permanent-mold casting

Example: die casting

.254   Centrifugal casting

.255   Investment casting

Variant names: cire perdue, lost-wax, precision casting

.256   Continuous casting

.3 **Mechanical working and related processes**

> 671.32–671.34 Mechanical working

Class here hot-working operations, cold-working operations, high-energy forming

Class comprehensive works in 671.3

For shot peening, see 671.36

.32   Rolling

.33   Pressing, stamping, forging

.332   Forging

.34	Extruding and drawing
.35	Machining

Including grinding

Class here cutting as a machining process, milling

Class comprehensive works on cutting metal in 671.53

.36	Heat treatment and hardening

Age-hardening, annealing, shot peening, tempering

.37	Powder metallurgical processes (Powder metallurgy)
.373	Sintering
.4	**Electroforming of metals**
.5	**Joining and cutting of metals**
.52	Welding
[.520 287]	Testing and measurement

Do not use; class in 671.520423

.520 4	Special topics
.520 42	Welds (Welded joints)
.520 422	Weldability, weld stability, weld defects
.520 423	Inspection and testing
.521	Electric welding
.521 2	Arc welding
.521 3	Resistance welding

Examples: flash, projection, seam, spot welding

.521 5	Induction welding
.522	Gas welding
.529	Forge, thermit, flow welding
.53	Cutting

Class cutting as a machining process in 671.35

.56	Soldering and brazing

Standard subdivisions are added for either or both of the topics named in the heading

.58	Bonding
.59	Riveting

.7	**Finishing and surface treatment of metals**

Examples: cleaning, deburring

.72   Buffing and polishing

.73   Coating

Example: cladding

Class enameling in 666.2

.732   Electroplating

.733   Hot-metal dipping

.734   Metal spraying

.735   Vapor plating (Vacuum deposition)

Examples: vacuum metalizing, vapor-phase deposition

.736   Diffusion coating

.8   **Primary products**

Class here comprehensive works on metal products

Class a specific metal product not provided for here with the product, e.g., metal furniture 684.105

.82   Rolled products

.821   Patternmaking

.823   Strips and sheets

.83   Forged, pressed, stamped products

.832   Pipes

.84   Extruded and drawn products

Example: cables

.842   Wires

.87   Powder metal products

672   Iron, steel, other iron alloys

Metalworking processes and primary products

Add to base number 672 the numbers following 671 in 671.2–671.8, e.g., heat treatment 672.36, galvanizing 672.732

Subdivisions are used for any or all of the topics named in the heading

For small forge work, see 682

673   Nonferrous metals

Metalworking processes and primary products

Class here alloys of nonferrous metals

Add to each subdivision identified by * the numbers following the numbers following 671 in 671.2–671.8, e.g., welding aluminum 673.72252

.2   **Precious, rare-earth, actinide-series metals**

.22   *Gold

.23   *Silver

.24   *Platinum

.29   Rare-earth and actinide-series metals

.290 01–.290 09   Standard subdivisions

.290 1–.294 9   Specific metals and groups of metals

Add to base number 673.29 the numbers following 546.4 in 546.401–546.44, e.g., uranium 673.2931

.3   ***Copper**

Class here brass, Muntz metal; bronze, gunmetal; copper-aluminum alloys; copper-beryllium alloys

.4   ***Lead**

.5   **Zinc and cadmium**

.52   *Zinc

For brass, Muntz metal, see 673.3

.56   *Cadmium

.6   ***Tin**

For bronze, gunmetal, see 673.3

.7   **Other nonferrous metals**

Examples: iridium, palladium, rhodium

See also 673.24 for platinum

.71   *Mercury

.72   Light, alkali, alkaline-earth metals

Standard subdivisions are added for light, alkali, alkaline-earth metals; for light metals alone

For titanium, see 673.7322; for zirconium, 673.735

.722   *Aluminum

For copper-aluminum alloys, see 673.3

*Add as instructed under 673

| .723 | *Magnesium |
| .724 | *Beryllium |

For copper-beryllium alloys, see 673.3

| .725 | Alkali and alkaline-earth metals |

Contains barium, calcium, cesium, francium, lithium, potassium, radium, rubidium, sodium, strontium

For magnesium, see 673.723; beryllium, 673.724

.73	Metals used in ferroalloys
.732	Titanium, vanadium, manganese
.732 2	*Titanium
.733	Nickel and cobalt
.733 2	*Nickel
.734	Chromium, molybdenum, tungsten
.735	Zirconium and tantalum
.75	Antimony, arsenic, bismuth
.79	Miscellaneous rare metals and metalloids

Limited to gallium, hafnium, indium, niobium, polonium, thallium; germanium, selenium, tellurium

674 Lumber processing, wood products, cork

Use 674.001–674.009 for standard subdivisions

SUMMARY

674.01–.09	Standard subdivisions of lumber technology
.1	Structure, chemical properties, types of lumber
.2	Sawmill operations
.3	Storage and seasoning of lumber
.4	Production of finished lumber
.5	Grading lumber
.8	Wood products
.9	Cork

.01	Philosophy and theory of lumber technology
.02	Miscellany of lumber technology
.021 2	Tables and formulas

Class specifications in 674.5

| .028 7 | Testing and measurement |

Class grading lumber in 674.5

| .03–.09 | Standard subdivisions of lumber technology |

*Add as instructed under 673

>   **674.1–674.5 Lumber technology**

               Class comprehensive works in 674

.1   **Structure, chemical properties, types of lumber**

.12   Structure

                 Gross and microscopic

.13   Chemical properties

                 Including chemical properties of wood extracts

[.132]   Physical properties

                 Relocated to 620.12

[.134]   Chemical properties

                 Number discontinued; class in 674.13

.14   Specific types

                 Class structure of specific types in 674.12, chemical properties of specific
                 types in 674.13

.142   Hardwoods

                 Examples: basswood, beech, cherry, chestnut, elm, maple, oak, poplar

.144   Softwoods

                 Examples: cedar, cypress, fir, hemlock, larch, pine, redwood, spruce

.2   **Sawmill operations**

                 Class wood waste and residues in 674.84

.202 8   Auxiliary techniques and procedures; apparatus, equipment, materials
                 [*formerly* 674.22]

[.22]   Techniques, procedures, apparatus, equipment, materials

                 Use of this number for basic techniques and procedures discontinued; class
                 in 674.2

                 Auxiliary techniques and procedures; apparatus, equipment, materials
                 relocated to 674.2028

.28   Rough lumber

                 Class here dimension stock (cut stock)

                 Use of this number for comprehensive works on rough lumber, wood waste
                 and residues discontinued; class in 674.2

.3   **Storage and seasoning of lumber**

.32   Storage in lumberyards

.38	Seasoning and drying
.382	By air
.384	In kiln
.386	By chemical treatment

.4 **Production of finished lumber**

.42   Production of surfaced lumber

     By planing mills

.43   Production of pattern lumber

     Examples: shiplap, sidings, tongue-and-groove products

.5 **Grading lumber**

     Including inspection and specifications

.8 **Wood products**

     Class here comprehensive works on wood-using technologies

     Class a specific product or wood-using technology not provided for here with the product or technology, e.g., wood as a fuel 662.65, finished lumber 674.4, pulp and paper technology 676, wooden furniture 684.104, carpentry 694

.82   Containers and pallets

     Examples: barrels, boxes, casks, crates

.83   Veneers and composite woods

.833   Veneers

>   674.834–674.836 Composites

     Class comprehensive works in 674.83

.834   Plywood

       See also 674.835 for specialty plywoods

.835   Laminated wood (Specialty plywoods, Sandwich panels)

.836   Particle board

.84   Wood waste and residues

     Examples: excelsior, sawdust, wood flour and shavings

     Class here pollution control

     Class utilization of wood waste and residues in making a specific product with the product, e.g., particle board 674.836

.88   Other products

     Examples: picture frames, signs, spools, toothpicks, wood-cased pencils, woodenware

.9	**Cork**

675   Leather and fur processing

For leather and fur goods, see 685

.2	**Processing of natural leather**
[.202 87]	Testing and measurement
	Do not use; class in 675.29
.22	Preliminary operations
	Examples: fleshing, unhairing (liming), bating hides and skins
.23	Tanning
.24	Dressing
.25	Finishing
	Examples: dyeing, embossing, glazing, production of patent leather
.29	Properties, tests, quality controls
.3	**Fur processing**
	Including manufacture of imitation furs
.4	**Manufacture of imitation leathers**

676   Pulp and paper technology

Class here comprehensive works on paper and paper products

See Manual at 676 vs. 676.1, 676.2

SUMMARY

676.04	**Special topics**
.1	**Pulp**
.2	**Conversion of pulp into paper, and specific types of paper and paper products**
.3	**Paper and paperboard containers**
.4	**Purified pulp**
.5	**Pulp by-products**
.7	**Paper from man-made and noncellulosic fibers**

.04	Special topics
.042	Waste control
	Class here comprehensive works on waste control for paper and paper products [*formerly* 676.26], pollution control
.1	**Pulp**
	Class by-products in 676.5
	See Manual at 676 vs. 676.1, 676.2
[.102 87]	Testing and measurement
	Do not use; class in 676.17

>   676.12–676.14 Specific pulps

Class comprehensive works in 676.1

For purified pulp, see 676.4

.12   Wood pulp

[.120 287]   Testing and measurement

           Do not use; class in 676.121

.121   Properties, tests, quality controls

>   676.122–676.127 Specific processes

Class comprehensive works in 676.12

See Manual at 676 vs. 676.1, 676.2

.122   Mechanical (Ground wood) process

.124   Soda process

.125   Sulfite process

.126   Sulfate (Kraft) process

.127   Semichemical process

.13   Rag pulp

.14   Other pulps

Examples: bagasse, bamboo, cornstalks, hemp, jute, straw

.142   Wastepaper

Class here paper recycling

.17   Properties, tests, quality controls

Class properties, tests, quality controls of specific pulps in 676.12–676.14

.18   Molded products and pulpboards

.182   Molded products

.183   Pulpboards

Examples: chip boards, fiberboards, wallboards

>   **676.2–676.5 Pulp products**

Class comprehensive works in 676

For molded products and pulpboards, see 676.18

.2   **Conversion of pulp into paper, and specific types of paper and paper products**

Use of this number for comprehensive works on paper and paper products discontinued; class in 676

Class paper recycling in 676.142

See Manual at 676 vs. 676.1, 676.2

[.202 87]   Testing and measurement

Do not use; class in 676.27

>   676.22–676.27 General topics

Class comprehensive works in 676.2, general topics of specific types of paper and paper products in 676.28

.22   Production by hand

.23   Specific processes of machine production

Materials and processes

Use of this number for comprehensive works on manufacture with machines discontinued; class in 676.2

See Manual at 676 vs. 676.1, 676.2

.232   Basic processes

.234   Finishing

Examples: calendering, coloring, creping, sizing

For coating, see 676.235

.235   Coating

[.26]   Waste control

Use of this number for waste control in conversion of pulp to paper discontinued; class in 676.2

Comprehensive works on waste control for paper and paper products relocated to 676.042

.27   Properties, tests, quality controls

.28   Specific types of paper and paper products

.280 27   Patents and identification marks

Example: watermarks

.282   Graphic arts paper

.282 3   Stationery

Including onionskin paper

.282 4   Book paper

           Class coated book paper in 676.283

.282 5   Drawing and art paper

.282 6   Currency paper

           Papers for printing money, bonds, securities

.283   Coated paper

.284   Specialty paper

.284 2   Tissue paper

           Examples: cleansing tissues, toilet paper

           Class onionskin paper in 676.2823

.284 4   Blotting and saturating paper

.284 5   Vulcanized and parchment papers

           See also 685 for parchment prepared from the skin of an animal

.284 8   Wallpaper

.286   Unsized paper

           Example: newsprint

.287   Wrapping and bag papers

           Examples: bogus wrapping, butcher paper, kraft wrapping, Manila paper

.288   Paperboard

           Examples: bristol board, cardboard, food board, pasteboard

.289   Roofing and building papers

.3   **Paper and paperboard containers**

.32   Boxes and cartons

           Examples: corrugated and solid paperboard boxes, folding boxes

           For food board containers, see 676.34

.33   Bags

.34   Food board containers

           Examples: food cartons, paper plates and cups

.4   **Purified pulp**

           Production of alpha cellulose from wood pulp and cotton linters

.5   **Pulp by-products**

           Examples: fatty acids, lignin, resins, tall oil, turpentine

.7   **Paper from man-made and noncellulosic fibers**

677   Textiles

Production of fibers, fabrics, cordage

Class here comprehensive works on manufacture of textiles and clothing

Class manufacture of clothing in 687

SUMMARY

677.001–.009	Standard subdivisions
.02	General topics
.1	Textiles of bast fibers
.2	Textiles of seed-hair fibers
.3	Textiles of animal fibers
.4	Textiles of man-made fibers
.5	Other textiles of specific fibers
.6	Special-process fabrics regardless of composition
.7	Cordage, trimmings and allied products
.8	Surgical gauze and cotton

.001   Philosophy and theory

.002   Miscellany

[.002 8]   Auxiliary techniques and procedures; apparatus, equipment

            Do not use; class in 677.028

.003–.009   Standard subdivisions

.02   General topics

.022   Designs (Working patterns)

.028   Techniques, procedures, apparatus, equipment, materials, products

.028 2   Operations

.028 21   Preliminary operations

            Examples: carding, combing

.028 22   Spinning, twisting, reeling

.028 24   Weaving, knitting, felting

.028 242   Weaving

.028 245   Knitting

.028 25   Basic finishing

            Physical and chemical processes

            Examples: beetling, calendering, creping, mercerizing, pressing, shearing, singeing, tentering

            For dyeing and printing, see 667.3

.028 3   Materials

.028 32   Fibers

.028 35   Textile chemicals

.028 5	Power equipment
.028 52	Spinning machines
.028 54	Looms and loom equipment
.028 55	Basic finishing machines
.028 6	Products

For tests and quality controls of products, see 677.0287

.028 62	Yarns and threads
.028 64	Fabrics
.028 7	Testing and measurement

Including tests and quality controls of products

| .029 | Waste control |

Class here pollution control

> ### 677.1–677.5 Textiles of specific composition

Class here specific kinds of textile fibers

Class comprehensive works in 677, special-process fabrics regardless of composition in 677.6

.1   **Textiles of bast fibers**

.11   Flax

[.110 28]   Auxiliary techniques and procedures; apparatus, equipment

Do not use; class in 677.112–677.117

.112–.117   Techniques, procedures, apparatus, equipment, materials, products

Add to base number 677.11 the numbers following 677.028 in 677.0282–677.0287, e.g., linen fabrics 677.1164

.12   Hemp

.13   Jute

.15   Ramie

.18   Coir

.2   **Textiles of seed-hair fibers**

.21   Cotton

[.210 28]   Auxiliary techniques and procedures; apparatus, equipment

Do not use; class in 677.212–677.217

.212–.217   Techniques, procedures, apparatus, equipment, materials, products

Add to base number 677.21 the numbers following 677.028 in 677.0282–677.0287, e.g., cotton ginning, carding, combing 677.2121

.23	Kapok

.3   **Textiles of animal fibers**

.31   Sheep wool

Class here comprehensive works on wool

For llama, alpaca, vicuña, guanaco wools, see 677.32

[.310 28]   Auxiliary techniques and procedures; apparatus, equipment

Do not use; class in 677.312–677.317

.312–.317   Techniques, procedures, apparatus, equipment, materials, products

Add to base number 677.31 the numbers following 677.028 in 677.0282–677.0287, e.g., sheep wool fibers 677.3132

.32   Llama, alpaca, vicuña, guanaco wools

.33   Goat hair

.34   Camel's hair

.35   Rabbit hair

.36   Waste and reused wool and hair

.39   Silk

.391   Cultivated silk

[.391 028]   Auxiliary techniques and procedures; apparatus, equipment

Do not use; class in 677.3912–677.3917

.391 2–.391 7   Techniques, procedures, apparatus, equipment, materials, products

Add to base number 677.391 the numbers following 677.028 in 677.0282–677.0287, e.g., beetling cultivated silk 677.39125

.392   Wild silk (Tussah silk)

.394   Waste and reused silk

.4   **Textiles of man-made fibers**

Class here chemistry of man-made fibers [*formerly also* 547.85]

.46   Cellulosics (Rayon and acetates)

Use 677.46001–677.46009 for standard subdivisions

For textiles of paper fibers, see 677.5

.460 1–.460 9   Standard subdivisions of rayon

\>   677.461–677.463 Rayon

Class comprehensive works in 677.46

.461   Nitrocellulose

.462	Cuprammonium rayon
.463	Viscose rayon
.464	Cellulose acetate
.47	Noncellulosics

For fiber glass, see 677.52

.472	Azlon
.473	Polyamides (Nylons)
.474	Other polymerization textiles
.474 2	Acrylics

Class here polyacrylics

.474 3	Polyesters
.474 4	Vinyls

Examples: nytrils, sarans, vinyons

Class here polyvinyls

.474 5	Olefins

Examples: polyethylene, polypropylene

.474 8	Polyfluoro hydrocarbons
.5	**Other textiles of specific fibers**
.51	Of asbestos fibers
.52	Of fiber glass
.53	Of metal fibers
.54	Of unaltered vegetable fibers

Examples: bamboo, cane, raffia, rattan, rush

.55	Of elastic fibers
[.57]	Of paper fibers

Number discontinued; class in 677.5

.6	**Special-process fabrics regardless of composition**

Class here nonwoven fabrics

.61	Fancy-weave fabrics

For tapestries, carpets, rugs, see 677.64; openwork fabrics, 677.65

.615	In dobby weave

Examples: bird's-eye, figured madras, huckaback, sharkskin

.616	In Jacquard weave

Examples: brocade, brocatelle, damask, lamé, upholstery fabrics

.617	In pile weave

Examples: chenille, corduroy, frieze, plush, terry cloth, velour, velvet, velveteen

.62	Woven felt

Class comprehensive works on felt in 677.63

.624	Flannel and swanskin yard goods
.626	Blankets, lap robes, coverlets
.63	Nonwoven felt

Class here comprehensive works on felt

For woven felt, see 677.62

.632	Yard goods and carpets
.64	Tapestries, carpets, rugs
.642	Tapestry yard goods
.643	Carpets and rugs

For nonwoven felt carpets, see 677.632

.65	Openwork fabrics

For chain-stitch and knotted fabrics, see 677.66

.652	In leno weave

Examples: marquisettes and grenadines

.653	Laces

Contains bobbin, needle, machine laces

.654	Tulles
.66	Chain-stitch and knotted fabrics
.661	Knitted fabrics
.662	Crocheted fabrics
.663	Tatted fabrics
.664	Netted fabrics
.68	Fabrics with functional finishes

Examples: drip-dry, durable press fabrics

Class specific types of special-process fabrics regardless of finish in 677.61−677.66

.681	Crease- and wrinkle-resistant fabrics

.682	Waterproof and water-repellent fabrics
.688	Shrinkage-controlled fabrics
.689	Flameproof and flame-resistant fabrics
.69	Bonded and laminated fabrics
.7	**Cordage, trimmings and allied products**
.71	Ropes, twines, strings

> *For passementerie, see 677.76*

.76	Passementerie

Examples: decorative bias bindings, braids, cords, gimps, lacings, ribbons, tapes, tinsel; upholstery trimmings

.77	Machine embroidery

Examples: clip spot, lappet, Schiffli, swivel (dotted swiss) embroidery

Class laces in 677.653

.8	**Surgical gauze and cotton**

Examples: bandages, sanitary napkins

678 Elastomers and elastomer products

SUMMARY

678.2	**Rubber**
.3	**Rubber products**
.4	**Properties of rubber**
.5	**Latexes**
.6	**Natural elastomers**
.7	**Synthetic elastomers**

.2	**Rubber**

> *For rubber products, see 678.3; properties of rubber, 678.4; natural rubber, 678.62; synthetic rubber, 678.72*

.202 8	Auxiliary techniques and procedures; apparatus, equipment

Class materials in 678.21

.21	Materials

> *For reclaimed rubber, see 678.29*

.22	Mastication
.23	Compounding

Examples: use of accelerators, antioxidants, pigments, solvents

.24	Vulcanization
.27	Molding, extruding, calendering

.29	Reclaimed rubber and waste control
	Including devulcanizing
	Class here pollution control
.3	**Rubber products**
	Class elastic fiber textiles in 677.55
	For natural rubber products, see 678.63; synthetic rubber products, 678.723
.32	Tires
.33	Overshoes
.34	Articles molded and vulcanized in presses
	Examples: doorstops, hollow ware, hot-water bottles, tiles
.35	Extruded articles
	Examples: inner tubes, rubber bands, weather stripping, windshield wipers
.36	Articles made by dipping, spreading, electrodeposition
	Examples: conveyor and driving belts, hose, sheeting
.4	**Properties of rubber**
.5	**Latexes**
	For natural latexes, see 678.61; synthetic latexes, 678.71
.502 8	Auxiliary techniques and procedures; apparatus, equipment
	Class materials in 678.521
.52	Techniques, procedures, apparatus, equipment, materials
.521	Materials
.522	Preliminary treatment
	Examples: preservation, concentration, creaming, centrifuging, preparation of latex biscuits
.524	Vulcanization
.527	Other operations
	Examples: casting, coating, dipping, electrodepositing, molding, spreading
.53	Products
.532	Foam articles
.533	Articles made by dipping and casting
	Example: feeding-bottle nipples
	Surgeons' gloves relocated to 685.43

.538   Articles made by extruding, spreading, spraying, electrodeposition

Use of this number for other products discontinued; class in 678.53

.54   Properties

.6   Natural elastomers

.61   Natural latexes

.62   Natural rubber

For natural rubber products, see 678.63; properties of natural rubber, 678.64

.63   Natural rubber products

.64   Properties of natural rubber

.68   Chemical derivatives of natural rubber

Examples: cyclo and halogenated rubber, rubber hydrochloride

.7   Synthetic elastomers

.71   Synthetic latexes [*formerly also* 547.8425]

.72   Synthetic rubber and derivatives

Examples: acrylonitrile rubber (GR-A), butadiene-styrene rubber (GR-S), chloroprene rubber (GR-M), isobutylene rubber (GR-I), polybutadiene rubber, polyurethane rubber

Standard subdivisions are added for synthetic rubber and derivatives, for synthetic rubber

Class comprehensive works on polyurethanes in 668.4239

.720 28   Auxiliary techniques and procedures; apparatus, equipment, materials

Class auxiliary techniques and procedures, apparatus, equipment, materials for synthetic rubber in 678.722

.722   Techniques, procedures, apparatus, equipment, materials for synthetic rubber

.723   Synthetic rubber products

.724   Properties of synthetic rubber

.728   Chemical derivatives of synthetic rubber

.73   High-styrene resins (Elastoplastics)

679   Other products of specific kinds of materials

.4   Products of keratinous and dentinal materials

.43   Ivory products

.47   Feather products

.6   **Products of fibers and bristles**

Examples: brooms, brushes, mops

.7   **Products of tobacco**

See also 688.4 for tobacco substitutes

.72   Cigars

.73   Cigarettes

680   Manufacture of products for specific uses

Not provided for elsewhere

General aspects: planning, design, fabrication

Class here interdisciplinary works on handicrafts

Class repairs of household equipment by members of household in 643.7; artistic handicraft work in 745.5; manufacture of products based on specific branches of engineering with engineering in 620, e.g., military engineering 623, automobile manufacture 629.2; and, except as provided for below, class manufacture of products of specific materials for specific uses in 671–679, e.g., manufacture of steel products 672, but manufacture of steel furniture 684.105

See Manual at 671–679 vs. 680; 680; 745.5 vs. 680

SUMMARY

681	Precision instruments and other devices
682	Small forge work (Blacksmithing)
683	Hardware and household appliances
684	Furnishings and home workshops
685	Leather and fur goods, and related products
686	Printing and related activities
687	Clothing and accessories
688	Other final products, and packaging technology

681   Precision instruments and other devices

SUMMARY

681.1	Instruments for measuring time, counting and calculating machines and instruments
.2	Testing and measuring instruments
.4	Optical instruments
.6	Printing, writing, duplicating machines and equipment
.7	Other scientific and technological instruments, machinery, equipment
.8	Musical instruments

.1   **Instruments for measuring time, counting and calculating machines and instruments**

For testing and measuring instruments, see 681.2

.11   Instruments for measuring time [*formerly also* 529.78]

.111   Ancient and primitive instruments

         Examples: hourglasses, sundials, water clocks

.112   Constituent parts (Clockwork)

         Examples: gears, escapements, bearings, regulating devices

.113   Clocks

         Class here interdisciplinary works on clocks

         Class clocks considered as works of art in 739.3

         For constituent parts, see 681.112; pneumatic clocks, 681.115; electric clocks, 681.116; chronographs, chronoscopes, chronometers, 681.118

.114   Watches

         Class here interdisciplinary works on watches

         Class watches considered as works of art in 739.3

         For constituent parts, see 681.112; chronographs, chronoscopes, chronometers, 681.118

.115   Pneumatic clocks

.116   Electric clocks

.118   Chronographs, chronoscopes, chronometers

         Examples: metronomes, stopwatches, tachometers, time clocks, time and date recorders, timers

.14   Counting and calculating machines and instruments

         Examples: calculators, cash registers, slide rules, sorting machines, voting machines

         For computers, see 621.39

.2   **Testing and measuring instruments**

         Examples: calorimeters [*formerly also* 536.62]; electrical instruments for measuring nonelectrical quantities [*formerly also* 621.379]; electronic gauges, indicators, meters, probes of general utility [*all formerly also* 621.381548]; measuring tools [*formerly* 621.994]; flowmeters

         Class here testing and measuring instruments of general application in science or technology, testing and measuring instruments for nontechnological application, instruments for measuring physical quantities

         Class testing and measuring instruments for a specific branch of science (other than instruments for measuring physical quantities) in 681.75; for a specific technological application with the manufacturing number, e.g., aircraft instrumentation 629.135, medical diagnostic equipment 681.761

         For instruments for measuring electrical quantities, see 621.37; for testing and measuring electronic signals, 621.381548; for measuring time, 681.11

.4   **Optical instruments [*formerly also* 535.33]**

.41   Specific instruments

Class component parts of specific instruments in 681.42–681.43

.411   Eyeglasses

.412   Telescopes, opera and field glasses

.413   Microscopes

.414   Spectroscopes

.414 2–.414 6   Optical and paraphotic spectroscopes

Add to base number 681.414 the numbers following 535.84 in 535.842–535.846, e.g., infrared spectroscopes 681.4142

.414 8   Other spectroscopes

Examples: magnetic resonance, microwave, radiofrequency, X- and gamma-ray spectroscopes

.415   Photometers

.416   Polarimeters

.418   Photographic equipment

Examples: cameras, projectors, accessories

Class film and other chemical photographic supplies in 661.808

For photometers, see 681.415; photocopying equipment, 681.65

\>   681.42–681.43 Component parts

Class comprehensive works in 681.4

.42   Lenses, prisms, mirrors

.423   Lenses

.428   Mirrors

.43   Frames and other housings

.6   **Printing, writing, duplicating machines and equipment**

Examples: computer output microform (COM) devices [*formerly* 621.3987], pens, mechanical pencils, rubber stamps

Class facsimile recorders in 621.38235, wood-cased pencils in 674.88

.61   Stenographic and composing machines, typewriters

.62   Printers and printing presses

Class here computer output printers [*formerly* 621.3987]

.65   Photocopying equipment

.7	**Other scientific and technological instruments, machinery, equipment**
	Not provided for elsewhere
.75	Scientific instruments and equipment
	Class here testing and measuring equipment for specific branches of science
	Class comprehensive works on scientific testing and measuring instruments in 681.2
.753	Physical instruments and equipment
	Including instruments with multiple applications based on physical principles, e.g., gyroscopes
	Class instruments for measuring physical quantities in 681.2
.754	Chemical instruments and equipment
.755	Geological instruments and equipment
.757	Biological instruments and equipment
.76	Technological instruments, machinery, equipment
	Examples: construction, pollution-control, mining, surveying equipment
	Class here testing and measuring instruments in specific branches of technology not provided for elsewhere
	Class comprehensive works on technological testing and measuring instruments in 681.2
.760 4	Special topics
.760 41	Pressure vessels
.761	Medical instruments, machinery, equipment
	Examples: condoms, diagnostic equipment, prosthetic devices
	For artificial legs, see 685.38
.763	Agricultural instruments, machinery, equipment
.763 1	For plant culture
.763 6	For animal culture
.766	For chemical and related technologies
.766 4	For food and beverage technology
.766 5	For petroleum and industrial gas technologies
.766 6	For ceramic technology
.766 8	For plastic and elastomer technologies
.766 9	For metallurgy
.767	For nonchemical manufactures
.767 1	For metal manufactures

.767 6	For wood and paper technologies
.767 7	For textile and clothing technologies

.8   **Musical instruments**

Class hand construction in 784.1923

[.81–.83]   Specific types of instruments

Relocated to 681.86–681.88

.86–.88   Specific types of instruments [*formerly* 681.81–681.83]

Add to base number 681.8 the numbers following 78 in 786–788, e.g., manufacture of pianos 681.862

Class hand construction in 786–788

682   Small forge work (Blacksmithing)

.1   **Horseshoeing**

.4   **Hand-forged tools and ironwork**

683   Hardware and household appliances

Class here comprehensive works on manufacture of hardware and building supplies

Class a specific hardware or building supply product not provided for here with the product, e.g., tools 621.9, paints 667.6

.3   **Locksmithing**

.31   Bolts and latches

.32   Locks and keys

.34   Safes and strongboxes

.4   **Small firearms**

Class here interdisciplinary works on small firearms, on gunsmithing

Class military small arms in 623.44

.400 1   Philosophy and theory

.400 2   Miscellany

[.400 288]   Maintenance and repair

Do not use; class in 683.403

.400 3–.400 9   Standard subdivisions

>   683.401–683.406 General topics

Class comprehensive works in 683.4

.401   Design

[.402]	Manufacture
	Number discontinued; class in 683.4
.403	Maintenance and repair
.406	Ammunition
.42	Rifles and shotguns
.422	Rifles
.426	Shotguns
.43	Handguns
.432	Pistols (Single-shot and automatic)
.436	Revolvers

.8 **Household utensils and appliances**

Class nonmetallic household utensils and appliances with the material, e.g., woodenware 674.88

.802 88   Maintenance and repair

Class maintenance and repair by members of household in 643.6

.82   Kitchen utensils

Examples: cutlery, pots, pans, pails

.83   Electrical appliances

Class comprehensive works on electrical equipment in 621.31042

For electrical equipment requiring special installation, see 683.88

.88   Heavy equipment

Electrical, gas, other equipment requiring special installation

Examples: dishwashers, dryers, garbage disposal units, ranges, stoves, washing machines, water heaters

Class heating, ventilating, air-conditioning equipment in 697

For refrigerators and freezers, see 621.57

684   Furnishings and home workshops

Use 684.001–684.009 for standard subdivisions for furnishings and home workshops, for furnishing alone

.08   Woodworking

Class here comprehensive works on home (amateur) workshops

For metalworking, see 684.09

.082   With hand tools

.083   With power tools

.084	Surface finishing
.09	Metalworking
.1	**Furniture**

Use 684.1001–684.1009 for standard subdivisions

>   684.104–684.106 General topics

Class comprehensive works in 684.1

.104	Wooden furniture
[.104 028 8]	Maintenance and repair

                Do not use; class in 684.1044

.104 2	Basic construction
.104 3	Surface finishing
.104 4	Maintenance and repair
.104 42	Body restoration
.104 43	Surface refinishing
.105	Metal furniture
.106	Furniture in other materials

Examples: composite materials, plastics, rattan, tiles

>   684.12–684.16 Specific kinds of furniture

Class comprehensive works in 684.1, outdoor furniture in 684.18

.12	Upholstered furniture

Examples: couches, sofas, upholstered chairs

.13	Chairs and tables

For upholstered chairs, see 684.12

.14	Desks
.15	Beds

Including frames, springs, mattresses

.16	Cabinets and built-in furniture

Examples: bookcases, chests, china and linen cabinets, dressers, file cabinets, shelving

Class built-in wooden shelves in 694.6

.18   Outdoor furniture

Examples: garden, patio, porch furniture

Class camping furniture in 685.53

.3   Fabric furnishings

Examples: curtains, draperies, hangings, slipcovers

For carpets and rugs, see 677.643

685   Leather and fur goods, and related products

Including parchment prepared from the skin of an animal

See also 676.2845 for parchment paper made from pulp

.1   Saddlery and harness making

.2   Leather and fur clothing and accessories

Class leather and fur footwear in 685.3, leather and fur gloves and mittens in 685.4

.22   Leather

Examples: aprons, belts, jackets, skirts, trousers

.24   Fur

Examples: coats, hats, jackets, muffs, neckpieces, stoles

.3   Footwear and related products

For overshoes, see 678.33; hosiery, 687.3

.31   Boots and shoes

Class wooden shoes and clogs in 685.32, shoes for specific activities in 685.36, for the disabled in 685.38

.310 01   Philosophy and theory

.310 02   Miscellany

[.310 028 8]   Maintenance and repair

Do not use; class in 685.3104

.310 03–.310 09   Standard subdivisions

.310 2   Design

.310 3   Construction

.310 4   Maintenance and repair

.32   Wooden shoes and clogs

.36   Footwear and related products for specific activities

.361   Ice skates

.362   Roller skates and skateboards

.363	Snowshoes
.364	Skis

> Class manufacture of equipment connected with snow skiing in 688.7693

.367	Stilts
.38	Footwear and related products for the disabled

> Examples: artificial legs, crutches, special shoes

.4   **Gloves and mittens**

> Regardless of material

.41	Conventional gloves
.43	Specialized gloves and mittens, gauntlets

> Examples: surgeons' gloves [*formerly also* 678.533], athletic gloves and mitts, protective gloves for industry

.47	Conventional mittens

.5   **Luggage, handbags, camping equipment**

.51	Luggage and handbags

> Including briefcases, attaché cases

.53	Camping equipment

> Examples: camp beds, campstools, sleeping bags, tents

686   Printing and related activities

> Class here design and manufacture of publications, book arts
>
> Class interdisciplinary works on the book in 002, book illustration in 741.64
>
> *See also 681.6 for manufacture of printing equipment*

SUMMARY

686.1	**Invention of printing**
.2	**Printing**
.3	**Bookbinding**
.4	**Photocopying (Photoduplication)**

.1   **Invention of printing**

.2   **Printing**

Including printing by museums [*formerly* 069.7]

Class here printing in the Latin alphabet

Class interdisciplinary works on print media in 302.232, comprehensive works on printing and publishing in 070.5

Works on "desktop publishing" that emphasize typography are classed in 686.22, e.g., microcomputer software for typesetting 686.2254436

See also 070.593 for self publishing

.209   Historical, geographical, persons treatment

Class invention of printing in 686.1

.21   Printing in specific non-Latin alphabets and characters

Class here typefounding, typecasting, typefaces for specific non-Latin alphabets and characters

Class other specific aspects of printing in non-Latin alphabets and characters with the aspect, e.g., letterpress printing 686.2312

[.212]   Braille and other raised characters

Relocated to 686.282

[.217]   Latin alphabet

Use of this number for comprehensive works on printing in the Latin alphabet discontinued; class in 686.2

Typefaces for the Latin alphabet relocated to 686.224

.218   Greek alphabet

.219   Other alphabets and characters

Add to base number 686.21 notation 91–99 from Table 6, e.g., Cyrillic alphabet 686.21918

.22   Typography

.221   Typefounding and typecasting

.224   Typefaces

Design, style, specimens of letters, ornaments, other characters and devices

Class here typefaces for the Latin alphabet [*formerly* 686.217]

Class typefaces for specific non-Latin alphabets and characters in 686.21, for braille and other raised characters in 686.282

.224 7   Specific typefaces and kinds of typefaces for the Latin alphabet

Examples: Gothic, italic, roman type; Bodoni, Garamond, Times Roman type

.225	Composition (Typesetting)

[.225 028 5]   Data processing   Computer applications

Do not use; class in 686.22544

.225 2   Page design

Including layout, paste-up

.225 3   Hand composition

.225 4   Machine composition

.225 42   By use of linotype and other human-operated equipment

.225 44   By use of computer-operated and other automatic equipment

Example: phototypesetting (photocomposition)

Class here computerized typesetting

Unless it is redundant, add to base number 686.22544 the numbers following 00 in 004–006, e.g., microcomputer programs for typesetting 686.22544536, the use of digital microcomputers 686.22544416, but the use of digital computers 686.22544 (*not* 686.225444)

.225 5   Proofreading

.225 6   Imposition and lockup

.23   Presswork (Impression)

Class interdisciplinary works on use of computer printers as low-volume output devices in 004.77; a specific use with the use, e.g., use in typesetting 686.22544477

For printing special graphic materials, see 686.28

See also 621.38235 for facsimile transmission, 681.6 for manufacture of printing equipment

.230 4   Special topics

.230 42   Color printing

.231   Mechanical techniques

Class photomechanical techniques in 686.232

.231 2   Printing from type

Class here comprehensive works on letterpress techniques

Class printing from plates in 686.2314

.231 4   Printing from plates

Printing from stereotypes, electrotypes, autotypes, engraved plates, paper mats

See also 686.2315 for printing from planographic plates

.231 5	Planographic (Flat-surface)

Class here lithography and offset (offset lithography)

For photolithography, photo-offset, collotype, see 686.2325

.231 6	Stencil techniques

Example: silk-screen

.232	Photomechanical techniques
.232 5	Photolithography, photo-offset, collotype (gelatin process)

See also 621.381531 for photolithography in manufacture of printed circuits (microlithography)

[.232 6]	Photometallography

Number discontinued; class in 686.232

.232 7	Photoengraving (Photointaglio)

Examples: photogravure, photoetching, line and halftone cuts

.233	Nonimpact techniques

Examples: electrographic, electrophotographic, ink jet, laser processes

See also 686.44 for electrophotographic processes in photocopying

.28	Printing special graphic materials
.282	Braille and other raised characters [*formerly also* 686.212]

Class comprehensive works on braille and other raised character alphabets in 411

.283	Maps
.284	Music
.288	Materials of direct monetary value

Examples: bank notes, postage stamps, securities

.3	**Bookbinding**

Processes and materials

Use 686.3001–686.3009 for standard subdivisions

.302	Hand and fine binding
.303	Specific kinds of commercial binding

Use of this number for comprehensive works on commercial binding discontinued; class in 686.3

.303 2	Individual-copy (Library) binding
.303 4	Edition binding
.34	Types of covers
.342	Leather

.343	Cloth and imitation leather
.344	Paper
.35	Methods of fastening

Examples: hand sewing, oversewing, side-sewing, wire-stitching; perfect binding and other kinds of gluing

.36	Ornamentation

Examples: gilding, lettering, marbling, tooling

.4 **Photocopying (Photoduplication)**

Class here interdisciplinary works on photocopying

Class telefax in 621.38235

See also 681.65 for manufacture of photocopying equipment

.42	Blueprinting
.43	Microphotography

Production of microfilm and other microreproductions

.44	Electrostatic and electrophotographic processes

Including xerography

.45	Production of photostats

687 **Clothing and accessories**

Class here casual clothes, sports clothes

Unless other instructions are given, class complex subjects with aspects in two or more subdivisions of this schedule in the one coming last, e.g., military headgear 687.4 (*not* 687.15)

Class interdisciplinary works on clothing in 391; interdisciplinary works on clothing construction in 646.4

For leather and fur clothing, see 685.2

SUMMARY

687.01–.09	Standard subdivisions
.1	Specific kinds of garments
.2	Underwear
.3	Hosiery
.4	Headgear
.8	Items auxiliary to clothing construction (Notions)

.04	General topics
.042	Patternmaking and grading
.043	Cutting
.044	Tailoring

[.045]	Dressmaking
	Relocated to 687.112
.081	Men's clothing
	Class here men's house garments [*formerly* 687.11042]
.082	Women's clothing
	Class here women's house garments [*formerly* 687.12]
.083	Young people's clothing
	Class here children's house garments [*formerly* 687.13]

.1   **Specific kinds of garments**

Use of this number for outer garments discontinued; class in 687

> *For footwear, see 685.3; gloves and mittens, 685.4; underwear, 687.2; hosiery, 687.3; headgear, 687.4*

.11   Miscellaneous kinds of garments

Limited to those provided for below

Use of this number for comprehensive works on house garments discontinued; class in 687

[.110 4]   Special topics

Use of this number discontinued; class in 687.11

[.110 42]   Men's house garments

Relocated to 687.081

.112   Dresses

Class here dressmaking [*formerly* 687.045]

.113   Suits, trousers, jackets

.115   Shirts, blouses, tops

.117   Skirts

[.12]   Women's house garments

Relocated to 687.082

[.13]   Children's house garments

Relocated to 687.083

.14   Outer coats and related garments

Class here comprehensive works on coats

Class suit coats, suit jackets in 687.113

[.140 81–.140 82]   For men and women

Do not use; class in 687.141–687.142

.140 83	For young adults

Class outer coats and related garments for children in 687.143, for young adult men aged twenty-one and over in 687.141, for young adult women twenty-one and over in 687.142

.140 84	For persons in specific stages of adulthood

Class outer coats and related garments for adult men regardless of age in 687.141, for adult women regardless of age in 687.142

.141	For men

Class outer coats and related garments for young adult men in 687.1408351

.142	For women

Class outer coats and related garments for young adult women in 687.1408352

.143	For children

> 687.144–687.147 Sweaters, wraps, specific types of outer coats

Class comprehensive works in 687.14

.144	Overcoats

Example: topcoats

.145	Raincoats
.146	Sweaters

Examples: pullovers and cardigans

.147	Stoles, cloaks, jackets
.15	Uniforms and symbolic garments

Examples: civil and military uniforms, ceremonial and academic robes, ecclesiastical vestments

.16	Garments for special purposes

Examples: athletic garments, costumes, evening and formal dress, fire-resistant and other protective clothing, maternity garments, wedding clothes

Use 687 for casual and sports clothes

For uniforms and symbolic garments, see 687.15

.165	Nightclothes

.19 Accessories

Examples: aprons, belts, cuffs, handkerchiefs, muffs, neckwear, scarves

Class interdisciplinary works on accessories in 391.44, on making jewelry in 739.27, on making costume jewelry in 688.2

For gloves and mittens, see 685.4; headgear 687.4

.2 Underwear

For hosiery, see 687.3

[.208 1–.208 3] Underwear for men, women, children

Do not use; class in 687.21–687.23

.208 4 Underwear for persons in specific stages of adulthood

Class underwear for adult men regardless of age in 687.21, for adult women regardless of age in 687.22

.208 7 Underwear for handicapped and ill persons

Class supporting undergarments worn for medical or health reasons in 687.25

.21 Men's underwear

.22 Women's underwear

Class here comprehensive works on lingerie

Class women's nightclothes in 687.165082

.23 Children's underwear

Class young men's underwear in 687.21, young women's underwear in 687.22

.25 Supporting undergarments worn for medical or health reasons

Examples: surgical corsets and belts

Use of this number for supporting undergarments not worn for medical or health reasons discontinued; class in 687.2

.3 Hosiery

.4 Headgear

Class here nonwoven felt hats

Class headscarves in 687.19

[.408 1–.408 3] Men's, women's, children's headgear

Do not use; class in 687.41–687.43

.408 4 Headgear for persons in specific stages of adulthood

Class headgear for adult men regardless of age in 687.41, for adult women regardless of age in 687.42

.41 Men's headgear

.42	Women's headgear
.43	Children's headgear

Class headgear for young men in 687.41, for young women in 687.42

.8   Items auxiliary to clothing construction (Notions)

Examples: buttons, hooks and eyes, needles, padding, pins, shields, slide fasteners, snaps, thread and yarn

688   Other final products, and packaging technology

.1   Models and miniatures

Class here interdisciplinary works on models and miniatures

Class interdisciplinary works on handcrafted models and miniatures in 745.5928; models and miniatures of a specific object with the object, using notation 0228 from Table 1, e.g., scale models of space stations 629.4420228

See Manual at 745.5928

.2   Costume jewelry

Class here interdisciplinary works on making costume jewelry

Class interdisciplinary works on costume jewelry in 391.7, on making jewelry in 739.27; handcrafted costume jewelry in 745.5942

.4   Smokers' supplies

Examples: ash trays, cigarette holders and cases, hookahs, lighters, tobacco pouches, tobacco substitutes

.42   Pipes

.5   Accessories for personal grooming

Examples: combs, electric shavers, nail-care tools, razors, razor blades, tweezers

For cosmetics, see 668.55; brushes, 679.6

.6   Nonmotor land vehicles

Examples: carriages, carts, wagons, wheelbarrows

For cycles, see 629.227

See Manual at 629.046 vs. 388

.7   Recreational equipment

.72   Toys

Class here interdisciplinary works on mass-produced and handcrafted toys

Class handcrafted toys in 745.592

.722	Dolls, puppets, marionettes
.722 1	Dolls
.722 4	Puppets and marionettes

.723	Doll houses and furniture
.724	Soft toys

Example: stuffed animals

Class stuffed dolls in 688.7221

.725   Educational toys

Examples: construction toys, science sets

.726   Novelties, ornaments, puzzles, tricks

Not provided for elsewhere

.728   Action toys

Mechanical, electrical, electronic, others

Class scale-model action toys in 688.1

>   688.74–688.79 Equipment for sports and games

Not provided for elsewhere

Class comprehensive works in 688.7

.74   Equipment for indoor games of skill

Add to base number 688.74 the numbers following 794 in 794.1–794.8, e.g., chessmen 688.741

.75   Equipment for games of chance

Add to base number 688.75 the numbers following 795 in 795.1–795.4, e.g., playing cards 688.754

.76   Equipment for outdoor sports and games

Add to base number 688.76 the numbers following 796 in 796.1–796.9, e.g., tennis rackets 688.76342; however, class skates, skateboards, skis in 685.36; camping equipment in 685.53

For equipment for equestrian sports and animal racing, see 688.78; equipment for fishing, hunting, shooting, 688.79

.78   Equipment for equestrian sports and animal racing

Example: hurdles

.79   Equipment for fishing, hunting, shooting

Add to base number 688.79 the numbers following 799 in 799.1–799.3, e.g., artificial flies 688.7912

For small firearms, see 683.4

.8　　**Packaging technology**

Materials, equipment, techniques

Class interdisciplinary works on packaging in 658.564; artistic aspects of containers in 700, e.g., vases 738.38; manufacture and use of containers made of a specific material with the material, e.g., paper containers 676.3

[689]　[Unassigned]

Most recently used in Edition 14

690　Buildings

General aspects: planning, analysis, engineering design, construction, destruction of habitable structures and their utilities

Class interdisciplinary works on design and construction of buildings in 721

See Manual at 643.7 vs. 690; 690 vs. 624; 721 vs. 690

SUMMARY

```
690.01–.09    Standard subdivisions
     .1–.8    [Specific structural elements, general activities, specific types of buildings]
     691      Building materials
     692      Auxiliary construction practices
     693      Construction in specific types of materials and for specific purposes
     694      Wood construction     Carpentry
     695      Roof covering
     696      Utilities
     697      Heating, ventilation, air-conditioning engineering
     698      Detail finishing
```

.01　　Philosophy and theory

.02　　Miscellany

.021 2　　Tables and formulas

Class specifications in 692.3

[.022 3]　　Maps and related forms, plans, diagrams

Do not use; class in 692.1

.028　　Auxiliary techniques and procedures; apparatus, equipment

Class materials in 691

[.028 8]　　Maintenance and repair

Do not use; class in 690.24

[.028 9]　　Safety measures

Do not use; class in 690.22

[.029 9]　　Estimates of labor, time, materials

Do not use; class in 692.5

.03–.09　　Standard subdivisions

.1   **Specific structural elements**

> Add to base number 690.1 the numbers following 721 in 721.1–721.8, e.g., auxiliary roof structures 690.15; however, class chimneys in 697.8, fireplaces in 697.1
>
> Class structural elements of specific types of buildings in 690.5–690.8, construction of structural elements in wood in 694

.2   **General activities**

> Including architectural acoustics
>
> Class application to specific structural elements in 690.1, to specific types of buildings in 690.5–690.8, interdisciplinary works on architectural acoustics in 729.29

.21   Structural analysis

> Statics, dynamics, stability, strength of buildings

.22   Provision for safety

> Engineering for safe buildings, safety during construction

.24   Maintenance and repair

> Class home repairs by members of household in 643.7

.26   Wrecking and razing

.5–.8   **Specific types of buildings**

> Add to base number 690 the numbers following 72 in 725–728, e.g., airport terminal buildings 690.539 [*formerly also* 629.1364]; however, class construction of buildings for defense against military action in 623.1, naval facilities in 623.64, military air facilities in 623.66, docks and port buildings in 627.3
>
> *See Manual at 629.226 vs. 643.2, 690.879, 728.79*

691   Building materials

> General aspects: selection, preservation, construction properties
>
> Class construction in a specific type of material in 693

.1   **Timber**

.12   Prevention of decay

> Examples: spraying, painting, impregnating with fungicides

.14   Prevention of termite damage

.15   Treatment for fire resistance

> Impregnation with monomagnesium, monoammonium, diammonium phosphates

.2   **Natural stones**

> Examples: granite, limestone, marble, sandstone, serpentine, slate, soapstone

.3   **Concretes and artificial stones**

Examples: concrete blocks, cinder blocks

.4   **Ceramic and clay materials**

Examples: brick, tile, terra cotta, sun-dried blocks

.5   **Masonry adhesives**

.6   **Glass**

.7   **Iron and steel (Ferrous metals)**

.8   **Metals**

Add to base number 691.8 the numbers following 669 in 669.2–669.7, e.g., aluminum 691.8722

For iron and steel, see 691.7

.9   **Other building materials**

.92   Plastics and their laminates

.95   Insulating materials

Examples: asbestos, corkboard, diatomaceous earth, kapok, rock wool

.96   Bituminous materials

Examples: asphalts, tar

.97   Prefabricated materials

.99   Adhesives and sealants

For masonry adhesives, see 691.5; plastics and their laminates, 691.92

692   Auxiliary construction practices

Class application of a specific auxiliary practice to a specific subject with the subject, e.g., construction specifications for air conditioning 697.93

.1   **Plans and drawings**

Interpretation and use of rough sketches, working drawings, blueprints

For detail drawings, see 692.2

.2   **Detail drawings**

Interpretation and use of large-scale drawings of trims, moldings, other details

.3   **Construction specifications**

.5   **Estimates of labor, time, materials**

Class here interdisciplinary works on quantity surveying

Class estimates for a specific subject in building with the subject, using notation 0299 from Table 1, e.g., estimates for air conditioning 697.930299

.8   **Contracting**

Provision of construction materials and services in accordance with
specifications

693   **Construction in specific types of materials and for specific
purposes**

Comprehensive works on construction in all types of materials is classed in 690

*For selection, preservation, construction properties of building materials, see
691; wood construction, 694; roofing materials, 695*

SUMMARY

693.1   Masonry
.2   Stabilized earth materials
.3   Tiles and terra cotta
.4   Artificial stones and hollow bricks
.5   Concrete
.6   Plaster-, stucco-, lathwork
.7   Metals
.8   Construction for specific purposes
.9   Construction in other materials

> **693.1–693.7 Construction in specific materials**

Class comprehensive works in 690, construction in specific materials for
specific purposes in 693.8

For construction in other materials, see 693.9

.1   **Masonry**

Including construction in natural stone

For masonry using materials other than natural stone, see 693.2–693.5

> **693.2–693.5 Masonry using materials other than natural stone**

Class comprehensive works in 693.1

.2   **Stabilized earth materials**

.21   Bricks

For hollow bricks, see 693.4

.22   Sun-dried blocks

Examples: adobe, cob, pisé, tabby, tapia

.3   **Tiles and terra cotta**

For hollow tiles, see 693.4

.4   **Artificial stones and hollow bricks**

Examples: concrete blocks, cinder blocks, hollow tiles

.5   **Concrete**

For concrete blocks, see 693.4

.52   Without reinforcement

.521   Poured concrete

.522   Precast concrete

.54   With reinforcement (Ferroconcrete)

.541   Poured concrete

.542   Prestressed concrete

.544   Precast concrete

.6   **Plaster-, stucco-, lathwork**

.7   **Metals**

.71   Iron and steel (Ferrous metals)

.72–.77   Nonferrous metals

Add to base number 693.7 the numbers following 669 in 669.2–669.7, e.g., tin 693.76

.8   **Construction for specific purposes**

.82   Fireproof construction

.83   Insulated construction

.832   Thermal insulation

.834   Acoustical insulation (Soundproofing)

.84   Pest-resistant construction

.842   Termite-resistant construction

.844   ,   Rodent-resistant construction

.85   Shock-resistant construction

.852   Earthquake-resistant construction

.854   Blast-resistant construction

.89   Waterproof, moistureproof, lightning-resistant construction

Use of this number for construction for other specific purposes discontinued; class in 693.8

.892   Waterproof construction

Class moistureproof construction in 693.893

.893   Moistureproof construction

.898   Lightning-resistant construction

.9		**Construction in other materials**
.91		Ice and snow
.92		Sandwich panels

Class sandwich panels in a specific substance with the substance, e.g., wood 694

.96	Glass
.97	Prefabricated materials

Class materials prefabricated in a specific substance with the substance, e.g., precast concrete 693.522

.98	Nonrigid materials

Example: pneumatic construction

.99	Miscellaneous materials

Add to base number 693.99 the numbers following 620.19 in 620.191–620.199, e.g., plastics 693.9923; however, class nonrigid materials in 693.98

694 Wood construction   Carpentry

.1   **Planning, analysis, engineering design**

> **694.2–694.6 Carpentry**

Class comprehensive works in 694

.2   **Rough carpentry (Framing)**

Construction of ceilings, floors, foundations, frames, openings, partition frames, posts, roofs, sidings, walls

.6   **Finish carpentry (Joinery)**

On-site construction of doors, doorways; blinds, shutters, windows; balconies, porches, verandas; balustrades, rails, ramps, stairs; trims, e.g., inlays, moldings, paneling; built-in cases and shelves

Class off-site manufacture of finishing items in 680

695 Roof covering

Class comprehensive works on roofs as structural elements in 690.15, wooden roofs in 694.2

696 Utilities

Class here comprehensive works on energy and environmental engineering of buildings

Class interior electric wiring in 621.31924; a specific aspect of energy and environmental engineering with the aspect, e.g., thermal insulation in 693.832

For heating, ventilating, air-conditioning engineering, see 697

.1   **Plumbing**

Design and installation of water fixtures and pipes

.12   Water supply

Including intake pipes, water receiving fixtures, water-softening equipment

For water supply in specific parts of buildings, see 696.18; hot-water supply, 696.6

.13   Water drainage

For water drainage in specific parts of buildings, see 696.18

.18   Water supply and drainage in specific parts of buildings

.182   Lavatories and bathrooms

.183   Laundries

.184   Kitchens

Including installation of garbage disposal units and dishwashers

.2   **Pipe fitting**

General aspects: design, installation

Example: gas pipes (gas fitting)

For water pipes, see 696.1; steam fitting, 696.3

.3   **Steam pipes (Steam fitting)**

General aspects: design, installation

.6   **Hot-water supply**

Design and installation of pipes, water heaters, water-softening equipment

697   Heating, ventilating, air-conditioning engineering

General aspects: design, manufacture, installation of systems and components

Use 697.0001–697.0009 for standard subdivisions

SUMMARY

697.001–.009	**Standard subdivisions of heating**
.02–.07	**[Local and central heating, heating with specific sources of energy, heating equipment]**
.1	**Heating with open fires (Radiative heating)**
.2	**Heating with space heaters (Convective heating)**
.3	**Hot-air heating**
.4	**Hot-water heating**
.5	**Steam heating**
.7	**Other heating methods**
.8	**Chimneys and flues**
.9	**Ventilation and air conditioning**

.001   Philosophy and theory of heating

.002   Miscellany of heating

.002 8	Auxiliary techniques and procedures; apparatus, materials of heating

Class heating equipment in 697.07

.003–.009	Standard subdivisions of heating
.02	Local heating

Class local heating by source of heat in 697.1–697.2

.03	Central heating

Class here comprehensive works on district heating

Class a specific type of central heating in 697.3–697.7, e.g., solar heating 697.78; district heating by hot water in 697.4, by steam in 697.54

.04	Heating with specific sources of energy

Class here specific fuels

Class a specific fuel used in local heating in 697.02, in central heating in 697.03

For solar heating, see 697.78; nuclear heating, 697.79

.042	Coal and coke heating
.043	Gas heating
.044	Oil heating
.045	Electric heating
.07	Heating equipment

Examples: boilers, furnaces, radiators, thermostats

> ### 697.1–697.8 Heating

Class comprehensive works in 697

> ### 697.1–697.2 Local heating

Class comprehensive works in 697.02, chimneys and flues for local heating in 697.8

.1	**Heating with open fires (Radiative heating)**

Including braziers, fireplaces

Class fireplace-like stoves that have visible fires but which are convective heaters in 697.2

.2	**Heating with space heaters (Convective heating)**
.22	Stationary stoves

Class cooking stoves in 683.88

.24	Portable heaters

> **697.3–697.7 Central heating**

Class comprehensive works in 697.03, chimneys and flues for central heating in 697.8

.3   Hot-air heating

Class radiant panel hot-air heating in 697.72

.4   Hot-water heating

Class hot-water supply in 696.6, radiant panel hot-water heating in 697.72, comprehensive works on district heating in 697.03

.5   Steam heating

Class steam fitting in 696.3, radiant panel steam heating in 697.72

.500 1   Philosophy and theory

.500 2   Miscellany

.500 28   Auxiliary techniques and procedures; apparatus, materials

Class equipment in 697.507

.500 3–.500 9   Standard subdivisions

.507   Equipment

Examples: boilers, furnaces, radiators

[.52]   Heating single buildings

Number discontinued; class in 697.5

.54   District heating

Heating a group of buildings from a central station

Class comprehensive works on steam and hot-water district heating in 697.03

See also 697.4 for hot-water district heating

.7   Other heating methods

.72   Radiant panel heating

.78   Solar heating

Class building of solar houses in 690.8370472

.79   Nuclear heating

.8   Chimneys and flues

.9   Ventilation and air conditioning

.92   Ventilation

.93	Air conditioning

Class heating in 697.1–697.8

.931	General topics

Class general topics applied to specific components in 697.932, to specific systems in 697.933–697.934, to specific types of buildings in 697.935–697.938

.931 2	Design principles
.931 5	Psychrometrics

Determination and control of enclosed atmospheric environments for optimum comfort

.931 6	Industrial and commercial applications

Determination and control of enclosed atmospheric environment for effective operations

.932	Components

Class here manufacturing

.932 2	Heating and cooling components

Examples: cooling and heating coils, thermostats

.932 3	Humidifying and dehumidifying components

Example: humidistats

.932 4	Air quality components

Devices for removing dust, pollen, other particulates

Class here filters

.932 5	Air circulation components

Example: blowers

.933	Air-conditioning systems

Class systems in specific types of buildings in 697.935–697.938, system components in 697.932

For unitary and combination systems, see 697.934

.933 2	Winter systems
.933 3	Summer systems
.933 4	Year-round systems
.934	Unitary and combination systems
.934 2	Unitary systems
.934 4	Combination systems

.935–.938   In specific types of buildings

Add to base number 697.93 the numbers following 72 in 725–728, e.g., air conditioning in hotels 697.9385

Class components for specific types of buildings in 697.932

698   Detail finishing

Examples: cladding, siding, suspended ceilings

Class plaster-, stucco-, lathwork in 693.6; wooden moldings, paneling, inlays in 694.6; roof covering in 695

.1   Painting

.102   Miscellany

.102 8   Auxiliary techniques and procedures; apparatus, equipment, materials

.102 82   Equipment

Examples: brushes, rollers, paints, diluents

.102 83   Paint mixing

.102 88   Application methods

Do not use for maintenance and repair; class in 698.1028

.12   Exteriors

.14   Interiors

Class painting woodwork in 698.35

.142   Walls

.146   Floors

.147   Ceilings

.2   Calcimining and whitewashing

.3   Finishing woodwork

.32   By staining

Including graining and marbling

.33   By polishing with wax and oil

.34   By varnishing and lacquering

.35   By painting

.5   Glazing and leading windows

.6   Paperhanging

.9   **Floor coverings**

General aspects: measuring, cutting, laying

Examples: carpets, rugs; linoleum, tiles

Class comprehensive works on floors in 690.16

[699]   [Unassigned]

Most recently used in Edition 14

[handwritten: Conceptual art]

[handwritten: Beware of difference between 700.1 and 701.01]

700 The arts   Fine and decorative arts

Description, critical appraisal, techniques, procedures, apparatus, equipment, materials of the fine, decorative, literary, performing, recreational arts

Class here conceptual art

Use 700 and standard subdivisions 700.1–700.9 for artists' books, performance and video art covering the arts in general; use 702.81 and 709 for artists' books, performance and video art limited to fine and decorative arts

For book arts, see 686; literature, 800

See Manual at 700

> **700.1–700.9 Standard subdivisions of the arts**

Use this standard subdivision span for material that includes two or more of the fine and decorative arts and one or more of the other arts, e.g., a work about a painter who is also a sculptor and a poet 700.92. If only one fine or decorative art and one of the other arts is involved, class in the number coming first in the schedule, e.g., a United States painter and poet 759.13

Class comprehensive works in 700

See Manual at 700

.1	**Philosophy and theory of the arts** *[handwritten: Public art]*
.103	Effects of social conditions and factors on the arts
.104	Effects of humanities on the arts
.105	Effects of science and technology on the arts
.108	Effects of other concepts on the arts
	Examples: humor, mythology, nature, parapsychology
.2–.6	**Standard subdivisions of the arts**
.7	**Education, research, related topics of the arts**
.74	Museums, collections, exhibits

Notation 074 from Table 1 is never added to the work of an individual artist whether the work falls in notation 092 from Table 1 (e.g., an exhibition of the work of a French sculptor 730.92) or in the number for the individual artist's country (e.g., an exhibition of the work of a Canadian painter 759.11)

See Manual at 700.74

.75   Museum activities and services   Collecting objects

Notation 075 from Table 1 is never added to the work of an individual artist whether the work falls in notation 092 from Table 1 (e.g., collecting the work of a French sculptor 730.92) or in the number for the individual artist's country (e.g., collecting the work of a Canadian painter 759.11)

.8   The arts with respect to kinds of persons

.9   Historical, geographical, persons treatment

.92   Persons

Class here the works themselves and critical appraisal and description of works of an artist or artists

See Manual at 700.92

701   Philosophy and theory of fine and decorative arts

.03–.08   Special topics

Add to base number 701.0 the numbers following 700.10 in 700.103–700.108, e.g., effects of social conditions and factors on fine and decorative arts 701.03

.1   Appreciative aspects

Including use of audiovisual aids

Class here works on art appreciation, including theory, history, and techniques

Do not use for systems; class in 701

See also 709 for history of the fine arts

.15   Psychological principles

Fine arts as products of creative imagination

.17   Aesthetics

Class interdisciplinary works in 111.85

.18   Criticism and appreciation

Class here theory, technique, history

Class works of critical appraisal in 709

.8   Inherent features

Examples: composition, form, style, decorative values, light, vision, space, time, movement, symmetry

.82   Perspective

See also 742 for the drawing aspects of perspective

.85   Color

See also 752 for the painting aspects of color

.9   **Methodology**

Do not use for psychological principles; class in 701.15

702   Miscellany of fine and decorative arts

.8   **Techniques, procedures, apparatus, equipment, materials**

Including testing and measurement, use of artists' models

.81   Mixed-media and composites

Including artists' books; performance, video art

Class finished works of mixed-media and composite art in 709, two-dimensional mixed-media art or composites in 760

See Manual at 700

.812   Collage

Class decoupage in 745.546

.813   Montage

.814   Assemblage

.87   Techniques of reproduction, execution, identification

Do not use for testing and measurement; class in 702.8

.872   Reproductions and copies

.874   Forgeries and alterations

.88   Conservation, preservation, restoration

Including expertizing

Do not use for routine maintenance and repair; class in 702.89

Class identification of reproductions, copies, forgeries, alterations in 702.87

.89   Safety measures and routine maintenance and repair

.9   **Commercial miscellany**

Class auction and sales catalogs in which an exhibition is involved in 707.4

703   Dictionaries, encyclopedias, concordances of fine and decorative arts

704   Special topics in fine and decorative arts   History and description with respect to kinds of persons

.03   History and description with respect to racial, ethnic, national groups

Add to base number 704.03 notation 01–99 from Table 5, e.g., art of North American native races 704.0397

Class the fine and decorative arts of nonliterate peoples in 709.011; history and description with respect to racial, ethnic, national groups in places where they predominate in 709.1, 709.3–709.9; history and description with respect to groups of specific kinds of persons of a specific racial, ethnic, national group in 704.04–704.87

.04–.87   History and description with respect to kinds of persons

Add to base number 704 notation 04–87 from Table 7, e.g., lawyers as artists 704.344; however, class art dealers in 380.1457; description, critical appraisal, works, biography of individual artists in 709.2

Class history and description with respect to racial, ethnic, national groups in 704.03, the fine and decorative arts of nonliterate peoples in 709.011

See Manual at 709.2 vs. 380.1457092

.9   **Iconography**

See Manual at 704.9

.94   Subjects

Development, description, critical appraisal, works

Do not use standard subdivisions

SUMMARY

704.942	Human figures and their parts
.943	Nature and still life
.944	Architectural subjects and cityscapes
.946	Symbolism and allegory
.947	Mythology and legend
.948	Religion and religious symbolism
.949	Other specific subjects

.942   Human figures and their parts

Not provided for in 704.946–704.948

Class here portraits

Observe the following table of precedence, e.g., groups of children 704.9425 (*not* 704.9426)

Erotica	704.9428
Specific kinds of persons	704.9423–.9425
Groups of figures	704.9426
According to attire	704.9421–.9422

Class works in which the human figure is not the center of interest with the subject, e.g., cityscapes 704.944

.942 092   Persons

Artists and critics

Works about the person portrayed are classed in 704.942

>   704.942 1–704.942 2 According to attire

      Class comprehensive works in 704.942

.942 1   Nudes

.942 2   Draped figures

>   704.942 3–704.942 5 Specific kinds of persons

      Class comprehensive works in 704.942

.942 3   Men

.942 4   Women

.942 5   Children

.942 6   Groups of figures

.942 8   Erotica

      Including pornography

.943   **Nature and still life**

      Not provided for in 704.946–704.948

      Standard subdivisions are added for nature and still life or for nature alone

.943 2   Animals

      Including hunting scenes

      Class symbolism of animals in 704.946; hunting scenes in which animals are not the center of interest with the subject, e.g., hunters 704.9426

      See Manual at 704.9

.943 4   Plants

      Class symbolism of plants in 704.946

      See Manual at 704.9

.943 5   Still life

.943 6   Landscapes

      Add to base number 704.9436 notation 1–9 from Table 2, e.g., landscapes of Utah 704.9436792

.943 7   Marine scenes and seascapes

.944	Architectural subjects and cityscapes
	Add to base number 704.944 notation 1–9 from Table 2, e.g., cityscapes of England 704.94442
[.945]	Abstractionism
	Relocated to 709.04052
.946	Symbolism and allegory
	For religious symbolism, see 704.948
.947	Mythology and legend
	Class religious mythology in 704.948
.948	Religion and religious symbolism
	Class here religious mythology
	Class significance and purpose of art in religion in 291.37, in Christianity in 246, in other religions in 292–299
(.948 1)	(Permanently unassigned)
	(Option: To give local emphasis and a shorter number to iconography of a specific religion, class it in this number)
.948 2	Christianity
	Including icons, santos, votive offerings
	For specific Christian subjects, see 704.9484–704.9487

> 704.948 4–704.948 7 Specific Christian subjects

Class here icons, santos, votive offerings

Class comprehensive works in 704.9482

.948 4	Biblical characters and events
	For Trinity and Holy Family and its members, see 704.9485; apostles, saints, angels, 704.9486; devils, 704.9487
.948 5	Trinity and Holy Family and its members
.948 52	Trinity
.948 53	Jesus Christ
.948 55	Madonna and Child
	Including Mary without Child
.948 56	Holy Family
	Presented as a group
	Class Jesus Christ in 704.94853, Mary with or without Child in 704.94855, Saint Joseph in 704.94863

.948 6	Apostles, saints, angels
.948 62	Apostles
.948 63	Saints

For Apostles, see 704.94862

.948 64	Angels
.948 7	Devils
.948 9	Other religions

Add to base number 704.9489 the numbers following 29 in 292–299, e.g., Buddhism in art 704.948943

Class Old Testament characters and events in 704.9484

.949   Other specific subjects

Add to base number 704.949 notation 001–999, e.g., industrial subjects 704.9496

705   Serial publications of fine and decorative arts

706.81 Art funding

706   Organizations and management of fine and decorative arts

707   Education, research, related topics of fine and decorative arts

.4   Temporary and traveling collections and exhibits

Class here permanent collections on tour, temporary exhibits of a private collection, auction and sales catalogs in which an exhibition is involved

Do not use for museums and permanent collections and exhibits; class in 708

Class a temporary in-house exhibit selected from a museum's or gallery's permanent collection with the museum or gallery in 708

708   Galleries, museums, private collections of fine and decorative arts

General art collections

Class here annual reports dealing with acquisitions, activities, programs, projects

Do not use for history and description of fine and decorative arts with respect to kinds of persons; class in 704.03–704.87

For temporary and traveling collections and exhibits, see 707.4

.001–.008   Standard subdivisions

.009   Historical and persons treatment

Class geographical treatment in 708.1–708.9

> **708.1–708.9 Geographical treatment**

Class here guidebooks and catalogs of specific galleries, museums, private collections

(Option: To give local emphasis and a shorter number to galleries, museums, private collections of a specific country, use one of the following:

(Option A: Place them first by use of a letter or other symbol, e.g., galleries, museums, private collections in Japan 708.J [preceding 708.1]

(Option B: Class them in 708.1; in that case class galleries, museums, private collections in North America in 708.97)

Class comprehensive works in 708

.1   **In North America**   *Use 708.97*

(Option: To give local emphasis and a shorter number to galleries, museums, private collections of a specific country other than United States and Canada, class them in this number; in that case class galleries, museums, private collections in North America in 708.97)

Class galleries, museums, private collections in Middle America in 708.972

.11   Canada

Add to base number 708.11 the numbers following —71 in notation 711–719 from Table 2, e.g., galleries, museums, private collections in British Columbia 708.111

.13–.19   United States

Add to base number 708.1 the numbers following —7 in notation 73–79 from Table 2, e.g., galleries, museums, private collections in Pennsylvania 708.148

Class galleries, museums, private collections in Hawaii in 708.9969

.2   **In British Isles**   **In England**

.21–.28   In England

Add to base number 708.2 the numbers following —42 in notation 421–428 from Table 2, e.g., galleries, museums, private collections in Manchester 708.2733

.29   In Scotland, Ireland, Wales

Add to base number 708.29 the numbers following —4 in notation 41–42 from Table 2, e.g., galleries, museums, private collections in Wales 708.2929

.3–.8   **In other European countries**

Add to base number 708 the numbers following —4 in notation 43–48 from Table 2, e.g., galleries, museums, private collections in France 708.4

Class comprehensive works, and galleries, museums, private collections in other European countries not provided for in notation 43–48 from Table 2 in 708.94, e.g., galleries, museums, private collections in Belgium 708.9493

.9   **In other geographical areas**   *use 708.97 for Americas AA*

> Add to base number 708.9 notation 1, 3–9 from Table 2, e.g., comprehensive works on galleries, museums, private collections in Islamic areas 708.917671, in European countries 708.94

709   Historical, geographical, persons treatment of fine and decorative arts

Development, description, critical appraisal, works

Class here finished works of experimental and mixed-media art that do not fit easily into a recognized medium

Class looting, plundering, theft, destruction of art as a crime in 364.162, two-dimensional experimental and mixed-media art in 760

See Manual at 700

SUMMARY

709.01	Arts of nonliterate peoples, and earliest times to 499
.02	500–1499
.03	1500–
.04	1900–1999
.05	2000–2099

.01   Arts of nonliterate peoples, and earliest times to 499

.011   Nonliterate peoples

> Regardless of time or place, but limited to nonliterate peoples of the past and nonliterate peoples clearly not a part of contemporary society

.011 2   Paleolithic art

.011 3   Rock art

>   709.012–709.05 Periods of development

> Class here schools and styles not limited by country or locality, European art limited by period, school, or style

> Class comprehensive works in 709

> *See Manual at 709.012–709.05 vs. 709.3–709.9*

.012   To 4000 B.C.

.013   3999–1000 B.C.

.014   999–1 B.C.

.015   1–499 A.D.

.02   500–1499

> Class here medieval art

.021	500–1199
.021 2	Early Christian art
	Class early Christian art before 500 in 709.015
.021 4	Byzantine art
	Class Byzantine art before 500 in 709.015
.021 6	Romanesque art
.022	1200–1299
	Class here Gothic art
	Class Gothic art of an earlier or later period with the specific period, e.g., 500–1199 709.021
.023	1300–1399
.024	1400–1499
	Class here Renaissance art
	Class Renaissance art of an earlier or later period with the period, e.g., 1500–1599 709.031
.03	1500–
	For 1900–1999, see 709.04; 2000–2099, 709.05
.031	1500–1599
.032	1600–1699
	Class here baroque art
	Class baroque art of 1700–1799 in 709.033
.033	1700–1799
	Including rococo art
.034	1800–1899
.034 1	Classical revival (Neoclassicism)
	Class classical revival of 1700–1799 in 709.033
.034 2	Romanticism
	Class romanticism of 1700–1799 in 709.033
.034 3	Naturalism and realism
	Class naturalism and realism of an earlier or later period with the specific period, e.g., 1700–1799 709.033
.034 4	Impressionism
	Including luminism, pleinairism
.034 5	Neo-impressionism
	Including divisionism, pointillism
.034 6	Postimpressionism

.034 7	Symbolism and synthetism
.034 8	Kitsch (Trash)
	Comprehensive works
	Class kitsch of 1900–1999 in 709.04013
.034 9	Art nouveau *Art Deco*
	Comprehensive works
	Class art nouveau of 1900–1999 in 709.04014
.04	1900–1999 *— 20th Century art – use amended schedules*
	Including artists' books; computer, mail, performance, video art
	Class here modern art
	For 1800–1899, see 709.034
.040 01–.040 07	Special topics
	Add to base number 709.0400 the numbers following 0 in notation 01–07 in table under —0901–0905 in Table 1, e.g., collecting modern art 709.040075
.040 1	Art deco, kitsch, art nouveau
.040 12	Art deco
.040 13	Kitsch (Trash)
	Class ~~comprehensive~~ works on kitsch in 709.0348
.040 14	~~Art nouveau~~
	Class ~~comprehensive~~ works on art nouveau in 709.0349
.040 2	Functionalism
.040 3	Cubism and futurism
	Including geometric design
.040 32	Cubism
.040 33	Futurism
.040 4	Expressionism and fauvism
.040 42	Expressionism
	Class abstract expressionism in 709.04052
.040 43	Fauvism
.040 5	Abstractionism, nonobjectivity, constructivism
.040 52	Abstractionism [*formerly also* 704.945]
	Including abstract expressionism, geometric abstractionism, neoplasticism
.040 56	~~Nonobjectivity~~ *Bauhaus*

.040 57	Constructivism
.040 6	Dadaism and surrealism
.040 62	Dadaism
.040 63	Surrealism
.040 7	Composite media and sensations
.040 71	Pop art
.040 72	Optical art (Op art)
.040 73	Kinetic art
.040 74	Happenings, environments, events
.040 75	Conceptual art
.040 76	Land art (Earthworks)
.040 77	Structuralism
.040 78	Multiple art
.040 79	Space art

[handwritten margin notes: Cybernetic, laser, light, psychedelic art; Installations, funk art, performance, body art, behaviour, environment, ecological, underground art, machine art; Analytical, multiple, minimal]

.041–.049   Periods

Add to base number 709.04 the numbers following —0904 in notation 09041–09049 from Table 1, e.g., arts of 1960–1969 709.046

Class a specific school or style in a specific period in 709.0401–709.0407

.05   2000–2099

.1   **Treatment by areas, regions, places in general**

Class history and description of fine and decorative arts with respect to kinds of persons in 704.03–704.87, art of nonliterate peoples regardless of place in 709.011

.2   **Persons**   *[handwritten: + suffix for individual artists name 'not limited to one specific form']*

Class here description, critical appraisal, biography, works of artists not limited to or chiefly identified with a specific form, e.g., painting, or group of forms, e.g., graphic arts

See Manual at 709.2 vs. 380.1457092

.22   Collected treatment

Class works of more than one artist in the same geographical area in 709.1, 709.3–709.9

[handwritten note at bottom:]
709.08 Realism
709.0409 Primitive art, Art Brut, Naive art
709.04091 Psychotic, outsider art

.3–.9   **Treatment by specific continents, countries, localities**

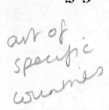

Class here art of specific periods, e.g., art of 1800–1899 in South America 709.809034

Class history and description of fine and decorative arts with respect to kinds of persons in 704.03–704.87; art of nonliterate peoples regardless of place in 709.011; comprehensive works on European art of specific periods in 709.01–709.05 (*not* 709.4), e.g., art of 1800–1899 in Europe 709.034 (*not* 709.409034)

See Manual at 709.012–709.05 vs. 709.3–709.9

710   Civic and landscape art

SUMMARY

711   **Area planning (Civic art)**
712   **Landscape architecture (Landscape design)**
713   **Landscape architecture of trafficways**
714   **Water features in landscape architecture**
715   **Woody plants in landscape architecture**
716   **Herbaceous plants in landscape architecture**
717   **Structures in landscape architecture**
718   **Landscape design of cemeteries**
719   **Natural landscapes**

711   Area planning (Civic art)

Design of physical environment for public welfare, convenience, pleasure

Unless other instructions are given, observe the following table of precedence, e.g., plans and planning of pedestrian malls in business districts 711.5522 (*not* 711.74)

Plans and planning for specific specific kinds of areas   711.5
Plans and planning of specific elements   711.6–.8
Plans and planning at specific levels   711.2–.4
Procedural and social aspects   711.1

Class interdisciplinary works on area planning in 307.12, comprehensive works on area planning and architecture in 720

For landscape architecture, see 712

See Manual at 711 vs. 307.12

SUMMARY

711.028   **Apparatus, equipment, materials**
.1   **Procedural and social aspects**
.2   **International and national plans and planning**
.3   **Interstate, state, provincial, county plans and planning**
.4   **Local community (City) plans and planning**
.5   **Plans and planning for specific kinds of areas**
.6   **Plans and planning of structural elements**
.7   **Plans and planning of transportation facilities**
.8   **Plans and planning of nontransportation utilities**

.028	Apparatus, equipment, materials
	Class auxiliary techniques and procedures in 711.1
.1	**Procedural and social aspects**
.12	Professional practice and technical procedures
	Examples: collection of data, preparation and presentation of plans and models
.13	Social factors affecting planning
.14	Economic factors affecting planning

> **711.2–711.4 Plans and planning at specific levels**

Class comprehensive works in 711

.2	**International and national plans and planning**
.3	**Interstate, state, provincial, county plans and planning**
	For metropolitan areas, see 711.43
.4	**Local community (City) plans and planning**
	Class here urban renewal (conservation, rehabilitation, redevelopment)
	For urban renewal of specific kinds of areas, see 711.5
.409	Historical, geographical, persons treatment
	Class here specific cities

> 711.41–711.45 Specific types of plans

Class complex subjects with aspects in two or more subdivisions of this schedule in the number coming last in the schedule, e.g., plans for small cities in cold climates 711.43 (*not* 711.42)

Class comprehensive works in 711.4, specific types of plans and planning for specific cities in 711.409

.41	Plans based on street patterns
	Examples: gridiron, radial, studied irregularity plans
.42	Plans based on environment
	Examples: plans based on topography and climate
.43	Plans based on size
	Examples: villages, small and large cities, metropolitan areas

.45	Plans based on function

Examples: cities serving primarily as governmental, industrial, residential centers

Including new towns

.5	**Plans and planning for specific kinds of areas**

Class here plans and planning for urban renewal (conservation, rehabilitation, redevelopment) of specific kinds of areas

Class interdisciplinary works on urban renewal in 307.3416

.55	Functional areas

Class here plazas, squares

> *For religious centers, see 711.56; cultural and educational areas, 711.57; residential areas, 711.58; parking areas, 711.73*

.551	Civic, administrative, governmental areas

Standard subdivisions are added for any or all of the topics named in the heading

.552	Commercial and industrial areas

Class plans and planning of transportation facilities in 711.7

.552 2	Commercial areas

Class here business districts, shopping centers

.552 4	Industrial areas

Class here industrial parks

.554	Agricultural areas
.555	Medical centers
.556	Prison and reformatory areas
.557	Hotel and restaurant areas

Including trailer camps for transients

.558	Recreational areas

Examples: parks, playgrounds, theatrical and performing arts centers

.56	Religious centers
.57	Cultural and educational areas

Examples: areas for libraries, museums, colleges and universities

Class theatrical and performing arts centers in 711.558

.58   **Residential areas**

Urban, suburban, rural areas

Examples: apartment-house districts, trailer parks for long-term residents

For housing renewal, see 711.59; hotel areas, 711.557

.59   **Housing renewal**

Class interdisciplinary works on housing renewal in 307.34

>   **711.6–711.8 Plans and planning of specific elements**

Class comprehensive works in 711.6

.6   **Plans and planning of structural elements**

Adaptation to site and use

Class here comprehensive works on plans and planning of specific elements

For utilities, see 711.7

.7   **Plans and planning of transportation facilities**

Class here comprehensive works on plans and planning of utilities

For plans and planning of nontransportation utilities, see 711.8

.72   **Bicycle transportation facilities**

.73   **Motor vehicle transportation facilities**

Including parking areas, motorcycle transportation facilities

.74   **Pedestrian transportation facilities**

Including pedestrian malls

.75   **Railroad transportation facilities**

Including rapid transit facilities

.76   **Marine transportation facilities**

.78   **Air transportation facilities**

.8   **Plans and planning of nontransportation utilities**

Examples: water, gas, electricity transmission and supply; communication lines; sanitation and flood control facilities

712   **Landscape architecture (Landscape design)**

Class engineering aspects of landscape architecture in 624

For specific elements in landscape architecture, see 714–717

.01   **Philosophy and theory**

Class aesthetics, composition, style in 712.2

.028   Apparatus, equipment, materials

Class auxiliary techniques and procedures in 712.3

>   **712.2–712.3 General considerations**

Class comprehensive works in 712, general considerations of design of specific kinds of land tracts in 712.5–712.7

.2   **Principles**

Examples: aesthetics, composition, effect, style

.3   **Professional practice and technical procedures**

Examples: collection of data, preparation and presentation of plans and models, supervision of operations

---

>   **712.5–712.7 Specific kinds of land tracts**

Class comprehensive works in 712

For trafficways, see 713; cemeteries, 718; natural landscapes, 719

.5   **Public parks and grounds**

Class here amusement parks, commons, fairgrounds, zoological and botanical gardens; comprehensive works on parks

Class parks of public reserved lands in 719.3

For private parks, see 712.6

.6   **Private parks and grounds**

Class here front yards and backyards, home gardens, penthouse gardens, estates

.7   **Semiprivate and institutional grounds**

Class here grounds of churches, country clubs, hospitals, hotels, industrial plants, schools

713   Landscape architecture of trafficways

>   **714–717 Specific elements in landscape architecture**

Class comprehensive works in 712

714   Water features in landscape architecture

Examples: cascades, fountains, natural and artificial pools

Class comprehensive works on fountains in 731.72

715   **Woody plants in landscape architecture**

Nonflowering and flowering

Class comprehensive works on woody and herbaceous plants in landscape architecture in 712

.1   **Topiary work**

>   **715.2–715.4 Specific kinds of plants**

Class comprehensive works in 715, topiary work on specific kinds of plants in 715.1

.2   **Trees**

.3   **Shrubs**

.4   **Vines**

716   **Herbaceous plants in landscape architecture**

Nonflowering and flowering

Including ground cover

Class here comprehensive works on flowering plants in landscape architecture

For flowering woody plants, see 715

717   **Structures in landscape architecture**

Relationship of buildings, terraces, fences, gates, steps, ornamental accessories to other elements of landscape architecture

Including pedestrian facilities, street furniture

718   **Landscape design of cemeteries**

.8   **National cemeteries**

719   **Natural landscapes**

Class natural water features in 714

.3   **Reserved lands**

.32   Public parks and natural monuments

Standard subdivisions are added for public parks and natural monuments, for public parks alone, or for natural monuments alone

.33   Forest and water-supply reserves

.36   Wildlife reserves

720   **Architecture**

Class here comprehensive works on architecture and civic and landscape art

For civic and landscape art, see 710

SUMMARY

720.1–.9	[Standard subdivisions]
721	Architectural structure
722	Architecture from earliest times to ca. 300
723	Architecture from ca. 300 to 1399
724	Architecture from 1400
725	Public structures
726	Buildings for religious and related purposes
727	Buildings for educational and research purposes
728	Residential and related buildings
729	Design and decoration of structures and accessories

.1   **Philosophy and theory**

.103–.108   Special topics

> Add to base number 720.10 the numbers following 700.10 in 700.103–700.108, e.g., effects of social conditions and factors on architecture 720.103

.2   **Miscellany**

.22   Illustrations, models, miniatures

[.221]   Drafting illustrations

> Do not use; class in 720.284

.222   Architectural drawings and related illustrations

> Add to base number 720.222 notation 1–9 from Table 2, e.g., architectural drawings from England 720.22242

> Class architectural drawings for one structure or a specific type of structure in 725–728, using notation 0222 from table under 721–729

.28   Auxiliary techniques and procedures; apparatus, equipment, materials

> Including site planning

.284   Architectural drawing

> Class drawings, illustrations, models in 720.222–720.228

.286   Remodeling

.288   Conservation, preservation, restoration

> Do not use for routine maintenance and repair; class in 720.289

> Class interdisciplinary works on conservation, preservation, restoration in 363.69

> *See Manual at 930–990: Historic preservation*

.289   Safety measures and routine maintenance and repair

.4   **Special topics**

> Unless other instructions are given, class complex subjects with aspects in two or more subdivisions of 720.4 in the one coming first, e.g., multiple-purpose skyscrapers 720.483 (*not* 720.49)

.42	Architecture for the handicapped
.43	Architecture for persons in late adulthood and ill persons
.47	Architecture and the environment
.472	Energy resources

> Example: use of solar energy
>
> Class here energy conservation

.473	Earth-sheltered buildings

> Class here underground architecture

.48	Buildings by shape

> Examples: atrium, circular, multistory, single-story buildings

.483	Tall buildings

> Class here skyscrapers

.49	Multiple-purpose buildings

> Class a multiple-purpose building with one primary purpose with single-purpose buildings of that type, e.g., an apartment building with a floor of commercial space 728.314

.8   Architecture with respect to kinds of persons

[.846]	Late adulthood

> Do not use; class in 720.43

.87	Gifted persons

> Class handicapped persons in 720.42, ill persons in 720.43

.9   Historical, geographical, persons treatment

> Class here Oriental architecture from ca. 300 limited to a specific country or locality [*formerly* 722], schools and styles limited to a specific country or locality, architectural aspects of historic buildings
>
> Class architectural drawings in 720.222, comprehensive works on specific schools and styles not limited to a specific country or locality in 722–724
>
> *See Manual at 913–919: Historic sites and buildings*

[.901–.905]	Historical periods

> Do not use; class in 722–724

[.93]	Ancient world

> Do not use; class in 722

.942 090 31	English architecture of 1500–1599

> Class here Elizabethan architecture [*formerly also* 724.1]

.942 090 32	English architecture of 1600–1699

> Including Jacobean architecture [*formerly also* 724.1]

.942 090 33	English architecture of 1700–1799
	Including Queen Anne architecture [*formerly also* 724.1]
.946 090 32	Spanish architecture of 1600–1699
	Class here Churrigueresque architecture [*formerly also* 724.19]
.95	Asia

Class here comprehensive works on Oriental architecture [*formerly* 722], Buddhist architecture [*formerly* 722.4]

Class Buddhist architecture of national styles not provided for here with the style, e.g., Japanese Buddhist architecture 720.952

.954	South Asia	India

Class here comprehensive works on Jain, Hindu architecture [*formerly* 722.4]

.97	North America

Class here comprehensive works on ancient American, ancient North American architecture [*formerly also* 722.91]

.98	South America

Class here ancient South American architecture [*formerly also* 722.91]

> ## 721–729 Specific aspects of architecture

Add to each term identified by * as follows:
01		Philosophy and theory
0103–0108		Special topics
		Add to 010 the numbers following 700.10 in 700.103–700.108, e.g., effects of social conditions and factors on architecture 0103
02		Miscellany
0222		Architectural drawings and related illustrations
		Add to 0222 notation 1–9 from Table 2, e.g., architectural drawings from England 022242
028		Auxiliary techniques and procedures; apparatus, equipment, materials
0286		Remodeling
0288		Conservation, preservation, restoration
		Do not use for routine maintenance and repair; class in 0289
0289		Safety measures and routine maintenance and repair
04		Special topics
		Add to 04 the numbers following 720.4 in 720.42–720.49, e.g., energy conservation 0472
09		Historical, geographical, persons treatment
		Class architectural drawings in 0222

Class comprehensive works in 720

721   Architectural structure

Class here interdisciplinary works on design and construction

Class architectural structure of specific types of structures in 725–728

For engineering design and construction, see 690; design and decoration, 729; structural engineering, 624.1

See Manual at 721; 721 vs. 690

SUMMARY

721.01–.09	**Standard subdivisions**
.1	**Foundations**
.2	**Walls**
.3	**Columnar constructions**
.4	**Curved constructions and details**
.5	**Roofs and roof structures**
.6	**Floors**
.7	**Ceilings**
.8	**Other elements**

.01–.02   Standard subdivisions

Notation from Table 1 as modified under 720.1–720.2, e.g., remodeling 721.0286; however, class materials in 721.044

.04   Special topics

.042   Buildings by shape

Examples: atrium, circular, multistory, single-story buildings

Class architectural construction of buildings of specific materials regardless of shape in 721.044

.044   Specific materials

.044 1–.044 6   Masonry

Add to base number 721.044 the numbers following 693 in 693.1–693.6, e.g., architectural construction in reinforced concrete 721.04454

.044 7   Metals

Add to base number 721.0447 the numbers following 669 in 669.1–669.7, e.g., architectural construction in aluminum 721.0447722

.044 8   Wood

.044 9   Other

Add to base number 721.0449 the numbers following 693.9 in 693.91–693.99, e.g., architectural construction in glass 721.04496

.046   Other special topics of architectural construction

> Add to base number 721.046 the numbers following 720.4 in 720.42–720.49, e.g., energy conservation 721.04672; however, class buildings by shape in 721.042

> **721.1–721.8 Structural elements**

Class here design [*formerly also* 729.3], decoration [*formerly* 729.3]

Class comprehensive works in 721, decoration of structural elements in specific mediums in 729.4–729.8

.1   **Foundations**

.2   **Walls**

> Including footings, entablatures; colonnades, partitions; bearing and retaining walls
>
> Arcades relocated to 721.41
>
> *See also 725.96 for free-standing walls*

.3   **Columnar constructions**

> Examples: abutments, colonnettes, columns, pedestals, piers, pilasters, posts
>
> *For colonnades, entablatures, see 721.2*

.36   Architectural orders

> *For entablatures, see 721.2*

.4   **Curved constructions and details**

.41   Arcades [*formerly* 721.2] and arches

> *For groined arches, see 721.44*
>
> *See also 725.96 for free-standing arches*

.43   Vaults

> *For specific types of vaults, see 721.44–721.45*

> 721.44–721.45 Specific types of vaults

Class comprehensive works in 721.43

.44   Groined vaults

> Including groined arches

.45   Other types of vaults

> Examples: expanding, fan, rib, tunnel vaults

.46   Domes

> Class cupolated roofs in 721.5

.48   Niches

.5   Roofs and roof structures

> Examples: dormers, gables; cornices, pediments; cupolas, pinnacles, spires, towers

> Including chimneys, skylights

.6   Floors

.7   Ceilings

.8   Other elements

> Examples: balustrades, fastenings, fireplaces

.82   Openings

> Class here blinds

.822   Doors and doorways

.823   Windows

> Class windows as parts of roof structures in 721.5

.83   Means of vertical access

> Example: ramps

.832   Stairs

> Including escalators

.833   Elevators

.84   Extensions

> Examples: balconies, decks, patios, porches

> ## 722–724 Architectural schools and styles

Class comprehensive works, schools and styles from ca. 300 limited to a specific country or locality in 720.9; architects of specific schools and styles not limited to a specific type of structure in 720.92; specific types of structures regardless of school or style in 725–728; details of construction of specific schools and styles in 721; design and decoration of structures of specific schools and styles in 729

722   Architecture from earliest times to ca. 300

Comprehensive works on Oriental architecture relocated to 720.95, Oriental architecture from ca. 300 limited to a specific country or locality relocated to 720.9, comprehensive works on Oriental architecture from ca. 300 to 1399 relocated to 723, comprehensive works on Oriental architecture from 1400 relocated to 724

.1   Ancient Chinese, Japanese, Korean architecture

Class here ancient Oriental architecture

Class ancient architecture of ancient south and southeast Asia in 722.4, of ancient Middle East in 722.5

.11   *Ancient Chinese architecture

Class ancient Tibetan architecture in 722.4

.12   *Ancient Japanese architecture

.13   *Ancient Korean architecture

.2   *Ancient Egyptian architecture

.3   *Ancient Semitic architecture

Class comprehensive works on Semitic architecture in 720.8992

.31   Phoenician architecture

Class here architecture of Tyre, Sidon, Beirut, Byblos

For colonial Phoenician, see 722.32

.32   Colonial Phoenician architecture

Examples: architecture of ancient Carthage, Utica, Cadiz, Cyprus

.33   Ancient Palestinian architecture

Including Israelite, Judean, Jewish architecture

.4   Ancient south and southeast Asian architecture

Comprehensive works on Buddhist architecture relocated to 720.95, on Jain, Hindu architecture relocated to 720.954

.44   *Ancient Indian architecture

.5   Ancient Middle Eastern architecture

For Semitic architecture, see 722.3; Egyptian architecture, 722.2; Aegean architecture, 722.61

.51   Mesopotamian architecture

.52   Ancient Persian architecture

.6   Ancient Western architecture

For Roman architecture, see 722.7; Greek (Hellenic) architecture, 722.8; other ancient Western architecture, 722.9

*Add as instructed under 721–729

.61   *Aegean, *Minoan, *Mycenaean architecture

.62   *Etruscan architecture

.7   *Roman architecture

.709 37   Architecture of Italian Peninsula and adjacent territories

             Class architecture of Roman empire in 722.7

.8   *Greek (Hellenic) architecture

         Class here comprehensive works on Greek and Roman architecture

         For Roman architecture, see 722.7

.809 38   Architecture of Greece

             Class architecture of Hellenistic world in 722.8

.9   Other ancient Western architecture

[.91]   Ancient American architecture

         Comprehensive works on ancient American, ancient North American architecture relocated to 720.97; on ancient South American architecture to 720.98

723   Architecture from ca. 300 to 1399

         Class here comprehensive works on Oriental architecture from ca. 300 to 1399 [*formerly* 722]; medieval architecture

[.09]   Historical, geographical, persons treatment

         Do not use notation 09 from Table 1 here or in any subdivision of 723; class architecture from ca. 300 to 1399 limited to a specific country or locality in 720.9, persons treatment in 720.92

.1   Early Christian architecture

.2   Byzantine architecture

.3   Saracenic architecture

         Class here Muslim, Moorish, Mudejar styles

.4   Romanesque and Norman architecture

.5   Gothic architecture

724   Architecture from 1400

         Class here comprehensive works on Oriental architecture from 1400 [*formerly* 722], modern architecture

[.09]   Historical, geographical, persons treatment

         Do not use notation 09 from Table 1 here or in any subdivision of 724; class architecture from 1400 limited to a specific country or locality in 720.9, persons treatment in 720.92

*Add as instructed under 721–729

.1   **1400–1800**

Class here colonial styles

Elizabethan architecture relocated to 720.94209031, Jacobean architecture to 720.94209032, Queen Anne architecture relocated to 720.94209033

Class colonial styles of a later period with the period, e.g., 1800–1899 724.5

.12   1400–1499

Class here Renaissance architecture

Class Renaissance architecture of an earlier or later period with the period, e.g., 1500–1599 724.14

.14   1500–1599

.16   1600–1699

Class here comprehensive works on baroque architecture [*formerly* 724.19]

Class baroque architecture of 1700–1799 in 724.19

.19   1700–1799

Class here Georgian, rococo architecture

Churrigueresque architecture relocated to 720.94609032, comprehensive works on baroque architecture relocated to 724.16

.2   **Classical revival architecture**

Class here neoclassical architecture [*formerly also* 724.5]

.22   Roman revival architecture

.23   Greek revival architecture

.3   **Gothic revival architecture**

.5   **1800–1899**

Class here eclecticism, revivals, Victorian architecture

Neoclassical architecture relocated to 724.2

Class eclecticism and revivals of another specific period with the period, e.g., 1700–1799 724.19

> *For classical revival architecture, see 724.2, gothic revival architecture, 724.3*

.52   Italianate revivals

Including Romanesque revival [*formerly* 724.8], Renaissance revival architecture

.6   **1900–1999 [*formerly* 724.91]**

Including art nouveau, expressionism, international style, functionalism

[.7]   **Swiss timber and half-timber**

Provision discontinued because without meaning in styles of architecture

| [.8] | **Romanesque revival architecture** |

Relocated to 724.52

| [.9] | **1900–** |

Use of this number discontinued; class in 724

| [.91] | 1900–1999 |

Relocated to 724.6

> ## 725–728 Specific types of structures

Class here development of architectural schools and styles, comprehensive works on specific structures and their interior design and decorations, interdisciplinary works on design and construction

Class comprehensive works in 720; engineering design and construction of specific types of habitable structures in 690.5–690.8; structures rehabilitated to a single new use with the new use, e.g., warehouses converted into apartments 728.314; structures rehabilitated to multiple new uses with the old use, e.g., warehouses converted into retail stores and apartments 725.35

For structural engineering, see 624.1; interior decoration, 747

725 Public structures

Not used primarily for religious, educational, research, residential purposes

SUMMARY

725.1	**Government buildings**
.2	**Commercial and communications buildings**
.3	**Transportation and storage buildings**
.4	**Industrial buildings**
.5	**Health and welfare buildings**
.6	**Prison and reformatory buildings**
.7	**Refreshment facilities and park structures**
.8	**Recreation buildings**
.9	**Other public structures**

| .1 | ***Government buildings** |

Class here international government, civic center buildings

| .11 | ***Legislative buildings** |

Class here capitols

| .12 | ***Executive buildings** |

Class here buildings containing branches of executive department

| .13 | ***County and *city government buildings** |

| .14 | ***Customs buildings** |

| .15 | ***Court, *record, *archive buildings** |

*Add as instructed under 721–729

.16	*Post offices
.17	*Official residences

Including embassy, legation, consulate buildings

Class here executive mansions, palaces of rulers

.18	*Military and *police buildings

Examples: barracks, forts, castles, fortresses, armory and arsenal buildings

Class engineering of forts and fortresses in 623.1, comprehensive works on castles in 728.81

.19	*Fire stations
.2	***Commercial and communications buildings**

For refreshment facilities, see 725.7

.21	*Retail trade buildings

Class here stores, shops; bazaars, shopping malls

.23	*Office and *communications buildings

Examples: medical office buildings and clinics, radio and television buildings and towers

.24	*Financial institutions

For exchanges, see 725.25

.25	*Exchanges

Examples: stock and commodity exchange, board of trade, chamber of commerce buildings

.3	***Transportation and storage buildings**
.31	*Railroad and *rapid transit stations

Class here passenger stations

For railroad freight stations, see 725.32

.32	*Railroad freight stations
.33	*Railroad and *rapid transit buildings

Examples: roundhouses, shops; tool storage, guard, signal buildings

For railroad and rapid transit stations, see 725.31

.34	*Marine transportation facilities

Examples: docks, piers

Class shipyards in 725.4; engineering of naval facilities in 623.64; engineering of harbors, ports, roadsteads in 627.2

*Add as instructed under 721–729

.35   *Warehouses

           Class here comprehensive works on storage buildings

           Class a specific kind of storage building other than warehouse with the kind, e.g., storage elevators 725.36

.36   *Storage elevators

.38   *Motor vehicle transportation buildings

           Examples: bus terminals, garages, filling stations

.39   *Air transportation buildings

           Examples: air terminals, hangars

           Class engineering of military air facilities in 623.66

.4   *Industrial buildings

           Examples: factories, mills, plants, shipyards

.5   *Health and welfare buildings

           For medical office buildings and clinics, see 725.23

.51   *General hospital and sanitarium buildings

           For children's hospital buildings, see 725.57

.52   *Psychiatric hospital buildings

.53   *Buildings of institutions for persons with mental handicaps

.54   *Buildings of institutions for persons with physical handicaps

.55   *Buildings of institutions for the poor

           Class buildings of institutions for indigent persons in late adulthood in 725.56

.56   *Buildings of institutions for persons in late adulthood

.57   *Child welfare institutions and *children's hospital buildings

.59   Other

.592   *Veterinary hospitals and shelters

.594   *Homes for veterans

.597   *Morgues and *crematories

.6   *Prison and *reformatory buildings

.7   Refreshment facilities and park structures

.71   *Restaurant buildings

.72   *Bars (Pubs)

.73   *Bathhouses and *saunas

*Add as instructed under 721–729

.74	*Swimming pools
.76	*Amusement park buildings and *casinos
.8	**Recreation buildings**

> *For refreshment facilities and park structures, see 725.7*

.804	General categories of recreation buildings
.804 2	Multiple-purpose complexes

> Class here cultural centers, recreation centers
>
> Class community centers for adult education in 727.9

.804 3	Sports complexes

> Variant names: sports centers, sports pavilions

.81	*Music halls and *concert halls

> *For opera houses, see 725.822*

.82	*Buildings for shows and spectacles
.822	*Theaters and *opera houses
.827	*Buildings for outdoor performances and *for outdoor sports

> Example: grandstands
>
> Class here amphitheaters, astrodomes, stadiums
>
> *For racetrack buildings, see 725.89*

.83	*Auditoriums

> Class here performing arts centers
>
> *For music halls and concert halls, see 725.81; theaters and opera houses, 725.822*

.84	*Buildings for indoor games

> Examples: bowling alleys; pool halls; halls for card games, checkers, chess
>
> *For gymnasiums, see 725.85*

.85	*Gymnasiums and *athletic club buildings
.86	*Rinks and *dance halls
.87	*Boathouses and *recreation pier buildings

> Including canoe club, yacht club buildings

.88	*Riding-club buildings
.89	*Racetrack buildings

*Add as instructed under 721–729

.9   **Other public structures**

.91   *Convention centers

Class here exhibition buildings

.94   *Memorial buildings

Class memorial buildings for a specific purpose with the purpose, e.g., memorial library buildings 727.8

.96   Arches, gateways, walls

Standard subdivisions are added for any or all of the topics in the heading

See also 721.2 for walls as structural elements, 721.41 for arches as structural elements

.97   *Towers

Examples: bell, clock towers

.98   Bridges, tunnels, moats

Class engineering of moats in 623.31, of tunnels in 624.193, of bridges in 624.2

726   Buildings for religious and related purposes

SUMMARY

726.1	**Temples and shrines**
.2	**Mosques and minarets**
.3	**Synagogues and Judaic temples**
.4	**Accessory houses of worship**
.5	**Buildings associated with Christianity**
.6	**Cathedrals**
.7	**Monastic buildings**
.8	**Mortuary chapels and tombs**
.9	**Other buildings for religious and related purposes**

> **726.1–726.3 Buildings associated with non-Christian religions**

Class comprehensive works in 726; a specific kind of building for religious purposes associated with a specific religion with the building, e.g., Buddhist monasteries 726.7843

See also 726.5 for buildings associated with Christianity

.1   ***Temples and *shrines**

Add to base number 726.1 the numbers following 29 in 292–299, e.g., Buddhist temples and shrines 726.143; however, class mosques and minarets in 726.2, synagogues and Judaic temples in 726.3

See Manual at 726.1

.2   ***Mosques and *minarets**

.3   ***Synagogues and *Judaic temples**

*Add as instructed under 721–729

.4   ***Accessory houses of worship**

> For all religions
>
> Examples: chapels, parish houses, Sunday school buildings
>
> Class here comprehensive works on baptistries
>
> Class baptistries as a part of church buildings in 726.596
>
> > *For mortuary chapels, see 726.8*
> >
> > *See also 726.595 for side chapels*

.5   ***Buildings associated with Christianity**

> Class here church buildings
>
> Class a specific kind of building not provided for here with the building, e.g., Franciscan monasteries 726.773
>
> > *For cathedrals, see 726.6*

.51   Design [*formerly also* 726.523], decoration [*formerly* 726.523], construction of structural elements

> Add to base number 726.51 the numbers following 721 in 721.1–721.8, e.g., design, decoration, construction of church vaulting 726.5143
>
> Class decoration of structural elements in specific mediums in 726.524–726.528

.52   Design and decoration of parts and built-in church furniture

[.523]   Design and decoration of structural elements

> Relocated to 726.51

.524–.528   Decoration in specific mediums

> Add to base number 726.52 the numbers following 729 in 729.4–729.8, e.g., decoration in relief 726.525
>
> Class decorations of built-in church furniture in 726.529; decoration in a specific medium not in an architectural context with the medium, e.g., sculpture 730

.529   Built-in church furniture [*formerly also* 729.9]

> Class built-in church furniture in a specific medium not in an architectural context with the medium, e.g., carved pew ends 731.54

.529 1   Sacramental furniture

> Examples: altars, baptismal fonts, confessionals, tabernacles

.529 2   Rostral furniture

> Examples: pulpits, lecterns, prayer desks

.529 3   Seats and canopies

> Examples: baldachins, bishops' thrones, choir stalls, pews

*Add as instructed under 721–729

.529 6		Screens and railings
		Examples: altar and rood screens, altar and chancel railings, reredoses
.529 7		Organ cases
.529 8		Lighting fixtures
.58		Buildings of specific denominations

Add to base number 726.58 the numbers following 28 in 281–289, e.g., Anglican church buildings 726.583

Class geographical treatment of buildings of specific denominations in 726.509, specific parts of church buildings of specific denominations in 726.59

.59		Parts

Class design and construction of parts in 726.51, design and decoration of parts in 726.52

.591		Entrances and approaches
.592		Naves and transepts
.593		Chancels, sanctuaries, choir lofts, pulpit platforms
.594		Clerestories
.595		Side chapels

See also 726.4 for chapels as separate buildings

.596		Sacristies and baptistries

Class comprehensive works on baptistries in 726.4

.597		Towers and steeples
.6	***Cathedrals**	

Class details and parts of cathedrals in 726.51–726.59

> 726.62–726.65 Cathedrals of specific denominations

Class comprehensive works in 726.6, geographical treatment of cathedrals of specific denominations in 726.609

.62	Cathedrals of Eastern churches

For Eastern Orthodox cathedrals, see 726.63

.63	Eastern Orthodox cathedrals
.64	Roman Catholic cathedrals
.65	Anglican cathedrals

*Add as instructed under 721–729

.69 Accessory structures

Examples: cathedral cloisters, chapter houses

Class here comprehensive works on cloisters

Class monastic cloisters in 726.79

.7 *Monastic buildings

Class here abbeys, convents, friaries, monasteries, priories

Class monastic churches either as a place of public worship or as a separate church building in 726.5

.77 Of specific Christian orders

Add to base number 726.77 the numbers following 271 in 271.1–271.9, e.g., Franciscan monasteries 726.773

Class geographical treatment of buildings of specific orders in 726.709

.78 Of orders of other religions

Add to base number 726.78 the numbers following 29 in 292–299, e.g., Buddhist monasteries 726.7843

.79 Parts and accessory structures

Examples: cells, cloisters, refectories

Class monastic libraries in 727.8

.8 *Mortuary chapels and *tombs

.9 Other buildings for religious and related purposes

Examples: episcopal palaces, missions, parsonages, buildings of religious associations, buildings housing roadside shrines

727 *Buildings for educational and research purposes

Class here school buildings

.1 *Elementary school buildings

.2 *Secondary school buildings

.3 *College and university buildings

Class specialized buildings of colleges and universities in 727.4–727.8

.38 Accessory structures

Examples: dining halls, dormitories, student unions

Music room buildings relocated to 727.478

.4 Professional and technical school buildings

Use 727.40001–727.40009 for standard subdivisions

Add to base number 727.4 notation 001–999, e.g., music room buildings 727.478 [*formerly also* 727.38], law school buildings 727.434

*Add as instructed under 721–729

.5   **Research buildings**

Examples: laboratory, observatory buildings

Use 727.50001–727.50009 for standard subdivisions

Add to base number 727.5 notation 001–999, e.g., physics laboratories 727.553

.6   **Museum buildings**

Use 727.60001–727.60009 for standard subdivisions

Add to base number 727.6 notation 001–999, e.g., science museum buildings 727.65

For art museum buildings, see 727.7

.7   ***Art museum and *gallery buildings***

.8   ***Library buildings***

>   727.82–727.84 Specific kinds of libraries

Class comprehensive works in 727.8, geographical treatment regardless of kind of library in 727.809

.82   General libraries

Add to base number 727.82 the numbers following 027 in 027.1–027.8, e.g., public library buildings 727.824; then add further as instructed under 721–729

For branch libraries, see 727.84

.83   Libraries devoted to specific subjects

.84   Branch libraries

.9   **Other buildings for educational and research purposes**

Examples: community centers for adult education, learned society buildings

728   *Residential and related buildings

Class here domestic architecture, conventional housing

Class residential educational buildings in 727.1–727.3

For official residences, see 725.17; episcopal palaces, parsonages, 726.9

.1   ***Low-cost housing**

Unit and multiple dwellings designed along simple lines to reduce construction costs

Class specific types of low-cost housing in 728.3–728.7

.3   **Specific kinds of conventional housing**

Use of this number for comprehensive works on conventional housing discontinued; class in 728

*Add as instructed under 721–729

.31	*Multiple dwellings
.312	*Row houses and *townhouses
	Including duplex houses
.314	*Apartments (Flats)
	Including apartment hotels, tenements
.37	*Separate houses
	Class here cottages
	Class farmhouses and farm cottages in 728.6, vacation houses in 728.72, large and elaborate private dwellings in 728.8
.370 472	Energy conservation
	Including solar houses [*formerly* 728.69]
.372	*Houses with two or more stories
.373	*Single-story houses
	Class here bungalows, ranch and split-level houses

> **728.4–728.7 Special-purpose housing**

Class comprehensive works in 728

.4   *Club houses

Country, city, fraternal clubs

Class a type of club house not provided for here with the type, e.g., racetrack club houses 725.89

.5   *Hotels and *motels

For apartment hotels, see 728.314

.6   *Farmhouses and *farm cottages

Class farm buildings other than human residences in 728.92

[.67]   Farmhouses and farm cottages

Use of this number discontinued; class in 728.6

[.69]   Solar houses

Relocated to 728.370472

.7   *Vacation houses, cabins, hunting lodges, houseboats, mobile homes

.72   *Vacation houses

.73   *Cabins

Class vacation cabins in 728.72

*Add as instructed under 721–729

.78   Houseboats

.79   Mobile homes

Examples: campers, trailers

For houseboats, see 728.78

See Manual at 629.226 vs. 643.2, 690.879, 728.79

.8   *Large and elaborate private dwellings

Class here chateaux, manor houses, mansions, plantation houses, villas

.81   *Castles

Fortified residences

Class here comprehensive works on architecture of castles

Class castles as military structures in 725.18

.82   *Palaces

Residences of the nobility

Use of this number for chateaux discontinued; class in 728.8

Class fortified palaces in 728.81

See also 725.17 for palaces of rulers, 726.9 for episcopal palaces

[.83–.84]   Mansions, manor houses, villas

Numbers discontinued; class in 728.8

.9   Accessory domestic structures

Examples: bathhouses, conservatories, garages, gatehouses, patios, saunas, swimming pools

.92   Farm buildings other than human residences

.922   *Barns

prefer 747 for interior design

729   Design and decoration of structures and accessories

Class here interior design (the art or practice of planning and supervising the design and execution of architectural interiors and their furnishings)

Class design and decoration of structures and accessories of specific types of buildings in 725–728

For interior decoration, see 747

See Manual at 729

>   **729.1–729.2 Design in specific planes**

Class comprehensive works in 729, design of structural elements in specific planes in 721.1–721.8

*Add as instructed under 721–729

.1   **Design in vertical plane**

Examples: facades, elevations, sections

.11   Composition

.13   Proportion

.19   Inscriptions and lettering

.2   **Design in horizontal plane (Plans and planning)**

As related to function and size of areas

Class here modular design

.23   Proportion

.24   *Interior arrangement

.25   *Lines of interior communication

.28   Lighting

.29   Acoustics

[.3]   **Design and decoration of structural elements**

Relocated to 721.1–721.8

>   **729.4–729.8 Decoration in specific mediums**

Class comprehensive works in 729; decoration in a specific medium not in an architectural context with the medium, e.g., sculpture 730

.4   **Decoration in paint**

As an adjunct to architecture

.5   **Decoration in relief**

Examples: carved and sculptured decoration and ornament, Gothic tracery

.6   **Decoration in veneer and incrustation**

Use of wood, stone, metal, enamel in architectural decoration

.7   **Decoration in mosaic**

Class comprehensive works on mosaics in 738.5

.8   **Decoration in ornamental glass**

[.9]   **Built-in church furniture**

Relocated to 726.529

*Add as instructed under 721–729

730   Plastic arts   Sculpture

Class kinetic, sound sculpture; mixed media and composites; assemblages, constructions; land art in 709.04

SUMMARY

.01   Philosophy and theory of plastic arts

.02   Miscellany of plastic arts

.028   Techniques, procedures, apparatus, equipment, materials of plastic arts

> Class here techniques of two or more of the plastic arts, e.g., firing of clays in sculpture and ceramics

.03–.09   Standard subdivisions of plastic arts

>   **730.1–730.9 Standard subdivisions of sculpture**

Class comprehensive works in 730

.1   **Philosophy and theory of sculpture**

.11   Appreciative aspects

> Do not use for systems; class in 730.1
>
> Class psychological principles in 730.19

.117   Aesthetics

.118   Criticism and appreciation

> Theory, technique, history
>
> Class works of critical appraisal in 730.9

.18   Inherent features

> Examples: color, composition, decorative values, form, movement, space, style, symmetry, vision

.2   **Miscellany of sculpture**

[.28]   Auxiliary techniques and procedures; apparatus, equipment, materials

> Do not use; class in 731.028

.3–.8	**Standard subdivisions of sculpture**
.9	**Historical, geographical, persons treatment of sculpture**

Class here Oriental sculpture from ca. 500 limited to a specific country or locality [*formerly* 732.3–732.9], schools and styles limited to a specific country or locality

Class comprehensive works on specific schools and styles not limited to country or locality in 732–735, sculpture of nonliterate peoples regardless of time or place in 732.2

[.901–.905]	Historical periods

Do not use; class in 732–735

.92	Sculptors

Description, critical appraisal, biography of sculptors and their works regardless of process, representation, style or school, period, place

Class sculptors who also work in the other plastic arts in 730.092

.922	Collected sculptors

Including works of sculptors from several geographical areas

Class works of more than one sculptor in the same geographical area in 730.91, 730.94–730.99, 732–735

[.93]	Ancient world

Do not use; class in 732–733

.95	Asia

Class here comprehensive works on Oriental sculpture [*formerly* 732.3–732.9], Buddhist sculpture [*formerly* 732.4]

Class Buddhist sculpture not provided for here with the style, e.g., Japanese Buddhist sculpture 730.952

.954	South Asia India

Class here comprehensive works on Jain, Hindu sculpture [*formerly* 732.4]

>	**731–735 Sculpture**

Class comprehensive works in 730

See Manual at 736–739 vs. 731–735

731   Processes, forms, subjects of sculpture

Class processes, forms, subjects of individual sculptors in 730.92; of specific periods and by specific schools in 732–735; of specific medieval or modern schools limited to a specific country or locality in 730.9

SUMMARY

.028   Techniques, procedures, apparatus, equipment, materials

Comprehensive works

Class techniques and procedures in 731.4, apparatus and equipment in 731.3, materials in 731.2

> **731.2–731.4 Techniques, procedures, apparatus, equipment, materials**

Class comprehensive works in 731.028; forms and subjects employing techniques, procedures, apparatus, equipment, materials in 731.5–731.8

.2   **Materials**

Examples: metals, wire, wood, stone, ceramic material, clay, glass, wax, rope, textiles, plastics, fiber glass, paper, papier-mâché, found objects

Class use of materials in specific techniques in 731.4

.3   **Apparatus and equipment**

Examples: tools, machines, accessories

Class use of apparatus and equipment in specific techniques in 731.4

.4   **Techniques and procedures**

.41   Direct-metal sculpture

Examples: beating, hammering, bending, shaping, cutting, welding, soldering metals (including pipe and wire)

Class art metalwork in 739

.42   Modeling

In clay, wax, other plastic materials with and without armatures

.43   Molding

Preparation of molds and models

Class use of molds in 731.45

.45   Casting

Example: sand casting

.452   In plaster and cement

.453   In plastics

.456   In bronze

            Including lost-wax casting

            Class here casting in metals

            For casting in other metals, see 731.457

.457   In other metals

.46   Carving and chiseling techniques in sculpture

.462   Sculpturing in wood

.463   Sculpturing in stone

.47   Firing and baking

            Including firing and baking clay models for molding

            Class techniques of firing and baking in ceramics in 738.143

.48   Conservation, preservation, restoration, routine maintenance and repair, safety measures

.5   **Forms**

            Not limited by time, place, person

            General aspects: development, description, critical appraisal, collections of works

            For sculpture in the round, see 731.7

.54   Sculpture in relief

            Class iconography of sculpture in relief in 731.8

.542   Portals and doors

.549   Monumental reliefs

            For monumental brasses, see 739.522

.55   Mobiles and stabiles

.7   **Specific types of sculpture in the round**

            Development, description, critical appraisal, collections of works

            Example: totem poles

            Class iconography of sculpture in the round in 731.8

.72   Decorative sculpture

            Examples: garden sculpture, fountains, sculptured vases and urns

.74   Busts

.75   Masks

.76   Monuments

            For monumental brasses, see 739.522

.8   **Iconography**

Not limited by time, place, person

General aspects: development, description, critical appraisal, works

.81   Equestrian sculpture

.82–.89   Other specific subjects

Add to base number 731.8 the numbers following 704.94 in 704.942–704.949, e.g., mythology and legend 731.87; however, class busts in 731.74, masks in 731.75

> **732–735 Schools and styles of sculpture**

Class comprehensive works, medieval and modern Western schools and styles limited to a specific country or locality in 730.9; sculptors associated with specific schools and styles in 730.92

732   Sculpture from earliest times to ca. 500, sculpture of nonliterate peoples

[.09]   Historical, geographical, persons treatment

Do not use; class persons treatment in 730.9, historical, geographical treatment in 732

.2   Sculpture of nonliterate peoples

Regardless of time or place

.22   Paleolithic sculpture

.23   Rock art (sculpture)

> **732.3–732.9 Ancient sculpture**

Do not use notation 092 from Table 1 in any subdivision of 732.3–732.9; class all persons treatment in 730.9

Comprehensive works on Oriental sculpture relocated to 730.95, Oriental sculpture from ca. 500 limited to a specific country or locality relocated to 730.9, comprehensive works on Oriental sculpture from ca. 500 to 1399 relocated to 734, comprehensive works on Oriental sculpture from 1400 relocated to 735

Class comprehensive works in 732

.3   Ancient Palestinian sculpture

Including Israelite, Judean, Jewish sculpture

.4   Ancient south and southeast Asian sculpture

Comprehensive works on Buddhist sculpture relocated to 730.95, on Jain, Hindu sculpture relocated to 730.954

.44   Ancient Indian sculpture

.5	**Mesopotamian and ancient Persian sculpture**
.6	**Ancient Germanic, Celtic, Slavic, Iberian, British sculpture**
.7	**Ancient Oriental sculpture**

Class ancient Oriental sculpture of a specific place not provided for here with the place, e.g., ancient Indian sculpture 732.44

.71	Ancient Chinese sculpture
.72	Ancient Japanese sculpture
.73	Ancient Korean sculpture
.8	**Ancient Egyptian sculpture**
.9	**Sculpture of other ancient areas**

Add to base number 732.9 the numbers following —39 in notation 391–398 from Table 2, e.g., Phoenician sculpture 732.944; however, ancient sculpture of Greek Archipelago relocated from 732.91 to 733.309391

For Greek, Etruscan, Roman sculpture, see 733

733 Greek, Etruscan, Roman sculpture

.3 Greek (Hellenic) sculpture

Comprehensive works on Greek and Roman sculpture is classed in 733

.309 38	Sculpture of Greece

Class sculpture of Hellenistic world in 733.3

.309 391	Sculpture of Greek Archipelago [*formerly* 732.91]
.4	**Etruscan sculpture**
.5	**Roman sculpture**
.509 37	Sculpture of Italian Peninsula and adjacent territories

Class sculpture of Roman Empire in 733.5

734 Sculpture from ca. 500 to 1399

Class here comprehensive works on Oriental sculpture from ca. 500 to 1399 [*formerly* 732.3–732.9]; medieval sculpture

Class sculpture from ca. 500 to 1399 limited to a specific country or locality in 730.9

[.09]	Historical, geographical, persons treatment

Do not use notation 09 from Table 1 here or in any subdivision of 734; class all geographical and persons treatment in 730.9

.2	**Styles**
.22	Early Christian and Byzantine sculpture
.222	Early Christian sculpture

.224	Byzantine sculpture
.24	Romanesque sculpture
.25	Gothic sculpture

735   Sculpture from 1400

Class here comprehensive works on Oriental sculpture from 1400 [*formerly* 732.3–732.9]; modern sculpture

Class sculpture from 1400 limited to a specific country or locality in 730.9

[.09]   Historical, geographical, persons treatment

Do not use notation 09 from Table 1 here or in any subdivision of 735; class all geographical and persons treatment in 730.9

.2   **Specific periods**

.21   1400–1799

Examples: Renaissance, baroque sculpture

.22   1800–1899

Examples: classical revival sculpture, romanticism, realism

.23   1900–1999

.230 4   Schools and styles

Add to base number 735.2304 the numbers following 709.040 in 709.0401–709.0407, e.g., abstractionism in sculpture 735.230452

.231–.239   Periods

Add to base number 735.23 the numbers following —0904 in notation 09041–09049 from Table 1, e.g., sculpture of 1960–1969 735.236

.24   2000–2099

> ## 736–739 Other plastic arts

Processes and products

Class comprehensive works in 730, other plastic arts not provided for here in 745–749

See also 731–735 for sculpture

See Manual at 736–739 vs. 731–735

736   Carving and carvings

.2   **Precious and semiprecious stones (Glyptics)**

Class engraved seals, stamps, signets in 737.6, setting of precious and semiprecious stones in 739.27

.202 8	Lapidary work
	Contains cutting, polishing, engraving gems
.22	Specific forms
	Class scarabs in 736.20932, carving in specific materials regardless of form in 736.23–736.28
.222	Cameos
.223	Intaglios
.224	Figurines

> **736.23–736.28 Specific stones**

Class comprehensive works in 736.2

.23	Diamonds
.24	Jade
	See also 731–735 for jade sculpture
.25	Sapphires
.28	Obsidian
.4	**Wood**
	Including whittling
	Example: butter prints and molds
	See also 731–735 for wood sculpture, 745.51 for wood handicrafts
.5	**Stone**
	Including lettering, inscriptions, designs
	Class here effigial and sepulchral slabs
.6	**Ivory, bone, horn, shell, amber**
.62	Ivory
	Class netsukes of ivory in 736.68
	See also 731–735 for ivory sculpture
.68	Netsukes
.7	**Ornamental fans**
	Class fans of a specific material with the material, e.g., ivory fans 736.62
.9	**Other materials**
.93	Wax
.94	Snow and ice

.95	Soap
.98	Paper cutting and folding
.982	Origami
.984	Silhouettes

Class comprehensive works on drawing and cutting silhouettes in 741.7

737   Numismatics and sigillography

For paper money, see 769.55

.2   Medals and related objects

.22   Medals

Class here medallions

.222   Commemorative medals

.223   Civilian and military medals

Including decorations, orders

.224   Religious medals

.23   Talismans and amulets

.24   Pins and buttons

.242   Political (Campaign) pins and buttons

.243   Sports pins and buttons

Example: baseball pins and buttons

.3   Counters and tokens

Standard subdivisions are added for counters and tokens, for counters alone, for tokens alone

.4   Coins

Class here counterfeit coins

.409   Historical, geographical, persons treatment

Class coins of specific countries in 737.49

.43   Gold coins

.430 9   Historical, geographical, persons treatment

Class gold coins of specific countries in 737.49

.49   Of specific countries

By place of origin

Add to base number 737.49 notation 3–9 from Table 2, e.g., Roman coins minted in Egypt 737.4932

See also 737.43094 for gold coins of Europe

.6 **Engraved seals, stamps, signets**

Class here sigillography

Standard subdivisions are added for any or all of the topics in the heading

738 Ceramic arts

Class here pottery

Class ceramic sculpture in 731–735

Works about "pottery" in the sense of porcelain and earthenware or stoneware are classed here, in the sense of only porcelain are classed in 738.2

For glass, see 748

SUMMARY

738.01–.09	**Standard subdivisions**
.1	**Techniques, procedures, apparatus, equipment, materials**
.2	**Porcelain**
.3	**Earthenware and stoneware**
.4	**Enameling and enamels**
.5	**Mosaics**
.6	**Ornamental bricks and tiles**
.8	**Other products**

[.028] Auxiliary techniques and procedures; apparatus, equipment, materials

Do not use; class in 738.1

.09 Historical, geographical, persons treatment

Class here brands of pottery [*formerly* 738.23]

.092 Potters

Description, critical appraisal, biography of potters regardless of material or product

Class here ceramic artists

Class enamelers in 738.4092, mosaicists in 738.5092

.1 **Techniques, procedures, apparatus, equipment, materials**

.12 Materials

Examples: clays, e.g., kaolin; glazes, e.g., petuntse; color materials

Class use of materials in specific techniques in 738.14

.13 Apparatus and equipment

Examples: kilns, potter's wheels

Class use of apparatus and equipment in specific techniques in 738.14

.14   Techniques and procedures

Class techniques of making specialized products in 738.4–738.8

For decorative treatment, see 738.15; conservation, preservation, restoration, safety measures, 738.18

.142   Modeling and casting

.143   Firing

Before and after glazing

.144   Glazing

.15   Decorative treatment

Examples: underglaze and overglaze painting, slip tracing, sgrafitto decoration, transfer painting

For glazing, see 738.144

.18   Conservation, preservation, restoration, safety measures

Including expertizing, routine maintenance and repair

>   **738.2–738.8 Products**

Development, description, critical appraisal, collections of works

Class comprehensive works in 738

.2   **Porcelain**

Use of this number for comprehensive works on pottery discontinued; class in 738

Class comprehensive works on porcelain, earthenware, stoneware in 738

[.202 8]   Auxiliary techniques and procedures; apparatus, equipment, materials

Do not use; class in 738.1

.209   Historical and geographical treatment of porcelain

Class here brands [*formerly* 738.27], geographical treatment of types and varieties [*formerly* 738.2709], geographical treatment of products [*formerly* 738.2809]

[.209 2]   Persons treatment

Do not use; class in 738.092

[.23]   Specific varieties and brands of pottery

Number discontinued; class in 738

Brands of pottery relocated to 738.09

[.24]   Specific products of pottery

Number discontinued; class in 738

.27	Specific types and varieties of porcelain
	Examples: blue and white, flow-blue
	Brands relocated to 738.209
.270 9	Historical treatment of porcelain
	Geographical treatment of types and varieties relocated to 738.209
.28	Specific porcelain products
	Class specific products of specific types or varieties in 738.27, specialized products in 738.4–738.8
.280 9	Historical treatment
	Geographical treatment of products relocated to 738.209
.3	**Earthenware and stoneware**
[.302 8]	Auxiliary techniques and procedures; apparatus, equipment, materials
	Do not use; class in 738.1
.309	Historical and geographical treatment
	Class here brands [*formerly* 738.37], geographical treatment of types and varieties [*formerly* 738.3709], geographical treatment of products [*formerly* 738.3809]
[.309 2]	Persons treatment
	Do not use; class in 738.092
.37	Specific types and varieties of earthenware and stoneware
	Examples: delft, faïence, majolica
	Brands relocated to 738.309
.370 9	Historical treatment
	Geographical treatment of types and varieties relocated to 738.309
.38	Specific earthenware and stoneware products
	Class specific products of specific types and varieties in 738.37; specialized products in 738.4–738.8
.380 9	Historical treatment
	Geographical treatment of products relocated to 738.309
.382	Middle Eastern and Western vessels
	Ancient and classical
	Standard subdivisions are added for a specific type of vessel, e.g., ancient Egyptian vases 738.3820932
	Use of this number for comprehensive works on vases discontinued; class in 738.38

[.383]   Other containers

Number discontinued; class in 738.38

>   **738.4–738.8 Specialized products and techniques of making them**

Class comprehensive works in 738

.4   **Enameling and enamels**

Examples: basse-taille, champlevé, ronde bosse

For nielloing, see 739.15; jewelry, 739.27

.42   Cloisonné

.46   Surface-painted enamels

.5   **Mosaics**

Class here mosaic painting, comprehensive works on mosaics in all materials

Class mosaics of a specific material not provided for here with the material, e.g., mosaic glass 748.5

.52   Mosaics used with architecture

Examples: walls, floors, pavements, fixed screens and panels

.56   Mosaics applied to portable objects

Examples: mosaic jewelry, ornaments, ornamental objects, movable panels

.6   **Ornamental bricks and tiles**

Standard subdivisions are added for bricks and tiles, for bricks alone, and for tiles alone

.8   **Other products**

Examples: braziers, candlesticks, lamps, lighting fixtures, stoves

.82   Figurines

Examples: figure groups, animals, plants

739   **Art metalwork**

For numismatics, see 737

SUMMARY

739.1	Techniques, procedures, apparatus, equipment, materials
.2	Work in precious metals
.3	Watches and clocks
.4	Ironwork
.5	Work in other metals
.7	Arms and armor

[.028]   Auxiliary techniques and procedures; apparatus, equipment, materials

Do not use; class in 739.1

.1   **Techniques, procedures, apparatus, equipment, materials**

Class techniques, procedures, apparatus, equipment, materials for a specific kind of metalwork with the kind, e.g., goldsmithing 739.22028

.12   Materials

Class use of materials in specific techniques in 739.14

.13   Apparatus and equipment

Examples: tools, machines, accessories

Class use of apparatus and equipment in specific techniques in 739.14

.14   Techniques and procedures

Examples: bending, casting, drawing, forging, rolling, shaping metals by hammering and beating (repoussé work), stamping, welding

For decorative treatment, see 739.15

.15   Decorative treatment

Examples: chasing, damascening, nielloing, painting, patinating

.16   Conservation, preservation, restoration, safety measures

Including routine maintenance and repair

.2   **Work in precious metals**

Class watches and clocks in precious metals in 739.3

>   739.22–739.24 In specific metals

Class comprehensive works in 739.2, jewelry in specific metals in 739.27

.22   Goldsmithing

Class comprehensive works on gold- and silversmithing in 739.2

.220 28   Techniques, procedures, apparatus, equipment, materials

Class techniques and procedures in 739.224, apparatus and equipment in 739.223, materials in 739.222

[.220 9]   Historical, geographical, persons treatment

Do not use; class in 739.227

(.220 92)   Goldsmiths

(Use of this number is optional; prefer 739.2272)

.222–.226   Techniques, procedures, apparatus, equipment, materials

> Add to base number 739.22 the numbers following 739.1 in
> 739.12–739.16, e.g., decorative treatment 739.225

> Class comprehensive works in 739.22028; historical, geographical,
> persons treatment in 739.227; techniques, apparatus, equipment,
> materials for specific products in 739.228

.227   Historical, geographical, persons treatment

> Add to base number 739.227 notation 01–9 from Table 2, e.g.,
> goldsmiths 739.2272
>> (Option: Class goldsmiths in 739.22092)

> Works about "goldsmiths" in the sense of both gold- and silversmiths
> are classed in 739.2092

.228   Products

> Gold and gold-plate

> Class historical, geographical, persons treatment of specific products in
> 739.227

.228 2   Religious articles

.228 3   Tableware

> Utensils used for setting a table or serving food and drink

> Including flatware, hollow ware

> Class tableware for religious use in 739.2282

.228 4   Receptacles

> Examples: boxes, loving cups, vases

> Class religious receptacles in 739.2282

.23   Silversmithing

> Add to base number 739.23 the numbers following 739.22 in
> 739.22028–739.228, e.g., silversmiths 739.2372, silver tableware 739.2383

.24   Platinumwork

.27   Jewelry

> Design of settings, mounting gems, repair work

> Class here interdisciplinary works on making fine and costume jewelry

> Class interdisciplinary works on jewelry in 391.7, on making costume
> jewelry in 688.2; making handcrafted costume jewelry in 745.5942; carving
> precious and semiprecious stones in 736.2; jewelry made in a material other
> than metal with the material, e.g., mosaic jewelry 738.56

.270 28   Techniques, procedures, apparatus, equipment, materials

> Class techniques and procedures in 739.274, apparatus and
> equipment in 739.273, materials in 739.272

.272–.276   Techniques, procedures, apparatus, equipment, materials

> Add to base number 739.27 the numbers following 739.1 in 739.12–739.16, e.g., techniques 739.274
>
> Class techniques, procedures, apparatus, equipment, materials for specific products in 739.278

.278   Specific products

> Examples: belt buckles, finger rings, shoe buckles, watch fobs

.3   Watches and clocks

> Class here clockcases regardless of material
>
> Add to base number 739.3 the numbers following 739.22 in 739.22028–739.227, e.g., decorative treatment 739.35
>
> Class clocks as furniture in 749.3; interdisciplinary works on clocks in 681.113, on watches in 681.114

>   **739.4–739.5 Work in base metals**

> Class comprehensive works in 739, watches and clocks in base metals in 739.3
>
> *For arms and armor, see 739.7*

.4   Ironwork

> Class here wrought iron, cast iron, stainless steel

.402 8–.47   Techniques, procedures, apparatus, equipment, materials; historical, geographical, persons treatment

> Add to base number 739.4 the numbers following 739.22 in 739.22028–739.227, e.g., decorative treatment 739.45

.48   Specific products

> Examples: balcony motifs, balustrades, grills, knockers, ornamental nails
>
> Class historical, geographical, persons treatment of specific products in 739.47

.5   Work in other metals

.51   Copper and its alloys

> *For brass, see 739.52*

.511   Copper

.512   Bronze

> Class bronze sculpture in 731–735

.52   Brass

.522   Monumental brasses

> Class here rubbing and rubbings for study and research of brasses
>
> Class rubbings as art form in 760

.53	Tin and its alloys
	For bronze, see 739.512
.532	Tin
.533	Pewter
.54	Lead
.55	Zinc and its alloys
	For brass, see 739.52
.56	Nickel
.57	Aluminum
.58	Chromium

.7   Arms and armor

Class here decorative treatment of shapes, handles, grips, metalwork

Class interdisciplinary works in 623.44

See also 623.441 for stone weapons

> 739.72–739.74 Arms

Class comprehensive works in 739.7

.72   Edged weapons

Examples: axes, bayonets, daggers, dirks, knives, spears

Class edged arrows in 739.73, interdisciplinary works on knives in 621.932

.722   Swords and sabers

Standard subdivisions are added for swords and sabers, for swords alone, for sabers alone

.73   Missile-hurling weapons

Examples: air guns, bows and arrows, spring guns

For firearms, see 739.74

.74   Firearms

Add to base number 739.74 the numbers following 623.4 in 623.42–623.44, e.g., pistols 739.7443

Class interdisciplinary works on small firearms in 683.4

.75   Armor

.752   Shields

740   Drawing and decorative arts

SUMMARY

741	Drawing and drawings
742	Perspective
743	Drawing and drawings by subject
745	Decorative arts
746	Textile arts
747	Interior decoration
748	Glass
749	Furniture and accessories

741   Drawing and drawings

Class comprehensive works on drawing and painting in 750, on two-dimensional art in 760

For drawing and drawings by subject, see 743

SUMMARY

741.01–.09	Standard subdivisions
.2	Techniques, procedures, apparatus, equipment, materials
.5	Cartoons, caricatures, comics
.6	Graphic design, illustration, commercial art
.7	Silhouettes
.9	Collections of drawings

.01   Philosophy and theory

.011   Appreciative aspects

Do not use for systems; class in 741.01

Class psychological principles in 741.019

.011 7   Aesthetics

.011 8   Criticism and appreciation

General aspects: theory, technique, history

Class works of critical appraisal in 741.09

.018   Inherent features

Examples: composition, color, form, style, decorative values, light, space, time, movement, symmetry

Class perspective in 742

[.028]   Auxiliary techniques and procedures; apparatus, equipment, materials

Do not use; class in 741.2

.074   Museums and exhibits

Class collections of drawings in 741.9

.09   Historical, geographical, persons treatment

Class collections of drawings of specific periods and places in
741.92–741.99

.092   Artists   *Use 741.9*

Description, critical appraisal, biography of artists regardless of medium,
process, subject, period, place

Description, critical appraisal, biography of artists working in special
applications relocated to 741.5–741.7

Class collections of drawings in 741.9

.2   Techniques, procedures, apparatus, equipment, materials

Including one-color washes highlighting drawings

Class techniques, procedures, apparatus, equipment, materials used in special
applications in 741.5–741.7; used in drawing specific subjects in 743.4–743.8;
used by individual artists in 741.092

For perspective, see 742

See also 751.422 for watercolor

.21   Techniques of reproduction and conservation

.217   Reproduction

Execution and identification

.217 2   Reproductions and copies

.217 4   Forgeries and alterations

.218   Conservation, preservation, restoration

Including expertizing

Class identification of reproductions, copies, forgeries, alterations in
741.217; routine maintenance and repair in 741.219

.219   Safety measures and routine maintenance and repair

>   741.22–741.29 Specific mediums

Class comprehensive works in 741.2

.22   Charcoal

.23   Chalk and crayon

.235   Pastel

.24   Pencil

.25   Silverpoint

.26   Ink with pen, brush, marker

.29   Scratchboard and airbrush drawing

> ### 741.5–741.7 Special applications

Techniques, procedures, apparatus, equipment, materials, description, critical appraisal, collections

Class here description, critical appraisal, biography of artists working in special applications [*formerly* 741.092]; collections by an individual artist devoted to special applications [*formerly* 741.9]

Class comprehensive works in 741.6

.5   **Cartoons, caricatures, comics**

Including fotonovelas

Class here cartoon fiction [*formerly also* with fiction with use of notation 306 from Table 3–B], graphic novels (visual novels)

Class cartoons or caricatures whose purpose is to inform or persuade with the subject of the cartoon or caricature, e.g., political cartoons 320.0207

.507 4   Museums and exhibits

Class collections in 741.59

.509 2   Artists

Class collections by individual artists in 741.593–741.599

.58   Animated cartoons

Class comprehensive works on cartoon films in 791.433, photographic techniques in 778.5347 — use this for cartoons

.59   Collections

Class here cartoons with subordinate text

.590 9   Historical and geographical treatment

Class treatment by specific continents, countries, localities in 741.593–741.599 (*not* 741.59093–741.59099)

.593–.599   Treatment by specific continents, countries, localities

Add to base number 741.59 notation 3–9 from Table 2, e.g., collections of cartoons from London 741.59421

Collections by individual artists are classed at country level only. Notation 074 from Table 1 for collections is not added. For example, a collection of an individual artist from London is classed in 741.5942 (*not* 741.95421, 741.9542074421)

[handwritten: printing, typography + papermaking 90 at 676/686]

.6   **Graphic design, illustration, commercial art**

Class here comprehensive works on special applications of drawing; on graphic design, illustration, commercial art

Class graphic arts, comprehensive works on two-dimensional art in 760; a specific type of illustration, a specific form of graphic design, a specific form of commercial art, not provided for here with the type or form, e.g., original oil paintings for book jackets 759

[handwritten: others - add 088 + Table 7 for specific commodities e.g. web sites 741.60886213]

See Manual at 800 vs. 741.6

.64   Books and book jackets

Standard subdivisions are added for books and book jackets, books alone, and for book jackets alone

Class illumination of manuscripts and books in 745.67

.642   Children's books

.65   Magazines and newspapers

.652   Magazines and magazine covers

Standard subdivisions are added for magazines and magazine covers, for magazines alone, and for magazine covers alone

.66   Covers for sheet music and recordings

.67   Advertisements and posters

Standard subdivisions are added for advertisements and posters, for advertisements alone

.672   Fashion drawing

Class fashion design in 746.92

[handwritten: .673 Trademarks, logos, corporate identity design]

.674   Posters

Class posters as a specific form of prints in 769.5

.68   Calendars, postcards, greeting and business cards

.682   Calendars

.683   Postcards

Class government-issued postcards without illustration in 769.566

.684   Greeting cards

.685   Business cards (Trade cards)

.69   Labels and match covers *[handwritten: – includes packaging design]*

.692   Labels

.694   Match covers [*formerly also* 769.5]

.7   **Silhouettes**

Class cut-out silhouettes in 736.984

.9 **Collections of drawings** *+ country no. + artists name suffix*

Regardless of medium or process

Class here exhibition catalogs

Preliminary drawings are classed with the finished work unless they are treated as works of art in their own right

Collections by an individual artist devoted to special applications relocated to 741.5–741.7

Class collections by more than one artist devoted to special applications in 741.5–741.7, collections of drawings by subject not from a specific period or place in 743.9

> 741.92–741.99 Collections of drawings from specific periods and places

Regardless of subject

Class comprehensive works in 741.9

.92 Historical periods

Not limited geographically

.921 Earliest times to 499 A.D.

.922 500–1399

.923 1400–1799

.924 1800–

.924 1 1800–1899

.924 2 1900–1999

.93–.99 Specific continents, countries, localities

Add to base number 741.9 notation 3–9 from Table 2, e.g., collections of drawings from London 741.9421

Collections by individual artists are classed at country level only. Notation 074 from Table 1 for collections is not added. For example, a collection of an individual artist from London is classed in 741.942 (*not* 741.9421, 741.942074421)

742 Perspective

General aspects: theory, principles, methods

Class perspective in drawing specific subjects in 743.4–743.8, in special applications in 741.5–741.7; comprehensive works on perspective in the arts in 701.82

743 Drawing and drawings by subject

.028 Techniques, procedures, apparatus, equipment, materials

Comprehensive works

Class specific subjects in 743.4–743.8

743.4–743.8 Techniques, procedures, apparatus, equipment, materials

Class comprehensive works in 743.028, artists regardless of subject in 741.092

.4 **Drawing human figures**

Class here nudes

For drawing draped figures, see 743.5

.42 Portraiture

Class portraiture of specific kinds of persons in 743.43–743.45

743.43–743.45 Specific kinds of persons

Class comprehensive works in 743.4, anatomy of specific kinds of persons in 743.49

.43 Men

.44 Women

.45 Children

.46 Bones (Skeletal system)

.47 Muscles (Muscular system)

.49 Anatomy for artists

Including parts and regions of body, e.g., head, abdomen, hands

For bones, see 743.46; muscles, 743.47

.5 **Drawing draperies and draped figures**

For fashion drawing, see 741.672

.6 **Drawing animals**

Specific animals

Add to base number 743.6 the numbers following 59 in 592–599, e.g., drawing birds 743.68

.62–.69 Specific animals

Add to base number 743.6 the numbers following 59 in 592–599, e.g., drawing birds 743.68

.7 **Drawing plants**

Including flowers, fruit

.8 **Drawing other subjects**

Add to base number 743.8 the numbers following 704.94 in 704.943–704.949, e.g., landscapes 743.836

.9   **Collections of drawings by subject (Iconography)**

Not limited by period or by place of production

Add to base number 743.9 the numbers following 704.94 in 704.942–704.949, e.g., collections of drawings of buildings 743.94

Class collections of drawings by subject from a specific period or place in 741.92–741.99

[744]   **[Unassigned]**

Most recently used in Edition 17

745   **Decorative arts**

Class here folk art

Class decorative arts not provided for here in 736–739, 746–749

For interior decoration, see 747

SUMMARY

745.1	**Antiques**
.2	**Industrial art and design**
.4	**Pure and applied design and decoration**
.5	**Handicrafts**
.6	**Calligraphy, illumination, heraldic design**
.7	**Decorative coloring**
.8	**Panoramas, cycloramas, dioramas**
.9	**Other decorative arts**

.1   **Antiques**

Class a specific kind of antique with the kind, e.g., brasses 739.52, passenger automobiles 629.222

See Manual at 745.1

.102 8	Techniques, procedures, apparatus, equipment, materials
.102 87	Techniques and reproduction
	Execution and identification
.102 872	Reproductions and copies
.102 874	Forgeries and alterations
.102 88	Conservation, preservation, restoration
	Including expertizing
	Do not use for routine maintenance and repair; class in 745.10289
	Class identification of reproductions, copies, forgeries, alterations in 745.10287
.102 89	Safety measures and routine maintenance and repair

.2   **Industrial art and design**   *add 088+ table 7 for specific commodities*

Creative design of mass-produced commodities

Class design of a specific commodity with the commodity, e.g., automobiles 629.231

.4   **Pure and applied design and decoration** — *use periods for general books but prefer geographical subdivisions if general*

Class here design source books

Class design in a specific art form with the form, e.g., design in architecture 729 *nor*

For industrial design, see 745.2

[.409]   Historical, geographical, persons treatment

Do not use; class in 745.44

(.409 2)   Artists

(Use of this number is optional; prefer 745.4492) *do not use*

.44   Historical, geographical, persons treatment

>   745.441–745.445 Periods of development

Class here schools and styles not limited by country or locality

Class comprehensive works in 745.44

.441   Nonliterate peoples, and earliest times to 499

Including paleolithic art

Class here design and decoration by nonliterate peoples regardless of time or place

.442   500–1399

Including early Christian, Byzantine, Romanesque, Gothic styles

.443   1400–1799

Including Renaissance, baroque, rococo styles

.444   1800–1999

.444 1   1800–1899

Including classical revival, romantic, art nouveau styles

.444 2   1900–1999

.445   2000–2099

.449   Geographical and persons treatment

Add to base number 745.449 notation 1−9 from Table 2, e.g., ~~artists~~ 745.4492
> (Option: Class artists in 745.4092)

Class design and decoration by nonliterate peoples regardless of place in 745.441

.5   **Handicrafts**

Creative work done by hand with aid of simple tools or machines

Including work in bread dough

Class home (amateur) workshops in 684.08, interdisciplinary works on handicrafts in 680

For decorative coloring, see 745.7; floral arts, 745.92

See Manual at 745.5 vs. 680

SUMMARY

745.51	**In woods**
.53	**In leathers and furs**
.54	**In papers**
.55	**In shells**
.56	**In metals**
.57	**In rubber and plastics**
.58	**From beads, found and other objects**
.59	**Making specific objects**

> **745.51−745.58 In specific materials**

Class comprehensive works in 745.5, specific objects made from specific materials in 745.59, glass handicrafts in 748

For textile handicrafts, see 746

.51   In woods

Examples: inlay trim, marquetry, ornamental woodwork, scrollwork

Including bamboo

Class treen (woodenware) in 674.88, cabinetmaking in 684.08, wooden furniture making in 684.104, artistic aspects of furniture in 749

For ornamental woodwork in furniture, see 749.5

.53   In leathers and furs

Class construction of clothing in 646.3

.531   Leathers

.537   Furs

.54 In papers

Examples: endpapers, paper boxes, tissue papers, wallpapers

Including gift wrapping, quilling

Class paper cutting and folding in 736.98

.542 Papier-mâché

Class papier-mâché used in sculpture in 731.2

.546 Decoupage

Including potichomania

.55 In shells

.56 In metals

Class art metalwork in 739

.57 In rubber and plastics

.572 Plastics

.58 From beads, found and other objects

Class specific objects made from other objects in 745.59

.582 Beads

For bead embroidery, see 746.5

.584 Found objects

Examples: cattails, scrap, stones, hosiery

.59 Making specific objects

Class here handicrafts in composite materials

.592 Toys, models, miniatures, related objects

Class interdisciplinary works on models and miniatures in 688.1, on mass-produced and handcrafted toys in 688.72

Including paper airplanes

> 745.592 2–745.592 4 Toys

Class comprehensive works in 745.592

For toy soldiers, see 745.59282

.592 2 Dolls, puppets, marionettes, and their clothing

.592 21 Dolls and their clothing

.592 24 Puppets and marionettes and their clothing

.592 3 Dollhouses and furniture

.592 4	Soft toys
	Example: stuffed animals
	Class stuffed dolls in 745.59221
.592 8	Models and miniatures
	Including ships in bottles
	Class here interdisciplinary works on handcrafted models and miniatures
	Class models and miniatures produced by assembly-line or mechanized manufacturing, interdisciplinary works on models and miniatures in 688.1; miniature and model educational exhibits, models for technical and professional use with the subject illustrated, e.g., handcrafted miniature anthropological exhibits 573.074
	See Manual at 745.5928
.592 82	Military models and miniatures
	Including toy soldiers
.593	Useful objects
	For toys, models, miniatures, related objects, see 745.592
.593 2	Lampshades
.593 3	Candles and candlesticks
.593 32	Candles
.593 4	Snuffboxes
.593 6	Decoys
	Class carved birds not used for hunting in 730
.594	Decorative objects
.594 1	For special occasions
	Examples: holidays, weddings
	Class here greeting cards
	For Easter eggs, see 745.5944
.594 12	Christmas
.594 2	Costume jewelry
	Class interdisciplinary works on costume jewelry in 391.7, on making jewelry in 739.27, on making costume jewelry in 688.2
.594 3	Artificial flowers
	Class arrangement of artificial flowers in 745.92
.594 4	Egg decorating
	Including Easter eggs

.6   Calligraphy, illumination, heraldic design

.61   Calligraphy

Class here artistic, decorative lettering

Class penmanship in 652.1, typography in 686.22

.619   Styles

.619 7   Latin (Western) styles

.619 74   Carolingian calligraphy

.619 75   Black-letter and Gothic calligraphy

.619 77   Italic calligraphy

.619 78   Roman calligraphy

.619 8   Greek calligraphy

.619 9   Other

Add to base number 745.6199 the numbers following —9 in —91–99 from Table 6, e.g., Chinese calligraphy 745.619951

.66   Heraldic design

.67   Illumination of manuscripts and books

Class here facsimiles of manuscripts reproduced for their illuminations

Standard subdivisions are added for manuscripts and books, for manuscripts alone, and for books alone

Class development, description, critical appraisal of manuscripts in 091, of illustrated books in 096.1

See also 741.64 for book illustration

See Manual at 745.67

.674   Illuminated manuscripts and books by language

Add to base number 745.674 notation 1–9 from Table 6, e.g., illuminated manuscripts in Byzantine Greek 745.67487; however, class illuminated manuscripts in Latin in 745.67094

Class illuminated manuscripts and books in specific languages produced in specific countries and localities in 745.67093–745.67099

.7   Decorative coloring

Class printing, painting, dyeing textiles in 746.6

.72   Painting and lacquering

.723   Painting

Examples: rosemaling, tolecraft

.726   Lacquering

Class here japanning

.73	Stenciling
.74	Decalcomania
.75	Gilding

Class gilding as an aspect of bookbinding in 686.36, of illumination of manuscripts and books in 745.67

.8 Panoramas, cycloramas, dioramas

.9 Other decorative arts

.92 Floral arts

Flower arrangement: selection and arrangement of plant materials and appropriate accessories

Class here arrangement of artificial flowers

Class making artificial flowers in 745.5943, potted plants as interior decorations in 747.98

> 745.922–745.926 Three-dimensional arrangements

Class comprehensive works in 745.92

> 745.922–745.925 Three-dimensional arrangements with specific materials

Class comprehensive works in 745.92, arrangements with specific materials for special occasions in 745.926

.922	Flower arrangements in containers
.922 4	Occidental compositions
.922 5	Oriental compositions
.922 51	Chinese flower arrangements
.922 52	Japanese flower arrangements
.923	Flower arrangements without containers

Examples: corsages, boutonnieres, set floral pieces

.924 Fruit and vegetable arrangements

Including carving of vegetables to produce artificial flowers

.925 Arrangements with other plant materials

Examples: driftwood, pods and cones, dried and gilded grasses and leaves

.926 Three-dimensional arrangements for special occasions

Examples: arrangements for church services, funerals, holidays, weddings

.928   Two-dimensional arrangements

Use of seeds and other dried plant materials in pictures, hangings, trays, for other decorative purposes

746   Textile arts

Class here textile handicrafts

Add to each subdivision identified by * as follows:

028	Auxiliary techniques and procedures; apparatus, equipment, materials
	Class techniques of reproduction and conservation in 048
0288	Routine maintenance and repair [*formerly also* 0489]
0289	Safety measures [*formerly also* 0489]
04	Special topics
041	Patterns
042	Stitches
048	Techniques of reproduction and conservation
0487	Reproductions, copies, forgeries, alterations
	Execution and identification
0488	Conservation, preservation, restoration
	Including expertizing
	Class identification of reproductions, copies, forgeries, alterations in 0487
[0489]	Routine maintenance and repair, safety measures
	Routine maintenance and repair relocated to 0288, safety measures relocated to 0289

Class domestic sewing and related operations in 646.2, a specific textile product not provided for here with the product, e.g., stuffed animals 745.5924

SUMMARY

746.04	**Specific materials**
.1	**Yarn preparation and weaving**
.2	**Laces and related fabrics**
.3	**Pictures, hangings, tapestries**
.4	**Needle- and handwork**
.5	**Bead embroidery**
.6	**Printing, painting, dyeing**
.7	**Rugs and carpets**
.9	**Other textile products**

.04   Specific materials

Add to base number 746.04 the numbers following 677 in 677.1–677.7, e.g., silk 746.0439, string art 746.0471

Class products in a specific material with the product, e.g., string pictures 746.3

>   746.1–746.9 Products and processes

Unless other instructions are given, observe the following table of precedence, e.g., embroidering tapestry 746.3 (*not* 746.44)

Laces and related fabrics	746.2
Pictures, hangings, tapestries	746.3
Rugs and carpets	746.7
Other textile products	746.9
Yarn preparation and weaving	746.1
Needle- and handwork	746.4
Bead embroidery	746.5
Printing, painting, dyeing	746.6

Class comprehensive works in 746, home sewing and clothing in 646, textile manufacturing in 677

.1   **Yarn preparation and weaving**

.11   Carding and combing

.12   Spinning, twisting, reeling

.13   Dyeing

.14   *Weaving

         Example: card weaving

           For weaving unaltered vegetable fibers, see 746.41; nonloom weaving, 746.42

.2   **Laces and related fabrics**

.22   *Laces

         Examples: crocheted, darned laces

           For tatting, see 746.436

.222   *Bobbin laces

.224   *Needlepoint laces

.226   *Knitted laces

.27   Passementerie

         Examples: braids, cords, fringes

.3   ***Pictures, hangings, tapestries**

[.309]   Historical, geographical, persons treatment

         Do not use; class in 746.39

(.309 2)   Artists

           (Use of this number is optional; prefer 746.392)

*Add as instructed under 746

.39	Historical, geographical, persons treatment

Add to base number 746.39 notation 01–9 from Table 2, e.g., artists 746.392 (Option: Class artists in 746.3092)

.4	**Needle- and handwork**
.41	Weaving, braiding, matting unaltered vegetable fibers

Examples: raffia work, rushwork

.412	Basketry
.42	Nonloom weaving and related techniques

Examples: braiding, plaiting, twining

Class nonloom weaving of unaltered vegetable fibers in 746.41

For card weaving, see 746.14

.422	Knotting
.422 2	*Macramé
.422 4	*Netting

Including knotless netting, sprang

.43	*Knitting, crocheting, tatting
.432	*Knitting

Class comprehensive works on knitting and crocheting in 746.43

.434	*Crocheting
.436	*Tatting
.44	*Embroidery

Examples: couching, cutwork, drawn work, hardanger, smocking

.440 28	Auxiliary techniques and procedures; apparatus, equipment, materials

Including machine embroidery

.442	*Canvas embroidery and needlepoint

Including bargello

Class cross-stitch and counted thread embroidery in 746.443

.443	*Cross-stitch

Class here counted thread embroidery

.445	*Appliqué
.446	*Crewelwork
.46	*Patchwork and quilting

Class quilts in 746.97

*Add as instructed under 746

.5	***Bead embroidery**
.6	**Printing, painting, dyeing**
	Examples: hand decoration, stenciling
.62	*Printing
	Block and silk-screen
.66	Resist-dyeing
.662	*Batik
.664	*Tie-dyeing
.7	***Rugs and carpets**
[.709]	Historical, geographical, persons treatment
	Do not use; class in 746.79
(.709 2)	Artists
	(Use of this number is optional; prefer 746.792)
.72	*Woven rugs and carpets
	Examples: Jacquard, plain, tapestry, twill weaves
	Including Navaho rugs
	For pile rugs and carpets, see 746.75
.73	*Crocheted, knitted, braided rugs and carpets
.74	*Hooked and embroidered rugs and carpets
.75	Pile rugs and carpets
.750 95	Asian pile rugs and carpets
	Class here Oriental-style rugs and carpets
	Class styles from specific Asian countries and localities in 746.751–746.758, from Caucasus region in 746.759

>   746.751–746.759 Oriental-style rugs and carpets

Class comprehensive works in 746.75095

.751–.758	Styles from specific Asian countries and localities
	Add to base number 746.75 the numbers following —5 in notation 51–58 from Table 2, e.g., Chinese rugs 746.751
.759	Styles from Caucasus region
.79	Historical, geographical, persons treatment
	Add to base number 746.79 notation 01–9 from Table 2, e.g., artists 746.792 (Option: Class artists in 746.7092)

*Add as instructed under 746

.9   **Other textile products**

.92   Costume

Including fashion design

Class interdisciplinary works on clothing in 391, on clothing construction in 646.4

See Manual at 391 vs. 646.3, 746.92

\>   746.94–746.98 Interior furnishings

Standard subdivisions are added for a single product, e.g., New England quilts 746.970974

Class comprehensive works in 746.9

.94   *Draperies and curtains

.95   *Furniture covers

Examples: antimacassars, kneelers, slipcovers, upholstery

.96   *Table linens

Examples: doilies, mats, napkins (serviettes), scarves, tablecloths; fair linens

.97   *Bedclothing

Examples: afghans, bedspreads, blankets, quilts; sheets, pillowcases

.98   *Towels and toweling

747   **Interior decoration**   *prefer this to 729 for interior design*

Design and decorative treatment of interior furnishings

Class here interior decoration of residential buildings [*formerly also* 645]

Class textile arts and handicrafts in 746, interior design in 729

Interior decoration of specific types of residential buildings is classed in 747.88

For furniture and accessories, see 749

SUMMARY

747.1	Decoration under specific limitations
.2	Historical, geographical, persons treatment
.3	Ceilings, walls, doors, windows
.4	Floors
.5	Draperies, upholstery, rugs and carpets
.7	Decoration of specific rooms of residential buildings
.8	Decoration of specific types of buildings
.9	Specific decorations

[.09]   Historical, geographical, persons treatment

Do not use; class in 747.2

*Add as instructed under 746

(.092)	Artists

> (Use of this number is optional; prefer 747.2)

.1   **Decoration under specific limitations**

Example: decorating on a budget

Class a specific aspect of decoration under limitations with the aspect, e.g., decorating dining rooms on a budget 747.76

.2   **Historical, geographical, persons treatment**   *— use for country style books eg Tuscan style*

Class here artists
(Option: Class artists in 747.092)

>   747.201–747.205 Periods of development

Class here schools and styles not limited by country or locality

Class comprehensive works in 747.2

.201   Earliest times to 499 A.D.

.202   500–1399

.203   1400–1799

.203 4   1400–1499

Class here Renaissance period

Class Renaissance decoration of an earlier or later period with the specific period, e.g., interior decoration in the 1500s 747.2035

.203 5   1500–1599

.203 6   1600–1699

.203 7   1700–1799

.204   1800–1999

.204 8   1800–1899

.204 9   1900–1999

Add to base number 747.2049 the numbers following —0904 in notation 09041–09049 from Table 1, e.g., interior decoration in the 1970s 747.20497

.205   2000–2099

.21–.29   Geographical treatment

Add to base number 747.2 the numbers following 708 in 708.1–708.9, e.g., interior decoration and artists in Islamic areas 747.2917671

Individual artists are classed in notation at country level only

> **747.3–747.4 Decoration of specific elements**

Class comprehensive works in 747, decoration of specific elements in specific types of buildings in 747.8, decoration of specific elements in specific rooms of residential buildings in 747.7, specific decorations of specific elements in 747.9

.3   **Ceilings, walls, doors, windows**

Including decorative hangings, painting, paneling, woodwork

Class here textile wall coverings, wallpapers

For draperies, see 747.5

.4   **Floors**

For rugs and carpets, see 747.5

.5   **Draperies, upholstery, rugs and carpets**

.7   **Decoration of specific rooms of residential buildings**

Standard subdivisions are added for individual rooms

Class specific decorations regardless of room in 747.9

.73   Home libraries and studies

.75   Living rooms, drawing rooms, parlors

Standard subdivisions are added for any or all of the topics in the heading

.76   Dining rooms

.77   Bedrooms and nurseries

.78   Bathrooms and powder rooms

.79   Other rooms

.791   Recreation and family rooms

.797   Kitchens

.8   **Decoration of specific types of buildings**

Class specific decorations regardless of type of building in 747.9

.85–.87   Decoration of public, religious, educational, research buildings

Add to base number 747.8 the numbers following 72 in 725–727, e.g., decoration of theaters 747.85822

.88   Decoration of specific types of residential buildings

> Add to base number 747.88 the numbers following 728 in 728.1–728.9, e.g., decoration of hotels 747.885
>
> Class decoration of residential buildings of institutions in 747.85–747.87
>
> Comprehensive works on decoration of residential buildings are classed in 747
>
> *For decoration of specific rooms of residential buildings, see 747.7*

.9   **Specific decorations**

> Observe the following table of precedence, e.g., decorative lighting for Christmas 747.92 (*not* 747.93)

Decorating with house plants	747.98
Decorative lighting	747.92
Decorating with color	747.94
Decorations for specific occasions	747.93

> *See also 747.5 for draperies, upholstery, rugs and carpets*

.92   Decorative lighting

.93   Decorations for specific occasions

> Examples: for parties, weddings, holidays

.94   Decorating with color

.98   Decorating with houseplants

748   Glass

SUMMARY

748.092		**Persons treatment**
.2		**Glassware**
.5		**Stained, painted, leaded, mosaic glass**
.6		**Methods of decoration**
.8		**Specific articles**

.092   Persons treatment

> Class here glassmakers
>
> The term ''glassmakers'' when referring only to makers of glassware is classed in 748.29

.2   **Glassware**

> Class here blown, cast, decorated, fashioned, molded, pressed glassware
>
> Class stained glass in 748.5
>
> *For methods of decoration, see 748.6; specific articles, 748.8*

.202 8   Techniques, procedures, apparatus, equipment, materials

.202 82   Glassblowing

.202 86   Bottle and jar cutting

.202 87	Reproductions, copies, forgeries, alterations
	Execution and identification
.202 88	Repair and restoration
	Including expertizing
	Safety measures relocated to 748.20289
	Class identification of reproductions, copies, forgeries, alterations in 748.20287
.202 89	Safety measures [*formerly also* 748.20288]
[.209]	Historical, geographical, persons treatment
	Do not use; class in 748.29
(.209 2)	Glassware makers
	(Use of this number is optional; prefer 748.29)
.29	Historical, geographical, persons treatment
	Class here glassware makers (Option: Class glassware makers in 748.2092)
.290 1–.290 5	Periods of development
	Class here schools and styles not limited by country or locality
	Add to base number 748.290 the numbers following 747.20 in 747.201–747.205, e.g., glassware of 1700–1799 748.29037; however, Greco-Roman glass relocated from 748.2901 to 748.29938
.291–.299	Geographical treatment
	Add to base number 748.29 the numbers following 708 in 708.1–708.9, e.g., Greco-Roman glass 748.29938 [*formerly* 748.2901], glassware and glassmakers of Pennsylvania 748.29148
	Individual glassmakers are classed in notation at country level only
.5	**Stained, painted, leaded, mosaic glass**
	Standard subdivisions are added for stained glass alone, for painted glass alone, and for leaded glass alone
	Class comprehensive works on mosaics in 738.5
	For specific articles, see 748.8
.502 8	Techniques, procedures, apparatus, equipment, materials
.502 82	Glass painting and staining
.502 84	Leaded glass craft
.502 85	Mosaic glass craft and making glass mosaics
.502 88	Conservation, preservation, restoration
	Do not use for routine maintenance and repair; class in 748.50289
.502 89	Safety measures and routine maintenance and repair

[.509]	Historical, geographical, persons treatment

Do not use; class in 748.59

(.509 2)	Artists

(Use of this number is optional; prefer 748.59)

.59	Historical, geographical, persons treatment

Class here artists
(Option: Class artists in 748.5092)

.590 1–.590 5	Periods of development

Class here schools and styles not limited by country or locality

Add to base number 748.590 the numbers following 747.20 in 747.201–747.205, e.g., 500–1399 748.5902

.591–.599	Geographical treatment

Add to base number 748.59 the numbers following 708 in 708.1–708.9, e.g., stained glass of Chartres 748.59451

Individual artists are classed in notation at country level only

.6	**Methods of decoration**

Examples: cutting, enameling, engraving, etching, sandblasting

Class methods of decoration of specific articles in 748.8

For painted glass, see 748.5

[.609 2]	Persons treatment

Do not use; class in 748.29

.8	**Specific articles**

Examples: mirrors, ornaments

Class mirrors as furniture in 749.3, glass lamps and lighting fixtures in 749.63

.82	Bottles

Bottles of artistic interest regardless of use

Class manufacture of glass bottles in 666.192

.83	Tableware

Class here drinking glasses

.84	Paperweights

.85	Glass beads

749   Furniture and accessories

For upholstery, see 747.5

[.09]	Historical, geographical, persons treatment

Do not use; class in 749.2

(.092)	Furniture makers
	(Use of this number is optional; prefer 749.2)

.1 Antique furniture

Class specific kinds of antique furniture in 749.3

.102 8	Auxiliary techniques and procedures; apparatus, equipment, materials
.102 87	Reproductions, copies, forgeries, alterations
	Execution and identification
.102 88	Conservation, preservation, restoration
	Including expertizing
	Do not use for routine maintenance and repair; class in 749.10289
	Class identification of reproductions, copies, forgeries, alterations in 749.10287
.102 89	Safety measures and routine maintenance and repair
[.109]	Historical, geographical, persons treatment
	Do not use; class in 749.2

.2 Historical, geographical, persons treatment

Class here antiques and reproductions, furniture makers
(Option: Class furniture makers in 749.092)

.201–.205	Periods of development
	Class here schools and styles not limited by country or locality
	Add to base number 749.20 the numbers following 747.20 in 747.201–747.205, e.g., Renaissance period 749.2034
.21–.29	Geographical treatment
	Add to base number 749.2 the numbers following 708 in 708.1–708.9, e.g., English furniture and furniture makers 749.22
	Individual furniture makers are classed in notation at country level only

.3 Specific kinds of furniture

Examples: beds, cabinets, chests, clockcases, desks, mirrors, screens, tables

Class outdoor furniture in 749.8

For built-in furniture, see 749.4; heating and lighting fixtures and furniture, 749.6; picture frames, 749.7

.32	Chairs

.4 Built-in furniture

Class built-in church furniture in architectural design in 726.529

For heating and lighting fixtures and furniture, see 749.6

.5   **Ornamental woodwork in furniture**

> Examples: inlay trim, lacquer work, marquetry, scrollwork
>
> Class ornamental woodwork in a specific kind of furniture with the kind, e.g., picture frames 749.7

.6   **Heating and lighting fixtures and furniture**

.62   Heating

> Examples: mantels, fireplace and inglenook fixtures and furniture

.63   Lighting

> Examples: chandeliers, lamps, sconces
>
> Class built-in church lighting fixtures in architectural design in 726.5298

.7   **Picture frames**

> Including shadow boxes
>
> Class here picture framing

.8   **Outdoor furniture**

> Class furniture used both in- and outdoors in 749.3

750   Painting and paintings

> Class here comprehensive works on painting and drawing
>
> Unless other instructions are given, observe the following table of precedence, e.g., Canadian painters of landscapes 759.11 (*not* 758.10971), landscape painting in Canada 758.10971 (*not* 759.11)

Individual painters and their work	759.1–.9
Techniques, procedures, apparatus, equipment, materials	751.2–.6
Iconography	753–758
Specific forms	751.7
Geographical treatment	759.1–.9
Periods of development	759.01–.07
Color	752

> Class comprehensive works on graphic arts, two-dimensional art in 760; painting in a specific decorative art with the art, e.g., illumination of manuscripts and books 745.67
>
> *For drawing and drawings, see 741*

SUMMARY

750.1–.9	**Standard subdivisions**
751	**Techniques, procedures, apparatus, equipment, materials, forms**
752	**Color**
753	**Symbolism, allegory, mythology, legend**
754	**Genre paintings**
755	**Religion and religious symbolism**
757	**Human figures and their parts**
758	**Other subjects**
759	**Historical, geographical, persons treatment**

.1	**Philosophy and theory**
.11	Appreciative aspects
	Do not use for systems; class in 750.1
	Class psychological principles in 750.19
.117	Aesthetics
.118	Criticism and appreciation
	General aspects: theory, technique, history
	Class works of critical appraisal in 759
.18	Inherent features
	Examples: composition, form, style, perspective, decorative values, light, vision, space, movement, symmetry
	Class color in 752
[.28]	Techniques, procedures, apparatus, equipment, materials
	Relocated to 751
[.9]	**Historical, geographical, persons treatment**
	Do not use; class in 759
(.92)	Painters
	(Use of this number is optional; prefer 759)

751 Techniques, procedures, apparatus, equipment, materials [*formerly* 750.28], forms

.2	**Materials**
	Examples: surfaces, pigments, mediums, fixatives, coatings
	Class use of materials in specific techniques in 751.4
.3	**Apparatus, equipment, artists' models**
	Class use of apparatus and equipment in specific techniques in 751.4

.4   **Techniques and procedures**

.42   Use of water-soluble mediums

For tempera painting, see 751.43

.422   Watercolor painting

Including casein painting, gouache

Class ink painting in color in 751.425

.422 4   Watercolor painting techniques by subject

Add to base number 751.4224 the numbers following 704.94 in 704.942–704.949, e.g., techniques of landscape painting in watercolor 751.422436

.425   Ink painting

.425 1   Chinese ink painting

.425 14   Chinese ink painting techniques by subject

Add to base number 751.42514 the numbers following 704.94 in 704.942–704.949, e.g., techniques of landscape painting in Chinese ink painting 751.4251436

.425 2   Japanese ink painting

.426   Acrylic painting

.43   Tempera painting

.44   Fresco painting

.45   Oil painting

.454   Oil painting techniques by subject

Add to base number 751.454 the numbers following 704.94 in 704.942–704.949, e.g., techniques of landscape painting in oils 751.45436

.46   Encaustic (Wax) painting

.49   Other methods

Examples: finger, polymer, roller (brayer), sand painting

Class mosaic painting in 738.5

.493   Collage

With painting as the basic technique

.494   Airbrush

.5   **Techniques of reproduction**

Execution, identification, determination of authenticity of reproductions, copies, forgeries, alterations

For printmaking and prints, see 760

.58   Forgeries and alterations

.6   **Conservation, preservation, restoration, safety measures, routine care**

.62   Conservation, preservation, restoration

Including expertizing

Class identification of reproductions, copies, forgeries, alterations in 751.5; routine care in 751.67

.67   Safety measures, routine care

.7   **Specific forms**

[.72]   Easel paintings

Number discontinued; class in 750

.73   Murals and frescoes

Class here painted graffiti, street art

.74   Panoramas, cycloramas, dioramas

.75   Scene paintings

Including theatrical scenery

.76   Glass underpainting

Class glass underpainting as a technique of glass decoration in 748.6

.77   Miniatures

Class miniatures done as illuminations in manuscripts and books in 745.67

See Manual at 745.67

752   **Color**

Class technology of color in 667, comprehensive works on color in the fine and decorative arts in 701.85

>   **753–758 Iconography**

General aspects: development, description, critical appraisal, works regardless of form

Class comprehensive works in 750

See Manual at 753–758

753   **Symbolism, allegory, mythology, legend**   *Subjects in painting*

.6   **Symbolism and allegory**

For religious symbolism, see 755

.7   **Mythology and legend**

Class religious mythology in 755

754   **Genre paintings**

755 Religion and religious symbolism

Add to base number 755 the numbers following 704.948 in 704.9482–704.9489, e.g., paintings of Holy Family 755.56

[756] Historical events

Relocated to 758.99

757 Human figures and their parts

Not provided for in 753–755, 758

Class here portraits

Observe the following table of precedence, e.g., groups of nude women 757.4 (*not* 757.22 or 757.6)

Erotica	757.8
Miniature portraits	757.7
Specific kinds of persons	757.3–.5
Groups of figures	757.6
According to attire	757.2

.2   **According to attire**

.22   Nudes

.23   Draped figures

> **757.3–757.5 Specific kinds of persons**

Class here portraits of individuals

Class comprehensive works in 757

.3   **Men**

.4   **Women**

.5   **Children**

.6   **Groups of figures**

.7   **Miniature portraits**

.8   **Erotica**

Including pornography

[.9]   **General collections of portraits**

Number discontinued; class in 757

758 Other subjects

.1   **Landscapes**

Add to base number 758.1 notation 1–9 from Table 2, e.g., landscapes of Utah 758.1792

.2   **Marine scenes and seascapes**

.3   **Animals**

Including hunting scenes

Class hunting scenes in which animals are not the center of interest with the subject, e.g., hunters 757.6

See Manual at 753–758

.4   **Still life**

.42   Flowers

.5   **Plants**

For flowers, see 758.42

See Manual at 753–758

.6   **Industrial and technical subjects**

.7   **Architectural subjects and cityscapes**

Add to base number 758.7 notation 1–9 from Table 2, e.g., cityscapes of England 758.742

.9   **Other**

Add to base number 758.9 notation 001–999, e.g., paintings of historical events 758.99 [*formerly also* 756]

For genre paintings, see 754; landscapes, 758.1; seascapes, 758.2; cityscapes, 758.7

759   Historical, geographical, persons treatment   *painters*

General aspects: development, description, critical appraisal, works

(Option: Class painters in 750.92)

Class exhibitions of paintings not limited by place, period, or subject in 750.74

>   759.01–759.07 Periods of development

Class here schools and styles not limited by country or locality, works on one or two periods of European painting

Class comprehensive works in 759; works on three or more periods of European painting in 759.94; schools associated with a specific locality in 759.1–759.9, e.g., Florentine school of Italian painting 759.551

.01   Nonliterate peoples, and earliest times to 499

.011   Nonliterate peoples

Regardless of time or place

Class paintings of both nonliterate and literate cultures in 759.1–759.9

.011 2   Paleolithic painting and paintings

.011 3	Rock art (painting and paintings)
.02	500–1399

Class here medieval painting and paintings

.021	500–1199
.021 2	Early Christian painting and paintings

Class early Christian painting and paintings before 500 in 759.01

.021 4	Byzantine painting and paintings

Class Byzantine painting and paintings before 500 in 759.01

.021 6	Romanesque painting and paintings
.022	1200–1399

Class here Gothic painting and paintings

Class Gothic painting and paintings of an earlier or later period with the specific period, e.g., 500–1199 759.021

.03	1400–1599

Class here Renaissance painting and paintings

Class Renaissance painting and paintings before 1400 in 759.022

.04	1600–1799
.046	1600–1699

Class here baroque painting and paintings

Class baroque painting and paintings of 1700–1799 in 759.047

.047	1700–1799

Including rococo painting and paintings

.05	1800–1899

Add to base number 759.05 the numbers following 709.034 in 709.0341–709.0349, e.g., romanticism in painting 759.052

.06	1900–1999

Class here modern painting

Add to base number 759.06 the numbers following 709.040 in 709.0401–709.0407, e.g., surrealist painting 759.0663

For 1800–1899, see 759.05

.07	2000–2099

> ### 759.1–759.9 Geographical treatment

Individual painters are classed in notation at country level only

(Option: To give local emphasis and a shorter number to painting and paintings of a specific country, use one of the following:

(Option A: Place them first by use of a letter or other symbol for the country, e.g., Burmese painting and paintings 759.B [preceding 759.1]

(Option B: Class them in 759.1; in that case class painting and paintings of North America in 759.97)

Class comprehensive works in 759, painting and paintings of nonliterate peoples in 759.011, Western painting of one or two specific periods in 759.02–759.07

.1 North America

(Option: To give local emphasis and a shorter number to painting and paintings of a specific country other than United States and Canada, class them in this number; in that case class painting and paintings of North America in 759.97)

Class painting and paintings of Middle America in 759.972

.11 Canada

Add to base number 759.11 the numbers following —71 in notation 711–719 from Table 2, e.g., painting and paintings of Toronto 759.113541

.13 United States

Class painting and paintings of specific states in 759.14–759.19

See also 759.97295 for painting and paintings of Puerto Rico

.14–.19 Specific states of United States

Add to base number 759.1 the numbers following —7 in notation 74–79 from Table 2, e.g., painting and paintings of San Francisco 759.19461

Class individual painters in 759.13, painting and paintings of Hawaii in 759.9969

.2 British Isles   England

For the purpose of classification, England, Scotland, Wales, and Northern Ireland are considered to be separate countries. Therefore, an English painter is classed in 759.2, a Scottish painter in 759.2911, a Welsh painter in 759.2929, and a Northern Ireland painter in 759.2916

.21–.28 England

Add to base number 759.2 the numbers following —42 in notation 421–428 from Table 2, e.g., painting and paintings of Manchester 759.2733

.29 Scotland, Ireland, Wales

Add to base number 759.29 the numbers following —4 in notation 41–42 from Table 2, e.g., painting and paintings of Scotland 759.2911

.3–.8   **Other European countries**

Add to base number 759 the numbers following —4 in notation 43–48 from Table 2, e.g., painting and paintings of France 759.4

Class comprehensive works, and painting and paintings of other European countries not provided for in notation 43–48 from Table 2 in 759.94, e.g., painting and paintings of Netherlands 759.9492

.9   **Other geographical areas**

.91   Areas, regions, places in general

Add to base number 759.91 the numbers following —1 in notation 11–19 from Table 2, e.g., Western Hemisphere 759.91812

Class individual painters in the notation for their respective countries

.93–.99   Continents, countries, localities

Class here painting and paintings of specific periods, e.g., painting and paintings of 1800–1899 in South America 759.9809034

Add to base number 759.9 notation 3–9 from Table 2, e.g., comprehensive works on painting and paintings of Europe 759.94, Etruscan painting and paintings 759.9375

Class works on one or two periods of European painting in 759.02–759.07, e.g., painting and paintings of 1800–1899 in Europe 759.05 (*not* 759.9409034); individual painters from Soviet Union in 759.7, individual Hawaiian painters in 759.13

760   Graphic arts   Printmaking and prints

Graphic arts: any and all nonplastic representations on flat surfaces, including painting, drawing, prints, and photographs

Including copy art made with photoduplication equipment, rubbings, typewriter art, typographical designs; two-dimensional mixed-media art and composites

Class here two-dimensional art; prints and at least one other of the graphic arts

Class comprehensive works on graphic and plastic arts in 701–709; rubbings used for study and research in a specific field with the field, e.g., monumental brasses 739.522

For drawing and drawings, see 741; painting and paintings, 750; photography and photographs, 770; printing, 686.2

See Manual at 700

SUMMARY

.01–.03	Standard subdivisions of graphic arts
.04	Special topics of graphic arts
.044	Iconography of graphic arts

Add to base number 760.044 the numbers following 704.94 in 704.942–704.949, e.g., landscapes in graphic arts 760.04436

.05–.08	Standard subdivisions of graphic arts
.09	Historical, geographical, persons treatment
.090 1–.090 5	Periods of development

Not limited by country or locality

Add to base number 760.090 the numbers following 709.0 in 709.01–709.05, e.g., graphic arts of the Renaissance 760.09024

.1   Philosophy and theory of printmaking and prints

.11   Appreciative aspects

Do not use for systems; class in 760.1

Class psychological principles in 760.19

.117   Aesthetics

.118   Criticism and appreciation

General aspects: theory, technique, history

Class works of critical appraisal in 769.9

.18   Inherent features

Examples: color, composition, decorative values, form, light, movement, perspective, style, space, symmetry, vision

.2   Miscellany of printmaking and prints

.28   Techniques, procedures, apparatus, equipment, materials of printmaking and prints

Class techniques, procedures, apparatus, equipment, materials for making specific kinds of prints in 761–767

.3–.6   Standard subdivisions of printmaking and prints

.7   Education, research, related topics of printmaking and prints

[.75]   Collecting prints

Do not use; class in 769.12

.8   History and description of printmaking and prints with respect to kinds of persons

[.9]   › **Historical, geographical, persons treatment of printmaking and prints**

> Do not use; class in 769.9

(.92)   Printmakers

> (Use of this number is optional; prefer 769.92)

> ## 761–769 Printmaking and prints

Class comprehensive works in 760

> ## 761–767 Printmaking

Fine art of executing a printing block or plate representing a picture or design conceived by the printmaker or copied from another artist's painting or drawing or from a photograph

General aspects: techniques, procedures, equipment, materials

Class comprehensive works in 760.28; techniques, procedures, apparatus, equipment, materials of reproduction, preservation, routine care in 769.1; techniques, procedures, apparatus, equipment, materials employed by individual printmakers in 769.92

761   Relief processes (Block printing)

Examples: raw potato printing, rubber-stamp printing

.2   **Wood engraving**

.3   **Linoleum-block printing**

.8   **Metal engraving**

[762]   [Unassigned]

Most recently used in Edition 14

763   Lithographic (Planographic) processes

For chromolithography, see 764.2

.2   **Surfaces**

.22   Stone lithography

.23   Aluminum lithography

.24   Zinc lithography

764   Chromolithography and serigraphy

.2   **Chromolithography**

.8   **Serigraphy**

Class here silk-screen printing

> **765–767 Intaglio processes**

Class comprehensive works in 765

765   Metal engraving

Class here comprehensive works on metal relief and metal intaglio processes, on intaglio processes

Class metal relief engraving in 761.8

For mezzotinting and aquatinting, see 766; etching and drypoint, 767

.2   **Line engraving**

.5   **Stipple engraving**

.6   **Criblé engraving**

766   Mezzotinting, aquatinting, related processes

.2   **Mezzotinting**

.3   **Aquatinting**

.7   **Composite processes**

Use of two or more processes in a single print

767   Etching and drypoint

.2   **Etching**

.3   **Drypoint**

[768]   [Unassigned]

Most recently used in Edition 14

769   Prints —

Works produced using a printing block, screen, or plate

General aspects: description, critical appraisal, collections regardless of process

SUMMARY

769.01–.08	**Standard subdivisions**
.1	**Collecting, reproduction, preservation, routine care of prints**
.4	**Iconography**
.5	**Forms of prints**
.9	**Historical, geographical, persons treatment of printmaking and prints**

.028 8   Maintenance and repair [*formerly also* 769.19]

Class conservation, preservation, restoration in 769.18

[.075]   Collecting prints

Do not use; class in 769.12

[.09]	Historical, geographical, persons treatment
	Do not use; class in 769.9

.1   **Collecting, reproduction, preservation, routine care of prints**

Class collecting, reproduction, preservation, routine care of specific forms of prints in 769.5

.12	Collecting prints
.17	Techniques of reproduction
.172	Reproductions and copies
.174	Forgeries and alterations
.18	Conservation, preservation, restoration

Including expertizing

Class identification of reproductions, copies, forgeries, alterations in 769.17

[.19]	Maintenance and repair
	Relocated to 769.0288

.4   **Iconography**

Add to base number 769.4 the numbers following 704.94 in 704.942–704.949, e.g., portrait prints 769.42

Class postage stamps by subject in 769.564, printmakers regardless of subject in 769.92

.5   **Forms of prints**

Examples: lettering, inscriptions, designs on name cards, diplomas, decorative prints, posters

Match covers relocated to 741.694

Class prints other than postage stamps on a specific subject regardless of form in 769.4, made by an individual printmaker regardless of form in 769.92; comprehensive works on posters in 741.674

.52	Bookplates
.53	Paper dolls
.55	Paper money

Class here counterfeit paper money

[.550 9]	Historical, geographical, persons treatment
	Do not use; class in 769.559
.559	Historical, geographical, persons treatment

Add to base number 769.559 notation 01–9 from Table 2, e.g., paper money of France 769.55944

.56	Postage stamps and related devices

Class here philately

Unless other instructions are given, class complex subjects with aspects in two or more subdivisions of this schedule in the one coming first, e.g., counterfeit stamps depicting birds 769.562 (*not* 769.56432)

Class stamps other than for prepayment of postage in 769.57

[.560 9]	Historical, geographical, persons treatment

Do not use; class in 769.569

.561	United Nations postage stamps, postal stationery, covers
.562	Counterfeit postage stamps, covers, cancellations
.563	Postage stamps commemorating persons and events
.564	Postage stamps depicting various specific subjects (Iconography)

Add to base number 769.564 the numbers following 704.94 in 704.943–704.949, e.g., postage stamps of birds of the world 769.56432

For stamps commemorating persons and events, see 769.563

.565	Covers
.566	Postal stationery

Postal-service-issued stationery (e.g., letter sheets, envelopes, postcards) bearing imprinted stamps

Class illustrated postcards in 741.683

.567	Postmarks, cancellations, cachets

Standard subdivisions may be added for postmarks, cancellations, cachets, for postmarks alone, for cancellations alone, and for cachets alone

See also 769.562 for counterfeit cancellations

.569	Historical, geographical, persons treatment

Add to base number 769.569 notation 01–9 from Table 2, e.g., postage stamps from San Marino 769.5694549

.57	Stamps other than for prepayment of postage

Examples: Christmas seals, officially sealed labels, ration coupons; postage-due, postal savings, revenue and savings stamps

.9   **Historical, geographical, persons treatment of printmaking and prints**

printers   Add to base number 769.9 notation 01–9 from Table 2, e.g., ~~printmakers~~

use   ~~769.92~~

country +   (Option: Class printmakers in 760.92)

suffix   Class the history of a specific process with the process, e.g., history of lithography 763.09

     See Manual at 769.92

770   Photography and photographs

Class technological photography in 621.367

SUMMARY

770.1–.9	**Standard subdivisions**
771	**Techniques, procedures, apparatus, equipment, materials**
772	**Metallic salt processes**
773	**Pigment processes of printing**
774	**Holography**
778	**Specific fields and special kinds of photography, and related activities**
779	**Photographs**

.1   **Philosophy and theory**

.11   Inherent features

       Examples: color, composition, decorative values, form, light, movement, perspective, space, style, symmetry, vision

       Do not use for systems; class in 770.1

.2   **Miscellany**

.23   Photography as a profession, occupation, hobby

.232   Photography as a profession and occupation

.233   Photography as a hobby

[.28]   Techniques, procedures, apparatus, equipment, materials

       Do not use for apparatus, equipment, materials; class in 771

       Techniques and procedures relocated to 771

.9   **Historical, geographical, persons treatment**

.92   ~~Photographers~~   *prefer 779 + suffix*

       Regardless of type of photography; however, class motion-picture photographers in 778.53092, television photographers in 778.59092

       Class photographs in 779

771 Techniques, procedures [*formerly also* 770.28], apparatus, equipment, materials

Including techniques of pinhole photography, of photography without camera

Class here interdisciplinary works on description, use, manufacture of apparatus, equipment, materials

Class techniques, procedures, apparatus, equipment, materials used in special processes in 772–774; in specific fields and special kinds of photography in 778; manufacture of a specific kind of apparatus, equipment, material with the subject, e.g., of cameras 681.418

.1 **Studios, laboratories, darkrooms**

Class laboratory and darkroom practice in 771.4

.2 **Furniture and fittings**

.3 **Cameras and accessories**

.31 Specific makes (brands) of cameras

Arrange alphabetically by trade name

.32 Specific types of cameras

Examples: 35mm single-lens reflex, automatic, instant, large format, miniature

Class specific makes of specific types of cameras in 771.31

.35 Optical parts of cameras

Class optical parts of specific makes of cameras in 771.31

For shutters, see 771.36; focusing and exposure apparatus, 771.37

.352 Lenses

.356 Filters

.36 Camera shutters

Class shutters of specific makes of cameras in 771.31

.37 Focusing and exposure apparatus

Examples: exposure meters, range finders, viewfinders

Class focusing and exposure apparatus of specific makes of cameras in 771.31

.38 Accessories

Examples: carrying cases, tripods

.4 **Darkroom and laboratory practice**

For chemical materials, see 771.5

.43 Preparation of negatives

.44   Preparation of positives

Examples: contact printing, enlarging, developing, mounting

.45   Preservation and storage of negatives and transparencies

.46   Preservation and storage of positives

For mounting, see 771.44

.47   Recovery of waste materials

.49   Developing and printing apparatus

Examples: enlargers, frames, trays, utensils

.5   Chemical materials

.52   Support materials

Examples: backings of cellulose compounds, ceramics, glass, metal, paper

.53   Photosensitive surfaces

.532   Specific photosensitive surfaces

.532 2   Plates

.532 3   Papers

.532 4   Films

.54   Developing and printing supplies

Examples: developing, fixing, intensifying, reducing, toning solutions

---

>   **772–774 Special processes**

Techniques, procedures, apparatus, equipment, materials

Class comprehensive works in 771, processing techniques in specific fields and special kinds of photography in 778

For photomechanical printing techniques, see 686.232

772   Metallic salt processes

.1   Direct positive and printing-out processes

Early photographic processes

For platinum printing-out process, see 772.3

.12   Daguerreotype process

.14   Wet-collodion, ferrotype, tintype processes

.16   Kallitype processes

.3   Platinotype processes

Including platinum printing-out process

.4   **Silver processes**

Use of silver halides in principal light-sensitive photographic emulsions

773   Pigment processes of printing

Early photographic printing processes

.1   **Carbon and carbro processes**

Examples: Mariotype, ozotype, ozobrome

.2   **Powder (Dusting-on) processes**

Including peppertype processes

Class xerography in 686.44

.3   **Imbibition processes**

.5   **Gum-bichromate processes**

.6   **Photoceramic and photoenamel processes**

.7   **Diazotype processes**

.8   **Oil processes**

Including bromoil process

774   Holography

[775]   [Unassigned]

Most recently used in Edition 14

[776]   [Unassigned]

Most recently used in Edition 14

[777]   [Unassigned]

Most recently used in Edition 14

778   Specific fields and special kinds of photography, and related activities

General aspects: techniques, procedures, apparatus, equipment, materials

Class here interdisciplinary works on use and manufacture of apparatus, equipment, materials of specific fields and specific kinds of photography

Class manufacture of a specific kind of apparatus, equipment, materials with the subject, e.g., of cameras 681.418

SUMMARY

778.2	**Photographic projection**
.3	**Special kinds of photography**
.4	**Stereoscopic photography and projection**
.5	**Motion-picture and television photography, and related activities**
.6	**Color photography and photography of colors**
.7	**Photography under specific conditions**
.8	**Special effects and trick photography**
.9	**Photography of specific subjects**

.2   **Photographic projection**

Including filmstrips, filmslides

For stereoscopic projection, see 778.4; motion-picture projection, 778.55

.3   **Special kinds of photography**

Not provided for elsewhere

Including Kirlian photography (high-voltage, high-frequency photopsychography)

Class a specific application of photography with the application, e.g., use of photography in astronomy 522.63

For technological photography and photo-optics, see 621.367

See also 133.8 for parapsychological aspects of Kirlian photography

See Manual at 778.3 vs. 621.367

.31   Photomicrography

For motion-picture photomicrography, see 778.56

.32   Photography in terms of focus

.322   Telephotography

For aerial and space photography, see 778.35; panoramic photography, 778.36

.324   Close-up photography

Including photomacrography

Class close-up motion-picture and television photography in 778.5

.34   Infrared photography

Interdisciplinary works

Class technological infrared photography in 621.3672

.35   Aerial and space photography

Including interpretation

For photogrammetry, see 526.982

.36   Panoramic photography

.37   High-speed photography

Including use of short-duration electronic flash

Class high-speed motion-picture photography in 778.56, use of normal photographic electronic flash (flashbulb photography) in 778.72

.4   **Stereoscopic photography and projection**

Class stereoscopic motion-picture projection in 778.5541

For stereoscopic motion-picture photography, see 778.5341

.5   **Motion-picture and television photography, and related activities**

.52   General topics of motion-picture and television photography

Add to base number 778.52 the numbers following 778.5 in 778.53–778.58, e.g., lighting for motion-picture and television photography 778.52343

>   778.53–778.58 Motion pictures

Class comprehensive works in 778.5

.53   Motion-picture photography (Cinematography) and editing

Class here comprehensive works on cinematography and projection

Class special kinds of motion-picture photography applicable to science and technology in 778.56, comprehensive works on motion-picture production and cinematography in 791.43

For motion-picture projection, see 778.55

.532   Darkroom and laboratory practice

.534   Specific types and elements of motion-picture photography

.534 1   Stereoscopic

.534 2   Color

.534 3   Lighting

.534 4   Sound

Including sound-picture recording, sound synchronization and scoring, postsynchronization

Film music relocated to 781.542

.534 5   Special effects

Examples: double-image, trick photography

.534 6   Time-lapse

.534 7   Animated cartoons   — use for cartoons

.534 9   Amateur

Class darkroom and laboratory practice for amateurs in 778.532; specific types and elements of amateur motion-picture photography in 778.5341–778.5347

.534 91   Specific types of cameras

.535	Editing films

Including titling

Class editing in a specific type or element of motion-picture photography in 778.534

.538	Photography of specific subjects

Add to base number 778.538 notation 001–999, e.g., motion-picture photography of birds 778.538598

Class specific types and elements of motion-picture photography regardless of subject in 778.534

.55	Motion-picture projection
.554	Of specific kinds of motion pictures
.554 1	Stereoscopic
.554 2	Color
.554 4	Sound
.554 9	Amateur
.56	Special kinds of motion-picture photography

Not provided for elsewhere

Examples: high-speed motion-picture photography, motion-picture photomicrography

Class a specific application with the application, e.g., use of motion-picture photography in diagnosis of diseases 616.075028

.58	Preservation and storage of motion-picture films
.59	Television photography

Television music relocated to 781.546

.599	Television recording and recorders

Tape, film, disc

.599 2	Recording
.599 3	Recorders
.6	**Color photography and photography of colors**

Class color photomicrography in 778.31

For color motion-picture photography, see 778.5342

.602 8	Auxiliary techniques and procedures; apparatus, equipment, materials

Class processing auxiliary techniques and procedures, apparatus, equipment, materials in color photography in 778.66

.62	Photography of colors in monochrome
	Orthochromatic and panchromatic
.63	Direct process reproduction in color photography
	Including Lippmann process
.65	Additive processes in color photography
.66	Processing techniques, procedures, apparatus, equipment, materials in color photography

Class here subtractive processes, production of color films and prints by subtractive analysis and subtractive synthesis, respectively

Class direct process reproduction in color photography in 778.63, additive processes in color photography in 778.65

.7	**Photography under specific conditions**
.71	Outdoors
.712	In sunlight
.719	At night

For infrared photography, see 778.34

.72	Indoors and by artificial light

Class here use of normal photographic electronic flash (flashbulb photography)

Class short-duration flash in high-speed photography in 778.37

For infrared photography, see 778.34

.73	Underwater
.75	Under extreme climatic conditions
.76	Available light

Class outdoor available light photography in 778.71, indoor available light photography in 778.72

.8	**Special effects and trick photography**

Examples: composite, high-contrast, tabletop photography; photomontage; photography of specters, distortions, multiple images, silhouettes

Class special effects motion-picture photography in 778.5345

.9	**Photography of specific subjects**

Class here comprehensive works on techniques of photographing, photographs of, and photographers of a specific subject

Add to base number 778.9 the numbers following 704.94 in 704.942–704.949, e.g., portrait photography 778.92

Class photographers in 770.92, photography by specific methods regardless of subject in 778.3–778.8

779   Photographs   + suffix for photographers

Add to base number 779 the numbers following 704.94 in 704.942–704.949, e.g., photographs of children 779.25

See Manual at 779

780   Music

This schedule is new and has been prepared with little or no reference to previous editions. Most numbers have been reused with new meanings.

A comparative table giving both old and new numbers for a substantial list of topics and equivalence tables showing the numbers in the old and new schedules appear in Volume 1 in this edition

(Option: Distinguish scores by prefixing a letter or other symbol to the number for treatises, e.g., music for violin M787.2 or &787.2, and distinguish miniature scores from other scores by a special prefix, e.g., MM787.2; distinguish recordings in a similar manner, e.g., violin recordings R787.2 or MR787.2. Alternatively, distinguish scores, texts, recordings by adding to the number for treatises the numbers following 78 in 780.26–780.269, e.g., miniature scores of music for violin 787.20265. Examples in this schedule do not distinguish scores, texts, or recordings)

In building numbers, do not add by use of 0 or 1 (alone or in combination) more than twice, e.g., history of rock protest songs 782.421661592 (*not* 782.42166159209)

(Option: Add as many times as desired)

See Manual at 780

SUMMARY

780.000 1–.099 9		Relation of music to other subjects
.1–.9		Standard subdivisions
781	**General principles and musical forms**	
.01–.09	Standard subdivisions	
.1	Basic principles	
.2	Elements of music	
.3	Composition	
.4	Techniques of music	
.5	Kinds of music	
.6	Traditions of music	
.7	Sacred music	
.8	Musical forms	
782	**Vocal music**	
.001–.009	Standard subdivisions	
.01–.08	[General principles and musical forms]	
.1	Dramatic vocal forms Operas	
.2	Nondramatic vocal forms	
.3	Services (Liturgy and ritual)	
.4	Secular forms	
.5	Mixed voices	
.6	Women's voices	
.7	Children's voices	
.8	Men's voices	
.9	Other types of voices	

783   Music for single voice   The voice
.001–.009   Standard subdivisions
.01–.09   [General principles and musical forms]
.1   Single voices in combination
.2   Solo voice
.3   High voice
.4   Middle voice
.5   Low voice
.6–.8   Woman's, child's, man's voice
.9   Other types of voice

784   Instruments and instrumental ensembles and their music
.01–.09   Standard subdivisions
.1   General principles, musical forms, instruments
.2   Full (Symphony) orchestra
.3   Chamber orchestra
.4   Light orchestra
.6   Keyboard, mechanical, electronic, percussion bands
.7   String orchestra
.8   Wind band
.9   Brass band

785   Ensembles with only one instrument per part
.001–.009   Standard subdivisions
.01–.09   [General principles, musical forms, instruments]
.1   Ensembles by size
.2   Ensembles with keyboard
.3   Ensembles without electrophones and with percussion and keyboard
.4   Ensembles without keyboard
.5   Ensembles without keyboard and with percussion
.6   Keyboard, electrophone, percussion ensembles
.7   String ensembles   Bowed string ensembles
.8   Woodwind ensembles
.9   Brass ensembles

786   Keyboard, mechanical, electrophonic, percussion instruments
.2   Pianos
.3   Clavichords
.4   Harpsichords
.5   Keyboard wind instruments   Organs
.6   Mechanical and aeolian instruments
.7   Electrophones   Electronic instruments
.8   Percussion instruments
.9   Drums and devices used for percussion effects

787   Stringed instruments (Chordophones)   Bowed stringed instruments
.2   Violins
.3   Violas
.4   Cellos (Violoncellos)
.5   Double basses
.6   Other bowed stringed instruments   Viols
.7   Plectral instruments
.8   Plectral lute family
.9   Harps and musical bows

788	**Wind instruments (Aerophones)**
.2	**Woodwind instruments and free aerophones**
.3	**Flute family**
.4	**Reed instruments**
.5	**Double-reed instruments**
.6	**Single-reed instruments**
.7	**Saxophones**
.8	**Free reeds**
.9	**Brass instruments (Lip-reed instruments)**

.000 1–.099 9   Relation of music to other subjects

Works in which the focus is music

Add to base number 780.0 three-digit notation 001–999, e.g., music and literature 780.08, music and Welsh literature 780.0891 (*not* 780.089166), music and the performing arts 780.079 (*not* 780.07902)

See Manual at 780.079 vs. 790.2

.1   Philosophy and theory

Class general principles, theory of music in 781

.14   Languages (Terminology) and communication

.148   Musical notation, abbreviations, symbols

Examples: staff notation, neumes, tablature, tonic sol-fa

Including braille musical notation

Class transcription from one form of notation to another in 780.149

.149   Editing

.15   Analytical guides and program notes

Do not use for scientific principles; class in 781.2

(.16)   Bibliographies, catalogs, indexes

(Optional number; prefer 016.78)

(.162)   *Bibliographies and catalogs of music literature

(.164)   *Bibliographies and catalogs of scores and parts

Example: bibliographies and catalogs of manuscript scores and parts

(.166)   *Discographies

Bibliographies and catalogs of music recorded on phonorecords (cylinders, discs, wires, tapes, films)

Example: biodiscographies

[.19]   Psychological principles

Do not use; class in 781.11

.2   Miscellany

*(Optional number; prefer 016.78)

.202   Synopses and outlines

Class synopses of stories and plots in 782.00269

.216   Lists, inventories, catalogs of music

Class here thematic catalogs

Class thematic catalogs of individual composers in 780.92

.26   Treatises on music scores, recordings, texts

(Option: Use this number and its subdivisions to distinguish scores and recordings within 780; see details in note under 780)

(Option: Class here law; prefer appropriate subdivisions of 340)

In other parts of the schedules, indicate scores, recordings, texts, and treatises about them by adding the numbers following 78 in 780.262–780.269, e.g., bibliography of musical manuscripts 016.780262, bibliography of manuscripts of violin music 016.78720262, discography of violin music 016.78720266

See Manual at 780: Standard subdivisions

>   780.262–780.265 Scores

Class comprehensive works in 780.26

For words and other vocal sounds to be sung or recited with music, see 780.268

.262   *Manuscripts

Including sketch books, autograph scores

.263   *Printed music

For performance scores, see 780.264; study scores 780.265

See also 070.5794 for music publishing, 686.284 for music printing

.264   *Performance scores and parts

Examples: full scores, conducting scores, piano-vocal scores

.265   *Study scores (Miniature scores, Pocket scores)

.266   *Sound recordings of music

Class here comprehensive works on music recordings

For video recordings, see 780.267

See also 781.49 for recording of music

.267   *Video recordings of music

*(Option: Use this standard subdivision to distinguish scores and recordings, see details in note under 780)

.268   Words and other vocal sounds to be sung or recited with music

Examples: librettos, lyrics, poems, screenplays

Class here texts

The words must be discussed in a musical context. Thus, if the words are presented as literature, folklore, or religious text, class the work in 800, 398, 200, respectively

Use this subdivision only for building other numbers; never use it by itself

Class comprehensive works in 782.00268

For stories plots, synopses, see 780.269

See Manual at 780.268

.269   Stories, plots, synopses

Example: scenarios

Use this subdivision only for building other numbers; never use it by itself

Class comprehensive works in 782.00269

See Manual at 780.269

.28   Auxiliary procedures; apparatus, equipment, materials

Class techniques of music in 781.4, instruments in 784

See also 780.26 for scores, 780.266 for recordings

.7   Education, research, performances, related topics

Including use of apparatus and equipment in study and teaching

.76   Review, exercises, examinations, works for self-instruction

.77   Special teaching and learning methods

Example: programmed teaching

Class techniques for acquiring musical skills and learning a repertoire in 781.42

.78   Performances

General aspects: concerts and recitals

Do not use for use of apparatus and equipment in study and teaching; class in 780.7

Add to base number 780.78 notation 3–9 from Table 2, e.g., concerts in London 780.78421

See also 781.43 for performance techniques

.79	Competitions, festivals, awards, financial support

Including adjudication

Add to base number notation 3–9 from Table 2, e.g., festivals in France 780.7944

Class performances at festivals and competitions in 780.78

.8	**History and description of music with respect to kinds of persons**

.89	Music with respect to specific racial, ethnic, national groups

Class folk music in 781.62

See Manual at 780.89 vs. 781.62

.9	**Historical, geographical, persons treatment**

General aspects: development, description, critical appraisal

Class critical appraisal in analytical guides and program notes in 780.15

> 780.901–780.905 Periods of stylistic development of music

Class here schools and styles not limited ethnically or by country or locality

Even though the periods are those of Western music, this does not limit the use of these numbers to Western or European music only. Any time period of any music transcending ethnic or country limitations is classed here

Class comprehensive works in 780.9

.901	Ancient times to 499

.902	500–1499

Examples: Gothic style, ars antiqua, ars nova, medieval music

.903	1450–

Class here modern music

For 1900–1999, see 780.904; 2000–2099, 780.905

.903 1	Ca. 1450–ca. 1600

Example: Renaissance music

.903 2	Ca. 1600–ca. 1750

Examples: baroque music, nuove musiche

.903 3	Ca. 1750–ca. 1825

Examples: preclassicism, classicism, rococo style, 18th century music

Class rococo style of earlier period, music of earlier part of 18th century in 780.9032

.903 4   Ca. 1825–ca. 1900

Examples: romanticism, nationalism, 19th century music

Class music of earlier part of 19th century in 780.9033, 20th century nationalism in 780.904

.904   1900–1999

Examples: impressionism, neoclassicism, avant-garde music

Class early impressionism in 780.9034

[.904 1–.904 9]   Individual decades

Do not use; class in 780.904

.905   2000–2099

.92   Persons associated with music

Examples: composers, performers, critics

Class here thematic catalogs of individual composers

(Option: Class individual composers in 789)

Class general thematic catalogs in 780.216

.94   European music

Use this number only for works that stress that they are discussing the European origin and character of music in contrast to music from other sources

---

> ## 781–788 Principles, forms, ensembles, voices, instruments

Class here music of all traditions

(Option: 781–788 may be used for only one tradition of music; in that case, class all other traditions in 789. For example, if it is desired to emphasize Western art music, class it here, and class all other traditions of music in 789, e.g., jazz 789.5; or, if it is desired to emphasize jazz, class it here, and class all other traditions of music in 789, e.g., Western art music 789.8)

Unless other instructions are given, class complex subjects with aspects in two or more subdivisions of 781–788 in the one coming last, e.g., Johann Sebastian Bach's cello sonatas 787.4183 (*not* 784.183), jazz mass 782.323165 (*not* 781.65)

Class comprehensive works in 780

781   General principles and musical forms

Class here music theory

Use the subdivisions of 781 only when the subject is not limited to voice, instrument, or ensemble. If voice, instrument, or ensemble is specified, class with voice, instrument, or ensemble; and then add as instructed. For example, rehearsal of music 781.44, rehearsal of opera (a form for the voice) 782.1144

SUMMARY

781.01–.09	**Standard subdivisions**
.1	**Basic principles**
.2	**Elements of music**
.3	**Composition**
.4	**Techniques of music**
.5	**Kinds of music**
.6	**Traditions of music**
.7	**Sacred music**
.8	**Musical forms**

.01–.09   Standard subdivisions

> Notation from Table 1 as modified under 780.1–780.9, e.g., music theory during the Renaissance 781.09031

.1   **Basic principles**

.11   Psychological principles

> *For aesthetics, appreciation, taste, see 781.17*

.12   Religious principles

.17   Artistic principles

> Including aesthetics, appreciation, taste

> .2   **781.2–781.8 Other principles and musical forms**

> Add to notation for each term identified by * as follows:
> 01–09 Standard subdivisions
> > Notation from Table 1 as modified at 780.1–780.9, e.g., performances 078
> 1   General principles
> > Add to 1 the numbers following 781 in 781.1–781.7, e.g., rock music 166, rehearsing rock music 166144

> Class comprehensive works in 781

.2   ***Elements of music**

> Class here scientific principles

SUMMARY

781.22	**Time**
.23	**Musical sound**
.24	**Melody**
.25	**Harmony**
.26	**Tonal systems**
.28	**Texture**

.22   *Time

> *For playing time, see 781.432*

.222   *Pulse

*Add as instructed under 781.2–781.8

.224	*Rhythm
.226	*Meter
.23	*Musical sound
.232	*Pitch
.233	*Volume
.234	*Timbre (Tone color)
.235	*Attack and decay
.236	*Silence

Including rests

.237	*Intervals

For consonance, see 781.238; dissonance, 781.239

.238	*Consonance
.239	*Dissonance
.24	*Melody
.246	*Scales and scalic formations
.247	*Ornaments

Examples: trills, embellishments

.248	*Themes

Examples: subject, countersubject, idée fixe, leitmotif

See also 780.216 for thematic catalogs

.25	*Harmony

Class here harmonic organization, comprehensive works on harmony and counterpoint

Class intervals in 781.237, figured bass in 781.47

For homophony, see 781.285; counterpoint, 781.286

.252	*Chords

Including arpeggios

.254	*Cadences
.256	*Harmonic rhythm
.258	*Tonality

Key relationships

For tonal systems, see 781.26

*Add as instructed under 781.2–781.8

.26	*Tonal systems

.262   *Diatonicism

.263   *Medieval church modes

Class here comprehensive works on modes, modes of Western folk music

For other modes, see 781.264

.264   Other modes

Examples: ancient Greek modes, Byzantine echoi, Indian rāgas

Class modes of Western folk music in 781.263

.265   *Macrotonality

Tonality based on units larger than the diatonic whole tone

Including pentatonicism

.266   *Whole tonality

Tonality based on scales of diatonic whole tones

.267   *Atonality

Music with no fixed tonic or key center

For dodecaphony, see 781.268

.268   *Dodecaphony (Twelve-tone system, Note rows)

Class comprehensive works on serialism in 781.33

.269   *Microtonality

Tonality based on melodic units smaller than the diatonic semitone

.28   *Texture

.282   *Monody

Music with a single melodic line

.283   *Heterophony

Music with a single melodic line simultaneously varied by two or more performers

.284   *Polyphony

Two or more melodic lines

For homophony, see 781.285; counterpoint, 781.286

.285   *Homophony

Two or more mutually dependent melodic lines

*Add as instructed under 781.2–781.8

.286   *Counterpoint

Two or more independent melodic lines

Class comprehensive works on harmony and counterpoint in 781.25

.3   *Composition

[.302 85]   Computer composition

Do not use; class in 781.34

.32   *Indeterminacy and aleatory composition

Forms of composition based on chance

.33   Serialism

.330 1–.330 9   Standard subdivisions

Notation from Table 1 as modified under 780.1–780.9, e.g., performances of serial music 781.33078

.331   Basic principles

.331 1   Psychological principles

For aesthetics, appreciation, taste, see 781.3317

.331 2   Religious principles

.331 7   Artistic principles

Including aesthetics, appreciation, taste

.332–.338   Specific elements

Add to base number 781.33 the numbers following 781.2 in 781.22–781.28, e.g., serialized rhythm 781.3324; however, class atonality in 781.267

.34   *Computer composition

.344–.346   Computer science aspects

Unless it is redundant, add to base number 781.34 the numbers following 00 in 004–006, e.g., use of digital microcomputers 781.34416, but use of digital computers 781.34 (*not* 781.344)

.36   *Extemporization (Improvisation)

.37   *Arrangement

Example: transcription

For arrangements, see 781.38

.374   *Orchestration

.377   *Paraphrase and parody

*Add as instructed under 781.2–781.8

.38   *Arrangements

.382–.388   By original voice, instrument, ensemble

Add to base number 781.38 the numbers following 78 in 782–788, e.g., arrangements of violin music 781.3872

Use these subdivisions only for building other numbers; never use them by themselves

See Manual at 781.382–781.388

.4   *Techniques of music

Class techniques of composition in 781.3

.42   *Techniques for acquiring musical skills and learning a repertoire

.423   *Sight and score reading

Class here visual techniques

.424   *Listening and ear training

Class here aural techniques

.426   *Memorizing

.43   *Performance techniques

For extemporization, see 781.36; specific performance techniques, 781.44–781.48

See also 784.193 for techniques for playing instruments

.432   *Playing time

.434   *Harmonization

.436   *Transposition

.438   *Ensemble technique

>   781.44–781.48 Specific performance techniques

Class comprehensive works in 781.43

.44   *Rehearsal and practice

.45   *Conducting

.46   *Interpretation

Including rubato

.47   *Accompaniment

Including continuo (thorough bass)

See Manual at 781.47

*Add as instructed under 781.2–781.8

.48   *Breathing and resonance

> *See also 784.1932 for breathing and resonance associated with instrumental performance*

.49   *Recording of music

> *See also 621.3893 for sound recording and reproducing equipment, 780.266 for treatises on music recordings*

.5   ***Kinds of music**

SUMMARY

781.52	**Music for specific times**
.53	**Music in specific settings**
.54	**Music for specific media**
.55	**Music accompanying public entertainments**
.56	**Program music**
.57	**Music accompanying activities**
.58	**Music accompanying stages of the life cycle**
.59	**Music reflecting other themes and subjects**

.52   *Music for specific times

.522   *For days of week

.522 2   *Sunday

.522 8   *Saturday

.523   *For times of day

> Examples: morning, noon, evening

.524   *For the seasons

.524 2   *Spring

.524 4   *Summer

.524 6   *Fall (Autumn)

> Including harvest

.524 8   *Winter

.53   *Music in specific settings

.532   *Outdoor

> Including street music

.534   *Indoor

> *For specific indoor settings, see 781.535–781.539*

>   781.535–781.539 Specific indoor settings

> Class music in religious settings in 781.7, comprehensive works in 781.534

*Add as instructed under 781.2–781.8

.535	*Domestic setting
.536	*Court setting
.538	*Theater setting
.539	*Concert hall setting
.54	*Music for specific media

To be classed here the music must be either background or mood music

.542	*Film music [*formerly also* 778.5344]

See also 778.5344 for sound synchronization of motion pictures

.544	*Radio music
.546	*Television music [*formerly also* 778.59]

See also 778.59 for sound synchronization of television programs

.55	*Music accompanying public entertainments
.552	*Dramatic music

Class here incidental dramatic music

Class dramatic vocal music in 782.1

.554	*Dance music

For ballet music, see 781.556

.556	*Ballet music
.56	*Program music

Music depicting extramusical concepts, e.g., music depicting the sea

Class musical forms depicting extramusical concepts in 784.18, e.g., nocturnes 784.18966

.57	*Music accompanying activities

Examples: inaugurations, initiations

Class music accompanying stages of the life cycle in 781.58, music reflecting other themes and subjects regardless of activity in 781.59

.58	*Music accompanying stages of the life cycle
.582	*Birth and infancy

Examples: music for infant baptisms and circumcisions

Class here music for confinements

.583	*Attainment of puberty

Example: music for bar mitzvahs

*Add as instructed under 781.2–781.8

.584	*Attainment of majority
	Example: music for debuts
.586	*Courtship and betrothal
.587	*Weddings and marriage
.588	*Dying and death

Examples: music for burials, cremations, funerals, mourning

.59	*Music reflecting other themes and subjects
.592	*Protest
.593	*Work
.594	*Sports and recreation
.595	*Sea life
.599	*Patriotic, *political, *military

Class here music commemorating historical events

.6   *Traditions of music

Works emphasizing a specific tradition

(Option: If 781–788 is used for only one tradition of music, class all other traditions in 789)

SUMMARY

781.62	**Folk music**
.63	**Popular music**
.64	**Western popular music**
.65	**Jazz**
.66	**Rock (Rock 'n' roll)**
.68	**Western art (Classical) music**
.69	**Non-Western art music**

| .62 | Folk music |

Music indigenous to the cultural group in which it occurs, usually evolved through aural transmission

See also 780.9 for music of and performed in a specific location

See Manual at 780.89 vs. 781.62

| .620 01–.620 07 | Standard subdivisions |

Notation from Table 1 as modified under 780.1–780.9, e.g., performances of folk music 781.620078

| .620 08 | History and description of folk music with respect to kinds of persons |
| [.620 089] | Treatment with respect to specific racial, ethnic, national groups |

Do not use; class in 781.621–781.629

*Add as instructed under 781.2–781.8

.620 09	Historical, geographical, persons treatment
.620 090 1–.620 090 5	Historical periods

> Add to base number 781.620090 the numbers following 780.90 in 780.901–780.905, e.g., folk music of the Renaissance 781.62009031

.620 091–.620 099	Geographical and persons treatment

> Class geographical treatment of folk music of specific racial, ethnic, national groups in 781.621–781.629

.620 1–.620 5	General principles

> Add to base number 781.620 the numbers following 781 in 781.1–781.5, e.g., folk music for springtime 781.6205242, rehearsing folk music for springtime 781.6205242144

.620 6	Stylistic influences of other traditions of music

> Add to base number 781.6206 the numbers following 781.6 in 781.63–781.69, e.g., influence of jazz on folk music 781.62065, performances of folk music influenced by jazz 781.62065078

.621–.629	Folk music of specific racial, ethnic, national groups

> Add to base number 781.62 notation 1–9 from Table 5, e.g., Spanish folk music 781.6261; then add further as follows:

001–008	Standard subdivisions	
	Notation from Table 1 as modified under 780.1–780.9, e.g., performances of Spanish folk music 781.62610078	
009	Historical, geographical, persons treatment	
00901–00905	Historical periods	
	Add to base number 0090 the numbers following 780.90 in 780.901–780.905, e.g., Spanish folk music of the Renaissance 781.6261009031	
[0093–0099]	Treatment by specific continents, countries, localities	
	Do not use; class in 03–09	
01	General principles	
	Add to 01 the numbers following 781 in 781.1–781.5, e.g., Spanish folk music for springtime 781.6261015242, rhythm in Spanish folk music for springtime 781.62610152421224	
02	Stylistic influence of other traditions of music	
	Add to 02 the numbers following 781.6 in 781.63–781.69, e.g., influence of jazz on Spanish folk music 781.6261025, performances of Spanish folk music influenced by jazz 781.6261025078	
03–09	Specific continents, countries, localities	
	Add to 0 notation 3–9 from Table 2, e.g., Spanish folk music in New York City 781.626107471	

> 781.63–781.69 Other traditions of music

Add to notation for each term identified by † as follows:
01–09   Standard subdivisions
Notation from Table 1 as modified under 780.1–780.9, e.g.,
performances 078
1   General principles and stylistic influences of other traditions of music
11–15   General principles
Add to 1 the numbers following 781 in 781.1–781.5, e.g.,
springtime music 15242, melody in springtime music
15242124
16   Stylistic influences of other traditions of music
Add to 16 the numbers following 781.6 in 781.62–781.69, e.g.,
influence of folk music 162, performances of influence of folk
music 162078

Class comprehensive works in 781.6

.63   †Popular music

For Western popular music, see 781.64

.64   †Western popular music

Examples: ragtime, reggae, skiffle

Most works on Western popular music are predominantly about popular
songs and are classed in 782.42164

For jazz, see 781.65; rock, 781.66

.642   †Country music

Class here bluegrass music

.643   †Blues

Class here rhythm and blues

.644   †Soul

.65   †Jazz

.652   †Early jazz

Class here origins of jazz

.653   †Traditional jazz

Examples: New Orleans, Dixieland, Southwest and Kansas City, Harlem,
white New York styles; Chicago breakdown

.654   †Mainstream jazz

Including swing

†Add as instructed under 781.63–781.69

.655   †Modern jazz

Examples: bop (bebop), hard bop, cool jazz, progressive jazz

For avant-garde jazz, see 781.656

.656   †Avant-garde jazz

.657   †Hybrid styles

Examples: Afro-Cuban, third stream, Indo-jazz

.66   †Rock (Rock 'n' roll)

Examples: acid, folk, hard, soft rock

.68   †Western art (Classical) music

Classical music as only one of many traditions

Class here comprehensive works on art music

Class general works on art (classical) music in 780

For non-Western art music, see 781.69

.69   †Non-Western art music

.7   Sacred music

Class sacred music accompanying stages of life cycle in 781.58

"Church music" usually means Christian church music and is classed in 781.71

See also 782.22 for sacred vocal music

SUMMARY

781.700 1–.700 9	**Standard subdivisions**
.701–.706	**General principles**
.71	**Christian sacred music**
.72	**Music of Christian church year**
.73	**Sacred music of classical (Greek and Roman) and Germanic religions**
.74–.79	**Sacred music of other specific religions**

.700 1–.700 9   Standard subdivisions

Notation from Table 1 as modified under 780.1–780.9, e.g., performances of sacred music 781.70078

.701–.706   General principles

Add to base number 781.70 the numbers following 781 in 781.1–781.6, e.g., harmonic rhythm in sacred music 781.70256, appreciation of harmonic rhythm in sacred music 781.70256117

.71   Christian sacred music

For music of Christian church year, see 781.72

†Add as instructed under 781.63–781.69

.710 01–.710 09   Standard subdivisions

> Notation from Table 1 as modified under 780.1–780.9, e.g., performances of Christian sacred music 781.70078

.710 1–.710 6   General principles

> Add to base number 781.710 the numbers following 781 in 781.1–781.6, e.g., harmonic rhythm in Christian sacred music 781.710256, appreciation of harmonic rhythm in Christian sacred music 781.710256117

.711–.718   Of specific denominations

> Add to base number 781.71 the numbers following —2 in notation 21–28 from Table 7, e.g., Baptist sacred music 781.7161; then add further as follows:
> 001–009   Standard subdivisions
>   Notation from Table 1 as modified under 780.1–780.9, e.g., performances of Baptist sacred music 781.71610078
> 01–06   General principles
>   Add to 0 the numbers following 781 in 781.1–781.6, e.g., harmonic rhythm in Baptist sacred music 781.71610256, appreciation of harmonic rhythm in Baptist sacred music 781.71610256117

.72   *Music of Christian church year

.722   *Advent

.723   *Christmas day

> Class here Christmas season

> *For Epiphany, see 781.724*

.724   *Epiphany

.725   *Lent

.725 5   *Passiontide

> *For Holy Week, see 781.726*

.726   *Holy Week

> Including Palm Sunday, Maundy Thursday, Good Friday

.727   *Easter Sunday

> Class here Eastertide (Easter season)

> *For Ascensiontide, see 781.728*

.728   *Ascensiontide

.729   *Pentecost and Trinity Sunday

.729 3   *Pentecost (Whitsunday)

.729 4   *Trinity Sunday

*Add as instructed under 781.2–781.8

.73   *Sacred music of classical (Greek and Roman) and Germanic religions

.74–.79   Sacred music of other specific religions

> Add to base number 781.7 the numbers following —29 in —294–299 from Table 7, e.g., Judaic sacred music 781.76; then add further as follows:
>
> 001–009   Standard subdivisions
> > Notation from Table 1 as modified under 780.1–780.9, e.g., performances of Judaic sacred music 781.760078
>
> 01–06   General principles
> > Add to base number 0 the numbers following 781 in 781.1–781.6, e.g., harmonic rhythm in Judaic sacred music 781.760256, appreciation of harmonic rhythm in Judaic sacred music 781.760256117

.8   ***Musical forms**

> Class here formal analysis; works that do not specify voice, instrument, or ensemble
>
> Class works for specific voice, instrument, or ensemble with the voice, instrument, or ensemble, e.g., Brahm's Variations on a theme by Schumann 786.21825 (*not* 781.825)
>
> *For vocal forms, see 782.1–782.4; instrumental forms, 784.183–784.189*

.82   Specific musical forms

.822   *Binary, ternary, da capo forms

.822 2   *Binary form

.822 3   *Ternary form

.822 5   *Da capo form

.823   *Strophic form

.824   *Rondo forms

> Example: sonata-rondo form

.825   *Variation forms

> Example: theme and variations

.826   *Paraphrase forms

> Including musical parody

.827   *Ground bass forms (Ostinato forms)

> Examples: chaconne, passacaglia

.828   *Cantus firmus forms

*Add as instructed under 781.2–781.8

782   Vocal music

Class orchestral music with vocal parts in 784.22

For music for single voices, see 783

SUMMARY

782.001–.009	**Standard subdivisions**
.01–.08	**[General principles and musical forms]**
.1	**Dramatic vocal forms Operas**
.2	**Nondramatic vocal forms**
.3	**Services (Liturgy and ritual)**
.4	**Secular forms**
.5	**Mixed voices**
.6	**Women's voices**
.7	**Children's voices**
.8	**Men's voices**
.9	**Other types of voices**

.001–.009   Standard subdivisions

Notation from Table 1 as modified under 780.1–780.9, e.g., performances of vocal music 782.0078

.01–.07   General principles

Add to base number 782.0 the numbers following 781 in 781.1–781.7, e.g., rehearsing vocal music 782.044, rhythm in patriotic vocal music 782.05991224

.08   Musical forms

Add to base number 782.08 the numbers following 784.18 in 784.182–784.189, e.g., vocal music in waltz form 782.08846

For vocal forms, see 782.1–782.4

> ### 782.1–782.4 Vocal forms

Class here treatises about and recordings of vocal forms for specific voices and ensembles

Add to notation for each term identified by * as follows:
   01–09   Standard subdivisions
                    Notation from Table 1 as modified under 780.1–780.9, e.g., performances 078
   1   General principles and musical forms
   11–17   General principles
                    Add to 1 the numbers following 781 in 781.1–781.7, e.g., rock music 166, rehearsing rock music 166144
   18   Musical forms
                    Add to 18 the numbers following 784.18 in 784.182–784.189, e.g., da capo form 1822, composition in da capo form 182213

Class comprehensive works in 782

.1   *Dramatic vocal forms   *Operas

Regardless of type of voice or vocal group

Operas and related forms: musical vocal forms in which the action is predominantly in the music, whether or not dialogue is involved

Example: operas for children

Class here concert versions

Stage presentations of dramatic vocal forms relocated to 792.5

See Manual at 792.5 vs. 782.1

.109 2   Persons associated with dramatic vocal forms, with operas

Class here biographies of singers known equally well as opera and recital singers, of conductors known primarily as opera conductors

Class biographies of singers known primarily as recital singers in 782.42168092, of conductors known equally well for conducting operas and orchestral music in 784.092

.109 4   European opera

Use this number only for works that stress that they are discussing European opera in contrast to operas from all other sources

.12   *Operettas

.13   *Singspiels

.14   *Musical plays

Musical vocal forms in which the action is predominantly outside the music

Examples: ballad operas, musicals, revues

For masques, see 782.15

.15   *Masques

.2   *Nondramatic vocal forms

For secular forms, see 782.4

.22   *Sacred vocal forms

For specific sacred vocal forms, see 782.23–782.29

>   782.23–782.29 Specific sacred vocal forms

Class comprehensive works in 782.22

For services, see 782.3

.23   *Oratorios

Example: passions

*Add as instructed under 782.1–782.4

.24	*Large-scale vocal works *Cantatas

Class here comprehensive works on cantatas

For oratorios, see 782.23; secular cantatas, 782.48

.25	*Sacred songs

Example: spirituals

Class here *small-scale sacred vocal forms

If the songs are called hymns, class them in 782.27; if called carols, class them in 782.28; otherwise, class them here

For motets, see 782.26; hymns, 782.27; carols, 782.28

.26	*Motets
.265	*Anthems
.27	*Hymns

Class texts of hymns without music in 245, comprehensive works on hymns without music in 264.2

For carols, see 782.28

.28	*Carols
.29	*Liturgical forms
.292	*Chant

Including responses, e.g., litanies, suffrages

Class here plainsong

Class Gregorian chant in 782.3222, Anglican chant in 782.3223

>	782.294–782.298 Specific texts

Class comprehensive works in 782.29

.294	*Psalms
.295	*Biblical texts

Examples: Lord's Prayer, amens, canticles

For psalms, see 782.294

.296	*Non-Biblical texts

Class parts of the mass in 782.323

.297	*Tropes

Accretions to the liturgy

For liturgical drama, see 782.298

.298	*Liturgical drama

*Add as instructed under 782.1–782.4

.3 ***Services (Liturgy and ritual)**

Musical settings of prescribed texts of specific religions

Class texts used by a specific religion with the religion, e.g., liturgy and ritual of a Christian church 264

.32 ***Christian services**

.322 Services of specific denominations

Add to base number 782.322 the numbers following —2 in notation 21–28 from Table 7, e.g., music for Methodist services 782.3227; then add further as follows:

001–009 Standard subdivisions
Notation from Table 1 as modified under 780.1–780.9, e.g., performances of music for Methodist services 782.32270078

01–07 General principles
Add to 0 the numbers following 781 in 781.1–781.7, e.g., music for Methodist Easter Sunday services 782.32270727, composition of music for Methodist Easter Sunday services 782.3227072713

08 Musical forms
Add to 08 the numbers following 784.18 in 784.182–784.189, e.g., preludes for Methodist services 782.322708928, composition of preludes for Methodist services 782.32270892813

Class specific liturgies of specific denominations in 782.323–782.326

> 782.323–782.326 Specific liturgies

Class comprehensive works in 782.32

.323 ***Mass (Communion service)**

This number is used for music including both the common and the proper of the mass. Masses written from 1350 to today are usually limited to the common and are thus classed in 782.3232. The major exception is the requiem mass, which is classed in 782.3238. Music for an individual part of the mass is classed with that part, e.g., gradual 782.3235

.323 2 ***Common (Ordinary) of the mass**

Contains Kyrie, Gloria, Credo, Sanctus, Benedictus, Agnus Dei

Class common of requiem mass in 782.3238

.323 5 ***Proper of the mass**

Contains introit, gradual, tract, sequence, offertory, communion

Class proper of requiem mass in 782.3238

.323 8 ***Requiem mass**

*Add as instructed under 782.1–782.4

.324   *Divine office

Contains matins, lauds, prime, terce, sext, none, vespers, compline

See also 782.325 for morning prayer, 782.326 for evening prayer

.325   *Morning prayer

Example: matins of the Anglican church

.326   *Evening prayer

Example: evensong of the Anglican church

.33   *Services of classical (Greek and Roman) and Germanic religions

.34–.39   Services of other specific religions

Add to base number 782.3 the numbers following —29 in notation 294–299 from Table 7, e.g., music for Judaic services 782.36; then add further as follows:

001–009   Standard subdivisions
              Notation from Table 1 as modified under 780.1–780.9, e.g., performances of music for Judaic services 782.360078

01–07   General principles
              Add to 0 the numbers following 781 in 781.1–781.7, e.g., music for Judaic spring services 782.3605242, composition of music for Judaic spring services 782.360524213

08   Musical form
              Add to 08 the numbers following 784.18 in 784.182–784.189, e.g., preludes for Judaic services 782.3608928, composition of preludes for Judaic services 782.360892813

.4   *Secular forms

.42   *Songs

Class here comprehensive works on songs

For sacred songs, see 782.25

.421 680 92   Persons associated with art songs

Class here biographies of singers known primarily as recital singers

Class biographies of singers known equally well as opera and recital singers in 782.1092

.43   *Forms derived from poetry   *Madrigals

Examples: frottole, balletts, chansons, ballads

.47   *Song cycles

.48   *Secular cantatas

*Add as instructed under 782.1–782.4

> ### 782.5–782.9 Vocal executants

Add to notation for each term identified by † as follows:
01–09   Standard subdivisions
             Notation from Table 1 as modified under 780.1–780.9, e.g.,
             performances 078
1   General principles and musical forms
11–17   General principles
             Add to 1 the numbers following 781 in 781.1–781.7, e.g., rock
             music 166, rehearsing rock music 166144
18   Musical forms
             Add to 18 the numbers following 784.18 in 784.182–784.189,
             e.g., da capo form 1822, composition in da capo form 182213
             Class dramatic vocal forms in 782.1
             For nondramatic vocal forms, see 2–4
2–4   Nondramatic vocal forms
             Add the numbers following 782 in 782.2–782.4, e.g., secular
             cantatas 48

Use 782.5–782.9 for scores and parts of vocal forms for specific vocal
ensembles. Use 782.1–782.4 for treatises about and recordings of vocal forms
for specific vocal ensembles. Class performance techniques for a specific
ensemble or form with the ensemble or form, e.g., breathing techniques for
choral music 782.5148, for opera 782.1148

Class comprehensive works in 782

.5   **†Mixed voices**

Class here choral music, music intended equally for choral or part-song
performance, choral music with solo parts, unison voices

For part songs, see 783.1

> ### 782.6–782.9 Types of voices

Class comprehensive works in 782

.6   **†Women's voices**

Class here music intended equally for women's or children's voices

Class music for children's voices in 782.7

.66   †Soprano (Treble) voices

.67   †Mezzo-soprano voices

.68   †Contralto (Alto) voices

.7   **†Children's voices**

Class music intended equally for women's or children's voices in 782.6

.76   †Soprano (Treble) voices

.77   †Mezzo-soprano voices

.78   †Contralto (Alto) voices

.79   †Changing voices

†Add as instructed under 782.5–782.9

.8	†**Men's voices**
.86	†Treble and alto voices

Class here countertenor, falsetto, castrato voices

.87	†Tenor voices
.88	†Baritone voices
.89	†Bass voices
.9	†**Other types of voices**
.96	†Speaking voices (Choral speech)
.97	†Sprechgesang
.98	†Whistle

783   Music for single voices   The voice

Use 783 for scores and parts of vocal forms for specific kinds or ensembles of single voice. Use 782.1–782.4 for treatises about and recordings of vocal forms for specific kinds or ensembles of single voice. Class performance techniques for a specific kind or ensemble of single voice or for a specific form with the kind, ensemble, or form, e.g., breathing techniques for part songs 783.1148, for opera 782.1148

SUMMARY

783.001–.009	**Standard subdivisions**
.01–.09	**[General principles and forms]**
.1	**Single voices in combination**
.2	**Solo voice**
.3	**High voice**
.4	**Middle voice**
.5	**Low voice**
.6–.8	**Woman's, child's, man's voice**
.9	**Other type of voice**

.001–.009   Standard subdivisions

Notation from Table 1 as modified under 780.1–780.9, e.g., performances of music for single voice 783.0078

.01–.07   General principles

Add to base number 783.0 the numbers following 781 in 781.1–781.7, e.g., patriotic music for single voices 783.0599, rhythm in patriotic music for single voices 783.05991224

.08   Musical forms

Add to base number 783.08 the numbers following 784.18 in 784.182–784.189, e.g., vocal music in waltz form for the single voice 783.08846

For dramatic vocal forms, see 782.1; nondramatic vocal forms, 783.09

†Add as instructed under 782.5–782.9

.09   Nondramatic vocal forms

Add to base number 783.09 the numbers following 782 in 782.2–782.4, e.g., carols for single voices 783.0928

.1   Single voices in combination

Class here part songs

Class music intended equally for choral or part-song performance in 782.5

.101–.109   Standard subdivisions

Notation from Table 1 as modified under 780.1–780.9, e.g., performances of part songs 783.1078

.11   General principles and musical forms

.111–.117   General principles

Add to base number 783.11 the numbers following 781 in 781.1–781.7, e.g., patriotic part songs 783.11599, rehearsing patriotic part songs 783.11599144

.118   Musical forms

Add to base number 783.118 the numbers following 784.18 in 784.182–784.189, e.g., part songs in waltz form 783.118846, rehearsing part songs in waltz form 783.118846144

For dramatic vocal forms, see 782.1; nondramatic vocal forms, 783.119

.119   Nondramatic vocal forms

Add to base number 783.119 the numbers following 782 in 782.2–782.4, e.g., carols for single voices in combination 783.11928

>   783.12–783.19 Ensembles by size

Add to each subdivision identified by † as follows:
   01–09   Standard subdivisions
           Notation from Table 1 as modified under 780.1–780.9, e.g., performances 078
   1   General principles and musical forms
   11–17   General principles
           Add to 1 the numbers following 781 in 781.1–781.7, e.g., rock music 166, rehearsing rock music 166144
   18   Musical forms
           Add to 18 the numbers following 784.18 in 784.182–784.189, e.g., da capo form 1822, composition in da capo form 182213
           Class dramatic vocal forms in 782.1
           For nondramatic vocal forms, see 2–4
   2–4 Nondramatic vocal forms
           Add the numbers following 782 in 782.2–782.4, e.g., secular cantatas 48

Class comprehensive works in 783.1

.12	†Duets
.13	†Trios
.14	†Quartets
.15	†Quintets
.16	†Sextets
.17	†Septets
.18	†Octets
.19	†Nonets and larger combinations

> ### 783.2–783.9 Solo voices

Add to each subdivision identified by ‡ notation 01–4 from table under 783.12–783.19, e.g., secular cantatas 48

Class comprehensive works in 783.2

.2 ‡Solo voice

Class here comprehensive works on types of single voices

Class specific types of single voices in 783.3–783.9

> ### 783.3–783.9 Specific types of single voices

Class comprehensive works in 783.2, single voices in ensembles in 783.12–783.19

.3 ‡High voice

Class woman's soprano voice in 783.66; child's soprano voice in 783.76; man's treble voice and alto voice in 783.86, tenor voice in 783.87

.4 ‡Middle voice

Class woman's mezzo-soprano voice in 783.67, child's mezzo-soprano voice in 783.77, baritone voice in 783.88

.5 ‡Low voice

Class woman's contralto voice in 783.68, child's contralto voice in 783.78, bass voice in 783.89

†Add as instructed under 783.12–783.19
‡Add as instructed under 783.2–783.9

.6–.8   Woman's, child's, man's voice

Add to base number 783 the numbers following 782 in 782.6–782.8, e.g., bass voice 783.89

.9   ‡Other types of voice

.96   ‡Speaking voice

.97   ‡Sprechgesang

.98   ‡Whistle

.99   ‡Voice instruments

Examples: didjeridu, mirliton (kazoo)

Including voice disguisers (sympathetic instruments relying on the human voice for their sound production) and roarers

> ## 784–788 Instruments and their music

Add to notation for each term identified by * as follows:
    01–09   Standard subdivisions
              Notation from Table 1 as modified under 780.1–780.9, e.g., performances 078
                See Manual at 784–788: Add table: 092
    1   General principles, musical forms, instruments
    11–17   General principles
              Add to 1 the numbers following 781 in 781.1–781.7, e.g., performance techniques 143
                For techniques for playing instruments, see 193
    18–19   Musical forms and instruments
              Add to 1 the numbers following 784.1 in 784.18–784.19, e.g., sonata form 183, techniques for playing instruments 193

Class comprehensive works in 784

784   Instruments and instrumental ensembles and their music

For specific instruments and their music, see 786–788

See also 787 for music for unspecified melody instrument

SUMMARY

784.01–.09	**Standard subdivisions**
.1	**General principles, musical forms, instruments**
.2	**Full (Symphony) orchestra**
.3	**Chamber orchestra**
.4	**Light orchestra**
.6	**Keyboard, mechanical, electronic, percussion bands**
.7	**String orchestra**
.8	**Wind band**
.9	**Brass band**

‡Add as instructed under 783.2–783.9

.01–.09   Standard subdivisions

> Notation from Table 1 as modified under 780.1–780.9, e.g., performances 078

.1   General principles, musical forms, instruments

SUMMARY

784.11–.17	General principles
.18	Musical forms
.19	Instruments

.11–.17   General principles

> Add to base number 784.1 the numbers following 781 in 781.1–781.7, e.g., performance techniques 784.143

> *For techniques for playing instruments, see 784.193*

.18   †Musical forms

SUMMARY

784.182	General musical forms
.183	Sonata forms
.184	Symphony forms
.185	Suite and related forms
.186	Concerto forms
.187	Contrapuntal forms
.188	Dance forms
.189	Other instrumental forms

.182   †General musical forms

.182 2   †Binary, ternary, da capo forms

.182 3   †Strophic form

.182 4   †Rondo forms

> Example: sonata-rondo form

.182 5   †Variation forms

> Example: theme and variations

.182 6   †Paraphrase forms

> Including musical parody

.182 7   †Ground bass forms (Ostinato forms)

> Examples: chaconne, passacaglia

>   784.183–784.189 Instrumental forms

> Class comprehensive works in 784.18

†Add as instructed under 781.2–781.8

.183	†Sonata forms
	Class sonata-rondo form in 784.1824
.183 2	†Sonatina form
.184	†Symphony forms
	Examples: sinfonietta, symphonic poem
.184 5	†Sinfonia concertante form
.185	†Suite and related forms
	Example: cassation
.185 2	†Divertimento form
.185 4	†Partita form
.185 6	†Serenade form
.185 8	†Suite form
.186	†Concerto forms

Use this subdivision only for concerto forms other than solo instruments with full orchestra, e.g., concerto forms for wind bands 784.8186, Bartok's Concerto for orchestra 784.2186

Examples: cadenza, concertante

Class comprehensive works on the concerto in 784.23

.186 2	†Concertino form
.187	†Contrapuntal forms
.187 2	†Fugue form
.187 4	†Invention form
.187 5	†Canzona form
.187 6	†Fancy and ricercar forms
	Examples: innomine, tiento
.187 8	†Canon form
.188	†Dance forms
.188 2	†European dance forms
	Examples: galliard, saltarello

For dances of the classical suite form, see 784.1883; European dance forms of the nineteenth and later centuries, 784.1884

.188 23	†Pavane form
.188 3	†Dances of the classical suite form
	Examples: gavotte, siciliano
.188 35	†Minuet form

†Add as instructed under 781.2–781.8

.188 4	†European dance forms of the nineteenth and later centuries
	Examples: galop, mazurka, polonaise
.188 44	†Polka form
.188 46	†Waltz form
.188 5	†Asian dance forms
.188 6	†African dance forms
.188 7	†North American dance forms
	Examples: cakewalk, hoedown
	For Latin-American dance forms, see 784.1888
.188 8	†Latin-American dance forms
	Examples: rumba, samba
.188 85	†Tango form
.188 9	†Dance forms of the Pacific Ocean islands and other parts of the world
.189	†**Other instrumental forms**
	Class here small-scale and character instrumental forms
.189 2	†Introductory forms
	Music preceding other music or other activities
.189 24	†Fanfare form
.189 26	†Overture form
.189 28	†Prelude form
.189 3	†Intermediate forms
	Music for between or after other activities
	Examples: intermezzo, interlude, postlude, voluntary
	Class incidental dramatic music in 781.552
.189 4	†Forms of music of an improvisatory or virtuoso nature
	Examples: arabesque, impromptu
.189 45	†Rhapsody form
.189 47	†Toccata form
.189 49	†Artistic étude form
.189 6	†Romantic and descriptive forms
	Examples: ballade, meditation, song without words
.189 64	†Elegy form
.189 66	†Nocturne form
.189 68	†Romance form

†Add as instructed under 781.2–781.8

.189 7	†March form
.189 9	†Forms derived from vocal music
.189 92	†From sacred music

Example: chorale prelude

Class instrumental forms derived from liturgical forms in 784.18993

.189 925	†Chorale form
.189 93	†From liturgical forms
.19	Instruments

For specific instruments, see 786–788

.190 28	Auxiliary techniques and procedures

Class description and design in 784.1922, construction in 784.1923

[.190 287]	Testing and measurement

Do not use; class in 784.1927

[.190 288]	Maintenance and repair

Do not use; class in 784.1928

[.190 94–.190 99]	Historical and geographical treatment by specific continents, countries, localities in modern world

Do not use; class in 784.194–784.199

.192	Specific techniques and procedures
.192 2	Description and design
.192 3	Construction

Class construction by machine in 681.8

.192 7	Testing, measurement, verification
.192 8	Maintenance, tuning, repair

Including temperament

.193	†Techniques for playing instruments

Class comprehensive works on performance techniques in 784.143

.193 2	†Breathing and resonance
.193 4	†Embouchure

Examples: lipping, tonguing

.193 6	†Arm techniques
.193 62	†Forearm techniques
.193 64	†Wrist techniques

†Add as instructed under 781.2–781.8

.193 65	†Hand techniques

> For left-hand techniques, see 784.19366; right-hand techniques, 784.19367

.193 66	†Left-hand techniques
.193 67	†Right-hand techniques
.193 68	†Finger techniques

Examples: touch, fingering, vibrato

.193 69	†Bowing techniques
.193 8	†Leg techniques

Example: pedaling

.194–.199	Geographical treatment

Add to base number 784.19 notation 4–9 from Table 2, e.g., instruments of Germany 784.1943

.2   *Full (Symphony) orchestra

Class here comprehensive works on orchestral combinations, music intended equally for orchestral or chamber performance

> For other orchestral combinations, see 784.3–784.9; chamber music, 785

.209 2	Persons associated with full (symphony) orchestras

Class here biographies of conductors known equally well for conducting operas and orchestral music

Class biographies of conductors known primarily as opera conductors in 782.1092

.22	*Orchestra with vocal parts
.23	*Orchestra with one or more solo instruments

Class here comprehensive works on concertos

> For orchestra with more than one solo instrument, see 784.24; orchestra with one solo instrument, 784.25

.24	*Orchestra with more than one solo instrument

Example: concerti grossi

.25	*Orchestra with one solo instrument

Class here comprehensive works on solo concertos

> For specific solo instruments, see 784.26–784.28

.26–.28	Specific solo instruments with orchestra

Add to base number 784.2 the numbers following 78 in 786–788, e.g., orchestra with solo piano 784.262, e.g., rehearsing orchestra with solo piano 784.262144

*Add as instructed under 784–788

†Add as instructed under 781.2–781.8

> **784.3–784.9 Other orchestral combinations and band**

Add to notation for each term identified by † as follows:
01–09   Standard subdivisions
                Notation from Table 1 as modified under 780.1–780.9, e.g.,
                performances 078
1   General principles, musical forms, instruments
11–17   General principles
                Add to 1 the numbers following 781 in 781.1–781.7, e.g.,
                sacred music 17, rehearsing sacred music 17044
18–19   Musical forms and instruments
                Add to 1 numbers following 784.1 in 784.18–784.19, e.g.,
                waltz form 18846, bowing techniques 19369
2   Featured voices, instruments, ensembles
                Add to 2 the numbers following 78 in 782–788, e.g., flutes 2832

Class comprehensive works on orchestral combinations and band, on band in
784; comprehensive works on orchestral combinations in 784.2

.3   **†Chamber orchestra**

For chamber music, see 785

.4   **†Light orchestra**

Class here salon orchestra

.44   †School orchestra

.46   †Orchestra with toy instruments

.48   †Dance orchestra (Dance band)

.6   **†Keyboard, mechanical, electronic, percussion bands**

.68   †Percussion band

Class here rhythm band

.7   **†String orchestra**

.8   **†Wind band**

Band consisting of woodwind instruments, brass instruments, or both

For brass band, see 784.9

.83   †Marching band

.84   †Military band

.89   †Woodwind band

.9   **†Brass band**

†Add as instructed under 784.3–784.9

785   Ensembles with only one instrument per part

Class here chamber music

Class works for solo melody instrument with keyboard or other accompaniment in 786–788

SUMMARY

785.001–.009	**Standard subdivisions**
.01–.09	**General principles, musical forms, instruments**
.1	**Ensembles by size**
.2	**Ensembles with keyboard**
.3	**Ensembles without electrophones and with percussion and keyboard**
.4	**Ensembles without keyboard**
.5	**Ensembles without keyboard and with percussion**
.6	**Keyboard, electrophone, percussion ensembles**
.7	**String ensembles Bowed string ensembles**
.8	**Woodwind ensembles**
.9	**Brass ensembles**

.001–.009   Standard subdivisions

> Notation from Table 1 as modified under 780.1–780.9, e.g., performances of chamber music 785.0078

.01–.07   General principles

> Add to base number 785.0 the numbers following 781 in 781.1–781.7, e.g., performance techniques 785.043
>
> *For techniques for playing instruments, see 785.093*

.08–.09   Musical forms and instruments

> Add to base number 785.0 the numbers following 784.1 in 784.18–784.19, e.g., waltz form 785.08846, techniques for playing instruments 785.093

.1   **Ensembles by size**

> These provisions, when applied throughout 785, refer to the number of instruments, except for percussion ensembles in 785.68, where they refer to the number of performers

.12   *Duets

.13   *Trios

.14   *Quartets

.15   *Quintets

.16   *Sextets

.17   *Septets

.18   *Octets

.19   *Nonets and larger ensembles

*Add as instructed under 784–788

> ### 785.2–785.9 Specific kinds of ensembles

Add to notation for each term identified by † as follows:
01–09   Standard subdivisions
             Notation from Table 1 as modified under 780.1–780.9, e.g.,
             performances 078
1   General principles, musical forms, size of ensemble
11–17   General principles
             Add to 1 the numbers following 781 in 781.1–781.7, e.g.,
             sacred music 17, conducting sacred music 17045
             Class instrumental techniques for mixed ensembles in 784.193,
             for specific instruments in 786–788, e.g., bowing techniques
             for violins 787.219369
18   Musical forms
             Add to 18 the numbers following 784.18 in 784.182–784.189,
             e.g., waltz form 18846
19   Size of ensemble
             Add to 19 the numbers following 785.1 in 785.12–785.19, e.g.,
             octets 198

Class comprehensive works in 785

> ### 785.2–785.5 Ensembles consisting of two or more instrumental groups

Class comprehensive works in 785

.2   †**Ensembles with keyboard**

*For ensembles without electrophones and with percussion and keyboard,
see 785.3*

.22   †Ensembles of woodwind, brass, strings, keyboard

.23   †Ensembles of woodwind, brass, keyboard

.24   †Ensembles of woodwind, strings, keyboard

.25   †Ensembles of brass, strings, keyboard

†Add as instructed under 785.2–785.9

.26	†Ensembles of woodwind and keyboard

Two or more woodwind instruments

See also 788.2 for ensembles of one woodwind instrument and keyboard

.27	†Ensembles of brass and keyboard

Two or more brass instruments

See also 788.9 for ensembles of one brass instrument and keyboard

.28	†Ensembles of strings and keyboard

Two or more stringed instruments

See also 787 for ensembles of one stringed instrument and keyboard

.29	†Ensembles with electrophones, percussion, keyboard
.292	†Ensembles of woodwind, brass, strings, electrophones, percussion, keyboard
.293	†Ensembles of woodwind, brass, electrophones, percussion, keyboard
.294	†Ensembles of woodwind, strings, electrophones, percussion, keyboard
.295	†Ensembles of brass, strings, electrophones, percussion, keyboard
.296	†Ensembles of woodwind, electrophones, percussion, keyboard
.297	†Ensembles of brass, electrophones, percussion, keyboard
.298	†Ensembles of strings, electrophones, percussion, keyboard
.299	†Ensembles with electrophones and keyboard
.299 2	†Ensembles of woodwind, brass, strings, electrophones, keyboard
.299 3	†Ensembles of woodwind, brass, electrophones, keyboard
.299 4	†Ensembles of woodwind, strings, electrophones, keyboard
.299 5	†Ensembles of brass, strings, electrophones, keyboard
.299 6	†Ensembles of woodwind, electrophones, keyboard
.299 7	†Ensembles of brass, electrophones, keyboard
.299 8	†Ensembles of strings, electrophones, keyboard
.299 9	†Ensembles of electrophones and keyboard

Two or more electrophones

See also 786.7 for ensembles of one electrophone and keyboard

.3	**†Ensembles without electrophones and with percussion and keyboard**
.32	†Ensembles of woodwind, brass, strings, percussion, keyboard
.33	†Ensembles of woodwind, brass, percussion, keyboard

†Add as instructed under 785.2–785.9

.34	†Ensembles of woodwind, strings, percussion, keyboard
.35	†Ensembles of brass, strings, percussion, keyboard
.36	†Ensembles of woodwind, percussion, keyboard
.37	†Ensembles of brass, percussion, keyboard
.38	†Ensembles of strings, percussion, keyboard
.39	†Ensembles of keyboard and percussion
.4	**†Ensembles without keyboard**

For ensembles without keyboard and with percussion, see 785.5

.42	†Ensembles of woodwind, brass, strings
.43	†Ensembles of woodwind and brass (Wind ensembles)
.44	†Ensembles of woodwind and strings
.45	†Ensembles of brass and strings
.46	†Ensembles with electrophones
.462	†Ensembles of woodwind, brass, strings, electrophones
.463	†Ensembles of woodwind, brass, electrophones
.464	†Ensembles of woodwind, strings, electrophones
.465	†Ensembles of brass, strings, electrophones
.466	†Ensembles of woodwinds and electrophones
.467	†Ensembles of brass and electrophones
.468	†Ensembles of strings and electrophones
.5	**†Ensembles without keyboard and with percussion**
.52	†Ensembles of woodwind, brass, strings, percussion
.53	†Ensembles of woodwind, brass, percussion
.54	†Ensembles of woodwind, strings, percussion
.55	†Ensembles of brass, strings, percussion
.56	†Ensembles of woodwind and percussion
.57	†Ensembles of brass and percussion
.58	†Ensembles of strings and percussion
.59	†Ensembles with electrophones and percussion
.592	†Ensembles of woodwind, brass, strings, electrophones, percussion
.593	†Ensembles of woodwind, brass, electrophones, percussion
.594	†Ensembles of woodwind, strings, electrophones, percussion

†Add as instructed under 785.2–785.9

.595	†Ensembles of brass, strings, electrophones, percussion
.596	†Ensembles of woodwind, electrophones, percussion
.597	†Ensembles of brass, electrophones, percussion
.598	†Ensembles of strings, electrophones, percussion
.599	†Ensembles of electrophones and percussion

> **785.6–785.9 Ensembles consisting of only one instrumental group**

The inclusion of "only one kind" in the 785.6–785.9 headings limits the subdivisions to individual kind of instruments, not to family of instruments. For example, a string quartet, which usually consists of two violins, a viola, and a cello is classed in 785.7194 string quartets, *not* 785.72194 violin quartets

When adding from 786–788 to indicate the instrument, add *only* the notation for the instrument; do not follow the footnote leading to add instructions. After indicating the instrument, add as instructed under 785.2–785.9, where notation 19 is used to indicate size of ensemble. For example, 785.7194 means string quartets, *not* string instruments of Europe (the meaning that would result from following the footnote instruction). The correct number for string quartets of Europe is 785.7194094

Class comprehensive works in 785

.6   †Keyboard, electrophone, percussion ensembles

.62–.65   Keyboard ensembles

Add to base number 785.6 the numbers following 786 in 786.2–786.5 for the instrument only, e.g., music for piano ensembles 785.62; then add further as instructed under 785.2–785.9, e.g., music for two pianos 785.62192

.67   †Electrophone ensembles

Class ensembles of a specific kind or group of electrically amplified or modified standard instruments with the instrument or group of instruments, e.g., electric guitar ensembles 785.787

See also 786.7 for electronic music for one performer

.673–.676   Ensembles with only one type of electrophone instrument

Add to base number 785.67 the numbers following 786.7 in 786.73–786.76 for the instrument only, e.g., music for synthesizers 785.674; then add further as instructed under 785.2–785.9, e.g., sextets for synthesizers 785.674196

.68   †Percussion ensembles

Class here ensembles for more than one performer; see note under 785.1

See also 786.8 for percussion music for one performer

†Add as instructed under 785.2–785.9

.7   †String ensembles   †Bowed string ensembles

.72–.79   Ensembles of only one kind of stringed instrument

> Add to base number 785.7 the numbers following 787 in 787.2–787.9 for the instrument only, e.g., music for guitar 785.787; then add further as instructed under 785.2–785.9, e.g., quartet for guitars 785.787194

.8   †Woodwind ensembles

.82–.88   Ensembles of only one kind of woodwind instrument

> Add to base number 785.8 the numbers following 788 in 788.2–788.8 for the instrument only, e.g., music for saxophones 785.87; then add further as instructed under 785.2–785.9, e.g., quartet for saxophones 785.87194

.9   †Brass ensembles

.92–.99   Ensembles of only one kind of brass instrument

> Add to base number 785.9 the numbers following 788.9 in 788.92–788.99 for the instrument only, e.g., music for trombones 785.93; then add further as instructed under 785.2–785.9, e.g., quartet for trombones 785.93194

> ## 786–788 Specific instruments and their music

> Class here music for solo instrument, music for solo instruments accompanied by one other instrument when accompanying instrument clearly has a subsidiary role

> Unless the forerunner of a modern instrument has its own notation, class it with the modern instrument. For example, the shawm, a forerunner of the oboe and an instrument without its own number, is classed with the oboe in 788.52; however, the vihuela, the forerunner of the guitar, is classed in 787.86 (its own number), *not* with the guitar in 787.87

> Class comprehensive works in 784, chamber music in 785, voice instruments in 783.99

786   *Keyboard, mechanical, electrophonic, percussion instruments

> Class here comprehensive works on keyboard instruments, on keyboard stringed instruments; music for unspecified keyboard instrument

SUMMARY

786.2	**Pianos**
.3	**Clavichords**
.4	**Harpsichords**
.5	**Keyboard wind instruments Organs**
.6	**Mechanical and aeolian instruments**
.7	**Electrophones Electronic instruments**
.8	**Percussion instruments**
.9	**Drums and devices used for percussion effects**

*Add as instructed under 784–788

†Add as instructed under 785.2–785.9

> **786.2–786.5 Keyboard instruments**

Class comprehensive works in 786, mechanical keyboard instruments in 786.66, keyboard idiophones in 786.83

> **786.2–786.4 Keyboard stringed instruments**

Class comprehensive works in 786

.2   ***Pianos**

.28   *Prepared pianos

.3   ***Clavichords**

.4   ***Harpsichords**

Class here virginals, spinets

.5   ***Keyboard wind instruments   *Organs**

Class concertinas in 788.84, accordions in 788.86

.55   *Reed organs and *regals

Variant names for reed organs: American organs, cabinet organs, harmoniums

.59   *Electronic organs

Class here comprehensive works on keyboard electrophones

Class a keyboard instrument whose sound is generated by conventional means, even though amplified or modified electronically, with the instrument, e.g., electric piano 786.2

See also 786.74 for synthesizers

.6   ***Mechanical and aeolian instruments**

> 786.64–786.68 Mechanical instruments

Class comprehensive works in 786.6

.64   *Mechanical struck idiophones

Examples: mechanized bells, carillons

Class here comprehensive works on mechanical idiophones

For mechanical plucked idiophones, see 786.65

.65   *Mechanical plucked idiophones

Examples: music boxes, symphonions

*Add as instructed under 784–788

.66   *Mechanical keyboard instruments

    Mechanical instruments with attached functional keyboard

    Example: player pianos (pianolas)

    Class mechanical wind keyboard instruments in 786.68

.67   *Mechanical stringed instruments

    Class mechanical stringed keyboard instruments in 786.66

.68   *Mechanical wind instruments

    Example: fair organs

.69   *Aeolian instruments

    Instruments activated by the blowing of the wind

.7   ***Electrophones**   ***Electronic instruments**

    Class here music made from electrically produced or manipulated sounds

    Class keyboard electrophones in 786.59; a specific electrically amplified or modified standard instrument other than keyboard instruments with the instrument, e.g., electric guitar 787.87

.73   *Monophonic electrophones

    Electronic sound producers capable of producing only one pitch at a time

    Examples: ondes martenot, theremins

.74   *Synthesizers

    Class here electronic music

    For tapes, see 786.75; computers, 786.76

.75   Tapes

    Class here musique concrète (concrete music)

.76   Computers

.8   ***Percussion instruments**

    For drums, see 786.92–786.98; struck stringed instruments, 787.7

.82   *Idiophones (Vibrating sonorous solids)

    Class here comprehensive works on percussion instruments of definite pitch

    Class percussion instruments of indefinite pitch in 786.88

    For mechanical idiophones, see 786.64; keyboard idiophones, 786.83; set idiophones, 786.84–786.87; single idiophones, 786.88

.83   *Keyboard idiophones

    Class here celestas

*Add as instructed under 784–788

>   786.84–786.87 Set idiophones

          Class comprehensive works in 786.84

.84   *Percussed idiophones

Sonorous solids struck by or against nonsonorous objects, e.g., sticks struck on ground

Class here comprehensive works on set idiophones (similar sonorous solids combined to form one instrument)

For plucked idiophones, see 786.85; friction idiophones, 786.86; concussion idiophones, 786.87

.842–.848   Sonorous solids of specific shapes

Add to base number 786.84 the numbers following 786.884 in 786.8842–786.8848, e.g., bar idiophones 786.843, performances on bar idiophones 786.843078

.85   *Plucked idiophones

Elastic bars or rods, usually of metal, fixed at one end and vibrated by plucking the free end

Example: sanzas (thumb pianos)

.86   *Friction idiophones

Objects rubbed to produce sounds of definite pitch

.862–.868   Sonorous solids of specific shapes

Add to base number 786.86 the numbers following 786.884 in 786.8842–786.8848, e.g., vessels 786.866, rehearsing on vessels 786.866144

.87   *Concussion idiophones

Two or more similar sonorous objects struck together to make both vibrate

.872–.878   Sonorous objects of specific shapes

Add to base number 786.87 the numbers following 786.884 in 786.8842–786.8848, e.g., blocks 786.873, rehearsing playing of blocks 786.873144

.88   *Single idiophones

Idiophones consisting of a single sonorous object

Class here comprehensive works on percussion instruments of indefinite pitch

Class a specific percussion instrument of indefinite pitch not provided for here with the instrument, e.g., cymbals 786.873

*Add as instructed under 784–788

.884		*Percussed idiophones
.884 2		*Sticks or rods

Example: triangles

.884 3		*Bars, plates, blocks

Examples: anvils, gongs

.884 4		*Troughs
.884 5		*Tubes
.884 6		*Vessels

For bells, see 786.8848

.884 8		*Bells
.884 85		*Hand bells
.885		*Rattled idiophones

Examples: maracas, sistrums

.886		*Scraped idiophones

Idiophones consisting of two objects, a notched one being scraped by the other to create vibrations in one or the other

Examples: washboards, football rattles

.887		*Plucked idiophones

Example: jew's harps

.888		*Friction idiophones

Example: musical saws

.9   *Drums and devices used for percussion effects

> 786.92–786.98 Drums (Membranophones, Vibrating stretched membranes)

Class comprehensive works in 786.9

.92	*Struck drums

For kettle-shaped drums, see 786.93; tubular drums, 786.94; frame-shaped drums, 786.95

.93	*Kettle-shaped drums

Examples: timpani (kettledrums), nakers (naqara), tabla

.94	*Tubular drums

Example: snare drums (side drums)

*Add as instructed under 784–788

.95   *Frame-shaped drums

Drums with depth of body not exceeding radius of membrane

Examples: bass drums, tambourines

.96   *Rattle drums

Drums whose membrane or membranes are struck by pellets or pendants

.97   *Plucked drums

Drums each with a string that when plucked transmits a vibration to the membrane through which the string passes

.98   *Friction drums

Drums whose membrane is made to vibrate by being rubbed either directly or by an attached stick or cord

Examples: quicas, rommelpots

.99   *Devices used for percussion effects

Examples: whips, motor horns, sirens, popguns

787   *Stringed instruments (Chordophones)   *Bowed stringed instruments

Class here music for unspecified melody instrument, comprehensive works on the lute family (instruments whose strings run from the resonating belly to the neck)

Class keyboard stringed instruments in 786, mechanical stringed instruments in 786.67

SUMMARY

787.2	Violins	
.3	Violas	
.4	Cellos (Violoncellos)	
.5	Double basses	
.6	Other bowed stringed instruments	Viols
.7	Plectral instruments	
.8	Plectral lute family	
.9	Harps and musical bows	

.2   *Violins

Class here comprehensive works on violin family

For violas, see 787.3; cellos, 787.4; double basses, 787.5

.3   *Violas

.4   *Cellos (Violoncellos)

.5   *Double basses

.6   *Other bowed stringed instruments   *Viols

For double basses, see 787.5

*Add as instructed under 784–788

.62	*Descant viols
.63	*Treble viols
.64	*Tenor viols
.65	*Bass viols (Viola da gambas)
.66	*Viola d'amores
.69	*Hurdy-gurdies (Vielles)
.7	***Plectral instruments**

Class here zithers, comprehensive works on struck stringed instruments

For plectral lute family, see 787.8; harps and musical bows, 787.9

> 787.72–787.75 Zithers

Class comprehensive works in 787.7

.72	*Stick, tube, trough zithers
.73	*Frame, ground, harp, raft zithers
.74	*Board zithers

Examples: cimbaloms, dulcimers, santirs, yang ch'ins

Class here struck board zithers

For plucked board zithers, see 787.75

| .75 | *Plucked board zithers |

Examples: Appalachian dulcimers, autoharps, concert zithers, psalteries, Tyrolean zithers

| .78 | *Lyres |
| **.8** | ***Plectral lute family** |

Class here long-necked, short-necked lutes

| .82 | *Round-backed lute family |

Examples: sitars, tamburas

For lutes, see 787.83; mandolins, 787.84

.83	*Lutes
.84	*Mandolins
.85	*Flat-backed lute family

Examples: biwas, citterns, shamisens

For vihuelas, see 787.86; guitars, 787.87; banjos, 787.88; ukuleles, 787.89

*Add as instructed under 784–788

.86   *Vihuelas

.87   *Guitars

.875   *Balalaikas

.88   *Banjos

.89   *Ukuleles

.9   *Harps and musical bows

.92   *Musical bows

Stringed instruments each with one or more strings stretched across a single flexible string bearer

Class pluriarcs in 787.93

.93   *Pluriarcs (Compound musical bows)

Stringed instruments with strings stretched across several string bearers

---

>   787.94–787.98 Harps

Class comprehensive works in 787.9

.94   *Bow (Arched) harps and *angle harps

Harps with neck forming an arch with the resonator

.95   *Frame harps

Harps with pillar joining end of neck to resonator

Examples: orchestral harps, Celtic harps

.98   *Bridge harps (Harp-lutes)

Lute-bodied harps with strings that are perpendicular to body of the harp and that pass through a bridge

Example: koras

788   *Wind instruments (Aerophones)

Class keyboard wind instruments in 786.5, mechanical wind instruments in 786.68

SUMMARY

788.2	**Woodwind instruments and free aerophones**
.3	**Flute family**
.4	**Reed instruments**
.5	**Double-reed instruments**
.6	**Single-reed instruments**
.7	**Saxophones**
.8	**Free reeds**
.9	**Brass instruments (Lip-reed instruments)**

*Add as instructed under 784–788

.2   *Woodwind instruments and free aerophones

> *For specific woodwind instruments, see 788.3–788.8*

.29   *Free aerophones

> Aerophones in which the airstream is not directed into or through a cavity or tube but directly into the outer air, or the air remains static and the instrument when moved vibrates through friction with the air
>
> Example: bull-roarers
>
> Class free aerophones used for percussion effects in 786.99

> **788.3–788.8 Specific woodwind instruments**
>
> Class comprehensive works in 788.2

.3   *Flute family

> Class here nose flutes

.32   *Transverse (Side-blown) flutes

> Variant name: flutes
>
> *For piccolos and fifes, see 788.33; bass flutes, 788.34*

.33   *Piccolos and *fifes

.34   *Bass flutes

.35   *Duct, *end-blown, *notched flutes

> Examples: flageolets, penny whistles, shakuhanchis
>
> *For recorders, see 788.36*

.36   *Recorders

.363   *Sopranino recorders

.364   *Descant (Soprano) recorders

.365   *Treble (Alto) recorders

.366   *Tenor recorders

.367   *Bass recorders

.37   *Multiple flutes   *Pan pipes

> Several flutes formed into one instrument

.38   *Vessel flutes

> Example: ocarinas

*Add as instructed under 784–788

.4   ***Reed instruments**

> *For double-reed instruments, see 788.5; single-reed instruments, 788.6; free reeds, 788.8*

.49   *Bagpipes

>> Examples: cornemuses; Northumbrian, uillean (union) pipes

>> Class here single- and double-reed bagpipes

.5   ***Double-reed instruments**

>> Examples: crumhorns, racketts

> *For bagpipes, see 788.49*

.52   *Oboes

.53   *Cors anglais (English horns)

.58   *Bassoons

> *For double bassoons, see 788.59*

.59   *Double bassoons (Contrabassoons)

.6   ***Single-reed instruments**

> *For bagpipes, see 788.49; saxophones, 788.7*

.62   *Clarinets

> *For bass clarinets, see 788.65*

.65   *Bass clarinets

.7   ***Saxophones**

.72   *Soprano saxophones

.73   *Alto saxophones

.74   *Tenor saxophones

.75   *Bass saxophones

.8   ***Free reeds**

>> Instruments consisting of sets of individual free reeds

.82   *Mouth organs   *Harmonicas

>> Example: shengs

.84   *Concertinas

>> Example: bandoneons

.86   *Accordions

.863   *Button accordions   *Melodeons

.865   *Piano accordions

*Add as instructed under 784–788

.9	***Brass instruments (Lip-reed instruments)**
.92	*Trumpets
.93	*Trombones
.94	*French horns (Horns)

> *See also 788.53 for English horns*

.95	*Bugles
.96	*Cornets
.97	*Flugelhorns (Saxhorns)
.974	*Tenor horns

> Examples: B-flat horns (also called baritones in United Kingdom and Germany) and E-flat horns (also called alto horns in North America and France)

.975	*Euphoniums and *baritones (American)
.98	*Tubas
.99	*Other brass instruments

> Examples: cornetts, ophicleides, serpents

(789)   Composers and traditions of music

(Optional number and subdivisions; prefer 780–788)

(Option A: Arrange treatises about all composers at 789 plus an alphabeting mark; then to the result add notation following 78 in 780–788

(Option B: Use 789 and its subdivisions for traditions of music

(If both options are used, class comprehensive works on traditions of music in 789.1)

Unless other instructions are given, class complex subjects with aspects in two or more subdivisions of 789 in the one coming last, e.g., Spanish folk music for springtime 789.26105242 (not 789.205242)

(.1)   †General principles of traditions of music

(If both options are used, class here comprehensive works on traditions of music)

Add to base number 789.1 the numbers following 781 in 781.1–781.5, e.g., treatment of springtime music in various traditions 789.15242

(.2)   †Folk music

Music indigenous to the cultural group in which it occurs, usually evolved through aural transmission

(.200 1–.200 7)   †Standard subdivisions

> Notation from Table 1 as modified under 780.1–780.9, e.g., performances of folk music 789.20078

*Add as instructed under 784–788

†(Optional number; prefer 781–788)

(.200 8)	†History and description of folk music with respect to kinds of persons
[.200 89]	Treatment with respect to specific racial, ethnic, national groups

Do not use; class in 789.21–789.29

(.200 9)	†Historical, geographical, persons treatment
(.200 901–.200 905)	†Historical periods

Add to base number 789.20090 the numbers following 780.90 in 780.901–780.905, e.g., Renaissance folk music 789.2009031

(.200 91–.200 99)	†Geographical and persons treatment

Class geographical treatment of folk music of specific racial, ethnic, national groups in 789.21–789.29

(.201)	†General principles, stylistic influences of other traditions, musical forms
(.201 1–.201 5)	†General principles

Add to base number 789.201 the numbers following 781 in 781.1–781.5, e.g., folk music for springtime 789.2015242, rhythm in folk music for springtime 789.20152421224

(.201 6)	†Stylistic influences of other traditions of music

Add to base number 789.2016 the numbers following 789 in 789.3–789.9, e.g., influence of jazz on folk music 789.20165, performances of folk music influenced by jazz 789.20165078

(.201 8)	†Musical forms

Add to base number 789.2018 the numbers following 784.18 in 784.182–784.189, e.g., march form in folk music 789.201897

(.202–.208)	†Voices, instruments, ensembles

Add to base number 789.20 the numbers following 78 in 782–788, e.g., folk songs for women singers 789.202642

(.21–.29)	†Folk music of specific racial, ethnic, national groups

Add to base number 789.2 notation 1–9 from Table 5, e.g., Spanish folk music 789.261; then add further as follows:

001–008   Standard subdivisions
        Notation from Table 1 as modified under 780.1–780.9,
        e.g., performances of Spanish folk music 789.2610078
009   Historical, geographical, persons treatment
00901–00905   Historical periods
        Add to 0090 the numbers following 780.90 in
        780.091–780.095, e.g., Spanish folk music of the
        Renaissance 789.261009031
[0093–0099]   Treatment by specific continents, countries, localities
        Do not use; class in 03–09

(continued)

†(Optional number; prefer 781–788)

(.21–.29)   †Folk music of specific racial, ethnic, national groups (continued)

01   General principles, stylistic influences of other traditions of
             music, musical forms
011–015   General principles
             Add to 01 the numbers following 781 in 781.1–781.5,
             e.g., Spanish folk music for springtime 789.261015242,
             rhythm in Spanish folk music for springtime
             789.2610152421224
016   Stylistic influences of other traditions of music
             Add to 016 the numbers following 789 in 789.3–789.9,
             e.g., influence of jazz on Spanish folk music
             789.2610165, performances of Spanish folk music
             influenced by jazz 789.2610165078
018   Musical forms
             Add to 018 the numbers following 784.18 in
             784.182–784.189, e.g., march form in Spanish folk
             music 789.26101897
02   Voices, instruments, ensembles
             Add to 02 the numbers following 78 in 782–788, e.g.,
             Spanish folk music for the guitar 789.26102787
03–09   Specific continents, countries, localities
             Add to 0 notation 3–9 from Table 2, e.g., Spanish folk
             music in New York City 789.26107471

>   (789.3–789.9) Other traditions of music

Add to notation for each term identified by * as follows:
001–009   Standard subdivisions
             Notation from Table 1 as modified under 780.1–780.9, e.g.,
             performance 0078
01   General principles, stylistic influences of other traditions of music,
             musical forms
011–015   General principles
             Add to 01 the numbers following 781 in 781.1–781.5, e.g.,
             springtime music 015242, melody in springtime music
             015242124
016   Stylistic influences of other traditions of music
             Add to 016 the numbers following 789 in 789.2–789.9, e.g.,
             influence of folk music 0162, performances of music
             influenced by folk music 0162078
018   Musical forms
             Add to 018 the numbers following 784.18 in
             784.182–784.189, e.g., march form 01897
1   Voices, instruments, ensembles
             Add to 1 the numbers following 78 in 782–788, e.g., guitar music
             1787
        Class comprehensive works in 789

(.3)   †*Popular music

           For Western popular music, see 789.4

*Add as instructed under 789.3–789.9
†(Optional number; prefer 781–788)

(.4)   †***Western popular music**

> Examples: ragtime, reggae, skiffle
>
> *For jazz, see 789.5; rock, 789.6*

(.42)   †*Country music

> Class here bluegrass music

(.43)   †*Blues

> Class here rhythm and blues

(.44)   †*Soul

(.5)   †***Jazz**

(.52)   †*Early jazz

> Class here origins of jazz

(.53)   †*Traditional jazz

> Examples: New Orleans, Dixieland, Southwest and Kansas City, Harlem, white New York styles; Chicago breakdown

(.54)   †*Mainstream jazz

> Including swing

(.55)   †*Modern jazz

> Examples: bop (bebop), hard bop, cool jazz, progressive jazz
>
> *For avant-garde jazz, see 789.56*

(.56)   †*Avant-garde jazz

(.57)   †*Hybrid styles

> Examples: Afro-Cuban, third stream, Indo-jazz

(.6)   †***Rock (Rock 'n' roll)**

> Examples: acid, folk, soft rock

(.8)   †***Western art (Classical) music**

> Class here comprehensive works on art music
>
> *For non-Western art music, see 789.9*

(.9)   †***Non-Western art music**

*Add as instructed under 789.3–789.9

†(Optional number; prefer 781–788)

790   Recreational and performing arts

Class here interdisciplinary works on recreation

Class the sociology of recreation in 306.48

For music, see 780

See Manual at 790

SUMMARY

790.01–.09	**Standard subdivisions of recreation**
.1–.2	**[Recreational activities and the performing arts in general]**
791	**Public performances**
792	**Stage presentations**
793	**Indoor games and amusements**
794	**Indoor games of skill**
795	**Games of chance**
796	**Athletic and outdoor sports and games**
797	**Aquatic and air sports**
798	**Equestrian sports and animal racing**
799	**Fishing, hunting, shooting**

.01   Philosophy and theory of recreation

.013   Value, influence, effect

.013 2   Psychological principles

.013 5   Effective use of leisure

[.019]   Psychological principles

Do not use; class in 790.0132

.02–.05   Standard subdivisions of recreation

.06   Organizations dealing with and management of recreation

.068   Recreation centers

Indoor and outdoor

Including parks and community centers as recreation centers

Add to base number 790.068 notation 1–9 from Table 2, e.g., recreation centers of California 790.068794

Do not use for management of recreation; class in 790.069

.069   Management of recreation

Add to base number 790.069 the numbers following —068 in notation 0681–0688 from Table 1, e.g., personnel management 790.0693

.07   Education, research, related topics of recreation

.08   History and description of recreation with respect to groups of persons

Class activities and programs for specific classes of people in 790.19

.09   Historical, geographical, persons treatment of recreation

.1   **Recreational activities**

> Class a specific activity with the subject, e.g., outdoor sports 796, piano playing 786.2143, paper cutting and folding 736.98

[.101–.109]   Standard subdivisions

> Do not use; class in 790.01–790.09

.13   Activities generally engaged in by individuals

> Class here hobbies

.132   Collecting

> Class collecting a specific kind of object with the object, using notation 075 from Table 1, e.g., stamp collecting 769.56075

.133   Play with mechanical and scientific toys

> Examples: electric trains, racing cars sets

> Class play with a specific toy provided for elsewhere with the toy, e.g., flying model airplanes 796.15

.134   Participation in contests

> Examples: writing jingles, matching numbers

> *See also 659.17 for advertising by means of contests*

.138   Passive (Spectator) activities

> Examples: reading, watching, listening

.15   Activities generally engaged in by groups

.19   Activities and programs for specific classes of people

> Class activities generally engaged in by individuals in 790.13, by groups other than families in 790.15

.191   For families

.192   For specific age levels

> Examples: young adults, mature adults

> Class activities for specific sexes regardless of age in 790.194; for invalids, convalescents, handicapped persons regardless of age in 790.196

.192 2   Children

.192 6   Adults aged 65 and over

.194   For groups by sex

> Class activities for invalids, convalescents, persons with handicaps regardless of sex in 790.196

.196   For invalids, convalescents, persons with handicaps

.2   **The performing arts in general**

Class a specific art with the subject, e.g., motion pictures 791.43, symphony orchestra performances 784.2078

Works that treat only public performances, e.g., stage, radio, television, music, are classed in 791. Works that also include athletic and outdoor sports and games are classed here

See Manual at 780.079 vs. 790.2

791   Public performances

Other than musical, sport, game performances

Class here performances at fairs

For stage presentations, see 792; magic, 793.8

See also 780 for musical performances, 793–796 for sport and game performances

SUMMARY

791.01–.09	**Standard subdivisions**
.1	**Traveling shows**
.3	**Circuses**
.4	**Motion pictures, radio, television**
.5	**Puppetry and toy theaters**
.6	**Pageantry**
.8	**Animal performances**

.06   Organizations and management

.068   Amusement parks

Add to base number 791.068 notation 1–9 from Table 2, e.g., amusement parks of United States 791.06873

Do not use for management; class in 791.069

.069   Management

Add to base number 791.069 the numbers following —068 in notation 0681–0688 from Table 1, e.g., management of marketing 791.0698

.092   Persons

See Manual at 791.092

.1   **Traveling shows**

Example: medicine shows

For circuses, see 791.3

.12   Minstrel shows and skits

See also 792.7 for vaudeville

.3　　　　**Circuses**

　　　　　Class here amateur circuses

.32　　　Animal performances

.33　　　Clowns

.34　　　Acrobatics and trapeze work

.35　　　Freaks and sideshows

.38　　　Parades

[.39]　　Amateur circuses

　　　　　Number discontinued; class in 791.3

.4　　　　**Motion pictures, radio, television**

　　　　　Unless other instructions are given, class complex subjects with aspects in two or more subdivisions of 791.4 in the one coming last, e.g., critical appraisal of a specific film 791.4372 (*not* 791.433)

　　　　　See also 302.234 for social aspects of motion pictures, radio, and television as mass media

　　　　　See Manual at 303.376 vs. 363.31, 791.4; 384.54, 384.55, 384.8 vs. 791.4

films on video — use this + country number. (except for UK
.43　　　Motion pictures *(no suffix)*

　　　　　Class here dramatic films

　　　　　Class photographic aspects of motion pictures in 778.53, made-for-TV movies in 791.45

　　　　　See also 384.8 for communication aspects of motion pictures

.430 1–.430 8　　Standard subdivisions　*— .43028 individual actors*

　　　　　Notation from Table 1 as modified under 792.01–792.02, e.g., makeup for motion pictures 791.43027; however, class programming (scheduling) in 384.84, types of presentation in 791.433

.430 9　　Historical, geographical, persons treatment

　　　　　Class here description, critical appraisal of specific companies and studios

　　　　　Class description, critical appraisal of specific films in 791.437

[.430 909]　　Special aspects

　　　　　Relocated to 791.436

.433　　　Types of presentation　*— Screenwriting now 808.23*

　　　　　Examples: home and amateur films, cartoon films, puppet films

　　　　　Class animation of films in 741.58

[.435]　　Kinds of motion pictures

　　　　　Number discontinued; class in 791.43

[.435 2]	Dramatic films
	Number discontinued; class in 791.43
[.435 3]	Educational and documentary films, newsreels
	Relocated to 070.18
.436	Special aspects [*formerly* 791.430909]
	Class here genres of, types of films
.436 1	Films displaying specific qualities
	Add to base number 791.4361 the numbers following —1 in notation 12–17 from Table 3–C, e.g., comedies 791.43617
.436 2–.436 8	Films dealing with specific themes and subjects
	Add to base number 791.436 the numbers following —3 in notation 32–38 from Table 3–C, e.g., films of the West and Westerns 791.436278
.437	Films
	General aspects: description, critical appraisal, screenplays
	Class texts of plays in 800, subject-oriented films themselves with the subject, e.g., films on flower gardening 635.9
	See Manual at 791.437 and 791.447, 791.457, 792.9
.437 2	Single films
	Arrange alphabetically by title of film
.437 5	Two or more films
	Class here collections of film reviews
	Class works which focus on a specific aspect of films with the aspect in 791.436, e.g., Westerns 791.436278; critical appraisal of films associated with a specific person with the person, e.g., films of a motion-picture photographer 778.5092, of a director 791.430233092
.44	Radio
	Class here dramatic programs
	See also 384.54 for communication aspects of radio
.440 1–.440 8	Standard subdivisions
	Notation from Table 1 as modified under 792.01–792.02, e.g., value of radio 791.44013; however, class programming (scheduling) in 384.5442, types of presentation in 791.443
.440 9	Historical, geographical, persons treatment
	Class here description, critical appraisal of specific companies and stations
	Class description, critical appraisal of specific programs in 791.447
[.440 909]	Special aspects
	Relocated to 791.446

.443	Types of presentation

Examples: live or recorded, network production, announcing, commercials

[.445]	Kinds of programs

Number discontinued; class in 791.44

Radio educational, expository, news programs relocated to 070.194, radio sports programs to 070.449796

.446	Special aspects [*formerly* 791.440909]

Class here genres of, types of programs

.446 1	Programs displaying specific qualities

Add to base number 791.4461 the numbers following —1 in notation 12–17 from Table 3–C, e.g., comedies 791.44617

.446 2–.446 8	Programs dealing with specific themes and subjects

Add to base number 791.446 the numbers following —3 in notation 32–38 from Table 3–C, e.g., programs of the West and Westerns 791.446278

.447	Programs

General aspects: description, critical appraisal, radio plays

Class texts of plays in 800, subject-oriented programs themselves with the subject, e.g., programs on flower gardening 635.9

See Manual at 791.437 and 791.447, 791.457, 792.9

.447 2	Single programs

Arrange alphabetically by name of program

.447 5	Two or more programs

Class here collections of program reviews

Class works which focus on a specific aspect of programs with the aspect in 791.446, e.g., Westerns 791.446278; critical appraisal of programs associated with a specific person with the person, e.g., programs of a director 791.440233092

.45	Television

Class here dramatic and audience programs, use of videotapes

Class use of videotapes not provided for here with the subject, e.g., video recordings of rock music 781.66

See also 384.55 for communication aspects of television

.450 1–.450 8	Standard subdivisions

Notation from Table 1 as modified under 792.01–792.02, e.g., scenery and lighting for television 791.45025; however, class programming (scheduling) in 384.5531, types of presentation in 791.453

.450 9   Historical, geographical, persons treatment

Class here description, critical appraisal of specific companies, stations, networks

Class description, critical appraisal of specific programs in 791.457

[.450 909]   Special aspects

Relocated to 791.456

.453   Types of presentation

Examples: live or filmed, color or black-and-white, network production, announcing, commercials

[.455]   Kinds of programs

Number discontinued; class in 791.45

Educational, expository, news television programs relocated to 070.195, television sports programs to 070.449796

.456   Special aspects [*formerly* 791.450909]

Class here genres of, types of programs

.456 1   Programs displaying specific qualities

Add to base number 791.4561 the numbers following —1 in notation 12–17 from Table 3–C, e.g., comedies 791.45617

.456 2–.456 8   Programs dealing with specific themes and subjects

Add to base number 791.456 the numbers following —3 in notation 32–38 from Table 3–C, e.g., programs of the West and Westerns 791.456278

.457   Programs

General aspects: description, critical appraisal, television plays

Class texts of plays in 800, subject-oriented programs themselves with the subject, e.g., programs on flower gardening 635.9

See Manual at 791.437 and 791.447, 791.457, 792.9

.457 2   Single programs

Arrange alphabetically by name of program

.457 5   Two or more programs

Class here collections of program reviews

Class works which focus on a specific aspect of programs with the aspect in 791.456, e.g., Westerns 791.456278; critical appraisal of programs associated with a specific person with the person, e.g., programs of a television photographer 778.59092, of a director 791.450233092

.5　　　　**Puppetry and toy theaters**

.53　　　　　Puppetry

>Class here marionettes, shadow puppets
>
>Class puppet films in 791.433

.538　　　　Production scripts of puppet plays

>Class texts of plays in 800

.6　　　　**Pageantry**

>Examples: processions, festivals, illuminations, parades, floats for parades
>
>*For water pageantry, see 797.203; circus parades, 791.38*
>
>*See Manual at 394.5 vs. 791.6*

.62　　　　　Pageants

.622　　　　Religious pageants

.624　　　　Historical and patriotic pageants

.64　　　　　Cheerleading

>Add to base number 791.64 the numbers following 796.3 in 796.31–796.35, e.g., cheerleading at American football games 791.6432

.8　　　　**Animal performances**

>Example: cockfighting
>
>*For circus animal performances, see 791.32; equestrian sports and animal racing, 798*

.82　　　　　Bullfighting

.84　　　　　Rodeos

>Class here Wild West shows

792　　Stage presentations

>Class here theater, dramatic presentation
>
>Class texts of plays in 800
>
>*For motion pictures, radio, television, see 791.4; puppetry and toy theaters, 791.5*

SUMMARY

792.01–.09	Standard subdivisions	
.1	Tragedy and serious drama	
.2	Comedy and melodrama	
.3	Pantomime	
.5	Opera	
.6	Musical plays	
.7	Variety shows	
.8	Ballet and modern dance	
.9	Stage productions	

.01	Philosophy, theory, aesthetics
.013	Value, influence, effect

> Class influence and effect on a specific subject with the subject, e.g., on crime 364.254

.015	Criticism and appreciation

> General aspects: theory, technique, history
>
> Do not use for scientific principles; class in 792.01

.02	Handbooks, techniques, procedures, apparatus, equipment, materials, miscellany
[.021]	Tabulated and related materials

> Do not use; class in 792.0291

> 792.022–792.028 Handbooks, techniques, procedures, apparatus, equipment, materials

> Use notation 01–09 (except —028) from Table 1 under each subdivision identified by *, e.g., periodicals on amateur theater 792.022205
>
> Do not use for miscellany; class in 792.029
>
> Class comprehensive works in 792.02

.022	*Types of stage presentation

> Examples: municipal theater, showboats, street theater

.022 2	*Amateur theater
.022 3	*Little theater
.022 4	*Summer theater
.022 6	*Children's theater
.022 8	*Arena theater (Theater-in-the-round)
.023	*Supervision
.023 2	*Production
.023 3	*Direction
.023 6	*Programming
.024	*Special effects

> Examples: sound effects, visual effects

.025	*Setting

> Contains scenery, lighting

.026	*Costuming
.027	*Makeup

*Add standard subdivisions as instructed under 792.022–792.028

.028		*Acting and performance
		Including impersonation, improvisation, use of expression and gestures
.029		Miscellany
		Do not use for commercial miscellany; class in 792.0299
.029 07		Humorous treatment
.029 08		Audiovisual treatment
.029 1–.029 7		Miscellaneous works

Add to base number 792.029 the numbers following —02 in notation 021–027 from Table 1, e.g., stage as a profession 792.0293

.029 9   Commercial miscellany

Examples: house organs, prospectuses, price lists, trade catalogs

.09   Historical, geographical, persons treatment

Class here description, critical appraisal of specific theaters and companies

Class specific productions in specific theaters or by specific companies in 792.9

[.090 9]   Special aspects

Number discontinued; class in 792.09

> **792.1–792.8 Specific kinds of performances**

Add to the notation for each notation identified by † the numbers following 792 in 792.01–792.09, e.g., costuming for ballet 792.8026

Class comprehensive works in 792

.1   **†Tragedy and serious drama**

.12   †Tragedy

.14   †Historical drama

.16   †Religious and morality plays

Examples: passion, miracle, mystery plays

See also 792.09 for treatment of religious concepts in the theater

.2   **†Comedy and melodrama**

.23   †Comedy

.27   †Melodrama

Including modern mystery (suspense) drama

.3   **†Pantomime**

*Add standard subdivisions as instructed under 792.022–792.028
†Add as instructed under 792.1–792.8

.5   †Opera

Class here comprehensive works on stage presentations of dramatic vocal forms [*formerly* 782.1]

For musical plays, see 792.6; variety shows, 792.7

See also 782.1 for comprehensive works on opera

See Manual at 792.5 vs. 782.1

.509   Historical, geographical, persons treatment

Class here description, critical appraisal of specific theaters and companies

Class specific productions in specific theaters or by specific companies in 792.54

.54   Opera productions

General aspects: description, critical appraisal, production and stage guides

.542   Single operas

Arrange alphabetically by title

.545   Two or more operas

Class here collections of reviews

Class critical appraisal of operas associated with a specific person with the person, e.g., operas associated with a singer 782.1092, with a director 792.50233092

.6   †Musical plays

See also 782.14 for comprehensive works on musical plays

See Manual at 792.5 vs. 782.1

.609   Historical, geographical, persons treatment

Class here description, critical appraisal of specific theaters and companies

Class specific productions in specific theaters or by specific companies in 792.64

.62   Dancing

Including choreography

.64   Musical play productions

General aspects: description, critical appraisal, production and stage guides

.642   Single musical plays

Arrange alphabetically by name

†Add as instructed under 792.1–792.8

.645   Two or more musical plays

Class here collections of reviews

Class critical appraisal of musical plays associated with a specific person with the person, e.g., musical plays associated with a singer 782.14092, with a director 792.60233092

.7   †Variety shows

Class here burlesque, cabaret, vaudeville, music hall and night club presentations

Including tap dancing [*formerly* 793.324]

Class stage productions in 792.9

See also 791.12 for minstrel shows and skits

.8   †Ballet and modern dance

Class here comprehensive works on dancing [*formerly* 793.3], theatrical dancing [*formerly* 793.32]

Class dancing in musical plays in 792.62

For tap dancing, see 792.7, social, folk, national dancing, 793.3

See Manual at 792.8 vs. 793.3

.809   Historical, geographical, persons treatment

Class here description, critical appraisal of specific theaters and companies

Class specific productions in specific theaters or by specific companies in 792.84

.82   Choreography

Class here choreology, e.g., Labanotation, Benesh

Use of this number for ballet dancing discontinued; class in 792.8

.84   Ballet productions

General aspects: description, critical appraisal, production scripts

Class here stories, plots, analyses, librettos, stage guides

.842   Single ballets

Arrange alphabetically by title

.845   Two or more ballets

Class here collections of reviews

Class critical appraisal of ballets associated with a specific person with the person, e.g., ballets associated with a director 792.80233092

†Add as instructed under 792.1–792.8

.9   **Stage productions**

General aspects: description, critical appraisal, production scripts and stage guides

Class here description, critical appraisal of specific theaters and companies

Class description, critical appraisal, production scripts of ballets in 792.84

See Manual at 791.437 and 791.447, 791.457, 792.9

.92   Single productions

Arrange alphabetically by title

.95   Two or more productions

Class here collections of reviews

Class critical appraisal of productions associated with a specific person with the person, e.g., productions associated with a director 792.0233092

793   Indoor games and amusements

For indoor games of skill, see 794; games of chance, 795

.01   Philosophy and theory

.019   Activities and programs for specific classes of people

Add to base number 793.019 the numbers following 790.19 in 790.191–790.196, e.g., indoor games and amusements for children 793.01922

Do not use for psychological principles; class 793.01

.08   History and description with respect to kinds of persons

Class activities and programs for specific classes of people in 793.019

.2   **Parties and entertainments**

.21   Children's parties

.22   Seasonal parties

Class children's seasonal parties in 793.21

.24   Charades and tableaux

.3   **Social, folk, national dancing**

Examples: belly, jazz dancing

Comprehensive works on dancing relocated to 792.8

See Manual at 792.8 vs. 793.3

.31   Folk and national dancing

[.310 9]   Historical, geographical, persons treatment

Do not use; class 793.319

.319	Historical, geographical, persons treatment

Add to base number 793.319 notation 01–9 from Table 2, e.g., folk dances of Germany 793.31943

.32	Clog dancing

Theatrical dancing relocated to 792.8

[.324]	Tap and clog dancing

Use of this number for clog dancing discontinued; class in 793.32

Tap dancing relocated to 792.7

.33	Ballroom dancing (Round dances)

Examples: fox trot, jitterbug, waltz

Including disco dancing

.34	Square dancing
.35	Dances with accessory features

Examples: cotillions, germans, sword dances

.38	Balls

Class ballroom dancing in 793.33

.4	**Games of action**

Examples: blind man's buff, musical chairs

.5	**Forfeit and trick games**
.7	**Games not characterized by action**

For charades and tableaux, see 793.24

.73	Puzzles and puzzle games

Examples: acrostics, anagrams, literary games, quizzes; jigsaw puzzles

Class puzzles as formal instructional devices for the teaching of a specific subject with the subject, using notation 07 from Table 1, e.g., puzzles teaching the use of the Bible 220.07

For mathematical games and recreations, see 793.74

.732	Crossword puzzles
.735	Riddles

See also 398.6 for riddles as folk literature

.74	Mathematical games and recreations

.8   Magic and related activities

> Example: scientific recreations
>
> Class here conjuring
>
> *For card tricks, see 795.438*

.87   Juggling

.89   Ventriloquism

.9   Other indoor diversions

> Example: making cat's cradles

.92   War games (Battle games)

> *See also 355.48 for military use of war games, 796.1 for outdoor war games*

.93   Adventure games   Fantasy games

> Examples: Dungeons and Dragons®, RuneQuest®
>
> Class here mystery games, role-playing games
>
> *See also 793.92 for war games (battle games)*

[.930 285]   Data processing   Computer applications

> Do not use; class in 793.932

.932   Computer adventure games   Computer fantasy games

> Unless it is redundant, add to base number 793.932 the numbers following 00 in 004–006, e.g., programs for digital microcomputers 793.932536, but use of digital computers 793.932 (*not* 793.9324)
>
> Class comprehensive works on computer games in 794.8

794   Indoor games of skill

> Example: go-moku
>
> Class here board games
>
> Class war games in 793.92, adventure, fantasy, mystery games in 793.93, games combining skill and chance in 795
>
> *For backgammon, see 795.15*

SUMMARY

794.1	**Chess**	
.2	**Checkers (Draughts)**	
.3	**Darts**	
.6	**Bowling**	
.7	**Ball games**	
.8	**Electronic games**	**Computer games**

.1   **Chess**

[.102 85]   Data processing   Computer applications

                         Do not use; class in 794.172

.12   Strategy and tactics

                  General aspects: combinations, sacrifices, traps, pitfalls, attack,
                  counterattack, defense

                  Class strategy and tactics with individual chessmen in 794.14

.122   Openings

.123   Middle games

.124   End games

.14   Individual chessmen

                  General aspects: position, moves, power, value

.142   Pawns

.143   Rooks (Castles)

.144   Knights

.145   Bishops

.146   Queen

.147   King

.15   Collections of games

.152   Master matches

                  Class master matches by individual players in 794.159

.157   Tournaments and championships

                  Class tournaments and championships of individual players in 794.159

.159   Games, matches, tournaments, championships of individual players

.17   Special forms of chess

                  Examples: blind play, simultaneous play, living chess; use of nonelectronic
                  mechanical chess players

.172   Electronic chess   Computer chess

                     Unless it is redundant, add to base number 794.172 the numbers
                     following 00 in 004–006, e.g., use of digital microcomputers
                     794.172416, but use of digital computers 794.172 (*not* 794.1724)

.18   Variants of chess

                  Examples: Chinese (chong-kie), Japanese (shogi), three-dimensional chess,
                  fairy chess, hexagonal chess

.2   **Checkers (Draughts)**

                  Use of this number for other board games discontinued; class in 794

[.22]	Checkers (Draughts)

Number discontinued; class in 794.2

.3   **Darts**

.6   **Bowling**

> *See also 796.315 for lawn bowling*

.7   **Ball games**

Class athletic ball games in 796.3

> *For bowling, see 794.6*

.72   Billiards

> *For pool, see 794.73*

.73   Pool (Pocket billiards)

.735   Snooker

.75   Pinball games [*formerly* 795.2]

.8   **Electronic games   Computer games**

Class computerized forms of a specific indoor game or amusement with the game in 793–795, using notation 0285 from Table 1, e.g., computerized checkers 794.20285

[.802 85]   Data processing   Computer applications

Do not use; class in 794.81

.81   Data processing   Computer applications

Unless it is redundant, add to base number 794.81 the numbers following 00 in 004–006, e.g., programs for digital microcomputers 794.81536, but use of digital computers 794.81 (*not* 794.814)

Class data processing for specific genres of computer games in 794.82, for computerized athletic and outdoor sports and games in 794.86–794.89

.82   Specific genres of computer games

Class computerized war games (battle games) in 793.920285; computerized adventure, fantasy, mystery games in 793.932; computerized athletic and outdoor sports and games in 794.86–794.89

> *See Manual at 794.82*

.822   Arcade games

Unless it is redundant, add to base number 794.822 the numbers following 00 in 004–006, e.g., programs for digital microcomputers 794.822536, but use of digital computers 794.822 (*not* 794.8224)

.86–.89   Computerized athletic and outdoor sports and games

Add to base number 794.8 the numbers following 79 in 796–799, e.g., computerized baseball 794.86357

795 · Games of chance

Class here gambling

Class gambling on a specific activity with the activity, e.g., on horse racing 798.401

See also 364.172 for gambling as a crime

.01   Theory

Including betting systems, probabilities of winning

See also 519.2 for statistical probability in games of chance

.1   Games with dice

.12   Craps

.15   Backgammon

.2   Wheel and top games

Examples: roulette, slot machines

Pinball games relocated to 794.75

.3   Games dependent on drawing numbers or counters

Examples: bingo, dominoes, mah-jongg

.4   Card games

.41   Games based chiefly on skill

Example: cribbage

.412   Poker

.413   Whist and bridge whist

.414   Auction bridge

.415   Contract bridge

Class here comprehensive works on bridge

For bridge whist, see 795.413; auction bridge, 795.414

.415 2   Bidding

.415 3   Play of the hand

.415 4   Scoring systems

.415 8   Collections of games and matches

.416   Pinochle

.418   Rummy and its variants

Examples: canasta, samba, bolivia

.42   Games based chiefly on chance

Examples: baccarat, faro, twenty-one (blackjack)

.43	Games and recreations based on position and skill

Examples: solitaire, patience

.438	Card tricks

796   Athletic and outdoor sports and games

For aquatic and air sports, see 797; equestrian sports and animal racing, 798; fishing, hunting, shooting, 799

See Manual at 613.71 vs. 646.75, 796; 796

SUMMARY

796.01–.09	Standard subdivisions
.1	Miscellaneous games
.2	Activities and games requiring equipment
.3	Ball games
.4	Weight lifting, track and field, gymnastics
.5	Outdoor life
.6	Cycling and related activities
.7	Driving motor vehicles
.8	Combat sports
.9	Ice and snow sports

.01	Philosophy and theory

.019	Activities and programs for specific classes of people

Add to base number 796.019 the numbers following 790.19 in 790.191–790.196, e.g., sports for girls 796.0194

Do not use for psychological principles; class in 796.01

.06	Organizations, facilities, management

.068	Facilities

Class here astrodomes, field houses, playgrounds, stadiums

Add to base number 796.068 notation 1–9 from Table 2, e.g., playgrounds of London 796.068421

Do not use for management; class in 796.069

.069	Management

Add to base number 796.069 the numbers following —068 in notation 0681–0688 from Table 1, e.g., financial management 796.0691

.07	Study and teaching

.077	Coaching

Do not use for programmed texts; class in 796.07

.08	History and description of sports and games with respect to groups of persons

Class activities and programs for specific classes of people in 796.019

.1   **Miscellaneous games**

         Not provided for elsewhere

.13   Singing and dancing games

.14   Active games

         Examples: leapfrog, hide-and-seek, puss in corner, prisoner's base

         For activities and games requiring equipment, see 796.2

.15   Play with kites, remote-controlled devices, similar devices

         Example: flying model airplanes

         See also 790.133 for play with mechanical and scientific toys

.2   **Activities and games requiring equipment**

         Not provided for elsewhere

         Examples: flying discs (Frisbees®), marbles, Yo-Yos®

.21   Roller skating

         Including skateboarding

.24   Pitching games

         Examples: quoits, horseshoes

.3   **Ball games**

SUMMARY

796.31	**Ball thrown or hit by hand**
.32	**Inflated ball thrown or hit by hand**
.33	**Inflated ball driven by foot**
.34	**Racket games**
.35	**Ball driven by club, mallet, bat**

.31   Ball thrown or hit by hand

.312   Handball

.315   Lawn bowling

         See also 794.6 for indoor bowling

.32   Inflated ball thrown or hit by hand

         Example: netball

.323   Basketball

.323 01–.323 09   Standard subdivisions

         Notation from Table 1 as modified under 796.3320202–796.332077, e.g., basketball courts 796.323068

.323 2   Strategy and tactics

.323 3   Refereeing

.323 6	Specific types of basketball

Class here games [*formerly* 796.3237]

Class strategy and tactics regardless of type in 796.3232, refereeing of specific types of basketball in 796.3233

.323 62	Precollege basketball
.323 63	College basketball
.323 64	Professional and semiprofessional basketball
[.323 7]	Games

Relocated to 796.3236

.323 8	Variants

Example: wheelchair basketball

.325	Volleyball
.33	Inflated ball driven by foot

Example: pushball

SUMMARY

796.332	**American football**
.333	**Rugby Union rugby**
.334	**Soccer (Association football)**
.335	**Canadian football**
.336	**Australian-rules football**

.332	American football
.332 02	Miscellany
.332 020 2	Handbooks and guides
.332 020 22	Official rules
.332 020 24	Spectators' guides
.332 028	Apparatus, equipment, materials

Examples: balls, goal posts

Class technique and procedures in 796.3322

.332 06	Organizations, facilities, management

Examples: clubs, leagues

.332 068	Grounds and their layout

Add to base number 796.332068 notations 1–9 from Table 2, e.g., football fields of Washington, D.C. 796.332068753

Do not use for management; class in 796.332069

.332 069	Management

Add to base number 796.332069 the numbers following —068 in notation 0681–0688 from Table 1, e.g., financial management 796.3320691

.332 07	Study and teaching
.332 077	Coaching

Do not use for programmed texts; class in 796.33207

.332 079	Competitions and awards [*formerly* 796.3327]
.332 2	Strategy and tactics
.332 22	Formations

Examples: T, split T, spread, single wingback

.332 23	Line play
.332 24	Backfield play
.332 25	Passing
.332 26	Blocking and tackling
.332 27	Kicking
.332 3	Refereeing and umpiring
.332 6	Specific types of American football

Class here games [*formerly* 796.3327]

Class strategy and tactics regardless of type in 796.3322, refereeing and umpiring of specific types of American football in 796.3323

.332 62	Precollege football
.332 63	College football

Example: bowl games

See also 796.332648 for Super Bowl

.332 64	Professional and semiprofessional football
.332 648	Super Bowl
[.332 7]	Games

Games relocated to 796.3326, competitions and awards to 796.332079

.332 8	Variants

Examples: six-man football, touch football

.333	Rugby Union rugby
.333 01–.333 09	Standard subdivisions

Notation from Table 1 as modified under 796.3320202–796.332077, e.g., official rules 796.33302022

.333 2	Strategy and tactics
.333 23	Forward play
	Including scrummaging, line-outs
.333 24	Halfback play
.333 25	Three-quarter play
.333 26	Back play
.333 3	Refereeing and umpiring
.333 6	Specific types of rugby
	Class here games [*formerly* 796.3337]
	Class strategy and tactics regardless of type in 796.3332, refereeing and umpiring of specific types of rugby in 796.3333
.333 62	Club
	Including college and university
.333 63	County
.333 64	Tours
.333 65	International
[.333 7]	Games
	Relocated to 796.3336
.333 8	Variants
	Example: league rugby

.334 Soccer (Association football)

.334 01–.334 09	Standard subdivisions
	Notation from Table 1 as modified under 796.3320202–796.332077, e.g., equipment 796.334028
.334 2	Strategy and tactics
.334 22	Formations
.334 23	Forward play
.334 24	Halfback play
.334 25	Back play
.334 26	Goalkeeping
.334 3	Refereeing and umpiring
.334 6	Specific types of soccer
	Class here games [*formerly* 796.3347]
	Class strategy and tactics regardless of type in 796.3342, refereeing and umpiring of specific types of soccer in 796.3343
.334 62	Amateur soccer

.334 63	League soccer
.334 64	Cup competition
	For World Cup competition, see 796.334668
.334 66	International
.334 668	World Cup competition
[.334 7]	Games
	Relocated to 796.3346
.334 8	Variants
.335	**Canadian football**
.335 01–.335 09	Standard subdivisions
	Notation from Table 1 as modified under 796.3320202–796.332077, e.g., coaching 796.335077
.335 2	Strategy and tactics
.335 3	Refereeing and umpiring
.335 6	Specific types of Canadian football
	Class here games [*formerly* 796.3357]
	Class strategy and tactics regardless of type in 796.3352, refereeing and umpiring of specific types of Canadian football in 796.3353
.335 62	Precollege Canadian football
.335 63	College Canadian football
.335 64	Professional and semiprofessional Canadian football
.335 648	Grey Cup
[.335 7]	Games
	Relocated to 796.3356
.335 8	Variants
	Example: touch football
.336	**Australian-rules football**
.34	**Racket games**
	Examples: court tennis (royal tennis), paddle tennis
.342	**Tennis (Lawn tennis)**
.342 01–.342 09	Standard subdivisions
	Notation from Table 1 as modified under 796.3320202–796.332077, e.g., layout of tennis courts 796.342068
.342 2	Strategy and tactics

.342 21	Service
.342 22	Forehand
.342 23	Backhand
.342 27	Singles
.342 28	Doubles
.342 3	Refereeing
.343	Rackets and squash
.345	Badminton
.346	Table tennis
.347	Lacrosse
.35	Ball driven by club, mallet, bat

SUMMARY

796.352	**Golf**
.353	**Polo**
.354	**Croquet**
.355	**Field hockey**
.357	**Baseball**
.358	**Cricket**

.352	Golf
.352 01–.352 09	Standard subdivisions
	Notation from Table 1 as modified under 796.3320202–796.332077, e.g., official rules 796.35202022
.352 2	Variants
	Example: miniature golf
.352 3	Tactics of play
	Class here grip, swing, adapting to specific golf courses
.352 32	Play with woods
.352 33	Play with distance irons
	Class here comprehensive works on play with irons
	For play with chipping or pitching irons, see 796.35234
.352 34	Play with chipping or pitching irons
.352 35	Putting
.352 4	Refereeing

.352 6	Specific types of golf
	Class here games and matches [*formerly* 796.3527]
	Class tactics of play regardless of type in 796.3523, refereeing of specific types of golf in 796.3524
.352 62	Amateur golf
	Class open games and matches in 796.35266
.352 64	Professional golf
	Class open games and matches in 796.35266
.352 66	Open games and matches
	Examples: British Open, Masters Tournament
[.352 7]	Games and matches
	Relocated to 796.3526
.353	Polo
.354	Croquet
.355	Field hockey
	Including indoor hockey
	See also 796.962 for ice hockey
.357	Baseball
.357 01–.357 09	Standard subdivisions
	Notation from Table 1 as modified under 796.3320202–796.332077, e.g., baseball leagues 796.35706
.357 2	Strategy and tactics
.357 22	Pitching
.357 23	Catching
.357 24	Infield play
	Class here comprehensive works on fielding
	For outfield play, see 796.35725
.357 25	Outfield play
.357 26	Batting
.357 27	Base running
.357 3	Umpiring
.357 6	Specific types of baseball
	Class here games [*formerly* 796.3577]
	Class strategy and tactics regardless of type in 796.3572, umpiring of specific types of baseball in 796.3573

.357 62	Precollege baseball
	Including sandlot baseball
	Class here Little league
.357 63	College baseball
.357 64	Professional and semiprofessional baseball
.357 646	World series games
.357 648	All-star games
[.357 7]	Games
	Relocated to 796.3576
.357 8	Variants
	Examples: softball, indoor baseball

.358 **Cricket**

.358 01–.358 09	Standard subdivisions
	Notation from Table 1 as modified under 796.3320202–796.332077, e.g., equipment 796.358028
.358 2	Strategy and tactics
.358 22	Bowling
.358 23	Fielding
.358 24	Wicketkeeping
.358 26	Batting
.358 3	Umpiring
.358 6	Specific types of cricket
	Class here matches [*formerly* 796.3587]
	Class strategy and tactics regardless of type in 796.3582, umpiring of specific types of cricket in 796.3583
.358 62	Amateur cricket
	Including school, college and university
.358 63	County
.358 65	International
[.358 7]	Matches
	Relocated to 796.3586
.358 8	Variants
	Example: single-wicket cricket

.4   **Weight lifting, track and field, gymnastics**

Exercise relocated to 613.71

.406   Organizations, facilities, management

.406 8   Gymnasiums and stadiums

Add to base number 796.4068 notation 1–9 from Table 2, e.g., gymnasiums of Japan 796.406852

Do not use for management; class in 796.4069

.406 9   Management

Add to base number 796.4069 the numbers following —068 in notation 0681–0688 from Table 1, e.g., financial management 796.40691

.407   Study and teaching

.407 7   Coaching

Do not use for programmed texts; class in 796.407

.41   Weight lifting

Weight lifting for fitness relocated to 613.713; calisthenics, gymnastic exercises to 613.714; sports gymnastics to 796.44

.42   Track and field

Class here running

For field events, see 796.43

See also 613.7172 for running as an exercise

.420 6   Organizations, facilities, management

.420 68   Athletic fields

Add to base number 796.42068 notation 1–9 from Table 2, e.g., athletic fields of Russia 796.4206847

Do not use for management; class in 796.42069

.420 69   Management

Add to base number 796.42069 the numbers following —068 in notation 0681–0688 from Table 1, e.g., personnel management 796.420693

.422   Sprints [*formerly* 796.426]

Class sprint relays in 796.427

.423   Middle-distance races

Class middle-distance relay races in 796.427

.424   Distance races

Class distance relay races in 796.427

For marathon, see 796.425; cross country races, 796.428

.425   Marathon

Class here comprehensive works on non-track races

For cross country races, see 796.427; race walking, 796.429

.426   Hurdles and steeplechase

Use of this number for comprehensive works on running discontinued; class in 796.42

Sprints relocated to 796.422

Class hurdle and steeplechase relay races in 796.427

.427   Relay races

.428   Cross-country races

.429   Race walking (Heel-and-toe races)

.43   Jumping, vaulting, throwing

Class here field events

.432   Jumping

Contains long jump (broad jump), triple jump (hop, step, and jump), high jump

.434   Pole vaulting

See also 796.44 for gymnastic vaulting

.435   Throwing

Examples: boomerang and discus throwing, javelin hurling, shot-putting

See also 796.24 for throwing games

.44   Sports gymnastics [*formerly* 796.41]

Examples: rhythmic gymnastics, use of horizontal and parallel bars, vaulting

For trapeze work, rope climbing, wire walking, see 796.46; acrobatics, tumbling, trampolining, contortion, 796.47

See also 613.714 for gymnastic exercises

.46   Trapeze work, rope climbing, wire walking

See also 791.34 for trapeze work and wire walking as circus acts

.47   Acrobatics, tumbling, trampolining, contortion

Including floor exercise

See also 791.34 for acrobatics as circus acts

.48   Olympic games

Arrange specific games chronologically

Class paralympics and special olympics in 796.0196, a specific activity with the subject, e.g., basketball 796.323, swimming 797.21

For winter Olympic games, see 796.98

.480 93–.480 99   Geographical treatment

Do not use for specific games; class in 796.48

.5   **Outdoor life**

Class a specific activity of outdoor life not provided for here with the activity, e.g., fishing 799.1

.51   Walking

Class here backpacking, hiking, orienteering

Walkers' guides that give only route details are classed here. Guides that also give description of things en route are classed in 914–919

For walking by kind of terrain, see 796.52

.52   Walking and exploring by kind of terrain

.522   Mountains, hills, rocks

Class here mountaineering

.522 3   Rock climbing

.525   Caves

Class here spelunking

See also 797.2 for cave swimming

.53   Beach activities

For aquatic sports, see 797.1–797.3

.54   Camping

Example: snow camping

.542   Kinds of camps

Class here camps operated for profit

Class activities in specific kinds of camps in 796.545

.542 2   Institutional camps

Examples: school, church, YMCA, scouts

Class institutional day camps in 796.5423

.542 3   Day camps

.545	Activities

Examples: woodcraft, campfires, games

For beach activities, see 796.53

.56	Dude ranching and farming
.6	**Cycling and related activities**

Use of wheeled vehicles not driven by motor or animal power

Examples: land sailing, soapbox racing

For roller skating, see 796.21

.62	Racing

Use of this number for soapbox racing discontinued; class in 796.6

.64	Touring
.7	**Driving motor vehicles**

For snowmobiling, see 796.94

> 796.72–796.76 Driving for competition

Class comprehensive works in 796.7

.72	Automobile racing

See also 790.133 for toy car racing

.720 6	Organizations, facilities, management
.720 68	Race tracks and speedways

Add to base number 796.72068 notation 1–9 from Table 2, e.g., Indianapolis Motor Speedway 796.7206877252

Do not use for management; class in 796.72069

.720 69	Management

Add to base number 796.72069 the numbers following —068 in notation 0681–0688 from Table 1, e.g., financial management 796.720691

.73	Automobile rallies
.75	Motorcycle and motor scooter racing
.756	Motocross
.76	Midget car racing (Karting)

> 796.77–796.79 Driving for pleasure

Class comprehensive works in 796.7

.77	Driving sports cars for pleasure
.78	Driving family cars for pleasure
.79	Travel for pleasure by mobile home

Examples: camper, trailer

.8 Combat sports

Class here martial arts

Class combat with animals in 791.8

.81	Unarmed combat

For boxing, see 796.83

.812	Wrestling

Including arm wrestling

.812 2	Continental (Greco-Roman) wrestling
.812 3	Freestyle (Catch-as-catch-can) wrestling
.812 5	Sumo
.815	Jujitsu and related martial arts forms

See also 613.7148 for related therapeutic exercises

.815 2	Judo

Class here jujitsus

.815 3	Karate
.815 4	Aikido
.815 5	Chinese forms T'ai chi ch'üan

For kempo and kung fu, see 796.8159

.815 9	Kempo and kung fu

Use of this number for other forms discontinued; class in 796.815

.83	Boxing
.86	Fencing

Including kendo, bojutsu

Class here sword fighting

.9 Ice and snow sports

For ice fishing, see 799.12

See also 796.54 for snow camping, 798.6 for horse-drawn sleighing

.91	Ice skating
.912	Figure skating

Examples: ice dancing, pair skating

.914	Speed skating
.92	Snowshoeing
.93	Skiing
.932	Cross-country skiing

Including biathlon

Class here Nordic skiing, Nordic combination

For jumping, see 796.933

.933	Jumping
.935	Alpine skiing

Contains downhill, giant slalom, slalom

Example: supergiant slalom

.937	Freestyle skiing

Examples: ballet, mogul, trick skiing

.94	Snowmobiling
.95	Sledding and coasting

Examples: bobsledding, lugeing, tobogganing

.96	Ice games

Example: curling

.962	Ice hockey

See also 796.355 for field hockey

.962 01–.962 09	Standard subdivisions

Notation from Table 1 as modified under 796.3320202–796.332077, e.g., equipment 796.962028

.962 2	Strategy and tactics

Including skating, stickhandling, passing

.962 27	Goalkeeping
.962 3	Refereeing
.962 6	Specific types of ice hockey

Class here games [*formerly* 796.9627]

Class strategy and tactics regardless of type in 796.9622

.962 62	Junior hockey
.962 63	College hockey
.962 64	Professional hockey
.962 648	Stanley Cup

.962 66	International hockey
	Class here specific tournaments
[.962 7]	Games
	Relocated to 796.9626
.97	Iceboating
.98	Winter Olympic games
	Arrange specific games chronologically
	Class a specific activity with the activity, e.g., skating 796.91
.980 93–.980 99	Geographical treatment
	Do not use for specific games; class in 796.98

797   Aquatic and air sports

.028 9	Safety measures
	Class comprehensive works on water safety in aquatic sports in 797.200289

>   **797.1–797.3 Aquatic sports**

Class comprehensive works in 797

For fishing, see 799.1

.1	**Boating**
.12	With specific types of vessels
	Class seamanship for specific types of vessels in 623.882, boat racing with specific types of vessels in 797.14
.122	Canoeing
.123	Rowboating
.124	Sailboating
	See also 797.33 for sailboarding
.124 6	Yachting
	Class here comprehensive works on yachting
	Class motor yachting in 796.1256
.125	Motorboating
.125 6	Yachting
.129	Houseboating
	See also 643.2 for houseboats as dwellings

.14   Boat racing and regattas

Standard subdivisions are added for any type of racing, e.g., yacht racing in Britain 791.140941

[.17]   Other aquatic sports

Relocated to 797.3

.2   Swimming and diving

Class here water parks

Use 797.2001–797.2009 for standard subdivisions

.203   Water pageantry

See also 797.21 for synchronized swimming

.21   Swimming

Example: synchronized swimming

For underwater swimming, see 797.23

.23   Underwater swimming

Examples: deep-sea, skin, scuba diving

.24   Springboard and precision diving

.25   Water games

Example: water polo

.3   Other aquatic sports [*formerly* 797.17]

.32   Surfing (Surf riding)

.33   Windsurfing (Boardsailing, Sailboarding)

.35   Water skiing

.37   Jet skiing

.5   Air sports

.51   Balloon flying

\>   797.52–797.54 Flying motor-driven aircraft

Class comprehensive works in 797.5

.52   Racing

.53   Flying for pleasure

.54   Stunt flying

Class here display aerobatics

.55   Gliding and soaring

               Example: hang gliding

.56   Parachuting (Skydiving)

798   Equestrian sports and animal racing

> **798.2–798.6 Equestrian sports**

Class comprehensive works in 798, hunting with aid of horses in 799.23

For polo, see 796.353

.2   **Horsemanship**

For horse racing, see 798.4

See Manual at 798.2

.23   Riding

Class here training of both horse and rider, dressage

Class training of the horse alone in 636.1088

For jumping, see 798.25

[.230 74]   Exhibitions

Do not use; class in 798.24

[.230 79]   Competitions and awards

Do not use; class in 798.24

.24   Riding exhibitions and competitions

Example: three-day events

Class jumping in 798.25

.25   Jumping

.4   **Horse racing   Flat racing**

.400 1–.400 5   Standard subdivisions

.400 6   Organizations, facilities, management

.400 68   Race tracks

Add to base number 798.40068 notation 1–9 from Table 2, e.g., race tracks of England 798.4006842

Do not use for management; class in 798.40069

.400 69   Management

Add to base number 798.40069 the numbers following —068 in notation 0681–0688 from Table 1, e.g., management of marketing 798.400698

.400 7–.400 9   Standard subdivisions

.401   Betting

Including pari-mutuel

[.43]   Flat racing

Number discontinued; class in 798.4

.45   Steeplechasing and hurdling

.46   Harness racing

.6   **Driving and coaching**

Including horse-drawn sleighing

For harness racing, see 798.46

.8   **Dog racing**

Use of this number for racing animals other than horses and dogs discontinued; class in 798

799   Fishing, hunting, shooting

See also 688.79 for the manufacture of both mass-produced and handcrafted equipment

.1   **Fishing**

Class commercial and sport fishing in 639.2

.11   Freshwater fishing

Class fishing for specific kinds of freshwater fish in 799.17

>   799.12–799.14 Specific methods of fishing

Class comprehensive works in 799.1; specific methods of freshwater fishing in 799.11, of saltwater fishing in 799.16, of fishing for specific kinds of fish in 799.17

.12   Angling

Examples: still fishing, fly casting, bait casting, spinning, trolling, ice fishing

See also 688.7912 for making artificial flies

.13   Net fishing

Example: seining

.14   Other methods of fishing

Example: spearfishing

.16   Saltwater fishing

Class fishing for specific kinds of saltwater fish in 799.17

[.160 916 3–.160 916 7]   In specific bodies of water

Do not use; class in 799.166

.166	In specific bodies of water

Add to base number 799.166 the numbers following 551.46 in 551.461–551.469, e.g., fishing in Gulf of Darien 799.16635

.17	Fishing for specific kinds of fish

Add to base number 799.17 the numbers following 597 in 597.2–597.5, e.g., trout fishing 799.1755

.2   **Hunting**

Class here comprehensive works on hunting and shooting sports

Class commercial and sport hunting in 639.1

For shooting other than game, see 799.3

.202	Miscellany
.202 8	Techniques, procedures, apparatus, equipment, materials

---

>   799.202 82–799.202 85 Ballistic devices in hunting and shooting

Class comprehensive works in 799.2028

.202 82	Blowpipes, boomerangs, spears, bolas, lassos, slings, nets
.202 83	Guns
.202 832	Rifles
.202 833	Pistols
.202 834	Shotguns
.202 85	Bows and arrows

Do not use for data processing or computers; class in 799.2028

[.209]	Historical, geographical, persons treatment

Do not use; class in 799.29

>   799.21–799.23 Methods

Class comprehensive works in 799.2, methods of hunting specific kinds of animals in 799.24–799.27

.21	Shooting game
.213	With guns
.215	With bows and arrows
.23	Hunting with aid of animals
.232	With falcons
.234	With dogs

>   799.24–799.27 Hunting specific kinds of animals

Class comprehensive works in 799.2

.24   Birds

>   799.242–799.244 Of specific habitats

Class comprehensive works in 799.24, birds of specific kinds regardless of habitat in 799.248

.242   Land birds

.243   Bay and shore birds

.244   Waterfowl

.248   Specific kinds

Add to base number 799.248 the numbers following 598 in 598.3–598.9, e.g., ducks 799.24841; however, class comprehensive works on hunting bay and shore birds in 799.243

.25   Small game hunting

For birds, see 799.24

.254–.259   Specific kinds

Add to base number 799.25 the numbers following 59 in 594–599, e.g., rabbits 799.259322

.26   Big game hunting

Class here comprehensive works on hunting big game mammals

For specific kinds, see 799.27

.27   Specific kinds of big game

For birds, see 799.24

.271–.278   Mammals

Add to base number 799.27 the numbers following 599 in 599.1–599.8, e.g., elephants 799.2761

Class comprehensive works in 799.26

.279   Reptiles

Add to base number 799.279 the numbers following 597.9 in 597.92–597.98, e.g., crocodiles 799.2798

.29   Historical, geographical, persons treatment

Add to base number 799.29 notation 01–9 from Table 2, e.g., hunting in Germany 799.2943

.3   **Shooting other than game**

For ballistic devices, see 799.20282–799.20285

.31   With guns

.312   At stationary targets

For biathlon, see 796.932

.313   At moving targets

Examples: trapshooting, skeet shooting

.32   With bow and arrow (Archery)

800

---

800   Literature (Belles-lettres) and rhetoric

Class here works of literature, works about literature

(Option: Class belletristic essays, speeches, letters, satire, humor, quotations, epigrams, anecdotes, diaries, journals, reminiscences on a specific subject with the subject, e.g., essays on architecture 720)

After general topics (800–809) the basic arrangement is literature by language, then literature of each language by form, then each form by historical period; however, miscellaneous writings are arranged first by historical period, then by form. More detailed instructions are given at the beginning of Table 3

Unless other instructions are given, observe the following table of precedence, e.g., collections of drama written in poetry from more than one literature 808.82 (*not* 808.81)

> Drama
> Poetry
>   Class epigrams in verse with miscellaneous writings
> Fiction
> Essays
> Speeches
> Letters
> Miscellaneous writings
> Satire and humor
>   Class here collections of satire and humor in two or more literary forms
>   (Option: Give precedence to satire and humor over all other forms)

Class interdisciplinary works on language and literature in 400, interdisciplinary works on the arts in 700, folk literature in 398.2; librettos, poems, words written to be sung or recited with music in 780

See Manual at 800; 800 vs. 398.2; 800 vs. 591, 636, 398.245; 800 vs. 741.6

801   Philosophy and theory

.3   **Value, influence, effect**

.9   **Nature and character**

.92   Psychology

     Including literature as a product of imagination

.93   Aesthetics

.95	Criticism

Class here theory, technique, history of literary criticism

Class works of critical appraisal in 809

_____

> 801.951–801.957 Criticism of specific literary forms

Observe table of precedence under 800

Class comprehensive works in 801.95, textual criticism of specific literary forms in 801.959

.951	Poetry
.952	Drama
.953	Fiction
.954	Essays
.955	Speeches
.956	Letters
.957	Satire and humor

Class here parody

.959	Textual criticism

802   Miscellany

803   Dictionaries, encyclopedias, concordances

[804]   [Unassigned]

Most recently used in Edition 16

805   Serial publications

Class collections of literary texts in serial form in 808.80005, history, description, critical appraisal in serial form in 809.005

806   Organizations

807   Education, research, related topics

808   Rhetoric and collections of literary texts from more than one literature

Rhetoric: the effective use of language

Class here composition, literary plagiarism

Do not use for history and description of literature and rhetoric with respect to kinds of persons; class history and description of rhetoric with respect to kinds of persons in 808.008, collections of literary texts from more than one literature with respect to kinds of persons in 808.89

Class general treatment of standard usage of language (prescriptive linguistics) in 418; treatment of standard usage in a specific language with the specific language, using notation 8 from Table 4, e.g., English usage 428; theory, technique, history of literary criticism in 801.95

See Manual at 808.001–808.7 vs. 070.52

SUMMARY

808.001–.009	**Standard subdivisions of rhetoric**
.02–.06	**General topics in rhetoric**
.1	**Rhetoric of poetry**
.2	**Rhetoric of drama**
.3	**Rhetoric of fiction**
.4	**Rhetoric of essays**
.5	**Rhetoric of speech**
.6	**Rhetoric of letters**
.7	**Rhetoric of satire and humor**
.8	**Collections of literary texts from more than one literature**

.001–.009   Standard subdivisions of rhetoric

>   808.02–808.06 General topics in rhetoric

Class comprehensive works in 808

.02   Authorship and editorial techniques

Writing in publishable form

Class here comprehensive works on preparation and submission of manuscripts

Authorship and editorial techniques for specific kinds of composition relocated to 808.06

Class submission of manuscripts to agents and publishers in 070.52

See also 001.4 for research

See Manual at 808.001–808.7 vs. 070.52

[.025]   Writing for publication

Number discontinued; class in 808.02

.027   Editorial techniques

Preparation of manuscripts in publishable form

Class here style manuals

.04   Rhetoric in specific languages

Class preparation of manuscripts regardless of language in 808.02, rhetoric of specific kinds of composition regardless of language in 808.06

.042   In English

.042 7   Study of rhetoric through critical reading

Including collections and single works for critical reading

See Manual at 808.0427

[.042 75]   Literature for learning rhetoric

Number discontinued; class in 808.0427

.043–.049   In other languages

Add to base number 808.04 notation 3–9 from Table 6, e.g., German rhetoric 808.0431; then to the result add the numbers following 808.042 in 808.04201–808.0427, e.g., study of German rhetoric through critical reading 808.04317

.06   Rhetoric of specific kinds of composition

Class here authorship and editorial techniques for specific kinds of composition [*formerly* 808.02]

Class rhetoric in specific literary forms in 808.1–808.7

.062   Abstracts and summaries

.066   Professional, technical, expository literature

Add to base number 808.066 three-digit numbers 001–999 (but no standard subdivisions), e.g., technical writing 808.0666, writing of technical dictionaries 808.0666 (*not* 808.066603), writing on bridge engineering 808.066624 (*not* 808.0666242); then, for writing in a foreign language, add 0 and to the result add notation 2–9 from Table 6, e.g., technical writing in Spanish for speakers of another language 808.0666061

Editorial mechanics in journalistic writing [*formerly* 070.415] are classed in 808.06607, style manuals for business writing in 808.06665 [*formerly* 651.7402], style of business letters in 808.066651 [*formerly* 651.75]

For expository writing for children, see 808.0688; abstracts and summaries, 808.062

See Manual at 651.7 vs. 808.06665, 658.45

.067   Adult easy literature

Works for adults learning to read or for adult beginners in foreign languages

.068	Children's literature
.068 1–.068 7	Specific literary forms

> Add to base number 808.068 the numbers following 808 in 808.1–808.7, e.g., drama 808.0682

.068 8	Expository writing

> **808.1–808.7 Rhetoric in specific literary forms**

Observe table of precedence under 800

Class comprehensive works in 808, specific forms for children in 808.0681–808.0687

.1   Rhetoric of poetry

Class here prosody

Add to base number 808.1 the numbers following —10 in notation 102–108 from Table 3–B, e.g., lyric poetry 808.14

See Manual at 808.1 vs. 414.6

.2   Rhetoric of drama    808.23 Screenwriting

Add to base number 808.2 the numbers following —20 in notation 202–205 from Table 3–B, e.g., one-act plays 808.241

.3   Rhetoric of fiction

Class here the rhetoric of novelettes and novels

Add to base number 808.3 the numbers following —30 in notation 301–308 from Table 3–B, e.g., science fiction 808.38762

.4   Rhetoric of essays

.5   Rhetoric of speech

Art or technique of oral expression

Class here voice, expression, gesture

.51   Public speaking (Oratory)

Examples: after-dinner, platform, radio speaking; making speeches and toasts for special occasions

For debating and public discussion, see 808.53; preaching, 251

.53   Debating and public discussion

.54   Recitation

Class here oral interpretation

Class choral speaking in 808.55

.543   Storytelling

.545   Reading aloud

.55   Choral speaking

.56	Conversation

[.59]   Listening

Number discontinued because without meaning in context

.6   Rhetoric of letters

.7   Rhetoric of satire and humor

Class here rhetoric of parody

.8   Collections of literary texts from more than one literature

By more than one author

Use of this number for general works consisting equally of literary texts and history, description, critical appraisal of literature discontinued; class in 800

Works consisting equally of literary texts and history, description, critical appraisal of literature are classed in subdivisions of 808.8 if limited to specific topics found in those subdivisions, e.g., texts and criticism of literature of the 18th century 808.80033, texts and criticism of drama 808.82

Class two or more literatures in the same language with the literature of that language

See Manual at 808.8

SUMMARY

808.800 01–.800 07	Standard subdivisions
.800 1–.800 5	Collections from specific periods
.801–.803	Collections displaying specific features
.81	Collections of poetry
.82	Collections of drama
.83	Collections of fiction
.84	Collections of essays
.85	Collections of speeches
.86	Collections of letters
.87	Collections of satire and humor
.88	Collections of miscellaneous writings
.89	Collections for and by specific kinds of persons

.800 01–.800 07   Standard subdivisions

[.800 08]   History and description with respect to kinds of persons

Do not use; class in 808.89

[.800 09]   Historical, geographical, persons treatment

Do not use; class in 809

.800 1–.800 5   Collections from specific periods

Add to base number 808.800 the numbers following —090 in notation 0901–0905 from Table 1, e.g., collections of 18th century literature 808.80033

.801–.803   Collections displaying specific features

>   Add to base number 808.80 notation 1–3 from Table 3–C, e.g.,
        collections of literature featuring classicism 808.80142, on death
        808.80354

>   808.81–808.88 Collections in specific forms

        Aside from additions, changes, deletions, exceptions shown under specific
        entries, add to the notation for each term identified by * as follows:
        001–008   Standard subdivisions
        009   Geographical treatment
                Class historical periods in 01–05; persons treatment in the
                number for the specific form, without adding notation from
                Table 1
        01–05   Historical periods
                Add to 0 the numbers following —090 in notation 0901–0905
                from Table 1, e.g., 18th century 033

        Observe the table of precedence under 800

        Class comprehensive works in 808.8

.81   *Collections of poetry

.812–.818   Specific kinds

        Add to base number 808.81 the numbers following —10 in notation
        102–108 from Table 3–B, e.g., collections of narrative poetry 808.813

.819   Poetry displaying specific features

        Add to base number 808.819 notation 1–3 from Table 3–C, e.g.,
        collections of poetry about animals 808.81936

        Class poetry of specific kinds regardless of feature in 808.812–808.818

.82   *Collections of drama

.822–.825   Specific media, scopes, kinds

        Add to base number 808.82 the numbers following —20 in notation
        202–205 from Table 3–B, e.g., collections of tragedies 808.82512

.829   Drama displaying specific features

        Add to base number 808.829 notation 1–3 from Table 3–C, e.g.,
        collections of plays about Abraham Lincoln 808.829351

        Class drama of specific media, scopes, kinds regardless of feature in
        808.822–808.825

.83   *Collections of fiction

.831–.838   Specific scopes and types

        Add to base number 808.83 the numbers following —30 in notation
        3ᴖ1–308 from Table 3–B, e.g., collections of love stories 808.8385

*Add as instructed under 808.81–808.88

.839	Fiction displaying specific features

Add to base number 808.839 notation 1–3 from Table 3–C, e.g., collections of fiction about animals 808.83936

Class fiction of specific scopes and types regardless of feature in 808.831–808.838

.84	*Collections of essays

.849	Essays displaying specific features

Add to base number 808.849 notation 1–3 from Table 3–C, e.g., collections of descriptive essays 808.84922

.85	*Collections of speeches

.851–.856	Specific kinds

Add to base number 808.85 the numbers following —50 in notation 501–506 from Table 3–B, e.g., debates 808.853

.859	Speeches displaying specific features

Add to base number 808.859 notation 1–3 from Table 3–C, e.g., collections of descriptive speeches 808.85922

Class speeches of specific kinds regardless of feature in 808.851–808.856

.86	*Collections of letters

.869	Letters displaying specific features

Add to base number 808.869 notation 1–3 from Table 3–C, e.g., collections of letters displaying classicism 808.869142

.87	*Collections of satire and humor

.879	Satire and humor displaying specific features

Add to base number 808.879 notation 1–3 from Table 3–C, e.g., collections of literary humor about holidays 808.87933

.88	*Collections of miscellaneous writings

.882	Jokes [*formerly* 808.887], quotations, epigrams, anecdotes, graffiti

.883	Diaries, journals, notebooks, reminiscences

.887	Works without identifiable form

Class here experimental and nonformalized works

Jokes relocated to 808.882

.888	Prose literature

Class a specific form of prose literature with the form, e.g., essays 808.84; prose without identifiable form in 808.887

*Add as instructed under 808.81–808.88

.89   Collections for and by specific kinds of persons

Add to base number 808.89 notation 8–9 from Table 3–C, e.g., collections of literature in more than one language by persons of African descent 808.89896

Class literature in specific forms for and by specific kinds of persons in 808.81–808.88, literature displaying specific features for and by specific kinds of persons in 808.801–808.803, literatures of specific languages for and by specific kinds of persons in 810–890

809   History, description, critical appraisal of more than one literature

Treating works by more than one author

Class here collected biography

Class theory, technique, history of literary criticism in 801.95; two or more literatures in the same language with the literature of that language

See Manual at 808.8

.001–.007   Standard subdivisions

[.008]   History and description with respect to kinds of persons

Do not use; class in 809.8

[.009]   Historical, geographical, persons treatment

Do not use; class persons in 809, historical periods in 809.01–809.05, geographical treatment in 809.89

.01–.05   Literature from specific periods

Add to base number 809.0 the numbers following —090 in notation 0901–0905 from Table 1, e.g, history, description, critical appraisal of 18th century literature 809.033

.1–.7   **Literature in specific forms**

Add to base number 809 the numbers following 808.8 in 808.81–808.87, e.g., history, description, critical appraisal of narrative poetry 809.13, of poetry about animals 809.136

.8   **Literature for and by specific kinds of persons**

Class here history and description of literature with respect to kinds of persons

Unless other instructions are given, observe the following table of precedence, e.g., history, description, critical appraisal of literature for or by American Roman Catholic girls 809.892827 (*not* 809.813, 809.89222, or 809.8973)

Persons of specific age groups	809.89282–.89285
Persons of specific sexes	809.89286–.89287
Persons occupied with geography, history, related disciplines	809.8929
Persons of other specific occupational and miscellaneous characteristics	809.89204–.89279
Persons of specific racial, ethnic, national groups	809.801–.889
Persons resident in specific continents, countries, localities	809.893–.899
Persons resident in specific regions	809.891

Class literature in specific forms for and by specific kinds of persons in 809.1–809.7, literature displaying specific features for and by specific kinds of persons in 809.9, literatures of specific languages for and by specific kinds of persons in 810–890

> 809.801–809.889 Literature for and by specific racial, ethnic, national groups

Class comprehensive works in 809.8

.801–.879   For and by general and larger Western racial, ethnic, national groups

Add to base number 809.8 notation 01–79 from Table 5, e.g., North Americans 809.81

.88   For and by other racial, ethnic, national groups

.881   Ancient Greeks

.888   Modern Greeks and Cypriots

.889   Other

Add to base number 809.889 the numbers following —9 in notation 91–99 from Table 5, e.g., Jewish literature 809.88924, African literature 809.8896

.89   For and by other specific kinds of persons

Add to base number 809.89 the numbers following —9 in notation 91–99 from Table 3–C, e.g., literature in more than one language by painters 809.89275, by residents of Canada 809.8971

.9   Literature displaying specific features

Class literature in specific forms regardless of feature in 809.1–809.7

.91–.92   Displaying specific qualities and elements

Add to base number 809.9 notation 1–2 from Table 3–C, e.g., history, description, critical appraisal of literature displaying tragedy and horror 809.916

Class literature dealing with specific themes and subjects regardless of quality or element displayed in 809.933

.93   Displaying other aspects

.933   Dealing with specific themes and subjects

Add to base number 809.93 notation 32–38 from Table 3–C, e.g., history, description, critical appraisal of literature dealing with marriage 809.93354

.935   Emphasizing subjects

Literary appraisal of works not basically belles-lettres

Add to base number 809.935 notation 001–999, e.g., religious works as literature 809.9352, biography and autobiography as literature 809.93592

> ## 810–890 Literatures of specific languages

Literature is classed by the language in which originally written, regardless of country
> (Option: Class translations into a language requiring local emphasis with the literature of that language)

Unless there is a specific provision for a dialect, literature in a dialect is classed with the literature of the basic language

Literature in a pidgin or creole is classed with the source language from which more of its vocabulary comes than from its other source language(s)

(Option: For any group of literatures, add 04 and then add notation 01–89 from Table 3–B, e.g., collections of lyric poetry written in African languages 896.0410408)

(Option: To give preferred treatment to, or make available more and shorter numbers for the classification of, literature of any specific language that it is desired to emphasize, use one of the following options:

> (Option A: Class in 810, where full instructions appear

> (Option B: Give preferred treatment by placing before 810 through use of a letter or other symbol, e.g., literature of Arabic language 8A0, for which the base number is 8A

> (Option C: Where two or more countries share the same language, either [1] use initial letters to distinguish the separate countries, or [2] use the special number designated for literatures of those countries that are *not* preferred. Full instructions appear under 810, 819, 820, 828.99, 840.1–848.9, 848.99, 860.1–868.9, 868.99, 869, 869.899)

Under each literature identified by *, add to designated base number notation 1–8 from Table 3–A for works by or about individual authors, notation 01–89 from Table 3–B for works by or about more than one author. If the base number is not identified in a note, it is the number given for the literature, e.g., for Dutch 839.31. Full instructions for building numbers are given at the start of Table 3

The numbers used in this schedule for literatures of individual languages do not necessarily correspond exactly with those in 420–490 or with the notation in Table 6. Use notation from Table 6 only when so instructed, e.g., at 899

Class comprehensive works in 800

810   *American literature in English

English-language literature of Western Hemisphere and Hawaii

Base number: 81

Special interpretations of and exceptions to notation from Table 3 for use with American literature in English:
> 810.8099 Collections for and by persons resident in Hawaii
> 810.999 History, description, critical appraisal of literature for and by persons resident in Hawaii

(continued)

810   *American literature in English (continued)

Assign period numbers for the United States (including Puerto Rico) and Canada only

PERIOD TABLES FOR AMERICAN LITERATURE IN ENGLISH
For Canada

3	Colonial period to 1867
4	1867–1900
5	1900–
52	1900–1945
54	1945–

For United States

1	Colonial period, 1607–1776
2	1776–1830
3	1830–1861
	Class here 19th century
	Class 1800–1830 in 2, 1861–1899 in 4
4	1861–1900
5	1900–
52	1900–1945
54	1945–

(Option: To give local emphasis and a shorter number to a specific literature other than American literature in English, e.g., Afrikaans literature, class it here; in that case class American literature in English in 820. Other options are described under 810–890)

(Option: Distinguish literatures of specific countries by initial letters, e.g., literature of Canada C810, of Jamaica J810, of United States U810; or class literatures not requiring local emphasis in 819. If literatures are identified by one of these methods, assign period numbers for Middle and South American literature as well as for United States and Canadian literature. Other options are described under 810–890)

Class comprehensive works on American literature in English and English literature in 820

811   ‡Poetry

812   ‡Drama

813   ‡Fiction

814   ‡Essays

815   ‡Speeches

816   ‡Letters

817   ‡Satire and humor

818   ‡Miscellaneous writings

*Add to base number as instructed at the beginning of Table 3
‡Add as instructed under 810 and at the beginning of Table 3

(819)   American literatures in English not requiring local emphasis

(Optional number and subdivisions; prefer 810–818 for all American literatures in English. Other options are described under 810–890)

Class here English-language literatures of specific American countries other than the country requiring local emphasis, e.g., libraries emphasizing United States literature class here Canadian literature, and libraries emphasizing Canadian literature class here United States literature

(.1)   *†Canada

(.3)   *†United States

(.5)   *†Mexico

(.7)   †Central America

(.700 1–.708 9)   †Subdivisions of Central American literature in English

Add to base number 819.70 as instructed at the beginning of Table 3, e.g., collections of Central American dramatic poetry in English 819.7010208

(.71–.77)   †Specific countries

Add to 819.7 the numbers following —728 in notation 7281–7287 from Table 2, e.g., English-language literature of Costa Rica 819.76; then to the base number thus derived add as instructed at the beginning of Table 3, e.g., collections of English-language literature of Costa Rica displaying naturalism 819.7608012

(.8)   †West Indies (Antilles) and Bermuda

(.800 1–.808 9)   †Subdivisions of English-language literatures of the West Indies (Antilles) and Bermuda

Add to base number 819.80 as instructed at the beginning of Table 3, e.g., collections of English-language literature of the West Indies for children 819.800809282

(.81)   *†Cuba

(.82)   *†Jamaica

(.83)   *†Dominican Republic

(.84)   *†Haiti

(.85)   *†Puerto Rico

(.86)   *†Bahama Islands

(.87)   *†Leeward Islands

(.88)   *†Windward and other southern islands

(.89)   *†Bermuda

*Add to base number as instructed at the beginning of Table 3
†(Optional number; prefer 810–818)

(.9)   †South America

(.900 1–.908)   †Subdivisions of English-language literatures of South America

> Add to base number 819.90 as instructed at the beginning of Table 3, e.g., collections of English-language one-act plays from South America 819.90204108

(.91–.99)   †Specific countries

> Add to 819.9 the numbers following —8 in notation 81–89 from Table 2, e.g., English-language literature of Brazil 819.91; then add further as instructed at the beginning of Table 3, e.g., history and critical appraisal of English-language literature of Brazil 819.9109

820   *English and Old English (Anglo-Saxon) literatures

Base number for English: 82

Assign period numbers for Great Britain and Ireland only

PERIOD TABLES FOR ENGLISH
For Great Britain and Ireland

1	Early English period, 1066–1400
	Class here medieval period
2	Pre-Elizabethan period, 1400–1558
3	Elizabethan period, 1558–1625
	Including Jacobean period
	Class here 16th century, Renaissance period
	Class 1500–1558, the pre-Elizabethan part of the Renaissance in 2
4	Post-Elizabethan period, 1625–1702
	Including Caroline and Restoration periods
5	Queen Anne period, 1702–1745
	Class here 18th century
	Class 1700–1702 in 4, 1745–1799 in 6
6	1745–1800
7	1800–1837
	Class here romantic period
8	Victorian period, 1837–1900
	Class here 19th century
	Class 1800–1837 in 7
9	1900–
91	1900–2000
912	1900–1945
914	1945–

(Option: Distinguish English-language literatures of specific countries by initial letters, e.g., literature of England E820, of Ireland Ir820, of Scotland S820, of Wales W820, or of all British Isles B820, of Australia A820, of India In820; or class literatures not requiring local emphasis in 828.99. If literatures are identified by one of these methods, assign optional period numbers for literature of Ireland, Africa, Asia, Australia, and New Zealand. Other options are described under 810–890

(continued)

†(Optional number; prefer 810–818)

820 *English and Old English (Anglo-Saxon) literatures (continued)

(For Ireland

(1   Medieval and early modern to 1660
(2   1660–1800
(3   1800–1900
(4   Irish literary revival, 1900–1945
(5   1945–

(For African countries other than South Africa

(1   To 1960
(2   1960–

(For Asian countries

(1   Early period to 1858
(2   1858–1947
(3   1947–

(For Australia

(1   Early period to 1890
(2   1890–1945
(3   1945–

(For New Zealand

(1   Early period to 1907
(2   1907–

(For South Africa

(1   To 1909
(2   1909–1961
(3   1961–   )

For American literature in English, see 810

821 ‡English poetry

822 ‡English drama

.3   **Elizabethan period, 1558–1625**

.33   William Shakespeare

(Option: Subarrange works about and by Shakespeare according to the following table, which may be adapted for use with any specific author:
A   Authorship controversies
        (Option: Class here bibliography; prefer 016.82233)
B   Biography
D   Critical appraisal
        Class critical appraisal of individual works in O-Z
E   Textual criticism
        Class textual criticism of individual works in O-Z
F   Sources, allusions, learning

(continued)

*Add to base number as instructed at the beginning of Table 3
‡Add as instructed under 820 and at the beginning of Table 3

.33   William Shakespeare (continued)
             G   Societies, concordances, miscellany
             H   Quotations, condensations, adaptations
             I   Complete works in English without notes
             J   Complete works in English with notes
             K   Complete works in translation
             L   Partial collections in English without notes
             M   Partial collections in English with notes
             N   Partial collections in translation
             >O–Z   Individual works
                        Use the first number of each pair for texts, the second for
                        description and critical appraisal
                        Class poems in 821.3
             >O–R   Comedies
             O1–2   All's well that ends well
             O3–4   As you like it
             O5–6   The comedy of errors
             O7–8   Love's labour's lost
             P1–2   Measure for measure
             P3–4   The merchant of Venice
             P5–6   The merry wives of Windsor
             P7–8   A midsummer night's dream
             Q1–2   Much ado about nothing
             Q3–4   The taming of the shrew
             Q5–6   The tempest
             Q7–8   Twelfth night
             R1–2   The two gentlemen of Verona
             R3–4   The winter's tale
             >S–V   Tragedies
             S1–2   Antony and Cleopatra
             S3–4   Coriolanus
             S5–6   Cymbeline
             S7–8   Hamlet
             T1–2   Julius Caesar
             T3–4   King Lear
             T5–6   Macbeth
             T7–8   Othello
             U1–2   Pericles
             U3–4   Romeo and Juliet
             U5–6   Timon of Athens
             U7–8   Titus Andronicus
             V1–2   Troilus and Cressida
             >W–X   Histories
             W1–2   Henry IV, parts 1–2
             W3–4   Henry V
             W5–6   Henry VI, parts 1–3
             W7–8   Henry VIII
             X1–2   King John
             X3–4   Richard II
             X5–6   Richard III
             Y   Poems
                        (Optional numbers; prefer 821.3)
             Y1–2   General works
             Y3–4   Venus and Adonis
             Y5–6   The rape of Lucrece
             Y7–8   Sonnets
             Z   Spurious and doubtful works)

823	**‡English fiction**
824	**‡English essays**
825	**‡English speeches**
826	**‡English letters**
827	**‡English satire and humor**
828	**‡English miscellaneous writings**

(.99)   English-language literatures not requiring local emphasis

> (Optional number and subdivisions; prefer 820–828 for all non-American English-language literatures. Other options are described under 810–890)

> Class here English-language literatures of specific non-American countries other than the country requiring local emphasis, e.g., libraries emphasizing British literature may class here Australian, Indian, other literatures, and libraries emphasizing Indian literature may class here British literature

(.991)   †Scotland and Ireland

> (Option: Class here all English-language literature of *United Kingdom, of *Great Britain, of *British Isles)

(.991 1)   *†Scotland

(.991 5)   *†Ireland

(.992)   *†England and Wales

(.992 9)   *†Wales

(.993)   †New Zealand, Australia, India, South Africa

(.993 3)   *†New Zealand

(.993 4)   *†Australia

(.993 5)   *†India

(.993 6)   *†South Africa

(.994–.999)   †Other parts of the world

> English-language literature except of British Isles, Western Hemisphere, Hawaii, New Zealand, Australia, India, South Africa

> Add to 828.99 notation 4–9 from Table 2, e.g., English-language literature of Israel 828.995694; then add 0 and to the base number thus derived add as instructed at the beginning of Table 3, e.g., English-language poetry of Israel 828.99569401

*Add to base number as instructed at the beginning of Table 3
†(Optional number; prefer 820–828)
‡Add as instructed under 820 and at the beginning of Table 3

829   *Old English (Anglo-Saxon)

Special interpretations of and exceptions to notation from Table 3 for use with Old English appear below under 829.2–829.8

.1   **Poetry**

> *For Caedmon, see 829.2; Beowulf, 829.3; Cynewulf, 829.4*

.2   **Caedmon**

.3   **Beowulf**

.4   **Cynewulf**

.8   **Prose literature**

830   Literatures of Germanic (Teutonic) languages   German literature

> *For English and Old English (Anglo-Saxon) literatures, see 820*

.01–.09   Standard subdivisions of literatures of Germanic (Teutonic) languages

*Add to base number as instructed at the beginning of Table 3

>

830.1–838.9 Subdivisions of *German literature

Class here literature in Alsatian, Franconian, Pennsylvania Dutch (Pennsylvania German), Swabian, Swiss-German dialects

Base number: 83

PERIOD TABLE

1	Early period to 1100
	Class here Old High German literature
	1100–1150 relocated to 21
2	1100–1350
	Class here medieval period, 750–1350; Middle High German literature
	Class 750–1100 in 1
21	1100–1250
	Including 1100–1150 [*formerly* 1]
	Class here Blütezeit
22	1250–1350
	Class here 1300–1350 [*formerly* 3]
3	1350–1517
	1350–1400 relocated to 22
4	Reformation period, 1517–1625
5	1625–1750
	Class here the baroque period
6	Classical period, 1750–1830
	Class here 18th century, the romantic period
	Class 1700–1750 in 5, the later romantic period in 7
7	Postclassical period, 1830–1856
	Class here 19th century
	Class 1800–1830 in 6, 1856–1899 in 8
8	1856–1900
9	1900–
91	1900–2000
912	1900–1945
914	1945–

Class comprehensive works in 830, Yiddish (Judeo-German) literature in 839.09, low German (Plattdeutsch) literature in 839.4

.1–.9 **Standard subdivisions; collections; history, description, critical appraisal of ‡German literature**

831   ‡German poetry

832   ‡German drama

833   ‡German fiction

834   ‡German essays

835   ‡German speeches

836   ‡German letters

*Add to base number as instructed at the beginning of Table 3

‡Add as instructed under 830.1–838.9 and at the beginning of Table 3

837   ‡German satire and humor

838   ‡German miscellaneous writings

839   Other Germanic (Teutonic) literatures

.09   *Yiddish

> PERIOD TABLE
> 1   Early period to 1700
> 2   Period of enlightenment, 1700–1860
> 3   Golden age and modern period, 1860–

> **839.1–839.4 West Germanic literatures**

Class comprehensive works in 839

.1   **Old Low Germanic literatures**

Examples: Old Frisian, Old Low Franconian, Old Low German, Old Saxon

---

> **839.2–839.4 Modern Low Germanic literatures**

Class comprehensive works in 839

.2   ***Frisian**

> PERIOD TABLE
> 1   Early period to 1609
> 2   1609–1800
> 3   1800–1900
> 4   1900–

.3   **Netherlandish literatures**

.31   *Dutch

Class here Flemish literature [*formerly* 839.32]

> PERIOD TABLE
> 1   Medieval period to 1450
> 2   Renaissance period, 1450–1600
> 3   1600–1700
> 4   1700–1800
> 5   1800–1900
> 6   1900–
> 62   1900–1945
> 64   1945–

[.32]   Flemish literature

Relocated to 839.31

*Add to base number as instructed at the beginning of Table 3
‡Add as instructed under 830.1–838.9 and at the beginning of Table 3

.36   *Afrikaans

PERIOD TABLE
1   Early period to 1875
2   1875–1904
3   1904–1924
4   1924–1961
     Class here 20th century
     Class 1900–1904 in 2, 1904–1924 in 3, 1961–1999 in 5
5   1961–

.4   **Low German (Plattdeutsch)**

PERIOD TABLE
1   Early period to 1600
2   1600–1900
3   1900–

.5   **Scandinavian (North Germanic) literatures**

For specific Scandinavian literatures, see 839.6–839.8

> **839.6–839.8 Specific Scandinavian literatures**

Class comprehensive works in 839.5

.6   **West Scandinavian literatures   Old Norse (Old Icelandic)**

.600 1–.600 9   Standard subdivisions of West Scandinavian literatures

.601–.68   Subdivisions of *Old Norse (Old Icelandic)

Base number: 839.6

.69   Modern West Scandinavian literatures   **Modern Icelandic**

.690 01–.690 09   Standard subdivisions of modern West Scandinavian literatures

.690 1–.698   Subdivisions of *Modern Icelandic

Base number: 839.69

PERIOD TABLE
1   Early period, 1500–1720
2   Age of enlightenment, 1720–1835
3   Renaissance, 1835–1900
     Class here 19th century
     Class 1800–1835 in 2
4   1900–

See also 839.699 for Faeroese

.699   *Faeroese

> **839.7–839.8 East Scandinavian literatures**

Class comprehensive works in 839.5

*Add to base number as instructed at the beginning of Table 3

.7   *Swedish

PERIOD TABLE
1   Medieval period to 1520
2   Reformation period, 1520–1640
3   Age of Stjernhjelm, 1640–1740
          Class here 17th century
          Class 1600–1640 in 2
4   Age of Dalin, 1740–1780
          Class here 18th century
          Class 1700–1740 in 3
5   Age of Gustavus, 1780–1800
6   1800–1900
7   1900–
72   1900–1945
74   1945–

.8   Danish and Norwegian

.81   *Danish

PERIOD TABLE
1   Medieval period to 1500
2   Reformation period, 1500–1560
3   Learned period, 1560–1700
4   Age of Holberg, 1700–1750
5   Period of enlightenment, 1750–1800
6   1800–1900
7   1900–
72   1900–1945
74   1945–

Class Dano-Norwegian literature in 839.82

.82   *Norwegian (Bokmal, Riksmal)

Class here Dano-Norwegian literature, comprehensive works on Norwegian literature

PERIOD TABLE
1   Medieval period to 1500
2   Reformation period, 1500–1560
3   Learned period, 1560–1700
4   1700–1750
5   Period of enlightenment, 1750–1800
6   1800–1900
7   1900–
72   1900–1945
74   1945–

For New Norse literature, see 839.83

*Add to base number as instructed at the beginning of Table 3

.83   *Norwegian (New Norse, Landsmal)

> PERIOD TABLE
> 6   1800–1900
> 7   1900–
> 72   1900–1945
> 74   1945–

Class comprehensive works on Norwegian literature in 839.82

.9   East Germanic literatures

Examples: Burgundian, Gothic, Vandalic

840   Literatures of Romance languages   French literature

Class comprehensive works on Italic languages in 870

For literatures of Italian, Romanian, Rhaeto-Romanic languages, see 850; of Spanish and Portuguese languages, 860

.01–.09   Standard subdivisions of literatures of Romance languages

---

>   **840.1–848.9 Subdivisions of *French literature**

Base number: 84

Assign period numbers only for European countries

PERIOD TABLE FOR FRENCH
For European countries

> 1   Early period to 1400
>   Class here medieval period
> 2   1400–1500
> 3   Renaissance period, 1500–1600
> 4   Classical period, 1600–1715
> 5   1715–1789
>   Class here 18th century, Enlightment, Age of Reason
>   Class 1700–1715 in 4, 1789–1799 in 6
> 6   Revolution and Empire, 1789–1815
> 7   Constitutional monarchy, 1815–1848
>   Class here 19th century
>   Class 1800–1815 in 6, 1848–1899 in 8
> 8   1848–1900
> 9   1900–
> 91   1900–2000
> 912   1900–1945
> 914   1945–

(Option: Distinguish French-language literatures of specific countries by initial letters, e.g., literature of Canada C840, of France F840; or class literatures not requiring local emphasis in 848.99. If literatures are identified by one of these methods, assign the following optional period numbers for Belgium and non-European countries. Other options are described under 810–890

(continued)

*Add to base number as instructed at the beginning of Table 3

> ### 840.1–848.9 Subdivisions of *French literature (continued)

(For Asian and African countries

(1	To 1960
(2	1960–

(For Belgium

(1	Early period to 1830
(2	1830–1900
	Class here 19th century
	Class 1800–1830 in 2
(3	1900–
(32	1900–1945
(34	1945–

(For Canada

(3	Colonial period to 1867
(4	1867–1900
(5	1900–
(52	1900–1945
(54	1945–)

Class comprehensive works in 840, Provençal literature in 849

.1–.9   **Standard subdivisions; collections; history, description, critical appraisal of ‡French literature**

841   ‡French poetry

842   ‡French drama

843   ‡French fiction

844   ‡French essays

845   ‡French speeches

846   ‡French letters

847   ‡French satire and humor

848   ‡French miscellaneous writings

(.99)   French-language literatures not requiring local emphasis

(Optional number and subdivisions; prefer 840–848 for all French-language literatures. Other options are described under 810–890)

Class here literatures of specific countries, e.g., libraries emphasizing literature of France may class here Belgian and Canadian literatures, and libraries emphasizing Canadian literature may class here literature of France

(.991)   *†France

*Add to base number as instructed at the beginning of Table 3
†(Optional number; prefer 840–848)
‡Add as instructed under 840.1–848.9 and at the beginning of Table 3

(.992)   *†Canada

(.993)   *†Belgium

(.994–.999)   †Other parts of the world

> French-language literature except of France, Belgium, Canada
>
> Add to 848.99 notation 4–9 from Table 2, e.g., French-language literature of Tahiti 848.9996211; then add 0 and to the base number thus derived add as instructed at the beginning of Table 3, e.g., French-language drama of Tahiti 848.999621102

849   *Provençal and Catalan

Base number for Provençal: 849

PERIOD TABLE FOR PROVENÇAL

1	Early period to 1100
2	Golden age, 1100–1300
3	1300–1500
4	Decline and revival, 1500–1900
5	1900–
52	1900–1945
54	1945–

.9   *Catalan

PERIOD TABLE

1	First period to 1350
2	Second period, 1350–1450
3	Golden age, 1450–1500
	Class here 15th century
	Class 1400–1450 in 3
4	Decline and revival, 1500–1900
5	1900–
52	1900–1945
54	1945–

*Add to base number as instructed at the beginning of Table 3

†(Optional number; prefer 840–848)

850   Literatures of *Italian, Romanian, Rhaeto-Romanic languages

Base number for Italian: 85

PERIOD TABLE FOR ITALIAN
1	Early period to 1375
2	Period of classical learning, 1375–1492
	Class here Renaissance period
	Class later Renaissance period in 3
3	1492–1542
4	1542–1585
	Class here 16th century
	Class 1500–1542 in 3, 1585–1599 in 5
5	Period of decline, 1585–1748
6	Period of renovation, 1748–1814
	Class here 18th century
	Class 1700–1748 in 5
7	1814–1859
	Class here 19th century
	Class 1800–1814 in 6, 1859–1899 in 8
8	1859–1900
9	1900–
91	1900–2000
912	1900–1945
914	1945–

Class comprehensive works on Romance languages in 840, on Italic languages in 870

851   ‡**Italian poetry**

852   ‡**Italian drama**

853   ‡**Italian fiction**

854   ‡**Italian essays**

855   ‡**Italian speeches**

856   ‡**Italian letters**

857   ‡**Italian satire and humor**

858   ‡**Italian miscellaneous writings**

*Add to base number as instructed at the beginning of Table 3
‡Add as instructed under 850 and at the beginning of Table 3

859 *Romanian and Rhaeto-Romanic

Base number for Romanian: 859

PERIOD TABLE FOR ROMANIAN
1 Early period to 1800
2 1800–1900
3 1900–
32   1900–1945
34   1945–

.9   **Rhaeto-Romanic languages**

Examples: Friulian, Ladin, Romansh

860   Literatures of Spanish and Portuguese languages

.01–.09   Standard subdivisions of literatures of Spanish and Portuguese languages

---

>   **860.1–868.9 Subdivisions of *Spanish literature**

Class here Judeo-Spanish (Ladino), Papiamento literature

Base number: 86

Assign period numbers only for Spain

PERIOD TABLES FOR SPANISH
For Spain

1 Early period to 1369
2 1369–1516
3 Golden Age, 1516–1700
4 1700–1800
5 1800–1900
6 1900–
62   1900–1945
64   1945–

(Option: Distinguish Spanish-language literatures of specific countries by initial letters, e.g., literature of Chile Ch860, of Colombia Co860, of Mexico M860 [or, of all American countries A860], of Spain S860; or class literatures not requiring local emphasis in 868.99. If literatures are identified by one of these methods, assign the following optional period numbers for literature of American countries. Other options are described under 810–890

(continued)

*Add to base number as instructed at the beginning of Table 3

>   **860.1–868.9 Subdivisions of *Spanish literature (continued)**

(For American countries

    (1   Colonial and revolutionary period, 1519–1826
    (2   1826–1888
           Class here 19th century
           Class 1800–1826 in 1, 1888–1899 in 3
    (3   Period of modernism and realism, 1888–1910
    (4   1910–
    (42   1910–1945
    (44   1945–   )

Class comprehensive works in 860

.1–.9   **Standard subdivisions; collections; history, description, critical appraisal of ‡Spanish literature**

861   **‡Spanish poetry**

862   **‡Spanish drama**

863   **‡Spanish fiction**

864   **‡Spanish essays**

865   **‡Spanish speeches**

866   **‡Spanish letters**

867   **‡Spanish satire and humor**

868   **‡Spanish miscellaneous writings**

(.99)   Spanish-language literatures not requiring local emphasis

(Optional number and subdivisions; prefer 860–868 for all Spanish-language literatures. Other options are described under 810–890)

Class here literatures of specific countries other than the country requiring local emphasis, e.g., libraries emphasizing literature of Spain may class here Hispanic-American literatures, and libraries emphasizing literature of Mexico may class here literatures of other Hispanic-American countries and of Spain

(.991)   *†Spain

(.992)   †Hispanic North America

Class here comprehensive works on Spanish-language literature of Hispanic America

For Hispanic South America, see 868.993

*Add to base number as instructed at the beginning of Table 3
†(Optional number; prefer 860–868)
‡Add as instructed under 860.1–868.9 and at the beginning of Table 3

(.992 001–.992 08)   †Subdivisions of Spanish-language literatures of Hispanic North America

> Add to base number 868.9920 as instructed at the beginning of Table 3, e.g., collections of Spanish-language one-act plays of Hispanic North America 868.99202041

(.992 1)   *†Mexico

(.992 2)   †Central America

(.992 200 1–.992 208)   †Subdivisions of Spanish-language literatures of Central America

> Add to base number 868.99220 as instructed at the beginning of Table 3, e.g., collections of Spanish-language one-act plays of Central America 868.992202041

(.992 21–.992 27)   †Specific countries

> Add to 868.9922 the numbers following —728 in notation 7281–7289 from Table 2, e.g., Spanish-language literature of Costa Rica 868.99226; then to the base number thus derived add as instructed at the beginning of Table 3, e.g., collections of Spanish-language literature of Costa Rica displaying naturalism 868.9922608012

(.992 3)   †West Indies (Antilles)

(.992 300 1–.992 308)   †Spanish-language literatures of the West Indies (Antilles)

> Add to base number 868.99230 as instructed at the beginning of Table 3, e.g., collections of Spanish-language one-act plays of the West Indies 868.99230204108

(.992 31)   *†Cuba

(.992 33)   *†Dominican Republic

(.992 35)   *†Puerto Rico

(.993)   †Hispanic South America

(.993 001–.993 08)   †Subdivisions of Spanish-language literatures of Hispanic South America

> Add to base number 868.9930 as instructed at the beginning of Table 3, e.g., collections of Spanish-language dramatic poetry of Hispanic South America 868.993010208

(.993 2–.993 9)   †Specific countries

> Add to 868.993 the numbers following —8 in notation 82–87, 89 from Table 2, e.g., Spanish-language literature of Chile 868.9933; then to the base number thus derived add as instructed at the beginning of Table 3, e.g., history and critical appraisal of Spanish-language literature of Chile 868.993309

*Add to base number as instructed at the beginning of Table 3

†(Optional number; prefer 860–868)

(.994–.999)   †Other parts of the world

> Spanish-language literature except of Spain, Hispanic America
>
> Add to 868.99 notation 4–9 from Table 2, e.g., Spanish-language literature of the United States 868.9973; then add 0 and to the base number thus derived add as instructed at the beginning of Table 3, e.g., Spanish-language poetry of the United States 868.997301

869   *Portuguese

> Class here Galician (Gallegan) literature
>
> Assign period numbers for Portugal only
>
> PERIOD TABLES FOR PORTUGUESE
> For Portugal
>
> | | |
> |---|---|
> | 1 | Early period to 1500 |
> | 2 | 1500–1800 |
> | | Including classical period |
> | 3 | 1800–1900 |
> | 4 | 1900– |
> | 41 | 1900–1945 |
> | 42 | 1945– |
>
> (Option: Distinguish Portuguese-language literatures of specific countries by initial letters, e.g., literature of Brazil B869, of Portugal P869; or class literatures not requiring local emphasis in 869.899. If literatures are identified by one of these methods, assign the following optional period numbers for literature of Brazil. Other options are described under 810–890
>
> > (For Brazil
> >
> > | | | |
> > |---|---|---|
> > | (1 | Period of formation, 1500–1750 | |
> > | (2 | Period of transformation, 1750–1830 | |
> > | (3 | 1830–1921 | |
> > | | Class here 19th century | |
> > | | Class 1800–1830 in 2 | |
> > | (4 | 1921–   ) | |
>
> *See also 860 for Papiamento literature*

(.899)   Portuguese-language literatures not requiring local emphasis

> (Optional number and subdivisions; prefer 869.01–869.8 for all Portuguese-language literatures. Other options are described under 810–890)
>
> Class here literatures of specific countries other than the country requiring local emphasis, e.g., libraries emphasizing literature of Portugal may class here Brazilian literature, and libraries emphasizing Brazilian literature may class here literature of Portugal

(.899 1)   *‡Portugal

(.899 2)   *‡Brazil

*Add to base number as instructed at the beginning of Table 3
†(Optional number; prefer 860–868)
‡(Optional number; prefer 869.01–869.8)

(.899 4–.899 9)	‡Other parts of world

Portuguese-language literature except of Portugal, Brazil

Add to 869.899 notation 4–9 from Table 2, e.g., Portuguese-language literature of India 869.89954; then add 0 and to the base number thus derived add as instructed at the beginning of Table 3, e.g., Portuguese-language drama of India 869.8995402

870   Literatures of Italic languages   Latin literature

Class comprehensive works of or on literatures of classical languages in 880

For literatures of Romance languages, see 840

.01–.09   Standard subdivisions of literatures of Italic languages

.1–.9   Standard subdivisions, collections, history, description, critical appraisal of *Latin literature

In more than one form by more than one author

Use the period table under 871–878

> ## 871–878 Specific forms of Latin literature

Add to base number 87 as instructed at the beginning of Table 3; however, observe the special interpretations of and exceptions to notation from Table 3 that appear below, e.g., collections of Latin poetry of the medieval period 871.0308, critical appraisal of Latin epic poetry and fiction of the Roman period 873.0109

PERIOD TABLE FOR LATIN
1   Roman period to ca. 500
2   Pre-Carolingian period, ca. 500–ca. 750
3   Medieval period, ca. 750–1350
4   Modern period, 1350–

Class comprehensive works in 870

871   ‡Latin poetry

For dramatic poetry, see 872; epic poetry, 873; lyric poetry, 874

.01–.04   Specific periods

Use the period table under 871–878

Do not use 871.02–871.08 for specific kinds

872   ‡Latin dramatic poetry and drama

.01–.04   Specific periods

Use the period table under 871–878

Do not use 872.02–872.05 for specific media, scopes, kinds

*Add to base number as instructed at the beginning of Table 3
‡(Optional number; prefer 869.01–869.8)

873   ‡Latin epic poetry and fiction

.01–.04   Specific periods

> Use the period table under 871–878
>
> Do not use 873.01–873.08 for specific scopes and types

874   ‡Latin lyric poetry

.01–.04   Specific periods

> Use the period table under 871–878

875   ‡Latin speeches

.01–.04   Specific periods

> Use the period table under 871–878
>
> Do not use 875.01–875.06 for specific kinds

876   ‡Latin letters

.01–.04   Specific periods

> Use the period table under 871–878

877   ‡Latin satire and humor

.01–.04   Specific periods

> Use the period table under 871–878

878   ‡Latin miscellaneous writings

.000 1–.000 9   Standard subdivisions

.002–.008   Specific kinds

.01–.04   Specific periods

> Use the period table under 871–878

879   Literatures of other Italic languages

.4   **Latinian literatures other than Latin**

.7   **Literatures of Sabellian languages**

.9   **Osco-Umbrian literatures**

880   Literatures of Hellenic languages   Classical Greek literature

> Class here comprehensive works of or on literatures of classical languages
>
> *For Latin literature, see 870*

.01–.09   Standard subdivisions of classical literatures

‡Add as instructed under 871–878 and at the beginning of Table 3

.1–.9   **Standard subdivisions, collections, history, description, critical appraisal of *classical Greek literature**

> In more than one form by more than one author

> Use the period table under 881–888

> ## 881–888 Specific forms of classical Greek literature

> Add to base number 88 as instructed at the beginning of Table 3; however, observe the special interpretations of and exceptions to notation from Table 3 that appear below, e.g., collections of classical Greek poetry of the medieval and Byzantine periods 881.0208, critical appraisal of classical Greek epic poetry and fiction of the ancient period 883.0109

> PERIOD TABLE FOR CLASSICAL GREEK
> 1   Ancient period to ca. 500
> 2   Medieval and Byzantine periods, ca. 500–1600
> 3   Modern period, 1600–

> Class comprehensive works in 880

881   **‡Classical Greek poetry**

> *For dramatic poetry, see 882; epic poetry, 883; lyric poetry, 884*

.01–.03   Specific periods

> Use the period table under 881–888

> Do not use 881.02–881.08 for specific kinds

882   **‡Classical Greek dramatic poetry and drama**

.01–.03   Specific periods

> Use the period table under 881–888

> Do not use 882.02–882.05 for specific media, scopes, kinds

883   **‡Classical Greek epic poetry and fiction**

.01–.03   Specific periods

> Use the period table under 881–888

> Do not use 883.01–883.08 for specific scopes and types

884   **‡Classical Greek lyric poetry**

.01–.03   Specific periods

> Use the period table under 881–888

*Add to base number as instructed at the beginning of Table 3
‡Add as instructed under 881–888 and at the beginning of Table 3

885   ‡Classical Greek speeches

.01–.03   Specific periods

> Use the period table under 881–888
>
> Do not use 885.01–885.06 for specific kinds

886   ‡Classical Greek letters

.01–.03   Specific periods

> Use the period table under 881–888

887   ‡Classical Greek satire and humor

.01–.03   Specific periods

> Use the period table under 881–888

888   ‡Classical Greek miscellaneous writings

.000 1–.000 9   Standard subdivisions

.002–.008   Specific kinds

.01–.03   Specific periods

> Use the period table under 881–888

889   *Modern Greek

> Class here Katharevusa and Demotic
>
> PERIOD TABLE
> 1   Early period to 1821
> 2   1821–1900
> 3   1900–
> 32   1900–1945
> 34   1945–

890   Literatures of other languages

SUMMARY

*Add to base number as instructed at the beginning of Table 3

‡Add as instructed under 881–888 and at the beginning of Table 3

891   East Indo-European and Celtic literatures

SUMMARY

891.1	**Indo-Iranian (Aryan) literatures**
.2	**Sanskrit**
.3	**Middle Indic literatures (Secondary Prakrits)**
.4	**Modern Indic literatures (Tertiary Prakrits)**
.5	**Iranian literatures**
.6	**Celtic literatures**
.7	**East Slavic literatures Russian**
.8	**Slavic literatures**
.9	**Baltic and other Indo-European literatures**

.1   Indo-Iranian (Aryan) literatures

> *For Indic (Indo-Aryan) literatures, see 891.2–891.4; Iranian literatures, 891.5*

> **891.2–891.4 Indic (Indo-Aryan) literatures**

Class comprehensive works in 891.1

.2   *Sanskrit

Class here Vedic (Old Indic) literature, classical Sanskrit literature

.3   Middle Indic literatures (Secondary Prakrits)

Class here comprehensive works on Prakrit literatures

Class tertiary Prakrit literatures in 891.4

.37   *Pali

.4   Modern Indic literatures (Tertiary Prakrits)

PERIOD TABLE FOR SPECIFIC MODERN INDIC LITERATURES
1   To 1345
2   1345–1645
3   1645–1845
4   1845–1895
        Class here 19th century
        Class 1800–1845 in 3, 1895–1899 in 5
5   1895–1920
6   1920–1940
7   1940–
        Class here 20th century
        Class 1900–1920 in 5, 1920–1940 in 6

(Option: Treat literatures of all *modern Indic languages as literature of one language, with base number 891.4)

.41   *Sindhi and Lahnda

Base number for Sindhi: 891.41

Use the period table under 891.4

*Add to base number as instructed at the beginning of Table 3

.419   *Lahnda

>   Use the period table under 891.4

.42   *Panjabi

>   Use the period table under 891.4

.43   Western Hindi literatures   Hindi

.430 01–.430 09   Standard subdivisions of Western Hindi literatures

.430 1–.438   Subdivisions of *Hindi

>   Base number: 891.43

>   Use the period table under 891.4

.439   *Urdu

>   Use the period table under 891.4

.44   *Bengali

>   Use the period table under 891.4

>   Class Assamese literature in 891.451

.45   Assamese, Bihari, Oriya

.451   *Assamese

>   Use the period table under 891.4

.454   *Bihari

>   Class here literatures in Bhojpuri, Magahi, Maithili

>   Use the period table under 891.4

.46   *Marathi

>   Class here Konkani literature

>   Use the period table under 891.4

.47   *Gujarati and Rajasthani

>   Base number for Gujarati: 891.47

>   Use the period table under 891.4

.479   *Rajasthani

>   Class here Jaipuri, Marwari literatures

>   Use the period table under 891.4

.48   *Sinhalese

>   Class here Mahl (Maldivian), Sinhalese-Maldivian literatures

>   Use the period table under 891.4

*Add to base number as instructed at the beginning of Table 3

.49	Other Indic (Indo-Aryan) literatures

Examples: Eastern Hindi, Nepali, Pahari

Including literatures in Awadhi, Bagheli, Chattisgarhi

See also 895.49 for literatures of Himalayan languages, e.g., Newari

.499	Dardic (Pisacha) literatures

Examples: Kashmiri, Khowar, Kohistani, Shina

Including Kafiri, Romany (Gypsy)

.5   Iranian literatures

.51	*Old Persian

Class here ancient West Iranian literatures

See also 891.52 for Avestan literature

.52	*Avestan

Class here ancient East Iranian literatures

.53	Middle Iranian literatures

Examples: Khotanese (Saka), Pahlavi (Middle Persian), Sogdian

.55	*Modern Persian (Farsi)

PERIOD TABLE
1   Period of formal development, ca. 1000–1389
2   Period of traditionalism, 1389–1900
3   1900–

Class Tajik literature in 891.59

.59	Other modern Iranian literatures

Examples: Baluchi, Kurdish, Ossetic, Tajik, Yaghnobi

.593	Pamir (Galcha) literatures Pashto (Afghan)

.593 001–.593 009	Standard subdivisions of Pamir (Galcha) literatures

.593 01–.593 8	Subdivisions of *Pashto (Afghan) literature

.6   Celtic literatures

Example: Gaulish

.62	*Irish Gaelic

PERIOD TABLE
1   Early period to 1171
2   Period of decline, 1171–1700
3   Period of renaissance, 1700–1850
4   Modern period, 1850–

*Add to base number as instructed at the beginning of Table 3

.63 *Scottish Gaelic

    PERIOD TABLE
    1 Early period to 1600
    2 Renaissance, 1600–1830
    3 Modern period, 1830–
      Including 19th century
      Class 1800–1830 in 2

.64 *Manx

.66 *Welsh (Cymric)

    PERIOD TABLE
    1 Early period to 1600
    2 1600–

.67 *Cornish

.68 *Breton

    PERIOD TABLE
    1 Early period to 1800
    2 1800–1900
    3 1900–

.7 East Slavic literatures Russian

.700 1–.700 9 Standard subdivisions of East Slavic literatures

.701–.78 Subdivisions of *Russian

    Base number: 891.7

    PERIOD TABLE
    1 Early period to 1700
    2 1700–1800
    3 1800–1917
    4 1917–
    42 1917–1945
    44 1945–

.79 *Ukrainian and Belorussian

    Base number for Ukrainian: 891.79

    PERIOD TABLE
    1 Early period to 1798
    2 1798–1917
    3 1917–

.799 *Belorussian

    PERIOD TABLE
    1 Early period to 1798
    2 1798–1917
    3 1917–

*Add to base number as instructed at the beginning of Table 3

.8 **Slavic literatures**

Class here comprehensive works on literatures of Balto-Slavic languages

For East Slavic literatures, see 891.7; Baltic literatures, 891.91–891.93

.81 South Slavic literatures Bulgarian

For Serbo-Croatian, see 891.82; Slovenian, 891.84

.810 01–.810 09 Standard subdivisions of South Slavic literatures

.810 1–.818 Subdivisions of *Bulgarian

Base number: 891.81

PERIOD TABLE
1 Early period to 1850
2 1850–1900
3 1900–

.819 *Macedonian

.82 *Serbo-Croatian

PERIOD TABLE
1 Early period to ca. 1550
2 Period of renaissance, ca. 1550–1700
3 1700–1800
4 1800–1900
5 1900–

.84 *Slovenian

PERIOD TABLE
1 Early period to ca. 1550
2 Period of renaissance, ca. 1550–1700
3 1700–1800
4 1800–1900
5 1900–

.85 West Slavic literatures Polish

Including Kashubian

For Czech, see 891.86; Slovak, 891.87; Wendish, 891.88; Polabian, 891.89

.850 01–.850 09 Standard subdivisions of West Slavic literatures

.850 1–.858 Subdivisions of *Polish

Base number: 891.85

PERIOD TABLE
1 Early period to 1400
2 Period of development, 1400–1500
3 Golden age, 1500–1600
4 Period of decline, 1600–1700
5 1700–1795
6 Period of renaissance, 1795–1919
7 1919–

*Add to base number as instructed at the beginning of Table 3

.86   *Czech

> *For literature in Moravian dialects, see 891.87*

> PERIOD TABLE
> 1   Early period to 1400
> 2   Reformation period, 1400–1450
> 3   Humanist period, 1450–1620
> 4   Period of decline, 1620–1900
> 5   1900–

.87   *Slovak

> Class here literature in Moravian dialects

.88   *Wendish (Sorbian, Lusatian)

.89   *Polabian

.9   Baltic and other Indo-European literatures

>   891.91–891.93 Baltic literatures

> Class comprehensive works in 891.9

.91   Old Prussian

.92   *Lithuanian

> PERIOD TABLE
> 1   Early period to 1800
> 2   1800–1900
> 3   1900–

.93   *Latvian (Lettish)

> PERIOD TABLE
> 1   Early period to 1800
> 2   1800–1900
> 3   1900–

.99   Other Indo-European literatures

.991   *Albanian

.992   *Armenian

> PERIOD TABLE
> 1   Early period to 600
> 2   600–1000
> 3   1000–1400
> 4   1400–1850
> 5   Modern period, 1850–

.993–.998   Other

> Add to 891.99 the numbers following —9199 in notation 91993–91998
> from Table 6, e.g., Hittite 891.998

*Add to base number as instructed at the beginning of Table 3

892   Afro-Asiatic (Hamito-Semitic) literatures   Semitic literatures

For non-Semitic Afro-Asiatic literatures, see 893

.1   East Semitic literatures   Akkadian literature

Class here literatures in Assyrian, Babylonian, Chaldean dialects of Akkadian

See also 892.2 for Aramaic, 899.95 for Sumerian

> **892.2–892.9 West Semitic literatures**

Class comprehensive works in 892

> **892.2–892.6 Northwest Semitic literatures**

Class comprehensive works in 892

.2   Aramaic literatures

For Eastern Aramaic literatures, see 892.3

.29   Western Aramaic literatures

Former heading: Biblical Aramaic (Chaldee) and Samaritan

.3   Eastern Aramaic literatures   Syriac

.4   *Hebrew

PERIOD TABLE
1   Early period to 700
2   Medieval period, 700–1700
3   1700–1820
4   1820–1885
      Class here 19th century
      Class 1800–1820 in 3, 1885–1899 in 5
5   1885–1947
6   1947–
      Class here 20th century
      Class 1900–1947 in 5

.6   Canaanite-Phoenician literatures

Examples: Eblaite, Ugaritic literatures

Class here comprehensive works on Canaanitic literatures

For Hebrew, see 892.4

See also 899.95 for Sumerian literature

> **892.7–892.9 Southwest Semitic literatures**

Class comprehensive works in 892

*Add to base number as instructed at the beginning of Table 3

.7   ***Arabic**

Class here Maltese literature

PERIOD TABLE
1   Pre-Islamic period to 622
2   Early Islamic and Mukhadrami period, 622–661
      Class here 7th century
      Class 600–622 in 1, 661–699 in 32
3   661–1258
32   Umayyad period, 661–750
34   Abbasid period, 750–1258
4   Period of decline, 1258–1800
5   Period of renaissance, 1800–1945
6   Contemporary period, 1945–

.8   **Ethiopic literatures**

Examples: Geez, Gurage, Harari, Tigre, Tigrinya

.87   ***Amharic**

.9   **South Arabic literatures**

Examples: Mahri, Qarawi, Shkhauri, Sokotri

893   Non-Semitic Afro-Asiatic literatures

Former heading: Hamitic and Chad literatures

Add to 893 the numbers following —93 in notation 931–937 from Table 6, e.g., Somali literature 893.5

Base number for *Coptic: 893.2

Base number for *Hausa: 893.72

894   Ural-Altaic, Paleosiberian, Dravidian literatures

.1–.3   **Altaic literatures**

Add to 894 the numbers following —94 in notation 941–943 from Table 6, e.g., Mongolian literature 894.2

Base number for *Turkish (Osmanli): 894.35

PERIOD TABLE FOR TURKISH (OSMANLI)
1   Early period to 1500
2   1500–1850
3   Modern period, 1850–
      Including 19th century
      Class 1800–1850 in 2

Base number for *Azerbaijani: 894.361

Class comprehensive works in 894; Japanese in 895.6; Korean in 895.7

*Add to base number as instructed at the beginning of Table 3

> ### 894.4–894.5 Uralic literatures

Class comprehensive works in 894

.4   Samoyedic literatures

.5   Finno-Ugric literatures

.51   Ugric literatures

Examples: Ostyak, Vogul

.511   *Hungarian (Magyar)

PERIOD TABLE
1   Early period to 1800
2   1800–1900
3   1900–

.53   Permian literatures

Contains Votyak (Udmurt), Zyrian

.54   Finnic literatures

Examples: Karelian, Livonian, Veps

For Lapp, see 894.55; Middle Volga literatures, 894.56

.541   *Finnish (Suomi)

PERIOD TABLE
1   Early period to 1800
2   1800–1900
3   1900–

.545   *Estonian

PERIOD TABLE
1   Early period to 1861
2   Modern period, 1861–

.55   *Lapp

.56   Middle Volga literatures

Examples: Mari, Mordvin

.6   Paleosiberian (Hyperborean) literatures

Including Ainu literature

*Add to base number as instructed at the beginning of Table 3

.8   **Dravidian literatures**

PERIOD TABLE FOR SPECIFIC DRAVIDIAN LITERATURES
1   To 1345
2   1345–1645
3   1645–1845
4   1845–1895
     Class here 19th century
     Class 1800–1845 in 3, 1895–1899 in 5
5   1895–1920
6   1920–1940
7   1940–
     Class here 20th century
     Class 1900–1920 in 5, 1920–1940 in 6

(Option: Treat literatures of all *Dravidian languages as literature of one language, with base number 894.8)

.81   South Dravidian literatures

Examples: Kota, Toda

Class here literatures of the Dravida group

Kurukh (Orâon), Malto literatures relocated to 894.83

.811   *Tamil

Use the period table under 894.8

.812   *Malayalam

Use the period table under 894.8

.814   *Kannada (Kanarese)

Use the period table under 894.8

.82   Central Dravidian literatures

Former heading: Andhra group

.823   *Gondi

Use the period table under 894.8

.824   *Khond (Kandh)

Use the period table under 894.8

.827   *Telugu

Use the period table under 894.8

.83   North Dravidian literatures   Brahui

Examples: Kurukh (Oraon), Malto [*both formerly* 894.81]

.830 01–.830 09   Standard subdivisions of North Dravidian literatures

*Add to base number as instructed at the beginning of Table 3

.830 1–.838   Subdivisions of *Brahui

Use the period table under 894.8

Base number: 894.83

895   Literatures of East and Southeast Asia   Sino-Tibetan literatures

Example: Miao (Hmong) literature

Here are classed literatures of South Asian languages closely related to the languages of East and Southeast Asia

Class literature of Malay languages in 899.2

.1   *Chinese

PERIOD TABLE

1	Origins, 15th century to 221 B.C.
	221–200 B.C. relocated to 22
	Class here the classical age
2	221 B.C.–618 A.D.
	Class here the middle epoch
	618–699 A.D. relocated to 3
22	Period of Chin and Han dynasties, 221 B.C.–220 A.D.
	Including 221–200 B.C. [*formerly* 1]
24	Period of Six Dynasties and Sui dynasty, 220–618 A.D.
3	Period of T'ang and Five dynasties, 618–960
	Including 618–699 [*formerly* 2]
	Class here renaissance and neoclassicism
4	960–1912
42	Period of Sung dynasty, 960–1279
44	Period of Yüan (Mongol) dynasty, 1271–1368
	Class period of Yüan dynasty during 1271–1279 in 42
46	Period of Ming dynasty, 1368–1644
48	Period of Ch'ing (Manchu) dynasty, 1644–1912
5	Modern Chinese literature, 1912–
51	1912–1949
52	1949–

.4   Tibeto-Burman literatures   Tibetan

Examples: literatures of the Bodo-Naga-Kachin, Kuki-Chin, Loloish languages

For Burmese, see 895.8

.400 1–.400 9   Standard subdivisions of Tibeto-Burman literatures

.401–.48   Subdivisions of *Tibetan

Base number: 895.4

.49   Literatures of Himalayan (Gyarung-Mishmi) languages

Example: Newari

See also 891.49 for Nepali literature

*Add to base number as instructed at the beginning of Table 3

.6   ***Japanese**

PERIOD TABLE
```
1     Early period to 1185
14      Heian period, 794–1185
2     Medieval period, 1185–1603
22      Kamakura period, 1185–1334
24      1334–1603
          Class here Muromachi period
3     Tokugawa (Edo) period, 1603–1868
32      1603–1770
          Including Genroku period
34      1770–1868
4     1868–1945
          Including Bunka-Bunsei period (1804–1830)
42      Meiji period, 1868–1912
44      1912–1945
          Class here 20th century
          Class 1900–1912 in 42, 1945–1999 in 5
5     1945–
```

.7   ***Korean**

PERIOD TABLE
```
1     Early period to 1392
2     Yi period, 1392–1910
28      Transition period, 1894–1910
3     1910–1945
4     1945–
          Class here 20th century
          Class 1900–1910 in 28, 1910–1945 in 3
```

.8   ***Burmese**

PERIOD TABLE
```
1     Early period to 1800
2     1800–1900
3     1900–
```

*Add to base number as instructed at the beginning of Table 3

.9   **Literatures of miscellaneous languages of Southeast Asia; Munda literatures**

Limited to the literatures named below

Class Malay literatures in 899.2

.91   Thai (Tai) literatures   Thai (Siamese)

Class Annam-Muong literatures in 895.92

.910 01–.910 09   Standard subdivisions of literatures of Thai languages

.910 1–.918   Subdivisions of *Thai (Siamese)

Base number: 895.91

PERIOD TABLE
1   Early period to 1800
2   1800–1900
3   1900–

.919   Other Thai (Tai) literatures

Examples: Ahom, Khamti, Lao, Shan

Use of this number for Karen discontinued; class in 895

Class Annam-Muong literatures in 895.92

.92–.95   Annam-Muong, Mon-Khmer, Munda literatures

Add to 895.9 the numbers following —959 in notation 9592–9595 from Table 6, e.g., Mundari literature 895.95

Base number for *Vietnamese (Annamese): 895.922

PERIOD TABLE FOR VIETNAMESE (ANNAMESE)
1   Early period to 1800
2   1800–1900
3   1900–

Base number for *Khmer (Cambodian): 895.932

*Add to base number as instructed at the beginning of Table 3

896 African literatures

Add to 896 the numbers following —96 in notation 961–965 from Table 6, e.g., Mandingo literature 896.34
(Option: Treat literatures of all *African languages as literature of one language, with base number 896)

Base number for *Wolof: 896.3214

Base number for *Fulani (Fulah): 896.322

Base number for *Ibo (Igbo): 896.332

Base number for *Yoruba: 896.333

Base number for *Ewe: 896.3374

Base number for *Akan: 896.3385

Base number for *Bemba: 896.3915

Base number for *Nyanja: 896.3918

Base number for *Swahili: 896.392

Base number for *Kongo: 896.3931

Base number for *Ruanda: 896.39461

Base number for *Rundi: 896.39465

Base number for *Kikuyu: 896.3954

Base number for *Ganda (Luganda): 896.3957

Base number for *Lingala: 896.39686

Base number for *Shona: 896.3975

Base number for *Northern Sotho: 896.39771

Base number for *Southern Sotho: 896.39772

Base number for *Tswana: 896.39775

Base number for *Xhosa: 896.3985

Base number for *Zulu: 896.3986

PERIOD TABLE FOR SPECIFIC AFRICAN LITERATURES
1   To 1960
2   1960–

For Ethiopic literatures, see 892.8; non-Semitic Afro-Asiatic literatures, 893

*Add to base number as instructed at the beginning of Table 3

897   Literatures of North American native languages

Example: Tarascan

Class here comprehensive works on literatures of North and South American native languages

Add to 897 the numbers following —97 in notation 971–979 from Table 6, e.g., Macro-Penutian literatures 897.4
> (Option: Treat literatures of all *North American native languages as literature of one language, with base number 897)

For literatures of South American native languages, see 898

898   Literatures of South American native languages

Examples: Hishkaryana; Penutian literatures of South America

Add to 898 the numbers following —98 in notation 982–984 from Table 6, e.g., Guaraní literature 898.3
> (Option: Treat literatures of all *South American native languages as literature of one language, with base number 898)

Base number for *Quechua: 898.323

Class comprehensive works on literatures of North and South American native languages in 897

899   Literatures of nonaustronesian languages of Oceania, of Austronesian languages, of miscellaneous languages

Add to 899 the numbers following —99 in notation 991–999 from Table 6, e.g., Polynesian literatures 899.4

Use of this number for literatures of other languages discontinued; class in 890

Base number for *Tagalog (Filipino): 899.211

PERIOD TABLE FOR TAGALOG (FILIPINO)
    1   Early period to 1800
    2   1800–1900
    3   1900–

Base number for *Indonesian (Bahasa Indonesia): 899.221

PERIOD TABLE FOR INDONESIAN (BAHASA INDONESIA)
    1   Early period to 1900
    2   1900–

Base number for *Javanese: 899.222

Base number for *Malay (Bahasa Malaysia): 899.28

Base number for *Malagasy: 899.3

Base number for *Basque: 899.92

Base number for *Sumerian: 899.95

Base number for *Esperanto: 899.992

Base number for *Interlingua: 899.993

*Add to base number as instructed at the beginning of Table 3

900

---

900 Geography, history, and auxiliary disciplines

Class here social situations and conditions; general political history; military, diplomatic, political, economic, social, welfare aspects of specific wars

History of witch crazes relocated to 133.4309, sociology of witch crazes to 306.4

Class historical and geographical treatment of a specific discipline or subject with the discipline or subject, using notation 09 from Table 1, e.g., historical and geographical treatment of natural sciences 509, of economic situations and conditions 330.9, of purely political situations and conditions 320.9, history of military science 355.009

Interdisciplinary works on ancient world, on specific continents, countries, localities are classed in 930–990

See also 303.49 for projected events (future history)

See Manual at 400 vs. 900; 900

.1–.9 **Standard subdivisions of geography and history**

901 Philosophy and theory of history

902 Miscellany of history

903 Dictionaries, encyclopedias, concordances of history

904 Collected accounts of events

Class here adventure

Class travel in 910; collections limited to a specific period in 909, to a specific area or region in 909.09, 930–990; history of a specific kind of event with the event, e.g., geological history of California earthquakes 551.2209794

See Manual at 900: Historic events vs. nonhistoric events

.5 **Events of natural origin**

.7 **Events induced by human activity**

905 Serial publications of history

906 Organizations and management of history

907   Education, research, related topics of history

.2   Historical research

Class here historiography

Class writing of history in 808.0669

.201–.209   Geographical and persons treatment

Add to base number 907.20 notation 1–9 from Table 2, e.g., historians and historiographers 907.202

Historians and historiographers who specialize in a specific area are classed with the area in 930–990, using notation 007202 from table under 930–990, e.g., the biography of a German who specializes in French history in general 944.007202. Those who specialize in specific historical periods of a specific area are classed with the historical period for the area studied, using notation 092 from Table 1, e.g., the biography of a German historian who specializes in the French Revolutionary period 944.04092

908   History with respect to kinds of persons

[.9]   Racial, ethnic, national groups

Do not use; class in 909.04

909   World history

Civilization and events not limited geographically

(Option: Class elementary textbooks on general history in 372.89045)

Class history of ancient world to ca. 499 in 930, history of specific continents, countries, localities in modern world in 940–990; collected accounts of events not limited by period, area, region, subject in 904

See Manual at 305 vs. 306, 909, 930–990; 320 vs. 909, 930–990; 910 vs. 909, 930–990

[.001–.008]   Standard subdivisions

Do not use; class in 901–908

[.009]   Historical treatment

Do not use; class in 907.2

.04   History with respect to racial, ethnic, national groups

Add to base number 909.04 notation 03–99 from Table 5, e.g., world history of Jews 909.04924; then add 0 and to the result add the numbers following 909 in 909.1–909.8, e.g., world history of Jews in 18th century 909.0492407

(Option: Class here general history of racial, ethnic, national groups in a specific continent, country, locality; prefer subdivision 004 from table under 930–990. If option is chosen, add notation 03–99 from Table 5 as above; then add 00 instead of 0 as above for world history by period, e.g., world history of Jews in 18th century 909.04924007; for specific areas add 0 and to the result add notation 3–9 from Table 2, e.g., history of Jews in Germany 909.04924043)

>   909.07–909.08 General historical periods

Class here general histories covering three or more continents (or three or more countries if not on the same continent)

Class comprehensive works in 909, ancient history in 930, specific historical periods in 909.1–909.8

.07   Ca. 500–1450/1500

Including Crusades

See also 940.18 for history of Europe during the Crusades

.08   Modern history, 1450/1500–

.09   Areas, regions, places in general

Not limited by continent, country, locality

Class here interdisciplinary works on areas, regions, places in general (other than land forms, oceans, seas)

Use 909.0901–909.0909 for standard subdivisions

Add to base number 909.09 the numbers following —1 in notation 11–19 from Table 2, e.g., history of tropical regions 909.093, of Caribbean Sea 909.096365; then add *0 and to the result add the numbers following 909 in 909.1–909.8, e.g., history of tropical regions in 1950–1959 909.0930825

Class interdisciplinary works on land forms, oceans, seas in 551.4

For geography of and travel in areas, regions, places in general, see 910.91

>   **909.1–909.8 Specific historical periods**

Class comprehensive works in 909, general historical periods in 909.07–909.08

.1   **6th-12th centuries, 500–1199**

.2   **13th century, 1200–1299**

.3   **14th century, 1300–1399**

.4   **15th century, 1400–1499**

.5   **16th century, 1500–1599**

.6   **17th century, 1600–1699**

.7   **18th century, 1700–1799**

.8   **1800–**

.81   19th century, 1800–1899

Class here Industrial Revolution

*Add 00 for standard subdivisions; see instructions at beginning of Table 1

.82	20th century, 1900–1999
.821	1900–1919
	For World War I, see 940.3
.822	1920–1929
.823	1930–1939
.824	1940–1949
	For World War II, see 940.53
.825	1950–1959
.826	1960–1969
.827	1970–1979
.828	1980–1989
.829	1990–1999
.83	21st century, 2000–2099

See also 303.49 for futurology

910   Geography and travel

(Option: Class elementary textbooks on general geography in 372.891045)

Class works on civilization, other than accounts of travel in 909, in ancient world and specific places in modern world in 930–990; geographical treatment of specific disciplines or subjects with the discipline or subject, e.g., geographical treatment of religion 200.9, of geomorphology 551.409

See Manual at 508 vs. 574, 910, 304.2; 550 vs. 910; 910 vs. 909, 930–990

.01	Philosophy and theory of geography and travel
.014	Language (Terminology) and communication

         Class here discourses on place names and their origin, history, meaning

         Class dictionaries and gazetteers of place names in 910.3

.02	The earth (Physical geography)

         Class specific features in 550, e.g., glaciers 551.312

         See also 551.4 for geomorphology

         See Manual at 550 vs. 910

.020 9	Historical and persons treatment

         Class physical geography of areas, regions, places in general in 910.021; of ancient world in 913.02; of specific continents, countries, localities in 913.1–919.9, using notation 02 from table under 913–919

.021	Of areas, regions, places in general

Add to base number 910.021 the numbers following −1 in notation 11−18 from Table 2, e.g., of forests 910.02152

[.09]	Geography of and travel in areas, regions, places in general

Relocated to 910.91

(.1)   Topical geography

(Optional number; prefer specific subject, e.g., economic geography 330.91−330.99)

Do not use for philosophy and theory of geography and travel; class 910.01

Add to base number 910.1 notation 001−899, e.g., economic geography 910.133; then add 0 and to the result add notation 1−9 from Table 2, e.g., economic geography of British Isles 910.133041

.2   Miscellany

.202	World travel guides

Class here guidebooks and tour books providing tourists updated information about places in many areas of the globe: how to travel, what to see, where to stay, how to plan a vacation

Class guides to areas, regions, places in general in 910.91, to specific continents, countries, localities in 913−919, using notation 04 from table under 913−919

.22	Illustrations, models, miniatures
.222	Pictures and related illustrations

Example: aerial photographs not limited to one specific area or region

.223	Diagrams

Class maps, plans, related forms in 912

.25	Directories of persons and organizations

Class here city directories, telephone books

Class city directories, telephone books of a specific place in 913−919

.3   Dictionaries, encyclopedias, concordances, gazetteers

Class here works on place names systematically arranged for ready reference

Class discourses on place names in 910.014; historical material associated with place names in general in 909, on specific places in 930−990

.4   **Accounts of travel**

Not geographically limited

Class travel accounts that emphasize civilization of places visited in 909

For discovery and exploration, see 910.9

See also 508 for scientific exploration and travel, 910.202 for world travel guides

.41   Trips around the world

.45   Ocean travel and seafaring adventures

Examples: pirates' expeditions, shipwrecks

Class ocean trips around the world in 910.41; travel in specific oceans in 910.9163–910.9167

[.453]   Collected voyages of adventure

Number discontinued; class in 910.45

.5–.8   **Standard subdivisions**

.9   **Historical, geographical, persons treatment**

Class here discovery, exploration, growth of geographic knowledge

.91   Geography of and travel in areas, regions, places in general [*formerly* 910.09]

(Option: Class elementary geography textbooks on specific areas, regions, places in general in 372.8911)

Class interdisciplinary works on land forms, oceans, seas in 551.4; physical geography of areas, regions, places in general in 910.02

.92   Geographers, travelers, explorers regardless of country of origin

.93–.99   Discovery and exploration by specific countries

Do not use for geography of and travel in specific continents, countries, localities; extraterrestrial worlds; class in 913–919

Add to base number 910.9 notation 3–9 from Table 2 for the country responsible, e.g., explorations by Great Britain 910.941

Class discovery and exploration by a specific country in areas, regions, places in general in 910.91, in specific continents, countries, localities, extraterrestrial worlds in 913–919, using notation 04 from table under 913–919; periods of discovery and exploration in history in 940–990

911   Historical geography

Growth and changes in political divisions

Class here historical atlases

.09   Historical treatment

Class geographical and persons treatment in 911.1–911.9

.1–.9   Geographical and persons treatment

> Add to base number 911 notation 1–9 from Table 2, e.g., historical geography of China 911.51

912   Graphic representations of surface of earth and of extraterrestrial worlds

> Class here atlases, maps, charts, plans

> Class map drawing in 526.0221

> *See Manual at T1—0223 vs. 912*

.01   Philosophy and theory

.014   Map reading

> Do not use for languages (terminology); class in 912.01

.014 8   Map scales, symbols, abbreviations

.09   Historical and persons treatment of maps and map making

> Class maps of specific areas, regions, places in general in 912.19; of specific continents, countries, localities, extraterrestrial worlds in 912.3–912.9

.1   Areas, regions, places in general

[.100 1–.189 9]   Specific subjects

> Relocated to subject with use of notation 0223 from Table 1

.19   Specific areas, regions, places in general

> Add to base number 912.19 the numbers following 1 in notation 11–19 from Table 2, e.g., maps of Western Hemisphere 912.19812

.3–.9   Specific continents, countries, localities, extraterrestrial worlds

> Class here land atlases of countries, tax maps that provide general descriptions of assessed land and structures

> Add to base number 912 notation 3–9 from Table 2, e.g., maps of Du Page County, Illinois 912.77324

> ## 913–919 Geography of and travel in ancient world and specific continents, countries, localities in modern world; extraterrestrial worlds

Class here comprehensive works on ancient and modern geography of and travel in specific continents, countries, localities

(Option: Class elementary geography textbooks on ancient world, on specific continents, countries, localities in 372.8913–372.8919)

Add to base number 91 notation 3–9 from Table 2, e.g., geography of England 914.2, of Norfolk, England 914.261; then add further as follows:

001	Philosophy and theory
0014	Language (Terminology) and communication
	Class here discursive works on place names and their origin, history, and meaning
	Class dictionaries and gazetteers of place names in 003
002	Miscellany
0022	Illustrations, models, miniatures
00222	Pictures and related illustrations
	Example: aerial photographs
	Class photographs reflecting the civilization of places in 930–990
0025	Directories of persons and organizations
	Class here city directories, telephone books
003	Dictionaries, encyclopedias, concordances, gazetteers
	Class here works on place names systematically arranged for ready reference
	Class discourses on place names in 0014, historical material associated with place names in 930–990
005–008	Standard subdivisions
01	Prehistoric geography
	Do not add to notation 4–6 from Table 2 if there is a corresponding notation 3 from Table 2, e.g., prehistoric geography of Greece 913.801 (*not* 914.9501), of Russia 914.701
	Class prehistoric geography of areas, regions, places in general in 09, prehistoric physical geography in 02
02	The earth (Physical geography)
	Class specific features in 550, e.g., glaciers of Canada 551.3120971
	See also 551.4 for geomorphology
	See Manual at 550 vs. 910

(continued)

> ## 913–919 Geography of and travel in ancient world and specific continents, countries, localities in modern world; extraterrestrial worlds (continued)

04   Travel
Class here discovery, exploration; guidebooks
Guidebooks emphasizing a specific subject relocated to the subject, e.g., a guidebook to holy places in Spain 263.04246
Class travel accounts that emphasize the civilization of country visited in 930–990, world travel guides in 910.202
See Manual at 913–919: Add table: 04

041–049   Historical periods
Add to 04 the historical period numbers following 0 that appear in subdivisions of 930–990, e.g., travel in England during Tudor period 914.2045
For United States historical periods, add to 04 the numbers following 973 in 973.1–973.9, e.g., travel in United States during the Nixon administration 917.304924

09   Areas, regions, places in general
Add to 09 the numbers following —1 in notation 11–18 from Table 2, e.g., geography of urban regions of England 914.209732
Class physical geography of areas, regions, places in 02; travel in 04; civilization in subdivisions 0091–0098 under 930–990

Class comprehensive works, geography of and travel in more than one continent in 910; historical geography in 911; graphic representations in 912; interdisciplinary works on geography and history of ancient world, of specific continents, countries, localities in 930–990; area studies in 940–990

See Manual at 913–919.

913   ***Geography of and travel in ancient world**

Class Biblical geography in 220.91

914   ***Geography of and travel in Europe**

915   ***Geography of and travel in Asia**

916   ***Geography of and travel in Africa**

917   ***Geography of and travel in North America**

918   ***Geography of and travel in South America**

919   ***Geography of and travel in other parts of world and extraterrestrial worlds**

*Add as instructed under 913–919

920   Biography, genealogy, insignia

Class here autobiographies, diaries, reminiscences, correspondence

Class biography of persons associated with a specific discipline or subject with the discipline or subject, using notation 092 from Table 1, e.g., biography of chemists 540.92

(Option: Class individual biography in 92 or B, collected biography in 92 or 920 undivided)

.001–.007	Standard subdivisions of biography
.008	History and description with respect to kinds of persons
[.008 1–.008 2]	Men and women

Do not use; class in 920.7

[.008 8]	Occupational and religious groups

Do not use; class in 920.1–928.9

[.008 9]	Racial, ethnic, national groups

Do not use; class in 920.0092

.009	General collections of biography by period, region, group

Class collections by specific continents, countries, localities in 920.03–920.09

.009 01–.009 05	Historical periods

Add to base number 920.0090 the numbers following —090 in notation 0901–0905 from Table 1, e.g., general biography of 19th century 920.009034

.009 1	Areas, regions, places in general

Add to base number 920.0091 the numbers following —1 in notation 11–19 from Table 2, e.g., biographies of suburbanites 920.0091733

.009 2	Racial, ethnic, national groups

Add to base number 920.0092 notation 03–99 from Table 5, e.g., biographies of Swedes 920.0092397

.02	General collections of biography

Not limited by period, place, group and not associated with a specific subject

.03–.09	General collections of biography by specific continents, countries, localities

Not associated with a specific subject

Add to base number 920.0 notation 3–9 from Table 2, e.g., collections of biographies of persons resident in England 920.042

Class collections by sex regardless of continent, country, locality in 920.7

> ### 920.1–928.9 Biography of specific classes of persons

(Option A: Use subdivisions identified by *

(Option B: Class individual biography in 92 or B, collected biography in 92 or 920 undivided

(Option C: Class individual biography of men in 920.71, of women in 920.72

(Prefer specific discipline or subject, using notation 092 from Table 1, e.g., collected biography of scientists 509.22)

Add to notation for each term identified by † notation 3–9 from Table 2, e.g., Baptists from Louisiana 922.6763

Class comprehensive works in 920.02

(.1) ***Bibliographers**

(.2) ***Librarians and book collectors**

(.3) ***Encyclopedists**

Class lexicographers in 924

(.4) ***Publishers and booksellers**

(.5) ***Journalists and news commentators**

.7   **Persons by sex**

Class here individual biography of persons not associated with a specific discipline or subject, collected biography of persons by sex

(Option: Class here all individual biography; prefer specific discipline or subject, using notation 092 from Table 1)

.71   Men

.72   Women

(.9) ***Persons associated with other subjects**

Not provided for in 920.1–920.5, 921–928

Add to base number 920.9 notation 001–999, e.g., astrologers 920.91335

(921) *Philosophers and psychologists

> (921.1–921.8) Modern Western philosophers and psychologists

Class comprehensive works in 921

(.1) ***United States and Canadian philosophers and psychologists**

(.2) ***British philosophers and psychologists**

Contains English, Scottish, Irish, Welsh philosophers and psychologists

(.3) ***German and Austrian philosophers and psychologists**

*(Optional number; prefer specific subject or discipline, as described under 920.1–928.9)

(.4)   ***French philosophers and psychologists**

(.5)   ***Italian philosophers and psychologists**

(.6)   ***Spanish and Portuguese philosophers and psychologists**

(.7)   ***Russian philosophers and psychologists**

(.8)   ***†Other modern Western philosophers and psychologists**

(.9)   ***Ancient, medieval, Oriental philosophers and psychologists**

> Add to base number 921.9 the numbers following 18 in 181–189, e.g., Aristotelian philosophers 921.95

(922)   *Religious leaders, thinkers, workers

>   (922.1–922.8) Christians

>   Class comprehensive works in 922

(.1)   ***†Early and Eastern churches**

(.2)   ***Roman Catholics**

(.21)   ***Popes**

(.22)   ***Saints**

(.24–.29)   ***†Other**

(.3)   ***†Anglicans**

(.4)   ***†Lutherans, Huguenots, continental Protestants**

(.5)   ***†Presbyterians, Congregationalists, American Reformed**

(.6)   ***†Baptists, Disciples of Christ, Adventists**

(.7)   ***†Methodists**

(.8)   ***Members of other Christian denominations and sects**

(.81)   ***†Unitarians and Universalists**

(.83)   ***†Latter-Day Saints**

(.84)   ***†Swedenborgians**

(.85)   ***†Christian Scientists**

(.86)   ***†Friends (Quakers)**

(.87)   ***†Mennonites**

(.88)   ***†Shakers**

(.89)   ***Others**

*(Optional number; prefer specific subject or discipline, as described under 920.1–928.9)
†Add as instructed under 920.1–928.9

(.9)	***Adherents of other religions**
(.91)	*Atheists and Deists

> Theosophists relocated to 922.99

(.94)	*Adherents of Indic religions
(.943)	*Buddhists
(.944)	*Jains
(.945)	*Hindus
(.946)	*Sikhs
(.95)	*Zoroastrians (Parsees)
(.96)	*Adherents of Judaism
(.97)	*Adherents of Islam
(.99)	*Others

> Example: Theosophists [*formerly* 922.91]

(923)   *Persons in social sciences

(.1)	***†Heads of state**

> Examples: kings, queens, presidents

(.2)	***†Persons in political science and politics**

> Examples: legislators, governors, politicians, statesmen, diplomats, nobility; political scientists
>
> *For heads of state, see 923.1*

(.3)	***Persons in economics**
(.31)	*†Labor leaders
(.33–.39)	*†Others
(.4)	***Criminals and persons in law**
(.41)	*†Criminals
(.43–.49)	*†Persons in law
(.5)	***†Public administrators and military persons**

> *For heads of state, see 923.1; governors, politicians, statesmen, 923.2*

(.6)	***†Philanthropists, humanitarians, social reformers**
(.7)	***†Educators**
(.8)	***†Persons in commerce, communication, transportation**
(.9)	***Explorers, geographers, pioneers, frontiersmen**

*(Optional number; prefer specific subject or discipline, as described under 920.1–928.9)
†Add as instructed under 920.1–928.9

(924)   ***Philologists and lexicographers**

> Add to base number 924 notation 1–9 from Table 6, e.g., lexicographers of Chinese 924.951

(925)   ***Scientists**

> Add to base number 925 the numbers following 5 in 510–590, e.g., botanists 925.8

(926)   ***Persons in technology**

> Add to base number 926 the numbers following 6 in 610–690, e.g., engineers 926.2
>
> *See also 920.4 for booksellers*

(927)   ***Persons in the arts and recreation**

> Add to base number 927 the numbers following 7 in 710–790, e.g., baseball players 927.96357
>
> *For persons in literature, see 928*

(928)   ***Persons in literature, history, biography, genealogy**

> Examples: historians, writers and critics of belles-lettres
>
> *See also 923.9 for explorers, geographers, pioneers, frontiersmen*

   (.1)   ***Americans**

   (.2–.9)   ***Others**

> Add to base number 928 notation 2–9 from Table 6 for language in which person has written, e.g., writers in Italian 928.51

929   **Genealogy, names, insignia**

   .1   **Genealogy**

> *For sources, see 929.3; family histories, 929.2*
>
> *See Manual at 929.1*

   [.102 8]   Auxiliary techniques and procedures; apparatus, equipment, materials

> Do not use; class genealogical techniques and procedures in 929.1072; equipment, apparatus, materials in 929.3

   .107 2   Research

> Class here the specific techniques and procedures involved in doing genealogical research in a specific area
>
> Class comprehensive works on genealogical research in 929.1

   [.109 4–.109 9]   Continents, countries, localities in modern world

> Do not use; class in 929.1072

*(Optional number; prefer specific subject or discipline, as described under 920.1–928.9)

.2   **Family histories**

(Option: Arrange alphabetically by name)

Class family histories emphasizing the contributions of the members of the family to a specific occupation with the occupation, e.g., the Rothschilds as a family of bankers 332.10922; family histories of a prominent person that emphasize the person's life with the biography number for the person, e.g., forebears, family, and life of Winston Churchill 941.082092

For royal houses, peerage, gentry, see 929.7

See Manual at 929.2; 929.2 vs. 929.7

.202 8   Auxiliary techniques and procedures; apparatus, equipment, materials

Class the techniques of compiling family histories in 929.1

.3   **Genealogical sources**

Examples: census records, court records, tax lists, wills

Use only for sources published by a genealogical organization or by a genealogist. Sources published by other agencies are classed with the subject of the publication, e.g., United States census records 317.3.

Standard subdivisions are added for miscellaneous collections and individual sources

Cemetery records relocated to 929.5

Class how to use sources in 929.1

For epitaphs, see 929.5

.309   Historical and geographical treatment

Class treatment by specific continents, countries, localities in 929.33–929.39 (*not* 929.3093–929.3099)

.33–.39   Treatment by specific continents, countries, localities

Regardless of form

Add to base number 929.3 notation 3–9 from Table 2, e.g., sources from New York 929.3747

.4   **Personal names**

See also 929.97 for names of houses, pets, ships

.42   Surnames

.44   Forenames

Class here lists of names for babies

.5   **Cemetery records [*formerly* 929.3]**

Regardless of form

Example: epitaphs

.6   **Heraldry**

Class here family coats of arms

Class comprehensive works on coats of arms in 929.82

> *For armorial bearings, see 929.82; royal houses, peerage, gentry, orders of knighthood, 929.7*

.7   **Royal houses, peerage, gentry, orders of knighthood**

Class here rank, precedence, titles of honor; genealogies tracing or establishing titles of honor; works emphasizing lineage or descent with respect to royalty, the peerage, or gentry; history and genealogy of royal families

Class histories of a royal family that include general historical events or biographies of members of the royal family in 930–990

> *See Manual at 929.2 vs. 929.7*

.709   Historical and geographical treatment

Class here countries outside Europe [*formerly* 929.7999]

Class historical and geographical treatment by specific countries of Europe in 929.72–929.79 (*not* 929.70941–929.70949)

.71   Orders of knighthood

Class Christian orders of knighthood in 255.791, Christian orders of knighthood in church history in 271.791

>   929.72–929.79 Treatment of royal houses, peerage, gentry by specific countries of Europe

Class comprehensive works in 929.7094

.72   Great Britain and Ireland

.73–.79   Other countries of Europe

Add to base number 929.7 the numbers following —4 in notation 43–49 from Table 2, e.g., royal houses of France 929.74

[.799 9]   Countries outside Europe

Relocated to 929.709

.8   **Awards, orders, decorations, armorial bearings, autographs**

.81   Awards, orders, decorations

> Standard subdivisions are added for awards, orders, or decorations considered alone

> Add to base number 929.81 notation 1–9 from Table 2, e.g., orders of Germany 929.8143

> Class awards, orders, decorations associated with a specific subject with the subject, using notation 079 from Table 1, e.g., American football awards 796.332079

> *For armorial bearings, see 929.82*

.82   Armorial bearings

> Contains coats of arms, crests, seals

> *For family coats of arms, see 929.6*

.88   Autographs

.9   **Forms of insignia and identification**

> Examples: motor vehicle registration plates, ownership and service marks, trademarks

> Class forms of insignia and identification not provided for here with the form, e.g., coats of arms 929.82; identification marks in a specific subject with the subject, using notation 027 from Table 1, e.g., airline insignia 387.70275

.92   Flags and banners

> Examples: national, state, provincial, ship, ownership flags and banners

> Class military use in 355.15

.97   Names

> Examples: names of houses, ships, pets

> *For place names, see 910.014; personal names, 929.4*

> ## 930–990 History of ancient world; of specific continents, countries, localities; of extraterrestrial worlds

Civilization and events

Class here interdisciplinary works on geography and history of ancient world, of specific continents, countries, localities

(Option: Class elementary history textbooks on ancient world, on specific continents, countries, localities in 372.893–372.899)

Add to base number 9 notation 3–9 from Table 2, e.g., general history of Europe 940, of England 942, of Norfolk, England 942.61; then add further as follows:

001–003	Standard subdivisions
004	Racial, ethnic, national groups
	(Option: Class in 909.04)
	Add to 004 notation 03–99 from Table 5, e.g., history and civilization of North American native peoples in New York 974.700497
	Class indigenous groups in the prehistoric period with the period, e.g., Inca empire before Spanish conquest 985.01; relation of racial, ethnic, national groups to a war with the war, e.g., relation of Jews to World War II 940.531503924
005–006	Standard subdivisions
007	Study and teaching
0072	Historical research
	Class here historiography
007202	Historians and historiographers
	Class historians and historiographers specializing in a specific historical period of a specific area with the historical period for the area studied, using notation 092 from Table 1; e.g., the biography of a Canadian historian who specializes in United States Revolutionary War 973.3092
008	History with respect to kinds of persons
[0089]	Racial, ethnic, national groups
	Do not use; class in 004
009	Areas, regions, places, persons
0091–0098	Areas, regions, places in general
	Add to 009 the numbers following —1 in notation 11–18 from Table 2, e.g., urban regions 009732

(continued)

> ## 930–990 History of ancient world; of specific continents, countries, localities; of extraterrestrial worlds (continued)

0099	Persons
	Description, critical appraisal, biography of persons associated with the history of the continent, country, locality but limited to no specific period
	Class persons of a specific period in 01–09, using notation 092 from Table 1; historians and historiographers in 007202
00992	Collected treatment
[00994]	Individual treatment
	Notation discontinued; class in 0099
01–09	Historical periods

Class here indigenous groups in the prehistoric period, e.g., Inca empire before Spanish conquest 985.01 (*not* 985.00498)

Add to 0 the period division numbers following 0 from the appropriate continent, country, locality in 930–990, e.g., period of 1760–1820 in British history 073 (from 941.073), period of 1815–1847 in German history 073 (from 943.073), period of 1815–1847 in Austrian history 042 (from 943.6042)

Unless other period notation is specified, add to each geographical subdivision of an area the period notation for the area as a whole, e.g., period of Ottoman Empire in Saudi Arabia 953.803 (based on period of Ottoman Empire in Arabian Peninsula 953.03)

Class areas, regions, places in general in a specific period in 0091–0098; racial, ethnic, national groups in a specific period in 004

See Manual at 930–990: Add table: 01–09

The schedules that follow do not enumerate all the countries and localities that appear in Table 2; however, the foregoing instructions apply to history of any place in notation 3–9 from Table 2

Class comprehensive works in 909; geography of ancient world, of specific continents, countries, localities in 913–919; sociology of war in 303.66, of military institutions in 306.27; social factors affecting war in 355.02, social causes of war in 355.0274

See Manual at 305 vs. 306, 909, 930–990; 320 vs. 909, 930–990; 355.009 vs. 930–990; 910 vs. 909, 930–990; 930–990

930   History of ancient world to ca. 499

SUMMARY

930.01–.09	**Standard subdivisions**
.1–.5	**[Archaeology and historical periods]**
931	**China to 420**
932	**Egypt to 640**
933	**Palestine to 70**
934	**India to 647**
935	**Mesopotamia and Iranian Plateau to 637**
936	**Europe north and west of Italian peninsula to ca. 499**
937	**Italian peninsula and adjacent territories to 476**
938	**Greece to 323**
939	**Other parts of ancient world to ca. 640**

.01–.09   Standard subdivisions

> As modified under 930–990; however, class archaeology in 930.1

.1   **Archaeology**

> Study of past civilizations through discovery, collection, interpretation of material remains
>
> Class here prehistoric archaeology; interdisciplinary works on archaeology
>
> Class archaeology of continents, countries, localities provided for in notation 3 from Table 2 in 931–939; archaeology of modern period, ancient and prehistoric archaeology of continents, countries, localities not provided for in notation 3 from Table 2 in 940–990; archaeology of specific oceans and seas in 909.0963–909.0967; industrial archaeology in 609
>
> *See also 700 for artistic aspects of archaeological objects*

.102   Miscellany

.102 8   Techniques, procedures, apparatus, equipment, materials

.102 804   Underwater archaeology

.102 82   Discovery of remains

.102 83   Excavation of remains

.102 85   Interpretation of remains

> Including dating techniques

>   930.11–930.16 Specific prehistoric ages
>
> Class comprehensive works in 930.1

.11   Eolithic Age

.12   Paleolithic (Old Stone) Age

> Class here comprehensive works on Stone Ages
>
> *For Mesolithic Age, see 930.13; Neolithic Age, 930.14*

.13   Mesolithic (Middle Stone) Age

.14	Neolithic (New Stone) Age
.15	Copper and Bronze Age
.16	Iron Age

.2–.5   **Historical periods**

Add to base number 930 the numbers following —0901 in notation 09012–09015 from Table 1, e.g., world history in 1st century A.D. 930.5; however, class specific archaeological ages in 930.11–930.16

> ## 931–939 Specific places

Class comprehensive works in 930; archaeology of modern period, ancient and prehistoric archaeology of continents, countries, localities not provided for in notation 3 from Table 2 in 940–990; archaeology of specific oceans and seas in 909.0963–909.0967

931   *China to 420

(Option: Class in 951.011–951.014)

.01	Earliest history to ca. 1523 B.C.
.02	Period of Shang (Yin) dynasty, ca. 1523–ca. 1028 B.C.
.03	Period of Chou dynasty and warring states, ca. 1028–222 B.C.
.04	Period of Ch'in to Chin (Tsin) dynasties, 221 B.C.–420 A.D.

932   *Egypt to 640

(Option: Class in 962.01)

.01	Earliest history to 332 B.C.
.011	Prehistoric period to ca. 3100 B.C.
.012	Protodynastic, Old Kingdom, first intermediate periods, ca. 3100–2052 B.C.
	Contains 1st-11th dynasties
.013	Middle Kingdom and second intermediate periods, 2052–1570 B.C.
	Contains 12th-17th dynasties
.014	Period of New Kingdom, 1570–1075 B.C.
	Contains 18th-20th dynasties
.015	Late and Saite periods, 1075–525 B.C.
	Contains 21st-26th dynasties
	Including period of sovereignty of Cush

*Add as instructed under 930–990

.016   Persian periods and last Egyptian kingdom, 525–332 B.C.

                  Contains 27th-31st dynasties

.02   Hellenistic, Roman, Byzantine periods, 332 B.C.–640 A.D.

.021   Hellenistic period, 332–30 B.C.

.022   Roman period, 30 B.C.–324 A.D.

.023   Byzantine (Coptic) period, 324–640

933   *Palestine to 70

                  (Option: Class in 956.9401, Jordan in 956.9501)

                  See also 220.93 for Biblical archaeology, 220.95 for history of Biblical events

.01   Earliest history to return of Jews from bondage in Egypt, ca. 1225 B.C.

.02   Great age of Twelve Tribes, ca. 1225–922 B.C.

                  Including rule of Judges, Saul, David, Solomon

.03   Periods of partition, conquest, foreign rule, 922–168 B.C.

                  Including periods of Assyrian, Babylonian, Persian, Hellenistic rule

.04   168–63 B.C.

                  Contains Hasmonean (Maccabean) period

.05   Period of Roman protectorate and rule to destruction of Jerusalem, 63 B.C.–70 A.D.

934   *India to 647

                  (Option: Class in 954.01)

.01   Pre-Aryan civilizations to ca. 1500 B.C.

.02   Indo-Aryan (Vedic) period, ca. 1500–ca. 600 B.C.

                  Including Iron Age culture in south India

.03   Ca. 600–ca. 322 B.C.

.04   Period of Mauryas, ca. 322–185 B.C.

.043   Ca. 322–ca. 274 B.C.

.045   Reign of Aśoka, ca. 274–ca. 237 B.C.

.047   Ca. 237–185 B.C.

.05   Period of changing dynasties, 185 B.C.–318 A.D.

.06   Period of Guptas, 318–500

.07   500–647

                  Including reign of Harsha, 606–647

*Add as instructed under 930–990

935   *Mesopotamia and Iranian Plateau to 637

(Option: Class Mesopotamia in 956.701, Iranian Plateau in 955.01)

.01   Elamite, Sumerian, Akkadian, Ur periods to ca. 1900 B.C.

.02   Period of Babylonian Empire and Kingdom of Mitanni, ca. 1900–ca. 900 B.C.

> Including reign of Hammurabi, ca. 1792–ca. 1750 B.C.

.03   Period of Assyrian Empire, ca. 900–625 B.C.

.04   Period of Median and Neo-Babylonian (Chaldean) Empires, 625–539 B.C.

> Including reign of Nebuchadnezzar II, 605–562 B.C.

.05   Period of Persian Empire, 539–332 B.C.

> *For Persian Wars, see 938.03*

.06   Hellenistic, Seleucid, Parthian periods, 332 B.C.–226 A.D.

.07   Period of Neo-Persian (Sassanian) Empire, 226–637

936   *Europe north and west of Italian Peninsula to ca. 499

Class here comprehensive works on ancient Europe

Class a specific part of ancient Europe not provided for here with the part, e.g., Italy 937, Russia 947.01

(Option: Class in 940.11)

.1   *British Isles to 410   Northern Britain and Ireland

(Option: Class British Isles in 941.012, northern Britain in 941.1012, Ireland in 941.5012)

Add to base number 936.1 the numbers following 936.2 in 936.201–936.204, e.g., Roman period 936.104

> *For southern Britain, see 936.2*

.2   *Southern Britain to 410   England

(Option: Class in 942.012)

.201   Earliest period to ca. 600 B.C.

.202   Celtic period, ca. 600–55 B.C.

.203   Period of early Roman contacts, 55 B.C.–43 A.D.

.204   Roman period, 43–410

.3   *Germanic regions to 481

(Option: Class general works in 943.012, Austria in 943.601, general works on Scandinavia in 948.012, Norway in 948.1012, Sweden in 948.5012, Denmark in 948.9012, Netherlands in 949.2012)

.301   Earliest period to 113 B.C.

*Add as instructed under 930–990

.302	Period of contacts with Roman Republic and Empire, 113 B.C.–481 A.D.

.4   ***Celtic regions to 486**

(Option: Class general works in 944.012, Belgium in 949.3012, Luxembourg in 949.3501, Switzerland in 949.4012)

For British Isles, see 936.1

.401	Earliest period to 125 B.C.
.402	Gallo-Roman period, 125 B.C.–486 A.D.

.6   ***Iberian Peninsula and adjacent islands to 415**

(Option: Class general works in 946.012, Portugal in 946.9012)

.601	Earliest period to ca. 1000 B.C.
.602	Period of Greek, Phoenician, and early Celtic and Germanic contacts, ca. 1000–218 B.C.
.603	Roman period, 218 B.C.–415 A.D.

937   *Italian Peninsula and adjacent territories to 476

(Option: Class in 945.012)

.01	Earliest period and Roman Kingdom to ca. 500 B.C.
.02	Period of Roman Republic, ca. 500–31 B.C.

For specific periods, see 937.03–937.05

>   937.03–937.05 Specific periods under the Republic

Class comprehensive works in 937.02

.03	Period of unification of Italy, ca. 500–264 B.C.
.04	Period of Punic Wars, 264–146 B.C.
.05	Period of civil strife, 146–31 B.C.
.06	Period of Roman Empire, 31 B.C.–476 A.D.

For specific periods, see 937.07–937.09

>   937.07–937.09 Specific periods under the Empire

Class comprehensive works in 937.06

.07	Early and middle periods, 31 B.C.–284 A.D.
.08	Period of absolutism, 284–395
.09	Final period, 395–476

*Add as instructed under 930–990

938   ***Greece to 323**

        (Option: Class in 949.5012)

.01   Earliest times to 775 B.C.

.02   775–500 B.C.

.03   Persian Wars, 500–479 B.C.

.04   Period of Athenian supremacy, 479–431 B.C.

.05   Period of Peloponnesian War, 431–404 B.C.

.06   Period of Spartan and Theban supremacy, 404–362 B.C.

.07   Period of Macedonian supremacy, 362–323 B.C.

.08   Hellenistic period, 323–146 B.C.

.09   Roman era, 146 B.C.–323 A.D.

.1   ***Macedonia to 323**

        (Option: Class comprehensive works in 949.56012, Albania in 949.65012)

939   ***Other parts of ancient world to ca. 640**

.1   ***Aegean Islands to 323**

        (Option: Class in 949.9012)

        Add to base number 939.1 the numbers following 938 in 938.01–938.09, e.g., Hellenistic period 939.108

.18   *Crete to 323

        (Option: Class in 949.98012)

.2   ***Western Asia Minor to ca. 640**

        Class here comprehensive works on Asia Minor

        (Option: Class in 956.1012)

        For eastern Asia Minor, see 939.3

.3   ***Eastern Asia Minor and Cyprus to ca. 640**

        (Option: Class in 956.1012)

.37   *Cyprus to ca. 640

        (Option: Class in 956.45012)

.4   ***Middle East to ca. 640**

        (Option: Class Middle East in 956.012)

        Class a specific part of Middle East not provided for here with the part, e.g., Egypt 932, Palestine 933

.43   *Syria

        Including Antioch

        (Option: Class Antioch in 956.4, Syria in 956.9101)

*Add as instructed under 930–990

.44   *Phoenicia to ca. 640

         (Option: Class in 956.9202)

.46   *Edom and Moab to 70

         (Option: Class Edom in 956.94901; Moab in 956.95601)

.47   *Arabia Deserta to 637

         (Option: Class in 956.701)

.48   *Arabia Petraea to 622

         Including Sinai Peninsula; Petra

         (Option: Class Arabia Petraea in 953.01; Sinai Peninsula in 953.101; Petra in 956.95701)

.49   *Arabia Felix to 622

         Class here comprehensive works on Arabia

         (Option: Class Arabia Felix, Arabia in 953.01)

         For Arabia Deserta, see 939.47; Arabia Petraea, 939.48

.6   ***Central Asia to ca. 640**

         Including earliest history of Afghanistan to ca. 640 [*formerly also* 958.101]

         (Option: Class in 958)

.7   ***North Africa to ca. 640**

         (Option: Class in 961.01)

         For Egypt, see 932

.71   *Mauretania to 647

         (Option: Class in 965.01, Morocco in 964.01)

.72   *Numidia to 647

         (Option: Class in 965.501)

.73   *Carthage to 647

         (Option: Class in 961.101)

.74   *Tripolis to 644

         Class here comprehensive works on ancient Libya

         (Option: Class in 961.201)

         For Cyrenaica, see 939.75; Marmarica, 939.76

*Add as instructed under 930–990

.75	*Cyrenaica to 644
	(Option: Class in 961.201)
.76	*Marmarica to 644
	(Option: Class in 961.201)
.77	*Gaetulia to 647
	(Option: Class in 965.701)
.78	*Ethiopia to 500
	(Option: Class in 962.501)

.8   ***Southeastern Europe to ca. 640**

(Option: Class Hungary in 943.9011, Turkey in Europe in 949.61012, Yugoslavia in 949.7012, Serbia in 949.71011, Bulgaria in 949.77012, Romania in 949.8012)

> ## 940–990 General history of modern world, of extraterrestrial worlds

Class here area studies; comprehensive works on ancient and modern history of specific continents, countries, localities

Class comprehensive works in 909

For general history of ancient world, see 930

940   General history of Europe   Western Europe

SUMMARY

940.01–.09	Standard subdivisions
.1	Early history to 1453
.2	1453–
.3	World War I, 1914–1918
.4	Military history of World War I
.5	1918–

941	British Isles
.01–.08	[Historical periods of British Isles]
.1	Scotland
.2	Northeastern Scotland
.3	Southeastern Scotland
.4	Southwestern Scotland
.5	Ireland
.6	Ulster Northern Ireland
.7	Republic of Ireland
.8	Leinster
.9	Munster

| 942 | England and Wales |
| .01–.08 | [Historical periods of England and Wales] |

*Add as instructed under 930–990

943　　　Central Europe　　Germany
　.000 1–.000 9　　　Standard subdivisions of central Europe
　.001–.009　　　Standard subdivisions of Germany
　.01–.08　　　Historical periods of Germany
　.1　　　　Northeastern Germany
　.6　　　　Austria and Liechtenstein
　.7　　　　Czechoslovakia
　.8　　　　Poland
　.9　　　　Hungary

944　　　France and Monaco
　.01–.08　　　Historical periods of France
　.9　　　　Southeastern France and Monaco　　Provence region

945　　　Italian Peninsula and adjacent islands　　Italy
　.01–.09　　　Historical periods of Italy
　.4　　　　Emilia-Romagna region and San Marino
　.6　　　　Central Italy and Vatican City
　.8　　　　Sicily and adjacent islands

946　　　Iberian Peninsula and adjacent islands　　Spain
　.000 1–.000 9　　　Standard subdivisions of Iberian Peninsula and adjacent islands
　.001–.009　　　Standard subdivisions of Spain
　.01–.08　　　Historical periods of Spain
　.7　　　　Eastern Spain and Andorra
　.8　　　　Andalusia autonomous community and Gibraltar
　.9　　　　Portugal

947　　　Eastern Europe　　Union of Soviet Socialist Republics (Soviet Union)
　.000 1–.000 9　　　Standard subdivisions of eastern Europe
　.001–.009　　　Standard subdivisions of Russia
　.01–.08　　　Historical periods of Russia

948　　　Northern Europe　　Scandinavia
　.01–.08　　　Historical periods of Scandinavia
　.1　　　　Norway
　.2　　　　Southeastern Norway
　.3　　　　Southwestern Norway
　.4　　　　Central and northern Norway
　.5　　　　Sweden
　.6　　　　Southern Sweden
　.7　　　　Central Sweden
　.8　　　　Northern Sweden
　.9　　　　Denmark and Finland

949　　　Other parts of Europe
　.1　　　　Northwestern islands
　.2　　　　Netherlands (Holland)
　.3　　　　Southern Low Countries　　Belgium
　.4　　　　Switzerland
　.5　　　　Greece
　.6　　　　Balkan Peninsula
　.7　　　　Yugoslavia and Bulgaria
　.8　　　　Romania
　.9　　　　Aegean Sea islands

.01–.09　　　Standard subdivisions

　　　As modified under 930–990

.1	**Early history to 1453**
	Class here Middle Ages, 476–1453
	Class ancient history to ca. 499 in 936
(.11)	Ancient history to ca. 499
	(Optional number; prefer 936)
.12	Ca. 500–799
	Class here Dark Ages
.14	Age of feudalism, 800–1099
.142	800–899
.144	900–999
.146	1000–1099
	For period of First Crusade, see 940.18
.17	1100–1453
	For period of Crusades, 1100–1299, see 940.18; 1300–1453, 940.19
.18	Period of Crusades, 1100–1299
	Including First Crusade, 1096–1099
	Class comprehensive works on Crusades in 909.07
.182	1100–1199
.184	1200–1299
.19	1300–1453
.192	1300–1399
	Including period of Black Death
.193	1400–1453
.2	**1453–**
	For World War I, see 940.3; 1918– , 940.5
.21	Renaissance period, 1453–1517
	Class here 15th century
	For 1400–1453, see 940.193
	See also 945.05 for Renaissance period in Italy
.22	1517–1789
	For Reformation period, 1517–1648, see 940.23; 1648–1789, 940.25
.23	Reformation period, 1517–1648
	For Thirty Years' War, see 940.24
.232	1517–1618

.24	Thirty Years' War, 1618–1648
.25	1648–1789
.252	1648–1715

Class here 17th century

Class 1600–1648 in 940.23

.252 5	1688–1701

Class here War of the League of Augsburg (War of the Grand Alliance), 1688–1697

Class North American aspects of the war in 973.25

.252 6	War of the Spanish Succession, 1701–1714

Class North American aspects of the war in 973.25

.253	1715–1789
.253 2	War of the Austrian Succession, 1740–1748

Class North American aspects of the war in 973.26

.253 4	Seven Years' War, 1756–1763

Class North American aspects of the war in 973.26

.27	Period of French Revolution and Napoleon I, 1789–1815

Class here Napoleonic Wars in specific European countries, e.g., war in Spain, 1807–1814

.28	1815–1914

Class here comprehensive works on 19th-20th centuries

Class comprehensive works on 20th century in 940.5

.282	1815–1829
.283	1830–1848
.284	Revolutions of 1848
.285	1848–1859
.286	1860–1869
.287	1870–1899
.288	1900–1914

.3   **World War I, 1914–1918**

> *For military history, see 940.4*

[.308]   World War I with respect to kinds of persons

> Do not use; class in 940.315

.31   Social, political, economic history

> Add to base number 940.31 the numbers following 940.531 in 940.5311–940.5317, e.g., internment camps 940.317 [*formerly* 940.472]
>
> *For diplomatic history, see 940.32*

.32   Diplomatic history

> Class diplomatic causes in 940.3112, efforts to preserve or restore peace in 940.312, diplomatic results in 940.314

.322   Allies and associated powers

> Add to base number 940.322 notation 4–9 from Table 2, e.g., diplomatic history of Great Britain 940.32241

.324   Central Powers

> Add to base number 940.324 notation 4–9 from Table 2, e.g., diplomatic history of Germany 940.32443

.325   Neutrals

> Add to base number 940.325 notation 4–9 from Table 2, e.g., diplomatic history of Switzerland 940.325494

.33   Participation of specific groups of countries

> Class a specific activity with the activity, e.g., diplomatic history among neutrals 940.325
>
> *For participation of specific countries and localities, see 940.34–940.39*

.332   Allies and associated powers

.334   Central Powers

.335   Neutrals

.34–.39   Participation of specific countries and localities

> Class here mobilization in specific countries and localities
>
> Add to base number 940.3 notation 4–9 from Table 2, e.g., participation of Great Britain 940.341
>
> Class a specific activity with the activity, e.g., efforts by a specific country to preserve or restore peace 940.312

.4   Military history of World War I

SUMMARY

940.400 1–.400 9	**Standard subdivisions**	
.401–.409	**[General aspects]**	
.41	**Operations and units**	
.42	**Land campaigns and battles of 1914–1916**	
.43	**Land campaigns and battles of 1917–1918**	
.44	**Air operations**	
.45	**Naval operations**	
.46–.48	**Celebrations, commemorations, memorials; prisoner-of-war camps;**	
	health and social services; other topics	

.400 1–.400 8   Standard subdivisions

.400 9   Historical, geographical, persons treatment

> Class military participation of specific countries in 940.409, personal narratives in 940.481–940.482

.401   Strategy

.401 2   Allies and associated powers

.401 3   Central Powers

.402   Mobilization

> *For mobilization in specific countries and localities, see 940.34–940.39*

.403   Racial minorities as troops

.405   Repressive measures and atrocities

> Class internment camps in 940.317

.409   Military participation of specific countries

> Add to base number 940.409 notation 4–9 from Table 2, e.g., military participation of Germany 940.40943

.41   Operations and units

> Class land campaigns and battles by year in 940.42–940.43
>
> *For air operations, see 940.44; naval operations, 940.45*

>   940.412–940.413 Military units and their operations

> Class here organization, history, rosters, service records
>
> Class comprehensive works in 940.41; units engaged in a special service with the service, e.g., ambulance companies 940.4753; operations in specific theaters in 940.414–940.416
>
> *For rolls of honor and lists of dead, see 940.467*

.412   Military units of Allies and associated powers

> Add to base number 940.412 notation 4–9 from Table 2, e.g., French units 940.41244

.413	Military units of Central Powers

> Add to base number 940.413 notation 4–9 from Table 2, e.g., Austrian units 940.413436

.414	Operations in Europe
.414 3	German fronts
.414 4	French front

> Class here western front
>
> Class German western front in 940.4143

.414 5	Italian front
.414 7	Russian front

> Class here eastern front
>
> Class German eastern front in 940.4143

.415	Operations in Asia
.416	Operations in Africa
.42	Land campaigns and battles of 1914–1916
.421	1914, western front
.422	1914, eastern front
.423	1914, other areas
.424	1915, western and Austro-Italian fronts
.425	1915, eastern Europe
.426	1915, other areas
.427	1916, European fronts
.427 2	Western and Austro-Italian fronts
.427 5	Eastern front
.429	1916, other areas
.429 1	Asia Minor
.43	Land campaigns and battles of 1917–1918
.431	1917, western and Austro-Italian fronts
.432	1917, eastern front
.433	1917, other areas
.434	1918, western and Austro-Italian fronts

> Including final German offensives
>
> Class final allied offensives in 940.435–940.436

.435	Allied offensives of July 18–September 24, 1918
.436	Allied offensives of September 25–November 11, 1918
.437	1918, eastern front
.438	1918, other areas
.439	Armistice, November 11, 1918
.44	Air operations

Including antiaircraft defenses

Class here combined air and naval operations

For naval operations, see 940.45

[.441]	Activities

Number discontinued; class in 940.44

.442	Air raids

Class specific events by year in 940.444–940.448

.443	Air bases

>   940.444–940.448 Events by year

Class comprehensive works in 940.44

.444	Events of 1914
.445	Events of 1915
.446	Events of 1916
.447	Events of 1917
.448	Events of 1918
.449	Operations of specific countries

Class here aircraft, fliers, units

Add to base number 940.449 notation 4–9 from Table 2, e.g., air operations of Germany 940.44943

Class events by year regardless of country in 940.444–940.448

.45	Naval operations
.451	Submarine warfare
.451 2	German use

Class events by year in 940.4514

.451 3	Allied use

> Add to base number 940.4513 notation 4–9 from Table 2, e.g., United States use of submarines 940.451373
>
> Class events by year in 940.4514

.451 4	Specific events
.451 6	Antisubmarine warfare

> Class events by year in 940.4514

.452	Blockades and blockade running

> *For events by year, see 940.454–940.458*

.453	Naval bases

> **940.454–940.458 Events by year**

> Class comprehensive works in 940.45, events in submarine warfare by year in 940.4514

.454	Events of 1914
.455	Events of 1915
.456	Events of 1916
.457	Events of 1917
.458	Events of 1918
.459	Naval operations of specific countries

> Class here ships, crews, units
>
> Add to base number 940.459 notation 4–9 from Table 2, e.g., naval operations of Italy 940.45945
>
> Class events by year regardless of country in 940.454–940.458

.46–.48	Celebrations, commemorations, memorials; prisoner-of-war camps; health and social services; other topics

> Add to base number 940.4 the numbers following 940.54 in 940.546–940.548, e.g., prisoner-of-war camps 940.472; however, internment camps relocated from 940.472 to 940.317

.5	**1918–**

SUMMARY

940.51	**1918–1929**
.52	**1930–1939**
.53	**World War II, 1939–1945**
.54	**Military history of World War II**
.55	**1945–**

.51	1918–1929

.52	1930–1939
	Class Holocaust in 940.5318
.53	World War II, 1939–1945
	Class here Sino-Japanese Conflict, 1937–1945
	Class Sino-Japanese Conflict during 1937–1941 in 951.042
	For military history, see 940.54
[.530 8]	World War II with respect to kinds of persons
	Do not use; class in 940.5315
.530 92	Persons
	Class personal narratives in 940.5481–940.5482
.531	Social, political, economic history
	For diplomatic history, see 940.532
.531 1	Causes
.531 12	Political and diplomatic
.531 13	Economic
.531 14	Social and psychological
.531 2	Efforts to preserve or restore peace
.531 4	Political, diplomatic, economic results
	Class results in and effects on a specific country with history of the country, e.g., on Norway 948.1045
.531 41	Conferences and treaties
	For consequences of conferences and treaties, see 940.53142
.531 42	Consequences of conferences and treaties
.531 422	Reparations
.531 424	Territorial questions
.531 425	Establishment of new nations
.531 426	Establishment of mandates
.531 44	Reconstruction
.531 5	Relation of kinds of persons to the war
	Class kinds of persons in relation to a specific aspect of the war and related events with the aspect or event, e.g., Jews and the Holocaust 940.5318
.531 503–.531 587	Classes by various characteristics
	Add to base number 940.5315 notation 03–87 from Table 7, e.g., scientists 940.53155; however, class refugees in 940.53159; children and other noncombatants, pacifists, enemy sympathizers in 940.5316

.531 59	Refugees
.531 6	Noncombatants, pacifists, enemy sympathizers
.531 61	Noncombatants
	Example: children
.531 62	Pacifists
.531 63	Enemy sympathizers
.531 7	Concentration and related camps

Examples: internment camps [*formerly* 940.5472], labor camps

Class the camps as a part of the Holocaust in 940.5318, prisoner-of-war camps in 940.5472

.531 709   Historical, geographical, persons treatment

Use area notation to indicate country maintaining the camps, e.g., internment camps maintained by the United States 940.53170973

Class camps by location in 940.53174–940.53179

.531 74–.531 79   Camps by location

Regardless of kind of camp

Add to base number 940.5317 notation 4–9 from Table 2, e.g., Manzanar internment camp for Japanese-Americans 940.531779487

Class extermination camps in 940.5318

.531 8	Holocaust

.532   Diplomatic history

Class diplomatic causes in 940.53112, efforts to preserve or restore peace in 940.5312, diplomatic results in 940.5314

.532 2   United Nations (Allies)

Add to base number 940.5322 notation 4–9 from Table 2, e.g., diplomatic history of Great Britain 940.532241

.532 4   Axis Powers

Add to base number 940.5324 notation 4–9 from Table 2, e.g., diplomatic history of Japan 940.532452

.532 5   Neutrals

Add to base number 940.5325 notation 4–9 from Table 2, e.g., diplomatic history of Switzerland 940.5325494

.533	Participation of specific groups of countries

Class here national groups, anti- and pro-Axis national groups, mobilization

Class a specific activity with the activity, e.g., diplomatic history among Axis Powers 940.5324

For participation of specific countries, see 940.534–940.539

.533 2	United Nations (Allies)
.533 4	Axis Powers
.533 5	Neutrals
.533 6	Occupied countries

Class here governments-in-exile, underground movements

For countries occupied by Axis Powers, see 940.5337; by United Nations (Allies) 940.5338

.533 7	Countries occupied by Axis Powers
.533 8	Countries occupied by United Nations (Allies)
.534–.539	Participation of specific countries

Class here mobilization in specific countries

Add to base number 940.53 notation 4–9 from Table 2, e.g., participation of Great Britain 940.5341

Class a specific activity with the activity, e.g., efforts by a specific country to preserve or restore peace 940.5312

.54	Military history of World War II

SUMMARY

940.540 01–.540 09	Standard subdivisions
.540 1–.540 9	[General aspects]
.541	Operations and units
.542	Campaigns and battles by theater
.544	Air operations
.545	Naval operations
.546	Celebrations, commemorations, memorials
.547	Prisoner-of-war camps; medical and social services
.548	Other topics

.540 01–.540 08	Standard subdivisions
.540 09	Historical, geographical, persons treatment

Class military participation of specific countries in 940.5409, personal narratives in 940.5481–940.5482

.540 1	Strategy
.540 12	United Nations (Allies)
.540 13	Axis Powers

.540 2	Mobilization
	For mobilization in specific countries, see 940.534–940.539
.540 3	Afro-Americans and American native peoples as troops
.540 4	Racial minorities as troops
	For Afro-Americans and American native peoples as troops, see 940.5403
.540 5	Repressive measures and atrocities
	Class concentration and related camps in 940.5317, Holocaust in 940.5318
.540 9	Military participation of specific countries
	Add to base number 940.5409 notation 4–9 from Table 2, e.g., military participation of Germany 940.540943
.541	Operations and units
	For campaigns and battles by theater, see 940.542; air operations, 940.544; naval operations, 940.545

> 940.541 2–940.541 3 Military units and their operations

Class here organization, history, rosters, service records

Class comprehensive works in 940.541; units engaged in a special service with the service, e.g., ambulance companies 940.54753

For rolls of honor and lists of dead, see 940.5467

.541 2	Military units of United Nations (Allies)
	Add to base number 940.5412 notation 4–9 from Table 2, e.g., French units 940.541244
.541 3	Military units of Axis Powers
	Add to base number 940.5413 notation 4–9 from Table 2, e.g., Japanese units 940.541352
.542	Campaigns and battles by theater
.542 1	In European theater
	Add to base number 940.5421 the numbers following —4 in —41–49 from Table 2, e.g., battles in France 940.542144
.542 3	In Middle East and African theaters
.542 5	In east and southeast Asian and East Indian theaters
	Examples: theaters covering Asian mainland, Japan, Netherlands East Indies, Philippines
	Class Sino-Japanese Conflict during 1937–1941 in 951.042

.542 6	In Pacific Ocean theater

Examples: theaters covering Hawaiian Islands, South Pacific Ocean islands

For East Indian theater, see 940.5425

See also 940.5425 for Japan and Philippines

.542 8	In American theater
.542 9	In other areas
.544	Air operations

Including antiaircraft defenses

Class here combined air and naval operations

For naval operations, see 940.545

[.544 1]	Activities

Number discontinued; class in 940.544

.544 2	Campaigns and battles

For campaigns and battles by theater, see 940.542

.544 3	Air bases

Add to base number 940.5443 notation 4–9 from Table 2, e.g., air bases in England 940.544342

.544 9	Operations of specific countries

Class here aircraft, fliers, units

Add to base number 940.5449 notation 4–9 from Table 2, e.g., operations of Germany 940.544943

Class campaigns and battles of specific countries in 940.5442

.545	Naval operations

For campaigns and battles by theater, see 940.542

.545 1	Submarine warfare
.545 16	Antisubmarine warfare
.545 2	Blockades and blockade running
.545 3	Naval bases
.545 9	Operations of specific countries

Class here ships, crews, units

Add to base number 940.5459 notation 4–9 from Table 2, e.g., Australian naval operations 940.545994

Class a specific kind of operation with the operation, e.g., blockades 940.5452

.546	Celebrations, commemorations, memorials

Including commemorative meetings, flag presentations, decorations and awards

Class celebrations, commemorations, memorials of a specific event with the event, e.g., Battle of the Coral Sea 940.5426

.546 5	Monuments and cemeteries

Add to base number 940.5465 notation 4–9 from Table 2, e.g., monuments and cemeteries in France 940.546544

.546 7	Rolls of honor and lists of dead

Add to base number 940.5467 notation 4–9 from Table 2, e.g., lists of Japanese dead 940.546752

.547	Prisoner-of-war camps; medical and social services
.547 2	Prisoner-of-war camps

Add to base number 940.5472 notation 4–9 from Table 2, e.g., prisoner-of-war camps maintained by Germany 940.547243

Internment camps relocated to 940.5317

.547 3	Prisoners exchange
.547 5	Medical services

For hospitals, see 940.5476

.547 52	Sanitary affairs
.547 53	Ambulance services
.547 54–.547 59	Services of specific countries

Add to base number 940.5475 notation 4–9 from Table 2, e.g., French medical services 940.547544

.547 6	Hospitals
.547 609	Historical and persons treatment

Class hospitals in specific places in 940.54763

.547 63	In specific places

Add to base number 940.54763 notation 4–9 from Table 2, e.g., hospitals in Rome 940.5476345632

Class hospitals maintained in specific places by specific countries in 940.54764–940.54769

.547 64–.547 69	Maintained by specific countries

Add to base number 940.5476 notation 4–9 from Table 2, e.g., hospitals maintained by Italy 940.547645

.547 7	Relief and welfare services
.547 709	Historical and persons treatment

Class activities in specific places in 940.54779

.547 71	Activities of Red Cross
.547 78	Activities conducted by specific countries

Add to base number 940.54778 notation 4–9 from Table 2, e.g., activities conducted by Switzerland 940.54778494

Class Red Cross activities conducted by specific countries in 940.54771

.547 79   Activities in specific places

Add to base number 940.54779 notation 4–9 from Table 2, e.g., welfare activities in Paris 940.5477944361

Class welfare activities conducted in specific places by specific countries in 940.54778, activities of Red Cross in specific places in 940.54771

.547 8	Religious life and chaplain services
.548	Other topics

>   940.548 1–940.548 2 Personal narratives

Class comprehensive works in 940.548, personal narratives on a specific subject with the subject, using notation 092 from Table 1, e.g., on blockade running 940.5452092

.548 1   Personal narratives of individuals from United Nations (Allies)

Add to base number 940.5481 notation 4–9 from Table 2, e.g., personal narratives of Britons 940.548141

.548 2   Personal narratives of individuals from Axis Powers

Add to base number 940.5482 notation 4–9 from Table 2, e.g., personal narratives of Germans 940.548243

.548 3   Military life and customs of United Nations (Allies)

Add to base number 940.5483 notation 4–9 from Table 2, e.g., military life in United States Navy 940.548373

.548 4   Military life and customs of Axis Powers

Add to base number 940.5484 notation 4–9 from Table 2, e.g., military life in Luftwaffe 940.548443

.548 5   Unconventional warfare

Examples: infiltration, intelligence, sabotage, subversion

For unconventional warfare of United Nations, see 940.5486; of Axis Powers, 940.5487; propaganda, 940.5488

.548 6   Unconventional warfare of United Nations (Allies)

Add to base number 940.5486 notation 4–9 from Table 2, e.g., intelligence operation of United States 940.548673

.548 7		Unconventional warfare of Axis Powers

Add to base number 940.5487 notation 4–9 from Table 2, e.g., intelligence operations of Germany 940.548743

.548 8   Propaganda

.548 809   Historical and persons treatment

Class propaganda in specific places in 940.54889

.548 86   By United Nations (Allies)

Add to base number 940.54886 notation 4–9 from Table 2, e.g., propaganda by United States 940.5488673

.548 87   By Axis Powers

Add to base number 940.54887 notation 4–9 from Table 2, e.g., propaganda by Germany 940.5488743

.548 89   Propaganda in specific places

Add to base number 940.54889 notation 4–9 from Table 2, e.g., propaganda in United States 940.5488973

Class propaganda by one side or one country regardless of location in 940.54886–940.54887

.55   1945–

.554   1945–1949

.555   1950–1959

.556   1960–1969

.557   1970–1979

.558   1980–1989

.559   1990–1999

941   *British Isles

Class here Great Britain, United Kingdom

See Manual at 941

SUMMARY

941.01–.08	[Historical periods of British Isles]
.1	Scotland
.2	Northeastern Scotland
.3	Southeastern Scotland
.4	Southwestern Scotland
.5	Ireland
.6	Ulster Northern Ireland
.7	Republic of Ireland
.8	Leinster
.9	Munster

*Add as instructed under 930–990

SUMMARY

941.01	**Early history to 1066**
.02–.05	**From Norman period through Tudor period, 1066–1603**
.06	**Stuart and Commonwealth periods, 1603–1714**
.07	**Period of House of Hanover, 1714–1837**
.08	**Period of Victoria and House of Windsor, 1837–**

.01   Early history to 1066

Class ancient history to 410 in 936.1

(.012)   Ancient history to 410

(Optional number; prefer 936.1)

Add to base number 941.012 the numbers following 936.20 in 936.201–936.204, e.g., 4th century 941.0124

.013–.019   From pre-Anglo-Saxon period through reign of Saxon kings, 410–1066

Add to base number 941.01 the numbers following 942.01 in 942.013–942.019, e.g., period of Danish kings 941.018

.02–.05   From Norman period through Tudor period, 1066–1603

Add to base number 941.0 the numbers following 942.0 in 942.02–942.05, e.g., reign of Henry VIII 941.052

.06   Stuart and Commonwealth periods, 1603–1714

(Option: Class here Anglo-Dutch Wars; prefer 949.204)

.061   Reign of James I, 1603–1625

.062   Reign of Charles I, 1625–1649

.063   Period as Commonwealth, 1649–1660

For Oliver Cromwell, see 941.064; Richard Cromwell, 941.065

.064   Protectorate of Oliver Cromwell, 1653–1658

.065   Protectorate of Richard Cromwell, 1658–1659

.066   Reign of Charles II, 1660–1685 (Restoration)

.067   1685–1689

Class here reign of James II, 1685–1688

.068   Reigns of William III (of Orange) and Mary II, 1689–1702

.069   Reign of Anne, 1702–1714

.07   Period of House of Hanover, 1714–1837

.071   Reign of George I, 1714–1727

.072   Reign of George II, 1727–1760

(Option: Class here War of Jenkins' Ear; prefer 946.055)

.073	Reign of George III, 1760–1820
	Including formation of United Kingdom
.074	Reign of George IV, 1820–1830
.075	Reign of William IV, 1830–1837
.08	Period of Victoria and House of Windsor, 1837–
.081	Reign of Victoria, 1837–1901

Class here 19th century

(Option: Class here Crimean War, South African [Second Anglo-Boer] War; prefer 947.073 for Crimean War, 968.048 for South African [Second Anglo-Boer] War)

Class 1800–1820 in 941.073, 1820–1830 in 941.074, 1830–1837 in 941.075

.082	1901–

For reign of George V, see 941.083; period of World War II, 941.084; 1945–   , 941.085

.082 3	Reign of Edward VII, 1901–1910
.083	Reign of George V, 1910–1936
.084	1936–1945

Class here reigns of Edward VIII, 1936, and George VI, 1936–1952; period of World War II, 1939–1945

Class reign of George VI during 1945–1949 in 941.0854, during 1950–1952 in 941.0855

.085	1945–

Class here reign of Elizabeth II, 1952–

.085 4	1945–1949
.085 5	1950–1959
.085 6	1960–1969
.085 7	1970–1979
.085 8	1980–1989
.085 9	1990–
.1	***Scotland**

For northeastern Scotland, see 941.2; southeastern Scotland, 941.3; southwestern Scotland, 941.4

.101	Early history to 1057

Class ancient history to 410 in 936.1

*Add as instructed under 930–990

(.101 2)	Ancient history of northern Britain to 410
	(Optional number; prefer 936.1)
.102	1057–1314
	Including Battle of Bannockburn, 1314
.103	1314–1424
.104	Reigns of James I-James V, 1424–1542
.105	Reformation period, 1542–1603
	Class here 16th century
	Class 1500–1542 in 941.104
.106–.108	From personal union with England to present time, 1603–
	Add to base number 941.10 the numbers following 941.0 in 941.06–941.08, e.g., reign of Edward VII 941.10823

.2 *Northeastern Scotland

Add to base number 941.2 the numbers following 941.1 in 941.101–941.108, e.g., Reformation period 941.205

.3 *Southeastern Scotland

Add to base number 941.3 the numbers following 941.1 in 941.101–941.108, e.g., Reformation period 941.305

.4 *Southwestern Scotland

Add to base number 941.4 the numbers following 941.1 in 941.101–941.108, e.g., Reformation period 941.405

.5 *Ireland

.501	Early history to 1086
	Including Battle of Clontarf, 1014
	Class ancient history to 410 in 936.1
(.501 2)	Ancient history to 410
	(Optional number; prefer 936.1)
.502	1086–1171
.503	Under House of Plantagenet, 1171–1399
.504	Under Houses of Lancaster and York, 1399–1485
.505	Under Tudors, 1485–1603
.506	Under Stuarts, 1603–1691
.507	1691–1799

*Add as instructed under 930–990

.508	1800–
.508 1	1800–1899
.508 2	1900–
.508 21	1900–1921

         Including Sinn Fein Rebellion (Easter Rebellion), 1916; Anglo-Irish War, 1919–1921

.508 22	1921–1949
.508 23	1950–1969
.508 24	1970–

.6   *Ulster   Northern Ireland

.608	1800–
.608 1	1800–1899
.608 2	1900–
.608 21	1900–1920

         Including Government of Ireland Act, 1920

.608 22	1921–1949
.608 23	1949–1968
.608 24	1969–

.7   *Republic of Ireland

For Leinster, see 941.8; Munster, 941.9

.708	1800–
.708 1	1800–1899
.708 2	1900–
.708 21	1900–1921
.708 22	1922–1949

         Including period as Irish Free State, 1922–1937; as Eire, 1937–1949

.708 23	1949–1969
.708 24	1970–

.8   *Leinster

.808	1800–

         Add to base number 941.808 the numbers following 941.708 in 941.7081–941.7082, e.g., 1949–1969 941.80823

*Add as instructed under 930–990

.9   *Munster

.908   1800–

>   Add to base number 941.908 the numbers following 941.708 in
>   941.7081–941.7082, e.g., 1949–1969 941.90823

942   *England and Wales

See Manual at 941

SUMMARY

942.01	Early history to 1066
.02	Norman period, 1066–1154
.03	Period of House of Plantagenet, 1154–1399
.04	Period of Houses of Lancaster and York, 1399–1485
.05	Tudor period, 1485–1603
.06–.08	From Stuart and Commonwealth periods to present time, 1603–

.01   Early history to 1066

>   Class ancient history to 410 in 936.2

(.012)   Ancient history of southern Britain to 410

>   (Optional number; prefer 936.2)

>   Add to base number 942.012 the numbers following 936.20 in
>   936.201–936.204, e.g., Celtic period 942.0122

.013   Pre-Anglo-Saxon period, 410–449

.014   449–ca. 600

>   Including reign of King Arthur

.015   Period of Heptarchy, ca. 600–829

>   Class supremacy of Wessex in 942.016

.015 3   Supremacy of Northumberland, 603–685

.015 7   Supremacy of Mercia, 757–796

.016   Supremacy of Wessex, 829–924

>   Class here 9th century

>   Class 800–829 in 942.015

.016 1   Reign of Egbert, 829–839

.016 2   Reign of Ethelwulf, 839–858

.016 3   Reigns of Ethelbald, Ethelbert, Ethelred I, 858–871

.016 4   Reign of Alfred the Great, 871–899

.016 5   Reign of Edward the Elder, 899–924

.017   Reigns of Saxon kings of England, 924–1016

.017 1   Reign of Athelstan, 924–940

*Add as instructed under 930–990

.017 2	Reigns of Edmund I, Edred, Edwy, 940–959
.017 3	Reigns of Edgar and Edward the Martyr, 959–978
.017 4	Reigns of Ethelred II and Edmund II, 978–1016
.018	**Reigns of Danish kings, 1016–1042**

Class here 11th century

Class 1000–1016 in 942.0174, 1042–1066 in 942.019, 1066–1099 in 942.02

.018 1	Reign of Canute, 1016–1035
.018 2	Reign of Harold I, 1035–1040
.018 3	Reign of Hardecanute, 1040–1042
.019	**1042–1066**

Contains reigns of Edward the Confessor, 1042–1066, and Harold II, 1066

.02	**Norman period, 1066–1154**

Class here 12th century

Class 1154–1199 in 942.03

.021	**Reign of William I, 1066–1087**

Including Battle of Hastings, 1066

.022	**Reign of William II, 1087–1100**
.023	**Reign of Henry I, 1100–1135**
.024	**Reign of Stephen, 1135–1154**
.03	**Period of House of Plantagenet, 1154–1399**
.031	**Reign of Henry II, 1154–1189**
.032	**Reign of Richard I, 1189–1199**
.033	**Reign of John, 1199–1216**
.034	**Reign of Henry III, 1216–1272**

Class here 13th century

Class 1200–1216 in 942.033, 1272–1299 in 942.035

.035	**Reign of Edward I, 1272–1307**
.036	**Reign of Edward II, 1307–1327**
.037	**Reign of Edward III, 1327–1377**

Class here 14th century

(Option: Class here Hundred Years' War; prefer 944.025)

Class 1300–1307 in 942.035, 1307–1327 in 942.036, 1377–1399 in 942.038

.038	Reign of Richard II, 1377–1399
.04	Period of Houses of Lancaster and York, 1399–1485

Class here Wars of the Roses, 1455–1485

.041	Reign of Henry IV, 1399–1413
.042	Reign of Henry V, 1413–1422
.043	Reign of Henry VI, 1422–1461
.044	Reign of Edward IV, 1461–1483
.045	Reign of Edward V, 1483
.046	Reign of Richard III, 1483–1485
.05	Tudor period, 1485–1603
.051	Reign of Henry VII, 1485–1509
.052	Reign of Henry VIII, 1509–1547
.053	Reign of Edward VI, 1547–1553
.054	Reign of Mary I, 1553–1558
.055	Reign of Elizabeth I, 1558–1603

Including Spanish Armada, 1588

.06–.08	From Stuart and Commonwealth periods to present time, 1603–

Add to base number 942.0 the numbers following 941.0 in 941.06–941.08, e.g., English Civil War 942.062

943   Central Europe   Germany

SUMMARY

.000 1–.000 9	Standard subdivisions of central Europe

As modified under 930–990

.001–.009	Standard subdivisions of Germany

As modified under 930–990

SUMMARY

>   943.01–943.08 Historical periods of Germany

Class comprehensive works in 943

.01   Early history to 843

Class ancient history to 481 in 936.3

(.012)   Ancient history to 481

(Optional number; prefer 936.3)

(.012 1)   Earliest period to 113 B.C.

(Optional number; prefer 936.301)

(.012 2)   Period of contacts with Roman Republic and Empire, 113 B.C.–481 A.D.

(Optional number; prefer 936.302)

.013   Period of Merovingian dynasty in Germany, 481–751

Class comprehensive works on Merovingian dynasty in France and Germany in 944.013

.014   751–843

Class here Carolingian dynasty in Germany, 751–911

Class comprehensive works on Carolingian dynasty in France and Germany in 944.014

For 843–911, see 943.021

.02   Period of early Holy Roman Empire, 843–1519

After Treaty of Verdun, 843

.021   843–911

.022   Period of Conrad I and Saxon emperors, 911–1024

.023   Period of Salian (Franconian) emperors and Lothair II, 1024–1137

.024	Hohenstaufen period, 1138–1254
	Including reign of Frederick I Barbarossa, 1152–1190
	Class here 12th century
	Class 1100–1137 in 943.023
	For later Hohenstaufen period, see 943.025
.025	Later Hohenstaufen period and Interregnum, 1198–1273
.026	Period of early Hapsburgs and others, 1273–1378
.027	Period of House of Luxemburg, 1378–1438
.028	Reigns of Albert II and Frederick III, 1438–1493
	Class here 15th century
	Class 1400–1438 in 943.027, 1493–1499 in 943.029
.029	Reign of Maximilian I, 1493–1519
.03	Period of Reformation and Counter-Reformation, 1519–1618
.031	Reign of Charles V, 1519–1556
	Including wars with France; Peasants' War, 1524–1525; Schmalkaldic War, 1546–1547
	(Option: Class wars with France in 944.028)
.032	Reign of Ferdinand I, 1556–1564
.033	Reign of Maximilian II, 1564–1576
.034	Reign of Rudolf II, 1576–1612
.035	Reign of Matthias, 1612–1619
.04	1618–1705
.041	Period of Thirty Years' War, 1618–1648
	Class reign of Matthias during Thirty Years' War in 943.035, of Ferdinand II in 943.042, of Ferdinand III in 943.043
.042	Reign of Ferdinand II, 1619–1637
.043	Reign of Ferdinand III, 1637–1657
.044	Reign of Leopold I, 1658–1705
.05	1705–1790
	Class here rise of Prussia
.051	Reign of Joseph I, 1705–1711
.052	Reign of Charles VI, 1711–1740

.053	**1740–1786**
	Class here reign of Frederick the Great, King of Prussia, 1740–1786
	For reign of Charles VII, see 943.054; Francis I, 943.055; Joseph II, 943.057
.054	Reign of Charles VII, 1742–1745
.055	Reign of Francis I, 1745–1765
	Including period of Seven Years' War, 1756–1763
.057	Reign of Joseph II, 1765–1790
.06	Period of Napoleonic Wars, 1790–1815
	Including Confederation of the Rhine
.07	Period of German Confederation, 1815–1866
	Class here 19th century
	Class 1800–1815 in 943.06, 1866–1899 in 943.08
.073	1815–1847
.076	1848–1866
	Including Schleswig-Holstein War, 1864; Austro-Prussian War (Seven Weeks' War), 1866
	(Option: Class Schleswig-Holstein War in 948.904)
.08	1866–
.081	1866–1871
	Class here period of North German Confederation
	For Franco-German War, see 943.082
.082	Franco-German War, 1870–1871
	(Option: Class in 944.07)
.083	Reign of William I, 1871–1888
	Class here German Empire, 1871–1918
	For reigns of Frederick III and William II, see 943.084
.084	Reigns of Frederick III and William II, 1888–1918
.085	Period of Weimar Republic, 1918–1933
.086	Period of Third Reich, 1933–1945
.087	1945–
	Class here Federal Republic, 1949–　　, comprehensive works on Federal and Democratic Republics
	Class German Democratic Republic in 943.1087
.087 4	1945–1949

.087 5	1950–1959
.087 6	1960–1969
.087 7	1970–1979
.087 8	1980–1989
.087 9	1990–

.1   ***Northeastern Germany**

.108 7   German Democratic Republic, 1949–

            Class here East Germany, 1945–

            Add to base number 943.1087 the numbers following 943.087 in 943.0874–943.0879, e.g., 1960–1969 943.10876

.6   ***Austria and Liechtenstein**

         Class ancient history to 481 in 936.3

(.601)   Ancient history of Austria to 481

         (Optional number; prefer 936.3)

\>   943.602–943.605 Historical periods of Austria

         Class comprehensive works in 943.6

.602   Medieval period, 481–1500

.602 2   481–976

.602 3   Period of Babenberg dynasty, 976–1246

.602 4   1246–1273

.602 5   Early period of Hapsburgs, 1273–1500

.603   1500–1815

            See also 940.2532 for War of the Austrian Succession

.604   1815–1919

            Class here Austrian Empire, 1804–1919

            Class Austrian Empire during 1804–1815 in 943.603

.604 2   1815–1847

.604 3   1848–1867

.604 4   Period of Austro-Hungarian Monarchy, 1867–1919

.605   1919–

.605 1   Period of Republic, 1919–1938

.605 2   1938–1955

.605 22   Anschluss and war periods, 1938–1945

*Add as instructed under 930–990

.605 23	1945–1955
.605 3	1955–
.64	*Western Austria, and Liechtenstein
.648	†Liechtenstein
	Class ancient history to 481 in 936.3

.7   *Czechoslovakia

.702	Early history to 1918
	Class here Kingdom of Bohemia
.702 1	To 907
	Including Great Moravian Empire
.702 2	907–1526
.702 23	Period of Přemyslid dynasty, 907–1306
.702 24	Period of Luxembourg dynasty, 1306–1526
	Including Hussite Wars, 1419–1436
.702 3	1526–1815
.702 32	1526–1620
.702 33	1620–1800
.702 34	1800–1815
.702 4	1815–1918
.703	1918–1945
.703 2	Period of Czechoslovak Republic, 1918–1939
.703 3	1939–1945
	Class here Protectorate of Bohemia and Moravia
	Slovak Republic relocated to 943.73033
.704	1945–
.704 2	1945–1968
	Including reform and repression, 1968
.704 3	1968–
.73	*Slovakia
	Add to base number 943.73 the numbers following 943.7 in 943.702–943.704, e.g., Slovak Republic 943.73033 [*formerly* 943.7033]

*Add as instructed under 930–990

†Add as instructed under 930–990; however, do not add historical periods

.8	***Poland**
.802	Early history to 1795
.802 2	To 1370
	Including period of Piast dynasty
.802 3	Period of Jagellonian dynasty, 1370–1572
.802 4	Period of elective kings, 1572–1697
.802 5	Period of Saxon dynasty and partitions, 1697–1795
	Including partitions of 1772, 1793, 1795
.803	Period of foreign rule, 1795–1918
.803 2	1795–1862
.803 3	1863–1918
.804	Period of Republic, 1918–1939
.805	1939–
.805 3	1939–1945
.805 4	1945–1956
.805 5	1956–1980
.805 6	1980–
.9	***Hungary**
.901	Early history to 894
	Class ancient history to ca. 640 in 939.8
(.901 1)	Ancient history to ca. 640
	(Optional number; prefer 939.8)
.902	Period of Arpad dynasty, 894–1301
.903	Period of elective kings, 1301–1526
.904	Turkish and Hapsburg periods, 1526–1918
.904 1	Turkish period, 1526–1686
.904 2	Hapsburg period, 1686–1918
	For period of Austro-Hungarian Monarchy, see 943.9043
.904 3	Period of Austro-Hungarian Monarchy, 1867–1918
.905	1918–
.905 1	1918–1941
.905 2	1942–1956
	Including uprising and suppression, 1956
.905 3	1956–

*Add as instructed under 930–990

944   *France and Monaco

SUMMARY

>   944.01–944.08 Historical periods of France

    Class comprehensive works in 944

.01   Early history to 987

    Class ancient history to 486 in 936.4

(.012)   Ancient history to 486

    (Optional number; prefer 936.4)

(.012 1)   Earliest period to 125 B.C.

    (Optional number; prefer 936.401)

(.012 2)   Gallo-Roman period, 125 B.C.–486 A.D.

    (Optional number; prefer 936.402)

.013   Period of Merovingian dynasty, 486–751

    Class here comprehensive works on Merovingian dynasty in France and Germany

    For Merovingian dynasty in Germany, see 943.013

.014   Period of Carolingian dynasty, 751–987

    Class here comprehensive works on Carolingian dynasty in France and Germany

    For Carolingian dynasty in Germany, see 943.014

.02   Period of growth of royal power, 987–1589

.021   Period of House of Capet, 987–1328

    Including reigns of Hugh Capet, Robert II, Henry I, 987–1060

    Class reigns of other Capetian kings in 944.022–944.024

.022   Reigns of Philip I, Louis VI, Louis VII, 1060–1180

.023   Reigns of Philip II, Louis VIII, Louis IX, 1180–1270

.024   Reigns of Philip III, Philip IV, Louis X, Jean I, Philip V, Charles IV, 1270–1328

*Add as instructed under 930–990

.025　　　　　Period of House of Valois, 1328–1589

　　　　　　　　Including reigns of Philip VI, Jean II, Charles V, 1328–1380

　　　　　　　　Class here Hundred Years' War, 1337–1453
　　　　　　　　(Option: Class Hundred Years' War in 942.037)

　　　　　　　　Class reigns of other Valois kings in 944.026–944.029

.026　　　　　Reigns of Charles VI and Charles VII, 1380–1461

.027　　　　　Reigns of Louis XI, Charles VIII, Louis XII, 1461–1515

　　　　　　　　Class here comprehensive works on French invasions of Italy,
　　　　　　　　1494–1559
　　　　　　　　(Option: Class French invasions of Italy in 945.06)

　　　　　　　　Class invasions during period of House of Angoulême in 944.028

.028　　　　　Period of House of Angoulême, 1515–1589

　　　　　　　　Including reigns of Francis I and Henry II, 1515–1559

　　　　　　　　(Option: Class here wars with Holy Roman Emperor Charles V; prefer
　　　　　　　　943.031)

　　　　　　　　For reigns of Francis II, Charles IX, Henry III, see 944.029

.029　　　　　Reigns of Francis II, Charles IX, Henry III, 1559–1589

.03　　　　　Bourbon period, 1589–1789

.031　　　　　Reign of Henry IV, 1589–1610

.032　　　　　Reign of Louis XIII, 1610–1643

.033　　　　　Reign of Louis XIV, 1643–1715

　　　　　　　　Including War of Devolution, 1667–1668

　　　　　　　　Class here 17th century

　　　　　　　　Class 1600–1610 in 944.031, 1610–1643 in 944.032

.034　　　　　Reign of Louis XV, 1715–1774

　　　　　　　　Class here 18th century

　　　　　　　　Class a specific part of 18th century not provided for here with the part,
　　　　　　　　e.g., Reign of Terror 944.044

.035　　　　　1774–1789

　　　　　　　　Class here period of Louis XVI, 1774–1792

　　　　　　　　Class period of Louis XVI during 1789–1792 in 944.041

.04　　　　　Revolutionary period, 1789–1804

.041　　　　　Period of Estates-General, National Assembly, Legislative
　　　　　　　　Assembly, 1789–1792

.042	Period of First Republic, 1792–1799
	For period of National Convention, see 944.043; Directory, 944.045
.043	Period of National Convention, 1792–1795
	For Reign of Terror, see 944.044
.044	Period of Reign of Terror, 1793–1794
.045	Period of Directory, 1795–1799
.046	Period of Consulate, 1799–1804
.05	Period of First Empire, 1804–1815
	Including reign of Louis XVIII, 1814–1815; Hundred Days, 1815
	Class here reign of Napoleon I, 1804–1814
	Class Napoleonic Wars in 940.27
.06	Period of restoration, 1815–1848
	Class here 19th century
	Class a specific part of 19th century not provided for here with the part, e.g., Second Empire 944.07
.061	Reign of Louis XVIII, 1815–1824
.062	Reign of Charles X, 1824–1830
.063	Period of Louis Philippe, 1830–1848 (July Monarchy)
.07	Period of Second Republic and Second Empire (period of Napoleon III), 1848–1870
	(Option: Class here Franco-German War; prefer 943.082)
.08	1870–
.081	Period of Third Republic, 1870–1945
.081 2	1870–1899
	Including Paris Commune, 1871
.081 3	1900–1914
.081 4	Period of World War I, 1914–1918
.081 5	1918–1939
.081 6	Period of World War II, 1939–1945
.082	Period of Fourth Republic, 1945–1958
.083	Period of Fifth Republic, 1958–
.083 6	1958–1969
.083 7	1970–1979
.083 8	1980–1989

.083 9   1990–

.9   ***Southeastern France and Monaco**   **Provence region**

.94   *Alpes-Maritimes, Corse, Monaco

.949   †Monaco

           Class ancient history to 486 in 936.4

945   *Italian Peninsula and adjacent islands   Italy

\>   945.01–945.09 Historical periods of Italy

         Class comprehensive works in 945

.01   Early history to 774

         Including Gothic and Lombard kingdoms, 476–774

         Class ancient history to 476 in 937

(.012)   Ancient history to 476

         (Optional number; prefer 937)

         Add to base number 945.012 the numbers following 937.0 in 937.01–937.09, e.g., Punic Wars 945.0124

.02   Period of Carolingian (Frankish) rule, 774–962

.03   Period of German emperors, 962–1122

.04   1122–1300

.05   Renaissance period, 1300–1494

.06   1494–1527

         (Option: Class here French invasions of Italy; prefer 944.027)

.07   Period of Spanish and Austrian domination, 1527–1796

.08   1796–1900

.082   Napoleonic period, 1796–1814

.083   Period of Risorgimento, 1814–1861

.084   Reigns of Victor Emmanuel II and Umberto I, 1861–1900

         Including 1870–1900 [*formerly* 945.09]

*Add as instructed under 930–990

†Add as instructed under 930–990; however, do not add historical periods

.09	1900–

               1870–1900 relocated to 945.084

.091	Reign of Victor Emmanuel III, 1900–1946

               Class here Fascist period

               (Option: Class here Ethiopian War and Italo-Ethiopian War; prefer 963.043 for Ethiopian War, 963.056 for Italo-Ethiopian War)

.092	Period of Republic, 1946–
.092 4	1946–1949
.092 5	1950–1959
.092 6	1960–1969
.092 7	1970–1979
.092 8	1980–1989
.092 9	1990–
.4	***Emilia-Romagna region and San Marino**
.49	†San Marino

               Class ancient history to 476 in 937.4

.6	***Central Italy and Vatican City**
.63	*Roma (Rome) province and Vatican City
.634	*Vatican City
.8	***Sicily and adjacent islands**
.85	†Malta

               Class ancient history to 476 in 937.8

946   Iberian Peninsula and adjacent islands   Spain

.000 1–.000 9	Standard subdivisions of Iberian Peninsula and adjacent islands

               As modified under 930–990

.001–.009	Standard subdivisions of Spain

               As modified under 930–990

>	946.01–946.08 Historical periods of Spain

               Class comprehensive works in 946

.01	Early history to 711

               Class here period of Visigothic domination, 415–711

               Class ancient history to 415 in 936.6

*Add as instructed under 930–990
†Add as instructed under 930–990; however, do not add historical periods

(.012)	Ancient history to 415
	(Optional number; prefer 936.6)
(.012 1)	Earliest period to ca. 1000 B.C.
	(Optional number; prefer 936.601)
(.012 2)	Period of Greek, Phoenician, early Celtic and Germanic contacts, ca. 1000–218 B.C.
	(Optional number; prefer 936.602)
(.012 3)	Roman period, 218 B.C.–415 A.D.
	(Optional number; prefer 936.603)
.02	Period of Moorish dynasties and reconquest, 711–1479
.03	Reign of Ferdinand V and Isabella I, 1479–1516
	Including union of Castile and Aragon
.04	Period of Hapsburg rulers, 1516–1700
	For period of later Hapsburg rulers, see 946.051
.042	Reign of Charles I, 1516–1556
.043	Reign of Philip II, 1556–1598
.05	Period of later Hapsburg rulers and Bourbon rulers, 1598–1808
.051	Period of later Hapsburg rulers, 1598–1700
	Including reign of Philip III, 1598–1621
	For reign of Philip IV, see 946.052; Charles II, 946.053
.052	Reign of Philip IV, 1621–1665
.053	Reign of Charles II, 1665–1700
.054	1700–1808
	Class here comprehensive works on Bourbon rulers in Spain
	Class the reign of a specific Bourbon ruler with the reign, e.g., reign of Isabella II 946.072
.055	Reign of Philip V, 1700–1746
	Including Anglo-Spanish War (War of Jenkins' Ear), 1739–1741 (Option: Class War of Jenkins' Ear in 941.072)
	See also 940.2526 for War of the Spanish Succession
.056	Reign of Ferdinand VI, 1746–1759
.057	Reign of Charles III, 1759–1788
.058	Reign of Charles IV, 1788–1808
.06	Period of Peninsular War and rule of Joseph Bonaparte, 1808–1814

.07	1814–1931
.072	Reigns of Ferdinand VII and Isabella II, 1814–1868

Including first Bourbon restoration

(Option: Class here Spanish-Moroccan War; prefer 964.03)

.073	1868–1874 [*formerly* 946.08]

Including revolution 1868–1871; second Bourbon restoration, 1871–1873; First Republic, 1873–1874

.074	Reigns of Alfonso XII and Alfonso XIII, 1874–1931 [*formerly* 946.08]

(Option: Class here Spanish-American War; prefer 973.89)

.08	1931–

Class here 20th century

1868–1874 relocated to 946.073; reigns of Alfonso XII and Alfonso XIII, 1874–1931 to 946.074

.081	Period of Second Republic, 1931–1939

Class here Civil War, 1936–1939

.082	Period of Francisco Franco, 1939–1975
.082 4	1939–1949
.082 5	1950–1959
.082 6	1960–1969
.082 7	1970–1975
.083	Reign of Juan Carlos I, 1975–
.7	***Eastern Spain and Andorra**
.79	†Andorra

Class ancient history to 415 in 936.6

.8	***Andalusia autonomous community and Gibraltar**
.89	†Gibraltar

Class ancient history to 415 in 936.6

.9	***Portugal**
.901	Early history to 1143

Class ancient history to 415 in 936.6

*Add as instructed under 930–990

†Add as instructed under 930–990; however, do not add historical periods

(.901 2)	Ancient history to 415
	(Optional number; prefer 936.6)
	Add to base number 946.9012 the numbers following 946.012 in 946.0121–946.0123, e.g., period of Greek contacts 946.90122
.902	Period of rise and fall of empire, 1143–1640
.903	Period of House of Braganza, 1640–1910
.903 2	1640–1750
	Including restoration of Portuguese monarchy
.903 3	1750–1807
	Including Pombaline reforms
.903 4	Period of monarchy in exile, 1807–1820
	Including period of Peninsular War
.903 5	1820–1847
.903 6	1847–1910
.904	1910–
.904 1	Period of Republic, 1910–1926
.904 2	1926–1968
	Including period of Salazar, 1933–1968
	Class here Novo Estado, 1933–1974
	Class Novo Estado during 1968–1974 in 946.9043
.904 3	1968–1974
.904 4	1974–

947   Eastern Europe   Union of Soviet Socialist Republics (Soviet Union)

.000 1–.000 9	Standard subdivisions of eastern Europe
	As modified under 930–990
.001–.009	Standard subdivisions of Russia
	As modified under 930–990

>	947.01–947.08 Historical periods of Russia
	Class comprehensive works in 947
.01	Early history to 862
.02	Kievan period, 862–1240
.03	Period of Tatar suzerainty, 1240–1462

.04	1462–1689
.041	Reign of Ivan III, 1462–1505
.042	Reign of Basil III, 1505–1533
.043	Reign of Ivan IV, (the Terrible), 1533–1584

Including Livonian War, 1557–1582
(Option: Class Livonian War in 948.502)

.044	Reigns of Theodore I and Boris Godunov, 1584–1605
.045	Time of Troubles, 1605–1613

Including reigns of Pseudo-Demetrius I and Pseudo-Demetrius II

.046	Period of House of Romanov, 1613–1917

Class reigns of specific Romanovs in 947.047–947.083

.047	Reign of Michael, 1613–1645
.048	Reign of Alexis, 1645–1676
.049	Reigns of Theodore III and regent Sophia, 1676–1689
.05	Reign of Peter I (the Great), 1689–1725

Including Great Northern War, 1700–1721
(Option: Class Great Northern War in 948.05 or 948.503)

.06	1725–1796
.061	Reigns of Catherine I, Peter II, Anne, Ivan VI, 1725–1741
.062	Reigns of Elizabeth and Peter III, 1741–1762
.063	Reign of Catherine II (the Great), 1762–1796
.07	1796–1855

Class here 19th century

Class 1855–1900 in 947.08

.071	Reign of Paul I, 1796–1801
.072	Reign of Alexander I, 1801–1825

Including period of invasion by Napoleon, 1812

.073	Reign of Nicholas I, 1825–1855

Including Crimean War, 1853–1856
(Option: Class Crimean War in 941.081)

.08	1855–
.081	Reign of Alexander II, 1855–1881

Including Russo-Turkish War, 1877–1878
(Option: Class Russo-Turkish War in 956.1015)

.082	Reign of Alexander III, 1881–1894
.083	Reign of Nicholas II, 1894–1917

> (Option: Class here Russo-Japanese War; prefer 952.031)

.084	1917–

> Class here Communist period; Union of Soviet Socialist Republics, 1923–
>
> *For 1953–   , see 947.085*

.084 1	Period of revolutions, Alexander Kerensky, V. I. Lenin, 1917–1924
.084 2	Period of Joseph Stalin, 1924–1953

> (Option: Class here Russo-Finnish War; prefer 948.97032)

.085	1953–
.085 2	Periods of Georgi Malenkov, Nikolay Aleksandrovich Bulganin, Nikita Sergeevich Khrushchev, 1953–1964
.085 3	Periods of Leonid Il'ich Brezhnev and Aleksey Nikolayevich Kosygin, 1964–1982
.085 4	Periods of IU. V. Andropov, K. U. Chernenko, and Mikhail Sergeevich Gorbachev, 1982–

948   *Northern Europe   Scandinavia

SUMMARY

948.01–.08	**Historical periods of Scandinavia**
.1	**Norway**
.2	**Southeastern Norway**
.3	**Southwestern Norway**
.4	**Central and northern Norway**
.5	**Sweden**
.6	**Southern Sweden**
.7	**Central Sweden**
.8	**Northern Sweden**
.9	**Denmark and Finland**

>	948.01–948.08 Historical periods of Scandinavia

> Class comprehensive works in 948

.01	Early history to 800

> Class ancient history to 481 in 936.3

(.012)	Ancient history to 481

> (Optional number; prefer 936.3)

.02	Period of migration and conquest, 800–1387
.022	Viking period, 800–1066

*Add as instructed under 930–990

.023	1066–1387
.03	1387–1523

> Class here period of Kalmar Union, 1397–1523

.04	Period of reformation and rise of Sweden, 1523–1648
.05	Period of conflict, 1648–1792

> (Option: Class here Great Northern War; prefer 947.05)

.06	1792–1814
.07	1814–1905
.08	1905–
.081	1905–1919
.082	1920–1929
.083	1930–1939
.084	1940–1949
.084 2	Period of World War II, 1940–1945
.084 3	1945–1949
.085	1950–1959
.086	1960–1969
.087	1970–1979
.088	1980–

.1   *Norway

> *For southeastern Norway, see 948.2; southwestern Norway, 948.3; central and northern Norway, 948.4*

.101	Early history to 1387

> Class ancient history to 481 in 936.3

(.101 2)	Ancient history to 481

> (Optional number; prefer 936.3)

.102	Period of union with Denmark, 1387–1814

> Including period of Kalmar Union, 1397–1523

.103	Period of union with Sweden, 1814–1905
.104	1905–
.104 1	1905–1945
.104 5	1945–1959
.104 6	1960–1969

*Add as instructed under 930–990

.104 7	1970–1979
.104 8	1980–1989
.104 9	1990–

.2   ***Southeastern Norway**

> Add to base number 948.2 the numbers following 948.1 in 948.101–948.104, e.g., period of Kalmar Union 948.202

.3   ***Southwestern Norway**

> Add to base number 948.3 the numbers following 948.1 in 948.101–948.104, e.g., period of Kalmar Union 948.302

.4   ***Central and northern Norway**

> Add to base number 948.4 the numbers following 948.1 in 948.101–948.104, e.g., period of Kalmar Union 948.402

.5   ***Sweden**

> *For southern Sweden, see 948.6; central Sweden, 948.7; northern Sweden, 948.8*

.501	Early history to 1523

> Including period of Kalmar Union, 1397–1523
>
> Class ancient history to 481 in 936.3

(.501 2)	Ancient history to 481

> (Optional number; prefer 936.3)

.502	Period of Vasa dynasty, 1523–1654

> (Option: Class here Livonian War; prefer 947.043)

.503	Period of decline of power, 1654–1818

> (Option: Class here Great Northern War; prefer 947.05)

.504	1818–1905
.505	1905–
.505 1	1905–1945
.505 5	1945–1959
.505 6	1960–1969
.505 7	1970–1979
.505 8	1980–1989
.505 9	1990–

.6   ***Southern Sweden**

> Add to base number 948.6 the numbers following 948.5 in 948.501–948.505, e.g., period of Vasa dynasty 948.602

*Add as instructed under 930–990

.7 ***Central Sweden**

> Add to base number 948.7 the numbers following 948.5 in 948.501–948.505, e.g., period of Vasa dynasty 948.702

.8 ***Northern Sweden**

> Add to base number 948.8 the numbers following 948.5 in 948.501–949.505, e.g., period of Vasa dynasty 948.802

.9 **Denmark and Finland**

.900 1–.900 9   Standard subdivisions of Denmark

> As modified under 930–990

> 948.901–948.905 Historical periods of Denmark

Class comprehensive works in 948.9

.901   Early history to 1387

> Class ancient history to 481 in 936.3

(.901 2)   Ancient history to 481

> (Optional number; prefer 936.3)

.902   Period of union with Norway and Sweden, 1387–1523

> Class here period of Kalmar Union, 1397–1523

.903   Period of union with Norway, 1523–1814

> *For Great Northern War, see 947.05*

.904   1814–1906

> (Option: Class here Schleswig-Holstein War; prefer 943.076)

.905   1906–

.905 1   1906–1945

.905 5   1945–1959

.905 6   1960–1969

.905 7   1970–1979

.905 8   1980–1989

.905 9   1990–

.97   ***Finland**

.970 1   Early history to end of Swedish rule, 1809

> *For Great Northern War, see 947.05*

.970 2   Period of Russian rule, 1809–1917

*Add as instructed under 930–990

.970 3	1917–
.970 31	1917–1939
.970 32	1939–1945

Including Russo-Finnish War, 1939–1940
(Option: Class Russo-Finnish War in 947.0842)

.970 33	1945–1982
.970 34	1982–

949   Other parts of Europe

SUMMARY

949.1	Northwestern islands	
.2	Netherlands (Holland)	
.3	Southern Low Countries	Belgium
.4	Switzerland	
.5	Greece	
.6	Balkan Peninsula	
.7	Yugoslavia and Bulgaria	
.8	Romania	
.9	Aegean Sea islands	

.1   ***Northwestern islands**

.12   *Iceland

.120 1   Early history to 1262

.120 2   Medieval period, 1262–1550

.120 3   1550–1848

.120 4   Modern period, 1848–1940

         Including independence under Danish crown, 1918–1944

         Class 1940–1944 in 949.1205

.120 5   1940–

         Class here period of Republic, 1944–

.15   †Faeroes

.2   ***Netherlands (Holland)**

.201   Early history to 1477

         Class ancient history to 481 in 936.3

(.201 2)   Ancient history to 481

         (Optional number; prefer 936.3)

.202   Period of Hapsburg rule, 1477–1568

.203   Period of struggle for independence, 1568–1648

*Add as instructed under 930–990

†Add as instructed under 930–990; however, do not add historical periods

.204	Period of Dutch Republic, 1648–1795
	Including Anglo-Dutch Wars, 1652–1653, 1665–1667; Great Wars against England, France, and allies, 1672–1678; Coalition War, 1690–1697
	(Option: Class Anglo-Dutch Wars in 941.06)
.205	1795–1830
	Including Batavian Republic, 1795–1806; Kingdom of Holland, 1806–1813
	Class here Napoleonic era
.206	1830–1901
	Class here 19th century
	Class 1800–1830 in 949.205
.207	1901–
.207 1	Reign of Wilhelmina, 1890–1948
	Class reign of Wilhelmina during 1890–1901 in 949.206
.207 2	Reign of Juliana, 1948–1980
.207 3	Reign of Beatrix, 1980–

.3   **Southern Low Countries**   **Belgium**

.300 01–.300 09	Standard subdivisions of southern Low Countries
	As modified under 930–990
.300 1–.300 9	Standard subdivisions of Belgium
	As modified under 930–990

>   949.301–949.304 Historical periods of Belgium

Class comprehensive works in 949.3

.301	Early history to 1477
	Class ancient history to 486 in 936.4
(.301 2)	Ancient history to 486
	(Optional number; prefer 936.4)
.302	Period of foreign rule, 1477–1830
.303	1830–1909
	Class here 19th century
	Class 1800–1830 in 949.302
.304	1909–
.304 1	Reign of Albert I, 1909–1934

.304 2	Reign of Léopold III, 1934–1951
.304 3	Reign of Baudouin I, 1951–
.35	*Luxembourg
.350 1	Early history to 1482
	Class ancient history to 486 in 936.4
(.350 12)	Ancient history to 486
	(Option: Class here ancient history; prefer 936.4)
.350 2	Period of foreign rule, 1482–1830
.350 3	1830–1890
	Class here 19th century
	Class 1800–1830 in 949.3502, 1890–1899 in 949.35041
.350 4	1890–
.350 41	1890–1918
.350 42	1918–1945
.350 43	1945–
.4	***Switzerland**
.401	Early history to 1291
	Class ancient history to 486 in 936.4
(.401 2)	Ancient history to 486
	(Optional number; prefer 936.4)
.402	1291–1499
.403	1499–1648
.404	1648–1798
	Including 1789–1798 [*formerly* 949.405]
.405	Napoleonic period, 1798–1815
	Class here Helvetic Republic, 1798–1803
	1789–1798 relocated to 949.404
.406	1815–1900
.406 2	Period of restoration, 1815–1848
.406 3	1848–1900
.407	1900–
.407 1	1900–1918
.407 2	1918–1945
.407 3	1945–

*Add as instructed under 930–990

.5   ***Greece**

Class here Byzantine Empire

.501   Early history to 717

Including wars against Avars and Persians

Class here Eastern Roman (Byzantine) Empire, 323–717

Class ancient history to 323 in 938

(.501 2)   Ancient history to 323

(Optional number; prefer 938)

Add to base number 949.5012 the numbers following 938.0 in 938.01–938.09, e.g., Persian Wars 949.50123

.502   Period of Byzantine prosperity, 717–1057

.503   Period of dissolution of Byzantine Empire, 1057–1204

.504   Period of Latin and Greek states and Turkish conquest, 1204–1453

.505   Period of Turkish domination, 1453–1821

.506   Period of monarchy, 1821–1924

Including Greco-Turkish War, 1896–1897
(Option: Class Greco-Turkish War in 956.1015)

For Balkan Wars, see 949.6

.507   1924–

.507 3   Period of Republic, 1924–1935

.507 4   Period of restoration of monarchy, 1935–1967

.507 5   Period of military junta, 1967–1974

.507 6   Period of restoration of democratic rule, 1974–

.56   ***Macedonia**

Add to base number 949.56 the numbers following 949.5 in 949.501–949.507, e.g., period of Republic 949.56073

Class ancient history to 323 in 938.1

.6   ***Balkan Peninsula**

Including Balkan Wars, 1912–1913

.61   ***Turkey in Europe (Turkish Thrace)**

.610 1   History to 1918

.610 11–.610 14   Early history to 1453

Add to base number 949.6101 the numbers following 949.50 in 949.501–949.504, e.g., period of Byzantine prosperity, 717–1057 949.61012

Class ancient history to 323 in 939.8

*Add as instructed under 930–990

.610 15	1453–1918

Class here period of Ottoman empire, 1453–1922

Class 1918–1922 in 949.61023

.610 2–.610 3	1918–

Add to base number 949.61 the numbers following 956.1 in 956.102–956.103, e.g., 1918–1923 949.61023

.65	*Albania

.650 1	Early history to 1912

Class ancient history to 323 in 938.1

(.650 12)	Ancient history to 323

(Optional number; prefer 938.1)

.650 2	1912–1946
.650 3	Period of People's Republic, 1946–

.7   Yugoslavia and Bulgaria

.700 01–.700 09	Standard subdivisions

As modified under 930–990

.700 1–.700 9	Standard subdivisions of Yugoslavia

As modified under 930–990

>   949.701–949.702 Historical periods of Yugoslavia

Class comprehensive works in 949.7

.701	Early history to 1918

Class ancient history to ca. 640 in 939.8

For Balkan Wars, see 949.6

(.701 2)	Ancient history to ca. 640

(Optional number; prefer 939.8)

.702	1918–
.702 1	Period of Kingdom, 1918–1939

Class 1939–1941 in 949.7022

.702 2	Period of World War II, 1939–1945

*Add as instructed under 930–990

.702 3	Administration of Josip Broz Tito, 1945–1980
.702 4	1980–
.71	*Serbia
.710 1	Early history to 1918
	Class ancient history to ca. 640 in 939.8
(.710 11)	Ancient history to ca. 640
	(Optional number; prefer 939.8)
.710 12	Ca. 640–1389
.710 13	Turkish period, 1389–1878
	For 1804–1878, see 949.71014
.710 14	Period of revolt and autonomy, 1804–1878
.710 15	Period of independence, 1878–1918
.710 2	1918–
	Class here 20th century
	Add to base number 949.7102 the numbers following 949.702 in 949.7021–949.7024, e.g., period of World War II 949.71022
	Class 1901–1918 in 949.71015
.77	*Bulgaria
.770 1	Early history to 1878
	Class ancient history to ca. 640 in 939.8
(.770 12)	Ancient history to ca. 640
	(Optional number; prefer 939.8)
.770 13	Ca. 640–1018
	Class here First Bulgarian Empire, ca. 680–1014
.770 14	Period of Byzantine rule and Second Bulgarian Empire, 1018–1396
.770 15	Turkish period, 1396–1878
.770 2	1878–1946
.770 22	1878–1918
	For Balkan Wars, see 949.6
.770 23	1918–1946
.770 3	Period of People's Republic, 1946–

*Add as instructed under 930–990

.8   ***Romania**

.801   Early history to 1861

              Class ancient history to ca. 640 in 939.8

(.801 2)   Ancient history to ca. 640

              (Optional number; prefer 939.8)

.801 3   Ca. 640–1250

.801 4   Period of Wallachia and Moldavia principalities, 1250–ca. 1500

.801 5   Turkish period, ca. 1500–1821

              Including reign of Michael the Brave, 1593–1601; Phanarist period, 1711–1821

.801 6   1821–1861

.802   Period of monarchy, 1861–1947

              Class here period of Kingdom, 1881–1947

              For Balkan Wars, see 949.6

.803   Period of People's Republic, 1947–

.9   ***Aegean Sea islands**

              Add to base number 949.9 the numbers following 949.5 in 949.501–949.507, e.g., early Byzantine period 949.901

              (Option: Class ancient history in 949.9012; prefer 939.1)

              Class ancient history to 323 in 939.1

.98   ***Crete**

.980 1   Early history to 961

              Class ancient history to 323 in 939.18

(.980 12)   Ancient history to 323

              (Optional number; prefer 939.18)

              Add to base number 949.98012 the numbers following 938.0 in 938.01–938.09, e.g., mythical age to 775 B.C. 949.980121

.980 2   961–1664

.980 3   Period of Turkish domination, 1664–1898

.980 4   1898–

.980 41   Period of autonomy, 1898–1913

.980 42   Period of incorporation into Greece, 1913–1924

.980 43–.980 46   1924–

              Add to base number 949.9804 the numbers following 949.507 in 949.5073–949.5076, e.g., restoration of monarchy 949.98044

*Add as instructed under 930–990

950   General history of Asia   Orient   Far East

SUMMARY

.01–.09   Standard subdivisions

> As modified under 930–990

.1   Early history to 1162

.2   Period of Mongol and Tatar Empires, 1162–1480

> Including reigns of Genghis Khan, ca. 1200–1227; Kublai Khan, ca. 1259–1294; Timur (Tamerlane), ca. 1336–1405

.3   Period of European exploration and penetration, 1480–1905

.4   1905–

.41   1905–1945

.42   1945–

.424   1945–1949

.425   1950–1959

.426   1960–1969

.427   1970–1979

.428   1980–1989

.429   1990–1999

951   China and adjacent areas

.000 1–.000 9   Standard subdivisions

> As modified under 930–990

.001–.009   Standard subdivisions of China

> As modified under 930–990

\>   951.01–951.05 Historical periods of China

Class comprehensive works in 951

.01	Early history to 960
	Class ancient history to 420 in 931
(.011–.014)	Ancient history to 420
	(Optional numbers; prefer 931)
	Add to base number 951.01 the numbers following 931.0 in 931.01–931.04, e.g., Shang dynasty 951.012
.015	Period of Northern and Southern dynasties, 420–581
.016	Period of Sui dynasty, 581–618
.017	Period of T'ang dynasty, 618–907
.018	Period of Five dynasties and Ten kingdoms, 907–960
.02	960–1644
.024	Period of Sung dynasty, 960–1279
.025	Period of Yüan (Mongol) dynasty, 1271–1368
	Class period of Yüan dynasty during 1271–1279 in 951.024
.026	Period of Ming dynasty, 1368–1644
.03	Period of Ch'ing (Manchu) dynasty, 1644–1912
.032	1644–1795
.033	1796–1850
	Including Opium War, 1840–1842
	Class here 19th century
	Class 1850–1864 in 951.034, 1864–1899 in 951.035
.034	Period of Taiping Rebellion, 1850–1864
.035	1864–1911
	Including Boxer Rebellion, 1899–1901
	(Option: Class here Sino-Japanese War, 1894–1895; prefer 952.031)
.036	Period of Revolution of 1911–1912
.04	Period of Republic, 1912–1949
.041	1912–1927
.042	Period of nationalist government, 1927–1949
	Including Sino-Japanese Conflict during 1937–1941 (Option: Class Sino-Japanese Conflict during 1937–1941 in 952.033)
	Class comprehensive works on Sino-Japanese Conflict, 1937–1945, in 940.53

.05	Period of People's Republic, 1949–

Class here 20th century

Class a specific part of 20th century not provided for here with the part, e.g., Revolution of 1911–1912 951.036

.055	1949–1959
.056	1960–1969

Including Cultural Revolution

.057	1970–1979
.058	1980–1989
.059	1990–
.2	***Southeastern China and adjacent areas**
.24	*East China Sea area
.249	*Taiwan (Formosa) and adjacent islands
.249 02	Early history to 1683
.249 03	Chinese period, 1683–1895
.249 04	Japanese period, 1895–1945
.249 05	Period of Republic of China (Nationalist China), 1945–
.25	*Hong Kong
.250 1–.250 3	Chinese period to 1843

Add to base number 951.250 the numbers following 951.0 in 951.01–951.03, e.g., period of Ming dynasty 951.25026

.250 4	Period as a British dependency, 1843–

For 1945–   , see 951.2505

.250 5	1945–
.26	†Macao

Class ancient history in 931

.7	***Mongolia**
.73	†Outer Mongolia (Mongolian People's Republic)
.9	***Korea**
.901	Early history to 1392
.902	Period of Yi dynasty, 1392–1910
.903	Japanese period, 1910–1945

*Add as instructed under 930–990

†Add as instructed under 930–990; however, do not add historical periods

.904	1945–
.904 1	1945–1950
.904 2	Korean War, 1950–1953
.904 3	1953–

952   *Japan

.01	Early history to 1185
.02	Feudal period, 1185–1868
.021	Kamakura period, 1185–1334
.022	Namboku period, 1334–1392
.023	Muromachi period, 1392–1573
.024	Momoyama period, 1573–1603
.025	Tokugawa (Edo) period, 1603–1868
.03	1868–1945
.031	Meiji period, 1868–1912

> Including Sino-Japanese War, 1894–1895; Russo-Japanese War, 1904–1905
>> (Option: Class Sino-Japanese War in 951.035, Russo-Japanese War in 947.083)

.032	Taishō period, 1912–1926
.033	Shōwa period, 1926–

> (Option: Class here Sino-Japanese Conflict, 1937–1941; prefer 951.042)

> *For 1945–   , see 952.04*

.04	1945–
.044	1945–1949
.045	1950–1959
.046	1960–1969
.047	1970–1979
.048	1980–1989
.049	1990–

953   *Arabian Peninsula and adjacent areas

> Class early history to 622 in 939.49

(.01)	Early history to 622

> (Optional number; prefer 939.49)

.02	622–1517

*Add as instructed under 930–990

.03	Period of Ottoman Empire, 1517–1740
	Class period of struggles to overthrow Turks in 953.04
.04	1740–1926
	Class here period of struggles to overthrow Turks, 1740–1918
.05	1926–
.052	1926–1964
.053	1964–

.1   *Sinai (Sinai Peninsula)

Governorate of Egypt

Add to base number 953.1 the numbers following 962 in 962.01–962.05, e.g., period of Ottoman Empire 953.103

Class ancient history in 939.48

.3   †Southwestern coast of Arabia

Class ancient history in 939.49

.32   †Yemen (Yemen Arab Republic)

Class ancient history in 939.49

.35   †Southern Yemen (People's Democratic Republic of Yemen)

Class ancient history in 939.49

.5   †Oman and United Arab Emirates

Class ancient history in 939.49

.53   †Oman

Class ancient history in 939.49

.57   †United Arab Emirates

Class ancient history in 939.49

.6   †Persian Gulf States

Class ancient history in 939.49

For Oman and United Arab Emirates, see 953.5

.63   †Qatar

Class ancient history in 939.49

.65   †Bahrain

Class ancient history in 939.49

.67   †Kuwait

Class ancient history in 939.49

*Add as instructed under 930–990

†Add as instructed under 930–99; however, do not add historical periods

.8   ***Saudi Arabia**

Class ancient history in 939.49

954   *South Asia   India

Class history of India to 647 in 934

(.01)   Early history to 647

(Optional number; prefer 934)

Add to base number 954.01 the numbers following 934.0 in 934.01–934.07, e.g., reign of Aśoka 954.0145

SUMMARY

954.02	647–1785
.03	**Period of British rule, 1785–1947**
.04	**1947–1971**
.05	**1971–**

.02   647–1785

.021   647–997

.022   Period of Muslim conquests, 997–1206

.022 3   Period of Ghazni dynasty, 997–1196

.022 5   Period of Ghor dynasty, 1196–1206

.023   1206–1414

.023 2   Period of slave kings of Delhi, 1206–1290

.023 4   Period of Khalji dynasty, 1290–1320

.023 6   Period of Tughluk dynasty, 1320–1414

.024   1414–1526

.024 2   Period of Sayyid dynasty, 1414–1451

.024 5   Period of Lodi dynasty, 1451–1526

.025   Period of Mogul Empire, 1526–1707

.025 2   Reign of Babur, 1526–1530

.025 3   Reign of Humayun, 1530–1556

.025 4   Reign of Akbar, 1556–1605

.025 6   Reign of Jahangir, 1605–1627

.025 7   Reign of Shahjahan, 1628–1658

.025 8   Reign of Aurangzeb, 1658–1707

.029   Period of European penetration, 1707–1785

.029 2   1707–1744

*Add as instructed under 930–990

.029 4	Period of Anglo-French conflict, 1744–1757
	Including Battle of Plassey, 1757
.029 6	1757–1772
	Including governorship of Lord Clive, 1757–1767
.029 8	Governorship of Warren Hastings, 1772–1785
.03	Period of British rule, 1785–1947
	Class governorship of Lord Clive in 954.0296, of Warren Hastings in 954.0298
.031	Period of East India Company, 1785–1858
.031 1	Governorships of Sir John Macpherson, Marquis Cornwallis (1st term), John Shore (Lord Teignmouth), 1785–1798
.031 2	Governorships of Marquess Wellesley, Marquess Cornwallis (2nd term), Sir George Barlow, 1798–1807
.031 3	Governorships of 1st Earl of Minto, Marquess of Hastings, Earl Amherst, 1807–1828
.031 4	Governorships of Lord Bentinck, Lord Metcalfe, Earl of Auckland, 1828–1842
.031 5	Governorships of Earl of Ellenborough and Viscount Hardinge, 1842–1848
.031 6	Governorship of Marquess of Dalhousie, 1848–1856
.031 7	Governorship of Earl Canning, 1856–1862
	Including Sepoy Mutiny, 1857–1858
	Class governorship of Earl Canning during 1858–1862 in 954.0351
.035	Period of control by crown, 1858–1947
.035 1	Governorships of Earl Canning, 8th Earl of Elgin, Baron Lawrence, 1858–1868
.035 2	Governorships of Earl of Mayo and Earl of Northbrook, 1869–1876
.035 3	Governorships of Earl of Lytton and Marquess of Ripon, 1876–1884
.035 4	Governorships of Marquis of Dufferin and Marquess of Lansdowne, 1884–1894
.035 5	Governorships of 9th Earl of Elgin and Marquis of Curzon, 1894–1905
.035 6	Governorships of 4th Earl of Minto and Baron Hardinge, 1905–1916
.035 7	Governorships of Viscount Chelmsford and Marquess of Reading, 1916–1926
.035 8	Governorships of Earl of Halifax and Marquess of Willingdon, 1926–1936
.035 9	Governorships of Marquess of Linlithgow, Earl of Wavell, Earl Mountbatten, 1936–1947

.04	1947–1971
.042	Prime ministership of Jawaharlal Nehru, 1947–1964
.043	Prime ministership of Lal Bahadur Shastri, 1964–1966
	(Option: Class here Indo-Pakistan War, 1965; prefer 954.9045)
.045	First prime ministership of Indira Gandhi, 1966–1977
	Class first prime ministership of Indira Gandhi during 1971–1977 in 954.051
.05	1971–
.051	Later half of first prime ministership of Indira Gandhi, 1971–1977
	(Option: Class here Indo-Pakistan War, 1971; prefer 954.9205)
.052	1977–
	Contains prime ministerships of Moraji Desai, 1977–1979, Charan Singh, 1979, Rajiv Gandhi, 1984– ; second prime ministership of Indira Gandhi, 1980–1984

.9   Other jurisdictions

Class here *Pakistan (West and East, 1947–1971)

.904	1947–1971
.904 2	Administration of Mahomed Ali Jinnah, 1947–1948
.904 3	1948–1958
.904 5	Administration of Mohammad Ayub Khan, 1958–1969
	Including Indo-Pakistan War, 1965 (Option: Class Indo-Pakistan War, 1965, in 954.043)
.904 6	Administration of Aga Muhammad Yahya Khan, 1969–1971
.91	*Pakistan
.910 4	Period of union of West and East Pakistan, 1947–1971
	Add to base number 954.9104 the numbers following 954.904 in 954.9042–954.9046, e.g., administration of Mohammad Ayub Khan 954.91045
.910 5	1971–
	For Indo-Pakistan War, 1971, see 954.9205
.92	*Bangladesh
.920 4	Period of union of East and West Pakistan, 1947–1971
	Add to base number 954.9204 the numbers following 954.904 in 954.9042–954.9046, e.g., administration of Mahomed Ali Jinnah 954.92042

*Add as instructed under 930–990

.920 5	1971–

> Including Indo-Pakistan War, 1971
> (Option: Class Indo-Pakistan War, 1971, in 954.051)

.93	*Sri Lanka
.930 1	Early history to 1795
.930 2	British period, 1795–1948
.930 3	1948–
.95	†Maldives
.96	†Nepal
.98	†Bhutan

955　　*Iran

Class ancient history to 637 in 935

(.01)	Early history to 637

> (Optional number; prefer 935)

> Add to base number 955.01 the numbers following 935.0 in 935.01–935.07, e.g., period of Sassanian Empire 955.017

.02	Period of Arab, Turkish, Mongol, Turkoman domination, 637–1499
.03	Period of Persian dynasties, 1499–1794
.04	1794–1906
.05	1906–
.051	1906–1925
.052	Reign of Reza Shah Pahlavi, 1925–1941
.053	Reign of Mohammed Reza Pahlavi, 1941–1979
.054	1979–

> Class here period of Ruhollah Khomeini; Iraqi-Iranian Conflict, 1980–
> (Option: Class Iraqi-Iranian Conflict, 1980–　　in 956.7043)

*Add as instructed under 930–990

†Add as instructed under 930–990; however, do not add historical periods

956 *Middle East (Near East)

SUMMARY

.01   Early history to 1900

> Class ancient history to ca. 640 in 939.4

(.012)   Ancient history to ca. 640

> (Optional number; prefer 939.4)

.013   640–1000

.014   Period of Seljuk supremacy, 1000–1300

.015   1300–1900

> Class here Ottoman Empire, ca. 1300–1922

> Class 1900–1918 in 956.02; 1918–1922 in 956.03; a specific part of the Ottoman Empire with the part, e.g., Ottoman Empire in Turkey 956.1015

.02   1900–1918

.03   1918–1945

.04   1945–1980

.042   Israel-Arab War, 1948–1949

.044   Sinai Campaign, 1956

.046   Israel-Arab War, 1967 (Six Days' War)

.048   Israel-Arab War, 1973 (Yom Kippur War)

.05   1980–

.052   Israel-Lebanon-Syria Conflict, 1982–1985

.053   1985–

.1   Turkey and Cyprus

> *For divisions of Turkey and Cyprus, see 956.2–956.6*

.100 01–.100 09   Standard subdivisions, groups, regions, persons

> As modified under 930–990

.100 1–.100 9   Standard subdivisions, groups, regions, persons of Turkey

> As modified under 930–990

*Add as instructed under 930–990

>   956.101–956.103 Historical periods of Turkey

     Class comprehensive works in 956.1

.101   Early history to 1918

     Class ancient history to ca. 640 in 939.2

(.101 2)   Ancient history to ca. 640

     (Optional number; prefer 939.2)

.101 3   640–1100

.101 4   Period of Seljuk rule, 1100–1300

.101 5   1300–1918

     Class here period of Ottoman Empire, 1300–1922

     (Option: Class here Russo-Turkish War of 1877–1878, Greco-Turkish War; prefer 947.081 for Russo-Turkish War of 1877–1878, 949.506 for Greco-Turkish War)

     Class 1918–1922 in 956.1023

.102   1918–1950

     Class here 20th century; Republic, 1923–

     Class 1900–1918 in 956.1015, 1950–   in 956.103

.102 3   1918–1923

.102 4   Administration of Kemal Ataturk, 1923–1938

.102 5   Administration of Ismet Inonu, 1938–1950

     Including 1945–1950 [*formerly also* 956.1035]

.103   1950–

.103 5   1950–1959

     1945–1950 relocated to 956.1025

.103 6   1960–1969

.103 7   1970–1979

.103 8   1980–1989

.103 9   1990–1999

>   **956.2–956.6 Divisions of Turkey and Cyprus**

     Class comprehensive works in 956.1

     For Turkey in Europe, see 949.61

.2   ***Western Turkey**

> Add to base number 956.2 the numbers following 956.1 in 956.101–956.103, e.g., period of Ottoman Empire 956.2015
>
> Class ancient history to ca. 640 in 939.2

.3   ***North central Turkey**

> Add to base number 956.3 the numbers following 956.1 in 956.101–956.103, e.g., period of Ottoman Empire 956.3015
>
> Class ancient Bithyia to ca. 640 in 939.25, ancient Paphlagonia in 939.31, ancient Galatia in 939.32

.4   ***South central Turkey and Cyprus**

> Add to base number 956.4 the numbers following 956.1 in 956.101–956.103, e.g., period of Ottoman Empire 956.4015
>
> Class ancient Pisidia to ca. 640 in 939.27, ancient Lycia in 939.28, ancient Pamphylia in 939.29, ancient Cappadocia in 939.34, ancient Cilicia in 939.35, ancient Commagene in 939.36

.45   *Cyprus

.450 1   Early history to 1571

> Class ancient history to ca. 640 in 939.37

(.450 12)   Ancient history to ca. 640

> (Optional number; prefer 939.37)

.450 2   1571–1878

.450 3   British period, 1878–1960

.450 4   1960–

.5   ***East central Turkey**

> Add to base number 956.5 the numbers following 956.1 in 956.101–956.103, e.g., period of Ottoman Empire 956.5015
>
> Class ancient history to ca. 640 in 939.33

.6   ***Eastern Turkey**

> Add to base number 956.6 the numbers following 956.1 in 956.101–956.103, e.g., period of Ottoman Empire 956.6015
>
> Class ancient Armenia to ca. 640 in 939.55

.7   ***Iraq**

> Class ancient history to 637 in 935

*Add as instructed under 930–990

(.701)	Ancient history to 637
	(Optional number; prefer 935 for Mesopotamia, 939.47 for Arabia Deserta)
	Add to base number 956.701 the numbers following 935.0 in 935.01–935.07, e.g., Hellenistic period 956.7016
.702	637–1553
.703	Period of Ottoman Empire, 1553–1920
.704	1920–
.704 1	Period of mandate, 1920–1932
	Class here reign of Faisal I, 1921–1933
	Class reign of Faisal I during 1932–1933 in 956.7042
.704 2	Period of independent monarchy, 1932–1958
	Contains reigns of Ghazi I, Faisal II
.704 3	Period of Republic, 1958–
	(Option: Class here Iraqi-Iranian Conflict, 1980– ; prefer 955.054)
.9	***Eastern Mediterranean**
.91	*Syria
	Class early history to ca. 640 in 939.43
(.910 1)	Early history to ca. 640
	(Optional number; prefer 939.43)
.910 2	640–1516
.910 3	Period of Ottoman Empire, 1516–1920
.910 4	1920–
.910 41	Period of mandate, 1920–1945
.910 42	Period of Republic, 1945–
	Including period as a part of United Arab Republic, 1958–1961
	Class Israel-Arab War, 1948–1949, in 956.042; Israel-Arab War, 1967, in 956.046; Israel-Arab War, 1973, in 956.048; Israel-Lebanon-Syria Conflict, 1982–1985, in 956.052
.92	*Lebanon
	Class early history to ca. 640 in 939.44
(.920 2)	Early history to ca. 640
	(Optional number; prefer 939.44)
.920 3	640–1926
.920 32	640–1517

*Add as instructed under 930–990

.920 34	Period of Ottoman Empire, 1517–1920
	Including period of autonomy, 1861–1918
.920 35	Period of mandate, 1920–1941
	Class 1926–1941 in 956.92042
.920 4	1926–
.920 42	1926–1941
.920 43	1941–
	Class Israel-Arab War, 1948–1949, in 956.042
	For 1975– , see 956.92044
.920 44	Period of civil war and religious strife, 1975–
	Class Israel-Lebanon-Syria Conflict, 1982–1985, in 956.052
.94	*Palestine Israel
	Class early history to 70 in 933
	See also 909.04924 for world history of Jews
[.940 01]	Zionism
	Relocated to 320.54095694
(.940 1)	Early history to 70
	(Optional number; prefer 933)
	Add to base number 956.9401 the numbers following 933.0 in 933.01–933.05, e.g., age of Solomon 956.94012
.940 2	Mishnaic and Talmudic periods, 70–640
.940 3	640–1917
	Including period of Ottoman Empire
.940 4	Period of British control, 1917–1948
.940 5	1948–
.940 52	1948–1967
	Class Israel-Arab War, 1948–1949, in 956.042; Sinai Campaign, 1956, in 956.044; Israel-Arab War, 1967, in 956.046
.940 53	1967–1974
	Class Israel-Arab War, 1973, in 956.048
.940 54	1974–
	Class Israel-Lebanon-Syria Conflict, 1982–1985, in 956.052

*Add as instructed under 930–990

.949	*Southern district

Add to base number 956.949 the numbers following 956.94 in 956.9401–956.9405, e.g., period of British control 956.94904

Class ancient Judah, Judea in 933; ancient Edom in 939.46

.95	*Jordan

Class early history to 70 in 933

(.950 1)	Early history to 70

(Optional number; prefer 933)

.950 2	70–640
.950 3	640–1923

Including period of Ottoman Empire

.950 4	1923–
.950 42	Period of mandate, 1923–1946
.950 43	Period of Hashemite Kingdom, 1946–

Class Israel-Arab War, 1948–1949, in 956.042; Israel-Arab War, 1967, in 956.046

For 1967–   , see 956.95044

.950 44	1967–
.956	*Karak district

Add to base number 956.956 the numbers following 956.95 in 956.9501–956.9504, e.g., period of Hashemite Kingdom 956.956043

Class ancient Moab to 70 in 939.46

.957	*Maan district

Add to base number 956.957 the numbers following 956.95 in 956.9501–956.9504, e.g., period of Hashemite Kingdom 956.957043

Class ancient Petra to 70 in 939.48

957   *Siberia (Asiatic Russia)

.03	Pre-Russian period to 1581
.07	1581–1855
.08	1855–

Add to base number 957.08 the numbers following 947.08 in 947.081–947.085, e.g., period of Siberia under Stalin 957.0842

958   *Central Asia

(Option: Class here early history to ca. 640; prefer 939.6)

Class early history to ca. 640 in 939.6

*Add as instructed under 930–990

.1   ***Afghanistan**

.101   Early history to 1221

        Earliest history to ca. 640 relocated to 939.6

.102   1221–1709

.103   1709–1919

.104   1919–

.104 2   1919–1933

.104 3   Reign of Muhammad Zahir Shah, 1933–1973

.104 4   Period of Republic, 1973–1978

.104 5   Period of Democratic Republic, 1978–

.4   ***Turkestan   Soviet Central Asia**

        For Turkmenistan, see 958.5, Tadzhikistan, 958.6; Uzbekistan, 958.7

.407   Pre-Russian period to 1855

        Class early history to ca. 640 in 939.6

.408   Russian period, 1855–

        Add to base number 958.408 the numbers following 947.08 in 947.081–947.085, e.g., later 20th century 958.4085

.5   ***Turkmenistan (Turkmen Soviet Socialist Republic)**

        Add to base number 958.5 the numbers following 958.4 in 958.407–958.408, e.g., pre-Russian period 958.507

.6   ***Tadzhikistan (Tadzhik Soviet Socialist Republic)**

        Add to base number 958.6 the numbers following 958.4 in 958.407–958.408, e.g., Russian period 958.608

.7   ***Uzbekistan (Uzbek Soviet Socialist Republic)**

        Add to base number 958.7 the numbers following 958.4 in 958.407–958.408, e.g., later 20th century 958.7085

959   *Southeast Asia

SUMMARY

959.01–.05	[Historical periods]
.1	Burma
.3	Thailand
.4	Laos
.5	Commonwealth of Nations territories Malaysia
.6	Cambodia (Khmer Republic, Kampuchea)
.7	Vietnam
.8	Indonesia
.9	Philippines

*Add as instructed under 930–990

.01	Early history to 1499
.02	1500–1699
.03	1700–1799
.04	1800–1899
.05	1900–
.051	1900–1941
.052	Period of Japanese occupation, 1941–1945
.053	1945–

.1   *Burma

.102	Early history to 1826
.103	Period of British conquest, 1826–1885
.104	Period of British rule, 1886–1948
.105	1948–

.3   *Thailand

.302	Early history to 1782
.302 1	Earliest history to 1219
.302 2	Sukhothai period, 1219–1350
.302 3	Ayutthaya period, 1350–1767
.302 4	Reign of Phraya Taksin, 1767–1782
.303	1782–1910
.303 1	Reign of Phutthayotfa Chulalok (Rama I), 1782–1809
.303 2	Reign of Phutthalœtla Naphalai (Rama II), 1809–1824
.303 3	Reign of Nangklao (Rama III), 1824–1851
.303 4	Reign of Mongkut (Rama IV), 1851–1868
.303 5	Reign of Chulalongkorn (Rama V), 1868–1910
.304	1910–
.304 1	Reign of Vajiravudh (Rama VI), 1910–1925
.304 2	Reign of Prajadhipok (Rama VII), 1925–1935
.304 3	Reign of Ananda Mahidol (Rama VIII), 1935–1946
.304 4	Reign of Bhumibol Adulyadej (Rama IX), 1946–

.4   *Laos

| .403 | Early history to 1949 |
| | Including period as a part of French Indochina, 1893–1954 |

*Add as instructed under 930–990

.404	1949–

Class here 20th century

Class 1900–1949 in 959.403, military operations in Laos during Vietnamese War in 959.70434

.5	***Commonwealth of Nations territories** **Malaysia**
.503	Early history to 1946
.504	1946–1963
.505	Period of federation, 1963–

Class here 20th century

Class 1900–1946 in 959.503, 1946–1963 in 959.504

.505 1	Prime ministership of Tunku Abdul Rahman Putra Al-Haj, 1963–1970

Including separation of Singapore, 1965

.505 2	Prime ministership of Tun Haji Abdul Razak bin Dato' Hussein, 1971–1976
.505 3	Prime ministership of Datuk Hussein Onn, 1976–1981
.505 4	Prime ministership of Mahathir bin Mohamad, 1981–
.55	***Brunei**
.550 3	Early history to 1946
.550 5	1946–

Class here 20th century

Class 1900–1946 in 959.5503

.57	***Singapore**
.570 3	Early history to 1946
.570 4	1946–1963
.570 5	Periods of federation with Malaysia, 1963–1965, and separate nationhood, 1965–

Class here 20th century

Class 1900–1946 in 959.5703, 1946–1963 in 959.5704

.6	***Cambodia (Khmer Republic, Kampuchea)**
.603	Early history to 1949

Including period as a part of French Indochina, 1863–1949

.604	1949–

Class here 20th century

Class 1900–1949 in 959.603, military operations in Cambodia during Vietnamese War in 959.70434

*Add as instructed under 930–990

.7   ***Vietnam**

.703   Early history to 1949

Including period as a part of French Indochina, 1883–1954

Class here comprehensive works on French Indochina

For Laos as a part of French Indochina, see 959.403; Cambodia as a part of French Indochina, 959.603; Indochinese War, 1946–1954, 959.7041

.704   1949–

.704 1   Indochinese War, 1946–1954

.704 2   1954–1961

.704 3   Vietnamese War, 1961–1975

[.704 308]   Vietnamese War with respect to kinds of persons

Do not use; class 959.70431

.704 309 2   Persons

Class personal narratives in 959.70438

.704 31   Social, political, economic history

Including causes, results, efforts to preserve or restore peace, relation of specific classes of persons to the war, internment camps

Class general diplomatic history in 959.70432; prisoner-of-war camps in 959.70437; results in and effects on a specific country with history of the country, e.g., on United States 973.923

.704 32   Diplomatic history

Class diplomatic causes, efforts to preserve or restore peace, diplomatic results in 959.70431

.704 33   Participation of specific countries, localities, groups

Class military participation of specific countries, localities, groups in 959.70434

.704 331   North Vietnam

.704 332   South Vietnam

.704 332 2   National Liberation Front

Class here Vietcong

.704 332 5   Government forces

.704 334–.704 339   Foreign participation

Add to base number 959.70433 notation 4–9 from Table 2, e.g., United States participation 959.7043373

Class a specific activity with the activity, e.g., efforts to preserve or restore peace 959.70431

*Add as instructed under 930–990

.704 34	Military operations
	Including military units
	Class units engaged in a specific type of operation or service with the operation or service, e.g., medical units 959.70437
.704 342	Land operations
.704 345	Naval operations
.704 348	Air operations
.704 36	Celebrations, commemorations, memorials
	Including decorations and awards, rolls of honor, cemeteries, monuments
.704 37	Prisoner-of-war camps, health and social services
.704 38	Other topics
	Including personal narratives, military life and customs, unconventional warfare, propaganda
	Class personal narratives on a specific subject with the subject, e.g., medical units 959.70437
.704 4	1975–

.8   ***Indonesia**

.801	Early history to 1602
.801 2	Earliest history to 1478
.801 5	Period of Muslim rule, 1478–1602
.802	Dutch period, 1602–1945
.802 1	Period of Dutch East India Company, 1602–1798
.802 2	Periods under control of British and Netherlands governments, 1798–1945
	Including Java War, 1825–1830
.803	Period of Republic, 1945–
	Class here 20th century
	Class 1900–1945 in 959.8022
.803 5	1945–1959
	Class here administration of Sukarno, 1945–1967
	Class administration of Sukarno during 1960–1967 in 959.8036
.803 6	1960–1969
.803 7	1970–1979
.803 8	1980–1989
.803 9	1990–

*Add as instructed under 930–990

.9	***Philippines**
.901	Early history to 1564
.902	Spanish period, 1564–1898
.902 7	Period of insurrection against Spanish, 1896–1898
.903	United States period, 1898–1946
.903 1	Philippine-American War, 1898–1901
.903 2	Period of United States rule, 1901–1935
.903 5	Period of Commonwealth, 1935–1946
.904	Period of Republic, 1946–
.904 1	Administration of Manuel Roxas, 1946–1948
.904 2	Administration of Elpidio Quirino, 1948–1954
.904 3	Administration of Ramon Magsaysay, 1954–1957
.904 4	Administration of Carlos Garcia, 1957–1961
.904 5	Administration of Diosdado Macapagal, 1961–1965
.904 6	Administration of Ferdinand Marcos, 1965–1986
.904 7	Administration of Corazon Cojuangco Aquino, 1986–

960   General history of Africa

SUMMARY

960.01–.09	**Standard subdivisions**
.1–.3	**[Historical periods]**
961	**Tunisia and Libya**
962	**Egypt and Sudan**
963	**Ethiopia**
964	**Northwest African coast and offshore islands** **Morocco**
965	**Algeria**
966	**West Africa and offshore islands**
967	**Central Africa and offshore islands**
968	**Southern Africa** **Republic of South Africa**
969	**South Indian Ocean islands**

.01–.09	Standard subdivisions
	As modified under 930–990
.1	**Early history to 640**
.2	**640–1885**
.21	640–1450
.22	1450–1799

*Add as instructed under 930–990

.23	1800–1885
	1885–1899 relocated to 960.312
.3	**1885–**
.31	1885–1945
.312	1885–1914
	Including 1885–1899 [*formerly* 960.23]
.314	1914–1918
.316	1918–1945
.32	1945–
.324	1945–1949
.325	1950–1959
.326	1960–1969
.327	1970–1979
.328	1980–1989
.329	1990–1999

961   *Tunisia and Libya

Class here North Africa

Class early history to ca. 640 in 939.7

(.01)	Early history to ca. 640
	(Optional number; prefer 939.7)
.02	Periods of Arab rule and Ottoman Empire, ca. 640–1830
.022	Period of Arab rule, ca. 640–ca. 1520
.023	Period of Ottoman Empire, ca. 1520–1830
	(Option: Class here Tripolitan War with the United States, United States War with Algiers; prefer 973.47 for Tripolitan War, 973.53 for War with Algiers)
.03	Period of European conquest and hegemony, 1830–1950
	Including 20th century
	Class 1950– in 961.04
.04	1950–
.045	1950–1959
.046	1960–1969
.047	1970–1979

*Add as instructed under 930–990

.048	1980–1989
.049	1990–1999

.1   ***Tunisia**

> Class early history to 647 in 939.73

(.101)	Early history to 647

> (Optional number; prefer 939.73)

.102	Period of Arab rule, 647–1516
.103	Period of Ottoman Empire, 1516–1881
.104	1881–1956
.105	1956–
.105 1	Administration of Habib Bourguiba, 1956–1987
.105 2	1987–

.2   ***Libya**

> Class early history to 644 in 939.74

(.201)	Early history to 644

> (Optional number; prefer 939.74)

.202	Periods of Arab rule and Ottoman Empire, 644–1911
.203	Period of Italian rule, 1911–1952
.204	1952–
.204 1	Reign of Idris I, 1952–1969
.204 2	Period of Muammar Qaddafi, 1969–

962   Egypt and Sudan

SUMMARY

962.000 1–.000 9	Standard subdivisions of Egypt and Sudan
.001–.009	Standard subdivisions of Egypt
.02–.05	Historical periods of Egypt
.4	Sudan
.5	Eastern and Northern regions of Sudan
.6	Khartoum province and Central region of Sudan
.7	Darfur region of Sudan
.8	Kordofan region of Sudan
.9	Southern regions of Sudan

.000 1–.000 9	Standard subdivisions of Egypt and Sudan

> As modified under 930–990

.001–.009	Standard subdivisions of Egypt

> As modified under 930–990

*Add as instructed under 930–990

(.01)	Early history to 640

(Optional number; prefer 932)

Add to base number 962.01 the numbers following 932.0 in 932.01–932.02, e.g., period of New Kingdom 962.0114

> 962.02–962.05 Historical periods of Egypt

Class comprehensive works in 962, early history in 932

(Option: Class early history in 962.01; prefer 932)

.02	Period of Arab rule, 640–1517
.03	Period of Ottoman Empire, 1517–1882
.04	Period of British occupation and protectorate, 1882–1922
.05	1922–
.051	Reign of Fuad I, 1922–1936
.052	Reign of Faruk I, 1936–1952, and regency (Fuad II), 1952–1953

> *For Israel-Arab War, 1948–1949, see 956.042*

.053	Administrations of Mohammed Naguib and Gamal Abdel Nasser, 1953–1970

Including United Arab Republic, 1958–1961

Class Syrian part of United Arab Republic in 956.91042

> *For Sinai Campaign, 1956, see 956.044; Israel-Arab War, 1967, 956.046*

.054	Administration of Anwar Sadat, 1970–1981

> *For Israel-Arab War, 1973, see 956.048*

.055	1981–

Including administration of Muhammad Hosni Mubarak, 1981–

.4	***Sudan**

> *For parts of Sudan, see 962.5–962.9*

.401	Early history to 500
.402	500–1820

Specific kingdoms relocated to area of the kingdom in 962.5–962.9, e.g., kingdom of Nobatia 962.5022, of Alwa 962.62022

.402 2	Period of Christian kingdoms, 500–1504
.402 3	Period of Funj Sultanate, 1504–1820

*Add as instructed under 930–990

.403	Period as Anglo-Egyptian Sudan, 1820–1956

Class here period of Egyptian and British rule

.404   1956–

Including administration of Jafar Muhammad Numayri, 1969–1985

> **962.5–962.9 Parts of Sudan**

Class comprehensive works in 962.4

.5   ***Eastern and Northern regions of Sudan**

Class early history to 500 in 939.78

(.501)   Early history to 500

Class here ancient Ethiopia

(Optional number; prefer 939.78)

.502   500–1820

.502 2   Period of Christian kingdoms, 500–1504

Examples: kingdoms of Mukhara, Nobatia [*both formerly* 962.402]

.502 3   Period of Funji Sultanate, 1504–1820

.503   Period as a part of Anglo-Egyptian Sudan, 1820–1956

.504   1956–

.6   ***Khartoum province and Central region of Sudan**

Add to base number 962.6 the numbers following 962.4 in 962.401–962.404, e.g., period as a part of Anglo-Egyptian Sudan 962.603

.7   ***Darfur region of Sudan**

Add to base number 962.7 the numbers following 962.4 in 962.401–962.404, e.g., period as a part of Anglo-Egyptian Sudan 962.703

.8   ***Kordofan region of Sudan**

Add to base number 962.8 the numbers following 962.4 in 962.401–962.404, e.g., period as a part of Anglo-Egyptian Sudan 962.803

.9   ***Southern regions of Sudan**

Add to base number 962.9 the numbers following 962.4 in 962.401–962.404, e.g., period as a part of Anglo-Egyptian Sudan 962.903

963   *Ethiopia

.01   Early history to 640

Kingdom of Axum relocated to 963.501

See also 939.78 for ancient Ethiopia (a part of what is now modern Sudan, not modern Ethiopia)

*Add as instructed under 930–990

.02	640–1543
.03	1543–1855
.04	1855–1913
.041	Reign of Theodore II, 1855–1868
.042	1868–1889

> Including reign of John IV, 1872–1889

.043	Reign of Menelik II, 1889–1913

> Including reign of Menelik II during 1889–1913 [*formerly* 963.052], Ethiopian War, 1895–1896
> (Option: Class Ethiopian War in 945.091)

.05	1913–1941

> Class here 20th century
>
> Class 1900–1913 in 963.043, 1941–1974 in 963.06, 1974–   in 963.07

[.052]	Reign of Menelik II during 1889–1913

> Relocated to 963.043

.053	Reign of Lij Yasu, 1913–1916
.054	Period of Jah Rastafari (Haile Selassie) as regent and king, 1917–1930
.055	Reign of Haile Selassie (Jah Rastafari) as emperor, 1930–1974

> Class reign of Haile Selassie during 1935–1974 in 963.056–963.06

.056	Italo-Ethiopian War, 1935–1936

> (Option: Class in 945.091)

.057	Period of Italian rule, 1936–1941
.06	1941–1974

> Including deposition of Haile Selassie, 1974

.07	1974–

> Including chairmanship of Mengistu Haile-Mariam, 1977–   ; Somali-Ethiopian conflicts, 1977–

.5	***Eritrea province**
.501	Early history to 640

> Including period of kingdom of Axum [*formerly* 963.01]

964   Northwest African coast and offshore islands   Morocco

.000 1–.000 9	Standard subdivisions of northwest African coast and offshore islands

> As modified under 930–990

*Add as instructed under 930–990

.001–.009   Standard subdivisions of Morocco

            As modified under 930–990

(.01)   Ancient history to 647

            (Optional number; prefer 939.71)

\>   964.02–964.05 Historical periods of Morocco

            Class comprehensive works in 964, early history to 647 in 939.71

            (Option: Class early history to 647 in 964.01; prefer 939.71)

.02   Periods of Arab and Berber rule, 647–1830

.03   1830–1899

            Including Spanish-Moroccan War, 1859–1860
               (Option: Class Spanish-Moroccan War in 946.072)

            Class here 19th century

            Class 1800–1830 in 964.02

.04   1900–1956

            Including reign of Muhammad V, 1927–1961

            Class here period of French and Spanish protectorates, 1912–1956

            Class reign of Muhammad V during 1956–1961 in 964.05

.05   1956–

            Including reign of Muhammad V during 1956–1961, Hassan II, 1961–

.9   ***Canary Islands**

.906   Early history to 1402

.907   Periods of French, Portuguese, Spanish rule, 1402–1927

.908   Period as Provinces of Spain, 1927–

.908 1   1927–1939

.908 2–.908 3   Periods of Francisco Franco and Juan Carlos I, 1939–

            Add to base number 964.908 the numbers following 946.08 in
            946.082–946.083, e.g., 1960–1969 964.90826

965   ***Algeria**

            Class early history to 647 in 939.71

(.01)   Early history to 647

            (Optional number; prefer 939.71)

.02   Periods of Arab and Berber rule and Ottoman Empire, 647–1830

*Add as instructed under 930–990

.03	Period of French rule, 1830–1962

For 1900–1962, see 965.04

.04	1900–1962
.05	1962–

Including administration of Chadli Bendjedid, 1979–

.5   *Northeastern departments

Add to base number 965.5 the numbers following 965 in 965.01–965.05, e.g., period of French rule 965.503

Class ancient Numidia to 647 in 939.72

.7   *Sahara departments

Add to base number 965.7 the numbers following 965 in 965.01–965.05, e.g., period of French rule 965.703

Class ancient Gaetulia to 647 in 939.77

966   *West Africa and offshore islands

SUMMARY

966.01–.03	Historical periods
.1	Mauritania
.2	Mali, Burkina Faso, Niger
.3	Senegal
.4	Sierra Leone
.5	Gambia, Guinea, Guinea-Bissau, Cape Verde
.6	Liberia and Ivory Coast
.7	Ghana
.8	Togo and Benin
.9	Nigeria

.01–.03	Historical periods

Add to base number 966.0 the numbers following 960 in 960.1–960.3, e.g., early history to 640 966.01

.1   *Mauritania

.101	Early history to 1903
.101 6	300–1200

Class here comprehensive works on period of Ghana Empire

Class period of Ghana Empire in Mali history in 966.2301

.101 7	1200–1500

Class here period of Mali Empire

.103	French period, 1903–1960
.105	1960–

*Add as instructed under 930–990

.2	***Mali, Burkina Faso, Niger**
.201	Early history to ca. 1900
.201 7	1200–1400
	Class here period of Mali Empire
	Class period of Mali Empire in Mauritanian history in 966.1017
.201 8	1400–1500
	Class here period of Songhai Empire
.202	French period, ca. 1900–1960
.203	1960–
.23	***Mali**
.230 1	Early history to 1902
	Class comprehensive works on Mali Empire in 966.2017
.230 3	Period as French Sudan, 1902–1960
	Class here French period
.230 5	1960–
	Class here administration of Moussa Traoré, 1968–
.25	***Burkina Faso**
	Former name: Upper Volta
.250 1	Early history to 1897
	Including kingdom of Mossi
.250 3	French period, 1897–1960
.250 5	1960–
	Including administration of Thomas Sankara, 1983–1987
.26	***Niger**
.260 1	Early history to 1900
.260 3	French period, 1900–1960
.260 5	1960–
	Including administration of Seyni Kountché, 1974–1987
.3	***Senegal**
.301	Early history to 1895
	Including kingdom of Tekrur
.303	French period, 1895–1960

*Add as instructed under 930–990

.305	1960–	

Including administration of Abdou Diouf, 1981–   ; Confederation of Senegambia, 1982–

Class Gambian part of Senegambia in 966.5103

.4	***Sierra Leone**
.401	Early history to 1787
.402	Period as a British colony, 1787–1896
.403	Period as both colony and protectorate, 1896–1961
.404	1961–
.5	***Gambia, Guinea, Guinea-Bissau, Cape Verde**
.51	*Gambia
.510 1	Early history to 1807
.510 2	Period as a British colony, 1807–1965
.510 3	Administration of Dawada Kairaba Jawara, 1965–

Including period as a part of Senegambia, 1982–

.52	*Guinea
.520 1	Early history to 1882
.520 3	Period as French Guinea, 1882–1958
.520 5	1958–
.57	*Guinea-Bissau
.570 1	Early history to 1879
.570 2	Period as Portuguese Guinea, 1879–1974
.570 3	1974–
.58	*Cape Verde
.580 1	Early history to 1900
.580 2	1900–1975
.580 3	Administration of Aristides Pereira, 1975–
.6	**Liberia and Ivory Coast**
.62	*Liberia
.620 1	Early history to 1847
.620 2	1847–1945
.620 3	1945–

Including administration of Samuel K. Doe, 1980–

*Add as instructed under 930–990

.68		*Ivory Coast
.680 1		Early history to 1904
.680 3		French period, 1904–1960
.680 5		Administration of Félix Houphouët-Boigny, 1960–
.7	***Ghana**	

See also 966.1016 for Ghana Empire

.701	Early history to 1874
.701 6	Period of Akan states, 1295–1740
	Examples: Akwamu, Bono kingdoms
.701 8	Period of Asante (Ashanti) empire, 1740–1874
.703	Period as Gold Coast, 1874–1957
	Class here British period
.705	1957–
	Including administration of Kwame Nkrumah, 1957–1966; of Jerry J. Rawlings, 1981–

.8	**Togo and Benin**	
.81		*Togo
.810 1		Early history to 1894
.810 2		German period, 1894–1914
.810 3		Anglo-French period, 1914–1960
.810 4		1960–
		Including administration of Gnassingbé Eyadéma, 1967–
.83		*Benin

See also 966.9301 for kingdom of Benin

.830 1	Early history to 1904
.830 18	Period of kingdom of Dahomey, 1600–1904
.830 3	French period, 1904–1960
.830 5	1960–

.9	***Nigeria**	
.901		Early history to 1886
[.901 3–.901 8]		Specific realms

Relocated to area of each realm in 966.91–966.98, e.g., kingdom of Benin 966.9301, Fulani empire 966.9501, kingdom of Kanem-Bornu 966.9801

*Add as instructed under 930–990

.903	Period as a British colony, 1886–1960
.905	1960–
.905 1	1960–1967
.905 2	Period of Nigerian Civil War, 1967–1970
.905 3	1970–

Including administration of Ibrahim Badamosi Babangida, 1983–

[.99]   Islands of Gulf of Guinea

Relocated to 967.1

967   *Central Africa and offshore islands

Class here Sub-Saharan Africa (Africa south of the Sahara)

Class each specific part of Sub-Saharan Africa not provided for here with the part, e.g., Nigeria 966.9

SUMMARY

967.01–.03	Historical periods
.1	Cameroon, Sao Tome and Principe, Equatorial Guinea
.2	Gabon and Republic of the Congo
.3	Angola
.4	Central African Republic and Chad
.5	Zaire, Rwanda, Burundi
.6	Uganda and Kenya
.7	Djibouti and Somalia
.8	Tanzania
.9	Mozambique

.01–.03   Historical periods

Add to base number 967.0 the numbers following 960 in 960.1–960.3, e.g., early history to 640 967.01

.1   *Cameroon, Sao Tome and Principe, Equatorial Guinea

Class here Islands of Gulf of Guinea [*formerly* 966.99], Lower Guinea area

.11   *Cameroon

.110 1   Early history to 1884

.110 2   Period as Kamerun, 1884–1916

Class here German period

.110 3   Anglo-French period, 1916–1959

.110 4   1960–

Including administration of Paul Biya, 1982–

.15   *Sao Tome and Principe

.150 1   Early history to 1975

*Add as instructed under 930–990

.150 2		Period of Republic, 1975–
.18		***Equatorial Guinea**
.180 1		Early history to 1469
.180 2		Portuguese, British, Spanish periods, 1469–1968
.180 3		1968–

> Including administration of Teodoro Obiang Nguema Mbasogo, 1979–

.2   ***Gabon and Republic of the Congo**

.201   Early history to 1910

.203   Period as French Equatorial Africa, 1910–1959

> Class here comprehensive works on French Equatorial Africa [*formerly* 967.2403]
>
> *For Ubangi-Shari as part of French Equatorial Africa, see 967.4103; Chad as part of French Equatorial Africa, 967.4302*

.205   1959–

.21   *Gabon

.210 1   Early history to 1839

.210 2   French period, 1839–1960

> Including period as a part of French Equatorial Africa

.210 4   1960–

> Including administration of Omar Bongo, 1967–

.24   *Republic of the Congo

.240 1   Early history to 1885

.240 3   Period as Middle Congo, 1885–1960

> Class here French period
>
> Comprehensive works on French Equatorial Africa relocated to 967.203

.240 5   1960–

> Including administration of Denis Sassou Nguesso, 1979–

.3   ***Angola**

.301   Early history to 1648

> Specific kingdoms relocated to area of the kingdom in 967.31–967.35, e.g., Lunda kingdom 967.3401

*Add as instructed under 930–990

.302	1648–1899
	Including 17th century
	Class 1600–1648 in 967.301
.303	1900–1975
.304	1975–
	Including administrations of António Agostinho Neto, José Eduardo dos Santos

.4   ***Central African Republic and Chad**

.41	*Central African Republic
.410 1	Early history to 1890
.410 3	Period as Ubangi-Shari, 1890–1960
	Class here French period, period as part of French Equatorial Africa
.410 5	1960–
.43	*Chad
.430 1	Early history to 1850
	Including kingdom of Kanem
	Class Kanem-Bornu in 966.9801
.430 2	Colonial period, 1850–1960
	Including period as part of French Equatorial Africa
.430 4	1960–
	Including administration of Hissein Habré, 1982–

.5   **Zaire, Rwanda, Burundi**

.51	*Zaire
.510 1	Early history to 1885
	Specific kingdoms relocated to specific area of kingdom in 967.511–967.518, , e.g., kingdom of Kongo 967.511401, of Luba 967.51801
.510 2	Belgian period, 1885–1960
.510 22	Period as Congo Free State, 1885–1908
.510 24	Period as Belgian Congo, 1908–1960
.510 3	1960–
	Class here administration of Mobutu Sese Seko, 1965–
.57	*Rwanda and Burundi
	Class here former Ruanda-Urundi
.570 1	Early history to 1899

*Add as instructed under 930–990

.570 2		German period, 1899–1917
.570 3		Belgian period, 1917–1962
.570 4		1962–
.571	*Rwanda	
.571 04		1962–
		Including administration of Juvénal Habyarimana, 1973–
.572	*Burundi	
.572 04		1962–
		Including administration of Jean-Baptiste Bagaza, 1976–1987

.6   *Uganda and Kenya

Class here East Africa

.601		Early history to 1894
.603		1894–1961
.604		1961–
.61	*Uganda	
.610 1		Early history to 1894
		Including kingdoms of Ankole, Buganda, Bunyoro, Busoga, Karagwe
.610 3		British period, 1894–1962
.610 4		1962–
		Including administrations of A. Milton Obote, Idi Amin, Yoweri Museveni
.62	*Kenya	
.620 1		Early history to 1895
.620 3		British period, 1895–1963
.620 4		Administrations of Jomo Kenyatta and Daniel Arap Moi, 1963–

.7   *Djibouti and Somalia

Class here Somaliland

.71	*Djibouti	
.710 1		Early history to 1881
.710 3		French period, 1881–1977
.710 32		Period as French Somaliland, 1881–1967
.710 34		Period as French Territory of the Afars and Issas, 1967–1977
.710 4		1977–

*Add as instructed under 930–990

.73	*Somalia
.730 1	Early history to 1884
	Including kingdom of Mogadishu
.730 3	Period of British and Italian control, 1884–1960
.730 5	1960–
	Including administration of Maxamed Siyaad Barre, 1969–
	Class Somali-Ethiopian conflicts, 1977– , in 963.07

.8   ***Tanzania**

.804	Period as United Republic, 1964–
	Including administration of Julius K. Nyerere, 1964–1985
.81	*Zanzibar and Pemba regions
.810 1	Early history to 1700
.810 2	Period of Arab rule, 1700–1890
.810 3	Period as a British protectorate, 1890–1963
.810 4	1963–
.82	*Tanganyika
.820 1	Early history to 1884
.820 2	German period, 1884–1916
.820 3	British period, 1916–1961
.820 4	1961–

.9   ***Mozambique**

.901	Early history to 1648
.902	1648–1900
	Including 17th century
	Class here Portugese period, 1648–1974
	Class 1600–1648 in 967.901
	For 1900–1975, see 967.903
.903	1900–1975
.905	1975–
	Including administration of Samora Machel, 1975–1986

*Add as instructed under 930–990

968   *Southern Africa   **Republic of South Africa**

See Manual at 968

SUMMARY

968.02–.06	**Historical periods of Republic of South Africa**
.2	**Transvaal**
.4	**Natal**
.5	**Orange Free State**
.7	**Cape of Good Hope**
.8	**Botswana, Lesotho, Swaziland, Namibia**
.9	**Zimbabwe, Zambia, Malawi**

\>   968.02–968.06 Historical periods of Republic of South Africa

Class comprehensive works in 968

.02   Early history to 1488

.03   Period of European exploration and settlement, 1488–1814

.04   1814–1910

.041   1814–1835

Class here Mfecane (Difaqane)

.042   Great Trek, 1835–1838

.044   1838–1854

.045   1854–1899

See also 968.2046 for First Anglo-Boer War

.048   South African (Second Anglo-Boer) War, 1899–1902

(Option: Class South African (Second Anglo-Boer) War in 941.081)

[.048 08]   South African War with respect to kinds of persons

Do not use; class 968.0481

.048 092   Persons

Class personal narratives in 968.0488

.048 1   Social, political, economic history

Including causes, results, efforts to preserve or restore peace, relation of specific classes of persons to the war, internment camps

Class general diplomatic history in 968.0482; prisoner-of-war camps in 968.0487; results in and effects on a specific country with history of the country, e.g., on Great Britain 941.0823

.048 2   Diplomatic history

Class diplomatic causes, efforts to preserve or restore peace, diplomatic results in 968.0481

.048 3	Participation of specific countries, localities, groups
	Class military participation of specific countries, localities, groups in 968.0484
.048 31	Great Britain
.048 32	Boer Republics
.048 4	Military operations
	Including military units
	Class units engaged in a specific type of operation or service with the operation or service, e.g., medical units 968.0487
.048 6	Celebrations, commemorations, memorials
	Including decorations and awards, rolls of honor, cemeteries, monuments
.048 7	Prisoner-of-war camps, health and social services
.048 8	Other topics
	Including personal narratives, military life and customs, unconventional warfare, propaganda
	Class personal narratives on a specific subject with the subject, e.g., medical units 968.0487
.049	1902–1910
.05	Period of Union, 1910–1961
.052	Prime ministership of Louis Botha, 1910–1919
.053	First prime ministership of Jan Christiaan Smuts, 1919–1924
.054	Prime ministership of James Barry Munnik Hertzog, 1924–1939
.055	Second prime ministership of Jan Christiaan Smuts, 1939–1948
.056	Prime ministership of Daniel François Malan, 1948–1954
.057	Prime ministership of Johannes Gerhardus Strijdom, 1954–1958
.058	Prime ministership of Hendrik Frensch Verwoerd, 1958–1966
	Including Sharpeville Massacre, 1960
	For 1961–1966, see 968.061
.06	Period as Republic, 1961–
.061	Period of prime ministership of Hendrik Frensch Verwoerd under republic, 1961–1966
.062	Prime ministership of B. J. Vorster, 1966–1978
.062 7	1976–1977
	Class here Soweto and related riots
.063	Prime ministership of P. W. Botha, 1978–

[.1]	**Botswana, Lesotho, Swaziland**	
	Relocated to 968.8	
.2	***Transvaal**	
.203	Early history to 1835	
.204	1835–1910	

Class here 19th century

Class 1800–1835 in 968.203

.204 2	Period of Great Trek and Boer settlement, 1835–1852
.204 5	Period as South African Republic, 1852–1877
.204 6	Period of British control, 1877–1881

Including First Anglo-Boer War, 1880–1881

.204 7	1881–1899
.204 75	Jameson raid, 1895–1896
.204 8	Period of South African (Second Anglo-Boer) War, 1899–1902
.204 9	Period as Transvaal Colony, 1902–1910
.205–.206	Periods of union and republic, 1910–

Add to base number 968.20 the numbers following 968.0 in 968.05–968.06, e.g., period of World War II 968.2055

.4	***Natal**
.403	Early history to 1824
.403 8	Period of early Nguni kingdoms, ca. 1500–1816

Examples: kingdoms of Mthethwa, Ndwandwe, Qwabe

.403 9   Reign of Shaka, 1816–1828

Including 1820–1824 [*formerly* 968.404]

Class reign of Shaka during 1824–1828 in 968.4041

.404   1824–1910

Class here period of Zululand, 1816–1879

1820–1824 relocated to 968.4039

For reign of Shaka, see 968.4039

.404 1   Period of early British settlement, 1824–1835

Class here reign of Dingaan, 1828–1840

Class reign of Dingaan during 1835–1840 in 968.4042

.404 2   Period of Great Trek and Boer settlement, 1835–1843

Including Battle of Blood River, 1838; republic of Natalia

*Add as instructed under 930–990

.404 5	Period as a British colony, 1843–1899
	Including reign of Cetewayo, 1872–1879; Zulu War, 1879; annexation of Zululand, 1897
.404 8	Period of South African (Second Anglo-Boer) War, 1899–1902
.404 9	1902–1910
.405–.406	Periods of union and republic, 1910–
	Add to base number 968.40 the numbers following 968.0 in 968.05–968.06, e.g., period of World War I 968.4052

.5   *Orange Free State

.503	Early history to 1828
.504	1828–1910
	Class here 19th century
	Class 1800–1828 in 968.503
.504 2	Periods of Great Trek and as Orange River Sovereignty, 1835–1854
.504 5	Period as Orange Free State, 1854–1899
.504 8	Period of South African (Second Anglo-Boer) War, 1899–1902
.504 9	Period as Orange River Colony, 1902–1910
.505–.506	Periods of union and republic, 1910–
	Add to base number 968.50 the numbers following 968.0 in 968.05–968.06, e.g., prime ministership of James Barry Munnik Hertzog 968.5054

.7   *Cape of Good Hope

.702	Early history to 1488
.703	Period of exploration and settlement, 1488–1814
.703 1	1488–1652
.703 2	Period of Dutch control, 1652–1795
	Including 1780–1795 [*formerly* 968.7033]
	Class period of control by Batavian Republic in 968.7033
.703 3	1795–1806
	Contains periods of British occupation, 1795–1803, control by Batavian Republic, 1803–1806
	1780–1795 relocated to 968.7032, 1806–1814 to 968.7042

*Add as instructed under 930–990

.704	1806–1910
.704 2	Period of British control, 1806–1854
	Including 1806–1814 [*formerly* 968.7033], period of Great Trek
	Class period of British occupation, 1795–1803, in 968.7033
.704 5	Period of self-government, 1854–1899
.704 8	Period of South African (Second Anglo-Boer) War, 1899–1902
.704 9	1902–1910
.705–.706	Union and republic, 1910–

Add to base number 968.70 the numbers following 968.0 in 968.05–968.06, e.g., first prime ministership of Jan Christiaan Smuts 968.7053

.8   ***Botswana, Lesotho, Swaziland [*all formerly* 968.1], Namibia**

.801–.803	Historical periods

Add to base number 968.80 the numbers following 960 in 960.1–960.3, e.g., 20th century 968.803

Historical periods of Namibia relocated to 968.8101–968.8103

.81	*Namibia

> 968.810 1–968.810 3 Historical periods of Namibia [*formerly* 968.801–968.803]

Class comprehensive works in 968.81

.810 1	Early history to 1884
.810 2	German period, 1884–1915
.810 3	South African period, 1915–
.83	*Botswana
.830 1	Early history to 1885
.830 2	Period as Bechuanaland, 1885–1966
	Class here British period
.830 3	1966–
	Including administration of Seretse Khama, 1966–1980
.85	*Lesotho
.850 1	Early history to 1868
.850 2	Period as Basutoland, 1868–1966
	Class here British period
.850 3	Reign of Moshoeshoe II, 1966–
	Including prime ministership of Leabua Jonathan, 1966–1986

*Add as instructed under 930–990

.87	*Swaziland
.870 1	Early history to 1840
.870 2	British period, 1840–1968
.870 3	1968–

Including reigns of Sobhuza II, 1968–1982; Mswari III, 1986–

.9 *Zimbabwe, Zambia, Malawi

.901	Early history to 1888
.902	Period of British control, 1888–1953
.903	Period as Federation of Rhodesia and Nyasaland (Central African Federation), 1953–1963

Class here prime ministership of Roy Welensky, 1956–1963

.904	1964–
.91	*Zimbabwe
.910 1	Early history to 1889

Including Karanga kingdoms of Changamire, the Monomotapas

.910 2	Period as Southern Rhodesia, 1889–1953

Class here British period

.910 3	Period of federation, 1953–1963
.910 4	Period as Rhodesia, 1964–1980

Class here prime ministership of Ian Douglas Smith, 1965–1979

.910 5	Period as Republic of Zimbabwe, 1980–

Class here prime ministership of Robert Gabriel Mugabe, 1980–

.94	*Zambia
.940 1	Early history to 1890

Including kingdoms of the Barotse, of the Bemba

.940 2	Period of British control, 1890–1953

Contains periods as North-eastern Rhodesia and North-western Rhodesia provinces, 1890–1911; as Northern Rhodesia, 1911–1953

.940 3	Period of federation, 1953–1963
.940 4	Period as Republic of Zambia, 1964–

Class here administration of Kenneth D. Kaunda, 1964–

.97	*Malawi
.970 1	Early history to 1891

Including kingdom of Malawi

*Add as instructed under 930–990

.970 2	Period as Nyasaland, 1891–1953
	Class here British period
.970 3	Period of federation, 1953–1963
.970 4	Administration of H. Kamuzu Banda, 1964–

969 †South Indian Ocean islands

.1   *Madagascar

.101	Early history to 1895
	Including kingdoms of Betsimisaraka, Boina, Menabe, Merina
.103	French period, 1895–1960
.105	1960–
	Including administration of Didier Ratsiraka, 1975–

.4   †Comoros (Federal and Islamic Republic of the Comoros)

.6   †Seychelles

.7   †Chagos Islands

.8   *Réunion and Mauritius

.81   *Réunion

.810 2	Early history to 1946
.810 4	Period as a Department of France, 1946–

.82   *Mauritius

.820 1	Early history to 1810
.820 2	Period of British rule, 1810–1968
.820 3	1968–

.9   †Isolated islands

Contains Amsterdam, Cocos (Keeling), Crozet, Kerguelen, Prince Edward, Saint Paul

*Add as instructed under 930–990

†Add as instructed under 930–990; however, do not add historical periods

970   General history of North America

SUMMARY

970.001–.009	**Standard subdivisions**	
.01–.05	**Historical periods**	
971	**Canada**	
972	**Middle America**	**Mexico**
973	**United States**	
974	**Northeastern United States (New England and Middle Atlantic states)**	
975	**Southeastern United States (South Atlantic states)**	
976	**South central United States**	**Gulf Coast states**
977	**North central United States**	
978	**Western United States**	
979	**Great Basin and Pacific Slope region of United States**	**Pacific Coast states**

.001–.003   Standard subdivisions

.004   Racial, ethnic, national groups

> Add to base number 970.004 notation 03–99 from Table 5, e.g., general history and civilization of North American native peoples in North America 970.00497
>> (Option: Class North American native peoples in North America in 970.1, specific native peoples in 970.3)

> Specific native peoples in a specific place relocated to the place in 971–979 with use of subdivision 00497 from table under 930–990, e.g., the Hopi in Arizona 979.1004974

> Class history and civilization of North American native peoples in a specific place before European discovery and conquest with the place, without using notation 00497, e.g., Aztecs before 1519 972.018

> *See Manual at 970.004*

.005–.009   Standard subdivisions

> As modified under 930–990

>   970.01–970.05 Historical periods

> Class comprehensive works in 970

.01   Early history to 1599

.011   Earliest history to 1492

> Including pre-Columbian claims

>> *For Chinese claims, see 970.012; Norse claims, 970.013; Welsh claims, 970.014*

.012   Chinese claims

.013   Norse claims

.014   Welsh claims

> 970.015–970.019 Period of European discovery and exploration

Class comprehensive works in 970.01

.015	Discoveries by Columbus
.016	Spanish and Portuguese explorations
.017	English explorations
.018	French explorations
.019	Explorations by other nations
.02	1600–1699
.03	1700–1799
.04	1800–1899
.05	1900–
.051	1900–1918

Class here period of World War I, 1914–1918

.052	1918–1945

Class here period of World War II, 1939–1945

.053	1945–
.053 4	1945–1949
.053 5	1950–1959
.053 6	1960–1969
.053 7	1970–1979
.053 8	1980–1989
.053 9	1990–1999

(.1) **North American native peoples**   **Indians of North America**

(Optional number; prefer 970.00497)

Class special topics in 970.3–970.5

(.3) **Specific native peoples**

(Optional number; prefer 971–979 with use of subdivision 00497 from table under 930–990, e.g., the Hopi in Arizona 979.1004974)

Arrange alphabetically by name of people

Class government relations with specific native peoples in 970.5

(.4)   **Native peoples in specific places in North America**

(Optional number; prefer 971–979 with use of subdivision 00497 from table under 930–990, e.g., native peoples in United States 973.0497, in Arizona 979.100497)

Add to base number 970.4 the numbers following —7 in notation 71–79 from Table 2, e.g., Indians in Arizona 970.491

Class government relations in specific places in 970.5, specific native peoples in specific places in 970.3

(.5)   **Government relations with North American native peoples**

History and policy

(Optional number; prefer 323.1197 for comprehensive works; a specific subject with the subject, e.g., Black Hawk War 973.56, relation to the state in Canada 323.1197071)

>   **971–979 Countries and localities**

Class specific native peoples in a specific place [*formerly* 970.00497] with the place in 971–979 with use of subdivision 00497 from table under 930–990, e.g., the Hopi in Arizona 979.1004974

     (Option: Class native peoples in specific places in North America in 970.4)

Class comprehensive works in 970

971   ***Canada**

SUMMARY

971.01–.06	Historical periods
.1	British Columbia
.2	Prairie Provinces
.3	Ontario
.4	Quebec
.5	Atlantic Provinces Maritime Provinces
.6	Nova Scotia
.7	Prince Edward Island
.8	Newfoundland and Labrador, Saint-Pierre and Miquelon
.9	Northern territories

SUMMARY

971.01	Early history to 1763
.02	Period of early British rule, 1763–1791
.03	Period of Upper and Lower Canada, 1791–1841
.04	Period of Province of Canada, 1841–1867
.05	Period of Dominion of Canada, 1867–1911
.06	1911–

*Add as instructed under 930–990

>   971.01–971.06 Historical periods

       Class comprehensive works in 971

.01   Early history to 1763

.011   Earliest history to 1632

.011 1   Period before European discovery and exploration

.011 2   Norse explorations

.011 3   French explorations

.011 4   English explorations

.016   Period of French and English expansion, 1632–1689

.016 2   Period of Company of New France, 1632–1663

.016 3   1663–1689

.018   Period of struggle of France and England for supremacy, 1689–1763

       Including periods of War of the League of Augsburg, 1688–1697; War of the Spanish Succession, 1701–1714; War of the Austrian Succession, 1740–1748

       Class here comprehensive works on period as a French royal province, 1663–1763

       (Option: Class here North American aspects of War of the League of Augsburg, War of the Spanish Succession, War of the Austrian Succession; prefer 973.25 for War of the League of Augsburg, War of the Spanish Succession, 973.26 for War of the Austrian Succession)

       Class comprehensive works on War of the League of Augsburg in 940.2525, War of the Spanish Succession in 940.2526, War of the Austrian Succession in 940.2532; North American aspects of War of the League of Augsburg, War of the Spanish Succession in 973.25, War of the Austrian Succession in 973.26

       For 1663–1689, see 971.0163

.018 7   Expulsion of Acadians, 1755

.018 8   Period of Seven Years' War, 1756–1763

       (Option: Class here North American aspects of Seven Years' War; prefer 973.26)

       Class comprehensive works on Seven Years' War in 940.2534, North American aspects in 973.26

.02   Period of early British rule, 1763–1791

.022   1763–1774

       Including Quebec Act, 1774

       (Option: Class here Pontiac's conspiracy, 1763–1764; prefer 973.27)

.024	Period of American Revolution, 1774–1783
	Including settlement of Loyalists from United States, 1774–1789
	Class settlement of Loyalists during 1783–1789 in 971.028
.028	1783–1791
	Class here Constitutional Act, 1791
.03	Period of Upper and Lower Canada, 1791–1841
.032	1791–1812
.034	Period of War of 1812, 1812–1814
	(Option: Class here War of 1812; prefer 973.52)
.036	1814–1837
.038	Period of rebellions of 1837–1838
	Including Family Compact of Upper Canada, Chateau Clique of Lower Canada
.039	1838–1841
	Class here Durham mission and report, 1838–1839; Act of Union, 1840
.04	Period of Province of Canada, 1841–1867
.042	1841–1864
.048	Period of Fenian activities, 1866–1871
.049	Period of Confederation, 1864–1867
	Including Charlottetown and Quebec Conferences, 1864; British North America Act, 1867
	For period of Fenian activities, see 971.048
.05	Period of Dominion of Canada, 1867–
	For 1911– , see 971.06
.051	First prime ministership of Sir John A. Macdonald, 1867–1873
	Including Riel's first (Red River) rebellion, 1869–1870
	Class Fenian activities during 1867–1871 in 971.048
.052	Prime ministership of Alexander Mackenzie, 1873–1878
.054	Second prime ministership of Sir John A. Macdonald, 1878–1891
	Including Riel's second (Northwest) rebellion, 1885
.055	1891–1896
	Including prime ministerships of Sir John J. C. Abbott, 1891–1892; of Sir John Sparrow Thompson, 1892–1894; of Sir Mackenzie Bowell, 1894–1896; of Sir Charles Tupper, 1896
.056	Prime ministership of Sir Wilfrid Laurier, 1896–1911

.06	1911–
.061	1911–1921
.061 2	Prime ministership of Sir Robert Laird Borden, 1911–1920
.061 3	First prime ministership of Arthur Meighen, 1920–1921
.062	1921–1935
.062 2	First and second prime ministerships of William Lyon Mackenzie King, 1921–1930
	Including second prime ministership of Arthur Meighen, 1926
.062 3	Prime ministership of Richard Bedford Bennett, 1930–1935
.063	1935–1957
.063 2	Third prime ministership of William Lyon Mackenzie King, 1935–1948
.063 3	Prime ministership of Louis Stephen Saint-Laurent, 1948–1957
.064	1957–
.064 2	Prime ministership of John G. Diefenbaker, 1957–1963
.064 3	Prime ministership of Lester B. Pearson, 1963–1968
.064 4	First prime ministership of Pierre Elliott Trudeau, 1968–1979
.064 5	Prime ministership of Joe (Charles Joseph) Clark, 1979–1980
.064 6	Second prime ministership of Pierre Elliott Trudeau, 1980–1984
	Including prime ministership of John Turner, 1984
.064 7	Prime ministership of Brian Mulroney, 1984–

>   **971.1–971.9 Specific provinces and territories**

    Class comprehensive works in 971

.1   ***British Columbia**

.101   Early history to 1790

.102   Period of settlement and colony, 1790–1871

     Including colony of New Caledonia

.103   Period as a Province of Canada, 1871–

     For 1945– , see 971.04

.104   1945–

.2   ***Prairie Provinces**

.201   Early history to 1869

     Including Rupert's Land

*Add as instructed under 930–990

.202	1869–1945
.203	1945–
.23	*Alberta

Add to base number 971.23 the numbers following 971.2 in 971.201–971.203, e.g., establishment as a Province of Canada, 1905, 971.2302

.24	*Saskatchewan

Add to base number 971.24 the numbers following 971.2 in 971.201–971.203, e.g., establishment as a Province of Canada, 1905, 971.2402

.27	*Manitoba

Add to base number 971.27 the numbers following 971.2 in 971.201–971.203, e.g., establishment as a Province of Canada, 1870, 971.2702

.3	***Ontario**
.301	Early history to 1791
.302	Period of Upper Canada and Act of Union, 1791–1867
.303	Period as a Province of Canada, 1867–

> *For 1945–   , see 971.304*

.304	1945–
.4	***Quebec**
.401	Early history to 1763
.401 2	Earliest history to 1608

> Including period of explorations by Jacques Cartier, 1534–1535

.401 4	French period, 1608–1763
.402	British period, 1763–1867

> Including period of Lower Canada, 1791–1841

.403	Period as a Province of Canada, 1867–

> *For 1945–   , see 971.404*

.404	1945–
.5	***Atlantic Provinces Maritime Provinces**

> *For Nova Scotia, see 971.6; Prince Edward Island, 971.7; Newfoundland and Labrador, 971.8*

[.501–.504]	Historical periods of New Brunswick

> Relocated to 971.5101–971.5104

*Add as instructed under 930–990

.51	*New Brunswick

> 971.510 1–971.510 4 Historical periods of New Brunswick [*formerly* 971.501–971.504]

Class comprehensive works in 971.51

.510 1	Early history to 1784
.510 2	Period as separate province, 1784–1867
.510 3	Period as a Province of Canada, 1867–

For 1945–   , see 971.5104

.510 4	1945–
.6	***Nova Scotia**
.601	Early history to 1763

Including Acadia

.602	Period as a British colony, 1763–1867
.603	Period as a Province of Canada, 1867–

For 1945–   , see 971.604

.604	1945–
.7	***Prince Edward Island**
.701	Early history to 1769
.702	Period as separate province, 1769–1873
.703	Period as a Province of Canada, 1873–

For 1945–   , see 971.704

.704	1945–
.8	***Newfoundland and Labrador, Saint-Pierre and Miquelon**
.801	Early history to 1855
.802	1855–1934
.803	Period of suspension of parliamentary government, 1934–1949
.804	Period as a Province of Canada, 1949–
.82	*Labrador
.820 1	Early history to 1763
.820 2	Period when claimed by Lower Canada (Quebec) and Newfoundland, 1763–1927
.820 3	Period as dependency of Newfoundland, 1927–1949

*Add as instructed under 930–990

.820 4	Period as part of Newfoundland, 1949–

.88   †Saint-Pierre and Miquelon

.9   *Northern territories

> Add to base number 971.9 the numbers following 971.2 in 971.201–971.203, e.g., 1945–   971.903

972   Middle America   Mexico

SUMMARY

972.000 1–.000 9	Standard subdivisions of Middle America
.001–.009	Standard subdivisions of Mexico
.01–.08	Historical periods of Mexico
.8	Central America
.9	West Indies (Antilles) and Bermuda

.000 1–.000 9   Standard subdivisions of Middle America

> As modified under 930–990

.001–.009   Standard subdivisions of Mexico

> As modified under 930–990

\>   972.01–972.08 Historical periods of Mexico

> Class comprehensive works in 972

.01   Early history to 1519

.016   Classical period, ca. 100–ca. 900

.017   Ca. 900–1325

> Class here period of Toltec empire, ca. 900–ca. 1200

.018   Aztec period, 1325–1519

> Including 1516–1519 [*formerly* 972.02]

.02   Conquest and colonial period, 1519–1810

> 1516–1519 relocated to 972.018

.03   Revolutionary period and period of independence, 1810–1822

.04   Periods of first empire and republic, 1822–1845

> Class here 19th century

> Class a part of 19th century not provided for here with the part, e.g., period of second empire 972.07

.05   Period of war with United States, 1845–1848

> (Option: Class here Mexican War; prefer 973.62)

*Add as instructed under 930–990

†Add as instructed under 930–990; however, do not add historical periods

.06	Period of reaction and reform, 1848–1861
.07	Period of European intervention, 1861–1867
	Class here period of second empire, 1864–1867
.08	Period of Republic, 1867–
.081	1867–1917
.081 2	1867–1876
.081 4	Porfiriato, 1876–1910
	Class here administrations of Porfirio Díaz, 1876–1880, 1884–1910
.081 6	Period of Mexican Revolution, 1910–1917
.082	1917–1964
.082 1	Administrations of Venustiano Carranza and Adolfo de la Huerta, 1917–1920
.082 2	Administration of Alvaro Obregón, 1920–1924
.082 3	Administration of Plutarco Elías Calles, 1924–1928
.082 4	Administrations of Emilio Portes Gil, Pascual Ortiz Rubio, Abelardo L. Rodríguez, 1928–1934
.082 42	Administration of Emilio Portes Gil, 1928–1930
.082 43	Administration of Pascual Ortiz Rubio, 1930–1932
.082 44	Administration of Abelardo L. Rodríguez, 1932–1934
.082 5	Administration of Lázaro Cárdenas, 1934–1940
.082 6	Administration of Manuel Avila Camacho, 1940–1946
.082 7	Administration of Miguel Alemán, 1946–1952
.082 8	Administration of Adolfo Ruiz Cortines, 1952–1958
.082 9	Administration of Adolfo López Mateos, 1958–1964
.083	1964–
.083 1	Administration of Gustavo Díaz Ordaz, 1964–1970
.083 2	Administration of Luis Echeverría Alvarez, 1970–1976
.083 3	Administration of José López Portillo, 1976–1982
.083 4	Administration of Miguel de la Madrid Hurtado, 1982–

> **972.8–972.9 Other parts of Middle America**

Class comprehensive works in 972

*Add as instructed under 930–990

.8   ***Central America**

.801   Early history to 1502

.802   Period of European discovery, exploration, conquest, 1502–1535

.803   Colonial period, 1535–1821

.804   1821–1899

>   Including period of United Provinces of Central America, 1823–1840

.805   1900–

.805 1   1900–1944

.805 2   1944–1979

.805 3   1979–

.81   ***Guatemala**

.810 1   Early history to 1502

.810 16   Mayan period, ca. 300–ca. 900

>   Class here comprehensive works on Mayan period in Middle America

>   Class a specific aspect of the Mayan period not provided for here with the aspect, e.g., Mayan period from ca. 900 to 1325 in Mexico 972.6017

.810 2   Period of European discovery, exploration, conquest, 1502–1524

>   1524–1535 relocated to 972.8103

.810 3   Colonial period, 1524–1821

>   Including 1524–1535 [*formerly* 972.8102]

.810 4   1821–1871

>   1871–1899 relocated to 972.81051

.810 42   1821–1839

>   Class here period as a part of United Provinces of Central America, 1823–1839

.810 44   1839–1871

>   Class here administration of Rafael Carrera, 1839–1865

.810 5   1871–

.810 51   1871–1931

>   Including 1871–1899 [*formerly* 972.8104]

>   1931–1945 relocated to 972.81052

.810 52   1931–1986

>   Including 1931–1945 [*formerly* 972.81051], 1979–1986 [*formerly* 972.81053]

*Add as instructed under 930–990

.810 53	1986–
	1979–1986 relocated to 972.81052
.82	*Belize
.820 1	Early history to 1502
.820 2	Period of Spanish discovery and colonization, 1502–1638
	Including 1535–1638 [*formerly* 972.8203]
.820 3	1638–1862
	Including 1821–1862 [*formerly* 972.8204]
	Class here period of British involvement, 1638–1963
	1535–1638 relocated to 972.8202
	For period as a British colony, see 972.8204
.820 4	Period as a British colony, 1862–1963
	Including 1900–1945 [*formerly* 972.82051], 1945–1963 [*formerly* 972.82052]
	1821–1862 relocated to 972.8203
.820 5	1964–
[.820 51]	1900–1945
	Relocated to 972.8204
[.820 52]	1945–1979
	Use of this number for 1964–1979 discontinued; class in 972.8205
	1945–1963 relocated to 972.8204
[.820 53]	1979–
	Number discontinued; class in 972.8205
.83	*Honduras
.830 1	Early history to 1502
.830 2	Period of Spanish discovery, exploration, conquest, 1502–1542
	Including 1535–1542 [*formerly* 972.8303]
.830 3	Colonial period, 1542–1821
	1535–1542 relocated to 972.8302
.830 4	1821–1838
	Class here period as a part of United Provinces of Central America, 1823–1838
	1838–1899 relocated to 972.83051

*Add as instructed under 930–990

.830 5	1838–
.830 51	1838–1924
	Including 1838–1899 [*formerly* 972.8304]
	1924–1945 relocated to 972.83052
.830 52	1924–1978
	Including 1924–1945 [*formerly* 972.83051]
.830 53	1978–
.84	*El Salvador
.840 1	Early history to 1524
	Including 1502–1524 [*formerly* 972.8402]
.840 2	Period of Spanish discovery, exploration, conquest, 1524–1542
	Including 1535–1542 [*formerly* 972.8403]
	1502–1524 relocated to 972.8401
.840 3	Colonial period, 1542–1821
	1535–1542 relocated to 972.8402
.840 4	1821–1859
	1859–1899 relocated to 972.84051
.840 42	1821–1839
	Class here period as a part of United Provinces of Central America, 1823–1839
.840 44	1839–1859
.840 5	1859–
.840 51	1859–1931
	Including 1859–1899 [*formerly* 972.8404]
	1931–1945 relocated to 972.84052
.840 52	1931–1979
	Including 1931–1945 [*formerly* 972.84051]
.840 53	1979–
.85	*Nicaragua
.850 1	Early history to 1502
.850 2	Period of Spanish discovery, exploration, conquest, 1502–1527
	1527–1535 relocated to 972.8503
.850 3	Colonial period, 1527–1821
	Including 1527–1535 [*formerly* 972.8502]

*Add as instructed under 930–990

.850 4	1821–1893
	1893–1899 relocated to 972.85051
.850 42	1821–1838
	Class here period as a part of United Provinces of Central America, 1823–1838
.850 44	1838–1893
.850 5	1893–
.850 51	1893–1934
	Including 1893–1899 [*formerly* 972.8504]
	Class here period of interventions by United States, 1909–1933
	1934–1945 relocated to 972.85052
.850 52	1934–1979
	Including 1934–1945 [*formerly* 972.85051]
.850 53	1979–
.86	*Costa Rica
.860 1	Early history to 1502
.860 2	Period of Spanish discovery, exploration, conquest, 1502–1560
	Including 1535–1560 [*formerly* 972.8603]
.860 3	Colonial period, 1560–1821
	1535–1560 relocated to 972.8602
.860 4	1821–1948
.860 42	1821–1838
	Class here period as a part of United Provinces of Central America, 1823–1838
.860 44	1838–1948
	Including 1900–1945 [*formerly* 972.86051], 1945–1948 [*formerly* 972.86052]
.860 5	1948–
[.860 51]	1900–1945
	Relocated to 972.86044
[.860 52]	1945–1979
	Use of this number for 1948–1979 discontinued; class in 972.8605
	1945–1948 relocated to 972.86044
[.860 53]	1979–
	Number discontinued; class in 972.8605

*Add as instructed under 930–990

.87	*Panama
.870 1	Early history to 1514
	1514–1550 relocated to 972.8702
.870 11	Early history to 1501
.870 12	Period of Spanish discovery, exploration, conquest, 1501–1514
.870 2	Colonial period, 1514–1821
	Including 1514–1550 [*formerly* 972.8701]; period as a part of Viceroyalty of New Granada, 1739–1810
.870 3	Period as a part of Gran Colombia, 1821–1903
[.870 4]	1903–1904
	Relocated to 972.87051
.870 5	1903–
.870 51	1903–1977
	Including 1903–1904 [*formerly* 972.8704], 1945–1977 [*formerly* 972.87052]
[.870 52]	1945–1977
	Relocated to 972.87051
.870 53	1977–

.9 *West Indies (Antilles) and Bermuda*

Class here Caribbean Area

Class a part of Caribbean Area not provided for here with the part, e.g., Venezuela 987

.901	Early history to 1492
.902	Period of European discovery and early colonial period, 1492–1608
.903	1608–1801
.904	1801–1902
.905	1902–
.905 1	1902–1945
.905 2	1945–
.91	*Cuba
.910 1	Early history to 1492
.910 2	Period of European discovery, exploration, conquest, 1492–1514
.910 3	1514–1763
.910 4	1763–1810

*Add as instructed under 930–990

.910 5	1810–1899
	For Spanish-American War, see 973.89
.910 6	1899–
	Class here period of Republic, 1902–
.910 61	Period of American military occupation, 1899–1902
.910 62	1902–1933
.910 63	1933–1958
.910 64	Period of Fidel Castro, 1959–
.92	*Jamaica and Cayman Islands

>   972.920 1–972.920 6 Historical periods of Jamaica

Class comprehensive works in 972.92

.920 1	Early history to 1494
.920 2	1494–1607
.920 3	1607–1832
.920 31	Last period of Spanish rule, 1607–1655
.920 32	1655–1692
	Including Great Earthquake, 1692
.920 33	1692–1782
.920 34	1782–1832
	Class here antislavery struggle and emancipation
.920 4	1832–1904
	Class here 19th century
	Class 1801–1832 in 972.92034
.920 5	1904–1962
	Class here 20th century
	Class 1901–1904 in 972.9204, 1962– in 972.9206
.920 6	Period of independence, 1962–
.921	†Cayman Islands
.93	*Dominican Republic
.930 1	Early history to 1492
.930 2	Period of European discovery and early colonial period, 1492–1608
.930 3	1608–1801

*Add as instructed under 930–990

†Add as instructed under 930–990; however, do not add historical periods

.930 4		1801–1902
.930 5		1902–
.930 52		1902–1930
.930 53		Period of Rafael Léonidas Trujillo Molina, 1930–1961
.930 54		1961–
.94	*Haiti	
.940 1		Early history to 1492
.940 2		Period of Spanish rule, 1492–1625
.940 3		Period as a French colony, 1625–1804
.940 4		1804–1915
.940 5		Period of American occupation, 1915–1934
.940 6		1934–1957
.940 7		1957–
.940 72		Periods of François Duvalier and Jean-Claude Duvalier, 1957–1986
.940 73		1986–
.95	*Puerto Rico	
.950 1		Early history to 1493
.950 2		Period of European discovery and early colonial period, 1493–1602
.950 3		1602–1804
.950 4		1804–1899
.950 5		1900–
.950 52		1900–1952
.950 53		Period of Commonwealth, 1952–
.96	†Bahama Islands	
.97	†Leeward Islands	
	For Dominica, see 972.9841	
.972	†Virgin Islands	
.973	†Anguilla and Saint Christopher-Nevis	
.974	†Antigua and Barbuda	
.975	†Montserrat	
.976	†Guadeloupe	
.977	†Leeward Netherlands islands	

*Add as instructed under 930–990

†Add as instructed under 930–990; however, do not add historical periods

.98	†Windward and other southern islands
.981	†Barbados
.982	†Martinique
.983	*Trinidad and Tobago
.983 01	Early history to 1498
.983 02	Spanish period, 1498–1797
.983 03	British period, 1797–1962
.983 04	Period of independence, 1962–
.984	†Windward Islands
.984 1	†Dominica
.984 3	†Saint Lucia
.984 4	†Saint Vincent and the Grenadines

For Carriacou, see 972.9845

.984 5	†Grenada and Carriacou
.986	†Netherlands islands

For Leeward Netherlands islands, see 972.977

.99	†Bermuda

973   United States

SUMMARY

973.01–.09	**Standard subdivisions**	
.1	**Early history to 1607**	
.2	**Colonial period, 1607–1775**	
.3	**Periods of Revolution and Confederation, 1775–1789**	
.4	**Constitutional period, 1789–1809**	
.5	**1809–1845**	
.6	**1845–1861**	
.7	**Administration of Abraham Lincoln, 1861–1865**	**Civil War**
.8	**Reconstruction period, 1865–1901**	
.9	**1901–**	

.01–.09	Standard subdivisions

As modified under 930–990

(If optional notation 734–739 from Table 2 is chosen, use 973.01–973.09 for historical periods, and 973.001–973.009 for standard subdivisions)

.1	**Early history to 1607**

Add to base number 973.1 the numbers following 970.01 in 970.011–970.019, e.g., French explorations 973.18

*Add as instructed under 930–990

†Add as instructed under 930–990; however, do not add historical periods

.2   **Colonial period, 1607–1775**

>   973.21–973.22 Period of early settlements, 1607–1643

Class comprehensive works in 973.21; specific European settlements with the settlement in 974–975, e.g., settlement of Jamestown 975.5425101

.21   Period of Virginia settlements, 1607–1620

.22   Period of other early settlements, 1620–1643

Including Pequot War, 1636–1638

.23   1643–1664

.24   1664–1689

Including King Philip's War, 1675–1676

.25   1689–1732

Including King William's War (North American aspect of War of the League of Augsburg), 1688–1697; Queen Anne's War (North American aspects of War of the Spanish Succession), 1701–1714
     (Option: Class North American aspects of King William's War, Queen Anne's War in 971.018)

Class comprehensive works on War of the League of Augsburg in 940.2525, on War of the Spanish Succession in 940.2526

.26   Period of extension of English rule, 1732–1763

Including King George's War (North American aspects of War of the Austrian Succession), 1740–1748; French and Indian War (North American aspects of Seven Year's War), 1756–1763
     (Option: Class North American aspects of War of the Austrian Succession in 971.018, of Seven Years' War in 971.0188)

Class comprehensive works on War of the Austrian Succession in 940.2532, on Seven Years' War in 940.2534

.27   End of colonial period, 1763–1775

Including Pontiac's Conspiracy, 1763–1764
     (Option: Class Pontiac's Conspiracy in 971.022)

Class events of 1763–1775 as causes of American Revolution in 973.311

.3   **Periods of Revolution and Confederation, 1775–1789**

.308   Kinds of persons during 1775–1789

Class relation of kinds of persons to the Revolution in 973.315

.309 2   Persons

Class personal narratives in 973.38

SUMMARY

973.31	**Social, political, economic history**
.32	**Diplomatic history**
.33	**Operations**
.34	**Military units**
.35	**Naval history**
.36	**Celebrations, commemorations, memorials**
.37	**Prisoner-of-war camps; health and social services**
.38	**Other topics**

.31   Social, political, economic history

> *For diplomatic history, see 973.32*

.311   Causes

.311 1   Stamp Act, 1765–1766

.311 2   Commercial restrictions

> Including Navigation Acts, Townshend Acts, burning of the Gaspée, 1772

> *For tax on tea, see 973.3115*

.311 3   Quartering of troops and Boston Massacre, 1770

.311 4   Taxation and representation

.311 5   Tax on tea and Boston Tea Party, 1773

.311 6   Boston Port Bill, 1774

.312   Continental Congress

.313   Declaration of Independence, 1776

.314   Loyalists (Tories)

> Class settlement of Loyalists in Canada in 971.024

.315   Relation of kinds of persons to the Revolution

> Add to base number 973.315 notation 03–99 from Table 7, e.g., doctors 973.31561

.316   Results

> *For Treaty of Peace, see 973.317*

.317   Treaty of Peace (Versailles Treaty), 1783

.318   Period of confederation, 1783–1789

\>   973.32–973.38 Aspects of American Revolution

> Class comprehensive works in 973.3

.32	Diplomatic history

Class here relations of United States with other nations

Add to base number 973.32 the numbers following —4 in notation 41–49 from Table 2, e.g., relations with France 973.324

For Treaty of Paris, see 973.317

.33	Operations

For naval operations, see 973.35

.331	Of 1775
.331 1	Battles of Lexington and Concord, 1775
.331 2	Battle of Bunker Hill, 1775
.332	Of 1776–January 3, 1777
.333	Of 1777

Class Battle of Princeton in 973.332

For winter at Valley Forge, see 973.3341

.334	Of 1778
.334 1	Winter at Valley Forge, 1777–1778
.335	Of 1779
.336	Of 1780
.337	Of 1781
.338	Of 1782
.339	Of 1783
.34	Military units

Class here organization, history, rosters, service records

Class operations of military units in 973.33, units engaged in a special service with the service, e.g., privateering 973.35

For naval units, see 973.35; rolls of honor, lists of dead, 973.36

.341	British troops

For mercenary troops, see 973.342; American native peoples as allies, 973.343

.342	Mercenary troops
.343	American native peoples as allies of British
.344–.345	American troops

Add to base number 973.34 the numbers following —7 in notation 74–75 from Table 2, e.g., Pennsylvania troops 973.3448

.346   Auxiliary troops on American side

           Including Polish, Spanish, Swedish

           For French troops, see 973.347

.347   French troops

.35   Naval history

           Class here operations, ships, units

           Including privateering

.36   Celebrations, commemorations, memorials

           Including rolls of honor, lists of dead

           Class celebrations, commemorations, memorials of a specific event with the event, e.g., Battle of Bunker Hill 973.3312

.37   Prisoner-of-war camps; health and social services

           Including exchange of prisoners

.371   British prisons and prison ships

.372   American prisons

.375   Medical services

           For hospitals, see 973.376

.376   Hospitals

.38   Other topics

           Including personal narratives, military life and customs

           Class personal narratives on a specific subject with the subject, e.g., on medical services 973.375

.381   Treason

           For treason of Benedict Arnold, see 973.382; of Charles Lee, 973.383

.382   Treason of Benedict Arnold

.383   Treason of Charles Lee

.385   American secret service and spies

           Class here comprehensive works on secret service and spies

           For British secret service and spies, see 973.386

.386   British secret service and spies

.388   Propaganda

.4	**Constitutional period, 1789–1809**
.41	Administration of George Washington, 1789–1797
	Including period of Indian wars, 1790–1791 [*formerly* 973.42]
	For second term, see 973.43
[.42]	Period of Indian wars, 1790–1791
	Relocated to 973.41
.43	Second term of the administration of George Washington, 1793–1797
.44	Administration of John Adams, 1797–1801
	Class here period of troubles with France, 1797–1800 [*formerly* 973.45]
[.45]	Period of troubles with France, 1797–1800
	Relocated to 973.44
.46	Administration of Thomas Jefferson, 1801–1809
	For Tripolitan War, see 973.47; second term, 973.48
.47	Tripolitan War, 1801–1805
	(Option: Class in 961.023)
.48	Second term of the administration of Thomas Jefferson, 1805–1809
.5	**1809–1845**
	Class here 19th century
	Class events of 1809–1845 as causes of Civil War in 973.711; a specific part of 19th century not provided for here with the part, e.g., Civil War 973.7
.51	Administration of James Madison, 1809–1817
	For War of 1812, see 973.52; war with Algiers, 973.53
.52	War of 1812, 1812–1814
	(Option: Class in 971.034)
.520 92	Persons
	Class personal narratives in 973.528
.521	Social, political, economic history
	Including causes, results
	For diplomatic history, see 973.522
.522	Diplomatic history
	Relations of United States with other nations
.523	Operations
	For naval operations, see 973.525
.523 8	In the South
	For Battle of New Orleans, see 973.5239

.523 9		Battle of New Orleans, 1814
.524		Military units

Class here organization, history, rosters, service records

Class operations of military units in 973.523, units engaged in a special service with the service, e.g., privateering 973.525

For naval units, see 973.525; rolls of honor, lists of dead, 973.526

.524 1		British troops
.524 2		American native peoples as allies of the British
.524 4–.524 7		American troops

Add to base number 973.524 the numbers following —7 in notation 74–77 from Table 2, e.g., Pennsylvania troops 973.52448

.525		Naval history

Class here operations, ships, units

Including privateering

.525 4		Battle of Lake Erie, 1813
.525 6		Battle of Lake Champlain, 1814
.526		Celebrations, commemorations, memorials

Including rolls of honor, lists of dead

Class celebrations, commemorations, memorials of a specific event with the event, e.g., Battle of Lake Erie 973.5254

.527		Prisoner-of-war camps; health and social services

Including exchange of prisoners

.527 5		Medical services

Including hospitals

.528		Other topics

Including personal narratives, military life and customs

Class personal narratives on a specific subject with the subject, e.g., on medical services 973.5275

.528 5		Secret service and spies
.53		War with Algiers, 1815

(Option: Class in 961.023)

.54		Administration of James Monroe, 1817–1825

Including First Seminole War, 1818; Missouri Compromise, 1820

.55		Administration of John Quincy Adams, 1825–1829

.56	Administration of Andrew Jackson, 1829–1837

Including Black Hawk War, 1832
(Option: Class Black Hawk War in 970.5)

.561	Nullification movement
.57	Administration of Martin Van Buren, 1837–1841

Including Second Seminole War, 1835–1842

.58	Administrations of William Henry Harrison and John Tyler, 1841–1845
.6	**1845–1861**

Class events of 1845–1861 as causes of Civil War in 973.711

.61	Administration of James Knox Polk, 1845–1849

Including Wilmot Proviso, 1847

For Mexican War, see 973.62

.62	Mexican War, 1845–1848

(Option: Class in 972.05)

.620 92	Persons

Class personal narratives in 973.628

.621	Social, political, economic history

Including causes, results

For diplomatic history, see 973.622

.622	Diplomatic history

Relations of United States with other nations

.623	Operations

For naval operations, see 973.625

.624	Military units

Class here organization, history, rosters, service records

Class operations of military units in 973.623, units engaged in a special service with the service, e.g., naval operations 973.625

For naval units, see 973.625; rolls of honor, lists of dead, 973.626

.625	Naval history

Operations, ships, units

.626	Celebrations, commemorations, memorials

Including rolls of honor, lists of dead

Class celebrations, commemorations, memorials of a specific event with the event, e.g., capture of Chapultepec 973.623

.627	Prisoner-of-war camps; health and social services
.627 5	Medical services
	Including hospitals
.628	Other topics
	Including personal narratives, military life and customs, unconventional warfare, propaganda
	Class personal narratives on a specific subject with the subject, e.g., on prisoner-of-war camps 973.627
.63	Administration of Zachary Taylor, 1849–1850
.64	Administration of Millard Fillmore, 1850–1853
	Including Compromise of 1850
.66	Administration of Franklin Pierce, 1853–1857
.68	Administration of James Buchanan, 1857–1861
	For Dred Scott decision, see 973.7115; John Brown's Raid, 973.7116
.7	**Administration of Abraham Lincoln, 1861–1865** **Civil War**
[.708]	Civil War with respect to kinds of persons
	Do not use; class 973.715
.709 2	Persons
	Class personal narratives in 973.781–973.782

SUMMARY

973.71	**Social, political, economic history**
.72	**Diplomatic history**
.73	**Operations**
.74	**Military units**
.75	**Naval history**
.76	**Celebrations, commemorations, memorials**
.77	**Prisoner-of-war camps; health and social services**
.78	**Other topics**

.71	Social, political, economic history
	For diplomatic history, see 973.72
.711	Causes
	For the South and secession, see 973.713
.711 2	Extension of slavery
.711 3	Wilmot Proviso, 1847, and compromises
	Examples: Missouri Compromise, 1820; Compromise of 1850
.711 4	Abolition movement
.711 5	Fugitive slaves
	Including underground railroad, Dred Scott decision

.711 6	John Brown's Raid, 1859
.712	Efforts to preserve or restore peace

For compromises, see 973.7113

.713	The South and secession

Confederate States of America in the war

.714	Results

Including Emancipation Proclamation, 1863; establishment of Freedmen's Bureau, 1865

Class a result as a specific event with the event, e.g., Reconstruction 973.8

.715	Relation of kinds of persons to the war
.715 03–.715 87	Occupational and miscellaneous groups

Add to base number 973.715 notation 03–87 from Table 7, e.g., doctors 973.71561; however, class refugees in 973.7159, southern Union sympathizers in 973.717, northern Confederate sympathizers in 973.718

.715 9	Refugees
.717	Southern Union sympathizers
.718	Northern Confederate sympathizers
.72	Diplomatic history
.721	Relations of Confederacy with other nations
.722	Relations of Union with other nations
.73	Operations

For naval operations, see 973.75

.730 1	Strategy

Do not use for philosophy and theory; class in 973.73

.730 12	Union side
.730 13	Confederate side
.731	Opening phase, 1861–April, 1862
.732	May-August, 1862
.733	September, 1862–May, 1863
.733 6	Lee's invasion of Maryland, 1862
.734	June-August, 1863
.734 4	Siege and fall of Vicksburg, 1863
.734 9	Battle of Gettysburg, 1863

.735	September-December, 1863
.735 9	Chattanooga campaign, 1863
.736	January-May, 1864
.737	June-December, 1864
.737 8	Sherman's March to the Sea and Savannah campaign, 1864
.738	1865
.74	Military units

Class here organization, history, rosters, service records

Class operations of military units in 973.73, units engaged in a special service with the service, e.g., privateering 973.75

For naval units, see 973.75; rolls of honor, lists of dead, 973.76

.741	Union troops

For state units, see 973.744–973.749

.741 5	Black troops
.742	Confederate troops

For state units, see 973.744–973.749

.744–.749	State units

Add to base number 973.74 the numbers following —7 in notation 74–79 from Table 2, e.g., Ohio troops 973.7471

.75	Naval history

Including operations, privateering, blockade running

.752	Battle of Monitor and Merrimac, 1862
.754	Battle of Kearsarge and Alabama, 1864
.757	Confederate Navy

Ships and units

.758	Union navy

Ships and units

.76	Celebrations, commemorations, memorials

Including rolls of honor, lists of dead

Class celebrations, commemorations, memorials of a specific event with the event, e.g., Battle of Antietam 973.7336

.77	Prisoner-of-war camps; health and social services

Including exchange of prisoners

.771	Confederate prisoner-of-war camps

.772	Union prisoner-of-war camps
.775	Medical services
	For hospitals, see 973.776
.776	Hospitals
.777	Welfare work
	Including United States Sanitary Commission
.778	Religious life and chaplain services
.78	Other topics

> 973.781–973.782 Personal narratives

Class comprehensive works in 973.78; personal narratives on a specific subject with the subject, e.g., on prisoner-of-war camps 973.77

.781	Personal narratives of individuals from Union side
.782	Personal narratives of individuals from Confederate side
.783	Military life and customs of Union side
	Class here comprehensive works on military life and customs
	For military life and customs of Confederate side, see 973.784
.784	Military life and customs of Confederate side
.785	Union secret service and spies
	Class here comprehensive works on secret service and spies
	For Confederate secret service and spies, see 973.786
.786	Confederate secret service and spies
.788	Propaganda
.8	**Reconstruction period, 1865–1901**
.81	Administration of Andrew Johnson, 1865–1869
.82	Administration of Ulysses Simpson Grant, 1869–1877
.83	Administration of Rutherford Birchard Hayes, 1877–1881
.84	Administrations of James Abram Garfield and Chester Alan Arthur, 1881–1885
.85	First administration of Grover Cleveland, 1885–1889
.86	Administration of Benjamin Harrison, 1889–1893
.87	Second administration of Grover Cleveland, 1893–1897

.88	Administration of William McKinley, 1897–1901
	For Spanish-American War, see 973.89
.89	Spanish-American War, 1898
	(Option: Class in 946.074)
.890 92	Persons
	Class personal narratives in 973.898
.891	Social, political, economic history
	Including causes, results
	For diplomatic history, see 973.892
.892	Diplomatic history
	Relations of United States with other nations
.893	Operations
	For naval operations, see 973.895
.893 3	Cuban campaign, 1898
.893 5	Puerto Rican campaign, 1898
.893 7	Philippine campaign, 1898
.894	Military units
	Class here organization, history, rosters, service records
	Class operations of military units in 973.893, units engaged in a special service with the service, e.g., naval operations 973.895
	For naval units, see 973.895; rolls of honor, lists of dead, 973.896
.895	Naval history
	Class here operations, ships, units
.896	Celebrations, commemorations, memorials
	Including rolls of honor, lists of dead
	Class celebrations, commemorations, memorials of a specific event with the event, e.g., Battle of Manila Bay 973.895
.897	Prisoner-of-war camps; health and social services
.897 5	Medical services
	Including hospitals
.898	Other topics
	Including personal narratives, military life and customs, unconventional warfare, propaganda
	Class personal narratives on a specific subject with the subject, e.g., on prisoner-of-war camps 973.897

.9	**1901–**
.91	1901–1953
.911	Administration of Theodore Roosevelt, 1901–1909
.912	Administration of William Howard Taft, 1909–1913
.913	Administration of Woodrow Wilson, 1913–1921
.914	Administration of Warren Gamaliel Harding, 1921–1923
.915	Administration of Calvin Coolidge, 1923–1929
.916	Administration of Herbert Clark Hoover, 1929–1933
.917	Administration of Franklin Delano Roosevelt, 1933–1945
.918	Administration of Harry S Truman, 1945–1953
.92	1953–
.921	Administration of Dwight David Eisenhower, 1953–1961
.922	Administration of John Fitzgerald Kennedy, 1961–1963
.923	Administration of Lyndon Baines Johnson, 1963–1969

> Class here period of Vietnamese War, 1961–1975
>
> Class 1961–1963 period of Vietnamese War in 973.922, 1969–1974 period in 973.924, 1974–1975 period in 973.925

.924	Administration of Richard Milhous Nixon, 1969–1974
.925	Administration of Gerald Rudolph Ford, 1974–1977
.926	Administration of Jimmy (James Earl) Carter, 1977–1981
.927	Administration of Ronald Reagan, 1981–

> ## 974–979 Specific states of United States

Class comprehensive works in 973

For Hawaii, see 996.9

> ## 974–975 Northeastern and southeastern United States

Add to notation for each term identified by † as follows:

01	Early history to 1620
02	Colonial period, 1620–1776
03	1776–1865
04	1865–
041	1865–1918
042	1918–1945
043	1945–

Class comprehensive works in 974

974   *†**Northeastern United States (New England and Middle Atlantic states)**

.1   *†**Maine**

.2   *†**New Hampshire**

.3   *†**Vermont**

.4   *†**Massachusetts**

.5   *†**Rhode Island**

.6   *†**Connecticut**

.7   *†**New York**

.8   *†**Pennsylvania**

.9   *†**New Jersey**

975   *†**Southeastern United States (South Atlantic states)**

.1   *†**Delaware**

.2   *†**Maryland**

.3   ***District of Columbia (Washington)**

.301   Early history to 1799

.302   1800–1865

.303   1865–1933

.304   1933–

.4   *†**West Virginia**

.5   *†**Virginia**

.6   *†**North Carolina**

.7   *†**South Carolina**

.8   *†**Georgia**

.9   ***Florida**

.901   Early history to 1763

.902   English period, 1763–1783

.903   Spanish period, 1783–1821

.904   Territorial period, 1821–1845

.905   Early statehood period, 1845–1865

*Add as instructed under 930–990

†Add historical periods as instructed under 974–975

.906	1865–
.906 1	1865–1918
.906 2	1918–1945
.906 3	1945–

976   *South central United States   Gulf Coast states

.01	Early history to 1700
.02	1700–1799
.03	1800–1865
.04	1865–
.041	1865–1918
.042	1918–1945
.043	1945–

.1   *Alabama

.101	Early history to 1701
.102	French period, 1701–1763
.103	British period, 1763–1783
.104	Spanish and territorial periods, 1783–1817
.105	Territorial and early statehood periods, 1817–1865
.106	1865–
.106 1	1865–1918
.106 2	1918–1945
.106 3	1945–

.2   *Mississippi

Add to base number 976.2 the numbers following 976.1 in 976.101–976.106, e.g., British period 976.203

.3   *Louisiana

.301	Early history to 1718
.302	French period, 1718–1763
.303	Spanish period, 1763–1803
.304	French and territorial periods, 1803–1812
.305	Early statehood period, 1812–1865
.306	1865–
.306 1	1865–1918

*Add as instructed under 930–990

.306 2	1918–1945
.306 3	1945–
.4	***Texas**
.401	Early history to 1680
.402	Spanish and French periods, 1680–1821
.403	Mexican period, 1821–1836
.404	Period of the Republic, 1836–1846
.405	Early statehood period, 1846–1865
.406	1865–
.406 1	1865–1918
.406 2	1918–1945
.406 3	1945–
.6	***Oklahoma**
.601	Early history to 1682
.602	French and Spanish periods, 1682–1803
.603	Period of Indian Territory, 1803–1866
.604	Territorial and early statehood periods, 1866–1907
.605	1907–
.605 2	1907–1945
.605 3	1945–
.7	***Arkansas**
.701	Early history to 1686
.702	French and Spanish periods, 1686–1803
.703	Preterritorial and territorial periods, 1803–1836
.704	Early statehood period, 1836–1865
.705	1865–
.705 1	1865–1918
.705 2	1918–1945
.705 3	1945–
.8	***Tennessee**
.801	Early history to 1682
.802	French, Spanish, English periods, 1682–1769

*Add as instructed under 930–990

.803	Early settlement and territorial periods, 1769–1796
	Including District of Washington, State of Franklin
.804	Early statehood period, 1796–1865
.805	1865–
.805 1	1865–1918
.805 2	1918–1945
.805 3	1945–

.9   *Kentucky

.901	Early history to 1736
.902	1736–1792
	Including periods of French, British, Virginian control; Transylvania Colony
.903	Early statehood period, 1792–1865
.904	1865–
.904 1	1865–1918
.904 2	1918–1945
.904 3	1945–

977   *North central United States

.01	Early history to 1787
.02	1787–1865
.03	1865–
.031	1865–1918
.032	1918–1945
.033	1945–

.1   *Ohio

.101	Early history to 1763
.102	British and early United States periods, 1763–1787
.103	Territorial and early statehood periods, 1787–1865
.104	1865–
.104 1	1865–1918
.104 2	1918–1945
.104 3	1945–

*Add as instructed under 930–990

.2   ***Indiana**

> Add to base number 977.2 the numbers following 977.1 in 977.101–977.104, e.g., territorial period 977.203

.3   ***Illinois**

> Add to base number 977.3 the numbers following 977.1 in 977.101–977.104, e.g., territorial period 977.303

.4   ***Michigan**

> Add to base number 977.4 the numbers following 977.1 in 977.101–977.104, e.g., territorial period 977.403

.5   ***Wisconsin**

> Add to base number 977.5 the numbers following 977.1 in 977.101–977.104, e.g., territorial period 977.503

.6   ***Minnesota**

.601   Early history to 1660

.602   French period, 1660–1783

.603   Preterritorial period, 1783–1849

.604   Territorial and early statehood periods, 1849–1900

.605   1900–

.605 1   1900–1918

.605 2   1918–1945

.605 3   1945–

.7   ***Iowa**

.701   Early history to 1838

.702   Territorial and early statehood periods, 1838–1899

.703   1900–

.703 1   1900–1918

.703 2   1918–1945

.703 3   1945–

.8   ***Missouri**

.801   Early history to 1750

.802   French and Spanish periods, 1750–1803

.803   Territorial and early statehood periods, 1803–1899

.804   1900–

.804 1   1900–1918

*Add as instructed under 930–990

.804 2	1918–1945
.804 3	1945–

978   *Western United States

.01	Early history to 1799
.02	1800–1899
.03	1900–
.031	1900–1918
.032	1918–1945
.033	1945–

.1   *Kansas

.101	Early history to 1803
.102	Territorial period, 1803–1861
.103	Statehood period, 1861–
.103 1	1861–1918
.103 2	1918–1945
.103 3	1945–

.2   *Nebraska

.201	Early history to 1854
.202	Territorial period, 1854–1867
.203	Statehood period, 1867–
.203 1	1867–1918
.203 2	1918–1945
.203 3	1945–

.3   *South Dakota

.301	Early history to 1861
.302	Territorial period, 1861–1889
.303	Statehood period, 1889–
.303 1	1889–1918
.303 2	1918–1945
.303 3	1945–

.4   *North Dakota

Add to base number 978.4 the numbers following 978.3 in 978.301–978.303, e.g., territorial period 978.402

*Add as instructed under 930–990

.6	***Montana**
.601	Early history to 1864
.602	Territorial period, 1864–1889
.603	Statehood period, 1889–
.603 1	1889–1918
.603 2	1918–1945
.603 3	1945–
.7	***Wyoming**
.701	Early history to 1868
.702	Territorial period, 1868–1890
.703	Statehood period, 1890–
.703 1	1890–1918
.703 2	1918–1945
.703 3	1945–
.8	***Colorado**
.801	Early history to 1803
.802	Acquisition and territorial periods, 1803–1876
.803	Statehood period, 1876–
.803 1	1876–1918
.803 2	1918–1945
.803 3	1945–
.9	***New Mexico**
.901	Early history to 1598
.902	Spanish period, 1598–1821
.903	Mexican period, 1821–1848
.904	Territorial period, 1848–1912
.905	Statehood period, 1912–
.905 2	1912–1945
.905 3	1945–

*Add as instructed under 930–990

979   *Great Basin and Pacific Slope region of United States   Pacific Coast states

Add to base number 979 the numbers following 978 in 978.01–978.03, e.g., 1900–   979.03

.1   *Arizona

Add to base number 979.1 the numbers following 978.9 in 978.901–978.905, e.g., territorial period 979.104

.2   *Utah

.201   Early history to 1848

.202   Territorial period, 1848–1896

.203   Statehood period, 1896–

.203 1   1896–1918

.203 2   1918–1945

.203 3   1945–

.3   *Nevada

.301   Early history to 1861

.302   Territorial and early statehood periods, 1861–1899

.303   1900–

.303 1   1900–1918

.303 2   1918–1945

.303 3   1945–

.4   *California

.401   Early history to 1769

.402   Spanish period, 1769–1822

.403   Mexican period, 1822–1848

.404   Territorial and early statehood periods, 1848–1899

.405   1900–

.405 1   1900–1918

.405 2   1918–1945

.405 3   1945–

*Add as instructed under 930–990

.5   ***Oregon**

.501   Early history to 1778

.502   Spanish and British periods, 1778–1819

.503   Preterritorial and territorial periods, 1819–1859

.504   Statehood period, 1859–

.504 1   1859–1918

.504 2   1918–1945

.504 3   1945–

.6   ***Idaho**

.601   Early history to 1863

.602   Territorial period, 1863–1890

.603   Statehood period, 1890–

.603 1   1890–1918

.603 2   1918–1945

.603 3   1945–

.7   ***Washington**

.701   Early history to 1818

.702   British and preterritorial periods, 1818–1853

.703   Territorial period, 1853–1889

.704   Statehood period, 1889–

.704 1   1889–1918

.704 2   1918–1945

.704 3   1945–

.8   ***Alaska**

.801   Early history to 1799

.802   Russian period, 1799–1867

.803   Preterritorial period, 1867–1912

.804   Territorial period, 1912–1959

.805   Statehood period, 1959–

*Add as instructed under 930–990

980   General history of South America

Class here Latin America

For Middle America, see 972

SUMMARY

980.001–.009		**Standard subdivisions**
.01–.03		**Historical periods**
981	**Brazil**	
982	**Argentina**	
983	**Chile**	
984	**Bolivia**	
985	**Peru**	
986	**Colombia and Ecuador**	
987	**Venezuela**	
988	**Guiana**	
989	**Paraguay and Uruguay**	

.001–.003   Standard subdivisions

.004   Racial, ethnic, national groups

> Add to base number 980.004 notation 03–99 from Table 5, e.g., general history and civilization of South American native peoples in South America 980.00498
>> (Option: Class South American native peoples in South America in 980.1, specific native peoples in 980.3)
>
> Specific native peoples in a specific place relocated to the place in 981–989 with use of subdivision 00498 from table under 930–990, e.g., the Arua in Pará state 981.15004984
>
> Class prehispanic history and civilization of South American native peoples in a specific place with the place, without using notation 00498, e.g., Incas before 1519 985.01

.005–.009   Standard subdivisions

> As modified under 930–990

>   980.01–980.03 Historical periods
>
> Class comprehensive works in 980

.01   Early history to 1806

.012   Prehispanic period to 1498

.013   Period of European discovery, exploration, colonization, 1498–1806

.02   Period of struggles for independence, 1806–1830

.03   1830–1999

.031   1830–1899

> Class here 19th century
>
> Class 1801–1806 in 980.013, 1806–1830 in 980.02

.032   1900–1918

.033	1918–1949

Class here 20th century

Class a specific part of 20th century not provided for here with the part, e.g., 1950–1959 980.035

.035	1950–1959
.036	1960–1969
.037	1970–1979
.038	1980–1989
.039	1990–1999

(.1) **South American native peoples (Indians)**

(Optional number; prefer 980.00498)

Class special topics in 980.3–980.5

(.3) **Specific native peoples**

(Optional number; prefer 981–989 with use of subdivision 00498 from table under 930–990, e.g., the Arua in Pará state 981.15004984)

Arrange alphabetically by name of people

Class government relations with specific native peoples in 980.5

(.4) **Native peoples in specific places in South America**

(Optional number; prefer 981–989 with use of subdivision 00498 from table under 930–990, e.g., native peoples in Brazil 981.00498)

Add to base number 980.4 the numbers following —8 in notation 81–89 from Table 2, e.g., native peoples in Brazil 980.41

Class government relations in specific places in 980.5, specific native peoples in specific places in 980.3

(.5) **Government relations with native South Americans**

(Optional number; prefer 323.1198 for comprehensive works; a specific subject with the subject, e.g., conquest of Incas by Pizarro 985.02, relation to state in Chile 323.1198083)

> ## 981–989 Countries and localities

Class a specific native people in a specific place [*formerly* 980.00498] with the place in 981–989 with use of subdivision 00498 from table under 930–990, e.g., the Arua in Pará state 981.15004984
(Option: Class South American native peoples in specific places in South America in 980.4)

Class comprehensive works in 980

981 *Brazil

.01 Early history to 1533

.012 Prehispanic period to 1500

.013 Period of European explorations, 1500–1533

.02 Period of hereditary captaincies, 1533–1549

.03 Colonial period, 1549–1822

.04 Period of Empire, 1822–1889

For Paraguayan War, see 989.205

.05 Period of First Republic, 1889–1930

.06 Period of Second Republic, 1930–

Class here 20th century

Class 1901–1930 in 981.05

.061 Period of Getúlio Vargas, 1930–1954

Including administrations of José Finol Linhares and Eurico Gaspar Dutra, 1945–1951

.062 1954–1967

Contains administrations of João Café Filho, Carlos Coimbra da Luz, Nereu Ramos, Juscelino Kubitschek, Jânio Quadros, João Belchior Marques Goulart, Humberto de Alencar Castelo Branco

.063 1967–

Contains administrations of Artur da Costa e Silva, Emílio Garrastazu Médici, Ernesto Geisel, João Baptista de Oliveira Figueiredo

982 *Argentina

.01 Prehispanic period to 1516

.02 Period of European discovery, conquest, colonization, 1516–1810

.022 Period of European discovery and conquest, 1516–1580

.023 Colonial period, 1580–1810

For period of viceroyalty of La Plata, 1776–1810, see 982.024

.024 Period of viceroyalty of La Plata, 1776–1810

.03 Period of struggle for independence, 1810–1829

.04 1829–1861

Class here 19th century

Class 1801–1810 in 982.024, 1810–1829 in 982.03, 1861–1900 in 982.05

.05 1861–1910

For Paraguayan War, see 989.205

*Add as instructed under 930–990

.06	1910–
.061	1910–1946
.062	First administration of Juan Domingo Perón, 1946–1955
.063	1955–1973
.064	1973–

> Including second administration of Juan Domingo Perón, 1973–1974; administration of Isabel Perón, 1974–1976

983   *Chile

.01	Prehispanic period to 1535
.02	Period of European discovery and conquest, 1535–1560
.03	Colonial period, 1560–1810
.04	Period of early republics, 1810–1861

> Class here 19th century
>
> Class a specific part of 19th century not provided for here with the part, e.g., 1879–1883 in 983.061
>
> *For period of autocratic republic, 1830–1861, see 983.05*

.05	Period of autocratic republic, 1830–1861
.06	Period of later republics, 1861–
.061	Period of liberal republic, 1861–1891

> Including War of the Pacific, 1879–1883
> (Option: Class War of the Pacific in 984.045)

.062	Revolution of 1891
.063	Period of parliamentary republic, 1891–1925
.064	1925–1973

> Class here 20th century
>
> Class 1901–1925 in 983.063, 1973–   in 983.065

.064 1	1925–1932
.064 2	1932–1946
.064 3	1946–1958
.064 4	Administration of Jorge Alessandrí Rodriguez, 1958–1964
.064 5	Administration of Eduardo Frei Montalva, 1964–1970
.064 6	Administration of Salvador Allende Gossens, 1970–1973
[.064 7]	Period of military rule, 1973–

> Relocated to 983.065

*Add as instructed under 930–990

.065   Period of military rule, 1973–   [*formerly* 983.0647]

984   *Bolivia

.01   Prehispanic period to 1532

Including period of Inca rule

.02   Period of European discovery and conquest, 1532–1559

.03   Colonial period, 1559–1809

.04   1809–1899

.041   Period of struggle for independence, 1809–1825

.042   Period of formation of the Republic, 1825–1831

.044   Administration of Andrés Santa Cruz, 1831–1839

Including Peru-Bolivian Confederation, 1836–1839

.045   1839–1883

(Option: Class here War of the Pacific; prefer 983.061)

.046   Period of conservative republic, 1883–1899

.05   1899–

.051   1899–1952

(Option: Class here Chaco War; prefer 989.2071)

.052   1952–

Including revolution of 1952

985   *Peru

.01   Prehispanic period to 1519

Including Incan rule

.02   Period of European discovery and conquest, 1519–1555

(Option: Class conquest in 980.5)

.03   Colonial period, 1555–1808

.04   Period of struggle for independence, 1808–1824

.05   1824–1867

Class here 19th century

Including Peru-Bolivian Confederation, 1836–1839

Class a specific part of 19th century not provided for here with the part, e.g., 1867–1883 985.061

.06   1867–

*Add as instructed under 930–990

.061	1867–1883
	For War of the Pacific, see 983.061
.062	Period of reconstruction, 1883–1895
.063	1895–
.063 1	1895–1933
.063 2	1933–1968
.063 3	1968–

986   *Colombia and Ecuador

.1   *Colombia

.101	Early history to 1550
.102	Colonial period, 1550–1810

Including periods as Viceroyalty of New Granada, 1718–1724 and 1740–1810

Class here comprehensive works on Viceroyalty of New Granada

For Panama as part of Viceroyalty of New Granada, see 972.8702; Ecuador as part of Viceroyalty of New Granada, 986.602; Venezuela as part of Viceroyalty of New Granada, 987.03

.103	Period of struggle for independence, 1810–1819
.104	Period of Gran Colombia, 1819–1830

Class here comprehensive works on Gran Colombia

For Panama as a part of Gran Colombia, see 972.8703; Ecuador as part of Gran Colombia, 986.604; Venezuela as part of Gran Colombia, 987.05

.105	1830–1863
.105 2	Period of Republic of New Granada, 1830–1858
.105 3	Period of Granadine Confederation, 1858–1863
.106	Period of later republics, 1863–
.106 1	Period of United States of Colombia, 1863–1886
.106 2	Period of Republic of Colombia, 1886–

                 For 1930–   , see 986.1063

.106 3	1930–

Class here 20th century

Class 1901–1930 in 986.1062

.106 31	Period of liberal domination, 1930–1946
.106 32	1946–

*Add as instructed under 930–990

.6	***Ecuador**
.601	Early history to 1562
.602	Colonial period, 1562–1810
	Including period as part of Viceroyalty of New Granada, 1740–1810
.603	Period of struggle for independence, 1810–1822
.604	Period as part of Gran Colombia, 1822–1830
	Class here Quito Presidency
.605	1830–1859
	Including period of formation of Republic
.606	1860–1895
.607	1896–
.607 1	1896–1925
.607 2	1925–1948
.607 3	1948–1960
.607 4	1960–

987   *Venezuela

.01	Prehispanic period to 1498
.02	Period of discovery and conquest, 1498–1528
.03	Colonial period, 1528–1810
	Including 1806–1810 [*formerly* 987.04], period as part of Viceroyalty, 1740–1810
.04	Period of struggle for independence, 1810–1821
	Including 1819–1821 [*formerly* 987.05]
	1806–1810 relocated to 987.03
.05	Period as part of Gran Colombia, 1821–1830
	1819–1821 relocated to 987.04
.06	Period of Republic, 1830–
.061	1830–1864
.062	1864–1899
	Class here period of Antonio Guzmán Blanco, 1870–1888
.063	1899–
.063 1	1899–1935
.063 12	Period of Cipriano Castro, 1899–1908

*Add as instructed under 930–990

.063 13	Period of Juan Vicente Gómez, 1908–1935
.063 2	1935–1959
.063 3	1959–

988   *Guiana

.01	Early history to 1815
.02	1815–1945
.03	1945–

> Class here 20th century
>
> Class 1901–1945 in 988.02

.1   *Guyana

.2   *French Guiana (Guyane)

.3   *Surinam

989   Paraguay and Uruguay

.2   *Paraguay

.201	Prehispanic period to 1524
.202	Period of European discovery, exploration, conquest, 1524–1537
.203	Colonial period, 1537–1811
.204	Period of struggle for independence, 1811–1814
.205	Period of dictatorship, 1814–1870

> Including Paraguayan War (War of the Triple Alliance), 1865–1870

.206	1870–1902
.207	1902–
.207 1	1902–1940

> Including Chaco War, 1933–1935
> (Option: Class Chaco War in 984.051)

.207 2	1940–1958
.207 3	1958–

.5   *Uruguay

.501	Prehispanic period to 1516
.502	Period of European discovery and conquest, 1516–1724
.503	Colonial period, 1724–1811
.504	Period of struggle for independence, 1811–1830

> Including 1825–1830 [*formerly* 989.505]

*Add as instructed under 930–990

.505	Period of Republic, 1830–

1825–1830 relocated to 989.504

For 1886–   , see 989.506; Paraguayan War, 989.205

[.505 5]	1830–1886

Number discontinued; class in 989.505

.506	1886–
.506 1	1886–1917
.506 2	1917–1933
.506 3	1933–1951
.506 4	1951–1966
.506 5	1966–

990   General history of other parts of world, of extraterrestrial worlds   Pacific Ocean islands

.01–.09   Standard subdivisions of Pacific Ocean islands

As modified under 930–990

[991]   [Unassigned]

Most recently used in Edition 17

[992]   [Unassigned]

Most recently used in Edition 17

993   *New Zealand

>   993.01–993.03 Historical periods [*formerly* 993.101–993.103]

Class comprehensive works in 993

.01	Early history to 1840

Including history of Maoris before European settlement, of European settlers

.02	Colonial period, 1840–1908

.021	Period as a Crown colony, 1840–1853

Including Maori Wars of 1843–1847

.022	Period of provincial governments, 1853–1876

Class here comprehensive works on Maori Wars

For Maori Wars of 1843–1847, see 993.021

.023	Period of centralized government, 1876–1908

*Add as instructed under 930–990

.03	Dominion period, 1908–
.031	1908–1918
.032	1918–1945
.035	1945–1969
.037	1970–

.1   **Specific islands**

> Use of this number for comprehensive works on New Zealand discontinued; class in 993

[.101–.103]   Historical periods

> Relocated to 993.01–993.03

[.2–.7]   **Melanesia**

> Relocated to 995

994   *Australia

.01	Early history to 1788
.02	Period of settlement and growth, 1788–1851
.03	Period of development of self government, 1851–1901
.031	Period of gold discovery and consolidation, 1851–1891
.032	1891–1901
.04	Period of Commonwealth, 1901–

> *For 1945–1966, see 994.05; 1966–   , 994.06*

.041	1901–1922
.042	1922–1945

> Including first prime ministership of Robert Gordon Menzies, 1939–1941

.05	1945–1966

> Class here second prime ministership of Robert Gordon Menzies, 1949–1966

.06	1966–
.061	1966–1972
.062	1972–1975
.063	1976–

*Add as instructed under 930–990

995   †Melanesia [*formerly also* 993.2–993.7]   New Guinea

Class here Oceania

Class Polynesia in 996

> ### 995.1–995.7 New Guinea

Class comprehensive works in 995

.1   ***Irian Jaya**

Add to base number 995.1 the numbers following 959.8 in 959.801–959.8103, e.g., period of administration of Sukarno 995.1035

.3   ***Papua New Guinea**   **New Guinea region**

For Papuan region, see 995.4; Highlands region, 995.6; Momase region, 995.7; Bismarck Archipelago, 995.8; North Solomons Province, 995.92

.301   Early history to 1884

.302   1884–1942

.302 1   1884–1921

        Class here German New Guinea

.302 2   1921–1942

        Class here period as Territory of New Guinea, 1921–1949

        Class 1942–1945 in 995.303, 1945–1949 in 995.304

.303   Period of World War II, 1942–1945

.304   1945–1975

        Class here Territory of Papua and New Guinea, 1949–1975

.305   Period of independence, 1975–

.4   ***Papuan region**

.401   Early history to 1884

.402   1884–1942

.402 1   Period as British New Guinea, 1884–1906

.402 2   1906–1942

        Class here period as Territory of Papua, 1906–1949

        Class 1942–1945 in 995.403, 1945–1949 in 995.404

.403   Period of World War II, 1942–1945

*Add as instructed under 930–990

†Add as instructed under 930–990; however, do not add historical periods

.404	1945–1975

Class here Papuan region as a part of Territory of Papua and New Guinea, 1949–1975

.405	Period of independence, 1975–

.6 *Highlands region

Add to base number 995.6 the numbers following 995.3 in 995.301–995.305, e.g., period of World War II 995.603

.7 *Momase (Northern coastal) region

Add to base number 995.7 the numbers following 995.3 in 995.301–995.305, e.g., period of World War II 995.703

.8 *Bismarck Archipelago

Add to base number 995.8 the numbers following 995.3 in 995.301–995.305, e.g., period of World War II 995.803

.9 †Other parts of Melanesia

.92	*North Solomons Province

Add to base number 995.92 the numbers following 995.3 in 995.301–995.305, e.g., period of World War II 995.9203

.93	†Solomon Islands
.95	†Vanuatu
.97	†New Caledonia

996 Other parts of Pacific   Polynesia

.001–.009	Standard subdivisions of Polynesia

As modified under 930–990

.1 †Southwest central Pacific, and isolated islands of southeast Pacific

.11	†Fiji
.12	†Tonga (Friendly Islands)
.13	†American Samoa
.14	†Western Samoa
.15	†Tokelau (Union Islands)
.18	†Isolated islands of southeast Pacific

.2 †South central Pacific

.3 †Southeast central Pacific

For isolated islands of southeast Pacific, see 996.18

.4 †Line Islands

*Add as instructed under 930–990

†Add as instructed under 930–990; however, do not add historical periods

.5	**†West central Pacific (Micronesia)**	**Trust Territory of the Pacific Islands**
.6	**†Federated States of Micronesia and Republic of Belau (Palau)**	
.7	**†Mariana Islands**	
.8	**†Islands of eastern Micronesia**	
.81	†Kiribati	
.82	†Tuvalu	
.83	†Marshall Islands	
.85	†Nauru (Pleasant Island)	
.9	**North central Pacific**	**Hawaii**

.900 01–.900 09   Standard subdivisions of north central Pacific

                     As modified under 930–990

.900 1–.900 9   Standard subdivisions of Hawaii

                     As modified under 930–990

>   996.902–996.904 Historical periods of Hawaii

            Class comprehensive works in 996.9

.902	Early history to 1898
.902 7	Period of kingdom, 1810–1893
.902 8	Period of republic, 1893–1898
.903	Territorial period, 1898–1959
.904	Statehood period, 1959–
.99	†Outlying islands

997   **†Atlantic Ocean islands**

        Class each specific island or group of islands not provided for here with the island or group of islands, e.g., Azores 946.99

.1	**†Falklands and Bouvet**
.3	**†Saint Helena and dependencies**

998   **†Arctic islands and Antartica**

.2	**†Greenland**

999   **Extraterrestrial worlds**

        Class here speculation on and the search for intelligent life on other worlds

        Do not add from table under 930–990

†Add as instructed under 930–990; however, do not add historical periods

The 20th edition of the Dewey Decimal Classification was designed by Lisa Hanifan of Albany, New York. Edition 20 is the first edition to be generated from an online database. Database design, technical support, and programming for this edition were provided by John J. Finni and Cora M. Arsenault from Inforonics, Inc., of Littleton, Massachusetts. Composition was done in Times Roman and Helvetica on a Linotronic L100 under the supervision of Inforonics, Inc. The book was printed and bound by Hamilton Printing Company of Rensselaer, New York.